THE MARX-ENGELS READER

SECOND EDITION

Books by Robert C. Tucker

Philosophy and Myth in Karl Marx
The Soviet Political Mind
The Great Purge Trial (*co-editor*)
The Marxian Revolutionary Idea
Stalin as Revolutionary, 1879–1929: A Study in History and Personality
The Lenin Anthology (*editor*)
Stalinism: Essays in Historical Interpretation (*editor*)

THE
MARX-ENGELS
READER

SECOND EDITION

Edited by

ROBERT C. TUCKER
PRINCETON UNIVERSITY

W · W · NORTON & COMPANY
New York · London

W. W. Norton & Company, Inc., 500 Fifth Avenue, New York, N.Y. 10110
W. W. Norton & Company Ltd., 10 Coptic Street, London, WC1A 1PU

Selections from *Grundrisse: Foundations of the Critique of Political Eonomy*, by
Karl Marx, translated by Martin Nicolaus. Copyright © 1973 by Martin Nicolaus.
Reprinted by permission of Random House, Inc. and Penguin Books Ltd.
Selection from *On Revolution*, by Karl Marx, edited by Saul K. Padover. Copy-
right © 1971 by Saul K. Padover. Used with permission of McGraw-Hill Book
Company.
Marx's 1837 letter to his father, and selections from Marx's doctoral dissertation,
from the "Contribution to the Critique of Hegel's *Philosophy of Right*, and
from "Critical Marginal Notes on the Article 'The King of Prussia and Social
Reform,' " are from Karl Marx and Frederick Engels, *Collected Works*, Volumes
1 and 3. Copyright © 1975 by International Publishers, Inc.

Library of Congress Cataloging in Publication Data
Main entry under title:
The Marx-Engels reader.
    Includes bibliographical references and index.
    1. Communism—Collected works. 2. Socialism—Collected works.
I. Marx, Karl, 1818–1883. Selections. English. 1978. II. Engels, Fried-
rich, 1820–1895. Selections. English. 1978. III. Tucker, Robert C.
HX39.5.M374 1978   335.4   77–16635

ISBN 0-393-09040-X

Contents

v

Part III. Revolutionary Program and Strategy

Part IV. Society and Politics in the Nineteenth Century

Part V. The Later Engels: Elaboration and
    Popularization

Preface to the Second Edition

A knowledge of the writings of Marx and Engels is virtually indispensable to an educated person in our time, whatever his political position or social philosophy. For classical Marxism, as the thought of Marx and Engels may be called, has profoundly affected ideas about history, society, economics, ideology, culture, and politics; indeed, about the nature of social inquiry itself. No other intellectual influence has so powerfully shaped the mind of modern left-wing radicalism in most parts of the world. Through classical Marxism, moreover, the left is linked to a greater intellectual tradition extending into the eighteenth-century French Enlightenment, German post-Kantian philosophy, English political economy, and early-nineteenth-century European socialism. Not to be well grounded in the writings of Marx and Engels is to be insufficiently attuned to modern thought, and self-excluded to a degree from the continuing debate by which most contemporary societies live insofar as their members are free and able to discuss the vital issues.

This book offers the original writings needed to acquire a thorough grounding in Marxist thought, together with introductory notes to each selection, a chronology of the careers of the two men, and a concluding bibliographic guide to some of the literature about them and their thought. I have aimed to place between the covers of one volume all or nearly all of what could be considered "the essential Marx and Engels." Since their published writings and correspondence fill more than forty volumes, such an undertaking involves difficult problems of selection. In resolving them I have followed certain established traditions in the anthologizing of Marx and Engels, but also have sought to break fresh ground. The main innovations are the inclusion of the principal early writings of Marx and substantial portions of *Capital* and the *Grundrisse*.

The inclusion of the early Marx is a response to the revolution that has taken place in "Marxology" in our time owing to the publication in the 1930s of some previously unknown writings of Marx's formative period. I shall say more about these writings and their significance in the Introduction. The outcome of the new Marx scholarship, as I shall argue, is a deeper and clearer understanding both of Marxism's origins in post-Kantian German philosophy and of its fundamental meaning. The new scholarship has also made plain the basic underlying continuity that exists between the early and later Marx. For these reasons, among others, the most important of the early writings deserve to be represented in any collection of the essential Marx and Engels, and have been included here.

Marx without *Capital* is Kant without *The Critique of Pure Reason* or Darwin without *The Origin of Species*. Even though he completed only the first volume of it, leaving the second and third volumes in unfinished form to be edited and published by Engels after he died, *Capital* was Marx's great work. When he completed and published Volume One in 1867, he described it in a letter to a friend as the book "to which I have sacrificed my health, my happiness and my family." When read closely and in the context of the remainder of his writings, *Capital* turns out to be not simply Marx's major treatise on political economy, but his principal work on man, society, and government—indeed, the fullest expression of his entire world-view. Clearly, there can be no "essential Marx and Engels" with *Capital* missing, yet the book is forbidding on account of its great size—about eight hundred pages—and its complexity. Feeling that token solutions of this problem through the inclusion mainly of Marx's prefaces to *Capital* are unsatisfactory, I have tried to resolve it by putting together sufficiently extensive extracts to convey the book's basic argument, the parts of greatest general interest.

The hospitable reception of this volume since its appearance five years ago has encouraged me to prepare a revised and enlarged edition to meet more fully the needs of teacher and student in the various disciplines for which Marxist thought is important.

No changes have been made in those respects in which the book seems to have proved sound: the five-part plan of organization; the idea of combining the thematic with the chronological in arranging the material; the integration of the early philosophical Marx with the later writings of both Marx and Engels; the inclusion of *Capital*; and the premise that Engels, in some measure, is quite indispensable—that a general anthology of classical Marxism cannot properly meet the needs of student and teacher unless it is a Marx-Engels reader. On the other hand, the material added in the new edition is mostly—but not exclusively—by Marx. The Marx portion of the reader, already predominant in the first edition, has been substantially increased in this one.

Additions are of two kinds: the inclusion of works, or material from works, not represented in the first edition; and the addition of more material to works that were included in less than the desirable measure. A small number of excisions, in no case involving a work as a whole, have been made in order to help accommodate voluminous additions without unduly increasing the book's bulk and cost.

Of the two parts that have been most heavily enlarged, one is Part I ("The Early Marx"), where I have added selections from Marx's commentary of 1843 on Hegel's *Philosophy of Right* (Marx's most extended work of strictly political analysis); the important section of the *Economic and Philosophical Manuscripts of 1844* on "The Meaning of Human Requirements"; selections from the student Marx's letter to his father in 1837, from Marx's doctoral dissertation, from the article "Critical Marginal Notes," and from Marx's early exposition of historical materialism in his 1846 letter to Annenkov.

The other part enlarged in greatest measure is Part II ("The Critique of Capitalism"), featuring Marx's economic writings. The chief innovation is the inclusion of extensive extracts from the *Grundrisse,* including the whole of its introductory part. Additions have been made to Volume One of *Capital*: the section on the "Industrial Reserve Army" and the chapters on "The Buying and Selling of Labour-Power" and "Modern Industry and Agriculture." The famous unfinished concluding chapter on "Classes" has been added to the short selection from Volume Three of *Capital,* and Marx's discussion of economic crises in his still little-known *Theories of Surplus Value* has been added for those with a specialized interest in Marxian economics. Other, brief additions to Part II are the concluding section of *The Poverty of Philosophy,* presenting Marx's 1847 preview of the violent revolutionary breakdown of capitalist society, and Marx's 1852 statement to Wedemeyer on what he considered his main innovation in the theory of history. *Wage Labour and Capital* has been preserved, although it is now given in somewhat condensed form. Engels' revealing discussion in *Anti-Dühring* on "The Division of Labour in Production," with added material, has been moved to Part V ("The Later Engels").

Part III ("Revolutionary Program and Strategy") has been enlarged by three short selections: Marx's speech of 1872 in Amsterdam allowing for the possibility of a peaceful road to socialism in certain countries; his discussion in a letter to Bolte in 1871 of the way in which economic issues should figure in revolutionary working-class politics; and his rebuttal of Bakunin's criticisms of Marxism (this occurs in Marx's conspectus, written in 1874–75, of Bakunin's work *Statehood and Anarchy*).

A classical historical pamphlet now included in Part IV ("Society and Politics in the Nineteenth Century"), Marx's *The Class Struggles in France 1848–1850,* is represented in extracts containing its passages of general bearing and interest. The key sections of *The Eighteenth Brumaire of Louis Bonaparte* and *The Civil War in France* are retained although some mainly narrative parts have been deleted. A short new section entitled "Europocentric World Revolution" presents thoughts of Marx and Engels on the problematic relation of the predicted European socialist revolution to future developments in the non-European parts of the world. Lastly, a key passage from Marx's letter of 1881 to Vera Zasulich has been added to the selection "On Social Relations in Russia."

The principal addition in Part V ("The Later Engels") is material on the past, present, and future of the family from Engels' *The Origin of the Family, Private Property, and the State*. This material constitutes classical Marxism's major statement on family history and the position of women. Finally, I have added material in Engels' letters on historical materialism, including his 1894 comments to Starkenburg on the role of "great men" in history.

The book's editorial apparatus has been, where necessary, revised and expanded. Revisions have been made in the headnotes, as needed, to make them more informative. A passage has been added to the Introduction. A "Note on Texts and Terminology" has been especially prepared for the new edition. Some minor revisions have been made in the Chronology. The Bibliographic Note has been amplified to include some new titles which have appeared in the intervening years and a listing of some books by major Marxist thinkers after Marx and Engels.

My thanks go first of all to two friends who have been instrumental in making this book a reality. My colleague Stephen Cohen convinced me of the need for the kind of comprehensive anthology of Marx and Engels that the book seeks to provide, and later was generous with his advice on many aspects of the work and gave me the benefit of a searching appraisal of my proposed choice of materials. James Mairs of W. W. Norton & Company was an unfailing source of encouragement, support, editorial judgment, and practical wisdom on all matters affecting the book.

I am also indebted to Emily Garlin for her editorial assistance; to Ronald Rogowski for translating Marx's letter to Arnold Ruge; to Norman Levine for critical comments and suggestions on the choice of materials; to Steven Marcus for suggesting the inclusion of Engels' description of working-class Manchester; to Lorna Giese for her able typing of portions of the manuscript; and to Jerome Nestor, Anthony Trenga, and Brian Kemple for help as research assistants.

Some of the ideas embodied in the new edition have come from persons who read the book in its first edition and thoughtfully brought one or another omission or imperfection to my attention. Among those who did so and to whom I wish to express gratitude are Gert H. Muller, Caroline B. Pierce, Dennis Dalton, Gary

Young, and Yasuyuki Owada. I am likewise indebted to Mihailo Markovic for his helpful advice.

Two colleagues exceptionally knowledgeable in areas covered by this book, Thomas Ferguson and Peter G. Stillman, were kind enough, in response to invitations from the publisher, to prepare searching, systematic critiques of the first edition and suggestions for additions and revisions in the second. If this volume is as improved now as I believe it to be, much of the credit goes to them, along with my deep thanks. Neither bears the responsibility for what inadequacies remain.

Unless otherwise indicated the texts are translations that have appeared in editions published by the Foreign Languages Publishing House or Progress Publishers in Moscow. Likewise, the editorial notes, save where specifically indicated, are those supplied by the original editor or translator.

Robert C. Tucker

The Lives of Marx and Engels

1818   (May 5) Karl Marx born at Trier, Prussia (now part of West Germany).

1820   (November 28) Friedrich Engels born at Barmen (incorporated into Wuppertal, 1929; now in West Germany).

1830–35   Marx studied in Trier high school.

1834–37   Engels studied in Elberfeld high school.

1835   Marx entered University of Bonn, faculty of law.

1836   Marx transferred to University of Berlin, faculty of law.

1836–38   Marx studied law, philosophy, history, and English and Italian languages at Berlin.

1839–41   Marx studied Greek philosophy and wrote doctoral dissertation, *The Difference Between the Democritean and Epicurean Philosophies of Nature*. Received Ph.D. from Jena, then moved to Bonn hoping to secure teaching position at University of Bonn.

1838–41   Sent to Bremen for business training, Engels worked as unsalaried clerk in an export business. Continued studies independently and wrote articles for press.

1841–42   Abandoning the idea of university teaching, Marx wrote articles for the Young Hegelian *Deutsche Jahrbücher* and the *Rheinische Zeitung*, an opposition newspaper published in Cologne. Became editor of *Rheinische Zeitung* in October, 1842. Moved to Cologne.

1841–42   Engels served in Household Artillery of Prussian Army, attended lectures at University of Berlin, and joined circle of Young Hegelian radicals, "The Free." Wrote articles for *Rheinische Zeitung*.

1842   (November) First meeting between Marx and Engels, in office of *Rheinische Zeitung* in Cologne. Engels stopped there on way to England.

1842–44   In Manchester to complete his business training in firm of Ermen and Engels, Engels studied English life and literature, read political economists, joined Chartist movement, published in Owenite paper *The New Moral World*, wrote "Outlines of a Critique of Political Economy."

1843   (March 17) Marx resigned as editor of *Rheinische Zeitung* after imposition of strict censorship on paper by Prussian government.

1843   (June 19) Marriage of Marx to Jenny von Westphalen.

1843   Marx undertook with Arnold Ruge to publish *Deutsch-Französische Jahrbücher* and worked on founding of the journal.

1843   (summer) Marx in Kreuznach worked on critique of Hegel's *Philosophy of Right*.

1843   (November) Marx moved to Paris.

1843   (fall and winter) Marx wrote "On the Jewish Question" and "Contribution to the Critique of Hegel's *Philosophy of Right*: Introduction" for *Jahrbücher*.

1843   (end of December) Marx became acquainted with Heinrich Heine.

1843–44   Marx studied history of French Revolution and began systematic study of classics of political economy.

1844   (January) Marx received articles from Engels for publication in *Jahrbücher*.

1844   Double issue of *Jahrbücher* published in Paris under editorship of Marx and Ruge. Publication of Engels' "Outlines of a Critique of Political Economy" in it led to correspondence between Marx and Engels.

1844   (April) Marx accused by Prussian government of high treason and *lese majesté* for his articles in *Jahrbücher* and ordered arrested in event of crossing Prussian border.

1844   (July) Marx became acquainted with Proudhon.

1844   (March–August) Marx wrote materials later published as *Economic and Philosophic Manuscripts of 1844*.

1844   (April–August) Engels gathered materials for a social history of England and on condition of English working class.

1844   (around August 28) Returning from Manchester to Germany, Engels visited Paris for second meeting with Marx. Commencement of their collaboration.

1844–45   Engels, in Barmen, wrote *Condition of the Working Class in England* (1845). Marx and Engels collaborated in writing *The Holy Family* (1845).

1845   (January) Banished from Paris by order of French government, acting under Prussian instigation, Marx moved to Brussels.

1845   (May–June) Marx wrote "Theses on Feuerbach."

1845   (April) Engels joined Marx in Brussels.

1845   (summer) Marx visited Manchester with Engels, returning to Brussels in late August.

1845–46   Marx and Engels wrote *The German Ideology*.

1845   Marx renounced Prussian citizenship under pressure from Prussian government.

1846–47   Marx wrote *The Poverty of Philosophy* (1847).

1847   Engels took part in First Congress of the Communist League in London. In November both Marx and Engels took part in Second Congress, also in London.

1847   (December) Marx, in Brussels, gave series of lectures later published as *Wage Labour and Capital* (1849).

1848   (February) *Communist Manifesto* published in London.

1848–49   Marx and Engels took active parts in revolution of 1848–49 in Germany, coediting *Neue Rheinische Zeitung* in Cologne.

1849   (June) Engels served as Willich's adjutant in unsuccessful Baden rising.

1849   (fall) Marx and family settled down in London.

1850   Marx resumed his economic studies in British Museum. Engels took up residence in Manchester, where he worked for twenty years in firm of Ermen and Engels, helping to support Marx as well as himself.

1851   Marx began an eleven-year period as regular contributor to *New York Daily Tribune*.

1851–52   Marx wrote *The Eighteenth Brumaire of Louis Bonaparte* (1852). Engels wrote articles on "Revolution and Counter-Revolution in Germany." Latter appeared in *New York Daily Tribune* under Marx's name.

1857   Marx and Engels wrote articles for *New American Encyclopedia*, Engels' on "The History of Artillery."

1857–58   Marx prepared manuscripts on criticism of political economy, the *Grundrisse* (1939–41).

1858–59   Marx wrote *A Contribution to the Critique of Political Economy* (1859).

1861–63   Marx wrote *Theories of Surplus Value*.

1863   Mary Burns, with whom Engels had lived for many years, died.

1864   Founding of International Working Men's Association in London.

1864–71   Marx active in affairs of General Council of International Working Men's Association.

1867   Publication of *Capital*, Volume One.

1867–80   Marx made some revisions on the texts of Volumes Two and Three of *Capital*, most of which were completed by 1867.

1871   Marx wrote *The Civil War in France* (1871).

1870–95   Engels lived in London.

1872   Appearance of Russian edition of *Capital*.

1874–80   Engels worked intermittently on *Dialectics of Nature*.

1878   Publication of Engels' *Anti-Dühring* in book form.

1881   Death of Jenny Marx.

1883   (March 14) Death of Karl Marx.

1884   Engels wrote *The Origin of the Family, Private Property and the State* (1884).

1885   Publication of Volume Two of *Capital*, edited by Engels.

1886   Engels wrote *Ludwig Feuerbach and the End of Classical German Philosophy* (1886).

1887   Publication of English translation of Volume One of *Capital*, edited by Engels. Publication in New York of first English edition of *The Condition of the Working Class in England in 1844*.

1888   (August–September) Engels traveled in the United States and Canada.

1889   Engels took part in the founding of the Second International.

1893   Engels attended International Socialist Workers' Congress in Zurich. Elected honorary president of Congress.

1894   Publication of Volume Three of *Capital*, edited by Engels.

1895   (August 5) Death of Engels.

Introduction

There is no royal road to science, and only those who do not dread the fatiguing climb of its steep paths have a chance of gaining the luminous summits.

—KARL MARX, 1872

I

Marx, like many writers, published considerably less than he wrote. His early writings, presented in Part I of this book, include some that were published in 1844, soon after he wrote them, and some not destined to appear in print until the 1930s.

The most important of the latter group are the *Economic and Philosophic Manuscripts of 1844* and *The German Ideology* (Part I of which appears to have been one of Marx's contributions to this book written jointly by himself and Engels), and the *Grundrisse*. Marx explained the non-publication of *The German Ideology* in the brief history of his opinions that he gave in the Preface to *A Contribution to the Critique of Political Economy*. As for the 1844 manuscripts, which were a very rough first sketch of his theory of history in notes and draft chapters of a projected treatise on the "criticism of political economy," these remained in a raw, unfinished state among his private papers. The papers came into Engels' possession after Marx's death in 1883, and went to the leaders of the German Social Democratic Party after Engels' death in 1895. After the Russian Revolution, the Marx-Engels Institute in Moscow acquired photocopies of the manuscript materials. Its director, the noted Marx scholar David Riazanov, took charge of the editing of the unpublished early writings, and, thanks largely to his labors, these writings finally came out in the 1920s and 1930s.[1] Later, Riazanov, like so many other prominent Russian Marxists, died in Stalin's purges.

Although reactions were somewhat slow in coming, the publication of the previously unknown early writings was a pivotal event in the history of Marxism and of scholarship about Marxism. Because they reflected the genesis and growth of the Marxist system of

[1]. For further particulars on the publishing history, see the Note on Texts and Terminology, below.

thought in the mind of its principal creator, the 1844 manuscripts and Part I of *The German Ideology* illuminated the origins of the system, its relation to post-Kantian German philosophy, and the meaning of some of Marx's basic concepts. Only then, in fact, did it become possible to trace in depth and detail, stage by stage, the emergence of Marxism.

The manner of Marxism's emergence was a subject that Marx and Engels left in some obscurity although they dealt with it now and then, for example in Engels' *Socialism: Utopian and Scientific*. But what they had to say was enigmatic. In Marxism, which has its foundation in what they variously called the "materialist conception of history" or "historical materialism,"[2] socialist thought had—they said—graduated from its earlier "utopian" stage and become "scientific." Whereas the "utopian" socialists had visualized a socialist reorganization of society as something that *ought* to be realized, the materialist conception of history had conclusively demonstrated that the human historical process was moving toward a worldwide anticapitalist revolution that would usher in socialism or communism (Marx and Engels tended to use these two words interchangeably).

Yet this "scientific socialism" of Marx and Engels was not in a direct line of descent from the teachings of the classical utopian socialists, the early-nineteenth-century fathers of modern socialist thought: Henri de Saint-Simon, Charles Fourier, and Robert Owen. Its immediate intellectual source was, rather, German philosophy, particularly that of Hegel. The materialist conception of history had originated in an inversion of Hegel's idealist conception of history, an intellectual operation whereby the Hegelian dialectic was, as Engels expressed it in one of his later writings, "placed

2. The notion that Marxism has its foundation in "dialectical materialism," a general world-view of which historical materialism is the application to human history, is a later growth particularly associated with Russian and subsequently Communist Marxism, and is not the classical Marxist position. For Marx the prime subject of Marxism was human history, hence historical materialism was the foundation of the teaching. Moreover, historical materialism was itself dialectical in that the human historical process showed a revolutionary pattern of development through opposition and conflict. To this it must be added that Engels, who more than Marx was interested in the progress of natural science in the nineteenth century, did give an initial impetus to the later emergence of a Marxist "dialectical materialism" by his speculations on the presence of dialectical laws in natural processes. He began but never completed a book on this subject, the manuscript of which was first published in the twentieth century under the title *Dialectics of Nature*. The term "dialectical materialism" was put into currency by the Russian Marxist Georgi Plekhanov in one of his writings of the late nineteenth century. For a long while the authoritative version of the viewpoint of Communist Marxism on this subject was the essay by Joseph Stalin, "Dialectical and Historical Materialism," published as a part of Chapter Four of the *History of the Communist Party of the Soviet Union (Bolsheviks). Short Course* (Moscow: Foreign Languages Publishing House, many editions).

upon its head; or rather, turned off its head, on which it was standing, and placed upon its feet."[3] This only repeated what Marx himself had written in 1873 in the Afterword to the second German edition of *Capital*, where he observed that thirty years earlier he had criticized the "mystifying side of Hegelian dialectic," and added: "The mystification which dialectic suffers in Hegel's hands, by no means prevents him from being the first to present its general form of working in a comprehensive and conscious manner. With him it is standing on its head. It must be turned right side up again, if you would discover the rational kernel within the mystical shell." So Marx and Engels.

The enigma mentioned above will now be apparent. Social theories normally do not originate through turning metaphysical systems of thought "right side up again." How could Marx's materialist conception of history arise by means of an inversion of Hegel's idealist conception? Hegel represents history as the self-realization of spirit (*Geist*) or God. The fundamental scheme of his theory is as follows. Spirit is self-creative energy imbued with a drive to become fully conscious of itself as spirit. Nature is spirit in its self-objectification in space; history is spirit in its self-objectification as culture—the succession of world-dominant civilizations from the ancient Orient to modern Europe. Spirit actualizes its nature as self-conscious being by the process of knowing. Through the mind of man, philosophical man in particular, the world achieves consciousness of itself as spirit. This process involves the repeated overcoming of spirit's "alienation" (*Entfremdung*) from itself, which takes place when spirit as the knowing mind confronts a world that appears, albeit falsely, as objective, i.e., as *other* than spirit. Knowing is recognition, whereby spirit destroys the illusory otherness of the objective world and recognizes it as actually subjective or *selbstisch*. The process terminates at the stage of "absolute knowledge," when spirit is finally and fully "at home with itself in its otherness," having recognized the whole of creation as spirit—Hegelianism itself being the scientific form of this ultimate self-knowledge on spirit's part. Such is the argument of Hegel's great work *The Phenomenology of Mind* (1807), on which he elaborated further in his later writings.

A philosophical tour de force this, but what does it have to do with Marxism? How could the materialist conception of history and "scientific socialism" be Hegelian in derivation? Marx and Engels asserted such a relationship in terms too clear for misunder-

3. *Ludwig Feuerbach and the End of Classical German Philosophy*, in Karl Marx and Frederick Engels, *Selected Works*, 2 vols. (Moscow: Foreign Languages Publishing House, 1962), vol. II, p. 387.

standing. Engels, to cite a further example, wrote the following about Hegel's system:

> Abstract and idealist though it was in form, yet the development of his thoughts always proceeded parallel with the development of world history and the latter is really meant to be only the test of the former. If, thereby, the real relation was inverted and stood on its head, nevertheless the *real content* entered everywhere into the philosophy; all the more so since Hegel—in contrast to his disciples—did not parade ignorance, but was one of the finest intellects of all time. . . . *This epoch-making conception of history was the direct theoretical premise for the new materialist outlook. . . .*[4]

But nowhere did Marx and Engels adequately explain just *how* Hegel's conception of history had served as the "direct theoretical premise" of Marxism. The materials needed for clarification of the matter did, however, exist—in Marx's desk drawer.

He alluded to this fact when he recalled in the 1873 Afterword to *Capital* that thirty years earlier he had criticized the "mystifying side of Hegelian dialectic." His reference could have been to either or both of two of his still-unpublished early writings: an unfinished commentary of 1843 on Hegel's *Philosophy of Right,* or the section of the 1844 manuscripts entitled "Critique of Hegel's Dialectic and Philosophy in General." Now that these and other early writings of Marx are available, Marxism's Hegelian derivation has ceased to be a mystery. Marx and Engels were correct in saying that Hegelianism had been the "direct theoretical premise" for the materialist conception of history. So great were the philosophical complexities of this transition, however, that the two men understandably refrained in their later years from offering a detailed explanation to their socialist followers, who in their majority were unversed and uninterested in post-Kantian German philosophy.

Briefly, Marx created his theory of history as a conscious act of *translation* of Hegel's theory into what he, Marx, took to be its valid or scientific form. In this he followed the procedure of the German philosopher Ludwig Feuerbach, author of *The Essence of Christianity* (1841), who had argued that Hegel's philosophy could reveal scientific truth if subjected to "transformational criticism." This consisted in the *inverting* of its principal propositions, meaning that one transposed subject and predicate in them. For Hegel man is spirit (or God) in the process of self-alienation and self-realization, i.e., man presents himself in history as self-alienated God. The truth, says Feuerbach, is just the reverse. Instead of seeing man as self-alienated God, we must see God as self-alienated man. That is, when man, the human species, projects an idealized

4. From a review, written in 1859, of   *of Political Economy.* Italics added.
Marx's *A Contribution to the Critique*

image of itself into heaven as "God" and worships this imaginary heavenly being, it becomes estranged from itself; its own ungodly earthly reality becomes alien and hateful. To overcome this alienation man must repossess his alienated being, take "God" back into himself, recognize in man—and specifically in other human individuals—the proper object of care, love, and worship. Such is the basic argument of Feuerbach's *Essence of Christianity*. Transformational criticism of Hegel yields the theme that religion is a phenomenon of human self-estrangement. The conception of history as the self-realization of God or spirit through man is transformed into the conception of history as the self-realization of the human species via the detour of alienation in the sphere of religion. Hegelian idealism undergoes a metamorphosis and becomes Feuerbachian "humanism."

For Marx, as for others on the Hegelian left in Germany, Feuerbach's "transformational criticism" of Hegel was an intellectual innovation of epochal importance. The message that Hegelian theory has truth-value if one applies the method of inversion came with a ring of revelation. It meant that one could go on making good use of Hegel while escaping the toils of his colossal and seemingly so otherworldly system. One could discover social reality, the reality of the human predicament in history, by turning Hegel "right side up." Man was not the personification of spirit; rather, spirit was the thought-process taking place in man. But as Feuerbach had shown, this thought-process as depicted by Hegel was a reflection of the actual movement of history. The Hegelian picture of spirit alienated from itself was, on this reading, simply the philosopher's upside-down and hence "mystified" vision of the real social process, namely, *man's* alienation from himself in the material world. Furthermore, man's alienation could be traced out in other spheres than religion. The state, for example, was a sphere of human alienation, and could be exposed as such by applying to Hegel's *political* philosophy the same method of transformational criticism that Feuerbach had applied to his general theory of history. Marx undertook this work in 1843 in a critical commentary on Hegel's *Philosophy of Right*. He did not complete the commentary, but summed up the most important parts of its message in two articles published in 1844. In one of them, the essay "On the Jewish Question," he portrayed the political life of man as analogous to the religious life, as treated in *The Essence of Christianity*. Just as man projects the idealized attributes of the species into his image of a transcendent deity, so he projects social power into a separate sphere—the state—which dominates him. Here, however, the resulting division of man against himself is not a matter of the imagination simply but of institutional reality; and the escape from political alienation, unlike that from religious alienation, requires a real revolution—a collective act whereby the citizens repossess the social power externalized in state institutions.

Applying "transformational criticism" to Hegel's political philosophy, Marx inverted the Hegelian proposition on the relation between the state and "civil society" (*bürgerliche Gesellschaft*, by which Hegel meant the realm of private economic endeavor). Civil society was not an outgrowth of the state, as in Hegel's view; rather, the state was an outgrowth of civil society. The primary sphere of man's being was not his life as a citizen of the state but rather his economic life in civil society; this was the foundation on which all else rested. Having reached this position via the critical commentary on Hegel's *Philosophy of Right*,[5] Marx was approaching the end of the strange road leading him to the formulation of the materialist conception of history. Now he posed for himself the task of investigating the economic life as a sphere of human self-alienation. In pursuit of this aim he undertook an intensive study of Adam Smith and other classical theorists of political economy. In these economic writings, read in conjunction with Hegel, he hoped to find a key to the understanding of man's alienation as a producer of material goods. At some point in the course of these studies he was struck by the thought that was to prove the cornerstone of the Marxian system: the fundamental human reality reflected in a mystified way in Hegel's philosophy of history was the reality of man's alienation in economic life. This was the underlying master theme of the papers that we now know as the *Economic and Philosophic Manuscripts of 1844*.

Deciphering what he conceived to be the hidden meaning-content of Hegel's *Phenomenology of Mind*, Marx here formulated his own conception of history as a process of self-development of the human species culminating in communism. Man, according to this conception, is essentially a producer; and material production is the primary form of his producing activity, industry being the externalized productive powers of the species. In the course of his history, which Marx described as a "history of production," a world of created objects gradually arises around man. Original nature is overlaid with a man-made or "anthropological nature." And Marx believed that this was the true or scientific restatement of the Hegelian conception. For had not Hegel seen the history of the world as a production-history on the part of spirit? His error had been to mystify the process by treating the productive activity as *spirit* activity. To move from mystification to reality, from philosophy to science, one had only to turn Hegel on his head. Then it

5. On this see Marx's own testimony in the Preface to *A Contribution to the Critique of Political Economy*, p. 4, below. For the commentary itself, see pp. 16–25, 53–65, below.

appeared that the Hegelian image of spirit creating a world was simply a philosopher's distorted picture of the reality of history, namely, that man—working man—creates a world in *material* productive activities over the centuries. Inevitably, therefore, Marx later named his transformed Hegelianism the "materialist conception of history."

Still following Hegel's basic scheme, Marx in the 1844 manuscripts visualized the human history of production as being also a history of estrangement (*Entfremdungsgeschichte*). Man's nature, he postulated, was to be a "free conscious producer," but so far he had not been able to express himself freely in productive activity. He had been driven to produce by need and greed, by a passion for accumulation which in the modern bourgeois age becomes accumulation of capital. His productive activity had always, therefore, been involuntary; it had been "labour." And since man, when he produces involuntarily, is estranged from his human nature, labour is "alienated labour."[6] Escape from alienated labour finally becomes materially possible in the stage of technological development created by modern machine industry. The way of escape lies in the revolutionary seizure and socialization of the productive powers by the proletariat. Repossessed through revolution of his organs of material production externalized in industry, man will at last be able to produce in freedom. Human self-realization will be attained on the scale of all humanity. So Marx defined communism in the 1844 manuscripts as "transcendence of human self-alienation" and "positive humanism." He saw it as the real future situation that Hegel had dimly adumbrated at the close of his *Phenomenology*, where spirit, having attained absolute knowledge, is beyond all alienation and fully "at home with itself in its otherness." Working man would no longer be confronted by an alienated world of objects appropriated as private property. He would dwell in aesthetic communion with an "anthropological nature" transformed into the common possession of all. Man would realize his human nature as a free conscious producer, engaging in a variety of creative activities no longer actuated by the drive to accumulate property.

Such was Marxism in its original formulation in Marx's manuscripts of 1844, for which Hegelianism was indeed the direct theoretical premise. This "original Marxism" was the foundation of the mature Marxist system, the matrix of the materialist conception of history as encountered in the later writings of Marx and Engels. We have evidence of this in the fact that there was no significant hiatus in time between the initial statement of the Marxist position in the manuscripts, which Marx completed in August of 1844, and

---

6. This is a main theme of the important section of the 1844 manuscripts on estranged labor. See below. pp. 70–81.

the systematic formulation of the materialist conception of history that he gave in Part One of *The German Ideology*. He laid out some of the underlying main themes of the latter in the spring of 1845 in a set of notes that have come down to us under the title "Theses on Feuerbach." He also expounded the theory to Engels, with whom he met in Brussels at that time. Marx had the theory of history "ready worked out" by then, recalled Engels in a note to the 1890 edition of the *Communist Manifesto*. The theory that Marx was able to set forth orally and in writing by the spring of 1845 must have been the one blocked out in his manuscripts of the previous year.

As the reader will see, there are numerous differences between these two early versions of Marxism. The German philosophical terminology, and therefore also the philosophical foundations, are far more clearly apparent in the manuscripts than in Part One of *The German Ideology*. The concept of man's alienation, which plays so central a part in the first formulation, is no longer an *explicit* centerpiece of the theory as reformulated. Now we are in the more impersonal world of Marxian social theory as made familiar in the later writings, with their characteristic emphasis upon class struggle as the driving force of history. The ethical themes so strikingly present in the manuscripts, such as the notion of "positive humanism" as the goal of human history, are not so salient now. All these changes have presented problems for contemporary scholarship in Marx studies, and should certainly not be dismissed as of small importance. But neither, on the other hand, should they be overemphasized, as though there were some profound rift between original and later Marxism. It appears, for example, that much of the content of the idea of man's alienation lives on in the mature Marx in the meaning that he and Engels assign to the concept "division of labour." The moral theme in Marxism arising out of its view of alienation as an evil, and something destined to be abolished by a final worldwide revolution, remains present in later Marxism's representation of the division of labour as an evil that has plagued man all through his history, in different ways, and will be ended by the proletarian revolution. Scholarly opinion is inclining, and in my opinion will increasingly incline, to the view that there is an underlying basic continuity of thought not only between the 1844 manuscripts and *The German Ideology*, but more broadly between the early Marx and the Marx of the later writings culminating in *Capital*.[7]

But the significance of the now-discovered early Marx goes far

7. The account given here of the origin and development of Marx's thought follows the lines of the interpretation presented in greater length and detail, with supporting evidence, in Robert C. Tucker, *Philosophy and Myth in Karl Marx* (New York: Cambridge University Press, 1961; 2nd ed., 1972).

beyond these questions of the intellectual development of Marxism and its exegesis. The early writings are of very considerable intrinsic interest. The 1844 manuscripts disclose a strangely modern youthful Marx speaking in accents almost of an existentialist philosopher, a Marx alive to psychological themes of interest to many in the second half of the twentieth century. Some European existentialists have recognized a kindred mind in Marx, and one influential thinker of the psychoanalytic school has made use of some of the ideas of the manuscripts in formulating a neo-Freudian philosophy of man.[8] Many in Russia and Eastern Europe, reacting against Stalinism and the dreary orthodoxy of official Communist Marxism, have found support and inspiration in the early Marx for a new, morally aware, critical Marxism—a Marxism that sees the possibility of alienation not only in bourgeois societies but in those officially called "socialist." For these reasons, among others, the early writings that Marx left unfinished and unpublished are widely read today.

II

The German word *Kritik*, which may be translated as either "criticism" or "critique," is a symbol of great importance for comprehending the mental world of Marx and Engels. It was the watchword of the circle of Young Hegelians with whom they were associated at the end of the 1830s and the beginning of the 1840s. Marx interpreted it in a spirit of radical negation of social reality, as reflected in his letter of 1843 to Arnold Ruge calling for a "ruthless criticism of everything existing." In his essay of 1844, "Contribution to the Critique of Hegel's *Philosophy of Right*," he elaborated his concept and program of criticism and pointed to the proletariat as the real social force destined to carry out criticism's verdict by overthrowing the existing order. In *The Holy Family: A Critique of Critical Criticism* (1845), Marx and Engels proclaimed their break with the Young Hegelian group. But no break with the idea of *Kritik* was intended.

In addition, as we have seen, Marx learned from Feuerbach a specific technique of critical thought involving the use of Hegel. By means of this technique Feuerbach had produced a criticism of religion as a phenomenon of human self-alienation. Taking up the critical enterprise in this sense, Marx produced, first, a criticism of the state as a phenomenon of human self-alienation, and then, in his

8. I am referring to Erich Fromm's *Man for Himself* (New York: Holt, Rinehart & Winston, 1947). See also his autobiographical study, *Beyond the Chains of Illusion: My Encounter with Marx and Freud* (New York: Simon & Schuster, 1962). For a discussion of Marx from an existentialist viewpoint, see F. H. Heinemann, *Existentialism and the Modern Predicament* (New York: Harper & Row, 1958).

manuscripts of 1844, the beginnings of what he called a "criticism of political economy." Engels, who acquired a deep interest in economics still earlier through working in his father's firm and being exposed to economic realities at the site of its English branch in Manchester, preceded Marx in undertaking a criticism of political economy. He produced an essay, "Outlines of a Critique of Political Economy," which appeared, along with Marx's essays on the Jewish question and the Hegelian *Philosophy of Right*, in the *Deutsch-Französische Jahrbücher* of 1844. Marx's references to this essay in the prefaces to his 1844 manuscripts and A *Contribution to the Critique of Political Economy* testify to the influence that it had upon him at the time it appeared.

"This political economy or science of enrichment born of the merchants' mutual envy and greed," wrote Engels at the beginning of his 1844 essay, "bears on its brow the mark of the most loathsome selfishness." The essay addressed itself to this argument through a systematic analysis of the categories of the "science of enrichment." In conclusion Engels referred to the factory system and announced his future intention to "expound in detail the despicable immorality of this system, and to expose mercilessly the economist's hypocrisy which here appears in all its glitter."[9] The projected work did not materialize, but Engels did publish in 1845, based on his English observations, *The Condition of the Working Class in England in 1844*. Strictly descriptive though this work was, it was obviously concerned with exposing the "despicable immorality of this system."[1] It was a work of *Kritik*.

Elsewhere I have suggested that Marx was a writer who spent the greater part of his life writing one important book under a number of different titles. In the 1844 manuscripts he set out to produce a *Kritik* of political economy, seeking to demonstrate, in terms of the categories of political economy, man's alienation as a worker in bourgeois society. Having achieved in these papers a sketch of his entire world-view, he set the manuscripts aside but in a few years time returned to the task he had posed for himself. *Wage Labour and Capital*, written in 1847, was a sort of prospectus for the full-scale *Kritik* of political economy that he was determined to write. In 1859 he published a not very successful beginning of the work under the title A *Contribution to the Critique of Political Economy*. Meanwhile, in 1857–58 he had written a huge new set of manuscripts that would one day be published under the

9. Karl Marx, *The Economic and Philosophic Manuscripts of 1844*, edited by Dirk J. Struik (New York: International Publishers, 1964), pp. 197, 226. Engels' "Outlines of a Critique of Political Economy" appears here as an appendix.

1. See in this connection the selection included here under the title "Working-Class Manchester" (pp. 579–585, below).

title *Fundamentals of the Critique of Political Economy*.[2] When he finally completed the work and published it in 1867 under the title of *Capital*, he subtitled it *Critique of Political Economy*. In short, *Capital* was the form in which Marx finally finished the book on the criticism of political economy that he had originally undertaken in his manuscripts of 1844.

The idea of *Kritik* is, then, a great unifying theme running through the writings of classical Marxism, and a key to the continuity of the thought of Marx and Engels from their youthful philosophical writings to the productions of their mature years. Although they devoted a great deal of energy to economic analysis and contributed writings—especially *Capital*—that constitute a significant and influential chapter in economic thought, they did so not as political economists in the ordinary sense but as *critics* of political economy. As such they wrote from a position that we can variously describe as moral, normative, or philosophical. It would be a great mistake, therefore, to think of the writings gathered in Part II of this volume as belonging to a compartment called "Marxian economics," separate from the remainder of their thought. These writings are in the mainstream of their thought about society and history, their revolutionary outlook, and their socialism. The serious student of Marx must get to know *Capital* as Marx's major book about man. As the attentive reader of these pages will discover, it is the book, too, into which he poured his views on a miscellany of topics of general interest, such as education, the family and its future, the implications of modern technological development, and so on.

For all its tortuous complexity and abstruseness of argument, *Capital* (I refer here to Volume One) is fairly simple in basic theme and design. It could be viewed as an eight-hundred-page elaboration of the passage from *The Holy Family*[3] speaking of private property and the proletariat as opposites forming an antagonistic "whole" that is moving toward its own ultimate dissolution because of private property's inherent tendency to generate more and more proletariat, which in turn is "conscious of itself as a dehumanization and hence abolishes itself." In *Capital* the antagonistic "whole" is presented as wage labour (*Lohnarbeit*) or, alternatively, as the capital-labour relationship—this being the relationship of production constitutive of capitalism itself as a mode of

---

2. *Grundrisse der Kritik der politischen Ökonomie* (Moscow, 1939–41). The full text in English is available in Karl Marx, *Grundrisse: Foundations of the Critique of Political Economy*, translated by Martin Nicolaus (New York: Vintage Books, 1973). (See below, pp. 221–293, for selections.)

3. See the selection entitled "Alienation and Social Classes," below.

production.[4] For Marx this relationship of production is the "basis" of bourgeois society, over which arises the institutional and ideological "superstructure." The real subject of the book, in his mind, is bourgeois society.

In wage labour, the argument runs, the worker sells to the capitalist employer the only commodity that he possesses, his labour power, and receives in recompense a wage reflecting this commodity's "value." Since, on Marx's assumptions about value, the value of any commodity is equivalent to the amount of average necessary labour time incorporated in it, the value of one day's labour power as a commodity is the monetary equivalent of the amount of resources required to keep the worker alive and at work and able to reproduce his kind, i.e., it is a subsistence wage. But when put to use by the capitalist for a day, this labour power is capable, Marx reasons, of producing a certain amount of value over and above its own value. This Marx calls "surplus value" (*Mehrwert*), and he characterizes capitalism as a system geared to the maximizing of surplus value through intense—and ever-intensifying—exploitation of labour power to the utmost extent sufferable by "that repellent yet elastic natural barrier, man." Further, surplus value has two forms. "Absolute surplus value," meaning the excess of new value created in a day over the value of the labour power bought by the capitalist, can be increased by lengthening the working day itself. "Relative surplus value," arising out of improvements in technology that reduce the necessary labour time invested in labour power, can be obtained by mechanization of production processes and therewith the degree of specialization in the factory, so that the worker becomes a detail labourer performing ever more minute and monotonous operations. The capitalists are driven willy-nilly by the imperatives of their situation to accumulate capital by increasing surplus value along both these lines, so that "in proportion as capital accumulates, the lot of the labourer, be his payment high or low, must grow worse." The "absolute general law of capitalist accumulation," as Marx christens it, "establishes an accumulation of misery, corresponding with accumulation of capital. Accumulation of wealth at one pole is, therefore, at the same time accumulation of misery, agony of toil, slavery, ignorance, brutality, mental degradation, at the opposite pole. . . ." This conclusion of the argument points to the violent breakdown of the "whole" that Marx heralds toward the end of the book, where he speaks of the coming "expropriation of a few usurpers by the mass of the people."

Capital was written by an angry man, and one can hardly read it without sensing the indignation that he felt in the face of the phe-

4. On Marx's use of the terms "mode of production" and "relations of production," see Robert C. Tucker, *The Marxian Revolutionary Idea* (New York: W. W. Norton, 1969), chapter 1.

nomena with which he was concerned. The great *Kritik* of political
economy is a work of analysis and description, but also of moral
condemnation and protest. The word "alienation" may be missing,
but the theme is not.[5] *Capital*'s proletarian is still *The Holy Family*'s "dehumanization which is conscious of itself as a dehumanization and hence abolishes itself." What was called "alienated
labour" in the manuscripts of 1844 appears here simply as "wage
labour." Now the object of study is subjected to endless analysis in
terms of the labour theory of value and to lavish documentation
out of the annals of British factory inspectors' reports, but it is the
same object, and the viewpoint taken toward it is also the same.

The basis of the moral condemnation of wage labour is not that
the wages are too low,[6] but that wage labour by its very nature
dehumanizes man. This means, for Marx, that it defeats his natural
human urge toward spontaneous productive activity, converts his
free creativity into forced labour and drudgery, and frustrates his
human need for a variety of occupations. The latter theme—the
division of labour or occupational specialization as an evil—is a salient one in *Capital*; and the history of the evolution of the modern
factory system that Marx gives in Part IV of the book is not presented out of an interest in economic history per se but as a means
of describing the horrifying extremes that the division of labour
attains under the "machinofacture" developed during the Industrial
Revolution. As he expresses his view here, ". . . constant labour of
one uniform kind disturbs the intensity and flow of a man's animal
spirits, which find recreation and delight in mere change of activity." That this was Engels' view as well, and more generally that
the condemnation of division of labour as an evil belongs to the
core of classical Marxism, is well illustrated in the section of
Engels' *Anti-Dühring* that has been included in the present volume
under the heading "On the Division of Labour in Production."

In their later writings, then, Marx and Engels are still writing
from the standpoint summed up in Marx's 1844 manuscripts as
"positive humanism." They are writing on behalf of a socialism
that means to them not a new system of distribution (though that,
too, they are sure, will come about) but a new mode of productive
activity that is to be achieved through the revolutionary liberation

5. Dirk J. Struik has pointed out that
Marx does not completely renounce the
term "alienation" in his later economic
writings. It makes a reappearance in
the *Grundrisse* and in the following
passage from *Capital*, Vol. III, Part I,
chapter 5, section 1: "The relations of
capital conceal indeed the inner connection (of the facts) in the complete indifference, exteriorization and alienation in which it places the worker in
relation to the conditions of the realization of his own labour" (*The Economic and Philosophic Manuscripts of
1844*, p. 235).
6. For Marx's scorn of the distributive
orientation in socialist thought, see
particularly his comments in *The Critique of the Gotha Program*, pp.
528–532, below. On the problem of distributive justice in Marx, see Tucker,
The Marxian Revolutionary Idea,
chapter 2.

of human productiveness from the bonds of factory toil for the accumulation of "surplus value." They advanced no particular name for this new mode of production, but described it in various places as the free activity of human beings producing in cooperative association. The socialization of the means of production was not, on this view, the essence of socialism or communism, but only its precondition.

III

Although born of German philosophy, Marxism from the beginning eschewed philosophy's contemplative attitude toward the world and adopted as its own the standpoint of the "unity of theory and practice." In the familiar words of Marx's eleventh thesis on Feuerbach, "The philosophers have only *interpreted* the world, in various ways; the point is to *change* it." Apart from being a critical comment on former philosophy, this statement had a biographical meaning. Not content with theorizing about a revolution in the abstract, Marx and Engels concerned themselves deeply with the strategy and tactics of a socialist revolution, the organizing of revolutionary activity, the politics of world-change. In the materials gathered in Part III of this volume, and also in the political journalism represented in Part IV, we see the reflection of this side of their activity.

In Marx's and Engels' own minds, it should be added, there was no clear demarcation line between their theoretical work and their practical and organizing activities. For various reasons they would hardly have agreed with the statement of their future Russian disciple, Lenin, that "without a revolutionary theory there can be no revolutionary movement."[7] They thought of a revolutionary movement as a spontaneous phenomenon of mass rebelliousness generated by conditions of existence that people find intolerable, hence not something dependent on a revolutionary theory for its emergence. Both *The German Ideology* and the *Communist Manifesto* offer unequivocal testimony on this point. But on the other hand, Marx and Engels believed that a correct revolutionary theory could powerfully *assist* a revolutionary movement by providing explanations and orienting its members to the movement's proper ends and means. Their own theorizing appeared to them an historic case in point. The Marxist theory was simply the contemporary proletarian revolutionary movement—an ongoing or incipient phenomenon in every industrial society—come to full programmatic consciousness.

7. *What Is to Be Done?*, in *The Lenin Anthology*, ed. Robert C. Tucker (New York: W. W. Norton, 1975), p. 19. By "movement" in this context Lenin meant an organized political movement led by a political party.

It was the prospectus of the revolutionary process taking place in bourgeois society, explaining its underlying causes and foretelling its preordained future course and outcome. By their theorizing as such, therefore, they were actively influencing historical events. Such, at any rate, was their view.

An obvious implication of this reasoning was that everything possible should be done to disseminate knowledge of the Marxist revolutionary theory and secure its acceptance by the organized workers' movement. The *Communist Manifesto* is an outstanding example of such effort. Marx's powerful polemical tract on *The Civil War in France*, an account of the Paris Commune and its suppression, may also be seen in this light. To explain the Paris Revolution of September, 1870–May, 1871, according to the canons of Marxist theory and assess its historic meaning in Marxist terms was to show Marxism's cogency as a mode of understanding contemporary historical reality and thereby to enhance its influence on educated minds. So successful was the pamphlet in achieving this purpose that one later historian of the socialist movement dates the widespread impact of Marxism from that time.[8] Much of the political journalism of Marx and Engels appears to have had, at least in part, a similar motivation. They propagated Marxism by seeking to demonstrate its applicability to current events. In *The Eighteenth Brumaire of Louis Bonaparte*, to take a particularly important example, Marx recounted the recent political history of France in a Marxist frame of reference. The result in this instance, as in some others, was a work of journalism that has taken its place also as a classic of Marxist historiography.

The nineteenth century was a birth-time of socialist theories and programs. Since Marxism at mid-century was only one of numerous available versions of socialist thought, its propagation by Marx and Engels was a highly competitive enterprise. In *The German Ideology* they attacked and ridiculed the doctrines of their fellow German "true socialists." A year later, in 1847, Marx published *The Poverty of Philosophy*, a polemic against the theories of the French socialist and anarchist thinker Pierre Joseph Proudhon. In the ensuing decades he and Engels waged a long-drawn-out struggle against Proudhonism and generally against the anarchist persuasion

8. "The work of Marx on the Civil War of 1871 has an extraordinary historical significance: for by this bold step Marx annexed the memory of the Commune. It is only since then that Marxism has possessed a revolutionary tradition in the eyes of mankind. By 1870 Marx had already acquired a reputation as an outstanding theoretician of the labour motivement, but the general public knew nothing of the political and revolutionary activity of the Marxists. . . . It is only since 1871 that Marxism has been clearly associated with the labour revolution. . . . In this manner Marx provided an important tradition for the future movements of the working class, and he placed his own doctrines in the centre of these movements" (Arthur Rosenberg, *Democracy and Socialism* [Boston: Beacon Press, 1965], pp. 204–205).

in socialism, one of whose leading proponents in the later nineteenth century was the Russian revolutionary Mikhail Bakunin.
Paradoxically, the Paris Commune of 1871 was, in its decentraliz-
ing measures, a victory of the Proudhonian influence, but this in no
way inhibited Marx and Engels from hailing the Commune as a
harbinger of the realization of the Marxist theory of history and
hence claiming it for Marxism.[9] Another arena of their competitive
struggle for the dominance of the Marxist theory was German
working-class politics, in which a prominent part was played by the
gifted political leader Ferdinand Lassalle. Their fight against Lassallean doctrinal influences continued unabated after Lassalle's death
in 1864 and finally was immortalized in a set of notes by Marx that
was published posthumously under the title *Critique of the Gotha
Program* and has since taken its place as one of Marxism's major
programmatic statements.

The International Working Men's Association, founded in
London in 1864 by representatives of the English, French,
German, and Italian workers as an international coordinating body
for the working-class movements of these and other countries,
offered an important forum for the propagation of Marxism.
Although he was present at the founding meeting of the association, now better known as the First International, Marx was not
one of its original organizers. Subsequently, however, he played a
leading part in its affairs. In drafting the rules of the association, he
prefaced them with an "Inaugural Address" written in his charac-
teristically forceful and incisive manner. Although he had to hold
the revolutionary rhetoric in check because of constraints arising
from the diverse membership of this loose federation of worker
groups from different countries, he managed to formulate the
Address in the spirit of Marxist doctrine and make of it a kind of
successor-document to the *Communist Manifesto*. Later, when the
fall of the Paris Commune made European revolutionary prospects
and hence those of the International appear dim for the time being,
Marx was concerned lest Bakunin and the anarchists acquire a decisive influence in the association. He therefore proposed, at its
Hague Congress in 1872, that the headquarters be moved to New
York. The ensuing transfer to America signaled the International's
demise.

Marxism was not a party doctrine in its inception, nor did Marx
and Engels originally envisage it as the formal ideology of a political party. The Communist League, on whose behalf they wrote the
Communist Manifesto, was not a political party but only a group
of a few hundred German journeymen workers living in Paris, Brus-

9. See Rosenberg, *Democracy and So-
cialism*, pp. 202–205, for further parti-   culars and a discussion of this issue.

sels, and London. In the *Manifesto*, moreover, Marx and Engels explicitly disclaimed the notion that the communists (i.e., the Marxists) should form themselves into a separate party, or that they should "set up any sectarian principles of their own, by which to shape and mould the proletarian movement." The communists, they went on, were simply the most consistently radical representatives of the proletarian movement and those with clear theoretical understanding of its conditions and aims. In later years, however, Marx and Engels shifted their ground in response to the rise of working-class political parties in a number of European countries, Germany in particular. A General German Workers' Society arose in 1863 under Lassalle. Three years later a German Social Democratic Workers' Party was founded under the leadership of Wilhelm Liebknecht, a longtime follower of Marx. The merger of the two groups in 1875 established the German Social Democrats as the leading working-class political party of Western Europe, with Marxist socialism as its ideology; and similar parties emerged in Italy, Austria, France, and elsewhere. Although the name "Social Democrat" did not please them,[1] Marx and Engels welcomed the rise of socialist working-class parties professing Marxism as their platform.

The irony of this development was that Marxism's very success in the struggle for supremacy in working-class politics of the later nineteenth century endangered what Lenin later called its "revolutionary soul." Although officially dedicated to Marxist principles of the revolutionary transformation of society, the Social Democratic parties were not really very radical. In some instances, such as in Germany, they were associated with organized trade union movements whose aims were basically reformist. Finally, increasing electoral success gave them both a place and a stake in the existing order, and encouraged the tendency of the party leaderships to look to the ballot box and the gradual conquest of political power by peaceful parliamentary means as the highroad to a socialist reshaping of society. The concern this aroused in Marx and Engels is clearly shown in their "Circular Letter" of September 17–18, 1879, to Bebel, Liebknecht, and other German Social Democratic leaders.

---

1. When informed in 1864 that the newspaper of the General German Workers' Society would be called *The Social Democrat,* Engels wrote to Marx: "What a disgusting title—*The Social Democrat!* Why don't those fellows frankly call the thing: *The Proletarian?*" Marx answered: "*Social Democrat* is a bad title. Yet one shouldn't immediately use the best title for something which may turn out to be a failure" (Rosenberg, *Democracy and Socialism,* p. 162). A Russian Social Democratic Workers' Party came into existence in 1898. In 1917, out of disgust with the behavior of the Social Democratic leaders of various countries who had supported their governments in World War I in contravention of Marxist internationalism, Lenin persuaded his Bolshevik branch of the Russian Social Democratic Party to change its name to "Communist Party."

It castigated the spirit of reformism spreading in the German party and insisted upon fidelity to the revolutionary class struggle as the only possible means of freeing the working classes.

It is a fact, however, that without renouncing his basic revolutionism and the related belief that the socialist revolution would in most countries have to take place by force, Marx envisaged the possibility of a nonviolent path to socialism in certain countries, like America and Britain, whose political institutions made radical change by democratic means conceivable. A very clear statement to this effect was made in a speech in Amsterdam in 1872.[2] In *The State and Revolution* (1917) Lenin contended that conditions in those countries had so changed in the interim that a Marxist could no longer recognize such potential exceptionalism. Meanwhile, the leading Social Democratic Marxist theorist, Karl Kautsky, held to and expanded upon Marx's position, and the split between Communist (i.e., Marxist-Leninist) and Social Democratic Marxism in the twentieth century turned largely on this issue. Much later, in 1956, Soviet Marxism under Nikita Khrushchev adopted a modified form of Marx's old position by positing that in certain (especially underdeveloped) countries with powerful Communist parties, socialist revolution could take place by a "peaceful parliamentary path."[3] Among revolutionaries and theorists of revolution, the question of the role of violence in social revolution remains controversial to this day.

Marx died in 1883 and Engels survived him by twelve years during which the German Social Democrats continued their advance at the polls. In an essay published in 1895 that proved to be his own valedictory to the Social Democratic movement,[4] Engels seemed to soften the Circular Letter's insistence on revolutionary class struggle as the only acceptable political strategy for a Marxist party. At any rate, he allowed that classic street-fighting on the barricades had largely been rendered obsolete by technological improvements favoring the military, and hailed the German Social Democrats' two million voters as "the decisive 'shock force' of the international proletarian army." But on close reading, particularly after restoration of those passages excised from the essay by the editors when it was originally published in 1895, Engels' concluding discourse on tactics turns out to be by no means an endorsement of Social Democratic reformism. His commitment to the Marxian

2. See the text of this speech. below.
3. For Lenin's argument see *The State and Revolution* in *The Lenin Anthology*, ed. Robert C. Tucker (New York: W. W. Norton, 1975), p. 337. For Kautsky's position and the Lenin-Kautsky conflict, see Karl Kautsky, *The Dictatorship of the Proletariat* (Ann Arbor: University of Michigan Press, 1964), and Tucker, *The Marxian Revolutionary Idea*, chapter 3. Soviet Marxism's espousal of the concept of a peaceful path is analyzed in chapter 6 of the latter work.
4. Engels, "The Tactics of Social Democracy," below.

revolutionary idea held firm to the end. For the older Engels, no less than for the younger Marx, the point was to change the world radically.

IV

The meetings between Marx and Engels in Paris in August, 1844, and in Brussels in April, 1845, inaugurated a partnership that continued unbroken to Marx's death nearly forty years after. Indeed, it continued beyond that time, for Engels devoted his final years to carrying forward the work on which he and his friend had been engaged together for so long. Intellectual history offers few if any comparable examples of lifelong collaboration between innovative minds. How shall we assess the relative weight of their contributions?

In a footnote to an essay of 1886, Engels answered this question as follows:

I cannot deny that both before and during my forty years' collaboration with Marx I had a certain independent share in laying the foundations of the theory, and more particularly in its elaboration. But the greater part of its leading basic principles, especially in the realm of economics and history, belong to Marx. What I contributed—at any rate with the exception of my work in a few special fields—Marx could very well have done without me. What Marx accomplished I would not have achieved. Marx stood higher, saw further, and took a wider and quicker view than all the rest of us. Marx was a genius; we others were at best talented. Without him the theory would not be by far what it is today. It therefore rightly bears his name.[5]

This generous tribute rightly recognized that Marx's mind was the forge of the system. True, Engels during his first sojourn in Manchester had independently and somewhat earlier than Marx come to the view that economics is the decisively important force in history, and his "Outlines of a Critique of Political Economy" had helped to inspire Marx's first attempt at such a critique. Yet Marxism as a transformed Hegelianism, a theory of history in the grand style, was essentially, as we have seen, Marx's creation. He was the seer and system-builder in relation to whom the merely talented Engels was bound to play a subordinate part.

But after acknowledging this, it must also be said that Engels was misleadingly modest concerning his own contributions. The Marx-Engels correspondence reflects a two-way process of collaboration in which Engels gave theoretical assistance to Marx—for

5. Engels, *Ludwig Feuerbach and the End of Classical German Philosophy*, p. 386.

example, on various problems encountered in the writing of *Capital*—as well as vice versa. Engels' independent contributions were substantial too, both in the works that he and Marx wrote jointly and in some that he produced on his own. One of the special fields of his expertise was military affairs and strategy. Another was natural science, and his writings on this subject—including the papers posthumously published under the title *Dialectics of Nature*—gave the impetus to the rise of "dialectical materialism," as a Marxist teaching about nature. Whether one feels that Marxism was enriched or vulgarized by the latter development, its importance is undeniable. Still another area of Engels' work was primitive society. He carried out Marx's unfulfilled plan of writing a treatise based upon the American anthropologist Lewis Henry Morgan's *Ancient Society*. The resulting work on *The Origin of the Family, Private Property, and the State*[6] provided Marxism with an anthropology, including a theory and history of the family and a viewpoint on the role of women in society.

As the writings gathered in Part V of this volume show, moreover, one of Engels' greatest services consisted in the systematizing and popularizing of Marxism. Marx was the great system-builder, yet he never managed in the writings published during his lifetime to set forth the fundamentals of the system in easily understandable terms in an essay or short book; *Capital* was not bedtime reading for the masses. Engels made good this deficiency. He lacked the supremely trenchant style of Marx, who wrote as though his pen were dipped in molten anger. But Engels' beautifully clear and free-flowing prose was ideally suited to the popularizing work to which he applied himself. In a number of letters on historical materialism[7] he attempted to clarify the economic interpretation of history and deal with certain questions that had arisen concerning it. His *Anti-Dühring* gave a running exposition of Marxism in the course of a polemic against one of its critics, and the portion of it published in 1880 under the title *Socialism: Utopian and Scientific* probably did more than any other single book to disseminate knowledge of Marxism. Engels even undertook to bring *Capital* to the wide public by writing nine different reviews of it, seven of which achieved publication at the time.

Paraphrasing Engels, one could say that without him Marxism would not be by far what it became. His gifts and Marx's were in large measure complementary. Classical Marxism is an amalgam in which Engels' work constitutes an essential and inalienable part.

Note on Texts and Terminology

The strange publishing history of Marx's writings was foreshadowed by their author when, late in his life, someone asked about his complete works. "They would first have to be written," he is said to have replied. Marx must have had in mind that much of what he had produced was still in unfinished manuscript and that his grand project of a multi-volume work, of which *Capital* would be only one part, was unlikely ever to be realized.[1] As it turned out, he did not live even to prepare Volumes Two and Three of *Capital* for publication.

In 1894, after putting out Volume Three of *Capital*, Engels began making arrangements for a complete edition of Marx's works and his own. But this project foundered upon his death in the following year, after which his papers and Marx's came into the possession of the German Social Democratic Party (SPD). For a long time, only limited efforts at publication were made. In 1902 Franz Mehring put out a collection of the earlier writings (1841–50), *Aus dem literarischen Nachlass von K. Marx, F. Engels und F. Lassalle* (Out of the Literary Legacy of Marx, Engels and Lassalle). Between 1905 and 1910 Marx's multi-volume *Theories of Surplus Value* came out under the editorship of Karl Kautsky. A heavily (and tendentiously) edited four volumes of correspondence between Marx and Engels appeared in 1913.

But systematic full-scale publication of their writings began only after the creation in 1921, under Lenin's personal sponsorship, of the Marx-Engels Institute in Moscow. The Institute had the financial backing of the Soviet Communist Party and, in its first decade, the able, dedicated direction of David B. Riazanov. Between 1923 and 1927 the Institute obtained photocopies of the manuscripts and correspondence of Marx and Engels in the SPD's archives, bought up manuscripts and letters owned by various individuals, and gathered early editions of individual works.[2] An institution of comparable importance, the International Institute of Social His-

---

1. For one of Marx's versions of the grand project, see the *Grundrisse*, below, p. 244. The successive versions are discussed by Joseph J. O'Malley in "Marx's 'Economics' and Hegel's *Philosophy of Right*: An Essay on Marx's Hegelianism," *Political Studies*, vol. XXIV, no. 1 (March 1976), pp. 48 ff.

2. For this and other particulars about the Institute I have drawn upon E. A. Stepanova, "O sobiranii i nauchnoi publikatsii v SSSR literaturnogo nasledstva osnovopolozhnikov marksizma," in *Iz istorii marksizma* (Moscow: Gospolitizdat, 1961), pp. 6–59.

tory, was founded in Amsterdam in 1935 and became the repository of the SPD's archives, which were endangered after the Nazis took power in Germany in 1933.

A first attempt at a full collection was the Marx-Engels Institute's three volumes, published between 1927 and 1932, Marx and Engels, *Historisch-Kritische Gesamtausgabe* (Historical-Critical Collected Works, generally known as *MEGA*). A fuller edition was published in Russian between 1928 and 1946, in thirty-four volumes: Marx and Engels, *Sochineniia* (Works). In the mid-1950's the Institute of Marxism-Leninism (as the Marx-Engels Institute had been renamed) commenced publication of a new, more complete edition in both German and Russian. The German edition is Marx and Engels, *Werke (Works)*, 41 volumes (Berlin; Dietz Verlag, 1957–68). But this edition is still far from complete. The first seven volumes of the English translation of it, covering the period up to and including 1848, are now (1977) available in Marx and Engels, *Collected Works* (Moscow: Progress Publishers; New York: International Publishers; London: Lawrence & Wishart). Multi-volume collections in English are presently coming out in the Marx Library series (New York; Vintage Books) and the Karl Marx Library series (New York: McGraw-Hill). Most of the principal writings of Marx and Engels are also available in individual editions in English. Still, the literary legacy is not yet entirely an open book. Thus the first full collection of the Marx-Engels correspondence for the New York *Daily Tribune* is only now coming out in English: Karl Marx and Friedrich Engels, *The Collected Writings in the New York "Daily Tribune,"* ed. T. Ferguson and S. J. O'Neil (New York: Urizen, 1977).

Meanwhile, a monumental effort at a truly complete edition in one hundred volumes—completion projected for the year 2000—has been announced as a collaborative project of the Moscow and East Berlin institutes of Marxism-Leninism. This new *MEGA*—its title is Marx and Engels, *Gesamtausgabe*—is to include all of Marx's still unpublished notebooks, the preparatory materials for *Capital*, even his miscellaneous jottings.[3]

Riazanov is said to have remarked that Marx had to be translated twice: first from his hard-to-decipher handwriting into legible German, and then from German into Russian. Translators of Marx from German into other languages have had to resolve some special problems, arising in part from Marx's use of Hegelian philosophical terminology. He made particularly heavy use of this terminology in his early writings, but it did not disappear from his later ones and those of Engels.

3. I am indebted to Professor Joseph J. O'Malley for this information.

Pervasive in the "original Marxism" of Marx's *Economic and Philosophic Manuscripts of 1844*, and recurrent in such later writings as the *Grundrisse* and even *Capital*, is the term *Entfremdung*, for which some translators have used "alienation" and others "estrangement." Correspondingly, Marx's *Selbstentfremdung* becomes either "self-alienation" or "self-estrangement." In the translation of the 1844 manuscripts used here, Martin Milligan has used "estrangement" and "self-estrangement." Thus the title of the famous section *Die entfremdete Arbeit* is rendered as "Estranged Labour."

What becomes estranged from man, notably the product of his labor and the surrounding material world as the aggregate of such products, must first be created. The process of creation is called by Marx *Entäusserung*, which is sometimes translated as "alienation" (as by Milligan in the 1844 manuscripts below), and sometimes, more literally, as "objectification." The latter translation may cause confusion because Marx also employs the term *Vergegenständlichung*, which quite literally means (and is translated) "objectification."

Another Hegelianism that Marx took over and that is central to an understanding of his thought—and that causes problems for the translator—is *Aufhebung* (from the verb *aufheben*), variously rendered in different translations (or even the same one) as "abolition," "annulment," "supercession," and "transcendence." Marx himself wrote "suspension" in a passage penned in English in the *Grundrisse*.[4]

The source of the problem is the richness and specificity of the concept to which the word is attached. For Hegel, *Aufhebung* is the culminating movement in a dialectical process that proceeds from an initial stage of affirmation or creation through a subsequent negation to a final synthesis via "negation of the negation," the latter being the nub of the dialectic. Hence Hegel emphasizes that the term has the twofold connotation of elimination and preservation: what undergoes *Aufhebung* is negated without being nullified. It is negated in its negative aspect but, thus transformed, continues to exist.[5] The same, *mutatis mutandis*, holds for Marx. Thus in the 1844 manuscripts he speaks of the future communist revolution as the *Aufhebung* of private property and of man's self-estrangement. Through its revolutionary appropriation by the proletarians, which Marx (at the close of *Capital*, Volume One, calls the "negation of the negation") private property is annuled or abolished *qua* private

---

4. See below, pp. 291–292, and Martin Nicolaus' discussion of the point in his Foreword to the full translation (Karl Marx, *Grundrisse: Foundations of the Critique of Political Economy* [New York: Vintage Books, 1973], p. 32).

5. The meaning of *Aufhebung* in the context of Hegel's philosophy of spirit is explicated in Robert C. Tucker, *Philosophy and Myth in Karl Marx* (New York: 1972), pp. 51–52, 59–60.

xlii · *Note on Texts and Terminology*

property, but preserved in a—for Marx—higher form: the socialized means of production. Because the term has this twofold meaning, some translators vary the translation according to context, as the negative or positive connotation seems uppermost. Milligan, for example, in his translation of the 1844 manuscripts, translates *Aufhebung* in one sentence as "transcendence" (of man's self-estrangement) and in another as "annulment" (of the state) (see p. 84, below).

One other term met very often in Marx yet often misunderstood—although not because of difficulty of translation—is "mode of production" (*Weise der Produktion,* alternatively *Produktionsweise*). One might easily suppose that it refers to instruments of production (Marx calls these *Produktionsmittels*) or state of technology, but such is not the case. Marx, to begin with, treats all forms of human activity under the aspect of production. So, in the 1844 manuscripts (see p. 85, below) he says that the family, state, law, morality, science, and art are so many *Weisen der Produktion*. And when he refers to "mode of production" in an economic context, he means a given way of carrying on production *as a social activity*—conditioned in every case, it is true, by a prevailing set of the means of production or state of technology. The mode of production is thus a form of productive activity, historically a form of labor, e.g., serf labor under feudalism or wage labor under capitalism. Marx's term for the new mode of production which he envisages arising on the yonder side of history, after the worldwide proletarian revolution, is "associated" production. "Labor" will have been abolished (see *The German Ideology,* below, p. 193), not in the sense that individuals will sink into indolent inactivity, but that their productive activities will take on the character of free creative self-expression not performed for wages or acquisitive purposes. Productive activity, having undergone *Aufhebung* as labor, will continue in a new mode.

As with any important thinker whose writings get translated, Marx presents not only particular translating problems but a more general issue: to what extent should felicity of expression be sought at the expense of closeness to the original text? There is no ideal solution; some compromise is the natural outcome. Yet when problems of exegesis are both difficult and stubbornly controversial, as here, there is something to be said for the position taken by Martin Nicolaus when he says of his translation of Marx's *Grundrisse* that it "aims at a tight fit to the original, including the roughness of grammar etc. To attempt to 'polish' this text would have been to tamper with an essential part of its significance." That applies with special force to a work that Marx left in raw manuscript. But then much of what he wrote finally came to light in that form.

The Early Marx

Marx on the History of His Opinions

This is the preface to Marx's book A *Contribution to the Critique of Political Economy*, first published in 1859. The passage setting forth the materialist conception of history—one of the few general statements of the theory that Marx gave in his middle and later years—is the *locus classicus* of historical materialism. But the preface is also important as an account by Marx himself of the formative period of Marxism. As such it forms an appropriate introduction to the writings of 1837–1846 gathered here in Part I. The "criticism of post-Hegelian philosophy" which he mentions in the third-to-last paragraph is a reference to his work *The German Ideology*, written jointly with Engels.

---

* * * I am omitting a general introduction which I had jotted down because on closer reflection any anticipation of results still to be proved appears to me to be disturbing, and the reader who on the whole desires to follow me must be resolved to ascend from the particular to the general. A few indications concerning the course of my own politico-economic studies may, on the other hand, appear in place here.

I was taking up law, which discipline, however, I only pursued as a subordinate subject along with philosophy and history. In the year 1842–44, as editor of the *Rheinische Zeitung*,[1] I experienced for the first time the embarrassment of having to take part in discussions on so-called material interests. The proceedings of the Rhenish Landtag on thefts of wood and parcelling of landed property, the official polemic which Herr von Schaper, then *Oberprasident* of the Rhine Province, opened against the *Rheinische Zeitung* on the conditions of the Moselle peasantry, and finally debates on free trade and protective tariffs provided the first occasions for occupying myself with economic questions. On the other hand, at that time when the good will "to go further" greatly outweighed knowledge of the subject, a philosophically weakly tinged echo of French socialism and communism made itself audible in the *Rheinische Zeitung*. I declared myself against this amateurism, but

1. *Rheinische Zeitung* (*Rhenish Gazette*): A daily radical newspaper published in Cologne in 1842–43; from October 15, 1842, to March 18, 1843, its editor was Marx.

3

frankly confessed at the same time in a controversy with the *All-gemeine Augsburger Zeitung*[2] that my previous studies did not permit me even to venture any judgement on the content of the French tendencies. Instead, I eagerly seized on the illusion of the managers of the *Rheinische Zeitung,* who thought that by a weaker attitude on the part of the paper they could secure a remission of the death sentence passed upon it, to withdraw from the public stage into the study.

The first work which I undertook for a solution of the doubts which assailed me was a critical review of the Hegelian philosophy of right, a work the introduction to which appeared in 1844 in the *Deutsch-Französische Jahrbücher,*[3] published in Paris. My investigation led to the result that legal relations as well as forms of state are to be grasped neither from themselves nor from the so-called general development of the human mind, but rather have their roots in the material conditions of life, the sum total of which Hegel, following the example of the Englishmen and Frenchmen of the eighteenth century, combines under the name of "civil society," that, however, the anatomy of civil society is to be sought in political economy. The investigation of the latter, which I began in Paris, I continued in Brussels, whither I had emigrated in consequence of an expulsion order of M. Guizot. The general result at which I arrived and which, once won, served as a guiding thread for my studies, can be briefly formulated as follows: In the social production of their life, men enter into definite relations that are indispensable and independent of their will, relations of production which correspond to a definite stage of development of their material productive forces. The sum total of these relations of production constitutes the economic structure of society, the real foundation, on which rises a legal and political superstructure and to which correspond definite forms of social consciousness. The mode of production of material life conditions the social, political and intellectual life process in general. It is not the consciousness of men that determines their being, but, on the contrary, their social being that determines their consciousness. At a certain stage of their development, the material productive forces of society come in conflict with the existing relations of production, or—what is but a legal expression for the same thing—with the property relations within which they have been at work hitherto. From forms of development of the productive forces these relations turn into their

2. Marx has in mind his article, "Der Kommunismus und die *Augsburger All-gemeine Zeitung*" (Communism and the *Augsburg General Journal*), *Marx-Engels Gesamtausgabe,* Abt. I, B. I, Halbband I, Frankfurt am Main, 1927, S. 260–65.

3. *Deutsch-Französische Jahrbücher* (*German-French Annals*): Organ of revolutionary and communist propaganda, published by Marx in Paris in 1844.

fetters. Then begins an epoch of social revolution. With the change of the economic foundation the entire immense superstructure is more or less rapidly transformed. In considering such transformations a distinction should always be made between the material transformation of the economic conditions of production, which can be determined with the precision of natural science, and the legal, political, religious, aesthetic or philosophic—in short, ideological forms in which men become conscious of this conflict and fight it out. Just as our opinion of an individual is not based on what he thinks of himself, so can we not judge of such a period of transformation by its own consciousness; on the contrary, this consciousness must be explained rather from the contradictions of material life, from the existing conflict between the social productive forces and the relations of production. No social order ever perishes before all the productive forces for which there is room in it have developed; and new, higher relations of production never appear before the material conditions of their existence have matured in the womb of the old society itself. Therefore mankind always sets itself only such tasks as it can solve; since, looking at the matter more closely, it will always be found that the task itself arises only when the material conditions for its solution already exist or are at least in the process of formation. In broad outlines Asiatic, ancient, feudal, and modern bourgeois modes of production can be designated as progressive epochs in the economic formation of society. The bourgeois relations of production are the last antagonistic form of the social process of production—antagonistic not in the sense of individual antagonism, but of one arising from the social conditions of life of the individuals; at the same time the productive forces developing in the womb of bourgeois society create the material conditions for the solution of that antagonism. This social formation brings, therefore, the prehistory of human society to a close.

Frederick Engels, with whom, since the appearance of his brilliant sketch on the criticism of the economic categories (in the *Deutsch-Französische Jahrbücher*), I maintained a constant exchange of ideas by correspondence, had by another road (compare his *The Condition of the Working Class in England in 1844*) arrived at the same result as I, and when in the spring of 1845 he also settled in Brussels, we resolved to work out in common the opposition of our view to the ideological view of German philosophy, in fact, to settle accounts with our erstwhile philosophical conscience. The resolve was carried out in the form of a criticism of post-Hegelian philosophy. The manuscript, two large octavo volumes, had long reached its place of publication in Westphalia when we received the news that altered circumstances did not allow of its being printed. We abandoned the manuscript to the gnawing criticism of the mice all the more willingly as we had achieved our main purpose—self-clarification. Of the scattered works in which we put our views before the public at that time, now from one aspect, now from another, I will mention only the *Manifesto of the Communist Party*, jointly written by Engels and myself, and *Discours sur le libre échange* published by me. The decisive points of our view were first scientifically, although only polemically, indicated in my work published in 1847 and directed against Proudhon: *Misère de la Philosophie*, etc. A dissertation written in German on *Wage Labour*, in which I put together my lectures on this subject delivered in the Brussels German Workers' Society, was interrupted, while being printed, by the February Revolution and my consequent forcible removal from Belgium.

The editing of the *Neue Rheinische Zeitung* in 1848 and 1849, and the subsequent events, interrupted my economic studies which could only be resumed in the year 1850 in London. The enormous material for the history of political economy which is accumulated in the British Museum, the favourable vantage point afforded by London for the observation of bourgeois society, and finally the new stage of development upon which the latter appeared to have entered with the discovery of gold in California and Australia, determined me to begin afresh from the very beginning and to work through the new material critically. These studies led partly of themselves into apparently quite remote subjects on which I had to dwell for a shorter or longer period. Especially, however, was the time at my disposal curtailed by the imperative necessity of earning my living. My contributions, during eight years now, to the first English-American newspaper, the *New York Tribune*, compelled an extraordinary scattering of my studies, since I occupy myself with newspaper correspondence proper only in exceptional cases. However, articles on striking economic events in England and on the Continent constituted so considerable a part of my contributions that I was compelled to make myself familiar with practical details which lie outside the sphere of the actual science of political economy.

This sketch of the course of my studies in the sphere of political economy is intended only to show that my views, however they may be judged and however little they coincide with the interested prejudices of the ruling classes, are the results of conscientious investigation lasting many years. But at the entrance to science, as at the entrance to hell, the demand must be posted:

> Qui si convien lasciare ogni sospetto;
> Ogni viltà convien che qui sia morta.[4]

4. Here all mistrust must be abandoned
   And here must perish every craven thought.
   (Dante, *The Divine Comedy*)

Discovering Hegel

KARL MARX

On November 10, 1837, soon after becoming a student at the University of Berlin, Marx wrote a long letter to his father. It shows that at nineteen he had formed two relationships of great importance: a personal one with Jenny von Westphalen of Trier and an intellectual one with the late philosopher Hegel. The love of Jenny led to marriage, the spell of Hegel to Marxism.

Dear Father,

There are moments in one's life which are like frontier posts marking the completion of a period but at the same time clearly indicating a new direction.

* * *

After my arrival in Berlin, I broke off all hitherto existing connections, made visits rarely and unwillingly, and tried to immerse myself in science and art.

In accordance with my state of mind at the time, lyrical poetry was bound to be my first subject, at least the most pleasant and immediate one. But owing to my attitude and whole previous development it was purely idealistic. My heaven, my art, became a world beyond, as remote as my love. Everything real became hazy and what is hazy has no definite outlines. All the poems of the first three volumes I sent to Jenny are marked by attacks on our times, diffuse and inchoate expressions of feeling, nothing natural, everything built out of moonshine, complete opposition between what is and what ought to be, rhetorical reflections instead of poetic thoughts, but perhaps also a certain warmth of feeling and striving for poetic fire. * * *

Poetry, however, could be and had to be only an accompaniment; I had to study law and above all felt the urge to wrestle with philosophy. * * *

From the idealism which, by the way, I had compared and nourished with the idealism of Kant and Fichte, I arrived at the point of seeking the idea in reality itself. If previously the gods had dwelt above the earth, now they became its centre.

I had read fragments of Hegel's philosophy, the grotesque craggy melody of which did not appeal to me. Once more I wanted to dive into the sea, but with the definite intention of establishing that the nature of the mind is just as necessary, concrete and firmly based as the nature of the body. My aim was no longer to practise tricks of

7

swordsmanship, but to bring genuine pearls into the light of day.

I wrote a dialogue of about 24 pages: "Cleanthes, or the Starting Point and Necessary Continuation of Philosophy." Here art and science, which had become completely divorced from each other, were to some extent united, and like a vigorous traveller I set about the task itself, a philosophical-dialectical account of divinity, as it manifests itself as the idea-in-itself, as religion, as nature, and as history. My last proposition was the beginning of the Hegelian system. * * *

For some days my vexation made me quite incapable of thinking; I ran about madly in the garden by the dirty water of the Spree, which "washes souls and dilutes the tea."[1] I even joined my landlord in a hunting excursion, rushed off to Berlin and wanted to embrace every street-corner loafer.

* * *

Owning to being upset over Jenny's illness and my vain, fruitless intellectual labours, and as the result of nagging annoyance at having had to make an idol of a view that I hated, I became ill, as I have already written to you, dear Father. When I got better I burnt all the poems and outlines of stories, etc., imagining that I could give them up completely, of which so far at any rate I have not given any proofs to the contrary.

While I was ill I got to know Hegel from beginning to end, together with most of his disciples. Through a number of meetings with friends in Stralow I came across a Doctors' Club,[2] which includes some university lecturers and my most intimate Berlin friend, Dr. Rutenberg. In controversy here, many conflicting views were expressed, and I became ever more firmly bound to the modern world philosophy from which I had thought to escape. * * *

* * *

Your ever loving son,
Karl

Please, dear father, excuse my illegible handwriting and bad style; it is almost 4 o'clock, the candle has burnt itself out, and my eyes are dim; a real unrest has taken possession of me, I shall not be able to calm the turbulent spectres until I am with you who are dear to me.

Please give greetings from me to my sweet, wonderful Jenny. I have read her letter twelve times already, and always discover new delights in it. It is in every respect, including that of style, the most beautiful letter I can imagine being written by a woman.

1. Heine.
2. The Doctors' Club was founded by representatives of the radical wing of the Hegelian school in Berlin in 1837. Among its members were lecturer on theology of Berlin University Bruno Bauer, gymnasium history teacher Karl Friedrich Köppen, and geography teacher Adolf Rutenberg. The usual meeting place was the small Hippel café. The Club, of which Marx was also an active member, played an important part in the Young Hegelian movement.

To Make the World Philosophical

KARL MARX

Marx's doctoral dissertation, "The Difference Between the Democritean and Epicurean Philosophics of Nature," written between 1839 and 1841, is chiefly of interest for the following excerpts arguing that after a great world philosophy—Aristotle's in antiquity and Hegel's now—the system's disciples feel an imperious urge to make the world "philosophical." What this would mean Marx hinted in the dissertation's foreword, where he saluted Prometheus' revolt against the gods as a proclamation of "human self-consciousness as the highest divinity." To transform the world in the image of Hegelian philosophy would mean to make of man in existential reality the divinity that, as Marx saw it, Hegel had already made him in thought.*

The last two paragraphs of the selection are taken from Marx's preparatory material for the dissertation, "Notebooks on Epicurean Philosophy."

* * *

Also in relation to Hegel it is mere ignorance on the part of his pupils, when they explain one or the other determination of his system by his desire for accommodation and the like, hence, in one word, explain it in terms of *morality*. They forget that only a short time ago they were enthusiastic about all his idiosyncrasies [*Einseitigkeiten*], as can be clearly demonstrated from their writings.

If they were really so affected by the ready-made science they acquired that they gave themselves up to it in naive uncritical trust, then how unscrupulous is their attempt to reproach the Master for a hidden intention behind his insight! The Master, to whom the science was not something received, but something in the process of becoming, to whose uttermost periphery his own intellectual heart's blood was pulsating! On the contrary, they rendered themselves suspect of not having been serious before. And now they oppose their own former condition, and ascribe it to Hegel, forgetting however that his relation to his system was immediate, substantial, while theirs is only a reflected one.

* * *

It is a psychological law that the theoretical mind, once liberated in itself, turns into practical energy, and, leaving the shadowy empire of Amenthes as *will*, turns itself against the reality of the world existing without it. (From a philosophical point of view, however, it is important to specify these aspects better, since from the

---

* For a fuller statement of this interpretation, see Robert C. Tucker, *Philosophy* and *Myth in Karl Marx*, pp. 75–80.

9

specific manner of this turn we can reason back towards the immanent determination and the universal historic character of a philosophy. We see here, as it were, its *curriculum vitae*[1] narrowed down
to its subjective point.) But the *practice* of philosophy is itself *theoretical*. It's the *critique* that measures the individual existence by
the essence, the particular reality by the Idea. But this *immediate
realisation* of philosophy is in its deepest essence afflicted with contradictions, and this its essence takes form in the appearance and
imprints its seal upon it.

When philosophy turns itself as will against the world of appearance, then the system is lowered to an abstract totality, that is, it
has become one aspect of the world which opposes another one. Its
relationship to the world is that of reflection. Inspired by the urge
to realise itself, it enters into tension against the other. The inner
self-contentment and completeness has been broken. What was
inner light has become consuming flame turning outwards. The
result is that as the world becomes philosophical, philosophy also
becomes worldly, that its realisation is also its loss, that what it
struggles against on the outside is its own inner deficiency, that in
the very struggle it falls precisely into those defects which it fights
as defects in the opposite camp, and that it can only overcome
these defects by falling into them. That which opposes it and that
which it fights is always the same as itself, only with factors
inverted.

This is the one side, when we consider this matter *purely objectively* as immediate realisation of philosophy. However, it has also a
subjective aspect, which is merely another form of it. This is *the
relationship of the philosophical system* which is realised *to its intellectual carriers*, to the individual self-consciousnesses in which its
progress appears. This relationship results in what confronts the
world in the realisation of philosophy itself, namely, in the fact that
these individual self-consciousnesses always carry *a double-edged
demand*, one edge turned against the world, the other against philosophy itself. Indeed, what in the thing itself appears as a relationship inverted in itself, appears in these self-consciousnesses as a
double one, a demand and an action contradicting each other.
Their liberation of the world from un-philosophy is at the same
time their own liberation from the philosophy that held them in
fetters as a particular system. * * *

* * *

As in the history of philosophy there are nodal points which raise
philosophy in itself to concretion, apprehend abstract principles in a
totality, and thus break off the rectilinear process, so also there are
moments when philosophy turns its eyes to the external world, and

1. Course of life.

no longer apprehends it, but, as a practical person, weaves, as it were, intrigues with the world, emerges from the transparent kingdom of Amenthes and throws itself on the breast of the worldly Siren. That is the carnival of philosophy, whether it disguises itself as a dog like the Cynic, in priestly vestments like the Alexandrian, or in fragrant spring array like the Epicurean. It is essential that philosophy should then wear character masks. As Deucalion, according to the legend, cast stones behind him in creating human beings, so philosophy casts its regard behind it (the bones of its mother are luminous eyes) when its heart is set on creating a world; but as Prometheus, having stolen fire from heaven, begins to build houses and to settle upon the earth, so philosophy, expanded to be the whole world, turns against the world of appearance. The same now with the philosophy of Hegel.

While philosophy has sealed itself off to form a consummate, total world, the determination of this totality is conditioned by the general development of philosophy, just as that development is the condition of the form in which philosophy turns into a practical relationship towards reality; thus the totality of the world in general is divided within itself, and this division is carried to the extreme, for spiritual existence has been freed, has been enriched to universality, the heart-beat has become in itself the differentiation in the concrete form which is the whole organism. The division of the world is total only when its aspects are totalities. The world confronting a philosophy total in itself is therefore a world torn apart. This philosophy's activity therefore also appears torn apart and contradictory; its objective universality is turned back into the subjective forms of individual consciousness in which it has life. But one must not let oneself be misled by this storm which follows a great philosophy, a world philosophy. Ordinary harps play under any fingers, Aeolian harps only when struck by the storm.

* * *

For a Ruthless Criticism
of Everything Existing

KARL MARX

The watchword of the young Karl Marx, as of his Young Hegelian associates generally, was *Kritik*—criticism. In this early article, printed in the *Deutsch-Französische Jahrbücher* in 1844 in the form of a letter to Arnold Ruge, Marx elaborated the idea of criticism into a program of this journal, of which he and Ruge were editors. His future strictures on utopian socialist plans, in the *Communist Manifesto* and other later writings, were prefigured in the dismissal here of the communist utopias of writers like Etienne Cabet as a "dogmatic abstraction." The *Deutsch-Französische Jahrbücher* (*German-French Annals*) came out in Paris in February, 1844, in the German language. Only one double issue of the journal was published.

The translation was made by Dr. Ronald Rogowski for this edition.

M. to R.
Kreuznach
September, 1843

I am delighted that you are resolved and turn your thoughts from backward glances at the past toward a new undertaking. In Paris, then, the old university of philosophy (*absit omen!*) and the new capital of the new world. What is necessary will arrange itself. I do not doubt, therefore, that all obstacles—whose importance I do not fail to recognize—will be removed.

The undertaking may succeed, however, or not; in any case I will be in Paris at the end of this month, since the air here makes one servile and I see no room at all in Germany for free activity.

In Germany, everything is being forcibly repressed, a true anarchy of the spirit has burst out, stupidity itself reigns supreme, and Zürich obeys commands from Berlin; hence it becomes ever clearer that a new gathering point must be sought for the really thinking and independent minds. I am convinced that our plan would meet

a real need, and real needs must surely also be able to find real fulfillment. I therefore have no doubts about the enterprise if only we
undertake it seriously.

The inner difficulties seem to be almost greater than the external
obstacles. For even if there is no doubt about the "whence," all the
more confusion reigns about the "whither." Apart from the general
anarchy which has erupted among the reformers, each is compelled
to confess to himself that he has no clear conception of what the
future should be. That, however, is just the advantage of the new
trend: that we do not attempt dogmatically to prefigure the future,
but want to find the new world only through criticism of the old.
Up to now the philosophers had the solution of all riddles lying
in their lectern, and the stupid uninitiated world had only to open
its jaws to let the roast partridges of absolute science fly into its
mouth. Now philosophy has become worldly, and the most incon
trovertible evidence of this is that the philosophical consciousness
has been drawn, not only externally but also internally, into the
stress of battle. But if the designing of the future and the proclamation of ready-made solutions for all time is not our affair, then
we realize all the more clearly what we have to accomplish in the
present—I am speaking of a *ruthless criticism of everything existing*,
ruthless in two senses: The criticism must not be afraid of its own
conclusions, nor of conflict with the powers that be.

I am therefore not in favor of setting up any dogmatic flag. On
the contrary, we must try to help the *dogmatics* to clarify to themselves the meaning of their own positions. Thus *communism*, to be
specific, is a dogmatic abstraction. I do not have in mind here some
imaginary, possible communism, but actually existing communism
in the form preached by Cabet, Dezamy,[1] Weitling,[2] etc. This
communism is only a special manifestation of the humanistic principle which is still infected by its opposite—private being. Elimination of private property is therefore by no means identical with this
communism, and it is not accidental but quite inevitable that communism has seen other socialist teachings arise in opposition to it,
such as the teachings of Fourier, Proudhon, etc., because it is itself
only a special, one-sided realization of the socialist principle.

And the socialist principle itself represents, on the whole, only
one side, affecting the *reality* of the true human essence. We have
to concern ourselves just as much with the other side, the theoretical existence of man, in other words to make religion, science, etc.,
the objects of our criticism. Moreover, we want to have an effect on
our contemporaries, and specifically on our German contemporaries. The question is, how is this to be approached? Two circum-

1. Theodore Dezamy, author of *Code de la nature* (1842). [R. T.]
2. Wilhelm Weitling, a German jour- neyman tailor whose *Guarantees of Harmony and Freedom* (1842) advo- cated communism. [R. T.]

stances cannot be denied. First, religion, and second, politics, arouse predominant interest in contemporary Germany. We must take these two subjects, however they are, for a starting-point, and not set up against them some ready-made system such as the *Voyage en Icarie*.[3]

Reason has always existed, only not always in reasonable form. The critic can therefore start out by taking any form of theoretical and practical consciousness and develop from the *unique* forms of existing reality the true reality as its norm and final goal. Now so far as real life is concerned, precisely the *political state* in all its *modern* forms contains, even where it is not yet consciously imbued with socialist demands, the demands of reason. Nor does the state stop at that. The state everywhere presupposes that reason has been realized. But in just this way it everywhere comes into contradiction between its ideal mission and its real preconditions.

Out of this conflict of the political state with itself, therefore, one can develop social truth. Just as *religion* is the catalogue of the theoretical struggles of mankind, so the *political state* is the catalogue of its practical struggles. The political state thus expresses, within the confines of its form *sub specie rei publicae*,[4] all social struggles, needs, truths. Thus it is not at all beneath the *hauteur des principes* to make the most specific political question—e.g., the difference between the corporative[5] and the representative system—the object of criticism. For this question only expresses in a *political* way the difference between the rule of man and the rule of private property. The critic therefore not only can but must go into these political questions (which the crass kind of socialists consider beneath anyone's dignity). By showing the superiority of the representative system over the corporative system, the critic *affects the practical interests* of a large party. By elevating the representative system from its political form to its general form and by bringing out the true significance underlying this system, the critic at the same time forces this party to go beyond its own confines, since its victory is at the same time its loss.

Nothing prevents us, then, from tying our criticism to the criticism of politics and to a definite party position in politics, and hence from identifying our criticism with real struggles. Then we shall confront the world not as doctrinaires with a new principle: "Here is the truth, bow down before it!" We develop new principles to the world out of its own principles. We do not say to the world: "Stop fighting; your struggle is of no account. We want to

---

3. This is the title of Cabet's utopian novel published in Paris in 1840. At that time Cabet's followers were called "communists." [*R. T.*]

4. From the political point of view. [*R. T.*]

5. The system of representation by estates (classes) as opposed to the system of representation by individuals. [*R. T.*]

shout the true slogan of the struggle at you." We only show the world what it is fighting for, and consciousness is something that the world *must* acquire, like it or not.

The reform of consciousness consists *only* in enabling the world to clarify its consciousness, in waking it from its dream about itself, in *explaining* to it the meaning of its own actions. Our whole task can consist only in putting religious and political questions into self-conscious human form—as is also the case in Feuerbach's criticism of religion.

Our motto must therefore be: Reform of consciousness not through dogmas, but through analyzing the mystical consciousness, the consciousness which is unclear to itself, whether it appears in religious or political form. Then it will transpire that the world has long been dreaming of something that it can acquire if only it becomes conscious of it. It will transpire that it is not a matter of drawing a great dividing line between past and future, but of carrying out the thoughts of the past. And finally, it will transpire that mankind begins no *new* work, but consciously accomplishes its old work.

So, we can express the trend of our journal in one word: the work of our time to clarify to itself (critical philosophy) the meaning of its own struggle and its own desires. This is work for the world and for us. It can only be the work of joint forces. It is a matter of *confession*, no more. To have its sins forgiven mankind has only to declare them to be what they really are.

Contribution to the Critique of Hegel's
Philosophy of Right

KARL MARX

In line with his program of effecting "a ruthless criticism of everything existing," Marx during 1843 took up the criticism of politics. He set about this by working on a commentary on Hegel's treatise on the state.* To the Hegelian political philosophy (which he called, following Feuerbach, "speculative philosophy") he applied the method of "transformational criticism" that Feuerbach had applied to the Hegelian philosophy of religion.** Although the work was left incomplete and unpublished, it was, as Marx later said (see p. 4, above), a milestone on his road to historical materialism: it led him to the view that instead of the state being the basis of "civil society," as Hegel held, civil or bourgeois society is the basis of the state.

Despite its incompleteness—the extant part of the commentary starts with paragraph 261 of Hegel's treatise and deals only with selected further sections up to paragraph 308—this work remains of interest as Marx's most extensive single piece of purely political writing, although his standpoint at the time of writing was no more than proto-Marxist.

The State and Civil Society[1]

* * *

The idea is made the subject and the *actual* relation of family and civil society to the state is conceived as its *internal imaginary* activity. Family and civil society are the premises of the state; they are the genuinely active elements, but in speculative philosophy things are inverted. When the idea is made the subject, however, the real subjects, namely, civil society, family, "circumstances, caprice, etc.," become *unreal* objective elements of the idea with a changed significance.

* * *

Rationally interpreted, Hegel's propositions would mean only this: The family and civil society are parts of the state. The mate-

---

* The treatise is available in English as *Hegel's Philosophy of Right,* translated with notes by T. M. Knox (Oxford: Oxford University Press, 1942). The complete text of Marx's commentary is available in Karl Marx, *Critique of Hegel's Philosophy of Right,* translated and edited by Jo-

seph J. O'Malley (Cambridge: Cambridge University Press, 1970).
** For more on transformational criticism and Marx's application of it in this commentary, see the Introduction, pp. xxiii–xxiv, above.
1. Subheadings supplied by R.C.T.

16

rial of the state is distributed amongst them "by circumstances, caprice and the individual's own choice of vocation." The citizens of the state are members of families and members of civil society.

"The actual idea, mind, *divides itself* into the two ideal spheres of its concept, family and civil society, that is, *its finite* phase"— hence, the division of the state into family and civil society is *ideal*, i.e., necessary as part of the essence of the state. Family and civil society are actual components of the state, actual spiritual existences of the will, they are modes of existence of the state. Family and civil society constitute *themselves* as the state. They are the driving force. According to Hegel, they are, on the contrary, *produced* by the actual idea. It is not the course of their own life which unites them in the state; on the contrary, it is the idea which in the course of its life has separated them off from itself. Indeed, they are the finiteness of this idea. They owe their presence to another mind than their own. They are entities determined by a third party, not self-determined entities. Accordingly, they are also defined as "finiteness," as the "actual idea's" own *finiteness*. The purpose of their being is not this being itself; rather, the idea separates these presuppositions off from itself "so as to emerge from their ideality as explicitly infinite actual mind." That is to say, there can be no political state without the natural basis of the family and the artificial basis of civil society; they are for it a *conditio sine qua non*. But the condition is postulated as the conditioned, the determinant as the determined, the producing factor as the product of its product. The actual idea only degrades itself into the "finiteness" of the family and civil society so as by transcending them to enjoy and bring forth its infinity. "*Accordingly*" (in order to achieve its purpose), it "assigns to these spheres the material of this, its finite actuality" (this? which? these spheres are indeed its "finite actuality," its "material"), "individuals as a multitude" ("the individuals, the multitude" are here the material of the state; "the state consists of them"; this composition of the state is here expressed as an act of the idea, as an "allocation" which it undertakes with its own material. The fact is that the state issues from the multitude in their existence as members of families and as members of civil society. Speculative philosophy expresses this fact as the idea's deed, not as the idea of the multitude, but as the deed of a subjective idea different from the fact itself), "in such a way that with regard to the individual this assignment" (previously the discussion was only about the assignment of individuals to the spheres of the family and civil society) "appears mediated by circumstances, caprice, etc." Empirical actuality is thus accepted as it is. It is also expressed as rational, but it is not rational on account of its own reason, but because the empirical fact in its empirical existence has a different significance from it itself. The fact which is taken as a point of departure is not conceived as such, but as a mystical result. The actual becomes a phenomenon, but the idea has no other content than this phenomenon. Nor has the idea any other purpose than the logical one of being "explicitly infinite actual mind." The entire mystery of the philosophy of law and of Hegel's philosophy as a whole is set out in this paragraph.

* * *

If Hegel had set out from real subjects as the bases of the state he would not have found it necessary to transform the state in a mystical fashion into a subject. "In its truth, however," says Hegel, "subjectivity exists only as *subject*, personality only as *person*." This too is a piece of mystification. Subjectivity is a characteristic of the subject, personality a characteristic of the person. Instead of conceiving them as predicates of their subjects. Hegel gives the predicates an independent existence and subsequently transforms them in a mystical fashion into their subjects.

The existence of predicates is the subject, so that the subject is the existence of subjectivity, etc.; Hegel transforms the predicates, the objects, into independent entities, but divorced from their actual independence, their subject. Subsequently the actual subject appears as a result, whereas one must start from the actual subject and look at its objectification. The mystical substance, therefore, becomes the actual subject, and the real subject appears as something else, as an element of the mystical substance. Precisely because Hegel starts from the predicates of the general description instead of from the real *ens* (ὑποχείμενον, subject), and since, nevertheless, there has to be a bearer of these qualities, the mystical idea becomes this bearer. The dualism consists in the fact that Hegel does not look upon the general as being the actual nature of the actual finite, i.e., of what exists and is determinate, or upon the actual *ens* as the *true subject* of the infinite.

Sovereignty

So in this case sovereignty, the essential feature of the state, is treated to begin with as an independent entity, is objectified. Then, of course, this objective entity has to become a subject again. This subject then appears, however, as a self-incarnation of sovereignty; whereas sovereignty is nothing but the objectifed mind of the subjects of the state.

* * *

As if the actual state were not the people. The state is an abstraction. The people alone is what is concrete. And it is remarkable that Hegel, who without hesitation attributes a living quality such as sovereignty to the abstraction, attributes it only with hesitation and reservations to something concrete. "The usual sense, however, in which men have recently begun to speak of the sovereignty of the people is in *opposition to the sovereignty existing in the monarch*. In this antithesis the sovereignty of the people is one of those confused notions which are rooted in the *wild* idea of the *people*."

The "confused notions" and the "*wild* idea" are here exclusively Hegel's. To be sure, if sovereignty *exists* in the monarch, then it is foolish to speak of an antithetical sovereignty in the people; for it is implied in the concept of sovereignty that sovereignty cannot have a double existence, still less one which is contradictory. However:

1) This is just the question: Is not that sovereignty which is claimed by the monarch an illusion? Sovereignty of the monarch or sovereignty of the people—that is the question.

2) One can also speak of a sovereignty of the people *in opposition to the sovereignty existing in the monarch*. But then it is not a question of *one and the same sovereignty* which has arisen on two sides, but two *entirely contradictory concepts of sovereignty*, the one a sovereignty such as can come to exist in a *monarch*, the other such as can come to exist only in a *people*. It is the same with the question: "Is God sovereign, or is man?" One of the two is an untruth, even if an existing untruth.

"Taken *without* its monarch and the *articulation* of the whole which is necessarily and directly *associated with the monarch*, the people is that formless mass which is no longer a state. It no longer possesses *any* of the attributes which are to be found only in an *internally organised* whole—sovereignty, government, courts of law, the administration, estates of the realm, etc. With the appearance in a nation of such factors, which relate to organisation, to the life of the state, a people ceases to be that indeterminate abstraction, which, as a purely general notion, is called the nation." All this is a tautology. If a people has a monarch and the structure that necessarily and directly goes with a monarch, i.e., if it is structured as a monarchy, then indeed, taken out of this structure, it is a formless mass and a purely general notion. "If by sovereignty of the people is understood a *republican* form of government and, more specifically, democracy . . . then . . . there can be no further discussion of such a notion in face of the developed idea." That is indeed right, if one has only "such a notion" and not a "developed idea" of democracy.

Democracy

Democracy is the truth of monarchy; monarchy is not the truth of democracy. Monarchy is necessarily democracy inconsistent with itself; the monarchical element is not an inconsistency in democracy. Monarchy cannot be understood in its own terms; democracy can. In democracy none of the elements attains a significance other than what is proper to it. Each is in actual fact only an element of the whole demos [people]. In monarchy one part determines the character of the whole. The entire constitution has to adapt itself to this fixed point. Democracy is the genus Constitution. Monarchy is one species, and a poor one at that. Democracy is content and form. Monarchy is *supposed* to be only a form, but it falsifies the content.

In monarchy the whole, the people, is subsumed under one of its particular modes of being, the political constitution. In democracy the *constitution itself* appears only as *one* determination, that is, the self-determination of the people. In monarchy we have the people of the constitution; in democracy the constitution of the people. Democracy is the solved *riddle* of all constitutions. Here, not merely *implicitly* and in essence but *existing* in reality, the constitution is constantly brought back to its actual basis, the *actual human being*, the *actual people*, and established as the people's *own* work. The constitution appears as what it is, a free product of man. It could be said that in a certain respect this applies also to constitutional monarchy; but the specific distinguishing feature of democracy is that here the *constitution* as such forms only *one* element in the life of the people—that it is not the *political constitution* by itself which forms the state.

Hegel starts from the state and makes man the subjectified state; democracy starts from man and makes the state objectified man. Just as it is not religion which creates man but man who creates religion, so it is not the constitution which creates the people but the people which creates the constitution. In a certain respect the relation of democracy to all other forms of state is like the relation of Christianity to all other religions. Christianity is the religion χατ' ἐξοχήν,[2] the *essence of religion*—deified man as a *particular* religion. Similarly, democracy is the *essence of all state constitutions*—socialised man as a *particular* state constitution. Democracy stands to the other constitutions as the genus stands to its species; except that here the genus itself appears as an existent, and therefore as one *particular* species over against the others whose existence does not correspond to their essence. To democracy all other forms of state stand as its Old Testament. Man does not exist for the law but the law for man—it is a *human manifestation*; whereas in the other forms of state man is a *legal manifestation*. That is the fundamental distinction of democracy.

All other *state forms* are definite, distinct, *particular forms of state*. In democracy the *formal* principle is at the same time the

2. *Par excellence*—i.e., "Christianity is the pre-eminent religion."

material principle. Only democracy, therefore, is the true unity of the general and the particular. In monarchy, for example, and in the republic as a merely particular form of state, political man has his particular mode of being alongside unpolitical man, man as a private individual. Property, contract, marriage, civil society, all appear here (as Hegel shows quite correctly with regard to these *abstract* state forms, but he *thinks* that he is expounding the idea of the state) as *particular* modes of existence alongside the *political* state, as the *content* to which the *political state* is related as *organising form*; properly speaking, the relation of the political state to this content is merely that of reason, inherently without content, which defines and delimits, which now affirms and now denies. In democracy the political state, which stands alongside this content and distinguishes itself from it, is itself merely a *particular* content and particular *form of existence* of the people. In monarchy, for example, this particular, the political constitution, has the significance of the *general* that dominates and determines everything particular. In democracy the state as particular is *merely* particular; as general, it is the truly general, i.e., not something determinate in distinction from the other content. The French have recently interpreted this as meaning that in true democracy the *political state is annihilated*. This is correct insofar as the political state *qua* political state, as constitution, no longer passes for the whole.

In all states other than democratic ones the *state*, the *law*, the *constitution* is what rules, without really ruling—i.e., without materially permeating the content of the remaining, non-political spheres. In democracy the constitution, the law, the state itself, insofar as it is a political constitution, is only the self-determination of the people, and a particular content of the people.

Incidentally, it goes without saying that all forms of state have democracy *for* their truth and that they are therefore untrue insofar as they are not democracy.

Politics: Ancient, Medieval, and Modern

In the states of antiquity the political state makes up the content of the state to the exclusion of the other spheres. The modern state is a compromise between the political and the unpolitical state.

In democracy the *abstract* state has ceased to be the dominant factor. The struggle between monarchy and republic is itself still a struggle within the abstract state. The *political* republic is democracy within the abstract state form. The abstract state form of democracy is therefore the republic; but here it ceases to be the *merely political* constitution.

Property, etc., in short, the entire content of the law and the state, is the same in North America as in Prussia, with few modifications. The *republic* there is thus a mere state *form*, as is the monarchy here. The content of the state lies outside these constitutions. Hegel is right, therefore, when he says: The political state is the constitution, i.e., the material state is not political. What obtains here is merely an external identity, a determination of changing forms. Of the various elements of national life, the one most difficult to evolve was the political state, the constitution. It developed as universal reason over against the other spheres, as ulterior to them. The historical task then consisted in its [the constitution's] reassertion, but the particular spheres do not realise that their private nature coincides with the other-worldly nature of the constitution or of the political state, and that the other-worldly existence of the political state is nothing but the affirmation of their own estrangement. Up till now the *political constitution* has been the *religious sphere*, the *religion* of national life, the heaven of its generality over against the *earthy existence* of its actuality. The political sphere has been the only state sphere in the state, the only sphere in which the content as well as the form has been species-content, the truly general; but in such a way that at the same time, because this sphere has confronted the others, its content has also become formal and particular. *Political life* in the modern sense is the *scholasticism* of national life. *Monarchy* is the perfect expression of this estrangement. The *republic* is the negation of this estrangement within its own sphere. It is obvious that the political constitution as such is brought into being only where the private spheres have won an independent existence. Where trade and landed property are not free and have not yet become independent, the political constitution too does not yet exist. The Middle Ages were the *democracy of unfreedom*.

The abstraction of the *state as such* belongs only to modern times, because the abstraction of private life belongs only to modern times. The abstraction of the *political state* is a modern product.

In the Middle Ages there were serfs, feudal estates, merchant and trade guilds, corporations of scholars, etc.: that is to say, in the Middle Ages property, trade, society, man are *political*; the material content of the state is given by its form; every private sphere has a political character or is a political sphere; that is, politics is a characteristic of the private spheres too. In the Middle Ages the political constitution is the constitution of private property, but only because the constitution of private property is a political constitution. In the Middle Ages the life of the nation and the life of the state are identical. Man is the actual principle of the state—but *unfree* man. It is thus the *democracy of unfreedom*—estrangement carried to completion. The abstract reflected antithesis belongs only to the modern world. The Middle Ages are the period of *actual* dualism; modern times, one of *abstract* dualism.

"We have already noted the stage at which the division of constitutions into democracy, aristocracy and monarchy has been made—the standpoint, that is, of that unity which is still *substantial, which still remains within itself and has not yet come to its process of infinite differentiation and inner deepening*: at that stage, the element of the *final self-determining resolution of the will* does not emerge explicitly into its *own proper actuality* as an *immanent* organic factor in the state." In the spontaneously evolved monarchy, democracy and aristocracy there is as yet no political constitution as distinct from the actual, material state or the other content of the life of the nation. The political state does not yet appear as the *form* of the material state. Either, as in Greece, the *res publica*[3] is the real private affair of the citizens, their real content, and the private individual is a slave; the political state, *qua* political state, being the true and only content of the life and will of the citizens; or, as in an Asiatic despotism, the political state is nothing but the personal caprice of a single individual; or the political state, like the material state, is a slave. What distinguishes the modern state from these states characterized by the substantial unity between people and state is not, as Hegel would have it, that the various elements of the constitution have been developed into *particular* actuality, but that the constitution itself has been developed into a *particular* actuality alongside the actual life of the people—that the political state has become the *constitution* of the rest of the state.

* * *

Bureaucracy

The "state formalism" which bureaucracy is, is the "state as formalism"; and it is as a formalism of this kind that Hegel has described bureaucracy. Since this "state formalism" constitutes itself as an actual power and itself becomes its own *material* content, it goes without saying that the "bureaucracy" is a web of *practical* illusions, or the "illusion of the state." The bureaucratic spirit is a jesuitical, theological spirit through and through. The bureaucrats are the jesuits and theologians of the state. The bureaucracy is *la république prêtre*.

Since by its *very nature* the bureaucracy is the "state as formalism," it is this also as regards its *purpose*. The actual purpose of the state therefore appears to the bureaucracy as an objective *hostile* to the state. The spirit of the bureaucracy is the "formal state spirit."

3. I.e., state, republic; etymologically, "public affairs."

The bureaucracy therefore turns the "formal state spirit" or the *actual* spiritlessness of the state into a categorical imperative. The bureaucracy takes itself to be the ultimate purpose of the state. Because the bureaucracy turns its "formal" objectives into its content, it comes into conflict everywhere with "real" objectives. It is therefore obliged to pass off the form for the content and the content for the form. State objectives are transformed into objectives of the department, and department objectives into objectives of the state. The bureaucracy is a circle from which no one can escape. Its hierarchy is a *hierarchy of knowledge*. The top entrusts the understanding of detail to the lower levels, whilst the lower levels credit the top with understanding of the general, and so all are mutually deceived.

The bureaucracy is the imaginary state alongside the real state— the spiritualism of the state. Each thing has therefore a double meaning, a real and a bureaucratic meaning, just as knowledge (and also the will) is both real and bureaucratic. The really existing, however, is treated in the light of its bureaucratic nature, its other-worldly, spiritual essence. The bureaucracy has the state, the spiritual essence of society, in its possession, as its *private property*. The general spirit of the bureaucracy is the *secret*, the mystery, preserved within itself by the hierarchy and against the outside world by being a closed corporation. Avowed political spirit, as also political-mindedness, therefore appear to the bureaucracy as *treason* against its mystery. Hence, *authority* is the basis of its knowledge, and the deification of authority is its *conviction*. Within the bureaucracy itself, however, *spiritualism* becomes *crass materialism*, the materialism of passive obedience, of faith in authority, of the *mechanism* of fixed and formalistic behaviour, and of fixed principles, views and traditions. In the case of the individual bureaucrat, the state objective turns into his private objective, into a *chasing after higher posts*, the *making of a career*. In the first place, he looks on actual life as something *material*, for the *spirit of this life has its distinctly separate existence* in the bureaucracy. The bureaucracy must therefore proceed to make life as material as possible. Secondly, actual life is material for the bureaucrat himself, i.e., so far as it becomes an object of bureaucratic manipulation; for his spirit is prescribed for him, his aim lies beyond him, and his existence is the existence of the department. The state only continues to exist as various fixed bureaucratic minds, bound together in subordination and passive obedience. *Actual* knowledge seems devoid of content, just as actual life seems dead; for this imaginary knowledge and this imaginary life are taken for the real thing. The bureaucrat must therefore deal with the actual state jesuitically, whether this jesuitry is conscious or unconscious. However, once its antithesis is knowledge, this jesuitry is likewise bound to achieve self-consciousness and then become deliberate jesuitry.

Whilst the bureaucracy is on the one hand this crass materialism, it manifests its crass spiritualism in the fact that it wants to *do everything*, i.e., by making the *will* the *causa prima*. For it is purely an *active* form of existence and receives its content from without and can prove its existence, therefore, only by shaping and restricting this content. For the bureaucrat the world is a mere object to be manipulated by him.

When Hegel calls the executive the *objective* aspect of the sovereignty dwelling in the monarch, that is right in the same sense in which the Catholic Church was the *real presence* of the sovereignty, substance and spirit of the Holy Trinity. In the bureaucracy the identity of state interest and particular private aim is established in such a way that the *state interest* becomes a *particular* private aim over against other private aims.

The abolition of the bureaucracy is only possible by the general interest *actually*—and not, as with Hegel, merely in thought, in *abstraction*—becoming the particular interest, which in turn is only possible as a result of the *particular* actually becoming the *general* interest. Hegel starts from an unreal antithesis and therefore achieves only an imaginary identity which is in truth again a contradictory identity. The bureaucracy is just such an identity.

* * *

On the Jewish Question

KARL MARX

In this essay, written in the autumn of 1843 and published in the
Deutsch-Französische Jahrbücher, Marx pursued his critical aims through a
review of two studies on the Jewish question by another Young Hegelian,
Bruno Bauer. The criticism of politics is developed in the first part, leading
to the conclusion that human emancipation requires the ending of the division between man as an egoistic being in "civil society" and man as abstract citizen in the state. In the second part, Marx proceeds to the criticism of economics or commerce, which he equates with "Judaism." His
concluding call for "the emancipation of society from Judaism" (which has
been seen on occasion as a manifesto of anti-Semitism) is in fact a call for
the emancipation of society from what he here calls "huckstering," or from
what he was subsequently to call "capitalism." This, however, is not to
deny that Marx, although he himself was of Jewish origin, harbored anti-
Jewish attitudes, nor is it to deny that such attitudes found expression in
this essay.

---

1. Bruno Bauer, *Die Judenfrage*[1]

The German Jews seek emancipation. What kind of emancipation do they want? *Civic, political* emancipation.

Bruno Bauer replies to them: In Germany no one is politically
emancipated. We ourselves are not free. How then could we liberate you? You Jews are *egoists* if you demand for yourselves, as Jews,
a special emancipation. You should work, as Germans, for the
political emancipation of Germany, and as men, for the emancipation of mankind. You should feel the particular kind of oppression
and shame which you suffer, not as an exception to the rule but
rather as a confirmation of the rule.

Or do the Jews want to be placed on a footing of equality with
the *Christian subjects?* If they recognize the *Christian state* as
legally established they also recognize the régime of general enslave-

1. The Jewish question. [Braunschweig, 1843.—*Marx*]

ment. Why should their particular yoke be irksome when they accept the general yoke? Why should the German be interested in the liberation of the Jew, if the Jew is not interested in the liberation of the German?

The *Christian* state recognizes nothing but *privileges*. The Jew himself, in this state, has the privilege of being a Jew. As a Jew he possesses rights which the Christians do not have. Why does he want rights which he does not have but which the Christians enjoy?

In demanding his emancipation from the Christian state he asks the Christian state to abandon its *religious* prejudice. But does he, the Jew, give up *his* religious prejudice? Has he then the right to insist that someone else should forswear his religion?

The *Christian* state, *by its very nature*, is incapable of emancipating the Jew. But, adds Bauer, the Jew, by his very nature, cannot be emancipated. As long as the state remains Christian, and as long as the Jew remains a Jew, they are equally incapable, the one of conferring emancipation, the other of receiving it.

With respect to the Jews the Christian state can only adopt the attitude of a Christian state. That is, it can permit the Jew, as a matter of privilege, to isolate himself from its other subjects; but it must then allow the pressures of all the other spheres of society to bear upon the Jew, and all the more heavily since he is in *religious* opposition to the dominant religion. But the Jew likewise can only adopt a Jewish attitude, i.e. that of a foreigner, towards the state, since he opposes his illusory nationality to actual nationality, his illusory law to actual law. He considers it his right to separate himself from the rest of humanity; as a matter of principle he takes no part in the historical movement and looks to a future which has nothing in common with the future of mankind as a whole. He regards himself as a member of the Jewish people, and the Jewish people as the chosen people.

On what grounds, then, do you Jews demand emancipation? On account of your religion? But it is the mortal enemy of the state religion. As citizens? But there are no citizens in Germany. As men? But you are not men any more than are those to whom you appeal.

Bauer, after criticizing earlier approaches and solutions, formulates the question of Jewish emancipation in a new way. What, he asks, is the nature of the Jew who is to be emancipated, and the *nature* of the Christian state which is to emancipate him? He replies by a critique of the Jewish religion, analyses the religious opposition between Judaism and Christianity, explains the essence of the Christian state; and does all this with dash, clarity, wit and profundity, in a style which is as precise as it is pithy and vigorous.

How then does Bauer resolve the Jewish question? What is the result? To formulate a question is to resolve it. The critical study of the Jewish question is the answer to the Jewish question. Here it is in brief: we have to emancipate ourselves before we can emancipate others.

The most stubborn form of the opposition between Jew and Christian is the *religious* opposition. How is an opposition resolved? By making it impossible. And how is *religious* opposition made impossible? By abolishing *religion*. As soon as Jew and Christian come to see in their respective religions nothing more than *stages in the development of the human mind*—snake skins which have been cast off by *history*, and *man* as the snake who clothed himself in them—they will no longer find themselves in religious opposition, but in a purely critical, *scientific* and human relationship. *Science* will then constitute their unity. But scientific oppositions are resolved by science itself.

The *German* Jew, in particular, suffers from the general lack of political freedom and the pronounced Christianity of the state. But in Bauer's sense the Jewish question has a general significance, independent of the specifically German conditions. It is the question of the relations between religion and the state, of the *contradiction between religious prejudice and political emancipation*. Emancipation from religion is posited as a condition, both for the Jew who wants political emancipation, and for the state which should emancipate him and itself be emancipated.

"Very well, it may be said (and the Jew himself says it) but the Jew should not be emancipated because he is a Jew, because he has such an excellent and universal moral creed; the *Jew* should take second place to the citizen, and he will be a *citizen* although he is and desires to remain a Jew. In other words, he is and remains a *Jew*, even though he is a *citizen* and as such lives in a universal human condition; his restricted Jewish nature always finally triumphs over his human and political obligations. The bias persists even though it is overcome by general principles. But if it persists, it would be truer to say that it overcomes all the rest." "It is only in a sophistical and superficial sense that the Jew could remain a Jew in political life. Consequently, if he wanted to remain a Jew, this would mean that the superficial became the essential and thus triumphed. In other words, his life *in the state* would be only a semblance, or a momentary exception to the essential and normal."[2]

Let us see also how Bauer establishes the role of the state.

"France," he says, "has provided us recently,[3] in connexion with

2. Bauer, "Die Fähigkeit der heutigen Juden und Christen, frei zu werden," *Einundzwanzig Bogen*, p. 57. [*Marx*]

Emphases added by Marx.
3. Chamber of Deputies. Debate of 26th December, 1840. [*Marx*]

the Jewish question (and for that matter all other *political* questions), with the spectacle of a life which is free but which revokes its freedom by law and so declares it to be merely an appearance; and which, on the other hand, denies its free laws by its acts."[4]

"In France, universal liberty is not yet established by law, nor is the *Jewish question as yet resolved*, because legal liberty, i.e. the equality of all citizens, is restricted in actual life, which is still dominated and fragmented by religious privileges, and because the lack of liberty in actual life influences law in its turn and obliges it to sanction the division of citizens who are by nature free into oppressors and oppressed."[5]

When, therefore, would the Jewish question be resolved in France?

"The Jew would really have ceased to be Jewish, for example, if he did not allow his religious code to prevent his fulfilment of his duties towards the state and his fellow citizens; if he attended and took part in the public business of the Chamber of Deputies on the sabbath. It would be necessary, further, to abolish all *religious priv-ilege*, including the monopoly of a privileged church. If, thereafter, some or many or *even the overwhelming majority felt obliged to fulfil their religious duties*, such practices should be left *to them as an absolutely* private matter."[6] "There is no longer any religion when there is no longer a privileged religion. Take away from religion its power to excommunicate and it will no longer exist."[7] "Mr. Martin du Nord has seen, in the suggestion to omit any mention of Sunday in the law, a proposal to declare that Christianity has ceased to exist. With equal right (and the right is well founded) the declaration that the law of the sabbath is no longer binding upon the Jew would amount to proclaiming the end of Judaism."[8]

Thus Bauer demands, on the one hand, that the Jew should renounce Judaism, and in general that man should renounce religion, in order to be emancipated as a citizen. On the other hand, he considers, and this follows logically, that the political abolition of religion is the abolition of all religion. The state which presupposes religion is not yet a true or actual state. "Clearly, the religious idea gives some assurances to the state. But to what state? *To what kind of state?*"[9]

At this point we see that the Jewish question is considered only from one aspect.

It was by no means sufficient to ask: who should emancipate? who should be emancipated? The critic should ask a third question:

4. Bauer, *Die Judenfrage*, p. 64. [*Marx*]
5. Ibid., p. 65. [*Marx*]
6. Loc. cit. [*Marx*]
7. Ibid., p. 71. [*Marx*]
8. Bauer, *Die Judenfrage*, p. 66. [*Marx*]
9. Ibid., p. 97. [*Marx*]

what kind of emancipation is involved? What are the essential conditions of the emancipation which is demanded? The criticism of *political emancipation* itself was only the final criticism of the Jewish question and its genuine resolution into the "*general question of the age.*"

Bauer, since he does not formulate the problem at this level, falls into contradictions. He establishes conditions which are not based upon the nature of *political* emancipation. He raises questions which are irrelevant to his problem, and he resolves problems which leave his question unanswered. When Bauer says of the opponents of Jewish emancipation that "Their error was simply to assume that the Christian state was the only true one, and not to subject it to the same criticism as Judaism,"[1] we see his own error in the fact that he subjects *only* the "Christian state," and not the "state as such" to criticism, that he does not examine *the relation between political emancipation and human emancipation,* and that he, therefore, poses conditions which are only explicable by his lack of critical sense in confusing political emancipation and universal human emancipation. Bauer asks the Jews: Have you, from your standpoint, the right to demand *political emancipation?* We ask the converse question: from the standpoint of *political* emancipation can the Jew be required to abolish Judaism, or man be asked to abolish religion?.

The Jewish question presents itself differently according to the state in which the Jew resides. In Germany, where there is no political state, no state as such, the Jewish question is purely *theological.* The Jew finds himself in *religious* opposition to the state, which proclaims Christianity as its foundation. This state is a theologian *ex professo.* Criticism here is criticism of theology; a double-edged criticism, of Christian and of Jewish theology. And so we move always in the domain of theology, however *critically* we may move therein.

In France, which is a *constitutional* state, the Jewish question is a question of constitutionalism, of the incompleteness *of political emancipation.* Since the *semblance* of a state religion is maintained here, if only in the insignificant and self-contradictory formula of a *religion of the majority,* the relation of the Jews to the state also retains a semblance of religious, theological opposition.

It is only in the free states of North America, or at least in some of them, that the Jewish question loses its *theological* significance and becomes a truly *secular* question. Only where the state exists in its completely developed form can the relation of the Jew, and of the religious man in general, to the political state appear in a pure form, with its own characteristics. The criticism of this relation

1. Bauer, *Die Judenfrage*, p. 3. [*Marx*]

ceases to be theological criticism when the state ceases to maintain a *theological* attitude towards religion, that is, when it adopts the attitude of a state, i.e. a *political* attitude. Criticism then becomes *criticism of the political state*. And at this point, where the question ceases to be *theological*, Bauer's criticism ceases to be critical.

"There is not, in the United States, either a state religion or a religion declared to be that of a majority, or a predominance of one religion over another. The state remains aloof from all religions."[2] There are even some states in North America in which "the constitution does not impose any religious belief or practice as a condition of political rights."[3] And yet, "no one in the United States believes that a man without religion can be an honest man."[4] And North America is pre-eminently the country of religiosity, as Beaumont,[5] Tocqueville[6] and the Englishman, Hamilton,[7] assure us in unison. However, the states of North America only serve as an example. The question is: what is the relation between *complete* political emancipation and religion? If we find in the country which has attained full political emancipation, that religion not only continues to *exist* but is *fresh* and *vigorous*, this is proof that the existence of religion is not at all opposed to the perfection of the state. But since the existence of religion is the existence of a defect, the source of this defect must be sought in the *nature* of the state itself. Religion no longer appears as the basis, but as the *manifestation* of secular narrowness. That is why we explain the religious constraints upon the free citizens by the secular constraints upon them. We do not claim that they must transcend their religious narrowness in order to get rid of their secular limitations. We claim that they will transcend their religious narrowness once they have overcome their secular limitations. We do not turn secular questions into theological questions; we turn theological questions into secular ones. History has for long enough been resolved into superstition; but we now resolve superstition into history. The question of the *relation between political emancipation and religion* becomes for us a question of the *relation between political emancipation and human emancipation*. We criticize the religious failings of the political state by criticizing the political state in its *secular* form, disregarding its religious failings. We express in human terms the contradiction between the state and a *particular religion*, for example *Judaism*, by showing the contradic-

2. Gustave de Beaumont, *Marie ou l'esclavage aux États-Unis*, Bruxelles, 1835, 2 vols., II, p. 207. [*Marx*] Marx refers to another edition, Paris, 1835.
3. Ibid., p. 216. Beaumont actually refers to *all* the States of North America.
4. Ibid., p. 217. [*Marx*]

5. G. de Beaumont, op. cit. [*Marx*]
6. A. de Tocqueville, *De la démocratie en Amérique*. [*Marx*]
7. Thomas Hamilton, *Men and Manners in North America*, Edinburgh, 1833, 2 vols. [*Marx*] Marx quotes from the German translation, Mannheim, 1834.

tion between the state and particular *secular elements*, between the state and *religion in general* and between the state and its general *presuppositions*.

The *political* emancipation of the Jew or the Christian—of the *religious* man in general—is the *emancipation of* the state from Judaism, Christianity, and *religion* in general. The *state* emancipates itself from religion in its own particular way, in the mode which corresponds to its nature, by emancipating itself from the *state religion*; that is to say, by giving recognition to no religion and affirming itself purely and simply as a state. To be *politically* emancipated from religion is not to be finally and completely emancipated from religion, because political emancipation is not the final and absolute form of *human* emancipation.

The limits of political emancipation appear at once in the fact that the *state* can liberate itself from a constraint without man himself being *really* liberated; that a state may be a *free state* without man himself being a *free man*. Bauer himself tacitly admits this when he makes political emancipation depend upon the following condition—

"It would be necessary, moreover, to abolish all religious privileges, including the monopoly of a privileged church. If some people, or even the *immense majority, still felt obliged to fulfil their religious duties*, this practice should be left to them as a *completely private matter*." Thus the state may have emancipated itself from religion, even though the *immense majority* of people continue to be religious. And the immense majority do not cease to be religious by virtue of being religious *in private*.

The attitude of the state, especially the *free state*, towards religion is only the attitude towards religion of the individuals who compose the state. It follows that man frees himself from a constraint in a *political* way, through the state, when he transcends his limitations, in contradiction with himself, and in an *abstract, narrow* and partial way. Furthermore, by emancipating himself *politically*, man emancipates himself in a *devious way*, through an intermediary, however *necessary* this intermediary may be. Finally, even when he proclaims himself an atheist through the intermediary of the state, that is, when he declares the state to be an atheist, he is still engrossed in religion, because he only recognizes himself as an atheist in a roundabout way, through an intermediary. Religion is simply the recognition of man in a roundabout fashion; that is, through an intermediary. The state is the intermediary between man and human liberty. Just as Christ is the intermediary to whom man attributes all his own divinity and all his religious *bonds*, so the state is the intermediary to which man confides all his non-divinity and all his *human freedom*.

The *political* elevation of man above religion shares the weaknesses and merits of all such political measures. For example, the state as a state abolishes *private property* (i.e. man decrees by *political* means the *abolition* of private property) when it abolishes the *property qualification* for electors and representatives, as has been done in many of the North American States. Hamilton interprets this phenomenon quite correctly from the political standpoint: *The masses have gained a victory over property owners and financial wealth.*[8] Is not private property ideally abolished when the non-owner comes to legislate for the owner of property? The *property qualification* is the last *political* form in which private property is recognized.

But the political suppression of private property not only does not abolish private property; it actually presupposes its existence. The state abolishes, after its fashion, the distinctions established by *birth, social rank, education, occupation,* when it decrees that birth, social rank, education, occupation are *non-political* distinctions; when it proclaims, without regard to these distinctions, that every member of society is an *equal* partner in popular sovereignty, and treats all the elements which compose the real life of the nation from the standpoint of the state. But the state, none the less, allows private property, education, occupation, to *act* after *their* own fashion, namely as private property, education, occupation, and to manifest their *particular* nature. Far from abolishing these *effective* differences, it only exists so far as they are presupposed; it is conscious of being a *political state* and it manifests its *universality* only in opposition to these elements. Hegel, therefore, defines the relation of the political state to religion quite correctly when he says: "In order for the state to come in to existence as the *self-knowing* ethical actuality of spirit, it is essential that it should be distinct from the forms of authority and of faith. But this distinction emerges only in so far as divisions occur within the ecclesiastical sphere itself. It is only in this way that the state, above the *particular* churches, has attained to the universality of thought—its formal principle—and is bringing this universality into existence."[9] To be sure! Only in this manner, *above* the *particular* elements, can the state constitute itself as universality.

The perfected political state is, by its nature, the *species-life*[1] of

8. Hamilton, op. cit., I, pp. 288, 306, 309. [*Marx*]
9. Hegel, *Grundlinien der Philosophie des Rechts*, I[er] Aufgabe, 1821, p. 346. [*Marx*] See the English translation by T. M. Knox, *Hegel's Philosophy of Right*, Oxford, 1942, p. 173.
1. The terms "species-life" (*Gattungsleben*) and "species-being" (*Gattungswesen*) are derived from Feuerbach. In the first chapter of *Das Wesen des Christentums* [*The Essence of Christianity*], Leipzig, 1841, Feuerbach discusses the nature of man, and argues that man is to be distinguished from animals not by "consciousness" as such, but by a particular kind of consciousness. Man is not only conscious of himself as an individual; he is also conscious of himself as a mem-

man as *opposed* to his material life. All the presuppositions of this egoistic life continue to exist in *civil society outside* the political sphere, as qualities of civil society. Where the political state has attained to its full development, man leads, not only in thought, in consciousness, but in *reality*, in *life*, a double existence—celestial and terrestrial. He lives in the *political community*, where he regards himself as a *communal being*, and in *civil society* where he acts simply as a *private individual*, treats other men as means, degrades himself to the role of a mere means, and becomes the plaything of alien powers. The political state, in relation to civil society, is just as spiritual as is heaven in relation to earth. It stands in the same opposition to civil society, and overcomes it in the same manner as religion overcomes the narrowness of the profane world; i.e. it has always to acknowledge it again, re-establish it, and allow itself to be dominated by it. Man, in his *most intimate* reality, in civil society, is a profane being. Here, where he appears both to himself and to others as a real individual he is an *illusory* phenomenon. In the state, on the contrary, where he is regarded as a species-being,[2] man is the imaginary member of an imaginary sovereignty, divested of his real, individual life, and infused with an unreal universality.

The conflict in which the individual, as the professor of a *particular* religion, finds himself involved with his own quality of citizenship and with other men as members of the community, may be resolved into the *secular* schism between the *political* state and *civil society*. For man as a *bourgeois*[3] "life in the state is only an appearance or a fleeting exception to the normal and essential." It is true that the *bourgeois*, like the Jew, participates in political life only in a sophistical way, just as the *citoyen*[4] is a Jew or a *bourgeois* only in a sophistical way. But this sophistry is not personal. It is the *sophistry of the political state* itself. The difference between the religious man and the citizen is the same as that between the shopkeeper and the citizens, between the day-labourer and the citizen, between the landed proprietor and the citizen, between the *living individual* and the *citizen*. The contradiction in which the religious man finds himself with the political man, is the same contradiction in which the *bourgeois* finds himself with the citizen, and the member of civil society with his *political lion's skin*.

---

ber of the human species, and so he apprehends a "human essence" which is the same in himself and in other men. According to Feuerbach this ability to conceive of "species" is the fundamental element in the human power of reasoning: "Science is the consciousness of species." Marx, while not departing from this meaning of the terms, employs them in other contexts; and he insists more strongly than Feuerbach that since this "species-consciousness" defines the nature of man, man is only living and acting authentically (i.e. in accordance with his nature) when he lives and acts deliberately as a "species-being," that is, as a *social* being.
2. See previous note.
3. I.e. as a member of civil society.
4. I.e. the individual with political rights.

This secular opposition, to which the Jewish question reduces itself—the relation between the political state and its presuppositions, whether the latter are material elements such as private property, etc., or spiritual elements such as culture or religion, the conflict between the *general interest* and *private interest*, the schism between the *political* state and *civil society*—these profane contradictions, Bauer leaves intact, while he directs his polemic against their *religious* expression. "It is precisely this basis—that is, the needs which assure the existence of *civil society* and *guarantee its necessity*—which exposes its existence to continual danger, maintains an element of uncertainty in civil society, produces this continually changing compound of wealth and poverty, of prosperity and distress, and above all generates change."[5] Compare the whole section entitled "Civil society,"[6] which follows closely the distinctive features of Hegel's philosophy of right. Civil society, in its opposition to this political state, is recognized as necessary because the political state is recognized as necessary.

Political emancipation certainly represents a great progress. It is not, indeed, the final form of human emancipation, but it is the final form of human emancipation *within* the framework of the prevailing social order. It goes without saying that we are speaking here of real, practical emancipation.

Man emancipates himself *politically* from religion by expelling it from the sphere of public law to that of private law. Religion is no longer the spirit of the *state*, in which man behaves, albeit in a specific and limited way and in a particular sphere, as a species-being, in community with other men. It has become the spirit of *civil society*, of the sphere of egoism and of the *bellum omnium contra omnes*. It is no longer the essence of *community*, but the essence of *differentiation*. It has become what it was at the *beginning*, an expression of the fact that man is *separated* from the *community*, from himself and from other men. It is now only the abstract avowal of an individual folly, a private whim or caprice. The infinite fragmentation of religion in North America, for example, already gives it the *external* form of a strictly private affair. It has been relegated among the numerous private interests and exiled from the life of the community as such. But one should have no illusions about the scope of political emancipation. The division of man into the *public person* and the *private person*, the *displacement* of religion from the state to civil society—all this is not a stage in political emancipation but its consummation. Thus political emancipation does not abolish, and does not even strive to abolish, man's *real* religiosity.

The *decomposition* of man into Jew and citizen, Protestant and citizen, religious man and citizen, is not a deception practised

5. Bauer, *Die Judenfrage*, p. 8. [*Marx*]   6. Ibid., pp. 8–9. [*Marx*]

against the political system nor yet an evasion of political emancipation. It is *political emancipation itself*, the *political* mode of emancipation from religion. Certainly, in periods when the political state as such comes violently to birth in civil society, and when men strive to liberate themselves through political emancipation, the state can, and must, proceed to *abolish and destroy religion*; but only in the same way as it proceeds to abolish private property, by declaring a maximum, by confiscation, or by progressive taxation, or in the same way as it proceeds to abolish life, by the *guillotine*. At those times when the state is most aware of itself, political life seeks to stifle its own prerequisites—civil society and its elements—and to establish itself as the genuine and harmonious species-life of man. But it can only achieve this end by setting itself in *violent* contradiction with its own conditions of existence, by declaring a *permanent* revolution. Thus the political drama ends necessarily with the restoration of religion, of private property, of all the elements of civil society, just as war ends with the conclusion of peace.

In fact, the perfected Christian state is not the so-called *Christian* state which acknowledges Christianity as its basis, as the state religion, and thus adopts an exclusive attitude towards other religions; it is, rather, the *atheistic* state, the democratic state, the state which relegates religion among the other elements of civil society. The state which is still theological, which still professes officially the Christian creed, and which has not yet dared to declare itself a *state*, has not yet succeeded in expressing in a human and *secular* form, in its political *reality*, the human basis of which Christianity is the transcendental expression. The so-called Christian state is simply a *non-state*; since it is not Christianity as a religion, but only the *human core* of the Christian religion which can realize itself in truly human creations.

The so-called Christian state is the Christian negation of the state, but not at all the political realization of Christianity. The state which professes Christianity as a religion does not yet profess it in a political form, because it still has a religious attitude towards religion. In other words, such a state is not the *genuine realization* of the human basis of religion, because it still accepts the *unreal, imaginary* form of this human core. The so-called Christian state is an *imperfect* state, for which the Christian religion serves as the *supplement* and *sanctification* of its imperfection. Thus religion becomes necessarily one of its *means*; and so it is the *hypocritical* state. There is a great difference between saying: (i) that the *perfect* state, owing to a deficiency in the general *nature* of the state, counts religion as one of its *prerequisites*, or (ii) that the *imperfect* state, owing to a deficiency in its *particular existence* as an imperfect state, declares that religion is its *basis*. In the latter, religion becomes *imperfect politics*. In the former, the imperfection even of perfected *politics* is revealed in religion. The so-called Christian state needs the Christian religion in order to complete itself *as a state*. The democratic state, the real state, does not need religion for its political consummation. On the contrary, it can dispense with religion, because in this case the human core of religion is realized in a profane manner. The so-called Christian state, on the other hand, has a political attitude towards religion, and a religious attitude towards politics. It reduces political institutions and religion equally to mere appearances.

In order to make this contradiction clearer we shall examine Bauer's model of the Christian state, a model which is derived from his study of the German-Christian state.

"Quite recently," says Bauer, "in order to demonstrate the *impossibility* or the *non-existence* of a Christian state, those passages in the Bible have been frequently quoted with which the state *does not conform* and *cannot conform unless it wishes to dissolve itself entirely*."

"But the question is not so easily settled. What do these Biblical passages demand? Supernatural renunciation, submission to the authority of revelation, turning away from the state, the abolition of profane conditions. But the Christian state proclaims and accomplishes all these things. It has assimilated the *spirit of the Bible*, and if it does not reproduce it exactly in the terms which the Bible uses, that is simply because it expresses this spirit in political forms, in forms which are borrowed from the political system of this world but which, in the religious rebirth which they are obliged to undergo, are reduced to simple appearances. Man turns away from the state and by this means realizes and completes the political institutions."[7]

Bauer continues by showing that the members of a Christian state no longer constitute a nation with a will of its own. The nation has its true existence in the leader to whom it is subjected, but this leader is, by his origin and nature, alien to it since he has been imposed by God without the people having any part in the matter. The laws of such a nation are not its own work, but are direct revelations. The supreme leader, in his relations with the real nation, the masses, requires privileged intermediaries; and the nation itself disintegrates into a multitude of distinct spheres which are formed and determined by chance, are differentiated from each other by their interests and their specific passions and preju-

7. Bauer, *Die Judenfrage*, p. 55. [*Marx*]

dices, and acquire as a privilege the permission to isolate themselves from each other, etc.[8]

But Bauer himself says: "Politics, if it is to be nothing more than religion, should not be politics; any more than the scouring of pans, if it is treated as a religious matter, should be regarded as ordinary housekeeping."[9] But in the German-Christian state religion is an "economic matter" just as "economic matters" are religion. In the German-Christian state the power of religion is the religion of power.

The separation of the "spirit of the Bible" from the "letter of the Bible" is an *irreligious* act. The state which expresses the Bible in the letter of politics, or in any letter other than that of the Holy Ghost, commits sacrilege, if not in the eyes of men at least in the eyes of its own religion. The state which acknowledges the Bible as its charter and Christianity as its supreme rule must be assessed according to the words of the Bible; for even the language of the Bible is sacred. Such a state, as well as the *human rubbish* upon which it is based, finds itself involved in a painful contradiction, which is insoluble from the standpoint of religious consciousness, when it is referred to those words of the Bible "with which it does not conform and *cannot conform unless it wishes to dissolve itself entirely.*" And why does it not wish to dissolve itself entirely? The state itself cannot answer either itself or others. In its own consciousness the official Christian state is an "ought" whose realization is imposible. It cannot affirm the *reality* of its own existence without lying to itself, and so it remains always in its own eyes an object of doubt, an uncertain and problematic object. Criticism is, therefore, entirely within its rights in forcing the state, which supports itself upon the Bible, into a total disorder of thought in which it no longer knows whether it is *illusion* or *reality*; and in which the infamy of its *profane* ends (for which religion serves as a cloak) enter into an insoluble conflict with the probity of its *religious* consciousness (for which religion appears as the goal of the world). Such a state can only escape its inner torment by becoming the *myrmidon* of the Catholic Church. In the face of this Church, which asserts that secular power is entirely subordinate to its commands, the state is powerless; powerless the secular power which claims to be the rule of the religious spirit.

What prevails in the so-called Christian state is not man but alienation. The only man who counts—the *King*—is specifically differentiated from other men and is still a religious being associated directly with heaven and with God. The relations which exist here are relations still based upon *faith*. The religious spirit is still not really secularized.

8. Ibid., p. 56. [*Marx*]   9. Ibid., p. 108. [*Marx*]

But the religious spirit cannot be *really* secularized. For what is it but the *non secular* form of a stage in the development of the human spirit? The religious spirit can only be realized if the stage of development of the human spirit which it expresses in religious form, manifests and constitutes itself in its *secular* form. This is what happens in the *democratic* state. The basis of this state is not Christianity but the *human basis* of Christianity. Religion remains the ideal, non-secular consciousness of its members, because it is the ideal form of the *stage of human development* which has been attained.

The members of the political state are religious because of the dualism between individual life and species-life, between the life of civil society and political life. They are religious in the sense that man treats political life, which is remote from his own individual existence, as if it were his true life; and in the sense that religion is here the spirit of civil society, and expresses the separation and withdrawal of man from man. Political democracy is Christian in the sense that man, not merely one man but every man, is there considered a sovereign being, a supreme being; but it is uneducated, unsocial man, man just as he is in his fortuitous existence, man as he has been corrupted, lost to himself, alienated, subjected to the rule of inhuman conditions and elements, by the whole organization of our society—in short man who is not yet a *real* species-being. Creations of fantasy, dreams, the postulates of Christianity, the sovereignty of man—but of man as an alien being distinguished from the real man—all these become, in democracy, the tangible and present reality, secular maxims.

In the perfected democracy, the religious and theological consciousness appears to itself all the more religious and theological in that it is apparently without any political significance or terrestrial aims, is an affair of the heart withdrawn from the world, an expression of the limitations of reason, a product of arbitrariness and fantasy, a veritable life in the beyond. Christianity here attains the *practical* expression of its universal religious significance, because the most varied views are brought together in the form of Christianity, and still more because Christianity does not ask that anyone should profess Christianity, but simply that he should have some kind of religion (*see* Beaumont, op. cit.). The religious consciousness runs riot in a wealth of contradictions and diversity.

We have shown, therefore, that political emancipation from religion leaves religion in existence, although this is no longer a privileged religion. The contradiction in which the adherent of a particular religion finds himself in relation to his citizenship is only *one aspect* of the universal *secular contradiction between the political state and* civil society. The consummation of the Christian state is a state which acknowledges itself simply as a state and ignores the religion of its members. The emancipation of the state from religion is not the emancipation of the real man from religion.

We do not say to the Jews, therefore, as does Bauer: you cannot be emancipated politically without emancipating yourselves completely from Judaism. We say rather: it is because you can be emancipated politically, without renouncing Judaism completely and absolutely, that *political emancipation* itself is not *human* emancipation. If you want to be politically emancipated, without emancipating yourselves humanly, the inadequacy and the contradiction is not entirely in yourselves but in the *nature* and the *category* of political emancipation. If you are preoccupied with this category you share the general prejudice. Just as the state *evangelizes* when, although it is a state, it adopts a Christian attitude towards the Jews, the Jew *acts politically* when, though a Jew, he demands civil rights.

But if a man, though a Jew, can be emancipated politically and acquire civil rights, can he claim and acquire what are called the *rights of man*? Bauer *denies* it. "The question is whether the Jew as such, that is, the Jew who himself avows that he is constrained by his true nature to live eternally separate from men, is able to acquire and to concede to others the *universal rights of man*."

"The idea of the rights of man was only discovered in the Christian world, in the last century. It is not an innate idea; on the contrary, it is acquired in a struggle against the historical traditions in which man has been educated up to the present time. The rights of man are not, therefore, a gift of nature, nor a legacy from past history, but the reward of a struggle against the accident of birth and against the privileges which history has hitherto transmitted from generation to generation. They are the results of culture, and only he can possess them who has merited and earned them."

"But can the Jew really take possession of them? As long as he remains Jewish the limited nature which makes him a Jew must prevail over the human nature which should associate him, as a man, with other men; and it will isolate him from everyone who is not a Jew. He declares, by this separation, that the particular nature which makes him Jewish is his true and supreme nature, before which human nature has to efface itself."

"Similarly, the Christian as such cannot grant the rights of man."[1]

According to Bauer man has to sacrifice the *"privilege of faith"* in order to acquire the general rights of man. Let us consider for a moment the so-called rights of man; let us examine them in their most authentic form, that which they have among those who dis-

1. Bauer, *Die Judenfrage*, pp. 19–20. [*Marx*]

covered them, the North Americans and the French! These rights of man are, in part, *political rights*, which can only be exercised if one is a member of a community. Their content is *participation* in the *community* life, in the *political* life of the community, the life of the state. They fall in the category of *political liberty*, of *civil rights*, which as we have seen do not at all presuppose the consistent and positive abolition of religion; nor consequently, of Judaism. It remains to consider the other part, namely the *rights of man* as distinct from the *rights of the citizen*.

Among them is to be found the freedom of conscience, the right to practise a chosen religion. The *privilege of faith* is expressly recognized, either as a *right of man* or as a consequence of a right of man, namely liberty. *Declaration of the Rights of Man and of the Citizen*, 1791, Article 10: "No one is to be disturbed on account of his opinions, even religious opinions." There is guaranteed, as one of the rights of man, "the liberty of every man to practise the *religion* to which he adheres."

The *Declaration of the Rights of Man, etc.* 1793, enumerates among the rights of man (Article 7): "The liberty of religious observance." Moreover, it is even stated, with respect to the right to express ideas and opinions, to hold meetings, to practise a religion, that: "The necessity of enunciating these *rights* presupposes either the existence or the recent memory of despotism." Compare the Constitution of 1795, Section XII, Article 354.

Constitution of Pennsylvania, Article 9, § 3: "All men have received from nature the imprescriptible *right* to worship the Almighty according to the dictates of their conscience, and no one can be legally compelled to follow, establish or support against his will any religion or religious ministry. No human authority can, in any circumstances, intervene in a matter of conscience or control the forces of the soul."

Constitution of New Hampshire, Articles 5 and 6: "Among these natural rights some are by nature inalienable since nothing can replace them. The rights of conscience are among them."[2]

The incompatibility between religion and the rights of man is so little manifest in the concept of the rights of man that the *right to be religious*, in one's own fashion, and to practise one's own particular religion, is expressly included among the rights of man. The privilege of faith is a *universal right of man*.

A distinction is made between the rights of man and the rights of the citizen. Who is this *man* distinct from the *citizen*? No one but the *member of civil society*. Why is the member of civil society called "man," simply man, and why are his rights called the "rights of man"? How is this fact to be explained? By the relation between

2. Beaumont, op. cit., II, pp. 206–7. [*Marx*]

the political state and civil society, and by the nature of political emancipation.

Let us notice first of all that the so-called *rights of man*, as distinct from the *rights of the citizen*, are simply the rights of a *member of civil society*, that is, of egoistic man, of man separated from other men and from the community. The most radical constitution, that of 1793, says: *Declaration of the Rights of Man and of the Citizen:* Article 2. "These rights, etc. (the natural and imprescriptible rights) are: *equality, liberty, security, property.*

What constitutes liberty?

Article 6. "Liberty is the power which man has to do everything which does not harm the rights of others."

Liberty is, therefore, the right to do everything which does not harm others. The limits within which each individual can act without harming others are determined by law, just as the boundary between two fields is marked by a stake. It is a question of the liberty of man regarded as an isolated monad, withdrawn into himself. Why, according to Bauer, is the Jew not fitted to acquire the rights of man? "As long as he remains Jewish the limited nature which makes him a Jew must prevail over the human nature which should associate him, as a man, with other men; and it will isolate him from everyone who is not a Jew." But liberty as a right of man is not founded upon the relations between man and man, but rather upon the separation of man from man. It is the right of such separation. The right of the *circumscribed* individual, withdrawn into himself.

The practical application of the right of liberty is the right of private property. What constitutes the right of private property?

Article 16 (Constitution of 1793). "The right of *property* is that which belongs to every citizen of enjoying and disposing *as he will* of his goods and revenues, of the fruits of his work and industry."

The right of property is, therefore, the right to enjoy one's fortune and to dispose of it as one will; without regard for other men and independently of society. It is the right of self-interest. This individual liberty, and its application, form the basis of civil society. It leads every man to see in other men, not the *realization*, but rather the *limitation* of his own liberty. It declares above all the right "to enjoy and to dispose *as one will*, one's goods and revenues, the fruits of one's work and industry."

There remain the other rights of man, equality and security.

The term "equality" has here no political significance. It is only the equal right to liberty as defined above; namely that every man is equally regarded as a self-sufficient monad. The Constitution of 1795 defines the concept of liberty in this sense.

Article 5 (*Constitution* of 1795). "Equality consists in the fact that the law is the same for all, whether it protects or punishes."

And security?

Article 8 (*Constitution* of 1793). "Security consists in the protection afforded by society to each of its members for the preservation of his person, his rights, and his property."

Security is the supreme social concept of civil society; the concept of the police. The whole society exists only in order to guarantee for each of its members the preservation of his person, his rights and his property. It is in this sense that Hegel calls civil society "the state of need and of reason."

The concept of security is not enough to raise civil society above its egoism. Security is, rather, the *assurance* of its egoism.

None of the supposed rights of man, therefore, go beyond the egoistic man, man as he is, as a member of civil society; that is, an individual separated from the community, withdrawn into himself, wholly preoccupied with his private interest and acting in accordance with his private caprice. Man is far from being considered, in the rights of man, as a species-being; on the contrary, species-life itself—society—appears as a system which is external to the individual and as a limitation of his original independence. The only bond between men is natural necessity, need and private interest, the preservation of their property and their egoistic persons.

It is difficult enough to understand that a nation which has just begun to liberate itself, to tear down all the barriers between different sections of the people and to establish a political community, should solemnly proclaim (*Declaration* of 1791) the rights of the egoistic man, separated from his fellow men and from the community, and should renew this proclamation at a moment when only the most heroic devotion can save the nation (and is, therefore, urgently called for), and when the sacrifice of all the interests of civil society is in question and egoism should be punished as a crime. (*Declaration of the Rights of Man, etc.* 1793). The matter becomes still more incomprehensible when we observe that the political liberators reduce citizenship, the *political community*, to a mere *means* for preserving these so-called rights of man; and consequently, that the citizen is declared to be the servant of egoistic "man," that the sphere in which man functions as a species-being is degraded to a level below the sphere where he functions as a partial being, and finally that it is man as a bourgeois and not man as a citizen who is considered the *true* and *authentic* man.

"The end of every *political association* is the *preservation* of the natural and imprescriptible rights of man." (*Declaration of the Rights of Man, etc.* 1791, Article 2.) "Government is instituted in

order to guarantee man's enjoyment of his natural and imprescriptible rights." (*Declaration, etc.* 1793, Article 1.) Thus, even in the
period of its youthful enthusiasm, which is raised to fever pitch by
the force of circumstances, political life declares itself to be only a
means, whose end is the life of civil society. It is true that its revolutionary practice is in flagrant contradiction with its theory.
While, for instance, security is declared to be one of the rights of
man, the violation of the privacy of correspondence is openly considered. While the "unlimited freedom of the Press" (*Constitution*
of 1793, Article 122), as a corollary of the right of individual liberty, is guaranteed, the freedom of the Press is completely
destroyed, since "the freedom of the Press should not be permitted
when it endangers public liberty."[3] This amounts to saying: the
right to liberty ceases to be a right as soon as it comes into conflict
with *political* life, whereas in theory political life is no more than
the guarantee of the rights of man—the rights of the individual
man—and should, therefore, be suspended as soon as it comes into
contradiction with its *end*, these rights of man. But practice is only
the exception, while theory is the rule. Even if one decided to
regard revolutionary practice as the correct expression of this relation, the problem would remain as to why it is that in the minds of
political liberators the relation is inverted, so that the end appears
as the means and the means as the end? This optical illusion of
their consciousness would always remain a problem, though a psychological and theoretical one.

But the problem is easily solved.

Political emancipation is at the same time the *dissolution* of the
old society, upon which the sovereign power, the alienated political
life of the people, rests. Political revolution is a revolution of civil
society. What was the nature of the old society? It can be characterized in one word: *feudalism*. The old civil society had a *directly
political* character; that is, the elements of civil life such as property, the family, and types of occupation had been raised, in the
form of lordship, caste and guilds, to elements of political life.
They determined, in this form, the relation of the individual to the
state as a whole; that is, his *political* situation, or in other words, his
separation and exclusion from the other elements of society. For
this organization of national life did not constitute property and
labour as social elements; it rather succeeded in *separating* them
from the body of the state, and made them *distinct* societies within
society. Nevertheless, at least in the feudal sense, the vital functions and conditions of civil society remained political. They
excluded the individual from the body of the state, and transformed the *particular* relation which existed between his corpora-

3. Buchez et Roux, "Robespierre jeune," *Histoire parlementaire de la Révolution française*, Tome XXVIII, p. 159. [*Marx*]

tion and the state into a general relation between the individual and social life, just as they transformed his specific civil activity and situation into a general activity and situation. As a result of this organization, the state as a whole and its consciousness, will and activity—the general political power—also necessarily appeared as the *private* affair of a ruler and his servants, separated from the people.

The political revolution which overthrew this power of the ruler, which made state affairs the affairs of the people, and the political state a matter of *general* concern, i.e. a real state, necessarily shattered everything—estates, corporations, guilds, privileges—which expressed the separation of the people from community life. The political revolution therefore *abolished* the *political character of civil society*. It dissolved civil society into its basic elements, on the one hand *individuals*, and on the other hand the *material and cultural elements* which formed the life experience and the civil situation of these individuals. It set free the political spirit which had, so to speak, been dissolved, fragmented and lost in the various culs-de-sac of feudal society; it reassembled these scattered fragments, liberated the political spirit from its connexion with civil life and made of it the community sphere, the *general* concern of the people, in principle independent of these particular elements of civil life. A *specific* activity and situation in life no longer had any but an individual significance. They no longer constituted the general relation between the individual and the state as a whole. Public affairs as such became the general affair of each individual, and political functions became general functions.

But the consummation of the idealism of the state was at the same time the consummation of the materialism of civil society. The bonds which had restrained the egoistic spirit of civil society were removed along with the political yoke. Political emancipation was at the same time an emancipation of civil society from politics and from even the *semblance* of a general content.

Feudal society was dissolved into its basic element, *man*; but into *egoistic* man who was its real foundation.

Man in this aspect, the member of civil society, is now the foundation and presupposition of the *political* state. He is recognized as such in the rights of man.

But the liberty of egoistic man, and the recognition of this liberty, is rather the recognition of the *frenzied* movement of the cultural and material elements which form the content of his life.

Thus man was not liberated from religion; he received religious liberty. He was not liberated from property; he received the liberty to own property. He was not liberated from the egoism of business; he received the liberty to engage in business.

The *formation of the political state*, and the dissolution of civil society into independent *individuals* whose relations are regulated by *law*, as the relations between men in the corporations and guilds were regulated by *privilege*, are accomplished by *one and the same act*. Man as a member of civil society—*non-political* man—necessarily appears as the *natural* man. The rights of man appear as natural rights because *conscious* activity is concentrated upon political *action*. Egoistic man is the *passive, given* result of the dissolution of society, an object of *direct apprehension* and consequently a *natural* object. The *political revolution* dissolves civil society into its elements without *revolutionizing* these elements themselves or subjecting them to criticism. This revolution regards civil society, the sphere of human needs, labour, private interests and civil law, as the *basis of its own existence*, as a self-subsistent *precondition*, and thus as its *natural basis*. Finally, man as a member of civil society is identified with *authentic man*, man as distinct from citizen, because he is man in his sensuous, individual and *immediate* existence, whereas *political* man is only abstract, artificial man, man as an *allegorical, moral* person. Thus man as he really is, is seen only in the form of *egoistic* man, and man in his *true* nature only in the form of the *abstract citizen*.

The abstract notion of political man is well formulated by Rousseau: "Whoever dares undertake to establish a people's institutions must feel himself capable of *changing*, as it were, *human nature* itself, of *transforming* each individual who, in isolation, is a complete but solitary whole, into a *part* of something greater than himself, from which in a sense, he derives his life and his being; [of changing man's nature in order to strengthen it;] of substituting a limited and moral existence for the physical and independent life [with which all of us are endowed by nature]. His task, in short, is to take from *a man his own powers*, and to give him in exchange alien powers which he can only employ with the help of other men."[4]

Every emancipation is a *restoration* of the human world and of human relationships to *man himself*.

Political emancipation is a reduction of man, on the one hand to a member of civil society, an *independent* and *egoistic* individual, and on the other hand, to a *citizen*, to a moral person.

Human emancipation will only be complete when the real, individual man has absorbed into himself the abstract citizen; when as an individual man, in his everyday life, in his work, and in his relationships, he has become a *species-being*; and when he has recognized and organized his own powers (*forces propres*) as *social* powers so that he no longer separates this social power from himself as *political* power.

4. J. J. Rousseau, *Du contrat social*, Book II. Chapter VII, "The Legislator." Marx quoted this passage in French, and added the emphases; he omitted the portions enclosed in square brackets.

2. Bruno Bauer, "Die Fähigkeit der heutigen Juden und Christen frei zu werden"[5]

It is in this form that Bauer studies the relation between the *Jewish and Christian religions*, and also their relation with modern criticism. This latter relation is their relation with "the capacity to become free."

He reaches this conclusion: "The Christian has only to raise himself one degree, to rise above his religion, in order to abolish religion in general," and thus to become free; but "the Jew, on the contrary, has to break not only with his Jewish nature, but also with the process towards the consummation of his religion, a process which has remained alien to him."[6]

Thus Bauer here transforms the question of Jewish emancipation into a purely religious question. The theological doubt about whether the Jew or the Christian has the better chance of attaining salvation is reproduced here in the more enlightened form: which of the two is more *capable of emancipation*? It is indeed no longer asked: which makes free—Judaism or Christianity? On the contrary, it is now asked: which makes free—the negation of Judaism or the negation of Christianity?

"If they wish to become free the Jews should not embrace Christianity as such, but Christianity in dissolution, religion in dissolution; that is to say, the Enlightenment, criticism, and its outcome, a free humanity."[7]

It is still a matter, therefore, of the Jews professing some kind of faith; no longer Christianity as such, but Christianity in dissolution.

Bauer asks the Jews to break with the essence of the Christian religion, but this demand does not follow, as he himself admits, from the development of the Jewish nature.

From the moment when Bauer, at the end of his *Judenfrage*, saw in Judaism only a crude religious criticism of Christianity, and, therefore, attributed to it only a religious significance, it was to be expected that he would transform the emancipation of the Jews into a philosophico-theological act.

Bauer regards the *ideal* and abstract essence of the Jew—his *religion*—as the *whole* of his nature. He, therefore, concludes rightly that "The Jew contributes nothing to mankind when he disregards his own limited law," when he renounces all his Judaism.[8]

The relation between Jews and Christians thus becomes the following: the only interest which the emancipation of the Jew presents for the Christian is a general human and *theoretical* interest.

5. The capacity of the present-day Jews and Christians to become free. [In *Einundzwanzig Bogen aus der Schweiz* (Ed. G. Herwegh), pp. 56–71.—*Marx*]

6. Loc. cit., p. 71. [*Marx*]
7. Ibid., p. 70. [*Marx*]
8. Loc. cit., p. 65. [*Marx*]

Judaism is a phenomenon which offends the religious eye of the Christian. As soon as the Christian's eye ceases to be religious the phenomenon ceases to offend it. The emancipation of the Jew is not in itself, therefore, a task which falls to the Christian to perform.

The Jew, on the other hand, if he wants to emancipate himself has to undertake, besides his own work, the work of the Christian—the "criticism of the gospels," of the "life of Jesus," etc.[9]

"It is for them to arrange matters; they will decide their own destiny. But history does not allow itself to be mocked."[1]

We will attempt to escape from the theological formulation of the question. For us, the question concerning the capacity of the Jew for emancipation is transformed into another question: what specific *social* element is it necessary to overcome in order to abolish Judaism? For the capacity of the present-day Jew to emancipate himself expresses the relation of Judaism to the emancipation of the contemporary world. The relation results necessarily from the particular situation of Judaism in the present enslaved world.

Let us consider the real Jew: not the *sabbath Jew*, whom Bauer considers, but the *everyday Jew*.

Let us not seek the secret of the Jew in his religion, but let us seek the secret of the religion in the real Jew.

What is the profane basis of Judaism? *Practical* need, *self-interest*. What is the worldly cult of the Jew? *Huckstering*. What is his worldly god? *Money*.

Very well: then in emancipating itself from *huckstering* and *money*, and thus from real and practical Judaism, our age would emancipate itself.

An organization of society which would abolish the preconditions and thus the very possibility of huckstering, would make the Jew impossible. His religious consciousness would evaporate like some insipid vapour in the real, life-giving air of society. On the other hand, when the Jew recognizes his *practical* nature as invalid and endeavours to abolish it, he begins to deviate from his former path of development, works for general *human emancipation* and turns against the *supreme practical* expression of human self-estrangement.

We discern in Judaism, therefore, a universal *antisocial* element of the *present time*, whose historical development, zealously aided in its harmful aspects by the Jews, has now attained its culminating point, a point at which it must necessarily begin to disintegrate.

9. Marx alludes here to Bruno Bauer, *Kritik der evangelischen Geschichte der Synoptiker*, Vols. I–II, Leipzig, 1841; Vol. III, Braunschweig, 1842, and David Friedrich Strauss, *Das Leben Jesu*, 2 vols. Tübingen, 1835–6. An English translation of Strauss' book by Marian Evans (George Eliot) was published in 1846 under the title *Life of Jesus Critically Examined*.
1. Bauer, "Die Fähigkeit . . . etc.," p. 71. [*Marx*]

In the final analysis, the *emancipation of* the Jews is the emancipation of mankind from *Judaism.*

The Jew has already emancipated himself in a Jewish fashion. "The Jew, who is merely tolerated in Vienna for example, determines the fate of the whole Empire by his financial power. The Jew, who may be entirely without rights in the smallest German state, decides the destiny of Europe. While the corporations and guilds exclude the Jew, or at least look on him with disfavour, the audacity of industry mocks the obstinacy of medieval institutions."[2]

This is not an isolated instance. The Jew has emancipated himself in a Jewish manner, not only by acquiring the power of money, but also because *money* has become, through him and also apart from him, a world power, while the practical Jewish spirit has become the practical spirit of the Christian nations. The Jews have emancipated themselves in so far as the Christians have become Jews.

Thus, for example, Captain Hamilton reports that the devout and politically free inhabitant of New England is a kind of Laocoon who makes not the least effort to escape from the serpents which are crushing him. *Mammon* is his idol which he adores not only with his lips but with the whole force of his body and mind. In his view the world is no more than a Stock Exchange, and he is convinced that he has no other destiny here below than to become richer than his neighbour. Trade has seized upon all his thoughts, and he has no other recreation than to exchange objects. When he travels he carries, so to speak, his goods and his counter on his back and talks only of interest and profit. If he loses sight of his own business for an instant it is only in order to pry into the business of his competitors.[3]

In North America, indeed, the effective domination of the Christian world by Judaism has come to be manifested in a common and unambiguous form; the *preaching of the Gospel* itself, Christian preaching, has become an article of commerce, and the bankrupt trader in the church behaves like the prosperous clergyman in business. "This man whom you see at the head of a respectable congregation began as a trader; his business having failed he has become a minister. This other began as a priest, but as soon as he had accumulated some money he abandoned the priesthood for trade. In the eyes of many people the religious ministry is a veritable industrial career."[4]

According to Bauer, it is "a hypocritical situation when, in theory, the Jew is deprived of political rights, while in practice he wields tremendous power and exercises on a wholesale scale the

2. Bauer, *Die Judenfrage,* p. 14. Marx paraphrases this passage. [*Marx*]
4. Beaumont, op. cit., II, p. 179. [*Marx*]
3. Hamilton, op. cit., I, p. 213. [*Marx*]

political influence which is denied him in minor matters."[5]

The contradiction which exists between the effective political power of the Jew and his political rights, is the contradiction between politics and the power of money in general. Politics is in principle superior to the power of money, but in practice it has become its bondsman.

Judaism has maintained itself *alongside* Christianity, not only because it constituted the religious criticism of Christianity and embodied the doubt concerning the religious origins of Christianity, but equally because the practical Jewish spirit—Judaism or commerce[6]—has perpetuated itself in Christian society and has even attained its highest development there. The Jew, who occupies a distinctive place in civil society, only manifests in a distinctive way the Judaism of civil society.

Judaism has been preserved, not in spite of history, but by history.

It is from its own entrails that civil society ceaselessly engenders the Jew.

What was, in itself, the basis of the Jewish religion? Practical need, egoism.

The monotheism of the Jews is, therefore, in reality, a polytheism of the numerous needs of man, a polytheism which makes even the lavatory an object of divine regulation. *Practical need, egoism,* is the principle of *civil society,* and is revealed as such in its pure form as soon as civil society has fully engendered the political state. The god of *practical need and self-interest* is *money.*

Money is the jealous god of Israel, beside which no other god may exist. Money abases all the gods of mankind and changes them into commodities. Money is the universal and self-sufficient *value* of all things. It has, therefore, deprived the whole world, both the human world and nature, of their own proper value. Money is the alienated essence of man's work and existence; this essence dominates him and he worships it.

The god of the Jews has been secularized and has become the god of this world. The bill of exchange is the real god of the Jew. His god is only an illusory bill of exchange.

The mode of perceiving nature, under the rule of private property and money, is a real contempt for, and a practical degradation of, nature, which does indeed exist in the Jewish religion but only as a creature of the imagination.

It is in this sense that Thomas Münzer declares it intolerable "that every creature should be transformed into property—the fishes in the water, the birds of the air, the plants of the earth: the

5. Bauer, *Die Judenfrage,* p. 14. [*Marx*]
6. The German word *Judentum* had, in the language of the time, the secondary meaning of "commerce," and in this and other passages Marx exploits the two senses of the word.

creature too should become free."[7]

That which is contained in an abstract form in the Jewish religion—contempt for theory, for art, for history, and for man as an end in himself—is the *real, conscious* standpoint and the virtue of the man of money. Even the species-relation itself, the relation between man and woman, becomes an object of commerce. Woman is bartered away.

The *chimerical* nationality of the Jew is the nationality of the trader, and above all of the financier.

The law, without basis or reason, of the Jew, is only the religious caricature of morality and right in general, without basis or reason; the purely *formal* rites with which the world of self-interest encircles itself.

Here again the supreme condition of man is his *legal* status, his relationship to laws which are valid for him, not because they are the laws of his own will and nature, but because they are dominant and any infraction of them will be *avenged*.

Jewish Jesuitism, the same practical Jesuitism which Bauer discovers in the Talmud, is the relationship of the world of self-interest to the laws which govern this world, laws which the world devotes its principal arts to circumventing.

Indeed, the operation of this world within its framework of laws is impossible without the continual supersession of law.

Judaism could not develop further as a *religion*, in a theoretical form, because the world view of practical need is, by its very nature, circumscribed, and the delineation of its characteristics soon completed.

The religion of practical need could not, by its very nature, find its consummation in theory, but only in *practice*, just because practice is its truth.

Judaism could not create a new world. It could only bring the new creations and conditions of the world within its own sphere of activity, because practical need, the spirit of which is self-interest, is always passive, cannot expand at will, but *finds* itself extended as a result of the continued development of society.

Judaism attains its apogee with the perfection of civil society; but civil society only reaches perfection in the Christian world. Only under the sway of Christianity, which *objectifies all* national, natural, moral and theoretical relationships, could civil society separate itself completely from the life of the state, sever all the species-bonds of man, establish egoism and selfish need in their place, and dissolve the human world into a world of atomistic, antagonistic individuals.

7. Quoted from Thomas Münzer's pamphlet against Luther, "Hochverrusachte Schutzrede und Antwort wider das geistlose, sanftlebende Fleisch zu Wittenberg, welches mit verkehrter Weise durch den Diebstahl der heiligen Schrift die erbärmliche Christenheit also ganz jammerlich besudelt hat." (p. B. iii. 1524.) [*Marx*]

Christianity issued from Judaism. It has now been re-absorbed into Judaism.

From the beginning, the Christian was the theorizing Jew; consequently, the Jew is the practical Christian. And the practical Christian has become a Jew again.

It was only in appearance that Christianity overcame real Judaism. It was too *refined*, too spiritual to eliminate the crudeness of practical need except by raising it into the ethereal realm.

Christianity is the sublime thought of Judaism; Judaism is the vulgar practical application of Christianity. But this practical application could only become universal when Christianity as perfected religion had accomplished, in a *theoretical* fashion, the alienation of man from himself and from nature.

It was only then that Judaism could attain universal domination and could turn alienated man and alienated nature into *alienable*, saleable objects, in thrall to egoistic need and huckstering.

Objectification is the practice of alienation. Just as man, so long as he is engrossed in religion, can only objectify his essence by an *alien* and fantastic being; so under the sway of egoistic need, he can only affirm himself and produce objects in practice by subordinating his products and his own activity to the domination of an alien entity, and by attributing to them the significance of an alien entity, namely money.

In its perfected practice the spiritual egoism of Christianity necessarily becomes the material egoism of the Jew, celestial need is transmuted into terrestrial need, subjectivism into self-interest. The tenacity of the Jew is to be explained, not by his religion, but rather by the human basis of his religion—practical need and egoism.

It is because the essence of the Jew was universally realized and secularized in civil society, that civil society could not convince the Jew of the *unreality* of his *religious* essence, which is precisely the ideal representation of practical need. It is not only, therefore, in the Pentateuch and the Talmud, but also in contemporary society, that we find the essence of the present-day Jew; not as an abstract essence, but as one which is supremely empirical, not only as a limitation of the Jew, but as the Jewish narrowness of society.

As soon as society succeeds in abolishing the *empirical* essence of Judaism—huckstering and its conditions—the Jew becomes *impossible*, because his consciousness no longer has an object. The subjective basis of Judaism—practical need—assumes a human form, and the conflict between the individual, sensuous existence of man and his species-existence, is abolished.

The *social* emancipation of the Jew is the *emancipation of society from Judaism*.

Contribution to the Critique of Hegel's *Philosophy of Right*: Introduction

KARL MARX

Written at the close of 1843 and published in the *Deutsch-Französische Jahrbücher* in 1844, this essay is a consummate expression of the radical mind. It proclaims the need for a "radical revolution" as the way to man's self-realization. Germany is taken as the focal point of this revolution, and the proletariat—the concept of which makes its first appearance in Marx's writings here—as its class vehicle. In August 1844 Marx sent a copy of the essay to Ludwig Feuerbach along with a long letter expressing love and respect for that thinker, whose writing had provided, he wrote, a "philosophical foundation for socialism" by bringing the idea of the human species from "the heaven of abstraction to the real earth." Feuerbach's influence, along with that of Hegel, is clearly visible in the essay.

For Germany, the *criticism of religion* has been largely completed; and the criticism of religion is the premise of all criticism.

The *profane* existence of error is compromised once its *celestial oratio pro aris et focis* has been refuted. Man, who has found in the fantastic reality of heaven, where he sought a supernatural being, only his own reflection, will no longer be tempted to find only the *semblance* of himself—a non-human being—where he seeks and must seek his true reality.

The basis of irreligious criticism is this: *man makes religion;* religion does not make man. Religion is indeed man's self-consciousness and self-awareness so long as he has not found himself or has lost himself again. But *man* is not an abstract being, squatting outside the world. Man *is the human world,* the state, society. This state, this society, produce religion which is an *inverted world consciousness,* because they are an *inverted world.* Religion is the general theory of this world, its encyclopedic compendium, its logic in popular form, its spiritual *point d'honneur,* its

53

enthusiasm, its moral sanction, its solemn complement, its general basis of consolation and justification. It is *the fantastic realization* of the human being inasmuch as the *human being* possesses no true reality. The struggle against religion is, therefore, indirectly a struggle against *that world* whose spiritual *aroma* is religion.

Religious suffering is at the same time an *expression* of real suffering and a *protest* against real suffering. Religion is the sigh of the oppressed creature, the sentiment of a heartless world, and the soul of soulless conditions. It is the *opium* of the people.

The abolition of religion as the *illusory* happiness of men, is a demand for their *real* happiness. The call to abandon their illusions about their condition is a *call to abandon a condition which requires illusions*. The criticism of religion is, therefore, *the embryonic criticism of this vale of tears* of which religion is the *halo*.

Criticism has plucked the imaginary flowers from the chain, not in order that man shall bear the chain without caprice or consolation but so that he shall cast off the chain and pluck the living flower. The criticism of religion disillusions man so that he will think, act and fashion his reality as a man who has lost his illusions and regained his reason; so that he will revolve about himself as his own true sun. Religion is only the illusory sun about which man revolves so long as he does not revolve about himself.

It is the *task of history*, therefore, once the *other-world of truth* has vanished, to establish the *truth of this world*. The immediate *task of philosophy*, which is in the service of history, is to unmask human self-alienation in its *secular form* now that it has been unmasked in its *sacred form*. Thus the criticism of heaven is transformed into the criticism of earth, the *criticism of religion* into the *criticism of law*, and the *criticism of theology* into the *criticism of politics*.

The following exposition[1]—which is a contribution to this undertaking—does not deal directly with the original but with a copy, the German *philosophy* of the state and of right, for the simple reason that it deals with Germany.

If one were to begin with the *status quo* itself in Germany, even in the most appropriate way, i.e. negatively, the result would still be an *anachronism*. Even the negation of our political present is already a dusty fact in the historical lumber room of modern nations. I may negate powdered wigs, but I am still left with unpowdered wigs. If I negate the German situation of 1843 I have,

---

1. Marx refers to his intention to publish a critical study of Hegel's *Philosophy of Right*, to which this essay was an introduction. One of Marx's preliminary manuscripts for such a study has been published entitled "Aus der Kritik der Hegelschen Rechtsphilosophie. Kritik des Hegelschen Staatsrechts" (*MEGA* I, 11, pp. 403–553).

according to French chronology, hardly reached the year 1789, and still less the vital centre of the present day.

German history, indeed, prides itself upon a development which no other nation had previously accomplished, or will ever imitate in the historical sphere. We have shared in the restorations of modern nations without ever sharing in their revolutions. We have been restored, first because other nations have dared to make revolutions, and secondly because other nations have suffered counter-revolutions; in the first case because our masters were afraid, and in the second case because they were not afraid. Led by our shepherds, we have only once kept company with liberty and that was on the *day of its internment*.

A school of thought, which justifies the infamy of today by that of yesterday, which regards every cry from the serf under the knout as a cry of rebellion once the knout has become time-honoured, ancestral and historical, a school for which history shows only its *a posteriori* as the God of Israel did for his servant Moses—the *Historical school of law*[2]—might be supposed to have invented German history, if it were not in fact itself an invention of German history, A Shylock, but a servile Shylock, it swears upon its bond, its historical, Christian-Germanic bond, for every pound of flesh cut from the heart of the people.

On the other hand, good-natured enthusiasts, German chauvinists by temperament and enlightened liberals by reflection, seek our history of liberty beyond our history, in the primeval Teutonic forests. But how does the history of our liberty differ from the history of the wild boar's liberty, if it is only to be found in the forests? And as the proverb has it: what is shouted into the forest, the forest echoes back. So peace upon the primeval Teutonic forests!

But *war* upon the state of affairs in Germany! By all means! This state of affairs is *beneath the level of history, beneath all criticism*; nevertheless it remains an object of criticism just as the criminal who is beneath humanity remains an object of the *executioner*. In its struggle against this state of affairs criticism is not a passion of the head, but the head of passion. It is not a lancet but a weapon. Its object is an *enemy* which it aims not to refute but to *destroy*. For the spirit of this state of affairs has already been refuted. It is not, in itself, an object worthy of our thought; it is an *existence* as

2. The principal representative of the Historical school was F. K. von Savigny (1779–1861) who outlined its programme in his book *Vom Beruf unserer Zeit für Gesetzgebung und Rechtswissenschaft* (On the Vocation of our Age for Legislation and Jurisprudence), Heidelberg, 1814. Marx attended Savigny's lectures at the University of Berlin in 1836–7; but he was more attracted by the lectures of Eduard Gans (1798–1839), a liberal Hegelian influenced by Saint-Simon, who emphasized in his teaching and writings the part played by reason in the development of law, and who was Savigny's principal opponent in Berlin.

contemptible as it is despised. Criticism itself has no need of any further elucidation of this object, for it has already understood it. Criticism is no longer an end in itself, but simply a means; *indignation* is its essential mode of feeling, and *denunciation* its principal task.

It is a matter of depicting the stifling pressure which the different social spheres exert upon other, the universal but passive ill-humour, the complacent but self-deluding narrowness of spirit; all this incorporated in a system of government which lives by conserving this paltriness, and is itself *paltriness in government*.

What a spectacle! Society is infinitely divided into the most diverse races, which confront each other with their petty antipathies, bad conscience and coarse mediocrity; and which, precisely because of their ambiguous and mistrustful situation, are treated without exception, though in different ways, as merely tolerated existences by their masters. And they are forced to recognize and acknowledge this fact of being *dominated, governed* and *possessed*, as a *concession from heaven*! On the other side are the rulers themselves, whose greatness is in inverse proportion to their number.

The criticism which deals with this subject-matter is criticism in a hand-to-hand fight; and in such a fight it is of no interest to know whether the adversary is of the same rank, is noble or *interesting*—all that matters is to *strike* him. It is a question of denying the Germans an instant of illusion or resignation. The burden must be made still more irksome by awakening a consciousness of it, and shame must be made more shameful still by rendering it public. Every sphere of German society must be depicted as the *partie honteuse* of German society; and these petrified social conditions must be made to dance by singing their own melody to them. The nation must be taught to be *terrified* of itself, in order to give it *courage*. In this way an imperious need of the German nation will be satisfied, and the needs of nations are themselves the final causes of their satisfaction.

Even for the modern nations this struggle against the limited character of the German *status quo* does not lack interest; for the German *status quo* is the open *consummation of the ancien régime*, and the *ancien régime* is the *hidden defect of the modern state*. The struggle against the political present of the Germans is a struggle against the past of the modern nations, who are still continually importuned by the reminiscences of this past. It is instructive for the modern nations to see the *ancien régime*, which has played a *tragic* part in their history, play a *comic* part as a German ghost. The *ancien régime* had a *tragic* history, so long as it was the established power in the world while liberty was a personal fancy; in short, so long as it believed and had to believe in its own validity. So long as the *ancien régime*, as an existing world order, struggled against a new world which was just coming into existence, there was on its side a historical error but no personal error. Its decline was, therefore, tragic.

The present German régime, on the other hand, which is an anachronism, a flagrant contradiction of universally accepted axioms—the nullity of the *ancien régime* revealed to the whole world—only imagines that it believes in itself and asks the world to share its illusion. If it believed in its own *nature* would it attempt to hide it beneath the *semblance* of an alien nature and look for its salvation in hypocrisy and sophistry? The modern *ancien régime* is the comedian of a world order whose *real heroes* are dead. History is thorough, and it goes through many stages when it conducts an ancient formation to its grave. The last stage of a world-historical formation is comedy. The Greek gods, already once mortally wounded in Aeschylus' tragedy *Prometheus Bound*, had to endure a second death, a comic death, in Lucian's dialogues. Why should history proceed in this way? So that mankind shall separate itself *gladly* from its past. We claim this *joyful* historical destiny for the political powers of Germany.

But as soon as criticism concerns itself with modern social and political reality, and thus arrives at genuine human problems, it must either go outside the German *status quo* or approach its object indirectly. For example, the relation of industry, of the world of wealth in general, to the political world is a major problem of modern times. In what form does this problem begin to preoccupy the Germans? In the form of *protective tariffs*, the *system of prohibition*, the *national economy*. German chauvinism has passed from men to matter, so that one fine day our knights of cotton and heroes of iron found themselves metamorphosed into patriots. The sovereignty of monopoly within the country has begun to be recognized since *sovereignty vis-à-vis foreign countries* was attributed to it. In Germany, therefore, a beginning is made with what came as the conclusion in France and England. The old, rotten order against which these nations revolt in their theories, and which they bear only as chains are borne, is hailed in Germany as the dawn of a glorious future which as yet hardly dares to move from a cunning[3] theory to a ruthless practice. While in France and England the problem is put in the form: *political economy* or the *rule of society over wealth*; in Germany it is put in the form: *national economy* or the *rule of private property over nationality*. Thus, in England and France it is a question of abolishing monop-

---

3. In German, *listigen*; Marx is punning upon the name of Friedrich List (1789–1846), the apostle of industrial capitalism in a nationalist and protec-tionist form, who published in 1840 his influential book, *Das nationale System der politischen Ökonomie*.

oly, which has developed to its final consequences; while in Germany it is a question of proceeding to the final consequences of monopoly. There it is a question of the solution; here, only a question of the collision. We can see very well from this example how modern problems are presented in Germany; the example shows that our history, like a raw recruit, has so far only had to do extra drill on old and hackneyed historical matters.

If the *whole* of German development were at the level of German *political* development, a German could have no greater part in contemporary problems than can a *Russian*. If the individual is not restricted by the limitations of his country, still less is the nation liberated by the liberation of one indivdual. The fact that a Scythian was one of the Greek philosophers[4] did not enable the Scythians to advance a single step towards Greek culture.

Fortunately, we Germans are not Scythians.

Just as the nations of the ancient world lived their pre-history in the imagination, in mythology, so we Germans have lived our post-history in thought, in *philosophy*. We are the *philosophical* contemporaries of the present day without being its *historical* contemporaries. German philosophy is the *ideal prolongation* of German history. When, therefore, we criticize, instead of the *oeuvres incomplètes* of our real history, the *oeuvres posthumes* of our ideal history—*philosophy*, our criticism stands at the centre of the problems of which the present age says: *that is the question*. That which constitutes, for the advanced nations, a *practical* break with modern political conditions, is in Germany where these conditions do not yet exist, virtually a *critical* break with their philosophical reflection.

The German *philosophy of right and of the state* is the only German history which is *al pari* with the *official* modern times. The German nation is obliged, therefore, to connect its dream history with its present conditions, and to subject to criticism not only these existing conditions but also their abstract continuation. Its future cannot be restricted either to the direct negation of its real juridical and political circumstances, or to the direct realization of its ideal juridical and political circumstances. The direct negation of its real circumstances already exists in its ideal circumstances, while it has almost outlived the realization of its ideal circumstances in the contemplation of neighbouring nations. It is with good reason, therefore, that the *practical* political party in Germany demands the *negation of philosophy*. Its error does not consist in formulating this demand, but in limiting itself to a demand which it does not, and cannot, make effective. It supposes that it can achieve this negation by turning its back on philosophy, looking

4. Anacharsis.

elsewhere, and murmuring a few trite and ill-humoured phrases. Because of its narrow outlook it does not take account of philosophy as part of *German* reality, and even regards philosophy as beneath the level of German practical life and its theories. You demand as a point of departure real germs of life, but you forget that the real germ of life of the German nation has so far sprouted only in its *cranium*. In short, *you cannot abolish philosophy without realizing it.*

The same error was committed, but in the opposite direction, by the *theoretical* party which originated in philosophy.

In the present struggle, this party saw *only* the *critical struggle of philosophy against the German world.* It did not consider that *previous philosophy* itself belongs to this world and is its complement, even if only an ideal complement. Critical as regards its counterpart, it was not self-critical. It took as its point of departure the *presuppositions* of philosophy; and either accepted the conclusions which philosophy had reached or else presented as direct philosophical demands and conclusions, demands and conclusions drawn from elsewhere. But these latter—assuming their legitimacy—can only be achieved by the *negation of previous philosophy*, that is, philosophy as philosophy. We shall provide later a more comprehensive account of this party. Its principal defect may be summarized as follows: *it believed that it could realize philosophy without abolishing it.*

The criticism of the *German philosophy of right and of the state* which was given its most logical, profound and complete expression by Hegel, is at once the critical analysis of the modern state and of the reality connected with it, and the definitive negation of all the past *forms of consciousness in German jurisprudence and politics,* whose most distinguished and most general expression, raised to the level of a *science,* is precisely the *speculative philosophy of right.* If it was only Germany which could produce the speculative philosophy of right—this extravagant and abstract thought about the modern state, the reality of which remains in the beyond (even if this beyond is only across the Rhine)—the *German* representative of the modern state, on the contrary, which leaves out of account the *real man* was itself only possible because, and to the extent that, the modern state itself leaves the *real man* out of account or only satisfies the *whole* man in an illusory way. In politics, the Germans have *thought* what other nations have *done.* Germany has been their *theoretical consciousness.* The abstraction and presumption of its philosophy was in step with the partial and stunted character of their reality. If, therefore, the *status quo* of the *German political system* expresses the *consummation of the ancien régime,* the thorn in the flesh of the modern state, the *status quo* of

German political science expresses the *imperfection of the modern state* itself, the degeneracy of its flesh.

As the determined adversary of the previous form of German political consciousness, the criticism of the speculative philosophy of right does not remain within its own sphere, but leads on to *tasks* which can only be solved by *means of practical activity*.

The question then arises: can Germany attain a practical activity *à la hauteur des principes*; that is to say, a revolution which will raise it not only to the *official level* of the modern nations, but to the *human level* which will be the immediate future of those nations.

It is clear that the arm of criticism cannot replace the criticism of arms. Material force can only be overthrown by material force; but theory itself becomes a material force when it has seized the masses. Theory is capable of seizing the masses when it demonstrates *ad hominem*, and it demonstrates *ad hominem* as soon as it becomes radical. To be radical is to grasp things by the root. But for man the root is man himself. What proves beyond doubt the radicalism of German theory, and thus its practical energy, is that it begins from the resolute *positive* abolition of religion. The criticism of religion ends with the doctrine that *man is the supreme being for man*. It ends, therefore, with the *categorical imperative to overthrow all those conditions* in which man is an abased, enslaved, abandoned, contemptible being—conditions which can hardly be better described than in the exclamation of a Frenchman on the occasion of a proposed tax upon dogs: "Wretched dogs! They want to treat you like men!"

Even from the historical standpoint theoretical emancipation has a specific practical importance for Germany. In fact Germany's *revolutionary* past is theoretical—it is the *Reformation*. In that period the revolution originated in the brain of a monk, today in the brain of the philosopher.

Luther, without question, overcame servitude through devotion but only by substituting servitude through *conviction*. He shattered the faith in authority by restoring the authority of faith. He transformed the priests into laymen by turning laymen into priests. He liberated man from external religiosity by making religiosity the innermost essence of man. He liberated the body from its chains because he fettered the heart with chains.

But if Protestantism was not the solution it did at least pose the problem correctly. It was no longer a question, thereafter, of the layman's struggle against the priest outside himself, but of his struggle against his *own internal priest*, against his own *priestly nature*. And if the Protestant metamorphosis of German laymen into priests emancipated the lay popes—the *princes* together with their clergy, the privileged and the philistines—the philosophical metamorphosis of the priestly Germans into men will emancipate the *people*. But just as emancipation will not be confined to princes, so the *secularization* of property will not be limited to the *confiscation of church property*, which was practised especially by hypocritical Prussia. At that time, the Peasant War, the most radical event in German history, came to grief because of theology.

Today, when theology itself has come to grief, the most unfree phenomenon in German history—our *status quo*—will be shattered by philosophy. On the eve of the Reformation official Germany was the most abject servant of Rome. On the eve of its revolution Germany is the abject servant of those who are far inferior to Rome; of Prussia and Austria, of petty squires and philistines.

But a *radical* revolution in Germany seems to encounter a major difficulty.

Revolutions need a *passive* element, a *material* basis. Theory is only realized in a people so far as it fulfils the needs of the people. Will there correspond to the monstrous discrepancy between the demands of German thought and the answers of German reality a similar discrepancy between civil society and the state, and within civil society itself? Will theoretical needs be directly practical needs? It is not enough that thought should seek to realize itself; reality must also strive towards thought.

But Germany has not passed through the intermediate stage of political emancipation at the same time as the modern nations. It has not yet attained in practice those stages which it has transcended in theory. How could Germany, in *salta mortale*, surmount not only its own barriers but also those of the modern nations, that is, those barriers which it must in reality experience and strive for as an emancipation from its own real barriers? A radical revolution can only be a revolution of radical needs, for which the conditions and breeding ground appear to be lacking.

But if Germany accompanied the development of the modern nations only through the abstract activity of thought, without taking an active part in the real struggles of this development, it has also experienced the *pains* of this development without sharing in its pleasures and partial satisfactions. The abstract activity on one side has its counterpart in the abstract suffering on the other. And one fine day Germany will find itself at the level of the European decadence, before ever having attained the level of European emancipation. It will be comparable to a fetishist who is sickening from the diseases of Christianity.

If the *German governments* are examined it will be found that the circumstances of the time, the situation of Germany, the outlook of German culture, and lastly their own fortunate instinct, all drive them to combine the *civilized deficiencies* of the *modern political world* (whose advantages we do not enjoy) with the *barbarous deficiencies* of the *ancien régime* (which we enjoy in full measure); so that Germany must participate more and more, if not in the reason at least in the unreason of those political systems which transcend its *status quo*. Is there, for example, any country in the whole world which shares with such naïveté as so-called constitutional Germany all the illusions of the constitutional régime without sharing its realities? And was it not, of necessity, a German government which had the idea of combining the torments of censorship with the torments of the French September laws[5] which presuppose the liberty of the Press? Just as the gods of all the nations were to be found in the Roman Pantheon, so there will be found in the Holy Roman German Empire all the *sins* of all the forms of State. That this eclecticism will attain an unprecedented degree is assured in particular by the *politico-aesthetic gourmandise* of a German king who proposes to play all the roles of royalty—feudal or bureaucratic, absolute or constitutional, autocratic or democratic—if not in the person of the people at least in his *own* person, and if not for the people, at least for *himself. Germany, as the deficiency of present-day politics constituted into a system,* will not be able to demolish the specific German barriers without demolishing the general barriers of present-day politics.

It is not *radical* revolution, *universal human* emancipation, which is a Utopian dream for Germany, but rather a partial, *merely* political revolution which leaves the pillars of the building standing. What is the basis of a partial, merely political revolution? Simply this: a *section of civil society* emancipates itself and attains universal domination; a determinate class undertakes, from its *particular situation*, a general emancipation of society. This class emancipates society as a whole, but only on condition that the whole of society is in the same situation as this class; for example, that it possesses or can easily acquire money or culture.

No class in civil society can play this part unless it can arouse, in itself and in the masses, a moment of enthusiasm in which it associates and mingles with society at large, identifies itself with it, and is felt and recognized as the *general representative* of this society. Its aims and interests must genuinely be the aims and interests of society itself, of which it becomes in reality the social head and heart. It is only in the name of general interests that a particular class can claim general supremacy. In order to attain this liberating position, and the political direction of all spheres of society, revolutionary energy and consciousness of its own power do

5. The laws of September, 1835, which increased the financial guarantees required from the publishers of news- papers and introduced heavier penalties for "subversive" publications.

not suffice. For a *popular revolution* and the *emancipation of a particular class* of civil society to coincide, for one class to represent the whole of society, another class must concentrate in itself all the evils of society, a particular class must embody and represent a general obstacle and limitation. A particular social sphere must be regarded as the *notorious crime* of the whole society, so that emancipation from this sphere appears as a general emancipation. For *one* class to be the liberating class *par excellence*, it is necessary that another class should be openly the oppressing class. The negative significance of the French nobility and clergy produced the positive significance of the bourgeoisie, the class which stood next to them and opposed them.

But in Germany every class lacks the logic, insight, courage and clarity which would make it a negative representative of society. Moreover, there is also lacking in every class the generosity of spirit which identifies itself, if only for a moment, with the popular mind; that genius which pushes material force to political power, that revolutionary daring which throws at its adversary the defiant phrase: *I am nothing and I should be everything*. The essence of German morality and honour, in classes as in individuals, is a *modest egoism* which displays, and allows others to display, its own narrowness. The relation between the different spheres of German society is, therefore, not dramatic, but epic. Each of these spheres begins to be aware of itself and to establish itself beside the others, not from the moment when it is oppressed, but from the moment that circumstances, without any action of its own, have created a new sphere which it can in turn oppress. Even the *moral sentiment of the German middle class* has no other basis than the consciousness of being the representative of the narrow and limited mediocrity of all the other classes. It is not only the German kings, therefore, who ascend their thrones *mal à propos*. Each sphere of civil society suffers a defeat before gaining the victory; it erects its own barrier before having destroyed the barrier which opposes it; it displays the narrowness of its views before having displayed their generosity, and thus every opportunity of playing an important role has passed before it properly existed, and each class, at the very moment when it begins its struggle against the class above it, remains involved in a struggle against the class beneath. For this reason, the princes are in conflict with the monarch, the bureaucracy with the nobility, the bourgeoisie with all of them, while the proletariat is already beginning its struggle with the bourgeoisie. The middle class hardly dares to conceive the idea of emancipation from its own point of view before the development of social conditions, and the progress of political theory, show that this point of view is already antiquated, or at least disputable.

In France it is enough to be something in order to desire to be everything. In Germany no one has the right to be anything without first renouncing everything. In France partial emancipation is a basis for complete emancipation. In Germany complete emancipation is a *conditio sine qua non* for any partial emancipation. In France it is the reality, in Germany the impossibility, of a progressive emancipation which must give birth to complete liberty. In France every class of the population is *politically idealistic* and considers itself first of all, not as a particular class, but as the representative of the general needs of society. The role of liberator can, therefore, pass successively in a dramatic movement to different classes in the population, until it finally reaches the class which achieves social freedom; no longer assuming certain conditions external to man, which are none the less created by human society, but organizing all the conditions of human life on the basis of social freedom. In Germany, on the contrary, where practical life is as little intellectual as intellectual life is practical, no class of civil society feels the need for, or the ability to achieve, a general emancipation, until it is forced to it by its *immediate* situation, by *material* necessity and by its *fetters themselves*.

Where is there, then, a *real* possibility of emancipation in Germany?

This is our reply. A class must be formed which has *radical chains*, a class in civil society which is not a class of civil society, a class which is the dissolution of all classes, a sphere of society which has a universal character because its sufferings are universal, and which does not claim a *particular redress* because the wrong which is done to it is not a *particular wrong* but *wrong in general*. There must be formed a sphere of society which claims no *traditional* status but only a human status, a sphere which is not opposed to particular consequences but is totally opposed to the assumptions of the German political system; a sphere, finally, which cannot emancipate itself without emancipating itself from all the other spheres of society, without, therefore, emancipating all these other spheres, which is, in short, a *total loss* of humanity and which can only redeem itself by a *total redemption of humanity*. This dissolution of society, as a particular class, is the *proletariat*.

The proletariat is only beginning to form itself in Germany, as a result of the industrial movement. For what constitutes the proletariat is not *naturally existing* poverty, but poverty *artificially produced*, is not the mass of people mechanically oppressed by the weight of society, but the mass resulting from the *disintegration* of society and above all from the disintegration of the middle class. Needless to say, however, the numbers of the proletariat are also increased by the victims of natural poverty and of Christian-Germanic serfdom.

When the proletariat announces the *dissolution of the existing social order*, it only declares the *secret of its* own existence, for it *is* the *effective* dissolution of this order. When the proletariat demands the *negation of private property* it only lays down as a *principle for society* what society has already made a principle *for the proletariat*, and what the *latter* already involuntarily embodies as the negative result of society. Thus the proletarian has the same right, in relation to the new world which is coming into being, as the *German king* has in relation to the existing world when he calls the people *his* people or a horse *his* horse. In calling the people his private property the king simply declares that the owner of private property is king.

Just as philosophy finds its *material* weapons in the proletariat, so the proletariat finds its *intellectual* weapons in philosophy. And once the lightning of thought has penetrated deeply into this virgin soil of the people, the *Germans* will emancipate themselves and become *men*.

Let us sum up these results. The emancipation of Germany is only possible *in practice* if one adopts the point of view of that theory according to which man is the highest being for man. Germany will not be able to emancipate itself from the *Middle Ages* unless it emancipates itself at the same time from the *partial* victories over the Middle Ages. In Germany *no* type of enslavement can be abolished unless *all* enslavement is destroyed. Germany, which likes to get to the bottom of things, can only make a revolution which upsets *the whole order* of things. The *emancipation of Germany* will be an *emancipation of man*. *Philosophy* is the *head* of this emancipation and the *proletariat* is its *heart*. Philosophy can only be realized by the abolition[6] of the proletariat, and the proletariat can only be abolished by the realization of philosophy.

When all the inner conditions ripen, *the day of German resurrection* will be proclaimed by *the crowing of the Gallic cock*.[7]

---

6. *Aufhebung* [R. T.]
7. I.e., the future German revolution will be sparked by revolutionary developments in France. (This last paragraph does not appear in the original Bottomore translation used here.) [R. T.]

Economic and Philosophic
Manuscripts of 1844

KARL MARX

Soon after moving to Paris in November, 1843, Marx applied himself to the criticism of political economy—the new phase of his critical program foreshadowed in his two essays in the *Deutsch-Französische Jahrbücher*. Between April and August of 1844 he produced the rough draft of what, judging by his preface, was to have been a book. He did not finish it for publication, however, and it lay unpublished for more than eighty years. The surviving parts, comprising four manuscripts, were given the name shown above. An incomplete version in Russian translation was published in Moscow in 1927. The first full edition in German, prepared by D. Riazanov of the Marx-Engels Institute in Moscow, was published in Berlin in 1932, in *Karl Marx, Friedrich Engels, Historisch-kritische Gesamtausgabe*.

The fundamentals of the Marxist interpretation of history are to be found in the 1844 manuscripts, including the notion of the proletarian revolution and future communism as the goal of the historical process. The theory is set forth, however, in terms of philosophical concepts drawn by Marx from Hegel and Feuerbach, most notably the concept of man's "self-alienation" or "self-estrangement." History, particularly under modern capitalism, is seen as a story of man's alienation in his life as producer, and communism is presented as the final transcendence of alienation via a revolution against private property. Because the 1844 manuscripts show us Marxism at the moment of its genesis in Marx's mind and because they help to clarify both the relation of Marxism to earlier German philosophy and its ethical significance, their publication has profoundly affected scholarship on Marx and Marxism in our time.

A part of the manuscripts consists largely of excerpts from writings of the political economists on such topics as wages of labor, profit of capital, and rent of land. The material reprinted here, comprising the extant portions in which Marx expounds his own position, consists of the preface and the sections entitled "Estranged Labour," "Private Property and Communism," "The Meaning of Human Requirements," "The Power of Money in Bourgeois Society," and "Critique of the Hegelian Dialectic and Philosophy as a Whole."

A number of passages in the manuscripts have been crossed out, apparently by Marx. There is no reason to think that the passages crossed out had ceased to represent what Marx thought. He may well have been guided by editorial considerations in working over the draft of a manuscript originally intended for publication.*

The translation and notes are by Martin Milligan.

---

* The cross-outs are indicated by pointed brackets in the complete text of the 1844 manuscripts as published in Karl Marx and Frederick Engels, *Collected Works*, vol. 3 (*Marx and Engels: 1843–44*) (London: Lawrence & Wishart, 1975), pp. 249–346. I am indebted to Thomas Ferguson for bringing the crossed-out material to my attention.

Preface

I have already given notice in the *Deutsch-Französische Jahrbücher* of the critique of jurisprudence and political science in the form of a critique of the *Hegelian* Philosophy of Right. In the course of elaboration for publication, the intermingling of criticism directed only against speculation with criticism of the various subjects themselves proved utterly unsuitable, hampering the development of the argument and rendering comprehension difficult. Moreover the wealth and diversity of the subjects to be treated, could have been compressed into *one* work only in a purely aphoristic style; whilst an aphoristic presentation of this kind, for its part, would have given the *impression* of arbitrary systematizing. I shall therefore issue the critique of law, ethics, politics, etc., in a series of distinct, independent pamphlets, and at the end try in a special work to present them again as a connected whole showing the interrelationship of the separate parts, and finally, shall make a critique of the speculative elaboration of that material. For this reason it will be found that the interconnection between political economy and the state, law, ethics, civil life, etc., is touched on in the present work only to the extent to which political economy itself *ex professo*[1] touches on these subjects.

It is hardly necessary to assure the reader conversant with political economy that my results have been won by means of a wholly empirical analysis based on a conscientious critical study of political economy.

[Whereas the uninformed reviewer who tries to hide his complete ignorance and intellectual poverty by hurling *the "utopian phrase"* at the positive critic's head, or again such phrases as "pure, resolute, utterly critical criticism," the "not merely legal but social—utterly social—society," the "compact, massy mass," the "oratorical orators of the massy mass,"[2] this reviewer has yet to furnish the first proof that besides his theological family-affairs he has anything to contribute to a discussion of *worldly* matters.][3]

It goes without saying that besides the French and English Socialists I have made use of German socialist works as well. The only *original* German works of substance in this science, however—other

---

1. Particularly.
2. Marx refers here to the Young Hegelian Bruno Bauer, who had published in *Allgemeine Literatur-Zeitung* two long reviews dealing with books, articles and pamphlets on the Jewish question. Most of the quoted phrases are taken from these reviews in *Allgemeine Literatur-Zeitung*, vol. 1, December, 1843; vol. 4, March, 1844. The expressions "utopian phrase" and "compact

mass" can be found in Bauer's article "Was ist jetzt der Gegenstand der Kritik?" published in *Allgemeine Literatur-Zeitung*, vol. 8, July, 1844.

Allgemeine Literatur-Zeitung (General Literary Gazette), a German monthly, was published by Bauer in Charlottenburg from December, 1843, to October, 1844.
3. Passages enclosed in brackets were crossed out by Marx in his manuscript.

than Weitling's writings—are the essays by Hess published in *Einundzwanzig Bogen*,[4] and Engels' *Umrisse zu einer Kritik der Nationalökonomie*[5] in the *Deutsch-Französische Jahrbücher* where, likewise, I indicated in a very general way the basic elements of this work.

[Besides being indebted to these authors who have given critical attention to political economy, positive criticism as a whole—and therefore also German positive criticism of political economy—owes its true foundation to the discoveries of *Feuerbach*, against whose *Philosophie der Zukunft*[6] and *Thesen zur Reform der Philosophie*[7] in the *Anecdotis*,[8] despite the tacit use that is made of them, the petty envy of some and the veritable wrath of others seem to have instigated a regular conspiracy of *silence*.]

It is only with *Feuerbach* that *positive*, humanistic and naturalistic criticism begins. The less noise they make, the more certain, profound, widespread and enduring is the effect of *Feuerbach's* writings, the only writings since Hegel's *Phänomenologie* and *Logik* to contain a real theoretical revolution.

In contrast to the *critical theologians*[9] of our day, I have deemed the concluding chapter of the present work—the settling of accounts with *Hegelian dialectic* and Hegelian philosophy as a whole—to be absolutely necessary, a task not yet performed. This *lack of thoroughness* is not accidental, since even the *critical* theologian remains a *theologian*. Hence, either he had to start from certain presuppositions of philosophy accepted as authoritative; or if in the process of criticism and as a result of other people's discoveries doubts about these philosophical presuppositions have arisen in him, he abandons them without vindication and in a cowardly fashion, *abstracts* from them showing his servile dependence on these presuppositions and his resentment at this dependence merely in a negative, unconscious and sophistical manner.

[In this connection the critical theologian is either forever repeating assurances about the *purity* of his own criticism, or tries to

4. The full title of this collection of articles is *Einundzwanzig Bogen aus der Schweiz* (*Twenty-One Sheets from Switzerland*), Erster Teil, Zürich and Winterthur, 1843.
5. Engels' "Outlines of a Critique of Political Economy."
6. Ludwig Feuerbach, *Grundsätze der Philosophie der Zukunft* (*Principles of the Philosophy of the Future*), Zürich and Winterthur, 1843.
7. Ludwig Feuerbach, *Vorläufige Thesen zur Reformation der Philosophie* (*Preliminary Theses on the Reformation of Philosophy*) published in *Anekdota*, vol. II.

8. Marx's abbreviation for *Anekdota zur neuesten deutschen Philosophie und Publicistik* (*Unpublished Materials Related to Modern German Philosophy and Writing*), a two-volume collection published by Arnold Ruge in Switzerland. It included Marx's *Notes on the Latest Prussian Instruction to Censors* and *Luther—the Arbiter Between Strauss and Feuerbach,* and articles by Bruno Bauer, Ludwig Feuerbach, Friedrich Köppen, Arnold Ruge, etc.
9. Marx has in mind Bauer and his followers, who were associated with the *Allgemeine Literatur-Zeitung*.

make it seem as though all that was left for criticism to deal with now was some other immature form of criticism outside itself—say eighteenth-century criticism—and the backwardness of the *masses*, in order to divert the observer's attention as well as his own from the *necessary* task of settling accounts between *criticism* and its point of origin—Hegelian *dialectic* and German philosophy as a whole—from this necessary raising of modern criticism above its own limitation and crudity. Eventually, however, whenever discoveries (such as *Feuerbach's*) are made about the nature of his own philosophic presuppositions, the critical theologian partly makes it appear as if he were the one who had accomplished this, producing that appearance by taking the results of these discoveries and, without being able to develop them, hurling them in the form of *catch-phrases* at writers still caught in the confines of philosophy; partly he even manages to acquire a sense of his own superiority to such discoveries by covertly asserting in a veiled, malicious and sceptical fashion elements of the Hegelian *dialectic* which he still finds lacking in the criticism of that dialectic (which have not yet been critically served up to him for his use) against such criticism—not having tried to bring such elements into their proper relation or having been capable of doing so, asserting, say, the category of mediating proof against the category of positive, self-originating truth, etc., in a way *peculiar* to Hegelian dialectic. For to the theological critic it seems quite natural that everything has to be *done* by philosophy, so that he can *chatter* away about purity, resoluteness, and utterly critical criticism; and he fancies himself the true *conqueror of philosophy* whenever he happens to *feel* some "moment" in Hegel[1] to be lacking in Feuerbach—for however much he practises the spiritual idolatry of *"self-consciousness"* and *"mind"* the theological critic does not get beyond feeling to consciousness.][2]

On close inspection *theological criticism*—genuinely progressive though it was at the inception of the movement—is seen in the final analysis to be nothing but the culmination and consequence of the old *philosophical*, and especially the *Hegelian*, *transcendentalism*, twisted into a *theological caricature*. This interesting example of the justice in history, which now assigns to theology, ever

---

1. "Moment" is a technical term in Hegelian philosophy meaning a vital element of thought. The term is used to stress that thought is a process, and thus that elements in a system of thought are also phases in a movement.
2. In Hegel, "feeling" (*Empfindung*) denotes a relatively low form of mental life in which the subjective and the objective are still confused together.

"Consciousness" (*Bewusstein*)—the name given by Hegel to the first major section of his *Phenomenology of Mind*—denotes those forms of mental activity where a subject first seeks to comprehend an object. "Self-consciousness" and "mind" denote subsequent, higher phases in the evolution of "absolute knowledge" or "the absolute."

philosophy's spot of infection, the further role of portraying in itself the negative dissolution of philosophy—i.e., the process of its decay—this historical nemesis I shall demonstrate on another occasion.

[How far, on the other hand, *Feuerbach's* discoveries about the nature of philosophy required still, for their *proof* at least, a critical settling of accounts with philosophical dialectic will be seen from my exposition itself.]

Estranged Labour[3]

We have proceeded from the premises of political economy. We have accepted its language and its laws. We presupposed private property, the separation of labour, capital and land, and of wages, profit of capital and rent of land—likewise division of labour, competition, the concept of exchange-value, etc. On the basis of political economy itself, in its own words, we have shown that the worker sinks to the level of a commodity and becomes indeed the most wretched of commodities; that the wretchedness of the worker is in inverse proportion to the power and magnitude of his production; that the necessary result of competition is the accumulation of capital in a few hands, and thus the restoration of monopoly in a more terrible form; that finally the distinction between capitalist and land-rentier, like that between the tiller of the soil and the factory-worker, disappears and that the whole of society must fall apart into the two classes—the property-*owners* and the propertyless *workers.*

Political economy proceeds from the fact of private property, but it does not explain it to us. It expresses in general, abstract formulae the *material* process through which private property actually passes, and these formulae it then takes for *laws.* It does not *comprehend* these laws—i.e., it does not demonstrate how they arise from the very nature of private property. Political economy does not disclose the source of the division between labour and capital, and between capital and land. When, for example, it defines the relationship of wages to profit, it takes the interest of the capitalists to be the ultimate cause; i.e., it takes for granted what it is supposed to evolve. Similarly, competition comes in everywhere. It is explained from external circumstances. As to how far these external and apparently fortuitous circumstances are but the expression of a necessary course of development, political economy teaches us nothing. We have seen how, to it, exchange itself appears to be a

3. *Die Entfremdete Arbeit.* See the Note on Texts and Terminology, p. xli, above, for a discussion of this term. [*R. T.*]

fortuitous fact. The only wheels which political economy sets in motion are *avarice* and the *war amongst the avaricious—competition*.

Precisely because political economy does not grasp the connections within the movement, it was possible to counterpose, for instance, the doctrine of competition to the doctrine of monopoly, the doctrine of craft-liberty to the doctrine of the corporation, the doctrine of the division of landed property to the doctrine of the big estate—for competition, craft-liberty and the division of landed property were explained and comprehended only as fortuitous, premeditated and violent consequences of monopoly, the corporation, and feudal property, not as their necessary, inevitable and natural consequences.

Now, therefore, we have to grasp the essential connection between private property, avarice, and the separation of labour, capital and landed property; between exchange and competition, value and the devaluation of men, monopoly and competition, etc.; the connection between this whole estrangement and the *money* system.

Do not let us go back to a fictitious primordial condition as the political economist does, when he tries to explain. Such a primordial condition explains nothing. He merely pushes the question away into a grey nebulous distance. He assumes in the form of fact, of an event, what he is supposed to deduce—namely, the necessary relationship between two things—between, for example, division of labour and exchange. Theology in the same way explains the origin of evil by the fall of man: that is, it assumes as a fact, in historical form, what has to be explained.

We proceed from an *actual* economic fact.

The worker becomes all the poorer the more wealth he produces, the more his production increases in power and range. The worker becomes an ever cheaper commodity the more commodities he creates. With the *increasing value* of the world of things proceeds in direct proportion the *devaluation* of the world of men. Labour produces not only commodities; it produces itself and the worker as a *commodity*—and does so in the proportion in which it produces commodities generally.

This fact expresses merely that the object which labour produces—labour's product—confronts it as *something alien*, as a *power independent* of the producer. The product of labour is labour which has been congealed in an object, which has become material: it is the *objectification* of labour. Labour's realization is its objectification. In the conditions dealt with by political economy this realization of labour appears as *loss of reality* for the workers; objectification as *loss of the object* and *object-bondage;* appropriation as *estrangement,* as *alienation.*[4]

So much does labour's realization appear as loss of reality that the worker loses reality to the point of starving to death. So much does objectification appear as loss of the object that the worker is robbed of the objects most necessary not only for his life but for his work. Indeed, labour itself becomes an object which he can get hold of only with the greatest effort and with the most irregular interruptions. So much does the appropriation of the object appear as estrangement that the more objects the worker produces the fewer can he possess and the more he falls under the dominion of his product, capital.

All these consequences are contained in the definition that the worker is related to the *product of his labour* as to an *alien* object. For on this premise it is clear that the more the worker spends himself, the more powerful the alien objective world becomes which he creates over-against himself, the poorer he himself—his inner world—becomes, the less belongs to him as his own. It is the same in religion. The more man puts into God, the less he retains in himself. The worker puts his life into the object; but now his life no longer belongs to him but to the object. Hence, the greater this activity, the greater is the worker's lack of objects. Whatever the product of his labour is, he is not. Therefore the greater this product, the less is he himself. The *alienation* of the worker in his product means not only that his labour becomes an object, an *external* existence, but that it exists *outside him,* independently, as something alien to him, and that it becomes a power of its own confronting him; it means that the life which he has conferred on the object confronts him as something hostile and alien.

Let us now look more closely at the *objectification,* at the production of the worker; and therein at the *estrangement,* the *loss* of the object, his product.

The worker can create nothing without *nature,* without the *sensuous external world.* It is the material on which his labor is manifested, in which it is active, from which and by means of which it produces.

But just as nature provides labor with the *means of life* in the sense that labour cannot *live* without objects on which to operate, on the other hand, it also provides the *means of life* in the more restricted sense—i.e., the means for the physical subsistence of the *worker* himself.

Thus the more the worker by his labour *appropriates* the external world, sensuous nature, the more he deprives himself of *means of life* in the double respect: first, that the sensuous external world

4. "Alienation"—*Entäusserung.*

more and more ceases to be an object belonging to his labour—to be his labour's *means of life*; and secondly, that it more and more ceases to be *means of life* in the immediate sense, means for the physical subsistence of the worker.

Thus in this double respect the worker becomes a slave of his object, first, in that he receives an *object of labour*, i.e., in that he receives *work*; and secondly, in that he receives *means of subsistence*. Therefore, it enables him to exist, first, as a *worker*; and, second, as a *physical subject*. The extremity of this bondage is that it is only as a *worker* that he continues to maintain himself as a *physical subject*, and that it is only as a *physical subject* that he is a *worker*.

(The laws of political economy express the estrangement of the worker in his object thus: the more the worker produces, the less he has to consume; the more values he creates, the more valueless, the more unworthy he becomes; the better formed his product, the more deformed becomes the worker; the more civilized his object, the more barbarous becomes the worker; the mightier labour becomes, the more powerless becomes the worker; the more ingenious labour becomes, the duller becomes the worker and the more he becomes nature's bondsman.)

Political economy conceals the estrangement inherent in the nature of labour by not considering the direct relationship between the worker (labour) *and production.* It is true that labour produces for the rich wonderful things—but for the worker it produces privation. It produces palaces—but for the worker, hovels. It produces beauty—but for the worker, deformity. It replaces labour by machines—but some of the workers it throws back to a barbarous type of labour, and the other workers it turns into machines. It produces intelligence—but for the worker idiocy, cretinism.

The direct relationship of labour to its produce is the relationship of the worker to the objects of his production. The relationship of the man of means to the objects of production and to production itself is only a *consequence* of this first relationship—and confirms it. We shall consider this other aspect later.

When we ask, then, what is the essential relationship of labour we are asking about the relationship of the *worker* to production.

Till now we have been considering the estrangement, the alienation of the worker only in one of its aspects, i.e., the worker's *relationship to the products of his labour*. But the estrangement is manifested not only in the result but in the *act of production*—within the *producing activity* itself. How would the worker come to face the product of his activity as a stranger, were it not that in the very act of production he was estranging himself from himself? The product is after all but the summary of the activity of production.

If then the product of labour is alienation, production itself must be active alienation, the alienation of activity, the activity of alienation. In the estrangement of the object of labour is merely summarized the estrangement, the alienation, in the activity of labour itself.

What, then, constitutes the alienation of labour?

First, the fact that labour is *external* to the worker, i.e., it does not belong to his essential being; that in his work, therefore, he does not affirm himself but denies himself, does not feel content but unhappy, does not develop freely his physical and mental energy but mortifies his body and ruins his mind. The worker therefore only feels himself outside his work, and in his work feels outside himself. He is at home when he is not working, and when he is working he is not at home. His labour is therefore not voluntary, but coerced; it is *forced labour*. It is therefore not the satisfaction of a need; it is merely a *means* to satisfy needs external to it. Its alien character emerges clearly in the fact that as soon as no physical or other compulsion exists, labour is shunned like the plague. External labour, labour in which man alienates himself, is a labour of self-sacrifice, of mortification. Lastly, the external character of labour for the worker appears in the fact that it is not his own, but someone else's, that it does not belong to him, that in it he belongs, not to himself, but to another. Just as in religion the spontaneous activity of the human imagination, of the human brain and the human heart, operates independently of the individual—that is, operates on him as an alien, divine or diabolical activity—in the same way the worker's activity is not his spontaneous activity. It belongs to another; it is the loss of his self.

As a result, therefore, man (the worker) no longer feels himself to be freely active in any but his animal functions—eating, drinking, procreating, or at most in his dwelling and in dressing-up, etc.; and in his human functions he no longer feels himself to be anything but an animal. What is animal becomes human and what is human becomes animal.

Certainly eating, drinking, procreating, etc., are also genuinely human functions. But in the abstraction which separates them from the sphere of all other human activity and turns them into sole and ultimate ends, they are animal.

We have considered the act of estranging practical human activity, labour, in two of its aspects. (1) The relation of the worker to the *product of labour* as an alien object exercising power over him. This relation is at the same time the relation to the sensuous external world, to the objects of nature as an alien world antagonistically opposed to him. (2) The relation of labour to the *act of production* within the *labour* process. This relation is the relation of the worker to his own activity as an alien activity not belonging to him; it is activity as suffering, strength as weakness, begetting as emasculating, the worker's own physical and mental energy, his personal life or what is life other than activity—as an activity which is turned against him, neither depends on nor belongs to him. Here we have *self-estrangement*, as we had previously the estrangement of the *thing*.

We have yet a third aspect of *estranged labour* to deduce from the two already considered.

Man is a species being, not only because in practice and in theory he adopts the species as his object (his own as well as those of other things), but—and this is only another way of expressing it—but also because he treats himself as the actual, living species; because he treats himself as a *universal* and therefore a free being.

The life of the species, both in man and in animals, consists physically in the fact that man (like the animal) lives on inorganic nature; and the more universal man is compared with an animal, the more universal is the sphere of inorganic nature on which he lives. Just as plants, animals, stones, the air, light, etc., constitute a part of human consciousness in the realm of theory, partly as objects of natural science, partly as objects of art—his spiritual inorganic nature, spiritual nourishment which he must first prepare to make it palatable and digestible—so too in the realm of practice they constitute a part of human life and human activity. Physically man lives only on these products of nature, whether they appear in the form of food, heating, clothes, a dwelling, or whatever it may be. The universality of man is in practice manifested precisely in the universality which makes all nature his *inorganic* body—both inasmuch as nature is (1) his direct means of life, and (2) the material, the object, and the instrument of his life-activity. Nature is man's *inorganic body*—nature, that is, in so far as it is not itself the human body. Man *lives* on nature—means that nature is his *body*, with which he must remain in continuous intercourse if he is not to die. That man's physical and spiritual life is linked to nature means simply that nature is linked to itself, for man is a part of nature.

In estranging from man (1) nature, and (2) himself, his own active functions, his life-activity, estranged labour estranges the *species* from man. It turns for him the *life of the species* into a means of individual life. First it estranges the life of the species and individual life, and secondly it makes individual life in its abstract form the purpose of the life of the species, likewise in its abstract and estranged form.

For in the first place labour, *life-activity, productive life* itself, appears to man merely as a *means* of satisfying a need—the need to maintain the physical existence. Yet the productive life is the life of the species. It is life-engendering life. The whole character of a species—its species character—is contained in the character of its life-activity; and free, conscious activity is man's species character. Life itself appears only as *a means to life*.

The animal is immediately identical with its life-activity. It does not distinguish itself from it. It is *its life-activity*. Man makes his life-activity itself the object of his will and of his consciousness. He has conscious life-activity. It is not a determination with which he directly merges. Conscious life-activity directly distinguishes man from animal life-activity. It is just because of this that he is a species being. Or it is only because he is a species being that he is a Conscious Being, i.e., that his own life is an object for him. Only because of that is his activity free activity. Estranged labour reverses this relationship, so that it is just because man is a conscious being that he makes his life-activity, his essential being, a mere means to his *existence*.

In creating an *objective world* by his practical activity, in *working-up* inorganic nature, man proves himself a conscious species being, i.e., as a being that treats the species as its own essential being, or that treats itself as a species being. Admittedly animals also produce. They build themselves nests, dwellings, like the bees, beavers, ants, etc. But an animal only produces what it immediately needs for itself or its young. It produces one-sidedly, whilst man produces universally. It produces only under the dominion of immediate physical need, whilst man produces even when he is free from physical need and only truly produces in freedom therefrom. An animal produces only itself, whilst man reproduces the whole of nature. An animal's product belongs immediately to its physical body, whilst man freely confronts his product. An animal forms things in accordance with the standard and the need of the species to which it belongs, whilst man knows how to produce in accordance with the standard of every species, and knows how to apply everywhere the inherent standard to the object. Man therefore also forms things in accordance with the laws of beauty.

It is just in the working-up of the objective world, therefore, that man first really proves himself to be a *species being*. This production is his active species life. Through and because of this production, nature appears as *his* work and his reality. The object of labour is, therefore, the *objectification of man's species life*: for he duplicates himself not only, as in consciousness, intellectually, but also actively, in reality, and therefore he contemplates himself in a world that he has created. In tearing away from man the object of his production, therefore, estranged labour tears from him his *species life*, his real species objectivity, and transforms his advantage over animals into the disadvantage that his inorganic body, nature, is taken from him.

Similarly, in degrading spontaneous activity, free activity, to a means, estranged labour makes man's species life a means to his physical existence.

The consciousness which man has of his species is thus transformed by estrangement in such a way that the species life becomes for him a means.

Estranged labour turns thus:

(3) *Man's species being*, both nature and his spiritual species property, into a being *alien* to him, into a *means* to his *individual existence*. It estranges man's own body from him, as it does external nature and his spiritual essence, his *human being*.

(4) An immediate consequence of the fact that man is estranged from the product of his labour, from his life-activity, from his species being is the *estrangement of man* from *man*. If a man is confronted by himself, he is confronted by the *other* man. What applies to a man's relation to his work, to the product of his labour and to himself, also holds of a man's relation to the other man, and to the other man's labour and object of labour.

In fact, the proposition that man's species nature is estranged from him means that one man is estranged from the other, as each of them is from man's essential nature.[5]

The estrangement of man, and in fact every relationship in which man stands to himself, is first realized and expressed in the relationship in which a man stands to other men.

Hence within the relationship of estranged labour each man views the other in accordance with the standard and the position in which he finds himself as a worker.

We took our departure from a fact of political economy—the estrangement of the worker and his production. We have formulated the concept of this fact—*estranged, alienated* labour. We have analysed this concept—hence analysing merely a fact of political economy.

Let us now see, further, how in real life the concept of estranged, alienated labour must express and present itself.

If the product of labour is alien to me, if it confronts me as an alien power, to whom, then, does it belong?

If my own activity does not belong to me, if it is an alien, a coerced activity, to whom, then, does it belong?

To a being *other* than me.

Who is this being?

The *gods*? To be sure, in the earliest times the principal produc-

5. "Species nature" (and, earlier, "species being")—*Gattungswesen*; "man's essential nature"—*menschlichen Wesen*.

tion (for example, the building of temples, etc., in Egypt, India
and Mexico) appears to be in the service of the gods, and the product belongs to the gods. However, the gods on their own were
never the lords of labour. No more was *nature*. And what a contradiction it would be if, the more man subjugated nature by his
labour and the more the miracles of the gods were rendered superfluous by the miracles of industry, the more man were to renounce
the joy of production and the enjoyment of the produce in favour
of these powers.

The *alien* being, to whom labour and the produce of labour
belongs, in whose service labour is done and for whose benefit the
produce of labour is provided, can only be *man* himself.

If the product of labour does not belong to the worker, if it confronts him as an alien power, this can only be because it belongs to
some *other man than the worker*. If the worker's activity is a torment to him, to another it must be *delight* and his life's joy. Not
the gods, not nature, but only man himself can be this alien power
over man.

We must bear in mind the above-stated proposition that man's
relation to himself only becomes *objective* and *real* for him through
his relation to the other man. Thus, if the product of his labour,
his labour *objectified*, is for him an *alien*, hostile, powerful object
independent of him, then his position towards it is such that someone else is master of this object, someone who is alien, hostile, powerful, and independent of him. If his own activity is to him an
unfree activity, then he is treating it as activity performed in the
service, under the dominion, the coercion and the yoke of another
man.

Every self-estrangement of man from himself and from nature
appears in the relation in which he places himself and nature to
men other than and differentiated from himself. For this reason
religious self-estrangement necessarily appears in the relationship of
the layman to the priest, or again to a mediator, etc., since we are
here dealing with the intellectual world. In the real practical world
self-estrangement can only become manifest through the real practical relationship to other men. The medium through which
estrangement takes place is itself *practical*. Thus through estranged
labour man not only engenders his relationship to the object and to
the act of production as to powers that are alien and hostile to
him; he also engenders the relationship in which other men stand
to his production and to his product, and the relationship in which
he stands to these other men. Just as he begets his own production
as the loss of his reality, as his punishment; just as he begets his
own product as a loss, as a product not belonging to him; so he
begets the dominion of the one who does not produce over produc-

tion and over the product. Just as he estranges from himself his own activity, so he confers to the stranger activity which is not his own.

Till now we have only considered this relationship from the standpoint of the worker and later we shall be considering it also from the standpoint of the non-worker.

Through *estranged, alienated labour*, then, the worker produces the relationship to this labour of a man alien to labour and standing outside it. The relationship of the worker to labour engenders the relation to it of the capitalist, or whatever one chooses to call the master of labour. *Private property* is thus the product, the result, the necessary consequence, of *alienated labour*, of the external relation of the worker to nature and to himself.

Private property thus results by analysis from the concept of *alienated labour*—i.e., of *alienated man*, of estranged labour, of estranged life, of. *estranged* man.

True, it is as a result of the *movement of private property* that we have obtained the concept of *alienated labour* (*of alienated life*) from political economy. But on analysis of this concept it becomes clear that though private property appears to be the source, the cause of alienated labour, it is really its consequence, just as the gods *in the beginning* are not the cause but the effect of man's intellectual confusion. Later this relationship becomes reciprocal.

Only at the very culmination of the development of private property does this, its secret, re-emerge, namely, that on the one hand it is the *product* of alienated labour, and that secondly it is the *means* by which labour alienates itself, the *realization of this alienation*.

This exposition immediately sheds light on various hitherto unsolved conflicts.

(1) Political economy starts from labour as the real soul of production; yet to labour it gives nothing, and to private property everything. From this contradiction Proudhon has concluded in favour of labour and against private property. We understand, however, that this apparent contradiction is the contradiction of *estranged labour* with itself, and that political economy has merely formulated the laws of estranged labour.

We also understand, therefore, that *wages* and *private property* are identical: where the product, the object of labour pays for labour itself, the wage is but a necessary consequence of labour's estrangement, for after all in the wage of labour, labour does not appear as an end in itself but as the servant of the wage. We shall develop this point later, and meanwhile will only deduce some conclusions.

A *forcing-up of wages* (disregarding all other difficulties, including the fact that it would only be by force, too, that the higher wages, being an anomaly, could be maintained) would therefore be nothing but *better payment for the slave*, and would not conquer either for the worker or for labour their human status and dignity.

Indeed, even the *equality of wages* demanded by Proudhon only transforms the relationship of the present-day worker to his labour into the relationship of all men to labour. Society is then conceived as an abstract capitalist.

Wages are a direct consequence of estranged labour, and estranged labour is the direct cause of private property. The downfall of the one aspect must therefore mean the downfall of the other.

(2) From the relationship of estranged labour to private property it further follows that the emancipation of society from private property, etc., from servitude, is expressed in the *political* form of the *emancipation of the workers*; not that *their* emancipation alone was at stake but because the emancipation of the workers contains universal human emancipation—and it contains this, because the whole of human servitude is involved in the relation of the worker to production, and every relation of servitude is but a modification and consequence of this relation.

Just as we have found the concept of *private property* from the concept of *estranged, alienated labour* by *analysis*, in the same way every *category* of political economy can be evolved with the help of these two factors; and we shall find again in each category, e.g., trade, competition, capital, money, only a *definite* and *developed expression* of the first foundations.

Before considering this configuration, however, let us try to solve two problems.

(1) To define the general *nature of private property*, as it has arisen as a result of estranged labour, in its relation to *truly human, social property*.

(2) We have accepted the *estrangement of labour*, its *alienation*, as a fact, and we have analysed this fact. How, we now ask, does *man* come to *alienate*, to estrange, *his labour*? How is this estrangement rooted in the nature of human development? We have already gone a long way to the solution of this problem by *transforming* the question as to the *origin of private property* into the question as to the relation of *alienated labour* to the course of humanity's development. For when one speaks of *private property*, one thinks of being concerned with something external to man. When one speaks of labour, one is directly concerned with man himself. This new formulation of the question already contains its solution.

As to (1): The general nature of private property and its relation to truly human property.

Alienated labour has resolved itself for us into two elements which mutually condition one another, or which are but different expressions of one and the same relationship. *Appropriation* appears as *estrangement*, as *alienation*; and *alienation* appears as *appropriation*, estrangement as true *enfranchisement*.

We have considered the one side—*alienated* labour in relation to the *worker* himself, i.e., the *relation of alienated labour to itself*. The *property-relation of the non-worker to the worker and to labour* we have found as the product, the necessary outcome of this relation of alienated labour. *Private property*, as the material, summary expression of alienated labour, embraces both relations—the *relation of the worker to work, to the product of his labour and to the non-worker*, and the relation of the *non-worker to the worker and to the product of his labour*.

Having seen that in relation to the worker who *appropriates* nature by means of his labour, this appropriation *appears* as estrangement, his own spontaneous activity as activity for another and as activity of another, vitality as a sacrifice of life, production of the object as loss of the object to an alien power, to an *alien* person—we shall now consider the relation to the worker, to labour and its object of this person who is *alien* to labour and the worker.

First it has to be noticed, that everything which appears in the worker as an *activity of alienation, of estrangement*, appears in the non-worker as a *state of alienation, of estrangement*.

Secondly, that the worker's *real, practical attitude* in production and to the product (as a state of mind) appears in the non-worker confronting him as a *theoretical* attitude.

Thirdly, the non-worker does everything against the worker which the worker does against himself; but he does not do against himself what he does against the worker.

Let us look more closely at these three relations.[6]

Private Property and Communism

Re. p. XXXIX. The antithesis of *propertylessness* and *property* so long as it is not comprehended as the antithesis of *labour* and *capital*, still remains an antithesis of indifference, not grasped in its *active connection*, its *internal* relation—an antithesis not yet grasped as a *contradiction*. It can find expression in this *first* form even without the advanced development of private property (as in ancient Rome, Turkey, etc.). It does not yet *appear* as having been established by private property itself. But labour, the subjective

6. At this point the first manuscript breaks off unfinished.

essence of private property as exclusion of property, and capital, objective labour as exclusion of labour, constitute *private property* as its developed state of contradiction—hence a dynamic relationship moving inexorably to its resolution.

Re. the same page. The transcendence of self-estrangement follows the same course as self-estrangement. *Private property* is first considered only in its objective aspect—but nevertheless with labour as its essence. Its form of existence is therefore *capital*, which is to be annulled "as such" (Proudhon). Or a *particular form* of labour—labour levelled down, parcelled, and therefore unfree—is conceived as the source of private property's *perniciousness* and of its existence in estrangement from men; for instance, *Fourier*, who, like the physiocrats, also conceived *agricultural labour* to be at least the *exemplary* type, whilst *Saint-Simon* declares in contrast that *industrial labour* as such is the essence, and now also aspires to the *exclusive* rule of the industrialists and the improvement of the workers' condition. Finally, *communism* is the *positive* expression of annulled private property—at first as *universal* private property. By embracing this relation as a *whole*, communism is:

(1) In its first form only a *generalization* and *consummation* of this relationship. It shows itself as such in a twofold form: on the one hand, the dominion of *material* property bulks so large that it wants to destroy *everything* which is not capable of being possessed by all as *private property*. It wants to abstract *by force* from talent, etc. For it the sole purpose of life and existence is direct, physical *possession*. The category of *labourer* is not done away with, but extended to all men. The relationship of private property persists as the relationship of the community to the world of things. Finally, this movement of counterposing universal private property to private property finds expression in the bestial form of counterposing to *marriage* (certainly a *form of exclusive private property*) the *community of women*, in which a woman becomes a piece of *communal* and *common* property. It may be said that this idea of the *community of women* gives away the *secret* of this as yet completely crude and thoughtless communism. Just as the woman passes from marriage to general prostitution,[7] so the entire world of wealth (that is, of man's objective substance) passes from the relationship of exclusive marriage with the owner of private property to a state of universal prostitution with the community. In negating the *personality* of man in every sphere, this type of communism is really nothing but the logical expression of private property, which

7. Prostitution is only a *specific* expression of the *general* prostitution of the *labourer*, and since it is a relationship in which falls not the prostitute alone, but also the one who prostitutes—and the latter's abomination is still greater—the capitalist, etc., also comes under this head. [*Marx*]

is this negation. General *envy* constituting itself as a power is the disguise in which *avarice* re-establishes itself and satisfies itself, only in *another* way. The thoughts of every piece of private property—inherent in each piece as such—are *at least* turned against all *wealthier* private property in the form of envy and the urge to reduce to a common level, so that this envy and urge even constitute the essence of competition. The crude communism is only the consummation of this envy and of this levelling-down proceeding from the *preconceived* minimum. It has a *definite, limited* standard. How little this annulment of private property is really an appropriation is in fact proved by the abstract negation of the entire world of culture and civilization, the regression to the *unnatural* simplicity of the *poor and undemanding* man who has not only failed to go beyond private property, but has not yet even attained to it.

The community is only a community of *labour*, and an equality of *wages* paid out by the communal capital—the *community* as the universal capitalist. Both sides of the relationship are raised to an *imagined* universality—*labour* as a state in which every person is put, and *capital* as the acknowledged universality and power of the community.

In the approach to *woman* as the spoil and handmaid of communal lust is expressed the infinite degradation in which man exists for himself, for the secret of this approach has its *unambiguous*, *decisive*, *plain* and undisguised expression in the relation of *man* to *woman* and in the manner in which the *direct* and *natural* procreative relationship is conceived. The direct, natural, and necessary relation of person to person is the *relation of man to woman*. In this *natural* relationship of the sexes man's relation to nature is immediately his relation to man, just as his relation to man is immediately his relation to nature—his own *natural* function. In this relationship, therefore, is *sensuously manifested*, reduced to an observable *fact*, the extent to which the human essence has become nature to man, or to which nature has to him become the human essence of man. From this relationship one can therefore judge man's whole level of development. It follows from the character of this relationship how much *man* as a *species being*, as *man*, has come to be himself and to comprehend himself; the relation of man to woman is *the most natural* relation of human being to human being. It therefore reveals the extent to which man's *natural* behaviour has become *human*, or the extent to which the *human* essence in him has become a *natural* essence—the extent to which his *human nature* has come to be *nature to him*. In this relationship is revealed, too, the extent to which man's *need* has become a *human* need; the extent to which, therefore, the *other* person as a person has become for him a need—the extent to which he in his individual existence is at the same time a social being. The first positive annulment of private property—*crude* communism—is thus merely one *form* in which the vileness of private property, which wants to set itself up as the *positive community, comes to the surface.*

(2) Communism (a) of a political nature still—democratic or despotic; (b) with the annulment of the state, yet still incomplete, and being still affected by private property (i.e., by the estrangement of man). In both forms communism already knows itself to be re-integration or return of man to himself, the transcendence of human self-estrangement; but since it has not yet grasped the positive essence of private property, and just as little the *human* nature of need, it remains captive to it and infected by it. It has, indeed, grasped its concept, but not its essence.

(3) *Communism* as the *positive* transcendence of *private property*, or *human self-estrangement*, and therefore as the real *appropriation of the human* essence by and for man; communism therefore as the complete return of man to himself as a *social* (i.e., human) being—a return become conscious, and accomplished within the entire wealth of previous development. This communism, as fully-developed naturalism, equals humanism, and as fully-developed humanism equals naturalism; it is the *genuine* resolution of the conflict between man and nature and between man and man—the true resolution of the strife between existence and essence, between objectification and self-confirmation, between freedom and necessity, between the individual and the species. Communism is the riddle of history solved, and it knows itself to be this solution.

The entire movement of history is, therefore, both its *actual* act of genesis (the birth act of its empirical existence) and also for its thinking consciousness the *comprehended* and *known* process of its *coming-to-be*. That other, still immature communism, meanwhile, seeks an *historical* proof for itself—a proof in the realm of the existent—amongst disconnected historical phenomena opposed to private property, tearing single phases from the historical process and focussing attention on them as proofs of its historical pedigree (a horse ridden hard especially by Cabet, Villegardelle, etc.). By so doing it simply makes clear that by far the greater part of this process contradicts its claims, and that, if it has once been, precisely its being in the *past* refutes its pretension to being *essential*.

That the entire revolutionary movement necessarily finds both its empirical and its theoretical basis in the movement of *private property*—in that of the economy, to be precise—is easy to see.

This *material*, immediately *sensuous* private property is the material sensuous expression of *estranged human* life. Its movement—production and consumption—is the *sensuous* revelation of the movement of all production hitherto—i.e., the realization or the reality of man. Religion, family, state, law, morality, science, art, etc., are only *particular* modes of production, and fall under its general law. The positive transcendence of *private property* as the appropriation of *human* life is, therefore, the positive transcendence of all estrangement—that is to say, the return of man from religion, family, state, etc., to his *human*, i.e., *social* mode of existence. Religious estrangement as such occurs only in the realm of *consciousness*, of man's inner life, but economic estrangement is that of *real life*; its transcendence therefore embraces both aspects. It is evident that the *initial* stage of the movement amongst the various peoples depends on whether the true and for them *authentic* life of the people manifests itself more in consciousness or in the external world—is more ideal or real. Communism begins from the outset (*Owen*) with atheism; but atheism is at first far from being *communism*; indeed, it is still mostly an abstraction.

The philanthropy of atheism is therefore at first only *philosophical*, abstract, philanthropy, and that of communism is at once *real* and directly bent on *action*.

We have seen how on the premise of positively annulled private property man produces man—himself and the other man; how the object, being the direct embodiment of his individuality, is simultaneously his own existence for the other man, the existence of the other man, and that existence for him. Likewise, however, both the material of labour and man as the subject, are the point of departure as well as the result of the movement (and precisely in this fact, that they must constitute the *point of departure*, lies the historical *necessity* of private property). Thus the *social* character is the general character of the whole movement: *just as* society itself produces *man as man*, so is society *produced* by him. Activity and consumption, both in their content and in their *mode of existence*, are *social*: *social* activity and *social* consumption; the *human* essence of nature first exists only for *social* man; for only here does nature exist for him as a *bond* with *man*—as his existence for the other and the other's existence for him—as the life-element of the human world; only here does nature exist as the *foundation* of his own *human* existence. Only here has what is to him his *natural* existence become his *human* existence, and nature become man for him. Thus *society* is the consummated oneness in substance of man and nature—the true resurrection of nature—the naturalism of man and the humanism of nature both brought to fulfilment.

Social activity and social consumption exist by no means *only* in the form of some *directly* communal activity and directly *commu-*

nal consumption, although *communal* activity and *communal* consumption—i.e., activity and consumption which are manifested and directly confirmed in *real association* with other men—will occur wherever such a *direct* expression of sociality stems from the true character of the activity's content and is adequate to the nature of consumption.

But again when I am active *scientifically*, etc.,—when I am engaged in activity which I can seldom perform in direct community with others—then I am *social*, because I am active as a *man*. Not only is the material of my activity given to me as a social product (as is even the language in which the thinker is active): my *own* existence *is* social activity, and therefore that which I make of myself, I make of myself for society and with the consciousness of myself as a social being.

My *general* consciousness is only the *theoretical* shape of that of which the *living* shape is the *real* community, the social fabric, although at the present day *general* consciousness is an abstraction from real life and as such antagonistically confronts it. Consequently, too, the *activity* of my general consciousness, as an activity, is my *theoretical* existence as a social being.

What is to be avoided above all is the re-establishing of "Society" as an abstraction *vis-à-vis* the individual. The individual *is the social being*. His life, even if it may not appear in the direct form of a *communal* life carried out together with others—is therefore an expression and confirmation of *social life*. Man's individual and species life are not *different*, however much—and this is inevitable—the mode of existence of the individual is a more *particular*, or more *general* mode of the life of the species, or the life of the species is a more *particular* or more *general* individual life.

In his *consciousness of species* man confirms his real *social life* and simply repeats his real existence in thought, just as conversely the being of the species confirms itself in species-consciousness and is for *itself* in its generality as a thinking being.

Man, much as he may therefore be a *particular* individual (and it is precisely his particularity which makes him an individual, and a real *individual* social being), is just as much the *totality*—the ideal totality—the subjective existence of thought and experienced society present for itself; just as he exists also in the real world as the awareness and the real enjoyment of social existence, and as a totality of human life-activity.

Thinking and being are thus no doubt *distinct*, but at the same time they are in *unity* with each other.

Death seems to be a harsh victory of the species over the *definite* individual and to contradict their unity. But the determinate individual is only a *determinate species being*, and as such mortal.

(4) Just as *private property* is only the sensuous expression of the fact that man becomes *objective* for himself and at the same time becomes to himself a strange and inhuman object; just as it expresses the fact that the assertion of his life is the alienation of his life, that his realization is his loss of reality, is an *alien* reality: conversely, the positive transcendence of private property—i.e., the *sensuous* appropriation for and by man of the human essence and of human life, of objective man, of human *achievements*—is not to be conceived merely in the sense of *direct*, one-sided *gratification*—merely in the sense of *possessing*, of *having*. Man appropriates his total essence in a total manner, that is to say, as a whole man. Each of his *human* relations to the world—seeing, hearing, smelling, tasting, feeling, thinking, being aware, sensing, wanting, acting, loving—in short, all the organs of his individual being, like those organs which are directly social in their form, are in their *objective* orientation or in their *orientation to the object*, the appropriation of that object, the appropriation of the *human* world; their orientation to the object is the *manifestation of the human world*;[8] it is human *efficaciousness* and human *suffering*, for suffering, apprehended humanly, is an enjoyment of self in man.

Private property has made us so stupid and one-sided that an object is only *ours* when we have it—when it exists for us as capital, or when it is directly possessed, eaten, drunk, worn, inhabited, etc.,—in short, when it is *used* by us. Although private property itself again conceives all these direct realizations of possession as *means of life*, and the life which they serve as means is the *life of private property*—labour and conversion into capital.

In place of *all* these physical and mental senses there has therefore come the sheer estrangement of *all* these senses—the sense of *having*. The human being had to be reduced to this absolute poverty in order that he might yield his inner wealth to the outer world. (On the category of "having," see Hess in the *Twenty-One Sheets*.)

The transcendence of private property is therefore the complete *emancipation* of all human senses and attributes; but it is this emancipation precisely because these senses and attributes have become, subjectively and objectively, *human*. The eye has become a *human* eye, just as its *object* has become a social, *human* object—an object emanating from man for man. The *senses* have therefore become directly in their practice *theoreticians*. They relate themselves to the *thing* for the sake of the thing, but the thing itself is an *objective human* relation to itself and to man,[9]

8. For this reason it is just as highly priced as the *determinations* of human *essence* and *activities*. [*Marx*]
9. In practice I can relate myself to a thing humanly only if the thing relates itself to the human being humanly. [*Marx*]

and vice versa. Need or enjoyment have consequently lost their *egotistical* nature, and nature has lost its mere *utility* by use becoming *human* use.

In the same way, the senses and enjoyments of other men have become my *own* appropriation. Besides these direct organs, therefore, *social* organs develop in the *form* of society; thus, for instance, activity in direct association with others, etc., has become an organ for *expressing* my own *life*, and a mode of appropriating *human life*.

It is obvious that the *human* eye gratifies itself in a way different from the crude, non-human eye; the human *ear* different from the crude ear, etc.

To recapitulate; man is not lost in his object only when the object becomes for him a *human* object or objective man. This is possible only when the object becomes for him a *social* object, he himself for himself a social being, just as society becomes a being for him in this object.

On the one hand, therefore, it is only when the objective world becomes everywhere for man in society the world of man's essential powers[1]—human reality, and for that reason the reality of his *own* essential powers—that all *objects* become for him the *objectification of himself*, become objects which confirm and realize his individuality, become *his* objects: that is, *man himself* becomes the object. The manner in which they become *his* depends on the *nature of the objects* and on the nature of the *essential power* corresponding *to it*; for it is precisely the *determinateness* of this relationship which shapes the particular, *real* mode of affirmation. To the *eye* an object comes to be other than it is to the *ear*, and the object of the eye is another object than the object of the *ear*. The peculiarity of each essential power is precisely its *peculiar essence*, and therefore also the peculiar mode of its objectification, of its *objectively actual* living *being*. Thus man is affirmed in the objective world not only in the act of thinking, but with *all* his senses.

On the other hand, looking at this in its subjective aspect: just as music alone awakens in man the sense of music, and just as the most beautiful music has *no* sense for the unmusical ear—is no object for it, because my object can only be the confirmation of one of my essential powers and can therefore only be so for me as my essential power is present for itself as a subjective capacity, because the sense of an object for me goes only so far as *my* senses go (has only sense for a sense corresponding to that object)—for this reason the *senses* of the social man are *other* senses than those of the non-social man. Only through the objectively unfolded rich-

---

1. "Essential powers"—*Wesenskräfte:*   my essential nature, my very being. i.e., powers belonging to me as part of

ness of man's essential being is the richness of subjective *human* sensibility (a musical ear, an eye for beauty of form—in short, *senses* capable of human gratifications, senses confirming themselves as essential powers of *man*) either cultivated or brought into being. For not only the five senses but also the so-called mental senses—the practical senses (will, love, etc.)—in a word, *human* sense—the humanness of the senses—comes to be by virtue of its object, by virtue of *humanized* nature. The *forming* of the five senses is a labour of the entire history of the world down to the present.

The *sense* caught up in crude practical need has only a *restricted* sense. For the starving man, it is not the human form of food that exists, but only its abstract being as food; it could just as well be there in its crudest form, and it would be impossible to say wherein this feeding-activity differs from that of *animals*. The care-burdened man in need has no sense for the finest play; the dealer in minerals sees only the mercantile value but not the beauty and the unique nature of the mineral: he has no mineralogical sense. Thus, the objectification of the human essence both in its theoretical and practical aspects is required to make man's *sense human*, as well as to create the *human sense* corresponding to the entire wealth of human and natural substance.

Just as resulting from the movement of *private property*, of its wealth as well as its poverty—or of its material and spiritual wealth and poverty—the budding society finds to hand all the material for this *development*: so *established* society produces man in this entire richness of his being—produces the *rich* man *profoundly endowed with all the senses*—as its enduring reality.

It will be seen how subjectivism and objectivism, spiritualism and materialism, activity and suffering, only lose their antithetical character, and thus their existence, as such antitheses in the social condition; it will be seen how the resolution of the *theoretical* antitheses is *only* possible *in a practical* way, by virtue of the practical energy of men. Their resolution is therefore by no means merely a problem of knowledge, but a *real* problem of life, which *philosophy* could not solve precisely because it conceived this problem as *merely* a theoretical one.

It will be seen how the history of *industry* and the established *objective* existence of industry are the *open* book of *man's essential powers*, the exposure to the senses of human *psychology*. Hitherto this was not conceived in its inseparable connection with man's *essential being*, but only in an external relation of utility, because, moving in the realm of estrangement, people could only think man's general mode of being—religion or history in its abstract-general character as politics, art, literature, etc.,—to be the reality of man's essential powers and *man's species-activity*. We have before us the *objectified essential powers* of man in the form of *sensuous, alien, useful objects*, in the form of estrangement, displayed in *ordinary material industry* (which can be conceived as a part of that general movement, just as that movement can be conceived as a particular part of industry, since all human activity hitherto has been labour—that is, industry—activity estranged from itself).

A *psychology* for which this, the part of history most contemporary and accessible to sense, remains a closed book, cannot become a genuine, comprehensive and *real* science. What indeed are we to think of a science which *airily* abstracts from this large part of human labour and which fails to feel its own incompleteness, while such a wealth of human endeavour unfolded before it means nothing more to it than, perhaps, what can be expressed in one word—*"need,"* *"vulgar need"*?

The *natural sciences* have developed an enormous activity and have accumulated a constantly growing mass of material. Philosophy, however, has remained just as alien to them as they remain to philosophy. Their momentary unity was only a *chimerical illusion*. The will was there, but the means were lacking. Even historiography pays regard to natural science only occasionally, as a factor of enlightenment and utility arising from individual great discoveries. But natural science has invaded and transformed human life all the more *practically* through the medium of industry; and has prepared human emancipation, however directly and much it had to consummate dehumanization. *Industry* is the *actual*, historical relation of nature, and therefore of natural science, to man. If, therefore, industry is conceived as the *exoteric* revelation of man's *essential powers*, we also gain an understanding of the *human* essence of nature or the *natural* essence of man. In consequence, natural science will lose its abstractly material—or rather, its idealistic— tendency, and will become the basis of *human* science, as it has already become the basis of actual human life, albeit in an estranged form. *One* basis for life and another basis for *science* is *a priori* a lie. The nature which comes to be in human history—the genesis of human society—is man's *real* nature; hence nature as it comes to be through industry, even though in an *estranged* form, is true *anthropological* nature.

Sense-perception (see Feuerbach) must be the basis of all science. Only when it proceeds from sense-perception in the twofold form both of *sensuous* consciousness and of *sensuous* need—that is, only when science proceeds from nature—is it *true* science. All history is the preparation for *"man"* to become the object of *sensuous* consciousness, and for the needs of "man as man" to become [natural, sensuous] needs. History itself is a *real* part of *natural his-*

tory—of nature's coming to be man. Natural science will in time subsume under itself the science of man, just as the science of man will subsume under itself natural science: there will be *one* science.

Man is the immediate object of natural science: for immediate, *sensuous nature* for man is, immediately, human sensuousness (the expressions are identical)— presented immediately in the form of the *other* man sensuously present for him. For his own sensuousness first exists as human sensuousness for himself through the *other* man. But *nature* is the immediate object of the *science of man*: the first object of man—man—is nature, sensuousness; and the particular human sensuous essential powers can only find their self-knowledge in the science of the natural world in general, since they can find their objective realization in *natural* objects only. The element of thought itself—the element of thought's living expression—*language*—is of a sensuous nature. The *social* reality of nature, and *human* natural science, or the *natural science about man*, are identical terms.

It will be seen how in place of the *wealth* and *poverty* of political economy come the *rich human being* and *rich human* need. The *rich* human being is simultaneously the human being *in need of* a totality of human life-activities—the man in whom his own realization exists as an inner necessity, as *need*. Not only *wealth*, but likewise the *poverty* of man—given socialism—receives in equal measure a *human* and therefore social significance. Poverty is the passive bond which causes the human being to experience the need of the greatest wealth—the *other* human being. The dominion of the objective being in me, the sensuous outburst of my essential activity, is *emotion*, which thus becomes here the *activity* of my being.

(5) A *being* only considers himself independent when he stands on his own feet; and he only stands on his own feet when he owes his *existence* to himself. A man who lives by the grace of another regards himself as a dependent being. But I live completely by the grace of another if I owe him not only the sustenance of my life, but if he has, moreover, *created* my *life*—if he is the *source* of my life; and if it is not of my own creation, my life has necessarily a source of this kind outside it. The *Creation* is therefore an idea very difficult to dislodge from popular consciousness. The self-mediated being of nature and of man is *incomprehensible* to it, because it contradicts everything *palpable* in practical life.

The creation of the *earth* has received a mighty blow from *geogeny*—i.e., from the science which presents the formation of the earth, the coming-to-be of the earth, as a process, as self-generation. *Generatio aequivoca*[2] is the only practical refutation of the theory of creation.

2. Spontaneous generation.

Now it is certainly easy to say to the single individual what Aristotle has already said. You have been begotten by your father and your mother; therefore in you the mating of two human beings—a species-act of human beings—has produced the human being. You see, therefore, that even physically, man owes his existence to man. Therefore you must not only keep sight of the *one* aspect—the *infinite* progression which leads you further to enquire: "Who begot my father? Who his grandfather?", etc. You must also hold on to the *circular movement* sensuously perceptible in that progression, by which *man* repeats himself in procreation, thus always remaining the subject. You will reply, however: I grant you this circular movement; now grant me the progression which drives me even further until I ask: Who begot the first man, and nature as a whole? I can only answer you: Your question is itself a product of abstraction. Ask yourself how you arrived at that question. Ask yourself whether your question is not posed from a standpoint to which I cannot reply, because it is a perverse one. Ask yourself whether that progression as such exists for a reasonable mind. When you ask about the creation of nature and man, you are abstracting, in so doing, from man and nature. You postulate them as *non-existent*, and yet you want me to prove them to you as *existing*. Now I say to you: Give up your abstraction and you will also give up your question. Or if you want to hold on to your abstraction, then be consistent, and if you think of man and nature as *non-existent*, then think of yourself as non-existent, for you too are surely nature and man. Don't think, don't ask me, for as soon as you think and ask, your *abstraction* from the existence of nature and man has no meaning. Or are you such an egoist that you postulate everything as nothing, and yet want yourself to be?

You can reply: I do not want to postulate the nothingness of nature. I ask you about *its genesis*, just as I ask the anatomist about the formation of bones, etc.

But since for the socialist man the *entire so-called history of the world* is nothing but the begetting of man through human labour, nothing but the coming-to-be of nature for man, he has the visible, irrefutable proof of his *birth* through himself, of his *process* of *coming-to-be*. Since the *real existence* of man and nature has become practical, sensuous and perceptible—since man has become for man as the being of nature, and nature for man as the being of man—the question about an *alien* being, about a being above nature and man—a question which implies the admission of the inessentiality of nature and of man—has become impossible in practice. *Atheism*, as the denial of this inessentiality, has no longer any meaning, for atheism is a *negation of God*, and postulates the *existence of man* through this negation; but socialism as socialism no longer stands in any need of such a mediation. It proceeds from the *practically and theoretically sensuous consciousness* of man and of nature as the *essence*. Socialism is man's *positive self-consciousness* no longer mediated through the annulment of religion, just as *real life* is man's positive reality, no longer mediated through the annulment of private property, through *communism*. Communism is the position as the negation of the negation, and is hence the *actual* phase necessary for the next stage of historical development in the process of human emancipation and recovery. *Communism* is the necessary pattern and the dynamic principle of the immediate future, but communism as such is not the goal of human development—the structure of human society.

The Meaning of Human Requirements

We have seen what significance, given socialism, the *wealth* of human needs has, and what significance, therefore, both a *new mode of production* and a new *object* of production have: a new manifestation of the forces of *human* nature and a new enrichment of *human* nature.[3] Under private property their significance is reversed: every person speculates on creating a *new* need in another, so as to drive him to a fresh sacrifice, to place him in a new dependence and to seduce him into a new mode of *gratification* and therefore economic ruin. Each tries to establish over the other an *alien* power, so as thereby to find satisfaction of his own selfish need. The increase in the quantity of objects is accompanied by an extension of the realm of the alien powers to which man is subjected, and every new product represents a new *potency* of mutual swindling and mutual plundering. Man becomes ever poorer as man; his need for *money* becomes ever greater if he wants to overpower hostile being; and the power of his *money* declines exactly in inverse proportion to the increase in the volume of production: that is, his neediness grows as the *power* of money increases.

The need for money is therefore the true need produced by the modern economic system, and it is the only need which the latter produces. The *quantity* of money becomes to an ever greater degree its sole *effective* attribute: just as it reduces everything to its abstract form, so it reduces itself in the course of its own movement to something merely *quantitative*. *Excess* and *intemperance* come to be its true norm. Subjectively, this is even partly manifested in that the extension of products and needs falls into *contriving* and ever-*calculating* subservience to inhuman, refined, unnatural and *imaginary* appetites.Private property does not know how to change crude

3. Forces of human nature: *menschlichen Wesenkraft*; human nature: *menschlichen Wesens*.

need into *human* need. Its *idealism* is *fantasy, caprice* and *whim*; and no eunuch flatters his despot more basely or uses more despicable means to stimulate his dulled capacity for pleasure in order to sneak a favour for himself than does the industrial eunuch—the producer—in order to sneak for himself a few pennies—in order to charm the golden birds out of the pockets of his Christianly beloved neighbours. He puts himself at the service of the other's most depraved fancies, plays the pimp between him and his need, excites in him morbid appetites, lies in wait for each of his weaknesses—all so that he can then demand the cash for this service of love. (Every product is a bait with which to seduce away the other's very being, his money; every real and possible need is a weakness which will lead the fly to the gluepot. General exploitation of communal human nature, just as every imperfection in man, is a bond with heaven—an avenue giving the priest access to his heart; every need is an opportunity to approach one's neighbour under the guise of the utmost amiability and to say to him: Dear friend, I give you what you need, but you know the *conditio sine qua non*; you know the ink in which you have to sign yourself over to me; in providing for your pleasure, I fleece you.)

And partly, this estrangement manifests itself in that it produces refinement of needs and of their means on the one hand, and a bestial barbarization, a complete, unrefined, abstract simplicity of need, on the other; or rather in that it merely resurrects itself in its opposite. Even the need for fresh air ceases for the worker. Man returns to living in a cave, which is now, however, contaminated with the mephitic breath of plague given off by civilization, and which he continues to occupy only *precariously*, it being for him an alien habitation which can be withdrawn from him any day—a place from which, if he does not pay, he can be thrown out any day. For this mortuary he has to *pay*. A dwelling in the *light*, which Prometheus in Aeschylus designated as one of the greatest boons, by means of which he made the savage into a human being, ceases to exist for the worker. Light, air, etc.—the simplest *animal* cleanliness—ceases to be a need for man. *Dirt*—this stagnation and putrefaction of man—the *sewage* of civilization (speaking quite literally)—comes to be the *element of life* for him. Utter, *unnatural* neglect, putrefied nature, comes to be his *life-element*. None of his senses exist any longer, and not only in his human fashion, but in an *inhuman* fashion, and therefore not even in an animal fashion. The crudest *modes* (and *instruments*) of human labour are coming back: the *tread mill* of the Roman slaves, for instance, is the means of production, the means of existence, of many English workers. It is not only that man has no human needs—even his *animal* needs are ceasing to exist. The Irishman no longer knows any need now but the need to *eat*, and indeed only the need to eat *potatoes*—and *scabby potatoes* at that, the worst kind of potatoes. But in each of their industrial towns England and France have already a *little* Ireland. The savage and the animal have at least the need to hunt, to roam, etc.—the need of companionship. Machine labour is simplified in order to make a worker out of the human being still in the making, the completely immature human being, the *child*—whilst the worker has become a neglected child. The machine accommodates itself to the *weakness* of the human being in order to make the *weak* human being into a machine.

How the multiplication of needs and of the means of their satisfaction breeds the absence of needs and of means is demonstrated by the political economist (and the capitalist: it should be noted that it is always *empirical* business men we are talking about when we refer to political economists—their *scientific* confession and mode of being). This he shows:

(1) By reducing the worker's need to the barest and most miserable level of physical subsistence, and by reducing his activity to the most abstract mechanical movement. Hence, he says: Man has no other need either of activity or of enjoyment. For he calls *even* this life *human* life and existence.

(2) By *counting* the *lowest* possible level of life (existence) as the standard, indeed as the general standard—general because it is applicable to the mass of men. He changes the worker into an insensible being lacking all needs, just as he changes his activity into a pure abstraction from all activity. To him, therefore, every *luxury* of the worker seems to be reprehensible, and everything that goes beyond the most abstract need—be it in the realm of passive enjoyment, or a manifestation of activity—seems to him a luxury. Political economy, this science of *wealth*, is therefore simultaneously the science of denial, of want, of *thrift*, of *saving*—and it actually reaches the point where it *spares* man the *need* of either fresh *air* or physical *exercise*. This science of marvellous industry is simultaneously the science of *asceticism*, and its true ideal is the *ascetic* but *extortionate* miser and the *ascetic* but *productive* slave. Its moral ideal is the *worker* who takes part of his wages to the savings bank, and it has even found ready-made an abject *art* in which to clothe this its pet idea: they have presented it, bathed in sentimentality, on the stage. Thus political economy—despite its worldly and wanton appearance—is a true moral science, the most moral of all the sciences. Self-denial, the denial of life and of all human needs, is its cardinal doctrine. The less you eat, drink and read books; the less you go to the theatre, the dance hall, the public-house; the less you think, love, theorize, sing, paint, fence, etc., the more you *save*—the *greater* becomes your treasure which neither

moths nor dust will devour—your *capital*. The less you *are*, the more you *have*; the less you express your own life, the greater is your *alienated* life—the greater is the store of your estranged being. Everything which the political economist takes from you in life and in humanity, he replaces for you in *money* and in *wealth*; and all the things which you cannot do, your money can do. It can eat and drink, go to the dance hall and the theatre; it can travel, it can appropriate art, learning, the treasures of the past, political power —all this it *can* appropriate for you—it can buy all this for you: it is the true *endowment*. Yet being all this, it is inclined to do nothing but create itself, buy itself; for everything else is after all its servant. And when I have the master I have the servant and do not need his servant. All passions and all activity must therefore be submerged in *avarice*. The worker may only have enough for him to want to live, and may only want to live in order to have [enough].

Of course a controversy now arises in the field of political economy. The one side (Lauderdale, Malthus, etc.) recommends *luxury* and execrates thrift. The other (Say, Ricardo, etc.) recommends thrift and execrates luxury. But the former admits that it wants luxury in order to produce *labour* (i.e., absolute thrift); and the latter admits that it recommends thrift in order to produce *wealth* (i.e., luxury). The Lauderdale-Malthus school has the *romantic* notion that avarice alone ought not to determine the consumption of the rich, and it contradicts its own laws in advancing *extravagance* as a direct means of enrichment. Against it, therefore, the other side very earnestly and circumstantially proves that I do not increase but reduce my *possessions* by being extravagant. The Say-Ricardo school, however, is hypocritical in not admitting that it is precisely whim and caprice which determine production. It forgets the "refined needs"; it forgets that there would be no production without consumption; it forgets that as a result of competition production can only become more extensive and luxurious. It forgets that it is use that determines a thing's value, and that fashion determines use. It wishes to see only "useful things" produced, but it forgets that production of too many useful things produces too large a *useless* population. Both sides forget that extravagance and thrift, luxury and privation, wealth and poverty are equal.

And you must not only stint the immediate gratification of your senses, as by stinting yourself of food, etc.: you must also spare yourself all sharing of general interest, all sympathy, all trust, etc.; if you want to be economical, if you do not want to be ruined by illusions.

You must make everything that is yours *saleable*, i.e., useful. If I ask the political economist: Do I obey economic laws if I extract money by offering my body for sale, by surrendering it to another's lust? (The factory workers in France call the prostitution of their wives and daughters the xth working hour, which is literally correct.)—Or am I not acting in keeping with political economy if I sell my friend to the Moroccans? (And the direct sale of men in the form of a trade in conscripts, etc., takes place in all civilized countries.)—Then the political economist replies to me: You do not transgress my laws; but see what Cousin Ethics and Cousin Religion have to say about it. My *political economic* ethics and religion have nothing to reproach you with, but— But whom am I now to believe, political economy or ethics? The ethics of political economy is *acquisition*, work, thrift, sobriety—but political economy promises to satisfy my needs. The political economy of ethics is the opulence of a good conscience, of virtue, etc.; but how can I live virtuously if I do not live? And how can I have a good conscience if I am not conscious of anything? It stems from the very nature of estrangement that each sphere applies to me a different and opposite yardstick—ethics one and political economy another; for each is a specific estrangement of man and focuses attention on a particular round of estranged essential activity, and each stands in an estranged relation to the other. Thus M. *Michel Chevalier* reproaches Ricardo with having abstracted from ethics. But Ricardo is allowing political economy to speak its own language, and if it does not speak ethically, this is not Ricardo's fault. M. Chevalier abstracts from political economy in so far as he moralizes, but he really and necessarily abstracts from ethics in so far as he practises political economy. The reference of political economy to ethics, if it is other than an arbitrary, contingent and therefore unfounded and unscientific reference, if it is not being put up as a *sham* but is meant to be *essential*, can only be the reference of the laws of political economy to ethics. If there is no such connection, or if the contrary is rather the case, can Ricardo help it? Besides, the opposition between political economy and ethics is only a *sham* opposition and just as much no opposition as it is an opposition. All that happens is that political economy expresses moral laws *in its own way*.

Needlessness as the principle of political economy is *most brilliantly* shown in its *theory of population*. There are *too many* people. Even the existence of men is a pure luxury; and if the worker is "*ethical*," he will be *sparing* in procreation. (Mill suggests public acclaim for those who prove themselves continent in their sexual relations, and public rebuke for those who sin against such barrenness of marriage. . . . Is not this the ethics, the teaching of asceticism?) The production of people appears in the form of public misery.

The meaning which production has in relation to the rich is seen *revealed* in the meaning which it has for the poor. At the top the manifestation is always refined, veiled, ambiguous—a sham; lower, it is rough, straightforward, frank—the real thing. The worker's *crude* need is a far greater source of gain than the *refined* need of the rich. The cellar-dwellings in London bring more to those who let them than do the palaces; that is to say, with reference to the landlord they constitute *greater wealth*, and thus (to speak the language of political economy) greater *social* wealth.

Industry speculates on the refinement of needs, but it speculates just as much on their *crudeness*, but on their artificially produced crudeness, whose true enjoyment, therefore, is *self-stupefaction*— this *seeming* satisfaction of need—this civilization contained *within* the crude barbarism of need; the English gin-shops are therefore the *symbolical embodiments* of private property. Their *luxury* reveals the true relation of industrial luxury and wealth to man. They are therefore rightly the only Sunday pleasures of the people, dealt with at least mildly by the English police.

We have already seen how the political economist establishes the unity of labour and capital in a variety of ways:—(1) Capital is *accumulated labour*. (2) The purpose of capital within production —partly, reproduction of capital with profit, partly, capital as raw material (material of labour), and partly, as itself a *working instrument* (the machine is capital directly equated with labour)—is *productive labour*. (3) The worker is a capital. (4) Wages belong to costs of capital. (5) In relation to the worker, labour is the reproduction of his life-capital. (6) In relation to the capitalist, labour is an aspect of his capital's activity.

Finally, (7) the political economist postulates the original unity of capital and labour in the form of the unity of the capitalist and the worker; this is the original state of paradise. The way in which these two aspects in the form of two persons leap at each other's throats is for the political economist a *contingent* event, and hence only to be explained by reference to external factors. (See Mill.)[4]

The nations which are still dazzled by the sensuous splendour of precious metals, and are therefore still fetish-worshippers of metal money, are not yet fully developed money-nations.—Contrast of France and England. The extent to which the solution of theoretical riddles is the task of practice and effected through practice, just as true practice is the condition of a real and positive theory, is shown, for example, in *fetishism*. The sensuous consciousness of the fetish-worshipper is different from that of the Greek, because his sensuous existence is still different. The abstract enmity between sense and spirit is necessary so long as the human feeling for nature,

4. James Mill, *Elements of Political Economy*.

the human sense of nature, and therefore also the *natural* sense of *man*, are not yet produced by man's own labour.

Equality is nothing but a translation of the German *"Ich=Ich"* into the French, i.e., political form. Equality as the *groundwork* of communism is its *political* justification, and it is the same as when the German justifies it by conceiving man as *universal self-consciousness*. Naturally, the transcendence of the estrangement always proceeds from that form of the estrangement which is the *dominant* power: in Germany, *self-consciousness*; in France, *equality*, because politics; in England, real, material, *practical* need taking only itself as its standard. It is from this standpoint that Proudhon is to be criticized and appreciated.

If we characterize *communism* itself because of its character as negation of the negation, as the appropriation of the human essence which mediates itself with itself through the negation of private property—as being not yet the *true*, self-originating position but rather a position originating from private property, [. . .][5]

Since in that case[6] the real estrangement of the life of man remains, and remains all the more, the more one is conscious of it as such, it may be accomplished solely by putting communism into operation.

In order to abolish the *idea* of private property, the *idea* of communism is completely sufficient. It takes *actual* communist action to abolish actual private property. History will come to it; and this movement, which in *theory* we already know to be a self-transcending movement, will constitute *in actual fact* a very severe and protracted process. But we must regard it as a real advance to have gained beforehand a consciousness of the limited character as well as of the goal of this historical movement—and a consciousness which reaches out beyond it.

When communist *workmen* associate with one another, theory, propaganda, etc., is their first end. But at the same time, as a result of this association, they acquire a new need—the need for society —and what appears as a means becomes an end. You can observe this practical process in its most splendid results whenever you see French socialist workers together. Such things as smoking, drinking, eating, etc., are no longer means of contact or means that bring together. Company, association, and conversation, which again has society as its end, are enough for them; the brotherhood of man is

5. In the manuscript the lower left corner of the page is torn off. Just the right-hand endings of the last six lines remain, making restorations of the text impossible. It is possible to surmise, however, that Marx here criticizes Hegel's idealistic "transcending" of estrangement (the words that have survived are cited in the next footnote). 6. In "transcending" estrangement "in the old German manner—the manner of the Hegelian phenomenology," i.e., in transcending it exclusively in the "consciousness" of the subject.

no mere phrase with them, but a fact of life, and the nobility of man shines upon us from their work-hardened bodies.

When political economy claims that demand and supply always balance each other, it immediately forgets that according to its own claim (theory of population) the supply of *people* always exceeds the demand, and that, therefore, in the essential result of the whole production process—the existence of man—the disparity between demand and supply gets its most striking expression.

The extent to which money, which appears as a means, constitutes true *power* and the sole *end*—the extent to which in general that means which gives me substance, which gives me possession of the objective substance of others, is an *end in itself*—can be clearly seen from the facts that landed property wherever land is the source of life, and *horse* and *sword* wherever these are the *true means of life*, are also acknowledged as the true political powers in life. In the middle ages a social class is emancipated as soon as it is allowed to carry the *sword*. Amongst nomadic peoples it is the *horse* which makes me a free man and a participant in the life of the community.

We have said above that man is regressing to the *cave dwelling* etc.—but that he is regressing to it in an estranged, malignant form. The savage in his cave—a natural element which freely offers itself for his use and protection—feels himself no more a stranger, or rather feels himself to be just as much at home as a *fish* in water. But the cellar-dwelling of the poor man is a hostile dwelling, "an alien, restraining power which only gives itself up to him in so far as he gives up to it his blood and sweat"—a dwelling which he cannot look upon as his own home where he might at last exclaim, "Here I am at home," but where instead he finds himself in *someone else's* house, in the house of a *stranger* who daily lies in wait for him and throws him out if he does not pay his rent. Similarly, he is also aware of the contrast in quality between his dwelling and a human dwelling—a residence in that *other* world, the heaven of wealth.

Estrangement is manifested not only in the fact that *my* means of life belong to *someone else*, that *my* desire is the inaccessible possession of *another*, but also in the fact that everything is in itself something *different* from itself—that my activity is *something else* and that, finally (and this applies also to the capitalist), all is under the sway of *inhuman* power. There is a form of inactive, extravagant wealth given over wholly to pleasure, the enjoyer of which on the one hand *behaves* as a mere *ephemeral* individual frantically spending himself to no purpose knows the slave-labour of others (human *sweat and blood*) as the prey of his cupidity, and therefore knows man himself, and hence also his own self, as a sacrificed and empty being. With such wealth the contempt of man makes its appearance, partly as arrogance and as the throwing-away of what can give sustenance to a hundred human lives, and partly as the infamous illusion that his own unbridled extravagance and ceaseless, unproductive consumption is the condition of the other's *labour* and therefore of his *subsistence*. He knows the realization of the *essential powers* of man only as the realization of his own excesses, his whims and capricious, bizarre notions. This wealth which, on the other hand, again knows wealth as a mere means, as something that is good for nothing but to be annihilated and which is therefore at once slave and master, at once generous and mean, capricious, presumptuous, conceited, refined, cultured and witty—this wealth has not yet experienced *wealth* as an utterly *alien power* over itself: it sees in it, rather, only its own power, and not wealth but *gratification* [is its][7] final aim and end.

* * *

Society, as it appears to the political economist, is *civil society*, in which every individual is a totality of needs and only exists for the other person, as the other exists for him, in so far as each becomes a means for the other. The political economist reduces everything (just as does politics in its *Rights of Man*) to man, i.e., to the individual whom he strips of all determinateness so as to class him as capitalist or worker.

The *division of labour* is the expression in political economy of the *social character of labour* within the estrangement. Or, since *labour* is only an expression of human activity within alienation, of the living of life as the alienating of life, the *division of labour*, too, is therefore nothing else but the *estranged, alienated* positing of human activity as *a real activity of the species* or as *activity of man as a species being*.

As for *the essence of the division of labour*—and of course the division of labour had to be conceived as a major driving force in the production of wealth as soon as *labour* was recognized as *the essence of private property*—i.e., about *the estranged and alienated form of human activity as an activity of the species*—the political economists are very unclear and self-contradictory about it.

* * *

The Power of Money in Bourgeois Society

If man's *feelings*, passions, etc., are not merely anthropological phenomena in the [narrower][8] sense, but truly *ontological* affirmations of essential being (of nature), and if they are only really affirmed because their *object* exists for them as an object of *sense*, then it is clear:

7. The bottom of the page is torn.   8. This word is illegible.
Three or four lines are missing.

(1) That they have by no means merely one mode of affirmation, but rather that the distinctive character of their existence, of their life, is constituted by the distinctive mode of their affirmation. In what manner the object exists for them, is the characteristic mode of their *gratification*.

(2) Whenever the sensuous affirmation is the direct annulment of the object in its independent form (as in eating, drinking, working up of the object, etc.), this is the affirmation of the object.

(3) In so far as man, and hence also his feeling, etc., are *human*, the affirmation of the object by another is likewise his own enjoyment.

(4) Only through developed industry—i.e., through the medium of private property—does the ontological essence of human passion come to be both in its totality and in its humanity; the science of man is therefore itself a product of man's establishment of himself by practical activity.

(5) The meaning of private property—liberated from its estrangement—is the *existence of essential objects* for man, both as objects of enjoyment and as objects of activity.

By possessing the *property* of buying everything, by possessing the property of appropriating all objects, *money* is thus the *object* of eminent possession. The universality of its *property* is the omnipotence of its being. It therefore functions as the almighty being. Money is the *pimp* between man's need and the object, between his life and his means of life. But that which mediates *my* life for me, also *mediates* the existence of other people *for me*. For me it is the *other* person.

> "What, man! confound it, hands and feet
> And head and backside, all are yours!
> And what we take while life is sweet,
> Is that to be declared not ours?
>   Six stallions, say, I can afford,
>   Is not their strength my property?
>   I tear along, a sporting lord,
>   As if their legs belonged to me."
>   (Mephistopheles, in *Faust*) [9]

Shakespeare in *Timon of Athens*:

> "Gold? Yellow, glittering, precious gold? No, Gods,
> I am no idle votarist! . . . Thus much of this will
>   make black white, foul fair,
> Wrong right, base noble, old young, coward valiant.
> . . . Why, this
> Will lug your priests and servants from your sides,
> Pluck stout men's pillows from below their heads:

9. Goethe, *Faust*, (Part I—Faust's (Penguin, 1949), p. 91. Study, III), translated by Philip Wayne

> This yellow *slave*
> Will knit and break religions, bless the accursed;
> Make the hoar leprosy adored, place thieves
> And give them title, knee and approbation
> With senators on the bench: This is it
> That makes the wappen'd widow wed again;
> She, whom the spital-house and ulcerous sores
> Would cast the gorge at, this embalms and spices
> To the April day again. . . . Damned earth,
> Thou common whore of mankind, that putt'st odds
> Among the rout of nations."[1]

And also later:

> "O thou sweet king-killer, and dear divorce
> Twixt natural son and sire! thou bright defiler
> Of Hymen's purest bed! thou valiant Mars!
> Thou ever young, fresh, loved and delicate wooer,
> Whose blush doth thaw the consecrated snow
> That lies on Dian's lap! Thou *visible God*!
> That solder'st *close impossibilities*,
> And mak'st them kiss! That speak'st with every tongue,
> To every purpose! O thou touch of hearts!
> Think thy slave man rebels, and by thy virtue
> Set them into confounding odds, that beasts
> May have the world in empire!"[2]

Shakespeare excellently depicts the real nature of *money*. To understand him, let us begin, first of all, by expounding the passage from Goethe.

That which is for me through the medium of *money*—that for which I can pay (i.e., which money can buy)—that am I, the possessor of the money. The extent of the power of money is the extent of my power. Money's properties are my properties and essential powers—the properties and powers of its possessor. Thus, what I *am* and *am capable* of is by no means determined by my individuality. I am ugly, but I can buy for myself the most *beautiful* of women. Therefore I am not *ugly*, for the effect of *ugliness*—its deterrent power—is nullified by money. I, in my character as an individual, am *lame*, but money furnishes me with twenty-four feet. Therefore I am not lame. I am bad, dishonest, unscrupulous, stupid; but money is honoured, and therefore so is its possessor. Money is the supreme good, therefore its possessor is good. Money, besides, saves me the trouble of being dishonest: I am therefore presumed honest. I am *stupid*, but money is the *real mind* of all things and how then should its possessor be stupid? Besides, he can buy talented people for himself, and is he who has

---

1. Shakespeare, *Timon of Athens*, Act 4, Scene 3. Marx quotes the Schlegel-Tieck German translation. (Marx's emphasis.)
2. Ibid.

power over the talented not more talented than the talented? Do not I, who thanks to money am capable of *all* that the human heart longs for, possess all human capacities? Does not my money therefore transform all my incapacities into their contrary?

If *money* is the bond binding me to *human* life, binding society to me, binding me and nature and man, is not money the bond of all *bonds*? Can it not dissolve and bind all ties? Is it not, therefore, the universal *agent of divorce*? It is the true *agent of divorce* as well as the true *binding agent*—the [universal][3] *galvano-chemical* power of Society.

Shakespeare stresses especially two properties of money:

(1) It is the visible divinity—the transformation of all human and natural properties into their contraries, the universal confounding and overturning of things: it makes brothers of impossibilities.

(2) It is the common whore, the common pimp of people and nations.

The overturning and confounding of all human and natural qualities, the fraternization of impossibilities—the *divine* power of money—lies in its *character* as men's estranged, alienating and self-disposing *species-nature*. Money is the alienated *ability of mankind*.

That which I am unable to do as a *man*, and of which therefore all my individual essential powers are incapable, I am able to do by means of *money*. Money thus turns each of these powers into something which in itself it is not—turns it, that is, into its *contrary*.

If I long for a particular dish or want to take the mail-coach because I am not strong enough to go by foot, money fetches me the dish and the mail-coach: that is, it converts my wishes from something in the realm of imagination, translates them from their meditated, imagined or willed existence into their *sensuous, actual* existence—from imagination to life, from imagined being into real being. In effecting this mediation, money is the *truly creative* power.

No doubt *demand* also exists for him who has no money, but his demand is a mere thing of the imagination without effect or existence for me, for a third party, for the others, and which therefore remains for me *unreal* and *objectless*. The difference between effective demand based on money and ineffective demand based on my need, my passion, my wish, etc., is the difference between *being* and *thinking*, between the imagined which *exists* merely within me and the imagined as it is for me outside me as a *real object*.

If I have no money for travel, I have no *need*—that is, no real and self-realizing need—to travel. If I have the *vocation* for study

3. An end of the page is torn out of the manuscript.

but no money for it, I have *no* vocation for study—that is, no *effective*, no *true* vocation. On the other hand, if I have really *no* vocation for study but have the will *and* the money for it, I have an *effective* vocation for it. Being the external, common *medium* and *faculty* for turning an *image* into *reality* and *reality* into a mere *image* (a faculty not springing from man as man or from human society as society), *money* transforms the *real essential powers of man and nature* into what are merely abstract conceits and therefore *imperfections*—into tormenting chimeras—just as it transforms *real imperfections and chimeras*—essential powers which are really impotent, which exist only in the imagination of the individual—into *real powers* and *faculties*.

In the light of this characteristic alone, money is thus the general overturning of *individualities* which turns them into their contrary and adds contradictory attributes to their attributes.

Money, then, appears as this *overturning* power both against the individual and against the bonds of society, etc., which claim to be *essences* in themselves. It transforms fidelity into infidelity, love into hate, hate into love, virtue into vice, vice into virtue, servant into master, master into servant, idiocy into intelligence and intelligence into idiocy.

Since money, as the existing and active concept of value, confounds and exchanges all things, it is the general *confounding* and *compounding* of all things—the world upside-down—the confounding and compounding of all natural and human qualities.

He who can buy bravery is brave, though a coward. As money is not exchanged for any one specific quality, for any one specific thing, or for any particular human essential power, but for the entire objective world of man and nature, from the standpoint of its possessor it therefore serves to exchange every property for every other, even contradictory, property and object: it is the fraternization of impossibilities. It makes contradictions embrace.

Assume *man* to be *man* and his relationship to the world to be a human one: then you can exchange love only for love, trust for trust, etc. If you want to enjoy art, you must be an artistically-cultivated person; if you want to exercise influence over other people, you must be a person with a stimulating and encouraging effect on other people. Every one of your relations to man and to nature must be a *specific expression*, corresponding to the object of your will, of your *real individual* life. If you love without evoking love in return—that is, if your loving as loving does not produce reciprocal love; if through a *living expression* of yourself as a loving person you do not make yourself a *loved person*, then your love is impotent—a misfortune.

Critique of the Hegelian Dialectic and Philosophy as a Whole

(6) This is perhaps the place at which, by way of explaining and justifying the ideas here presented, we might offer some considerations in regard to the Hegelian dialectic generally and especially its exposition in the *Phenomenology* and *Logic*, and also, lastly, the relation to it of the modern critical movement.

So powerful was modern German criticism's preoccupation with the past—so completely was it possessed in its development by its subject-matter—that there prevailed a completely uncritical attitude to the method of criticizing, together with a complete lack of awareness about the *seemingly formal*, but really *vital* question: how do we now stand as regards the Hegelian *dialectic*? This lack of awareness about the relationship of modern criticism to the Hegelian philosophy as a whole and especially to the Hegelian dialectic has been so great that critics like *Strauss* and *Bruno Bauer* still remain wholly within the confines of the Hegelian Logic; the former completely so and the latter at least implicitly so in his *Synoptics*[4] (where, in opposition to Strauss, he replaces the substance of "abstract nature" by the "self-consciousness" of abstract man) and even in *Christianity Discovered*.[5] Thus in *Christianity Discovered*, for example, you get:

"As though in positing the world, self-consciousness posits that which is different from itself, and in what it posits it posits itself, because it in turn annuls the difference between what it has posited and itself, inasmuch as it itself has being only in the positing and the movement.—How then can it not have its purpose in this movement?" etc.; or again: "They" (the French materialists) "have not yet been able to see that it is only as the movement of self-consciousness that the movement of the universe has actually come to be for itself, and achieved unity with itself."

Such expressions do not even show any verbal divergence from the Hegelian approach, but on the contrary, repeat it word for word.

How little consciousness there was in relation to the Hegelian dialectic during the act of criticism (Bauer, *The Synoptics*), and

4. Bruno Bauer, *Kritik der evangelischen Geschichte der Synoptiker* (*Critique of the Synoptic Gospels*), vol. 1–2, Leipzig, 1841; vol. 3, Braunschweig, 1842. In religious literature the authors of the first three Gospels are known as the Synoptics.
5. Bruno Bauer, *Das Entdeckte Christentum. Eine Erinnerung des Achtzehnten Jahrhundert und eine Beitrag zur Krisis des Neunzehnten* (*Christianity Discovered: A Memorial of the Eighteenth Century and a Contribution to the Crisis of the Nineteenth*), Zürich and Winterthur, 1843.

how little this consciousness came into being even after the act of material criticism is proved by Bauer when, in his *The Good of Freedom*,[6] he dismisses the brash question put by Herr Gruppe— "What about logic now?"—by referring him to future critics.

But even now—now that *Feuerbach* both in his *Theses* in the *Anecdotis* and, in detail, in *The Philosophy of the Future*, has in principle overthrown the old dialectic and philosophy; now that that school of criticism, on the other hand, which was incapable of accomplishing this has all the same seen it accomplished and has proclaimed itself pure, resolute, absolute criticism—criticism that has come into the clear with itself; now that this criticism, in its spiritual pride, has reduced the whole process of history to the relation between the rest of the world and itself (the rest of the world, in contrast to itself, falling under the category of "the masses") and dissolved all dogmatic antithesis into the *single* dogmatic antithesis of its own cleverness and the stupidity of the world—the antithesis of the critical Christ and Mankind, the *rabble*; now that daily and hourly it has demonstrated its own excellence against the dullness of the masses; now, finally, that it has proclaimed the critical *Last Judgement* in the shape of an announcement that the day is approaching when the whole of expiring humanity will assemble before it and be sorted by it into groups, each particular mob receiving its *testimonium paupertatis*;[7] now that it has made known in print[8] its superiority to human feelings as well as its superiority to the world, over which it sits enthroned in sublime solitude, only letting fall from time to time from its sarcastic lips the ringing laughter of the Olympian Gods—even now, after all these delightful antics of moribund idealism in the guise of criticism (i.e., of Young-Hegelianism)—even now it has not expressed the suspicion that the time was ripe for a critical settling of accounts with the mother of Young-Hegelianism—the Hegelian dialectic—and even had [nothing] to say about its critical attitude towards the Feuerbachian dialectic. Criticism with a completely uncritical attitude to itself!

Feuerbach is the only one who has a *serious, critical* attitude to the Hegelian dialectic and who has made genuine discoveries in this field. He is in fact the true conqueror of the old philosophy. The extent of his achievement, and the unpretentious simplicity with which he, Feuerbach, gives it to the world, stand in striking contrast to the reverse.

Feuerbach's great achievement is:

(1) The proof that philosophy is nothing else but religion rendered into thoughts and thinking expounded, and that it has there-

6. Bruno Bauer, *Die Gute Sache der Freiheit und meine Eigene Angelegenheit (The Good of Freedom and My Own Affair)*, Zürich and Winterthur, 1842.

7. Certificate of poverty.

8. A reference to the *Allgemeine Literatur-Zeitung*.

fore likewise to be condemned as another form and manner of existence of the estrangement of the essence of man;

(2) The establishment of *true materialism* and of *real science*, since Feuerbach also makes the social relationship "of man to man" the basic principle of the theory;

(3) His opposing to the negation of the negation, which claims to be the absolute positive, the self-supporting positive, positively grounded on itself.

Feuerbach explains the Hegelian dialectic (and thereby justifies starting out from the positive, from sense-certainty) as follows:

Hegel sets out from the estrangement of Substance (in Logic, from the Infinite, the abstractly universal)—from the absolute and fixed abstraction; which means, put popularly, that he sets out from religion and theology.

Secondly, he annuls the infinite, and establishes the actual, sensuous, real, finite, particular (philosophy—annulment of religion and theology).

Thirdly, he again annuls the positive and restores the abstraction, the infinite—restoration of religion and theology.

Feuerbach thus conceives the negation of the negation *only* as a contradiction of philosophy with itself—as the philosophy which affirms theology (the transcendent, etc.) after having denied it, and which it therefore affirms in opposition to itself.

The position or self-affirmation and self-confirmation contained in the negation of the negation is taken to be a position which is not yet sure of itself, which is therefore burdened with its opposite, which is doubtful of itself and therefore in need of proof, and which, therefore, is not a position establishing itself by its existence—not a position that justifies itself; hence it is directly and immediately confronted by the self-grounded position of sense-certainty.[9]

But because Hegel has conceived the negation of the negation from the point of view of the positive relation inherent in it as the true and only positive, and from the point of view of the negative relation inherent in it as the only true act and self-realizing act of all being, he has only found the *abstract, logical, speculative* expression for the movement of history; and this historical process is not yet the *real* history of man—of man as a given subject, but only man's *act of genesis*—the *story* of man's *origin*. We shall explain both the abstract form of this process, and the difference between this process as it is in Hegel in contrast to modern criticism, that is, in contrast to the same process in Feuerbach's *Wesen des Christentums* (*Essence of Christianity*), or rather the *critical* form of this in Hegel still uncritical process.

9. Feuerbach views negation of negation, the definite concept as thinking surpassing itself in thinking and as thinking wanting to be directly aware-ness, nature, reality. [*Marx*] Marx is referring to Feuerbach's critical observations about Hegel in § 29–30 of his *Grundsätze der Philosophie zer Zukunft.*

Let us take a look at the Hegelian system. One must begin with Hegel's *Phenomenology*, the true point of origin and the secret of the Hegelian philosophy.

PHENOMENOLOGY[1]

A. *Self-Consciousness*

I. *Consciousness.* (a) Certainty at the level of sense experience; or the "This" and *Meaning.* (b) *Perception,* or the Thing with Its Properties, and *Deception.* (c) Force and Understanding, Appearance and the Super-sensible World.

II. *Self-Consciousness.* The Truth of Certainty of Self. (a) Independence and Dependence of Self-Consciousness; Lordship and Bondage. (b) Freedom of Self-Consciousness: Stoicism, Scepticism, the Unhappy Consciousness.

III. *Reason.* Reason's Certainty and Reason's Truth. (a) Observation as a Process of Reason. Observation of Nature and of Self-Consciousness. (b) Realization of Rational Self-Consciousness through its own Activity. Pleasure and Necessity. The Law of the Heart and the Frenzy of Self-Conceit. Virtue and the Course of the World. (c) The Individuality Which is Real In and For Itself. The Spiritual Animal Kingdom and the Deception, or the Real Fact. Reason as Lawgiver. Reason Which Tests Laws.

B. *Mind*

I. *True* Mind; the Ethical Order.
II. Mind in Self-Estrangement—Culture.
III. Mind Certain of Itself, Morality.

C. *Religion*

Natural Religion; *Religion in the Form of Art*; *Revealed* Religion.

D. *Absolute Knowledge*

Hegel's *Encyclopaedia*,[2] beginning as it does with Logic, with *pure speculative thought*, and ending with *Absolute Knowl-*

---

1. What follows here are the main chapter and section-headings of Hegel's *Phenomenology of Mind*. Here and in later quotations from the *Phenomenology*, the translator has followed Baillie's translation very closely, departing from it only on the few occasions where this was necessary to keep the terminology in line with that used throughout the present volume.
2. G. W. F. Hegel, *Enzyklopädie der Philosophischen Wissenschaften* (Heidelberg, 1st ed., 1817, 3rd ed., 1830).

Hegel's *Encyclopaedia of the Philosophical Sciences* is a single volume falling into three main parts: the subject of the first is Logic (cf. *The Logic of Hegel*, trans. William Wallace, 2nd ed., Oxford, 1892); the subject of the second part is the Philosophy of Nature (of which no English translation has been published), and that of the third the Philosophy of Mind. (Cf. Hegel's *Philosophy of Mind*, trans. William Wallace, Oxford, 1894.)

edge—with the self-conscious, self-comprehending, philosophic or absolute (i.e., superhuman) abstract mind—is in its entirety nothing but the *display*, the self-objectification, of the *essence* of the philosophic mind, and the philosophic mind is nothing but the estranged mind of the world thinking within its self-estrangement—i.e., comprehending itself abstractly. *Logic* (mind's *coin of the realm*, the speculative or *thought-value* of man and nature—their essence grown totally indifferent to all real determinateness, and hence their unreal essence) is *alienated thinking*, and therefore thinking which abstracts from nature and from real man: *abstract* thinking. Then: *The externality of this abstract thinking . . . nature*, as it is for this abstract thinking. Nature is external to it—its self-loss; and it apprehends nature also in an external fashion, as abstract thinking—but as alienated abstract thinking. Finally, *Mind*, this thinking returning home to its own point of origin—the thinking which, as the anthropological, phenomenological, psychological, ethical, artistic and religious mind, is not valid for itself, until ultimately it finds itself, and relates itself to itself, as *absolute* knowledge in the hence absolute, i.e., abstract mind, and so receives its conscious embodiment in a mode of being corresponding to it. For its real mode of being is *abstraction*.

There is a double error in Hegel.

The first emerges most clearly in the *Phenomenology*, the Hegelian philosophy's place of origin. When, for instance, wealth, state-power, etc., are understood by Hegel as entities estranged from the *human* being, this only happens in their form as thoughts. . . . They are thought-entities, and therefore merely an estrangement of *pure*, i.e., abstract, philosophical thinking. The whole process therefore ends with Absolute Knowledge. It is precisely abstract thought from which these objects are estranged and which they confront with their arrogation of reality. The *philosopher* sets up himself (that is, one who is himself an abstract form of estranged man) as the *measuring-rod* of the estranged world. The whole *history of the alienation-process* and the whole *process of the retraction* of the alienation is therefore nothing but the *history of the production* of abstract (i.e., absolute) thought—of logical, speculative thought. The *estrangement*, which therefore forms the real interest of this alienation and of the transcendence of this alienation, is the opposition of *in itself* and *for itself*, of *consciousness* and *self-consciousness*, of *object* and *subject*—that is to say, it is the opposition, within thought itself, between abstract thinking and sensuous reality or real sensuousness. All other oppositions and movements of these oppositions are but the *semblance, the cloak, the exoteric* shape of these oppositions which alone matter, and which constitute the *meaning* of these other, profane oppositions. It is not the fact that the human being *objectifies himself inhumanly*, in opposition to himself, but the fact that he *objectifies himself* in *distinction* from and in *opposition* to abstract thinking, that is the posited essence of the estrangement and the thing to be superseded.

The appropriation of man's essential powers, which have become objects—indeed, alien objects—is thus in the *first place* only an *appropriation* occurring in *consciousness*, in *pure thought*—i.e., in *abstraction*: it is the appropriation of these objects as *thoughts* and as *movements of thought*. Consequently, despite its thoroughly negative and critical appearance and despite the criticism really contained in it, which often anticipates far later development, there is already latent in the *Phenomenology* as a germ, a potentiality, a secret, the uncritical positivism and the equally uncritical idealism of Hegel's later works—that philosophic dissolution and restoration of the existing empirical world. In the *second place*: the vindication of the objective world for man—for example, the realization that *sensuous* consciousness is not an *abstractly* sensuous consciousness but a *humanly* sensuous consciousness—that religion, wealth, etc., are but the estranged world of *human* objectification, of *man's* essential powers given over to work and that they are therefore but the *path* to the true *human* world—this appropriation or the insight into this process consequently appears in Hegel in this form, that *sense, religion,* state-power, etc., are *spiritual* entities; for only *mind* is the *true* essence of man, and the true form of mind is thinking mind, the logical, speculative mind. The *humanness* of nature and of the nature begotten by history—the humanness of man's products—appears in the form that they are *products* of abstract mind and as such, therefore, phases of *mind*—*thought entities*. The *Phenomenology* is, therefore, an occult critique—still to itself obscure and mystifying criticism; but inasmuch as it keeps steadily in view man's *estrangement*, even though man appears only in the shape of mind, there lie concealed in it *all* the elements of criticism, already *prepared* and *elaborated* in a manner often rising far above the Hegelian standpoint. The "Unhappy Consciousness," the "Honest Consciousness," the struggle of the "Noble and Base Consciousness,"[3] etc., etc.,—these separate sections contain, but still in an estranged form, the *critical* elements of whole spheres such as religion, the state, civil life, etc. Just as *entities, objects,* appear as *thought-entities,* so the *subject* is always *consciousness* or *self-consciousness;* or rather the object appears only as *abstract* consciousness, man only as *self-consciousness:* the distinct forms of estrangement which make their appearance are, therefore, only various forms of consciousness and self-consciousness. Just as *in itself* abstract consciousness (the form in which the object is con-

---

3. "The unhappy consciousness," etc.—forms of mind, and phases and factors in human history, distinguished and analysed in particular sections of Hegel's *Phenomenology.*

ceived) is merely a moment of distinction of self-consciousness, what appears as the result of the movement is the identity of self-consciousness with consciousness—absolute knowledge—the movement of abstract thought no longer directed outwards but going on now only within its own self: that is to say, the dialectic of pure thought is the result.

The outstanding thing in Hegel's *Phenomenology* and its final outcome—that is, the dialectic of negativity as the moving and generating principle—is thus first that Hegel conceives the self-genesis of man as a process, conceives objectification as loss of the object, as alienation and as transcendence of this alienation; that he thus grasps the essence of *labour* and comprehends objective man—true, because real man—as the outcome of man's *own labour*. The *real*, active orientation of man to himself as a species being, or his manifestation as a real species being (i.e., as a human being), is only possible by his really bringing out of himself all the *powers* that are his as the *species* man—something which in turn is only possible through the totality of man's actions, as the result of history—is only possible by man's treating these generic powers as objects: and this, to begin with, is again only possible in the form of estrangement.

We shall now demonstrate in detail Hegel's one-sidedness and limitations as they are displayed in the final chapter of the *Phenomenology*, "Absolute Knowledge"—a chapter which contains the concentrated spirit of the *Phenomenology*, the relationship of the *Phenomenology* to speculative dialectic, and also Hegel's *consciousness* concerning both and their relationship to one another.

Let us provisionally say just this much in advance: Hegel's standpoint is that of modern political economy. He grasps *labour* as the *essence* of man—as man's essence in the act of proving itself: he sees only the positive, not the negative side of labour. Labour is man's *coming-to-be for himself* within *alienation*, or as *alienated* man. The only labour which Hegel knows and recognizes is *abstractly mental* labour. Therefore, that which constitutes the *essence* of philosophy—the *alienation of man in his knowing of himself*, or *alienated* science *thinking itself*—Hegel grasps as its essence; and he is therefore able *vis-à-vis* preceding philosophy to gather together its separate elements and phases, and to present his philosophy as the philosophy. What the other philosophers did— that they grasped separate phases of nature and of human life as phases of self-consciousness, and indeed of abstract self-consciousness—is *known* to Hegel as the *doings* of philosophy. Hence his science is absolute.

Let us now turn to our subject.

Absolute Knowledge. The last chapter of the "Phenomenology."

The main point is that the *object of consciousness* is nothing else but *self-consciousness*, or that the object is only *objectified self-consciousness*—self-consciousness as object.

(Positing of man=self-consciousness.)

The issue, therefore, is to surmount the *object of consciousness*. *Objectivity* as such is regarded as an *estranged* human relationship which does not correspond to the *essence of man*, to self-consciousness. The *re-appropriation* of the objective essence of man, begotten in the form of estrangement as something alien, has the meaning therefore not only to annul *estrangement*, but *objectivity* as well. Man, that is to say, is regarded as a *non-objective*, *spiritual* being.

The movement of *surmounting the object of consciousness* is now described by Hegel in the following way:

The *object* reveals itself not merely as *returning into the self*—for Hegel that is the *one-sided* way of apprehending this movement, the grasping of only one side. Man is posited as equivalent to self. The self, however, is only the *abstractly* conceived man—man begotten by abstraction. Man *is* egotistic. His eye, his ear, etc., are *egotistic*. In him every one of his essential powers has the quality of *selfhood*. But it is quite false to say on that account *"Self-consciousness* has eyes, ears, essential powers." Self-consciousness is rather a quality of human nature, of the human eye, etc.; it is not human nature that is a quality of *self-consciousness*.

The self-abstracted and fixed for itself is man as *abstract egoist*—egoism raised in its pure abstraction to the level of thought. (We shall return to this point later.)

For Hegel the *essence of man*—*man*—equals *self-consciousness*. All estrangement of the human essence is therefore *nothing but estrangement of self-consciousness*. The estrangement of self-consciousness is not regarded as an *expression* of the *real* estrangement of the human being—its expression reflected in the realm of knowledge and thought. Instead, the *real* estrangement—that which appears real—is from its *innermost*, hidden nature (a nature only brought to light by philosophy) nothing but the *manifestation* of the estrangement of the real essence of man, of *self-consciousness*. The science which comprehends this is therefore called *Phenomenology*. All re-appropriation of the estranged objective essence appears, therefore, as a process of incorporation into self-consciousness: The man who takes hold of his essential being is *merely* the self-consciousness which takes hold of objective essences. Return of the object into the self is therefore the re-appropriation of the object.

The *surmounting of the object of consciousness*, comprehensively expressed, means:[4]

(1) That the object as such presents itself to consciousness as

---

4. The paragraph which follows is a transcript of the second and third paragraphs of the last chapter of Hegel's *Phenomenology*, trans. Baillie, 2nd ed., p. 789.

something vanishing. (2) That it is the alienation of self-consciousness which establishes thinghood. (3) That this externalization[5] of self-consciousness has not merely a *negative* but a *positive* significance. (4) That it has this meaning not merely *for us* or *intrinsically*, but *for self-consciousness itself.* (5) For *self-consciousness*, the negative of the object, its annulling of itself, has *positive* significance—self-consciousness *knows* this nullity of the object—because self-consciousness itself alienates itself; for in this alienation it establishes *itself* as object, or, for the sake of the indivisible unity of *being-for-self*, establishes the object as itself. (6) On the other hand, there is also this other moment in the process, that self-consciousness has also just as much annulled and superseded this alienation and objectivity and resumed them into itself, being thus at home with *itself* in *its* other-being *as such.* (7) This is the movement of *consciousness* and in this movement consciousness is the totality of its moments. (8) Consciousness must similarly have taken up a relation to the object in all its aspects and phases, and have comprehended it from the point of view of each of them. This totality of its determinate characteristics makes the object *intrinsically a spiritual being*; and it becomes so in truth for consciousness through the apprehending of each single one of them as *self* or through what was called above the *spiritual* attitude to them.

As to (1): That the object as such presents itself to consciousness as something vanishing—this is the above-mentioned *return of the object into the self.*

As to (2): *The alienation of self-consciousness establishes thinghood.* Because man equals self-consciousness, his alienated, objective essence, or *thinghood, equals alienated self-consciousness*, and *thinghood* is thus established through this alienation (thinghood being *that* which is an *object for man* and an object for him is really only that which is to him an essential object, therefore his *objective essence.* And since it is not *real Man*, nor therefore *Nature*—Man being *human Nature*—who as such is made the subject, but only the abstraction of man—self-consciousness—thinghood cannot be anything but alienated self-consciousness). It is only to be expected that a living, natural being equipped and endowed with objective (i.e., material) essential powers should have *real natural objects* of his essence; as is the fact that his self-alienation should lead to the establishing of a *real*, objective world—but a world in the form of *externality*—a world, therefore, not belonging to his own essential being, and an overpowering world. There is nothing incomprehensible or mysterious in this. It would be mysterious, rather, if it were otherwise. But it is equally clear that a *self-consciousness* can only establish *thinghood*

5. "Externalization"—*Entäusserung.*

through its alienation—i.e., establish something which itself is only an abstract thing, a thing of abstraction and not a *real* thing. It is clear, further, that thinghood is therefore utterly without any *independence*, any *essentiality* *vis-à-vis* self-consciousness; that on the contrary, it is a mere creature—something *posited* by self-consciousness. And what is posited, instead of confirming itself, is but a confirmation of the act of positing in which is concentrated for a moment the energy of the act as its product, *seeming* to give the de-posit—but only for a moment—the character of an independent, real substance.[6]

Whenever real, corporeal *man*, man with his feet firmly on the solid ground, man exhaling and inhaling all the forces of nature, *establishes* his real, objective *essential powers* as alien objects by his externalization, it is not the *act of positing* which is the subject in this process: it is the subjectivity of *objective* essential powers, whose action, therefore, must also be something *objective*. A being who is objective acts objectively, and he would not act objectively if the objective did not reside in the very nature of his being. He creates or establishes only *objects, because* he is established by objects—because at bottom he is *nature*. In the act of establishing, therefore, this objective being does not fall from his state of "pure activity" into a *creating of the object*; on the contrary, his *objective* product only confirms his *objective* activity, establishing his activity as the activity of an objective, natural being.

Here we see how consistent naturalism or humanism distinguishes itself both from idealism and materialism, constituting at the same time the unifying truth of both. We see also how only naturalism is capable of comprehending the act of world history.

Man is directly a *natural being*. As a natural being and as a living natural being he is on the one hand furnished with *natural powers of life*—he is an *active* natural being. These forces exist in him as tendencies and abilities—as *impulses*. On the other hand, as a natural, corporeal, sensuous, objective being he is a *suffering*, conditioned and limited creature, like animals and plants. That is to say, the *objects* of his impulses exist outside him, as *objects* independent of him; yet these objects are *objects* of his *need*—essential *objects*, indispensable to the manifestation and confirmation of his essential powers. To say that man is a *corporeal*, living, real, sensuous, objective being full of natural vigour is to say that he has *real, sensuous, objects* as the objects of his being or of his life, or that he can only *express* his life in real, sensuous objects. To be objective, natural and sensuous, and at the same time to have object, nature and sense outside oneself, or oneself to be object, nature and sense for a third party, is one and the same thing. *Hunger* is a natural *need*; it therefore needs a *nature* outside itself,

6. "Substance"—*Wesen*.

an *object* outside itself, in order to satisfy itself, to be stilled. Hunger is an acknowledged need of my body for an *object* existing outside it, indispensable to its integration and to the expression of its essential being. The sun is the *object* of the plant—an indispensable object to it, confirming its life—just as the plant is an object of the sun, being an *expression* of the life-awakening power of the sun, of the sun's *objective* essential power.

A being which does not have its nature outside itself is not a *natural* being, and plays no part in the system of nature. A being which has no object outside itself is not an objective being. A being which is not itself an object for some third being has no being for its *object*; i.e., it is not objectively related. Its be-ing is not objective.[7]

An unobjective being is a *nullity*—an *un-being*.

Suppose a being which is neither an object itself, nor has an object. Such a being, in the first place, would be the *unique* being: there would exist no being outside it—it would exist solitary and alone. For as soon as there are objects outside me, as soon as I am not *alone*, I am *another*—*another reality* than the object outside me. For this third object I am thus an *other reality* than it; that is, I am *its* object. Thus, to suppose a being which is not the object of another being is to presuppose that *no* objective being exists. As soon as I have an object, this object has me for an object. But a *non-objective* being is an unreal, nonsensical thing—something merely thought of (merely imagined, that is)—a creature of abstraction. To be *sensuous*, that is, to be an object of sense, to be a *sensuous* object, and thus to have sensuous objects outside oneself—objects of one's sensuousness. To be sensuous is to *suffer*.[8]

Man as an objective, sensuous being is therefore a *suffering* being—and because he feels what he suffers, a *passionate* being. Passion is the essential force of man energetically bent on its object.

But man is not merely a natural being: he is a *human* natural being. That is to say, he is a being for himself. Therefore he is a *species being*, and has to confirm and manifest himself as such both in his being and in his knowing. Therefore, *human* objects are not natural objects as they immediately present themselves, and neither is *human sense* as it immediately *is*—as it is objectively—*human* sensibility, human objectivity. Neither nature objectively nor nature subjectively is directly given in a form adequate to the *human* being. And as everything natural has to have its *beginning*, *man* too has his act of coming-to-be—*history*—which, however, is for him a known history, and hence as an act of coming-to-be it is a conscious self-transcending act of coming-to-be. History is the true

7. "Being"—*Wesen*; "nature"—*Natur*; "system"—*Wesen*; "be-ing"—*Sein*.
8. "To be sensuous is to suffer" —*Sinnlich sein ist leidend sein*. Here "to suffer" should probably be understood in the sense of "to undergo"—to be the object of another's action. Note the transition in the next sentence from *Leiden* (suffering) to *leidenschaftlich* (passionate).

natural history of man (on which more later).

Thirdly, because this establishing of thinghood is itself only sham, an act contradicting the nature of pure activity, it has to be cancelled again and thinghood denied.

Re. 3, 4, 5 *and* 6. (3) This externalization of consciousness has not merely a *negative* but a *positive* significance, and (4) it has this meaning not merely *for us* or intrinsically, but for consciousness itself.[9] (5) *For consciousness* the negative of the object, its annulling of itself, has *positive* significance—consciousness *knows* this nullity of the object because it alienates *itself*; for in this alienation it *knows* itself as object, or, for the sake of the indivisible unity of *being-for-itself*, the object as itself. (6) On the other hand, there is also this other moment in the process, that consciousness has also just as much annulled and superseded this alienation and objectivity and resumed them into itself, being thus *at home with itself* in its *other-being as such*.

As we have already seen: the appropriation of what is estranged and objective, or the annulling of objectivity in the form of *estrangement* (which has to advance from indifferent foreignness to real, antagonistic estrangement) means equally or even primarily for Hegel that it is *objectivity* which is to be annulled, because it is not the *determinate* character of the object, but rather its *objective* character that is offensive and constitutes estrangement for self-consciousness. The object is therefore something negative, self-annulling—a *nullity*. This nullity of the object has not only a negative but a *positive* meaning for consciousness, for such a *nullity* of the object is precisely the *self-confirmation* of the non-objectivity, of the *abstraction* of itself. For *consciousness itself* this nullity of the object has a positive meaning because it *knows* this nullity, the objective being, as its *self-alienation*; because it knows that it exists only as a result of its own *self-alienation*. . . .

The way in which consciousness is, and in which something is for it, is *knowing*. Knowing is its sole act. Something therefore comes to be for consciousness in so far as the latter *knows* this *something*. Knowing is its sole objective relation. Consciousness, then, knows the nullity of the object (i.e., knows the non-existence of the distinction between the object and itself, the non-existence of the object for it) because it knows the object as its *self-alienation*; that is, it knows itself—knows knowing as the object—because the object is only the *semblance* of an object, a piece of mystification, which in its essence, however, is nothing else but knowing itself, which has confronted itself with itself and in so

9. Here Marx has taken the impersonal pronoun *es* (it) to represent *Bewusstsein* (consciousness); but it seems that Baillie is more correct in reading this as standing for *Selbstbewusstsein* (self-consciousness). In the first quotation of this passage (p. 114) Marx simply uses *es* without specifying what it represents, and the translation has followed Baillie in interpreting it as "self-consciousness." In the present repetition of the passage, Marx's specification of the "it" as "consciousness," has been followed in the translation.

doing has confronted itself with a *nullity*—a something which has *no* objectivity outside the knowing. Or: knowing knows that in relating itself to an object it is only *outside itself*—that it only externalizes itself; that *it itself* appears to itself only *as an object*—or that that which appears to it as an object is only it itself.

On the other hand, says Hegel, there is at the same time this other moment in this process, that consciousness has just as much annulled and superseded this externalization and objectivity and resumed them into itself, being thus *at home* in its *other-being as such*.

In this discussion are brought together all the illusions of speculation.

First of all: consciousness—self-consciousness—is *at home with itself in its other-being as such*. It is therefore—or if we here abstract from the Hegelian abstraction and put the self-consciousness of man instead of Self-consciousness—*it is at home with itself in its other-being, as such*. This implies, for one thing, that consciousness (knowing as knowing, thinking as thinking) pretends to be directly the *other* of itself—to be the world of sense, the real world, life—thought over-reaching itself in thought (Feuerbach).[1] This aspect is contained herein, inasmuch as consciousness as mere consciousness takes offence not at estranged objectivity, but at *objectivity as such*.

Secondly, this implies that self-conscious man, in so far as he has recognized and annulled and superseded the spiritual world (or his world's spiritual, general mode of being) as self-alienation, nevertheless again confirms this in its alienated shape and passes it off as his true mode of being—re-establishes it, and pretends to be *at home in his other-being as such*. Thus, for instance, after annulling and superseding religion, after recognizing religion to be a product of self-alienation, he yet finds confirmation of himself in *religion as religion*. Here *is* the root of Hegel's *false* positivism, or of his merely *apparent* criticism: this is what Feuerbach designated as the positing, negating and re-establishing of religion or theology—but it has to be grasped in more general terms. Thus reason is at home in unreason as unreason. The man who has recognized that he is leading an alienated life in politics, law, etc., is leading his true human life in this alienated life as such. Self-affirmation, *in contradiction* with itself—in contradiction both with the knowledge of and with the essential being of the object—is thus true *knowledge* and *life*.

There can therefore no longer be any question about an act of accommodation on Hegel's part *vis-à-vis* religion, the state, etc.,

1. Marx refers to § 30 of Feuerbach's *Grundsätze der Philosophie der Zukunft*, which says: "Hegel is a thinker who transcends himself in thinking."

since this lie is *the* lie of his principle.

If I *know* religion as *alienated* human self-consciousness, then what I know in it as religion is not my self-consciousness, but my alienated self-consciousness confirmed in it. I therefore know my own self, the self-consciousness that belongs to its very nature, confirmed not in *religion* but rather in *annihilated* and *superseded* religion.

In Hegel, therefore, the negation of the negation is not the confirmation of the true essence, effected precisely through negation of the pseudo-essence. With him the negation of the negation is the confirmation of the pseudo-essence, or of the self-estranged essence in its denial; or it is the denial of this pseudo-essence as an objective being dwelling outside man and independent of him, and its transformation into the subject.

A peculiar role, therefore, is played by the act of *superseding* in which denial and preservation—denial and affirmation—are bound together.

Thus, for example, in Hegel's *Philosophy of Right*, *Private Right* superseded equals *Morality*, Morality superseded equals the *Family*, the Family superseded equals *Civil Society*, Civil Society superseded equals the *State*, the State superseded equals *World History*. In the *actual world* private right, morality, the family, civil society, the state, etc., remain in existence, only they have become *moments* of man—state of his existence and being—which have no validity in isolation, but dissolve and engender one another, etc. They have become *moments of motion*.

In their actual existence this *mobile* nature of theirs is hidden. It first appears and is made manifest in thought, in philosophy. Hence my true religious existence is my existence in the *philosophy of religion*; my true political existence is my existence within the *philosophy of right*; my true natural existence, existence in the *philosophy of nature*; my true artistic existence, existence in the *philosophy of art*; my true *human* existence, my existence in *philosophy*. Likewise the true existence of religion, the state, nature, art is the *philosophy* of religion, of nature, of the state and of art. If, however, the philosophy of religion, etc., is for me the sole true existence of religion, then, too, it is only as a *philosopher of religion* that I am truly religious, and so I deny *real* religious sentiment and the really *religious* man. But at the same time I *assert* them, in part within my own existence or within the alien existence which I oppose to them—for this *is* only their *philosophic* expression—and in part I assert them in their own original shape, for they have validity for me as merely the *apparent* other-being, as allegories, forms of their own true existence (i.e., of my *philosophical* existence) hidden under sensuous disguises.

In just the same way, *Quality* superseded equals *Quantity*, Quantity superseded equals *Measure*, Measure superseded equals

Essence, Essence superseded equals *Appearance*, Appearance superseded equals *Actuality*, Actuality superseded equals the *Concept*, the Concept superseded equals *Objectivity*, Objectivity superseded equals the *Absolute Idea*, the Absolute Idea superseded equals *Nature*, Nature superseded equals *Ethical* Objective Mind, Ethical Mind superseded equals *Art*, Art superseded equals *Religion*, Religion superseded equals *Absolute Knowledge*.[2]

On the one hand, this act of superseding is a transcending of the thought entity; thus, Private Property *as a thought* is transcended in the *thought* of morality. And because thought imagines itself to be directly the other of itself, to be *sensuous reality*—and therefore takes its own action for *sensuous, real action*—this superseding in thought, which leaves its object standing in the real world, believes that it has really overcome it. On the other hand, because the object has now become for it a moment of thought, thought takes it in its reality too to be self-confirmation of itself—of self-consciousness, of abstraction.

From the one point of view the existent which Hegel *supersedes* in philosophy is therefore not *real* religion, the *real* state, or *real* nature, but religion itself already become an object of knowledge, i.e., *Dogmatics*; the same with *Jurisprudence, Political Science* and *Natural Science*. From the one point of view, therefore, he stands in opposition both to the *real* thing and to immediate, unphilosophic *science* or the unphilosophic *conceptions* of this thing. He therefore contradicts their conventional conceptions.[3]

On the other hand, the religious man, etc., can find in Hegel his final confirmation.

It is now time to lay hold of the *positive* aspects of the Hegelian dialectic within the realm of estrangement.

(a) *Annulling* as an objective movement of *retracting* the alienation *into self*. This is the insight, expressed within the estrangement, concerning the *appropriation* of the objective essence through the annulment of its estrangement; it is the estranged insight into the *real objectification* of man, into the real appropriation of his objective essence through the annihilation of the *estranged* character of the objective world, through the annulment of the objective world in its estranged mode of being—just as atheism, being the annulment of God, is the advent of theoretic humanism, and communism, as the annulment of private property, is the justification of real human life as man's possession and thus the advent of practical humanism (or just as atheism is humanism mediated with itself through the annulment of religion, whilst com-

2. This sequence gives the major "categories" or "thought-forms" of Hegel's *Encyclopaedia* in the order in which they occur and are superseded. Similarly, the sequence above from "private right" to "world history" gives the major categories of Hegel's *Philosophy of Right* in the order in which they appear there.

3. The conventional conception of theology, jurisprudence, political science, natural science, etc.

munism is humanism mediated with itself through the annulment of private property). Only through the annulment of this mediation—which is itself, however, a necessary premise—does positively self-deriving humanism, *positive humanism,* come into being.

But atheism and communism are no flight, no abstraction; they are not a losing of the objective world begotten by man—of man's essential powers given over to the realm of objectivity; they are not a returning in poverty to unnatural, primitive simplicity. On the contrary, they are but the first real coming-to-be, the realization become real for man, of man's essence—of the essence of man as something real.

Thus, by grasping the *positive* meaning of self-referred negation (if even again in estranged fashion) Hegel grasps man's self-estrangement, the alienation of man's essence, man's loss of objectivity and his loss of realness as finding of self, change of his nature, his objectification and realization. In short, within the sphere of abstraction, Hegel conceives labour as man's act of *self-genesis*—conceives man's relation to himself as an alien being and the manifesting of himself as an alien being to be the coming-to-be of *species-consciousness* and *species-life.*

(b) However, apart from, or rather in consequence of, the perverseness already described, this act appears in Hegel:

First of all as a *merely formal,* because abstract, act, because the human essence itself is taken to be only an *abstract, thinking essence,* conceived merely as self-consciousness. And,

secondly, because the conception is *formal* and *abstract,* the annulment of the alienation becomes a confirmation of the alienation; or again, for Hegel this movement of *self-genesis* and *self-objectification* in the form of *self-alienation* and *self-estrangement* is the *absolute,* and hence final, *expression of human life*—of life with itself as its aim, of life at rest in itself, of life that has attained oneness with its essence.

This movement, in its abstract form as dialectic, is therefore regarded as *truly human life,* and because it is nevertheless an abstraction—an estrangement of human life—it is regarded as a *divine process,* but as the divine process of man, a process traversed by man's abstract, pure, absolute essence that is distinct from him.

Thirdly, this process must have a bearer, a subject. But the subject first emerges as a result. This result—the subject knowing itself as absolute self-consciousness—is therefore *God—absolute Spirit—the self-knowing and self-manifesting Idea.* Real man and real nature become mere predicates—symbols of this esoteric, unreal man and of this unreal nature. Subject and predicate are therefore related to each other in absolute inversion—a *mystical subject-object* or a *subjectivity reaching beyond the object*—the *absolute subject* as a *process,* as *subject alienating* itself and returning from alienation into itself, but at the same time retracting this alienation into itself, and the subject as this process; a pure, *restless* revolving within itself.

First, the *formal and abstract* conception of man's act of self-genesis or self-objectification.

Hegel having posited man as equivalent to self-consciousness, the estranged object—the estranged essential reality of man—is nothing but *consciousness,* the thought of estrangement merely—estrangement's *abstract* and therefore empty and unreal expression, *negation.* The annulment of the alienation is therefore\ likewise nothing but an abstract, empty annulment of that empty abstraction—the *negation of the negation.* The rich, living, sensuous, concrete activity of self-objectification is therefore reduced to its mere abstraction, *absolute negativity*—an abstraction which is again fixed as such and thought of as an independent activity—as sheer activity. Because this so-called negativity is nothing but the *abstract, empty* form of that real living act, its content can in consequence be merely a *formal* content begotten by abstraction from all content. As a result there are general, abstract *forms of abstraction* pertaining to every content and on that account indifferent to, and, consequently, valid for, all content—the thought-forms or logical categories torn from *real* mind and from *real* nature. (We shall unfold the *logical* content of absolute negativity further on.)

Hegel's positive achievement here, in his speculative logic, is that the *determinate concepts,* the universal *fixed thought-forms* in their independence *vis-à-vis* nature and mind are a necessary result of the general estrangement of the human essence and therefore also of human thought, and that Hegel has therefore brought these together and presented them as moments of the abstraction-process. For example, superseded Being is Essence, superseded Essence is Concept, the Concept superseded is . . . the Absolute Idea. But what, then, is the Absolute Idea? It supersedes its own self again, if it does not want to traverse once more from the beginning the whole act of abstraction, and to acquiesce in being a totality of abstractions or in being the self-comprehending abstraction. But abstraction comprehending itself as abstraction knows itself to be nothing: it must abandon itself—abandon abstraction—and so it arrives at an entity which is its exact contrary —at *nature.* Thus, the entire *Logic* is the demonstration that abstract thought is nothing in itself; that the Absolute Idea is nothing in itself; that only *Nature* is something.

The absolute idea, the *abstract* idea, which "*considered* with regard to its unity with itself is *intuiting,*"[4] (Hegel's *Encyclopae-*

---

4. *The Logic of Hegel,* trans. Wallace, ¶ 244. "Intuiting" is here used to render *Anschauen.* In popular usage *Anschauen* means "to contemplate," but Hegel is here using the word, like Kant, as a technical term in philosophy meaning, roughly, "to be aware through the senses." "Intuiting," likewise, should be understood here not in its popular sense but as the philosophical term which is the recognized English equivalent of *Anschauen.*

dia, 3rd edition, p. 222), and which "in its own absolute truth *resolves* to let the moment of its particularity or of initial characterization and other-being—the *immediate idea,* as its reflection, *go forth freely from itself as nature*" (l.c.)—this whole idea which behaves in such a strange and singular way, and which has given the Hegelians such terrible headaches, is from beginning to end nothing else but *abstraction* (i.e., the abstract thinker)— abstraction which, made wise by experience and enlightened concerning its truth, resolves under various (false and themselves still abstract) conditions to *abandon itself* and to replace its self-absorption, nothingness, generality and indeterminateness by its other-being, the particular, and the determinate; resolves to let *nature,* which it held hidden in itself only as an abstraction, as a thought-entity, *go forth freely from itself*: that is to say, abstraction resolves to forsake abstraction and to have a look at nature *free* of abstraction. The abstract idea, which without mediation becomes *intuiting,* is nothing else through-and-through but abstract thinking that gives itself up and resolves on *intuition.* This entire transition from Logic to Natural Philosophy is nothing else but the transition—so difficult to effect for the abstract thinker and therefore so queer in his description of it—from *abstracting* to *intuiting.* The *mystical* feeling which drives the philosopher forward from abstract thinking to intuiting is *boredom*—the longing for a content.

(The man estranged from himself is also the thinker estranged from his *essence*—that is, from the natural and human essence. His thoughts are therefore fixed mental shapes or ghosts dwelling outside nature and man. Hegel has locked up all these fixed mental forms together in his *Logic,* laying hold of each of them first as negation—that is, as an *alienation* of *human* thought—and then as negation of the negation—that is, as a superseding of this alienation, as a *real* expression of human thought. But as even this still takes place within the confines of the estrangement, this negation of the negation is in part the restoring of these fixed forms in their estrangement; in part a stopping-short at the last act—the act of self-reference in alienation—as the true mode of being of these fixed mental forms;[5] and in part, to the extent that this abstraction apprehends itself and experiences an infinite weariness with itself, there makes its appearance in Hegel, in the form

---

5. This means that what Hegel does is to put in place of these fixed abstractions the act of abstraction which revolves in its own circle. In so doing, he has the merit, in the first place, of having indicated the source of all these inappropriate concepts which, as originally presented, belonged to disparate philosophies; of having brought them together; and of having created the entire compass of abstraction exhaustively set out as the object of criticism, instead of some specific abstraction. (Why Hegel separates thought from the *subject* we shall see later: at this stage it is already clear, however, that when man is not, his characteristic expression also cannot be human, and so neither could thought be grasped as an expression of man as a human and natural subject endowed with eyes, ears, etc., and living in society, in the world, and in nature.) [*Marx*]

of the resolution to recognize *nature* as the essential being and to go over to intuition, the abandonment of abstract thought—the abandonment of thought revolving solely within the orbit of thought, of thought devoid of eyes, of teeth, of ears, of everything.)

But *nature* too, taken abstractly, for itself—nature fixed in isolation from man—is *nothing* for man. It goes without saying that the abstract thinker who has committed himself to intuiting, intuits nature abstractly. Just as nature lay enclosed in the thinker in the form of the absolute idea, in the form of a thought-entity—in a shape which is his and yet is esoteric and mysterious even to him—so what he has let go forth from himself in truth is only this *abstract nature*, only nature as a *thought-entity*—but with the significance now of being the other-being of thought, of being real, intuited nature—of being nature distinguished from abstract thought. Or, to talk a human language, the abstract thinker learns in his intuition of nature that the entities which he thought to create from nothing, from pure abstraction—the entities he believed he was producing in the divine dialectic as pure products of the labour of thought forever weaving in itself and never looking outward—are nothing else but *abstractions* from *characteristics of nature*. To him, therefore, the whole of nature merely repeats the logical abstractions in a sensuous, external form. He *analyses* it and these abstractions over again. Thus, his intuition of nature is only the act of confirming his abstraction from the intuition of nature—is only the conscious repetition by him of the process of begetting his abstraction. Thus, for example, Time equals Negativity referred to itself (l.c., p. 238): to the superseded Becoming as Being there corresponds, in natural form, superseded Movement as Matter. Light is *Reflection-in-Itself*, in *natural* form. Body as *Moon* and *Comet* is the *natural* form of the *antithesis* which according to the *Logic* is on the one side the *Positive resting on itself* and on the other side the *Negative* resting on itself. The Earth is the *natural* form of the logical *Ground*, as the negative unity of the antithesis, etc.[6]

Nature as nature—that is to say, in so far as it is still sensuously distinguished from that secret sense hidden within it—nature isolated, distinguished from these abstractions, is *nothing*—a nothing *proving itself to be nothing*—is *devoid of sense*, or has only the sense of being an externality which has to be annulled.

"In the finite-*teleological* position is to be found the correct premise that nature does not contain within itself the absolute purpose" (p. 225).

Its purpose is the confirmation of abstraction.

---

6. Time, Motion, Matter, Light, etc., are forms distinguished within Hegel's *Philosophy of Nature*. Becoming, etc., are of course categories of the *Logic*.

"Nature has shown itself to be the Idea in the *form* of *other-being*. Since the *Idea* is in this form the negative of itself or *external to itself*, nature is not just relatively external *vis-à-vis* this idea," but *externality* constitutes the form in which it exists as nature" (p. 227).

Externality here is not to be understood as the *self-externalizing world of sense* open to the light, open to the man endowed with senses. It is to be taken here in the sense of alienation—a mistake, a defect, which ought not to be. For what is true is still the Idea. Nature is only the *form of the Idea's other-being*. And since abstract thought is the *essence*, that which is external to it is by its essence something merely *external*. The abstract thinker recognizes at the same time that *sensuousness—externality* in contrast to thought weaving *within itself*—is the essence of nature. But he expresses his contrast in such a way as to make this *externality of nature*, its *contrast* to thought, its *defect*, so that inasmuch as it is distinguished from abstraction, nature is something defective. Something which is defective not merely for me or in my eyes but in itself—intrinsically—has something outside itself which it lacks. That is, its being is something other than it itself. Nature has therefore to supersede itself for the abstract thinker, for it is already posited by him as a potentially *superseded* being.

"*For us*, Mind has *nature* for its *premise*, being nature's *truth* and for that reason its *absolute prius*. In this truth nature *has vanished*, and mind has resulted as the Idea arrived at being-for-itself, the *object* of which, as well as the *subject*, is the *concept*. This identity is *absolute negativity*, for whereas in nature the concept has its perfect external objectivity, this its alienation has been superseded, and in this alienation the concept has become identical with itself. But it is this identity, therefore, only in being a return out of nature" (p. 392).
"As the *abstract* idea, *revelation* is unmediated transition to, the *coming-to-be* of, nature; as the revelation of the mind, which is free, it is the *establishing* of nature as the *mind's* world—an establishing which at the same time, being reflection, is a *presupposing* of the world as independently-existing nature. Revelation in conception is the creation of nature as the mind's being, in which the mind procures the *affirmation* and the *truth* of its freedom."[7] "*The absolute is mind*. This is the highest definition of the absolute."

7. Cf. Hegel's *Philosophy of Mind*, trans. Wallace, ¶ 381. But in rendering these passages from the *Encyclopaedia*, the present translator has not followed Wallace closely.

Critical Marginal Notes on the Article "The King of Prussia and Social Reform"

KARL MARX

Apart from showing Marx's pride in being the socialist spokesman of a revolutionarily "philosophical people," the Germans, and his sense of the theoretical preeminence of German socialist thought because of its philosophical depth, this early article is especially notable for its discussion of the relation between social and political revolution. The "Prussian" who wrote the article Marx attacks was Arnold Ruge. The event under discussion was the Silesian weavers' uprising of June 1844. The essay was written in July 1844 and published the following month in the newspaper *Vorwärts*.

No. 60 of *Vorwärts* contains an article headed "Der König von Preussen und die Sozialreform," signed "A *Prussian*."

First of all this alleged Prussian sets out the content of the royal Prussian Cabinet order on the *uprising of the Silesian workers* and the opinion of the French newspaper *La Réforme* on the Prussian Cabinet order. The *Réforme*, he writes, considers that the King's "*alarm* and *religious feeling*" are the source of the Cabinet order. It even sees in this document a *presentiment* of the great reforms which are in prospect for bourgeois society. The "Prussian" lectures the *Réforme* as follows:

> The King and German society has not yet arrived at the 'presentiment of their reform," even the Silesian and Bohemian uprisings have not aroused this feeling. It is impossible to make such an *unpolitical* country as Gemany regard the *partial* distress of the factory districts as a matter of general concern, let alone as an affliction of the whole civilised world. The Germans regard this event as if it were of the same nature as any *local* distress due to flood or famine. Hence the King regards it as due to *deficiencies in the administration or in charitable activity*. For this reason, and because a few soldiers sufficed to cope with the feeble weavers, the destruction of factories and machinery, too, did not inspire any "alarm" either in the King or the authorities. Indeed, the Cabinet order was not prompted even by *religious feeling*: it is a very sober expression of the Christian art of statesmanship and of a doctrine which considers that no difficulties can withstand its sole medicine—"the well-disposed Christian hearts." Poverty and crime are two great evils; who can cure them? The state and the authorities? No, but the union of all Christian hearts can.

The alleged Prussian denies the King's *"alarm"* on the grounds, among others, that a few soldiers sufficed to cope with the feeble weavers.

Therefore, in a country where ceremonial dinners with liberal toasts and liberally foaming champagne—recall the Düsseldorf festival—inspired a royal Cabinet order;[1] where *not a single* soldier was needed to shatter the desires of the *entire* liberal bourgeoisie for freedom of the press and a constitution; in a country where passive obedience is the order of the day—can it be that in such a country the necessity to employ armed force against feeble weavers is *not an event*, and not an *alarming* event? Moreover, at the first encounter the feeble weavers were victorious. They were suppressed only by subsequent troop reinforcements. Is the uprising of a body of workers less dangerous because it did not require a whole army to suppress it? Let the wise Prussian compare the uprising of the Silesian weavers with the revolts of the English workers, and the Silesian weavers will be seen by him to be strong weavers.

Starting out from the *general* relation of *politics* to *social ills*, we shall show why the uprising of the weavers could not cause the King any special *"alarm."* For the time being we shall say only the following: the uprising was not aimed directly against the King of Prussia, but against the bourgeoisie. As an aristocrat and absolute monarch, the King of Prussia cannot love the bourgeoisie; still less can he be alarmed if the submissiveness and impotence of the bourgeoisie is increased because of a tense and difficult relationship between it and the proletariat. Further: the orthodox Catholic is more hostile to the orthodox Protestant than to the atheist, just as the Legitimist is more hostile to the liberal than to the Communist. This is not because the atheist and the Communist are more akin to the Catholic or Legitimist, but because they are more foreign to him than are the Protestant and the liberal, being *outside* his circle. In the sphere of politics, the King of Prussia, as a politician, has his direct opposite in liberalism. For the King, the proletariat is as little an antithesis as the King is for the proletariat. The proletariat would have to have already attained considerable power for it to stifle the other antipathies and political antitheses and to divert to itself all political enmity. Finally: in view of the well-known character of the King, avid for anything *interesting* and *significant*, it must have been a joyful surprise for him to discover this *"interesting"* and *"much discussed"* *pauperism* in his own territory and consequently a new opportunity for making people talk about him. How pleasant for him must have been the news that henceforth he posseses his *"own,"* royal Prussian *pauperism!*

* * *

1. A royal order of July 18, 1843, prohibiting government officials from taking part in events such as an official banquet arranged by the liberals in Düsseldorf.

Let us suppose * * * that the "Prussian's" remarks about the German Government and the German bourgeoisie—after all, the latter is included in "German society"—are entirely well founded. Is this section of society more at a loss in Germany than in England and France? Can one be more at a loss than, for example, in England, where *perplexity* has been made into a system? When today workers' revolts break out throughout England, the bourgeoisie and government there know no better what to do than in the last third of the eighteenth century. Their sole expedient is material force, and since this material force diminishes in the same proportion as the spread of pauperism and the understanding of the proletariat increase, England's perplexity inevitably grows in geometrical progression.

Finally, it is *untrue, actually untrue*, that the German bourgeoisie totally fails to understand the general significance of the Silesian uprising. In several towns the masters are trying to act jointly with the apprentices. All the *liberal* German newspapers, the organs of the liberal bourgeoisie, teem with articles about the organisation of labour, the reform of society, criticism of monopolies and competition, etc. All this is the result of the movements among the workers.* * *

* * *

Let us pass now to the oracular pronouncements of the "Prussian" on the *German workers.* "*The German poor,*" he says wittily, "*are no wiser than the poor Germans,* i.e., *nowhere* do they see beyond their own hearth and home, their own factory, their own district; the whole question has *so far still* been ignored by the all-penetrating *political soul.*"

In order to be able to compare the condition of the German workers with the condition of the French and English workers, the "Prussian" would have had to compare the *first form*, the *start*, of the English and French workers' movement with the *German* movement that is *just beginning.* He failed to do so. Consequently, his arguments lead to trivialities, such as that *industry* in Germany is not yet so developed as in England, or that a movement at its start looks different from the movement in its subsequent progress. He wanted to speak about the *specific character* of the German workers' movement, but he has not a word to say on this subject of his.

On the other hand, suppose the "Prussian" were to adopt the correct standpoint. He will find that *not one* of the French and English workers' uprisings had such a *theoretical* and *conscious* character as the uprising of the Silesian weavers.

First of all, recall the *song of the weavers*,[2] that bold *call* to

2. This refers to the song *Das Blutgericht*, which was popular among the weavers on the eve of the revolt.

struggle, in which there is not even a mention of hearth and home, factory or district, but in which the proletariat at once, in a striking, sharp, unrestrained and powerful manner, proclaims its opposition to the society of private property. The Silesian uprising *begins* precisely with what the French and English workers' uprisings *end*, with consciousness of the nature of the proletariat. The action itself bears the stamp of this *superior* character. Not only machines, these rivals of the workers, are destroyed, but also *ledgers*, the titles to property. And while all other movements were aimed primarily only against the *owner of the industrial enterprise*, the visible enemy, this movement is at the same time directed against the banker, the hidden enemy. Finally, not a single English workers' uprising was carried out with such courage, thought and endurance.

As for the educational level or capacity for education of the German workers in general, I call to mind Weitling's brilliant writings, which as regards theory are often superior even to those of Proudhon, however much they are inferior to the latter in their execution. Where among the bourgeoisie—including its philosophers and learned writers—is to be found a book about the emancipation of the bourgeoisie—*political* emancipation—similar to Weitling's work: *Garantien der Harmonie und Freiheit*? It is enough to compare the petty, faint-hearted mediocrity of German political literature with this *vehement* and brilliant literary debut of the German workers, it is enough to compare these gigantic *infant shoes* of the proletariat with the dwarfish, worn-out political shoes of the German bourgeoisie, and one is bound to prophesy that the *German Cinderella* will one day have the *figure of an athlete*. It has to be admitted that the German proletariat is the *theoretician* of the European proletariat, just as the English proletariat is its *economist*, and the French proletariat its *politician*. It has to be admitted that Germany is just as much *classically* destined for a *social* revolution as it is incapable of a *political* one. For, just as the impotence of the German bourgeoisie is the *political* impotence of Germany, so also the capability of the German proletariat—even apart from German theory—represents the *social* capability of Germany. The disparity between the philosophical and the political development of Germany is not an *anomaly*. It is an inevitable disparity. A philosophical people can find its corresponding practice only in socialism, hence it is only in the *proletariat* that it can find the dynamic elements of its emancipation.

* * *

Why does the "Prussian" judge the German workers so contemptuously? Because he finds that the "whole question"—namely, the question of the distressed state of the workers—has *"so far still"* been ignored by the "all-penetrating *political* soul." He expounds his platonic love for the *political soul* in more detail as follows: "All uprisings which break out in this disastrous *isolation of people from the community*, and of their *thoughts from social principles*, will be smothered in blood and incomprehension; but when distress produces understanding, and the *political* understanding of the Germans discovers the roots of social distress, then in Germany too these events will be appreciated as symptoms of a great revolution."

* * *

That *social distress* produces *political* understanding is so incorrect that, on the contrary, what is correct is the opposite: *social well-being* produces *political* understanding. *Political* understanding is a spiritualist, and is given to him who already has, to him who is already comfortably situated. Let our "Prussian" listen to a French economist, M. *Michel Chevalier*, on this subject: "When the bourgeoisie rose up in 1789, it lacked—in order to be free—only participation in governing the country. Emancipation consisted for it in wresting the control of public affairs, the principal civil, military and religious functions, from the hands of the privileged who had the monopoly of these functions. *Rich* and *enlightened*, capable of being self-sufficient and of managing its own affairs, it wanted to escape from the system of arbitrary rule."[3]

We have already shown the "Prussian" how incapable *political* understanding is of discovering the source of social distress. Just *one* word more on this view of his. The more developed and universal the *political* understanding of a people, the more does the *proletariat*—at any rate at the beginning of the movement—squander its forces in senseless, useless revolts, which are drowned in blood. Because it thinks in the framework of politics, the proletariat sees the cause of all evils in the *will*, and all means of remedy in *violence* and in the *overthrow* of a *particular* form of state. The proof: the first uprisings of the *French* proletariat.[4] The Lyons workers believed that they were pursuing only political aims, that they were only soldiers of the republic, whereas actually they were soldiers of socialism. Thus their political understanding concealed from them the roots of social distress, thus it falsified their insight into their real aim, thus their *political understanding deceived* their *social instinct*.

But if the "Prussian" expects understanding to be produced by distress, why does he lump together "*smothering in blood*" and "*smothering in incomprehension*"? If distress is in general a means of producing understanding, then *bloody* distress is even a *very acute* means to this end. The "Prussian" therefore should have said:

3. M. Chevalier, *Des intérêts matériels en France*, p. 3 (Marx gives a free translation).

4. Marx is referring to the revolts of the Lyons weavers in November 1831 and April 1834.

smothering in blood will smother incomprehension and procure a proper current of air for the understanding.

The "Prussian" prophesies the smothering of uprisings which break out in *"disastrous isolation of people from the community,* and in the *separation of their thoughts from social principles."*

We have shown that the Silesian uprising occurred by no means in circumstances of the separation of thoughts from social principles. It only remains for us to deal with the *"disastrous isolation of people from the community."* By community here is meant the *political community, the state.* This is the old story about *unpolitical* Germany.

But do not *all* uprisings, without exception, break out in a *disastrous isolation of man from the community?* Does not *every* uprising necessarily presuppose isolation? Would the 1789 revolution have taken place without the disastrous isolation of French citizens from the community? It was intended precisely to abolish this isolation.

But the *community* from which the worker is *isolated* is a community the real character and scope of which is quite different from that of the *political* community. The community from which the worker is isolated by *his own labour* is *life* itself, physical and mental life, human morality, human activity, human enjoyment, *human* nature. *Human nature* is the *true community* of men. The disastrous isolation from this essential nature is incomparably more universal, more intolerable, more dreadful, and more contradictory, than isolation from the political community. Hence, too, the *abolition* of this isolation—and even a partial reaction to it, an *uprising* against it—is just as much more infinite as *man* is more infinite than the *citizen,* and *human life* more infinite than *political life.* Therefore, however *partial* the uprising of the *industrial workers* may be, it contains within itself a *universal* soul; however universal a *political* uprising may be, it conceals even in its *most grandiose* form a *narrow-minded* spirit.

The "Prussian" worthily concludes his article with the following sentence: *"A social revolution without a political soul* (i.e., without an organising idea from the point of view of the whole) is impossible."

We have already seen that a *social* revolution is found to have the point of view of the *whole* because—even if it were to occur in only *one* factory district—it represents man's protest against a dehumanised life, because it starts out from the *point of view of a separate real individual,* because the *community,* against the separation of which from himself the individual reacts, is man's *true* community, *human* nature. The *political soul* of revolution, on the other hand, consists in the *tendency* of classes having no political influence to abolish their *isolation* from *statehood* and *rule*. Its point of view is that of the state, of an *abstract* whole, which exists only through *separation* from real life, and which is *inconceivable* without the *organised* contradiction between the universal idea of man and the individual existence of man. Hence, too, a revolution with a *political soul*, in accordance with the *limited* and *dichoto-mous* nature of this soul, organises a ruling stratum in society at the expense of society itself.

We want to divulge to the "Prussian" what a "*social revolution* with a *political* soul" actually is; we shall thereby at the same time confide the secret to him that he himself is unable, even in *words*, to rise above the narrow-minded political point of view.

A "*social*" revolution with a *political* soul is either a nonsensical concoction, if by "social" revolution the "Prussian" means a "social" as *opposed* to a political revolution, and nevertheless endows the social revolution with a political soul instead of a social one; or else a "*social revolution with a political soul*" is only a *para-phrase* for what was usually called a "*political revolution*," or "*simply a revolution*." Every revolution dissolves the *old society* and to that extent it is *social*. Every revolution overthrows *the old power* and to that extent it is *political*.

Let the "Prussian" choose between the *paraphrase* and the *non-sense*! But whereas a *social revolution* with a *political soul* is a para-phrase or nonsense, a *political revolution* with a *social* soul has a rational meaning. *Revolution* in general—the *overthrow* of the existing power and *dissolution* of the old relationships—is a *politi-cal act*. But *socialism* cannot be realised without *revolution*. It needs this *political* act insofar as it needs *destruction* and *dissolu-tion*. But where its *organising activity* begins, where its *proper object*, its *soul*, comes to the fore—there socialism throws off the *political* cloak.

* * *

Alienation and Social Classes

KARL MARX

A meeting between Marx and Engels in Paris at the end of August, 1844, inaugurated their lifelong collaboration. Their first jointly written work, published in 1845, was *The Holy Family: A Critique of Critical Criticism*, a heavily satirical polemic against Bruno Bauer and the Young Hegelians. The following passage, probably written by Marx, shows the alienation doctrine of the 1844 manuscripts merging into the class struggle doctrine as we encounter it in *The German Ideology* and later Marxist writings. It is also of value as a revelation of Marx's special way of conceiving and explaining historical necessity.

The translation for this edition is by R. C. Tucker.

---

* * * The proletariat and wealth are opposites. As such they form a whole. They are both products of the world of private property. The whole question is what position each of these two elements occupies within the opposition. It does not suffice to proclaim them two sides of one whole.

Private property as private property, as wealth, is compelled to preserve *its own existence* and thereby the existence of its opposite, the proletariat. This is the *positive* side of the antagonism, private property satisfied with itself.

The proletariat, on the other hand, is compelled to abolish[1] itself and thereby its conditioning opposite—private property—which makes it a proletariat. This is the *negative* side of the antagonism, its disturbance within itself, private property abolished and in the process of abolishing itself.

The possessing class and the proletarian class represent one and the same human self-alienation.[2] But the former feels satisfied and affirmed in this self-alienation, experiences the alienation as a sign *of its own power*, and possesses in it the *appearance* of a human existence. The latter, however, feels destroyed in this alienation, seeing in it its own impotence and the reality of an inhuman existence. To use Hegel's expression, this class is, within depravity, an

1. I.e., *qua* proletariat. The verb is *aufheben* [R. T.]

2. The term used here is *Selbstentfremdung*. [R. T.]

indignation against this depravity, an indignation necessarily aroused in this class by the contradiction between its human *nature* and its life-situation, which is a blatant, outright and all-embracing denial of that very nature.

Within the antagonism as a whole, therefore, private property represents the *conservative* side and the proletariat the *destructive* side. From the former comes action aimed at preserving the antagonism; from the latter, action aimed at its destruction.

In its economic movement, it is true, private property presses towards its own dissolution, but it does this only by means of a developmental course that is unconscious and takes place independently of it and against its will, a course determined by the nature of the thing itself. It does this only by giving rise to the proletariat *as* proletariat—this poverty conscious of its own spiritual and physical poverty, this dehumanization which is conscious of itself as a dehumanization and hence abolishes itself.[3] The proletariat executes the sentence that proletariat-producing private property passes upon itself, just as it executes the sentence that wage labour passes upon itself by producing others' wealth and its own poverty. When the proletariat wins victory, it by no means becomes the absolute side of society, for it wins victory only by abolishing itself and its opposite. Both the proletariat itself and its conditioning opposite— private property—disappear with the victory of the proletariat.

If socialist writers attribute this world-historical role to the proletariat, this is by no means, as critical criticism assures us, because they regard the proletarians as *gods*. On the contrary. Since the fully formed proletariat represents, practically speaking, the completed abstraction from everything human, even from the *appearance* of being human; since all the living conditions of contemporary society have reached the acme of inhumanity in the living conditions of the proletariat; since in the proletariat man has lost himself, although at the same time he has both acquired a theoretical consciousness of this loss and has been directly forced into indignation against this inhumanity by virtue of an inexorable, utterly unembellishable, absolutely imperious *need*, that practical expression of *necessity*—because of all this the proletariat itself can and must liberate itself. But it cannot liberate itself without destroying its own living conditions. It cannot do so without destroying *all* the inhuman living conditions of contemporary society which are concentrated in its own situation. Not in vain does it go through the harsh but hardening school of *labour*. It is not a matter of what this or that proletarian or even the proletariat as a whole *pictures* at present as its goal. It is a matter of *what the proletariat is in actuality* and what, in accordance with this *being*, it will historically be

3. Here and further on in this paragraph, the word translated as "abolish" is *aufheben*. [*R. T.*]

compelled to do. Its goal and its historical action are prefigured in
the most clear and ineluctable way in its own life-situation as well
as in the whole organization of contemporary bourgeois society.
There is no need to harp on the fact that a large part of the English and French proletariat is already *conscious* of its historic task
and is continually working to bring this consciousness to full clarity.

Society and Economy in History

KARL MARX

This selection comes from Marx's letter of December 28, 1846, to P. V. Annenkov, who had asked for his opinion of Pierre-Joseph Proudhon's new book *The Philosophy of Poverty*. Marx subsequently expanded his critique of the book into a book-length polemic, *The Poverty of Philosophy* (the meat of which is succinctly stated in this letter).

The material here presented is of interest as a trenchant statement of the materialist conception of history, Marx's enlarged understanding of the division of labor as a ubiquitous fact of human historical development, his view on the evolution of machinery, and his notion of dialectics as a process that finds final resolution in a social condition beyond conflict ("contradictions"). Since this document appeared at the close of Marx's early period, it conclusively disproves the notion of a hiatus between a Hegelian-Feuerbachian philosophical early Marx who hadn't reached historical materialism, and a scientific mature Marx who had.* It was *in and through* the early writings represented in this section of our reader that Marx created historical materialism.

* * *

* * * M. Proudhon sees in history a series of social developments; he finds progress realised in history; finally he finds that men, as individuals, did not know what they were doing and were mistaken about their own movement, that is to say, their social development seems at the first glance to be distinct, separate and independent of their individual development. He cannot explain these facts, and so the hypothesis of universal reason manifesting itself comes in very handy. Nothing is easier than to invent mystical causes, that is to say, phrases which lack common sense.

But when M. Proudhon admits that he understands nothing about the historical development of humanity—he admits this by using such high-sounding words as: Universal Reason, God, etc.—is he not implicitly and necessarily admitting that he is incapable of understanding *economic development*?

What is society, whatever its form may be? The product of men's reciprocal action. Are men free to choose this or that form of society? By no means. Assume a particular state of development in the productive faculties of man and you will get a particular form of commerce and consumption. Assume particular stages of

* A recent exponent of the hiatus theory is Louis Althusser. See his *For* *Marx*, translated by Ben Brewster (New York: Pantheon, 1969), e.g., p. 47.

development in production, commerce and consumption and you will have a corresponding social constitution, a corresponding organisation of the family, of orders or of classes, in a word, a corresponding civil society. Assume a particular civil society and you will get particular political conditions which are only the official expression of civil society. M. Proudhon will never understand this because he thinks he is doing something great by appealing from the state to civil society that is to say, from the official résumé of society to official society.

It is superfluous to add that men are not free to choose *their productive forces*—which are the basis of all their history—for every productive force is an acquired force, the product of former activity. The productive forces are therefore the result of practical human energy; but this energy is itself conditioned by the circumstances in which men find themselves, by the productive forces already acquired, by the social form which exists before they do, which they do not create, which is the product of the preceding generation. Because of this simple fact that every succeeding generation finds itself in possession of the productive forces acquired by the previous generation, which serve it as the raw material for new production, a coherence arises in human history, a history of humanity takes shape which is all the more a history of humanity as the productive forces of man and therefore his social relations have been more developed. Hence it necessarily follows that the social history of men is never anything but the history of their individual development, whether they are conscious of it or not. Their material relations are the basis of all their relations. These material relations are only the necessary forms in which their material and individual activity is realised.

M. Proudhon mixes up ideas and things. Men never relinquish what they have won, but this does not mean that they never relinquish the social form in which they have acquired certain productive forces. On the contrary, in order that they may not be deprived of the result attained and forfeit the fruits of civilisation, they are obliged, from the moment when their mode of carrying on commerce no longer corresponds to the productive forces acquired, to change all their traditional social forms. I am using the word "commerce" here in its widest sense, as we use *Verkehr* in German. For example: the privileges, the institution of guilds and corporations, the regulatory regime of the Middle Ages, were social relations that alone corresponded to the acquired productive forces and to the social condition which had previously existed and from which these institutions had arisen. Under the protection of the regime of corporations and regulations, capital was accumulated, overseas trade was developed, colonies were founded. But the fruits of this men would have forfeited if they had tried to retain the forms under whose shelter these fruits had ripened. Hence burst two thunderclaps—the Revolutions of 1640 and 1688. All the old economic forms, the social relations corresponding to them, the political conditions which were the official expression of the old civil society, were destroyed in England. Thus the economic forms in which men produce, consume, and exchange, are *transitory and historical*. With the acquisition of new productive faculties, men change their mode of production and with the mode of production all the economic relations which are merely the necessary relations of this particular mode of production.

This is what M. Proudhon has not understood and still less demonstrated. M. Proudhon, incapable of following the real movement of history, produces a phantasmagoria which presumptuously claims to be dialectical. He does not feel it necessary to speak of the seventeenth, the eighteenth or the nineteenth century, for his history proceeds in the misty realm of imagination and rises far above space and time. In short, it is not history but old Hegelian junk, it is not profane history—a history of man—but sacred history—a history of ideas. From his point of view man is only the instrument of which the idea or the eternal reason makes use in order to unfold itself. The *evolutions* of which M. Proudhon speaks are understood to be evolutions such as are accomplished within the mystic womb of the absolute idea. If you tear the veil from this mystical language, what it comes to is that M. Proudhon is offering you the order in which economic categories arrange themselves inside his own mind. It will not require great exertion on my part to prove to you that it is the order of a very disorderly mind.

The series of economic evolutions of the eternal reason begins with *division of labour*. To M. Proudhon division of labour is a perfectly simple thing. But was not the caste regime also a particular division of labour? Was not the regime of the corporations another division of labour? And is not the division of labour under the system of manufacture, which in England begins in the middle of the seventeenth century and comes to an end in the last part of the eighteenth, also totally different from the division of labour in large-scale, modern industry?

M. Proudhon is so far from the truth that he neglects what even the profane economists attend to. When he talks about division of labour he does not feel it necessary to mention the world *market*. Good. Yet must not the division of labour in the fourteenth and fifteenth century, when there were still no colonies, when America did not as yet exist for Europe, and Eastern Asia only existed for her through the medium of Constantinople, have been fundamentally different from what it was in the seventeenth century when colonies were already developed.

And that is not all. Is the whole inner organisation of nations, are all their international relations anything else than the expression of a particular division of labour? And must not these change when the division of labour changes?

M. Proudhon has so little understood the problem of the division of labour that he never even mentions the separation of town and country, which took place in Germany, for instance, from the ninth to the twelfth century. Thus, to M. Proudhon, this separation is an eternal law since he knows neither its origin nor its development. All through his book he speaks as if this creation of a particular mode of production would endure until the end of time. All that M. Proudhon says about the division of labour is only a summary, and moreover a very superficial and incomplete summary, of what Adam Smith and a thousand others have said before him.

The second evolution is *machinery*. The connection between the division of labour and machinery is entirely mystical to M. Proudhon. Each kind of division of labour had its specific instruments of production. Between the middle of the seventeenth and the middle of the eighteenth century, for instance, people did not make everything by hand. They had instruments, and very complicated ones at that, such as looms, ships, levers, etc.

Thus there is nothing more absurd than to derive machinery from division of labour in general.

I may also remark, by the way, that M. Proudhon has understood very little the historical origin of machinery, but has still less understood its development. One can say that up to the year 1825—the period of the first general crisis—the demands of consumption in general increased more rapidly than production, and the development of machinery was a necessary consequence of the needs of the market. Since 1825, the invention and application of machinery has been simply the result of the war between workers and employers. But this is only true of England. As for the European nations, they were driven to adopt machinery owing to English competition both in their home markets and on the world market. Finally, in North America the introduction of machinery was due both to competition with other countries and to lack of hands, that is, to the disproportion between the population of North America and its industrial needs. From these facts you can see what sagacity Monsieur Proudhon develops when he conjures up the spectre of competition as the third evolution, the antithesis to machinery!

Lastly and in general, it is altogether absurd to make *machinery* an economic category alongside with division of labour, competition, credit, etc.

Machinery is no more an economic category than the ox which draws the plough. The application of machinery in the present day is one of the relations of our present economic system, but the way in which machinery is utilised is totally distinct from the machinery itself. Powder is powder whether used to wound a man or to dress his wounds.

* * *

M. Proudhon, mainly because he lacks the historical knowledge, has not perceived that as men develop their productive faculties, that is, as they live, they develop certain relations with one another and that the nature of these relations must necessarily change with the change and growth of the productive faculties. He has not perceived that *economic categories* are only *abstract expressions* of these actual relations and only remain true while these relations exist. He therefore falls into the error of the bourgeois economists, who regard these economic categories as eternal and not as historical laws which are only laws for a particular historical development, for a definite development of the productive forces. Instead, therefore, of regarding the political-economic categories as abstract expressions of the real, transitory, historic social relations, Monsieur Proudhon, thanks to a mystic inversion, sees in the real relations only embodiments of these abstractions. These abstractions themselves are formulas which have been slumbering in the heart of God the Father since the beginning of the world.

* * *

Monsieur Proudhon has very well grasped the fact that men produce cloth, linen, silks, and it is a great merit on his part to have grasped this small amount! What he has not grasped is that these men, according to their abilities, also produce the *social relations* amid which they prepare cloth and linen. Still less has he understood that men, who produce their social relations in accordance with their material productivity, also produce *ideas, categories,* that is to say the abstract ideal expressions of these same social relations. Thus the categories are no more eternal than the relations they express. They are historical and transitory products. To M. Proudhon, on the contrary, abstractions, categories are the primordial cause. According to him they, and not men, make history. The *abstractio*n, the *category taken as such,* i.e., apart from men and their material activities, is of course immortal, unchangeable, unmoved; it is only one form of the being of pure reason; which is only another way of saying that the abstraction as such is abstract. An admirable tautology!

Thus, regarded as categories, economic relations for M. Proudhon are eternal formulas without origin or progress.

* * *

M. Proudhon is therefore necessarily *doctrinaire*. To him the historical movement, which is turning the present-day world upside down, reduces itself to the problem of discovering the correct equilibrium, the synthesis, of two bourgeois thoughts. And so the clever fellow by virtue of his subtlety discovers the hidden thought of God, the unity of two isolated thoughts—which are only isolated because M. Proudhon has isolated them from practical life, from present-day production, which is the combination of the realities which they express. In place of the great historical movement arising from the conflict between the productive forces already acquired by men and their social relations, which no longer correspond to these productive forces; in place of the terrible wars which are being prepared between the different classes within each nation and between different nations; in place of the practical and violent action of the masses by which alone these conflicts can be resolved—in place of this vast, prolonged and complicated movement, Monsieur Proudhon supplies the whimsical motion of his own head. So it is the men of learning that make history, the men who know how to purloin God's secret thoughts. The common people have only to apply their revelations. You will now understand why M. Proudhon is the declared enemy of every political movement. The solution of present problems does not lie for him in public action but in the dialectical rotations of his own head. Since to him the categories are the motive force, it is not necessary to change practical life in order to change the categories. Quite the contrary. One must change the categories and the consequence will be a change in the existing society.

In his desire to reconcile the contradictions Monsieur Proudhon does not even ask if the very basis of those contradictions must not be overthrown. He is exactly like the political doctrinaire who wants to have the king and the chamber of deputies and the chamber of peers as integral parts of social life, as eternal categories. All he is looking for is a new formula by which to establish an equilibrium between these powers whose equilibrium consists precisely in the actual movement in which one power is now the conqueror and now the slave of the other. Thus in the eighteenth century a number of mediocre minds were busy finding the true formula which would bring the social estates, nobility, king, parliament, etc., into equilibrium, and they woke up one morning to find that there was in fact no longer any king, parliament or nobility. The true equilibrium in this antagonism was the overthrow of all the social relations which served as a basis for these feudal existences and for the antagonisms of these feudal existences.

Because M. Proudhon places eternal ideas, the categories of pure reason, on the one side and human beings and their practical life, which, according to him is the application of these categories, on the other, one finds with him from the beginning a *dualism* between life and ideas, between soul and body, a dualism which recurs in many forms. You can see now that this antagonism is nothing but the incapacity of M. Proudhon to understand the profane origin and the profane history of the categories which he deifies.

My letter is already too long for me to speak of the absurd case which M. Proudhon puts up against communism. For the moment you will grant me that a man who has not understood the present state of society may be expected to understand still less the movement which is tending to overthrow it, and the literary expressions of this revolutionary movement.

The *sole* point on which I am in complete agreement with Monsieur Proudhon is in his dislike for sentimental socialistic daydreams. I had already, before him, drawn much enmity upon myself by ridiculing this sentimental, utopian, mutton-headed socialism. But is not M. Proudhon strangely deluding himself when he sets up his petty-bourgeois sentimentality—I am referring to his declamations about home, conjugal love and all such banalities—in opposition to socialist sentimentality, which in Fourier, for example goes much deeper than the pretentious platitudes of our worthy Proudhon? * * *

Theses on Feuerbach

KARL MARX

Marx wrote the "Theses on Feuerbach" in the spring of 1845 as he and Engels were starting their collaborative work *The German Ideology*. More than forty years later, Engels found them in one of the notebooks that had come into his possession after his friend died. He published them as an appendix to his essay of 1888 on *Ludwig Feuerbach and the End of Classical German Philosophy*, and described them in the foreword to this essay as "the brilliant germ of the new world outlook." They have fascinated Marx scholars ever since, and an extensive literature of exegesis of the "Theses" has accumulated. The eleventh thesis, in which Marx proclaims it the task of philosophy not simply to interpret but to change the world, is one of his most frequently quoted statements.

Before resorting to commentaries, however, the reader should apply himself to Marx's own amplification of the "Theses" in Part I of *The German Ideology*, which follows this selection.

Engels made a few small changes in the "Theses" when he published them in 1888: he added the phrase "in Robert Owen, for example," in parentheses, at the end of the first paragraph of Thesis III; italicized "social product" in Thesis VII; italicized "contemplative" and placed quotation marks around "civil society" in Thesis IX. The version presented below is Marx's.

I

The chief defect of all hitherto existing materialism—that of Feuerbach included—is that the thing, reality, sensuousness, is conceived only in the form of the object or of *contemplation*, but not as *human sensuous activity*, *practice*, not subjectively. Hence it happened that the *active* side, in contradistinction to materialism, was developed by idealism—but only abstractly, since, of course, idealism does not know real, sensuous activity as such. Feuerbach wants sensuous objects, really distinct from the thought objects, but he does not conceive human activity itself as *objective* activity. Hence, in *Das Wesen des Christentums*, he regards the theoretical attitude as the only genuinely human attitude, while practice is conceived and fixed only in its dirty-judaical manifestation. Hence he does not grasp the significance of "revolutionary," of practical-critical, activity.

143

II

The question whether objective truth can be attributed to human thinking is not a question of theory but is a *practical* question. Man must prove the truth, that is, the reality and power, the this-sidedness of his thinking in practice. The dispute over the reality or non-reality of thinking which is isolated from practice is a purely *scholastic* question.

III

The materialist doctrine that men are products of circumstances and upbringing, and that, therefore, changed men are products of other circumstances and changed upbringing, forgets that it is men who change circumstances and that it is essential to educate the educator himself. Hence, this doctrine necessarily arrives at dividing society into two parts, one of which is superior to society.

The coincidence of the changing of circumstances and of human activity can be conceived and rationally understood only as revolutionising practice.

IV

Feuerbach starts out from the fact of religious self-alienation, of the duplication of the world into a religious, imaginary world and a real one. His work consists in resolving the religious world into its secular basis. He overlooks the fact that after completing this work, the chief thing still remains to be done. For the fact that the secular basis detaches itself from itself and establishes itself in the clouds as an independent realm can only be explained by the cleavage and self-contradictions within this secular basis. The latter must itself, therefore, first be understood in its contradiction and then, by the removal of the contradiction, revolutionised in practice. Thus, for instance, after the earthly family is discovered to be the secret of the holy family, the former must then itself be criticised in theory and revolutionised in practice.

V

Feuerbach, not satisfied with *abstract thinking*, appeals to *sensuous contemplation*; but he does not conceive sensuousness as practical, human-sensuous activity.

VI

Feuerbach resolves the religious essence into the human essence. But the human essence is no abstraction inherent in each single individual. In its reality it is the ensemble of the social relations.

Feuerbach, who does not enter upon a criticism of this real essence, is consequently compelled:

(1) To abstract from the historical process and to fix the religious sentiment as something by itself and to presuppose an abstract—*isolated*—human individual.

(2) The human essence, therefore, can with him be comprehended only as "genus," as an internal, dumb generality which merely *naturally* unites the many individuals.

VII

Feuerbach, consequently, does not see that the "religious sentiment" is itself a social product, and that the abstract individual whom he analyses belongs in reality to a particular form of society.

VIII

Social life is essentially *practical*. All mysteries which mislead theory into mysticism find their rational solution in human practice and in the comprehension of this practice.

IX

The highest point attained by contemplative materialism, that is, materialism which does not comprehend sensuousness as practical activity, is the contemplation of single individuals in civil society.

X

The standpoint of the old materialism is *"civil"* society; the standpoint of the new is *human* society, or socialised humanity.

XI

The philosophers have only *interpreted* the world, in various ways; the point, however, is to *change* it.

The German Ideology: Part I

KARL MARX

Marx and Engels wrote *The German Ideology* in 1845–46 in order (as Marx later recalled) "to settle accounts with our erstwhile philosophical conscience." He further explained: "The manuscript, two large octavo volumes, had long reached its place of publication in Westphalia when we received the news that altered circumstances did not allow of its being printed. We abandoned the manuscript to the gnawing criticism of the mice, all the more willingly as we had achieved our main purpose—self-clarification."* The work was first published in 1932 by the Marx-Engels Institute in Moscow.

The original difficulty of publication was very probably connected with the fact that most of this very bulky work consisted of satirically written, rather arid polemics against Bruno Bauer, Max Stirner, Karl Grün, and others. But Part I (here presented in full) is a different matter. Although polemical at various points, it is basically a work of exposition. It gives every appearance of being the work for which the "Theses on Feuerbach" served as an outline; hence we may infer that it was written by Marx. It is, in essence, a restatement, minus much of the German philosophical terminology, of the theory of history adumbrated in the manuscripts of 1844. Marx now calls it the "materialist conception of history." It is particularly valuable and important to the student of Marxist thought because Marx never again set down a comprehensive statement of his theory of history at such length and in such detail. This point is not contradicted by Engels' remark in the 1888 foreword that the exposition of the materialist conception of history in *The German Ideology* "proves only how incomplete our knowledge of economic history still was at that time."

The German Ideology has recently appeared in a re-edited version containing several previously unknown pages of the manuscript that were discovered in the International Institute of Social History in Amsterdam, where the original manuscript is kept. Part I appears here in this new and fuller version as translated from the German and edited by S. Ryazanskaya, and published in English by the Foreign Languages Publishing House, Moscow, in 1964. In preparing this new translation, the translator made use of an earlier English translation made by W. Lough and edited by R. Pascal.

---

* Preface to *A Contribution to the Critique of Political Economy*. See above, pp. 5–6.

Feuerbach: Opposition of the Materialistic and Idealistic Outlook

As we hear from German ideologists, Germany has in the last few years gone through an unparalleled revolution. The decomposition of the Hegelian philosophy, which began with Strauss, has developed into a universal ferment into which all the "powers of the past" are swept. In the general chaos mighty empires have arisen only to meet with immediate doom, heroes have emerged momentarily only to be hurled back into obscurity by bolder and stronger rivals. It was a revolution beside which the French Revolution was child's play, a world struggle beside which the struggles of the Diadochi appear insignificant. Principles ousted one another, heroes of the mind overthrew each other with unheard-of rapidity, and in the three years 1842–45 more of the past was swept away in Germany than at other times in three centuries.

All this is supposed to have taken place in the realm of pure thought.

Certainly it is an interesting event we are dealing with: the putrescence of the absolute spirit. When the last spark of its life had failed, the various components of this *caput mortuum*[1] began to decompose, entered into new combinations and formed new substances. The industrialists of philosophy, who till then had lived on the exploitation of the absolute spirit, now seized upon the new combinations. Each with all possible zeal set about retailing his apportioned share. This naturally gave rise to competition, which, to start with, was carried on in moderately staid bourgeois fashion. Later when the German market was glutted, and the commodity in spite of all efforts found no response in the world market, the business was spoiled in the usual German manner by fabricated and fictitious production, deterioration in quality, adulteration of the raw materials, falsification of labels, fictitious purchases, bill-jobbing and a credit system devoid of any real basis. The competition turned into a bitter struggle, which is now being extolled and interpreted to us as a revolution of world significance, the begetter of the most prodigious results and achievements.

If we wish to rate at its true value this philosophic charlatanry, which awakens even in the breast of the honest German citizen a glow of national pride, if we wish to bring out clearly the pettiness, the parochial narrowness of this whole Young-Hegelian movement

1. Literally: "dead head"; a term used in chemistry for the residuum left after distillation; here: "remainder," "residue."

and in particular the tragicomic contrast between the illusions of these heroes about their achievements and the actual achievements themselves, we must look at the whole spectacle from a standpoint beyond the frontiers of Germany.

A. IDEOLOGY IN GENERAL, GERMAN IDEOLOGY IN PARTICULAR

German criticism has, right up to its latest efforts, never quitted the realm of philosophy. Far from examining its general philosophic premises, the whole body of its inquiries has actually sprung from the soil of a definite philosophical system, that of Hegel. Not only in their answers but in their very questions there was a mystification. This dependence on Hegel is the reason why not one of these modern critics has even attempted a comprehensive criticism of the Hegelian system, however much each professes to have advanced beyond Hegel. Their polemics against Hegel and against one another are confined to this—each extracts one side of the Hegelian system and turns this against the whole system as well as against the sides extracted by the others. To begin with they extracted pure unfalsified Hegelian categories such as "substance" and "self-consciousness," later they desecrated these categories with more secular names such as "species," "the Unique," "Man," etc.

The entire body of German philosophical criticism from Strauss to Stirner is confined to criticism of *religious* conceptions. The critics started from real religion and actual theology. What religious consciousness and a religious conception really meant was determined variously as they went along. Their advance consisted in subsuming the allegedly dominant metaphysical, political, juridical, moral and other conceptions under the class of religious or theological conceptions; and similarly in pronouncing political, juridical, moral consciousness as religious or theological, and the political, juridical, moral man—"*man*" in the last resort—as religious. The dominance of religion was taken for granted. Gradually every dominant relationship was pronounced a religious relationship and transformed into a cult, a cult of law, a cult of the State, etc. On all sides it was only a question of dogmas and belief in dogmas. The world was sanctified to an ever-increasing extent till at last our venerable Saint Max was able to canonise it *en bloc* and thus dispose of it once for all.

The Old Hegelians had *comprehended* everything as soon as it was reduced to an Hegelian logical category. The Young Hegelians *criticised* everything by attributing to it religious conceptions or by pronouncing it a theological matter. The Young Hegelians are in agreement with the Old Hegelians in their belief in the rule of religion, of concepts, of a universal principle in the existing world. Only, the one party attacks this dominion as usurpation, while the other extols it as legitimate.

Since the Young Hegelians consider conceptions, thoughts, ideas, in fact all the products of consciousness, to which they attribute an independent existence, as the real chains of men (just as the Old Hegelians declared them the true bonds of human society) it is evident that the Young Hegelians have to fight only against these illusions of the consciousness. Since, according to their fantasy, the relationships of men, all their doings, their chains and their limitations are products of their consciousness, the Young Hegelians logically put to men the moral postulate of exchanging their present consciousness for human, critical or egoistic consciousness, and thus of removing their limitations. This demand to change consciousness amounts to a demand to interpret reality in another way, i.e., to recognise it by means of another interpretation. The Young-Hegelian ideologists, in spite of their allegedly "world-shattering" statements, are the staunchest conservatives. The most recent of them have found the correct expression for their activity when they declare they are only fighting against *"phrases."* They forget, however, that to these phrases they themselves are only opposing other phrases, and that they are in no way combating the real existing world when they are merely combating the phrases of this world. The only results which this philosophic criticism could achieve were a few (and at that thoroughly one-sided) elucidations of Christianity from the point of view of religious history; all the rest of their assertions are only further embellishments of their claim to have furnished, in these unimportant elucidations, discoveries of universal importance.

It has not occurred to any one of these philosophers to inquire into the connection of German philosophy with German reality, the relation of their criticism to their own material surroundings.

The premises from which we begin are not arbitrary ones, not dogmas, but real premises from which abstraction can only be made in the imagination. They are the real individuals, their activity and the material conditions under which they live, both those which they find already existing and those produced by their activity. These premises can thus be verified in a purely empirical way.

The first premise of all human history is, of course, the existence of living human individuals. Thus the first fact to be established is the physical organisation of these individuals and their consequent relation to the rest of nature. Of course, we cannot here go either into the actual physical nature of man, or into the natural conditions in which man finds himself—geological, orohydrographical, climatic and so on. The writing of history must always set out from these natural bases and their modification in the course of history through the action of men.

Men can be distinguished from animals by consciousness, by religion or anything else you like. They themselves begin to distinguish themselves from animals as soon as they begin to *produce* their means of subsistence, a step which is conditioned by their physical organisation. By producing their means of subsistence men are indirectly producing their actual material life.

The way in which men produce their means of subsistence depends first of all on the nature of the actual means of subsistence they find in existence and have to reproduce. This mode of production must not be considered simply as being the reproduction of the physical existence of the individuals. Rather it is a definite form of activity of these individuals, a definite form of expressing their life, a definite *mode of life* on their part. As individuals express their life, so they are. What they are, therefore, coincides with their production, both with *what* they produce and with *how* they produce. The nature of individuals thus depends on the material conditions determining their production.

This production only makes its appearance with the *increase of population*. In its turn this presupposes the *intercourse* [*Verkehr*] of individuals with one another. The form of this intercourse is again determined by production.

The relations of different nations among themselves depend upon the extent to which each has developed its productive forces, the division of labour and internal intercourse. This statement is generally recognised. But not only the relation of one nation to others, but also the whole internal structure of the nation itself depends on the stage of development reached by its production and its internal and external intercourse. How far the productive forces of a nation are developed is shown most manifestly by the degree to which the division of labour has been carried. Each new productive force, insofar as it is not merely a quantitative extension of productive forces already known (for instance the bringing into cultivation of fresh land), causes a further development of the division of labour.

The division of labour inside a nation leads at first to the separation of industrial and commercial from agricultural labour, and hence to the separation of *town* and *country* and to the conflict of their interests. Its further development leads to the separation of commercial from industrial labour. At the same time through the division of labour inside these various branches there develop various divisions among the individuals co-operating in definite kinds of labour. The relative position of these individual groups is determined by the methods employed in agriculture, industry and commerce (patriarchalism, slavery, estates, classes). These same conditions are to be seen (given a more developed intercourse) in the relations of different nations to one another.

The various stages of development in the division of labour are just so many different forms of ownership, i.e., the existing stage in the division of labour determines also the relations of individuals to one another with reference to the material, instrument, and product of labour.

The first form of ownership is tribal [*Stammeigentum*] ownership. It corresponds to the undeveloped stage of production, at which a people lives by hunting and fishing, by the rearing of beasts or, in the highest stage, agriculture. In the latter case it pre supposes a great mass of uncultivated stretches of land. The division of labour is at this stage still very elementary and is confined to a further extension of the natural division of labour existing in the family. The social structure is, therefore, limited to an extension of the family; patriarchal family chieftains, below them the members of the tribe, finally slaves. The slavery latent in the family only develops gradually with the increase of population, the growth of wants, and with the extension of external relations, both of war and of barter.

The second form is the ancient communal and State ownership which proceeds especially from the union of several tribes into a *city* by agreement or by conquest, and which is still accompanied by slavery. Beside communal ownership we already find movable, and later also immovable, private property developing, but as an abnormal form subordinate to communal ownership. The citizens hold power over their labouring slaves only in their community, and on this account alone, therefore, they are bound to the form of communal ownership. It is the communal private property which compels the active citizens to remain in this spontaneously derived form of association over against their slaves. For this reason the whole structure of society based on this communal ownership, and with it the power of the people, decays in the same measure as, in particular, immovable private property evolves. The division of labour is already more developed. We already find the antagonism of town and country; later the antagonism between those states which represent town interests and those which represent country interests, and inside the towns themselves the antagonism between industry and maritime commerce. The class relation between citizens and slaves is now completely developed.

This whole interpretation of history appears to be contradicted by the fact of conquest. Up till now violence, war, pillage, murder and robbery, etc., have been accepted as the driving force of history. Here we must limit ourselves to the chief points and take, therefore, only the most striking example—the destruction of an old civilisation by a barbarous people and the resulting formation of an entirely new organisation of society. (Rome and the barbarians; feudalism and Gaul; the Byzantine Empire and the Turks.) With the conquering barbarian people war itself is still, as indicated above, a regular form of intercourse, which is the more eagerly exploited as the increase in population together with the traditional and, for it, the only possible, crude mode of production gives rise to the need for new means of production. In Italy, on the other hand, the concentration of landed property (caused not only by buying-up and indebtedness but also by inheritance, since loose living being rife and marriage rare, the old families gradually died out and their possessions fell into the hands of a few) and its conversion into grazing-land (caused not only by the usual economic forces still operative today but by the importation of plundered and tribute corn and the resultant lack of demand for Italian corn) brought about the almost total disappearance of the free population. The very slaves died out again and again, and had constantly to be replaced by new ones. Slavery remained the basis of the whole productive system. The plebeians, midway between freemen and slaves, never succeeded in becoming more than a proletarian rabble. Rome indeed never became more than a city; its connection with the provinces was almost exclusively political and could, therefore, easily be broken again by political events.

With the development of private property, we find here for the first time the same conditions which we shall find again, only on a more extensive scale, with modern private property. On the one hand, the concentration of private property, which began very early in Rome (as the Licinian agrarian law proves) and proceeded very rapidly from the time of the civil wars and especially under the Emperors; on the other hand, coupled with this, the transformation of the plebeian small peasantry into a proletariat, which, however, owing to its intermediate position between propertied citizens and slaves, never achieved an independent development.

The third form of ownership is feudal or estate property. If antiquity started out from the town and its little territory, the Middle Ages started out from the *country*. This different starting-point was determined by the sparseness of the population at that time, which was scattered over a large area and which received no large increase from the conquerors. In contrast to Greece and Rome, feudal development at the outset, therefore, extends over a much wider territory, prepared by the Roman conquests and the spread of agriculture at first associated with them. The last centuries of the declining Roman Empire and its conquest by the barbarians destroyed a number of productive forces; agriculture had declined, industry had decayed for want of a market, trade had died out or been violently suspended, the rural and urban population had decreased. From these conditions and the mode of organisation of the conquest determined by them, feudal property developed under the influence of the Germanic military constitution. Like tribal and communal ownership, it is based again on a community; but the directly producing class standing over against it is not, as in the case of the ancient community, the slaves, but the enserfed small peasantry. As soon as feudalism is fully developed, there also arises antagonism to the towns. The hierarchical structure of landownership, and the armed bodies of retainers associated with it, gave the nobility power over the serfs. This feudal organisation was, just as much as the ancient communal ownership, an association against a subjected producing class; but the form of association and the relation to the direct producers were different because of the different conditions of production.

This feudal system of landownership had its counterpart in the *towns* in the shape of corporative property, the feudal organisation of trades. Here property consisted chiefly in the labour of each individual person. The necessity for association against the organised robber nobility, the need for communal covered markets in an age when the industrialist was at the same time a merchant, the growing competition of the escaped serfs swarming into the rising towns, the feudal structure of the whole country: these combined to bring about the *guilds*. The gradually accumulated small capital of individual craftsmen and their stable numbers, as against the growing population, evolved the relation of journeyman and apprentice, which brought into being in the towns a hierarchy similar to that in the country.

Thus the chief form of property during the feudal epoch consisted on the one hand of landed property with serf labour chained to it, and on the other of the labour of the individual with small capital commanding the labour of journeymen. The organisation of both was determined by the restricted conditions of production—the small-scale and primitive cultivation of the land, and the craft type of industry. There was little division of labour in the heyday of feudalism. Each country bore in itself the antithesis of town and country; the division into estates was certainly strongly marked; but apart from the differentiation of princes, nobility, clergy and peasants in the country, and masters, journeymen, apprentices and soon also the rabble of casual labourers in the towns, no division of importance took place. In agriculture it was rendered difficult by the strip-system, beside which the cottage industry of the peasants themselves emerged. In industry there was no division of labour at all in the individual trades themselves, and very little between them. The separation of industry and commerce was found already in existence in older towns; in the newer it only developed later, when the towns entered into mutual relations.

The grouping of larger territories into feudal kingdoms was a necessity for the landed nobility as for the towns. The organisation of the ruling class, the nobility, had, therefore, everywhere a monarch at its head.

The fact is, therefore, that definite individuals who are productively active in a definite way enter into these definite social and political relations. Empirical observation must in each separate instance bring out empirically, and without any mystification and speculation, the connection of the social and political structure with production. The social structure and the State are continually evolving out of the life process of definite individuals, but of individuals, not as they may appear in their own or other people's imagination, but as they *really* are; i.e., as they operate, produce materially, and hence as they work under definite material limits, presuppositions and conditions independent of their will.

The production of ideas, of conceptions, of consciousness, is at first directly interwoven with the material activity and the material intercourse of men, the language of real life. Conceiving, thinking, the mental intercourse of men, appear at this stage as the direct efflux of their material behaviour. The same applies to mental production as expressed in the language of politics, laws, morality, religion, metaphysics, etc., of a people. Men are the producers of their conceptions, ideas, etc.—real, active men, as they are conditioned by a definite development of their productive forces and of the intercourse corresponding to these, up to its furthest forms. Consciousness can never be anything else than conscious existence, and the existence of men is their actual life-process. If in all ideology men and their circumstances appear upside-down as in a *camera obscura*, this phenomenon arises just as much from their historical life-process as the inversion of objects on the retina does from their physical life-process.

In direct contrast to German philosophy which descends from heaven to earth, here we ascend from earth to heaven. That is to say, we do not set out from what men say, imagine, conceive, nor from men as narrated, thought of, imagined, conceived, in order to arrive at men in the flesh. We set out from real, active men, and on the basis of their real life-process we demonstrate the development of the ideological reflexes and echoes of this life-process. The phantoms formed in the human brain are also, necessarily, sublimates of their material life-process, which is empirically verifiable and bound to material premises. Morality, religion, metaphysics, all the rest of ideology and their corresponding forms of consciousness, thus no longer retain the semblance of independence. They have no history, no development; but men, developing their material production and their material intercourse, alter, along with this their real existence, their thinking and the products of their thinking. Life is not determined by consciousness, but consciousness by life. In the first method of approach the starting-point is consciousness taken as the living individual; in the second method, which conforms to real life, it is the real living individuals themselves, and consciousness is considered solely as *their* consciousness.

This method of approach is not devoid of premises. It starts out from the real premises and does not abandon them for a moment. Its premises are men, not in any fantastic isolation and rigidity, but in their actual, empirically perceptible process of development under definite conditions. As soon as this active life-process is described, history ceases to be a collection of dead facts as it is with the empiricists (themselves still abstract), or an imagined activity of imagined subjects, as with the idealists.

Where speculation ends—in real life—there real, positive science begins: the representation of the practical activity, of the practical process of development of men. Empty talk about consciousness ceases, and real knowledge has to take its place. When reality is depicted, philosophy as an independent branch of knowledge loses its medium of existence. At the best its place can only be taken by a summing-up of the most general results, abstractions which arise from the observation of the historical development of men. Viewed apart from real history, these abstractions have in themselves no value whatsoever. They can only serve to facilitate the arrangement of historical material, to indicate the sequence of its separate strata. But they by no means afford a recipe or schema, as does philosophy, for neatly trimming the epochs of history. On the contrary, our difficulties begin only when we set about the observation and the arrangement—the real depiction—of our historical material, whether of a past epoch or of the present. The removal of these difficulties is governed by premises which it is quite impossible to state here, but which only the study of the actual life-process and the activity of the individuals of each epoch will make evident. We shall select here some of these abstractions, which we use in contradistinction to the ideologists, and shall illustrate them by historical examples.

1. History

Since we are dealing with the Germans, who are devoid of premises, we must begin by stating the first premise of all human existence and, therefore, of all history, the premise, namely, that men must be in a position to live in order to be able to "make history."[2] But life involves before everything else eating and drink-ing, a habitation, clothing and many other things. The first histori-cal act is thus the production of the means to satisfy these needs, the production of material life itself. And indeed this is an histori-cal act, a fundamental condition of all history, which today, as thousands of years ago, must daily and hourly be fulfilled merely in order to sustain human life. Even when the sensuous world is reduced to a minimum, to a stick as with Saint Bruno, it presup-poses the action of producing the stick. Therefore in any interpreta-tion of history one has first of all to observe this fundamental fact in all its significance and all its implications and to accord it its due importance. It is well known that the Germans have never done this, and they have never, therefore, had an *earthly* basis for history and consequently never a historian. The French and the English, even if they have conceived the relation of this fact with so-called history only in an extremely one-sided fashion, particularly as long as they remained in the toils of political ideology, have nevertheless made the first attempts to give the writing of history a materialistic basis by being the first to write histories of civil society, of com-merce and industry.

The second point is that the satisfaction of the first need (the action of satisfying, and the instrument of satisfaction which has been acquired) leads to new needs; and this production of new needs is the first historical act. Here we recognise immediately the spiritual ancestry of the great historical wisdom of the Germans who, when they run out of positive material and when they can serve up neither theological nor political nor literary rubbish, assert that this is not history at all, but the "prehistoric era." They do not, however, enlighten us as to how we proceed from this nonsen-sical "prehistory" to history proper; although, on the other hand, in their historical speculation they seize upon this "prehistory" with especial eagerness because they imagine themselves safe there from interference on the part of "crude facts," and, at the same time, be-cause there they can give full rein to their speculative impulse and set up and knock down hypotheses by the thousand.

The third circumstance which, from the very outset, enters into historical development, is that men, who daily remake their own life, begin to make other men, to propagate their kind: the relation between man and woman, parents and children, the *family*. The family, which to begin with is the only social relationship, becomes later, when increased needs create new social relations and the increased population new needs, a subordinate one (except in Ger-many), and must then be treated and analysed according to the

2. Marginal note by Marx: "*Hegel*. Geological, hydrographical, etc., condi- tions. Human bodies. Needs, labour."

existing empirical data, not according to "the concept of the family," as is the custom in Germany.³ These three aspects of social activity are not of course to be taken as three different stages, but just as three aspects or, to make it clear to the Germans, three "moments," which have existed simultaneously since the dawn of history and the first men, and which still assert themselves in history today.

The production of life, both of one's own in labour and of fresh life in procreation, now appears as a double relationship: on the one hand as a natural, on the other as a social relationship. By social we understand the co-operation of several individuals, no matter under what conditions, in what manner and to what end. It follows from this that a certain mode of production, or industrial stage, is always combined with a certain mode of co-operation, or social stage, and this mode of co-operation is itself a "productive force." Further, that the multitude of productive forces accessible to men determines the nature of society, hence, that the "history of humanity" must always be studied and treated in relation to the history of industry and exchange. But it is also clear how in Germany it is impossible to write this sort of history, because the Germans lack not only the necessary power of comprehension and the material but also the "evidence of their senses," for across the Rhine you cannot have any experience of these things since history has stopped happening. Thus it is quite obvious from the start that there exists a materialistic connection of men with one another, which is determined by their needs and their mode of production, and which is as old as men themselves. This connection is ever taking on new forms, and thus presents a "history" independently of the existence of any political or religious nonsense which would especially hold men together.

Only now, after having considered four moments, four aspects of

3. The building of houses. With savages each family has as a matter of course its own cave or hut like the separate family tent of the nomads. This separate domestic economy is made only the more necessary by the further development of private property. With the agricultural peoples a communal domestic economy is just as impossible as a communal cultivation of the soil. A great advance was the building of towns. In all previous periods, however, the abolition of individual economy, which is inseparable from the abolition of private property, was impossible for the simple reason that the material conditions governing it were not present. The setting-up of a communal domestic economy presupposes the development of machinery, of the use of natural forces and of many other productive forces—e.g., of water-supplies, of gas-lighting, steam-heating, etc., the removal [of the antagonism] of town and country. Without these conditions a communal economy would not in itself form a new productive force; lacking any material basis and resting on a purely theoretical foundation, it would be a mere freak and would end in nothing more than a monastic economy.—What was possible can be seen in the towns brought about by condensation and the erection of communal buildings for various definite purposes (prisons, barracks, etc.). That the abolition of individual economy is inseparable from the abolition of the family is self-evident. [*Marx*]

the primary historical relationships, do we find that man also possesses "consciousness";[4] but, even so, not inherent, not "pure" consciousness. From the start the "spirit" is afflicted with the curse of being "burdened" with matter, which here makes its appearance in the form of agitated layers of air, sounds, in short, of language. Language is as old as consciousness, language is practical consciousness that exists also for other men, and for that reason alone it really exists for me personally as well; language, like consciousness, only arises from the need, the necessity, of intercourse with other men. Where there exists a relationship, it exists for me: the animal does not enter into "relations" with anything, it does not enter into any relation at all. For the animal, its relation to others does not exist as a relation. Consciousness is, therefore, from the very beginning a social product, and remains so as long as men exist at all. Consciousness is at first, of course, merely consciousness concerning the immediate sensuous environment and consciousness of the limited connection with other persons and things outside the individual who is growing self-conscious. At the same time it is consciousness of nature, which first appears to men as a completely alien, all-powerful and unassailable force, with which men's relations are purely animal and by which they are overawed like beasts; it is thus a purely animal consciousness of nature (natural religion).

We see here immediately: this natural religion or this particular relation of men to nature is determined by the form of society and vice versa. Here, as everywhere, the identity of nature and man appears in such a way that the restricted relation of men to nature determines their restricted relation to one another, and their restricted relation to one another determines men's restricted relation to nature, just because nature is as yet hardly modified historically; and, on the other hand, man's consciousness of the necessity of associating with the individuals around him is the beginning of the consciousness that he is living in society at all. This beginning is as animal as social life itself at this stage. It is mere herd-consciousness, and at this point man is only distinguished from sheep by the fact that with him consciousness takes the place of instinct or that his instinct is a conscious one. This sheep-like or tribal consciousness receives its further development and extension through increased productivity, the increase of needs, and, what is fundamental to both of these, the increase of population. With these there develops the division of labour, which was originally nothing but the division of labour in the sexual act, then that division of labour which develops spontaneously or "naturally" by

4. Marginal note by Marx: "Men have history because they must *produce* their life, and because they must produce it moreover in a *certain* way: this is determined by their physical organisation; their consciousness is determined in just the same way."

virtue of natural predisposition (e.g., physical strength), needs, accidents, etc., etc. Division of labour only becomes truly such from the moment when a division of material and mental labour appears.[5] From this moment onwards consciousness *can* really flatter itself that it is something other than consciousness of existing practice, that it *really* represents something without representing something real; from now on consciousness is in a position to emancipate itself from the world and to proceed to the formation of "pure" theory, theology, philosophy, ethics, etc. But even if this theory, theology, philosophy, ethics, etc., comes into contradiction with the existing relations, this can only occur because existing social relations have come into contradiction with existing forces of production; this, moreover, can also occur in a particular national sphere of relations through the appearance of the contradiction, not within the national orbit, but between this national consciousness and the practice of other nations,[6] i.e., between the national and the general consciousness of a nation (as we see it now in Germany).

Moreover, it is quite immaterial what consciousness starts to do on its own: out of all such muck we get only the one inference that these three moments, the forces of production, the state of society, and consciousness, can and must come into contradiction with one another, because the *division of labour* implies the possibility, nay the fact that intellectual and material activity—enjoyment and labour, production and consumption—devolve on different individuals, and that the only possibility of their not coming into contradiction lies in the negation in its turn of the division of labour. It is self-evident, moreover, that "spectres," "bonds," "the higher being," "concept," "scruple," are merely the idealistic, spiritual expression, the conception apparently of the isolated individual, the image of very empirical fetters and limitations, within which the mode of production of life and the form of intercourse coupled with it move.

With the division of labour, in which all these contradictions are implicit, and which in its turn is based on the natural division of labour in the family and the separation of society into individual families opposed to one another, is given simultaneously the *distribution*, and indeed the *unequal* distribution, both quantitative and qualitative, of labour and its products, hence property: the nucleus, the first form, of which lies in the family, where wife and children are the slaves of the husband. This latent slavery in the family, though still very crude, is the first property, but even at this early stage it corresponds perfectly to the definition of modern econo-

5. Marginal note by Marx: "The first form of ideologists, *priests*, is concurrent."

6. Marginal note by Marx: "*Religion.* The Germans and *ideology* as such."

mists who call it the power of disposing of the labour-power of others. Division of labour and private property are, moreover, identical expressions: in the one the same thing is affirmed with reference to activity as is affirmed in the other with reference to the product of the activity.

Further, the division of labour implies the contradiction between the interest of the separate individual or the individual family and the communal interest of all individuals who have intercourse with one another. And indeed, this communal interest does not exist merely in the imagination, as the "general interest," but first of all in reality, as the mutual interdependence of the individuals among whom the labour is divided. And finally, the division of labour offers us the first example of how, as long as man remains in natural society, that is, as long as a cleavage exists between the particular and the common interest, as long, therefore, as activity is not voluntarily, but naturally, divided, man's own deed becomes an alien power opposed to him, which enslaves him instead of being controlled by him. For as soon as the distribution of labour comes into being, each man has a particular, exclusive sphere of activity, which is forced upon him and from which he cannot escape. He is a hunter, a fisherman, a shepherd, or a critical critic, and must remain so if he does not want to lose his means of livelihood; while in communist society, where nobody has one exclusive sphere of activity but each can become accomplished in any branch he wishes, society regulates the general production and thus makes it possible for me to do one thing today and another tomorrow, to hunt in the morning, fish in the afternoon, rear cattle in the evening, criticise after dinner, just as I have a mind, without ever becoming hunter, fisherman, shepherd or critic. This fixation of social activity, this consolidation of what we ourselves produce into an objective power above us, growing out of our control, thwarting our expectations, bringing to naught our calculations, is one of the chief factors in historical development up till now.

And out of this very contradiction between the interest of the individual and that of the community the latter takes an independent form as the *State*, divorced from the real interests of individual and community, and at the same time as an illusory communal life, always based, however, on the real ties existing in every family and tribal conglomeration—such as flesh and blood, language, division of labour on a larger scale, and other interests—and especially, as we shall enlarge upon later, on the classes, already determined by the division of labour, which in every such mass of men separate out, and of which one dominates all the others. It follows from this that all struggles within the State, the struggle between democracy, aristocracy, and monarchy, the struggle for the franchise, etc., etc., are merely the illusory forms in which the real struggles of the different classes are fought out among one another (of this the German theoreticians have not the faintest inkling, although they have received a sufficient introduction to the subject in the *Deutsch-Französische Jahrbücher* and *Die heilige Familie*). Further, it follows that every class which is struggling for mastery, even when its domination, as is the case with the proletariat, postulates the abolition of the old form of society in its entirety and of domination itself, must first conquer for itself political power in order to represent its interest in turn as the general interest, which in the first moment it is forced to do. Just because individuals seek *only* their particular interest, which for them does not coincide with their communal interest (in fact the general is the illusory form of communal life), the latter will be imposed on them as an interest "alien" to them, and "independent" of them, as in its turn a particular, peculiar "general" interest; or they themselves must remain within this discord, as in democracy. On the other hand, too, the *practical* struggle of these particular interests, which constantly *really* run counter to the communal and illusory communal interests, makes *practical* intervention and control necessary through the illusory "general" interest in the form of the State. The social power, i.e., the multiplied productive force, which arises through the co-operation of different individuals as it is determined by the division of labour, appears to these individuals, since their co-operation is not voluntary but has come about naturally, not as their own united power, but as an alien force existing outside them, of the origin and goal of which they are ignorant, which they thus cannot control, which on the contrary passes through a peculiar series of phases and stages independent of the will and the action of man, nay even being the prime governor of these.

This *"estrangement"* (to use a term which will be comprehensible to the philosophers) can, of course, only be abolished given two *practical* premises. For it to become an "intolerable" power, i.e., a power against which men make a revolution, it must necessarily have rendered the great mass of humanity "propertyless," and produced, at the same time, the contradiction of an existing world of wealth and culture, both of which conditions presuppose a great increase in productive power, a high degree of its development. And, on the other hand, this development of productive forces (which itself implies the actual empirical existence of men in their *world-historical*, instead of local, being) is an absolutely necessary practical premise because without it *want* is merely made general, and with *destitution* the struggle for necessities and all the old filthy business would necessarily be reproduced; and furthermore, because only with this universal development of productive forces is a *universal* intercourse between men established, which produces in all nations simultaneously the phenomenon of the "propertyless" mass (universal competition), makes each nation dependent on the revolutions of the others, and finally has put *world-historical*, empirically universal individuals in place of local ones. Without this, (1) communism could only exist as a local event; (2) the *forces* of intercourse themselves could not have developed as *universal*, hence intolerable powers: they would have remained home-bred conditions surrounded by superstition; and (3) each extension of intercourse would abolish local communism. Empirically, communism is only possible as the act of the dominant peoples "all at once" and simultaneously, which presupposes the universal development of productive forces and the world intercourse bound up with communism. How otherwise could for instance property have had a history at all, have taken on different forms, and landed property, for example, according to the different premises given, have proceeded in France from parcellation to centralisation in the hands of a few, in England from centralisation in the hands of a few to parcellation, as is actually the case today? Or how does it happen that trade, which after all is nothing more than the exchange of products of various individuals and countries, rules the whole world through the relation of supply and demand—a relation which, as an English economist says, hovers over the earth like the fate of the ancients, and with invisible hand allots fortune and misfortune to men, sets up empires and overthrows empires, causes nations to rise and to disappear—while with the abolition of the basis of private property, with the communistic regulation of production (and, implicit in this, the destruction of the alien relation between men and what they themselves produce), the power of the relation of supply and demand is dissolved into nothing, and men get exchange, production, the mode of their mutual relation, under their own control again?

Communism is for us not a *state of affairs* which is to be established, an *ideal* to which reality [will] have to adjust itself. We call communism the *real* movement which abolishes the present state of things. The conditions of this movement result from the premises now in existence. Moreover, the mass of *propertyless* workers—the utterly precarious position of labour-power on a mass scale cut off from capital or from even a limited satisfaction and, therefore, no longer merely temporarily deprived of work itself as a secure source of life—presupposes the *world market* through competition. The proletariat can thus only exist *world-historically*, just as communism, its activity, can only have a "world-historical" existence. World-historical existence of individuals, i.e., existence of individuals which is directly linked up with world history.

The form of intercourse determined by the existing productive forces at all previous historical stages, and in its turn determining these, is *civil society*. The latter, as is clear from what we have said above, has as its premises and basis the simple family and the multiple, the so-called tribe, and the more precise determinants of this society are enumerated in our remarks above. Already here we see how this civil society is the true source and theatre of all history, and how absurd is the conception of history held hitherto, which neglects the real relationships and confines itself to high-sounding dramas of princes and states.

Civil society embraces the whole material intercourse of individuals within a definite stage of the development of productive forces. It embraces the whole commercial and industrial life of a given stage and, insofar, transcends the State and the nation, though, on the other hand again, it must assert itself in its foreign relations as nationality, and inwardly must organise itself as State. The term "civil society" [*bürgerliche Gesellschaft*][7] emerged in the eighteenth century, when property relationships had already extricated themselves from the ancient and medieval communal society. Civil society as such only develops with the bourgeoisie; the social organisation evolving directly out of production and commerce, which in all ages forms the basis of the State and of the rest of the idealistic superstructure, has, however, always been designated by the same name.

2. Concerning the Production of Consciousness

In history up to the present it is certainly an empirical fact that separate individuals have, with the broadening of their activity into world-historical activity, become more and more enslaved under a power alien to them (a pressure which they have conceived of as a dirty trick on the part of the so-called universal spirit, etc.), a power which has become more and more enormous and, in the last instance, turns out to be the *world market*. But it is just as empirically established that, by the overthrow of the existing state of society by the communist revolution (of which more below) and the abolition of private property which is identical with it, this power, which so baffles the German theoreticians, will be dissolved; and that then the liberation of each single individual will be accomplished in the measure in which history becomes transformed into world history. From the above it is clear that the real intellectual wealth of the individual depends entirely on the wealth of his real connections. Only then will the separate individuals be liberated from the various national and local barriers, be brought into

7. *Bürgerliche Gesellschaft* can mean either "bourgeois society" or "civil society."

practical connection with the material and intellectual production of the whole world and be put in a position to acquire the capacity to enjoy this all-sided production of the whole earth (the creations of man). *All-round* dependence, this natural form of the *world-historical* co-operation of individuals, will be transformed by this communist revolution into the control and conscious mastery of these powers, which, born of the action of men on one another, have till now overawed and governed men as powers completely alien to them. Now this view can be expressed again in speculative-idealistic, i.e., fantastic, terms as "self-generation of the species" ("society as the subject"), and thereby the consecutive series of interrelated individuals connected with each other can be conceived as a single individual, which accomplishes the mystery of generating itself, It is clear here that individuals certainly make *one another*, physically and mentally, but do not make themselves either in the nonsense of Saint Bruno, or in the sense of the "Unique," of the "made" man.

This conception of history depends on our ability to expound the real process of production, starting out from the material production of life itself, and to comprehend the form of intercourse connected with this and created by this mode of production (i.e., civil society in its various stages), as the basis of all history; and to show it in its action as State, to explain all the different theoretical products and forms of consciousness, religion, philosophy, ethics, etc., etc., and trace their origins and growth from that basis; by which means, of course, the whole thing can be depicted in its totality (and therefore, too, the reciprocal action of these various sides on one another). It has not, like the idealistic view of history, in every period to look for a category, but remains constantly on the real *ground* of history; it does not explain practice from the idea but explains the formation of ideas from material practice; and accordingly it comes to the conclusion that all forms and products of consciousness cannot be dissolved by mental criticism, by resolution into "self-consciousness" or transformation into "apparitions," "spectres," "fancies," etc., but only by the practical overthrow of the actual social relations which gave rise to this idealistic humbug; that not criticism but revolution is the driving force of history, also of religion, of philosophy and all other types of theory. It shows that history does not end by being resolved into "self-consciousness" as "spirit of the spirit," but that in it at each stage there is found a material result: a sum of productive forces, a historically created relation of individuals to nature and to one another, which is handed down to each generation from its predecessor; a mass of productive forces, capital funds and conditions, which, on the one hand, is indeed modified by the new generation, but also on the other prescribes for it its conditions of life and gives it a definite development, a special character. It shows that circumstances make men just as much as men make circumstances. This sum of productive forces, capital funds and social forms of intercourse, which every individual and generation finds in existence as something given, is the real basis of what the philosophers have conceived as "substance" and "essence of man," and what they have deified and attacked: a real basis which is not in the least disturbed, in its effect and influence on the development of men, by the fact that these philosophers revolt against it as "self-consciousness" and the "Unique." These conditions of life, which different generations find in existence, decide also whether or not the periodically recurring revolutionary convulsion will be strong enough to overthrow the basis of the entire existing system. And if these material elements of a complete revolution are not present (namely, on the one hand the existing productive forces, on the other the formation of a revolutionary mass, which revolts not only against separate conditions of society up till then, but against the very "production of life" till then, the "total activity" on which it was based), then, as far as practical development is concerned, it is absolutely immaterial whether the *idea* of this revolution has been expressed a hundred times already, as the history of communism proves.

In the whole conception of history up to the present this real basis of history has either been totally neglected or else considered as a minor matter quite irrelevant to the course of history. History must, therefore, always be written according to an extraneous standard; the real production of life seems to be primeval history, while the truly historical appears to be separated from ordinary life, something extra-superterrestrial. With this the relation of man to nature is excluded from history and hence the antithesis of nature and history is created. The exponents of this conception of history have consequently only been able to see in history the political actions of princes and States, religious and all sorts of theoretical struggles, and in particular in each historical epoch have had to *share the illusion of that epoch.* For instance, if an epoch imagines itself to be actuated by purely "political" or "religious" motives, although "religion" and "politics" are only forms of its true motives, the historian accepts this opinion. The "idea," the "conception" of the people in question about their real practice, is transformed into the sole determining, active force, which controls and determines their practice. When the crude form in which the division of labour appears with the Indians and Egyptians calls forth the caste-system in their State and religion, the historian believes that the caste-system is the power which has produced this crude social form. While the French and the English at least hold by the political illusion, which is moderately close to reality, the Germans move in the realm of the "pure spirit," and make religious illusion the driving force of history. The Hegelian philosophy of history is the last consequence, reduced to its "finest expression," of all this German historiography, for which it is not a question of real, nor even of political, interests, but of pure thoughts, which consequently must appear to Saint Bruno, as a series of "thoughts" that devour one another and are finally swallowed up in "self-consciousness";[8] and even more consistently the course of history appears to the Blessed Max Stirner, who knows not a thing about real history, as a mere tale of "knights," robbers and ghosts, from whose visions he can, of course, only save himself by "unholiness." This conception is truly religious: it postulates religious man as the primitive man, the starting-point of history; and in its imagination puts the religious production of fancies in the place of the real production of the means of subsistence and of life itself. This whole conception of history, together with its dissolution and the scruples and qualms resulting from it, is a purely *national* affair of the Germans and has only *local* interest for the Germans, as for instance the important question treated several times of late: how really we "pass from the realm of God to the realm of Man"—as if this "realm of God" had ever existed anywhere save in the imagination, and the learned gentlemen, without being aware of it, were not constantly living in the "realm of Man" to which they are now seeking the way; and as if the learned pastime (for it is nothing more) of explaining the mystery of this theoretical bubble-blowing did not on the contrary lie in demonstrating its origin in actual earthly conditions. Always, for these Germans, it is simply a matter of resolving the nonsense of earlier writers into some other freak, i.e., of presupposing that all this nonsense has a special *sense* which can be discovered; while really it is only a question of explaining this theoretical talk from the actual existing conditions. The real, practical dissolution of these phrases, the removal of these notions from the consciousness of men, will, as we have already said, be effected by altered circumstances, not by theoretical deductions. For the mass of men, i.e., the proletariat, these theoretical notions do not exist and hence do not require to be dissolved, and if this mass ever had any theoretical notions, e.g., religion, etc., these have now long been dissolved by circumstances.

The purely national character of these questions and solutions is shown again in the way these theorists believe in all seriousness that chimeras like "the God-Man," "Man," etc., have presided over

8. Marginal note by Marx: "So-called *objective* historiography just consists in treating the historical conditions inde- pendent of activity. Reactionary character."

individual epochs of history (Saint Bruno even goes so far as to assert that "only criticism and critics have made history") and when they themselves construct historical systems, they skip over all earlier periods in the greatest haste and pass immediately from "Mongolism" to history "with meaningful content," that is to say, to the history of the *Hallische* and *Deutsche Jahrbücher* and the dissolution of the Hegelian school into a general squabble. They forget all other nations, all real events, and the *theatrum mundi* is confined to the Leipzig Book Fair and the mutual quarrels of "Criticism," "Man," and "the Unique." If these theorists treat really historical subjects, as for instance the eighteenth century, they merely give a history of the ideas of the times, torn away from the facts and the practical development fundamental to them; and even that merely in order to represent that period as an imperfect preliminary stage, the as yet limited predecessor of the real historical age, i.e., the period of the German philosophic struggle from 1840 to 1844. As might be expected when the history of an earlier period is written with the aim of accentuating the brilliance of an unhistoric person and his fantasies, all the really historic events, even the really historic invasion of politics into history, receive no mention. Instead we get a narrative based not on research but on arbitrary constructions and literary gossip, such as Saint Bruno provided in his now forgotten history of the eighteenth century. These high-falutin and haughty hucksters of ideas, who imagine themselves infinitely exalted above all national prejudices, are thus in practice far more national than the beer-quaffing philistines who dream of a united Germany. They do not recognise the deeds of other nations as historical: they live in Germany, to Germany, and for Germany; they turn the Rhine-song into a religious hymn and conquer Alsace and Lorraine by robbing French philosophy instead of the French State, by Germanising French ideas instead of French provinces. Herr Venedey is a cosmopolitan compared with the Saints Bruno and Max, who, in the universal dominance of theory, proclaim the universal dominance of Germany.

It is also clear from these arguments how grossly Feuerbach is deceiving himself when (*Wigand's Vierteljahrsschrift*, 1845, Volume 2) by virtue of the qualification "common man" he declares himself a communist, transforms the latter into a predicate of "man," and thereby thinks it possible to change the word "communist," which in the real world means the follower of a definite revolutionary party, into a mere category. Feuerbach's whole deduction with regard to the relation of men to one another goes only so far as to prove that men need and *always have needed* each other. He wants to establish consciousness of this fact, that is to say, like the other theorists, merely to produce a correct consciousness about an *existing* fact; whereas for the real communist it is a question of overthrowing the existing state of things. We thoroughly appreciate, moreover, that Feuerbach, in endeavouring to produce consciousness of just *this* fact, is going as far as a theorist possibly can, without ceasing to be a theorist and philosopher. It is characteristic, however, that Saint Bruno and Saint Max seize on Feuerbach's conception of the communist and put it in place of the real communist—which occurs, partly, in order that they can combat communism too as "spirit of the spirit," as a philosophical category, as an equal opponent and, in the case of Saint Bruno, partly also for pragmatic reason. As an example of Feuerbach's acceptance and at the same time misunderstanding of existing reality, which he still shares with our opponents, we recall the passage in the *Philosophie der Zukunft* where he develops the view that the existence of a thing or a man is at the same time its or his essence, that the conditions of existence, the mode of life and activity of an animal or human individual are those in which its "essence" feels itself satisfied. Here every exception is expressly conceived as an unhappy chance, as an abnormality which cannot be altered. Thus if millions of proletarians feel by no means contented with their living conditions, if their "existence" does not in the least correspond to their "essence," then, according to the passage quoted, this is an unavoidable misfortune, which must be borne quietly. The millions of proletarians and communists, however, think differently and will prove this in time, when they bring their "existence" into harmony with their "essence" in a practical way, by means of a revolution. Feuerbach, therefore, never speaks of the world of man in such cases, but always takes refuge in external nature, and moreover in *nature* which has not yet been subdued by men. But every new invention, every advance made by industry, detaches another piece from this domain, so that the ground which produces examples illustrating such Feuerbachian propositions is steadily shrinking. The "essence" of the fish is its "existence," water—to go no further than this one proposition. The "essence" of the freshwater fish is the water of a river. But the latter ceases to be the "essence" of the fish and is no longer a suitable medium of existence as soon as the river is made to serve industry, as soon as it is polluted by dyes and other waste products and navigated by steamboats, or as soon as its water is diverted into canals where simple drainage can deprive the fish of its medium of existence. The explanation that all such contradictions are inevitable abnormalities does not essentially differ from the consolation which the Blessed Max Stirner offers to the discontented, saying that this contradiction is their own contradiction and this predicament their own predicament, whereupon they should either set their minds at ease, keep their disgust to themselves, or revolt against it in some fantastic way. It differs just as little from Saint Bruno's allegation that these unfortunate circumstances are due to the fact that those concerned are stuck in the muck of "substance," have not advanced to "absolute self-consciousness," and do not realise that these adverse conditions are spirit of their spirit.

We shall, of course, not take the trouble[9] to enlighten our wise philosophers by explaining to them that the "liberation" of "man" is not advanced a single step[1] by reducing philosophy, theology, substance and all the trash to "self-consciousness"[2] and by liberating man from the domination of these phrases,[3] which have never held him in thrall.[4] Nor will we explain to them that it is only possible to achieve real liberation in the real world and by employing real means, that slavery cannot be abolished without the steam-engine and the mule and spinning-jenny, serfdom cannot be abolished without improved agriculture, and that, in general, people cannot be liberated as long as they are unable to obtain food and drink, housing and clothing in adequate quality and quantity. "Liberation" is a historical and not a mental act, and it is brought about by historical conditions, the [development] of industry, commerce, [agri]culture, the [conditions of intercourse] * * * * [5]

In Germany,[6] a country where only a trivial historical development is taking place, these mental developments, these glorified and ineffective trivialities, naturally serve as a substitute for the lack of historical development, and they take root and have to be combated. But this fight is of local importance.[7]

* * * [8] in reality and for the *practical* materialist, i.e., the *communist*, it is a question of revolutionising the existing world, of practically attacking and changing existing things. When occasionally we find such views with Feuerbach, they are never more than isolated surmises and have much too little influence on his general outlook to be considered here as anything else than embryos capable of development. Feuerbach's "conception" of the sensuous world is confined on the one hand to mere contemplation of it, and on the other to mere feeling; he says "Man" instead of "real historical man." "Man" is really "the German." In the first case, the *contemplation* of the sensuous world, he necessarily lights on things which

9. Marginal note by Marx: *"Feuerbach."*
1. Marginal note by Marx: "Philosophic liberation and real liberation."
2. Marginal note by Marx: *"Man. The Unique one. The individual."*
3. Marginal note by Marx: "Geological, hydrographical, etc., conditions."
4. Marginal note by Marx: "The human body. Need and labour."
5. The following lines cannot be deciphered, for the sheet of paper is badly damaged.
6. Marginal note by Marx: "The importance of phrases in Germany."
7. Marginal note by Marx: "Language is the language of reality."
8. A gap in the manuscript.

contradict his consciousness and feeling, which disturb the harmony he presupposes, the harmony of all parts of the sensuous world and especially of man and nature.[9] To remove this disturbance, he must take refuge in a double perception, a profane one which only perceives the "flatly obvious" and a higher, philosophical, one which perceives the "true essence" of things. He does not see how the sensuous world around him is, not a thing given direct from all eternity, remaining ever the same, but the product of industry and of the state of society; and, indeed, in the sense that it is an historical product, the result of the activity of a whole succession of generations, each standing on the shoulders of the preceding one, developing its industry and its intercourse, modifying its social system according to the changed needs. Even the objects of the simplest "sensuous certainty" are only given him through social development, industry and commercial intercourse. The cherry-tree, like almost all fruit-trees, was, as is well known, only a few centuries ago transplanted by *commerce* into our zone, and therefore only *by* this action of a definite society in a definite age it has become "sensuous certainty" for Feuerbach.

Incidentally, when we conceive things thus, as they really are and happened, every profound philosophical problem is resolved, as will be seen even more clearly later, quite simply into an empirical fact. For instance, the important question of the relation of man to nature (Bruno goes so far as to speak of "the antitheses in nature and history" (p. 110), as though these were two separate "things" and man did not always have before him an historical nature and a natural history) out of which all the "unfathomably lofty works" on "substance" and "self-consciousness" were born, crumbles of itself when we understand that the celebrated "unity of man with nature" has always existed in industry and has existed in varying forms in every epoch according to the lesser or greater development of industry, just like the "struggle" of man with nature, right up to the development of his productive powers on a corresponding basis. Industry and commerce, production and the exchange of the necessities of life, themselves determine distribution, the structure of the different social classes and are, in turn, determined by it as to the mode in which they are carried on; and so it happens that in Manchester, for instance, Feuerbach sees only factories and machines, where a hundred years ago only spinning-wheels and weaving-looms were to be seen, or in the Campagna of Rome he finds only pasture lands and swamps, where in the time of Augus-

9. N.B. Feuerbach's failing is not that he subordinates the flatly obvious, the sensuous *appearance*, to the sensuous reality established by more accurate investigation of the sensuous facts, but that he cannot in the last resort cope with the sensuous world except by looking at it with the "eyes," i.e., through the "spectacles" of the philosopher. [*Marx*]

tus he would have found nothing but the vineyards and villas of Roman capitalists. Feuerbach speaks in particular of the perception of natural science; he mentions secrets which are disclosed only to the eye of the physicist and chemist; but where would natural science be without industry and commerce? Even this "pure" natural science is provided with an aim, as with its material, only through trade and industry, through the sensuous activity of men. So much is this activity, this unceasing sensuous labour and creation, this production, the basis of the whole sensuous world as it now exists, that, were it interrupted only for a year, Feuerbach would not only find an enormous change in the natural world, but would very soon find that the whole world of men and his own perceptive faculty, nay his own existence, were missing. Of course, in all this the priority of external nature remains unassailed, and all this has no application to the original men produced by *generatio aequivoca*; [1] but this differentiation has meaning only insofar as man is considered to be distinct from nature. For that matter, nature, the nature that preceded human history, is not by any means the nature in which Feuerbach lives, it is nature which today no longer exists anywhere (except perhaps on a few Australian coral-islands of recent origin) and which, therefore, does not exist for Feuerbach.

Certainly Feuerbach has a great advantage over the "pure" materialists in that he realises how man too is an "object of the senses." But apart from the fact that he only conceives him as an "object of the senses," not as "sensuous activity," because he still remains in the realm of theory and conceives of men not in their given social connection, not under their existing conditions of life, which have made them what they are, he never arrives at the really existing active men, but stops at the abstraction "man," and gets no further than recognising "the true, individual, corporeal man" emotionally, i.e., he knows no other "human relationships" "of man to man" than love and friendship, and even then idealised. He gives no criticism of the present conditions of life. Thus he never manages to conceive the sensuous world as the total living sensuous *activity* of the individuals composing it; and therefore when, for example, he sees instead of healthy men a crowd of scrofulous, overworked and consumptive starvelings, he is compelled to take refuge in the "higher perception" and in the ideal "compensation in the species," and thus to relapse into idealism at the very point where the communist materialist sees the necessity, and at the same time the condition, of a transformation both of industry and of the social structure.

As far as Feuerbach is a materialist he does not deal with history, and as far as he considers history he is not a materialist. With him

1. Spontaneous generation.

materialism and history diverge completely, a fact which incidentally is already obvious from what has been said.

History is nothing but the succession of the separate generations, each of which exploits the materials, the capital funds, the productive forces handed down to it by all preceding generations, and thus, on the one hand, continues the traditional activity in completely changed circumstances and, on the other, modifies the old circumstances with a completely changed activity. This can be speculatively distorted so that later history is made the goal of earlier history, e.g., the goal ascribed to the discovery of America is to further the eruption of the French Revolution. Thereby history receives its own special aims and becomes "a person ranking with other persons" (to wit: "Self-Consciousness, Criticism, the Unique," etc.), while what is designated with the words "destiny," "goal," "germ," or "ideal" of earlier history is nothing more than an abstraction formed from later history, from the active influence which earlier history exercises on later history.

The further the separate spheres, which act on one another, extend in the course of this development, the more the original isolation of the separate nationalities is destroyed by the developed mode of production and intercourse and the division of labour between various nations naturally brought forth by these, the more history becomes world history. Thus, for instance, if in England a machine is invented, which deprives countless workers of bread in India and China, and overturns the whole form of existence of these empires, this invention becomes a world-historical fact. Or again, take the case of sugar and coffee which have proved their world-historical importance in the nineteenth century by the fact that the lack of these products, occasioned by the Napoleonic Continental System, caused the Germans to rise against Napoleon, and thus became the real basis of the glorious Wars of Liberation of 1813. From this it follows that this transformation of history into world history is not indeed a mere abstract act on the part of the "self-consciousness," the world spirit, or of any other metaphysical spectre, but a quite material, empirically verifiable act, an act the proof of which every individual furnishes as he comes and goes, eats, drinks and clothes himself.

The ideas of the ruling class are in every epoch the ruling ideas: i.e., the class which is the ruling *material* force of society, is at the same time its ruling *intellectual* force. The class which has the means of material production at its disposal, has control at the same time over the means of mental production, so that thereby, generally speaking, the ideas of those who lack the means of mental production are subject to it. The ruling ideas are nothing more than the ideal expression of the dominant material relationships, the dom-

inant material relationships grasped as ideas; hence of the relationships which make the one class the ruling one, therefore, the ideas
of its dominance. The individuals composing the ruling class possess
among other things consciousness, and therefore think. Insofar,
therefore, as they rule as a class and determine the extent and compass of an epoch, it is self-evident that they do this in its whole
range, hence among other things rule also as thinkers, as producers
of ideas, and regulate the production and distribution of the ideas
of their age: thus their ideas are the ruling ideas of the epoch. For
instance, in an age and in a country where royal power, aristocracy
and bourgeoisie are contending for mastery and where, therefore,
mastery is shared, the doctrine of the separation of powers proves
to be the dominant idea and is expressed as an "eternal law."

The division of labour, which we have already seen above as
one of the chief forces of history up till now, manifests itself also
in the ruling class as the division of mental and material labour, so
that inside this class one part appears as the thinkers of the class
(its active, conceptive ideologists, who make the perfecting of the
illusion of the class about itself their chief source of livelihood),
while the others' attitude to these ideas and illusions is more passive and receptive, because they are in reality the active members of
this class and have less time to make up illusions and ideas about
themselves. Within this class this cleavage can even develop into a
certain opposition and hostility between the two parts, which, however, in the case of a practical collision, in which the class itself is
endangered, automatically comes to nothing, in which case there
also vanishes the semblance that the ruling ideas were not the ideas
of the ruling class and had a power distinct from the power of this
class. The existence of revolutionary ideas in a particular period presupposes the existence of a revolutionary class; about the premises
for the latter sufficient has already been said above.

If now in considering the course of history we detach the ideas
of the ruling class from the ruling class itself and attribute to them
an independent existence, if we confine ourselves to saying that
these or those ideas were dominant at a given time, without bother-
ing ourselves about the conditions of production and the producers
of these ideas, if we thus ignore the individuals and world conditions which are the source of the ideas, we can say, for instance,
that during the time that the aristocracy was dominant, the concepts honour, loyalty, etc., were dominant, during the dominance
of the bourgeoisie the concepts freedom, equality, etc. The ruling
class itself on the whole imagines this to be so. This conception of
history, which is common to all historians, particularly since the
eighteenth century, will necessarily come up against the phenomenon that increasingly abstract ideas hold sway, i.e., ideas which

increasingly take on the form of universality. For each new class which puts itself in the place of one ruling before it, is compelled, merely in order to carry through its aim, to represent its interest as the common interest of all the members of society, that is, expressed in ideal form: it has to give its ideas the form of universality, and represent them as the only rational, universally valid ones. The class making a revolution appears from the very start, if only because it is opposed to a *class*, not as a class but as the representative of the whole of society; it appears as the whole mass of society confronting the one ruling class.[2] It can do this because, to start with, its interest really is more connected with the common interest of all other non-ruling classes, because under the pressure of hitherto existing conditions its interest has not yet been able to develop as the particular interest of a particular class. Its victory, therefore, benefits also many individuals of the other classes which are not winning a dominant position, but only insofar as it now puts these individuals in a position to raise themselves into the ruling class. When the French bourgeoisie overthrew the power of the aristocracy, it thereby made it possible for many proletarians to raise themselves above the proletariat, but only insofar as they became bourgeois. Every new class, therefore, achieves its hegemony only on a broader basis than that of the class ruling previously, whereas the opposition of the non-ruling class against the new ruling class later develops all the more sharply and profoundly. Both these things determine the fact that the struggle to be waged against this new ruling class, in its turn, aims at a more decided and radical negation of the previous conditions of society than could all previous classes which sought to rule.

This whole semblance, that the rule of a certain class is only the rule of certain ideas, comes to a natural end, of course, as soon as class rule in general ceases to be the form in which society is organised, that is to say, as soon as it is no longer necessary to represent a particular interest as general or the "general interest" as ruling.

Once the ruling ideas have been separated from the ruling individuals and, above all, from the relationships which result from a given stage of the mode of production, and in this way the conclusion has been reached that history is always under the sway of ideas, it is very easy to abstract from these various ideas "*the* idea," the notion, etc., as the dominant force in history, and thus to understand all these separate ideas and concepts as "forms of self-determination" on the part of *the* concept developing in history. It

2. Marginal note by Marx: "Universality corresponds to (1) the class versus the estate, (2) the competition, world-wide intercourse, etc., (3) the great numerical strength of the ruling class, (4) the illusion of the *common* interests (in the beginning this illusion is true), (5) the delusion of the ideologists and the division of labour."

follows then naturally, too, that all the relationships of men can be derived from the concept of man, man as conceived, the essence of man, *Man*. This has been done by the speculative philosophers. Hegel himself confesses at the end of the *Geschichtsphilosophie* that he "has considered the progress of the *concept* only" and has represented in history the "true *theodicy*." Now one can go back again to the producers of the "concept," to the theorists, ideologists and philosophers, and one comes then to the conclusion that the philosophers, the thinkers as such, have at all times been dominant in history: a conclusion, as we see, already expressed by Hegel. The whole trick of proving the hegemony of the spirit in history (hierarchy Stirner calls it) is thus confined to the following three efforts.

No. 1. One must separate the ideas of those ruling for empirical reasons, under empirical conditions and as empirical individuals, from these actual rulers, and thus recognise the rule of ideas or illusions in history.

No. 2. One must bring an order into this rule of ideas, prove a mystical connection among the successive ruling ideas, which is managed by understanding them as "acts of self-determination on the part of the concept" (this is possible because by virtue of their empirical basis these ideas are really connected with one another and because, conceived as *mere* ideas, they become self-distinctions, distinctions made by thought).

No. 3. To remove the mystical appearance of this "self-determining concept" it is changed into a person—"Self-Consciousness"— or, to appear thoroughly materialistic, into a series of persons, who represent the "concept" in history, into the "thinkers," the "philosophers," the ideologists, who again are understood as the manufacturers of history, as the "council of guardians," as the rulers.[3] Thus the whole body of materialistic elements has been removed from history and now full rein can be given to the speculative steed.

Whilst in ordinary life every shopkeeper is very well able to distinguish between what somebody professes to be and what he really is, our historians have not yet won even this trivial insight. They take every epoch at its word and believe that everything it says and imagines about itself is true.

This historical method which reigned in Germany and especially the reason why, must be understood from its connection with the illusion of ideologists in general, e.g., the illusions of the jurists, politicians (of the practical statesmen among them, too), from the dogmatic dreamings and distortions of these fellows; this is explained perfectly easily from their practical position in life, their job, and the division of labour.

3. Marginal note by Marx: "Man = the 'rational human spirit.'"

[B. THE REAL BASIS OF IDEOLOGY][4]

1. *Intercourse and Productive Forces*

The greatest division of material and mental labour is the separation of town and country. The antagonism between town and country begins with the transition from barbarism to civilisation, from tribe to State, from locality to nation, and runs through the whole history of civilisation to the present day (the Anti-Corn Law League).

The existence of the town implies, at the same time, the necessity of administration, police, taxes, etc., in short, of the municipality, and thus of politics in general. Here first became manifest the division of the population into two great classes, which is directly based on the division of labour and on the instruments of production. The town already is in actual fact the concentration of the population, of the instruments of production, of capital, of pleasures, of needs, while the country demonstrates just the opposite fact, isolation and separation. The antagonism between town and country can only exist within the framework of private property. It is the most crass expression of the subjection of the individual under the division of labour, under a definite activity forced upon him—a subjection which makes one man into a restricted town-animal, the other into a restricted country-animal, and daily creates anew the conflict between their interests. Labour is here again the chief thing, power *over* individuals, and as long as the latter exists, private property must exist. The abolition of the antagonism between town and country is one of the first conditions of communal life, a condition which again depends on a mass of material premises and which cannot be fulfilled by the mere will, as anyone can see at the first glance. (These conditions have still to be enumerated.) The separation of town and country can also be understood as the separation of capital and landed property, as the beginning of the existence and development of capital independent of landed property—the beginning of property having its basis only in labour and exchange.

In the towns which, in the Middle Ages, did not derive ready-made from an earlier period but were formed anew by the serfs who had become free, each man's own particular labour was his only property apart from the small capital he brought with him, consisting almost solely of the most necessary tools of his craft. The competition of serfs constantly escaping into the town, the con-

4. Brackets indicate a sub-heading added by the editors. [*R. T.*]

stant war of the country against the towns and thus the necessity of an organised municipal military force, the bond of common ownership in a particular kind of labour, the necessity of common buildings for sale of their wares at a time when craftsmen were also traders, and the consequent exclusion of the unauthorised from these buildings, the conflict among the interests of the various crafts, the necessity of protecting their laboriously acquired skill, and the feudal organisation of the whole of the country: these were the causes of the union of the workers of each craft in guilds. We have not at this point to go further into the manifold modifications of the guild-system, which arise through later historical developments. The flight of the serfs into the towns went on without interruption right through the Middle Ages. These serfs, persecuted by their lords in the country, came separately into the towns, where they found an organised community, against which they were powerless and in which they had to subject themselves to the station assigned to them by the demand for their labour and the interest of their organised urban competitors. These workers, entering separately, were never able to attain to any power, since, if their labour was of the guild type which had to be learned, the guild-masters bent them to their will and organised them according to their interest; or if their labour was not such as had to be learned, and therefore not of the guild type, they became day-labourers and never managed to organise, remaining an unorganised rabble. The need for day-labourers in the towns created the rabble.

These towns were true "associations," called forth by the direct need, the care of providing for the protection of property, and of multiplying the means of production and defence of the separate members. The rabble of these towns was devoid of any power, composed as it was of individuals strange to one another who had entered separately, and who stood unorganised over against an organised power, armed for war, and jealously watching over them. The journeymen and apprentices were organised in each craft as it best suited the interest of the masters. The patriarchal relationship existing between them and their masters gave the latter a double power—on the one hand because of their influence on the whole life of the journeymen, and on the other because, for the journeymen who worked with the same master, it was a real bond which held them together against the journeymen of other masters and separated them from these. And finally, the journeymen were bound to the existing order by their simple interest in becoming masters themselves. While, therefore, the rabble at least carried out revolts against the whole municipal order, revolts which remained completely ineffective because of their powerlessness, the journeymen never got further than small acts of insubordination within separate guilds, such as belong to the very nature of the guild system. The great risings of the Middle Ages all radiated from the country, but equally remained totally ineffective because of the isolation and consequent crudity of the peasants.

In the towns, the division of labour between the individual guilds was as yet [quite naturally derived] and, in the guilds themselves, not at all developed between the individual workers. Every workman had to be versed in a whole round of tasks, had to be able to make everything that was to be made with his tools. The limited commerce and the scanty communication between the individual towns, the lack of population and the narrow needs did not allow of a higher division of labour, and therefore every man who wished to become a master had to be proficient in the whole of his craft. Thus there is found with medieval craftsmen an interest in their special work and in proficiency in it, which was capable of rising to a narrow artistic sense. For this very reason, however, every medieval craftsman was completely absorbed in his work, to which he had a contented, slavish relationship, and to which he was subjected to a far greater extent than the modern worker, whose work is a matter of indifference to him.

Capital in these towns was a naturally derived capital, consisting of a house, the tools of the craft, and the natural, hereditary customers; and not being realisable, on account of the backwardness of commerce and the lack of circulation, it descended from father to son. Unlike modern capital, which can be assessed in money and which may be indifferently invested in this thing or that, this capital was directly connected with the particular work of the owner, inseparable from it and to this extent *estate* capital.

The next extension of the division of labour was the separation of production and commerce, the formation of a special class of merchants; a separation which, in the towns bequeathed by a former period, had been handed down (among other things with the Jews) and which very soon appeared in the newly formed ones. With this there was given the possibility of commercial communications transcending the immediate neighbourhood, a possibility, the realisation of which depended on the existing means of communication, the state of public safety in the countryside, which was determined by political conditions (during the whole of the Middle Ages, as is well known, the merchants travelled in armed caravans), and on the cruder or more advanced needs (determined by the stage of culture attained) of the region accessible to intercourse.

With commerce the prerogative of a particular class, with the extension of trade through the merchants beyond the immediate surroundings of the town, there immediately appears a reciprocal action between production and commerce. The towns enter into relations *with one another*, new tools are brought from one town into the other, and the separation between production and commerce soon calls forth a new division of production between the individual towns, each of which is soon exploiting a predominant branch of industry. The local restrictions of earlier times begin gradually to be broken down.

In the Middle Ages the citizens in each town were compelled to unite against the landed nobility to save their skins. The extension of trade, the establishment of communications, led the separate towns to get to know other towns, which had asserted the same interests in the struggle with the same antagonist. Out of the many local corporations of burghers there arose only gradually the burgher *class*. The conditions of life of the individual burghers became, on account of their contradiction to the existing relationships and of the mode of labour determined by these, conditions which were common to them all and independent of each individual. The burghers had created the conditions insofar as they had torn themselves free from feudal ties, and were created by them insofar as they were determined by their antagonism to the feudal system which they found in existence. When the individual towns began to enter into associations, these common conditions developed into class conditions. The same conditions, the same contradiction, the same interests necessarily called forth on the whole similar customs everywhere. The bourgeoisie itself, with its conditions, develops only gradually, splits according to the division of labour into various fractions and finally absorbs all propertied classes it finds in existence[5] (while it develops the majority of the earlier propertyless and a part of the hitherto propertied classes into a new class, the proletariat) in the measure to which all property found in existence is transformed into industrial or commercial capital. The separate individuals form a class only insofar as they have to carry on a common battle against another class; otherwise they are on hostile terms with each other as competitors. On the other hand, the class in its turn achieves an independent existence over against the individuals, so that the latter find their conditions of existence predestined, and hence have their position in life and their personal development assigned to them by their class, become subsumed under it. This is the same phenomenon as the subjection of the separate individuals to the division of labour and can only be removed by the abolition of private property and of labour itself. We have already indicated several times how this subsuming of individuals under the class brings with it their subjection to all kinds of ideas, etc.

5. Marginal note by Marx: "To begin with it absorbs the branches of labour directly belonging to the State and then all ± [more or less] ideological estates."

It depends purely on the extension of commerce whether the productive forces achieved in a locality, especially inventions, are lost for later development or not. As long as there exists no commerce transcending the immediate neighbourhood, every invention must be made separately in each locality, and mere chances such as irruptions of barbaric peoples, even ordinary wars, are sufficient to cause a country with advanced productive forces and needs to have to start right over again from the beginning. In primitive history every invention had to be made daily anew and in each locality independently. How little highly developed productive forces are safe from complete destruction, given even a relatively very extensive commerce, is proved by the Phoenicians,[6] whose inventions were for the most part lost for a long time to come through the ousting of this nation from commerce, its conquest by Alexander and its consequent decline. Likewise, for instance, glass-painting in the Middle Ages. Only when commerce has become world commerce and has as its basis large-scale industry, when all nations are drawn into the competitive struggle, is the permanence of the acquired productive forces assured.

The immediate consequence of the division of labour between the various towns was the rise of manufactures, branches of production which had outgrown the guild-system. Manufactures first flourished, in Italy and later in Flanders, under the historical premise of commerce with foreign nations. In other countries, England and France for example, manufactures were at first confined to the home market. Besides the premises already mentioned manufactures depend on an already advanced concentration of population, particularly in the countryside, and of capital, which began to accumulate in the hands of individuals, partly in the guilds in spite of the guild regulations, partly among the merchants.

That labour which from the first presupposed a machine, even of the crudest sort, soon showed itself the most capable of development. Weaving, earlier carried on in the country by the peasants as a secondary occupation to procure their clothing, was the first labour to receive an impetus and a further development through the extension of commerce. Weaving was the first and remained the principal manufacture. The rising demand for clothing materials, consequent on the growth of population, the growing accumulation and mobilisation of natural capital through accelerated circulation, the demand for luxuries called forth by the latter and favoured generally by the gradual extension of commerce, gave weaving a quantitative and qualitative stimulus, which wrenched it out of the form of production hitherto existing. Alongside the peas-

6. Marginal note by Marx: "and the manufacture of glass in the Middle Ages."

ants weaving for their own use, who continued, and still continue, with this sort of work, there emerged a new class of weavers in the towns, whose fabrics were destined for the whole home market and usually for foreign markets too.

Weaving, an occupation demanding in most cases little skill and soon splitting up into countless branches, by its whole nature resisted the trammels of the guild. Weaving was, therefore, carried on mostly in villages and market centres without guild organisation, which gradually became towns, and indeed the most flourishing towns in each land.

With guild-free manufacture, property relations also quickly changed. The first advance beyond naturally derived estate capital was provided by the rise of merchants whose capital was from the beginning movable, capital in the modern sense as far as one can speak of it, given the circumstances of those times. The second advance came with manufacture, which again made mobile a mass of natural capital, and altogether increased the mass of movable capital as against that of natural capital.

At the same time, manufacture became a refuge of the peasants from the guilds which excluded them or paid them badly, just as earlier the guild-towns had [served] as a refuge for the peasants from [the oppressive landed nobility].

Simultaneously with the beginning of manufactures there was a period of vagabondage caused by the abolition of the feudal bodies of retainers, the disbanding of the swollen armies which had flocked to serve the kings against their vassals, the improvement of agriculture, and the transformation of great strips of tillage into pasture land. From this alone it is clear how this vagabondage is strictly connected with the disintergration of the feudal system. As early as the thirteenth century we find isolated epochs of this kind, but only at the end of the fifteenth and beginning of the sixteenth does this vagabondage make a general and permanent appearance. These vagabonds, who were so numerous that, for instance, Henry VIII of England had 72,000 of them hanged, were only prevailed upon to work with the greatest difficulty and through the most extreme necessity, and then only after long resistance. The rapid rise of manufactures, particularly in England, absorbed them gradually.

With the advent of manufactures, the various nations entered into a competitive relationship, the struggle for trade, which was fought out in wars, protective duties and prohibitions, whereas earlier the nations, insofar as they were connected at all, had carried on an inoffensive exchange with each other. Trade had from now on a political significance.

With the advent of manufacture the relationship between worker and employer changed. In the guilds the patriarchal relationship between journeyman and master continued to exist; in manufacture its place was taken by the monetary relation between worker and capitalist—a relationship which in the countryside and in small towns retained a patriarchal tinge, but in the larger, the real manufacturing towns, quite early lost almost all patriarchal complexion.

Manufacture and the movement of production in general received an enormous impetus through the extension of commerce which came with the discovery of America and the sea-route to the East Indies. The new products imported thence, particularly the masses of gold and silver which came into circulation and totally changed the position of the classes towards one another, dealing a hard blow to feudal landed property and to the workers; the expeditions of adventurers, colonisation; and above all the extension of markets into a world market, which had now become possible and was daily becoming more and more a fact, called forth a new phase of historical development, into which in general we cannot here enter further. Through the colonisation of the newly discovered countries the commercial struggle of the nations amongst one another was given new fuel and accordingly greater extension and animosity.

The expansion of trade and manufacture accelerated the accumulation of movable capital, while in the guilds, which were not stimulated to extend their production, natural capital remained stationary or even declined. Trade and manufacture created the big bourgeoisie; in the guilds was concentrated the petty bourgeoisie, which no longer was dominant in the towns as formerly, but had to bow to the might of the great merchants and manufacturers.[7] Hence the decline of the guilds, as soon as they came into contact with manufacture.

The intercourse of nations took on, in the epoch of which we have been speaking, two different forms. At first the small quantity of gold and silver in circulation involved the ban on the export of these metals; and industry, for the most part imported from abroad and made necessary by the need for employing the growing urban population, could not do without those privileges which could be granted not only, of course, against home competition, but chiefly against foreign. The local guild privilege was in these original prohibitions extended over the whole nation. Customs duties originated from the tributes which the feudal lords exacted as protective levies against robbery from merchants passing through their territories, tributes later imposed likewise by the towns, and which, with the

7. Marginal note by Marx: "Petty bourgeoisie—Middle class—Big bourgeoisie."

rise of the modern states, were the Treasury's most obvious means of raising money.

The appearance of American gold and silver on the European markets, the gradual development of industry, the rapid expansion of trade and the consequent rise of the non-guild bourgeoisie and of money, gave these measures another significance. The State, which was daily less and less able to do without money, now retained the ban on the export of gold and silver out of fiscal considerations; the bourgeois, for whom these masses of money which were hurled on to the market became the chief object of speculative buying, were thoroughly content with this; privileges established earlier became a source of income for the government and were sold for money; in the customs legislation there appeared the export duty, which, since it only [placed] a hindrance in the way of industry, had a purely fiscal aim.

The second period began in the middle of the seventeenth century and lasted almost to the end of the eighteenth. Commerce and navigation had expanded more rapidly than manufacture, which played a secondary role; the colonies were becoming considerable consumers; and after long struggles the separate nations shared out the opening world market among themselves. This period begins with the Navigation Laws and colonial monopolies. The competition of the nations among themselves was excluded as far as possible by tariffs, prohibitions and treaties; and in the last resort the competitive struggle was carried on and decided by wars (especially naval wars). The mightiest maritime nation, the English, retained preponderance in trade and manufacture. Here, already, we find concentration in one country.

Manufacture was all the time sheltered by protective duties in the home market, by monopolies in the colonial market, and abroad as much as possible by differential duties. The working-up of home-produced material was encouraged (wool and linen in England, silk in France), the export of home-produced raw material forbidden (wool in England), and the [working-up] of imported material neglected or suppressed (cotton in England). The nation dominant in sea trade and colonial power naturally secured for itself also the greatest quantitative and qualitative expansion of manufacture. Manufacture could not be carried on without protection, since, if the slightest change takes place in other countries, it can lose its market and be ruined; under reasonably favourable conditions it may easily be introduced into a country, but for this very reason can easily be destroyed. At the same time through the mode in which it is carried on, particularly in the eighteenth century, in the countryside, it is to such an extent interwoven with the vital relationships of a great mass of individuals, that no country dare jeopardise its existence by permitting free competition. Insofar as it manages to export, it therefore depends entirely on the extension or restriction of commerce, and exercises a relatively very small reaction [on the latter]. Hence its secondary [importance] and the influence of [the merchants] in the eighteenth century. It was the merchants and especially the shippers who more than anybody else pressed for State protection and monopolies; the manufacturers also demanded and indeed received protection, but all the time were inferior in political importance to the merchants. The commercial towns, particularly the maritime towns, became to some extent civilised and acquired the outlook of the big bourgeoisie, but in the factory towns an extreme petty-bourgeois outlook persisted. Cf. Aiken, etc. The eighteenth century was the century of trade. Pinto says this expressly: "*Le commerce fait la marotte du siècle*";[8] and: "*Depuis quelque temps il n'est plus question que de commerce, de navigation et de marine.*"[9]

This period is also characterised by the cessation of the bans on the export of gold and silver and the beginning of the trade in money; by banks, national debts, paper money; by speculation in stocks and shares and stockjobbing in all articles; by the development of finance in general. Again capital lost a great part of the natural character which had still clung to it.

The concentration of trade and manufacture in one country, England, developing irresistibly in the seventeenth century, gradually created for this country a relative world market, and thus a demand for the manufactured products of this country, which could no longer be met by the industrial productive forces hitherto existing. This demand, outgrowing the productive forces, was the motive power which, by producing big industry—the application of elemental forces to industrial ends, machinery and the most complex division of labour—called into existence the third period of private ownership since the Middle Ages. There already existed in England the other pre-conditions of this new phase: freedom of competition inside the nation, the development of theoretical mechanics, etc. (Indeed, the science of mechanics perfected by

8. "Commerce is the rage of the century."
9. "For some time now people have been talking only about commerce, navigation and the navy." [The movement of capital, although considerably accelerated, still remained, however, relatively slow. The splitting-up of the world market into separate parts, each of which was exploited by a particular nation, the exclusion of competition among themselves on the part of the nations, the clumsiness of production itself and the fact that finance was only evolving from its early stages, greatly impeded circulation. The consequence of this was a haggling, mean and niggardly spirit which still clung to all merchants and to the whole mode of carrying on trade. Compared with the manufacturers, and above all with the craftsmen, they were certainly big bourgeois; compared with the merchants and industrialists of the next period they remain petty bourgeois. Cf. Adam Smith.—*Marx*]

Newton was altogether the most popular science in France and England in the eighteenth century.) (Free competition inside the nation itself had everywhere to be conquered by a revolution—1640 and 1688 in England, 1789 in France.) Competition soon compelled every country that wished to retain its historical role to protect its manufactures by renewed customs regulations (the old duties were no longer any good against big industry) and soon after to introduce big industry under protective duties. Big industry universalised competition in spite of these protective measures (it is practical free trade; the protective duty is only a palliative, a measure of defence *within* free trade), established means of communication and the modern world market, subordinated trade to itself, transformed all capital into industrial capital, and thus produced the rapid circulation (development of the financial system) and the centralisation of capital. By universal competition it forced all individuals to strain their energy to the utmost. It destroyed as far as possible ideology, religion, morality, etc., and where it could not do this, made them into a palpable lie. It produced world history for the first time, insofar as it made all civilised nations and every individual member of them dependent for the satisfaction of their wants on the whole world, thus destroying the former natural exclusiveness of separate nations. It made natural science subservient to capital and took from the division of labour the last semblance of its natural character. It destroyed natural growth in general, as far as this is possible while labour exists, and resolved all natural relationships into money relationships. In the place of naturally grown towns it created the modern, large industrial cities which have sprung up overnight. Wherever it penetrated, it destroyed the crafts and all earlier stages of industry. It completed the victory of the commercial town over the countryside. [Its first premise] was the automatic system. [Its development] produced a mass of productive forces, for which private [property] became just as much a fetter as the guild had been for manufacture and the small, rural workshop for the developing craft. These productive forces received under the system of private property a one-sided development only, and became for the majority destructive forces; moreover, a great multitude of such forces could find no application at all within this system. Generally speaking, big industry created everywhere the same relations between the classes of society, and thus destroyed the peculiar individuality of the various nationalities. And finally, while the bourgeoisie of each nation still retained separate national interests, big industry created a class, which in all nations has the same interest and with which nationality is already dead; a class which is really rid of all the old world and at the same time stands pitted against it. Big industry makes for the worker not only the relation to the capitalist, but labour itself, unbearable.

It is evident that big industry does not reach the same level of development in all districts of a country. This does not, however, retard the class movement of the proletariat, because the proletarians created by big industry assume leadership of this movement and carry the whole mass along with them, and because the workers excluded from big industry are placed by it in a still worse situation than the workers in big industry itself. The countries in which big industry is developed act in a similar manner upon the more or less non-industrial countries, insofar as the latter are swept by universal commerce into the universal competitive struggle.[1]

These different forms are just so many forms of the organisation of labour, and hence of property. In each period a unification of the existing productive forces takes place, insofar as this has been rendered necessary by needs.

2. The Relation of State and Law to Property

The first form of property, in the ancient world as in the Middle Ages, is tribal property, determined with the Romans chiefly by war, with the Germans by the rearing of cattle. In the case of the ancient peoples, since several tribes live together in one town, the tribal property appears as State property, and the right of the individual to it as mere "possession" which, however, like tribal property as a whole, is confined to landed property only. Real private property began with the ancients, as with modern nations, with movable property.—(Slavery and community) (*dominium ex jure Quiritum*[2]). In the case of the nations which grew out of the Middle Ages, tribal property evolved through various stages—feudal landed property, corporative movable property, capital invested in manufacture—to modern capital, determined by big industry and universal competition, i.e., pure private property, which has cast off all semblance of a communal institution and has shut out the State from any influence on the development of property. To this

1. Competition separates individuals from one another, not only the bourgeois but still more the workers, in spite of the fact that it brings them together. Hence it is a long time before these individuals can unite, apart from the fact that for the purposes of this union—if it is not to be merely local—the necessary means, the great industrial cities and cheap and quick communications, have first to be produced by big industry. Hence every organised power standing over against these isolated individuals, who live in relationships daily reproducing this isolation, can only be overcome after long struggles. To demand the opposite would be tantamount to demanding that competition should not exist in this definite epoch of history, or that the individuals should banish from their minds relationships over which in their isolation they have no control. [*Marx*]

2. Ownership in accordance with the law applying to full Roman citizens.

modern private property corresponds the modern State, which, purchased gradually by the owners of property by means of taxation, has fallen entirely into their hands through the national debt, and its existence has become wholly dependent on the commercial credit which the owners of property, the bourgeois, extend to it, as reflected in the rise and fall of State funds on the stock exchange. By the mere fact that it is a *class* and no longer an *estate*, the bourgeoisie is forced to organise itself no longer locally, but nationally, and to give a general form to its mean average interest. Through the emancipation of private property from the community, the State has become a separate entity, beside and outside civil society; but it is nothing more than the form of organisation which the bourgeois necessarily adopt both for internal and external purposes, for the mutual guarantee of their property and interests. The independence of the State is only found nowadays in those countries where the estates have not yet completely developed into classes, where the estates, done away with in more advanced countries, still have a part to play, and where there exists a mixture; countries, that is to say, in which no one section of the population can achieve dominance over the others. This is the case particularly in Germany. The most perfect example of the modern State is North America. The modern French, English and American writers all express the opinion that the State exists only for the sake of private property, so that this fact has penetrated into the consciousness of the normal man.

Since the State is the form in which the individuals of a ruling class assert their common interests, and in which the whole civil society of an epoch is epitomised, it follows that the State mediates in the formation of all common institutions and that the institutions receive a political form. Hence the illusion that law is based on the will, and indeed on the will divorced from its real basis— on *free* will. Similarly, justice is in its turn reduced to the actual laws.

Civil law develops simultaneously with private property out of the disintegration of the natural community. With the Romans the development of private property and civil law had no further industrial and commercial consequences, because their whole mode of production did not alter.[3] With modern peoples, where the feudal community was disintegrated by industry and trade, there began with the rise of private property and civil law a new phase, which was capable of further development. The very first town which carried on an extensive maritime trade in the Middle Ages, Amalfi, also developed maritime law. As soon as industry and trade developed private property further, first in Italy and later in other coun-

3. Marginal note by Engels: "(Usury!)"

tries, the highly developed Roman civil law was immediately adopted again and raised to authority. When later the bourgeoisie had acquired so much power that the princes took up its interests in order to overthrow the feudal nobility by means of the bourgeoisie, there began in all countries—in France in the sixteenth century —the real development of law, which in all countries except England proceeded on the basis of the Roman Codex. In England, too, Roman legal principles had to be introduced to further the development of civil law (especially in the case of movable property). (It must not be forgotten that law has just as little an independent history as religion.)

In civil law the existing property relationships are declared to be the result of the general will. The *jus utendi et abutendi*[4] itself asserts on the one hand the fact that private property has become entirely independent of the community, and on the other the illusion that private property itself is based solely on the private will, the arbitrary disposal of the thing. In practice, the *abuti*[5] has very definite economic limitations for the owner of private property, if he does not wish to see his property and hence his *jus abutendi* pass into other hands, since actually the thing, considered merely with reference to his will, is not a thing at all, but only becomes a thing, true property in intercourse, and independently of the law (a *relationship,* which the philosophers call an idea[6]). This juridical illusion, which reduces law to the mere will, necessarily leads, in the further development of property relationships, to the position that a man may have a legal title to a thing without really having the thing. If, for instance, the income from a piece of land is lost owing to competition, then the proprietor has certainly his legal title to it along with the *jus utendi et abutendi.* But he can do nothing with it: he owns nothing as a landed proprietor if in addition he has not enough capital to cultivate his ground. This illusion of the jurists also explains the fact that for them, as for every code, it is altogether fortuitous that individuals enter into relationships among themselves (e.g., contracts); it explains why they consider that these relationships [can] be entered into or not at will, and that their content rests purely on the individual [free] will of the contracting parties.

Whenever, through the development of industry and commerce, new forms of intercourse have been evolved (e.g., ensurance companies, etc.), the law has always been compelled to admit them among the modes of acquiring property.

4. The right of using and consuming (also: abusing), i.e., of disposing of a thing at will.
5. Consuming or abusing.
6. Marginal note by Marx: *"For the philosophers relationship = idea.* They only know the relation of 'Man' to himself and hence for them all real relations become ideas."

[3. *Natural and Civilised Instruments of Production and Forms
of Property*]

* * *[7] From the first, there follows the premise of a highly developed division of labour and an extensive commerce; from the
second, the locality. In the first case the individuals must be
brought together, in the second they find themselves alongside the
given instrument of production as instruments of production themselves. Here, therefore, arises the difference between natural instruments of production and those created by civilisation. The field
(water, etc.) can be regarded as a natural instrument of production. In the first case, that of the natural instrument of production,
individuals are subservient to nature; in the second, to a product of
labour. In the first case, therefore, property (landed property)
appears as direct natural domination, in the second, as domination
of labour, particularly of accumulated labour, capital. The first case
presupposes that the individuals are united by some bond: family,
tribe, the land itself, etc.; the second, that they are independent of
one another and are only held together by exchange. In the first
case, what is involved is chiefly an exchange between men and
nature in which the labour of the former is exchanged for the products of the latter; in the second, it is predominantly an exchange of
men among themselves. In the first case, average, human common
sense is adequate—physical activity is as yet not separated from
mental activity; in the second, the division between physical and
mental labour must already be practically completed. In the first
case, the domination of the proprietor over the propertyless may be
based on a personal relationship, on a kind of community; in the
second, it must have taken on a material shape in a third party—
money. In the first case, small industry exists, but determined by
the utilisation of the natural instrument of production and therefore without the distribution of labour among various individuals;
in the second, industry exists only in and through the division of
labour.

Our investigation hitherto started from the instruments of production, and it has already shown that private property was a necessity for certain industrial stages. In *industrie extractive* private property still coincides with labour; in small industry and all agriculture
up till now property is the necessary consequence of the existing
instruments of production; in big industry the contradiction
between the instrument of production and private property appears
for the first time and is the product of big industry; moreover, big
industry must be highly developed to produce this contradiction.

7. Four pages of the manuscript are missing here.

And thus only with big industry does the abolition of private property become possible.

In big industry and competition the whole mass of conditions of existence, limitations, biases of individuals, are fused together into the two simplest forms: private property and labour. With money every form of intercourse, and intercourse itself, is considered fortuitous for the individuals. Thus money implies that all previous intercourse was only intercourse of individuals under particular conditions, not of individuals as individuals. These conditions are reduced to two: accumulated labour or private property, and actual labour. If both or one of these ceases, then intercourse comes to a standstill. The modern economists themselves, e.g., Sismondi, Cherbuliez, etc., oppose "association of individuals" to "association of capital." On the other hand, the individuals themselves are entirely subordinated to the division of labour and hence are brought into the most complete dependence on one another. Private property, insofar as within labour itself it is opposed to labour, evolves out of the necessity of accumulation, and has still, to begin with, rather the form of the communality; but in its further development it approaches more and more the modern form of private property. The division of labour implies from the outset the division of the *conditions* of labour, of tools and materials, and thus the splitting-up of accumulated capital among different owners, and thus, also, the division between capital and labour, and the different forms of property itself. The more the division of labour develops and accumulation grows, the sharper are the forms that this process of differentiation assumes. Labour itself can only exist on the premise of this fragmentation.

Thus two facts are here revealed.[8] First the productive forces appear as a world for themselves, quite independent of and divorced from the individuals, alongside the individuals: the reason for this is that the individuals, whose forces they are, exist split up and in opposition to one another, whilst, on the other hand, these forces are only real forces in the intercourse and association of these individuals. Thus, on the one hand, we have a totality of productive forces, which have, as it were, taken on a material form and are for the individuals no longer the forces of the individuals but of private property, and hence of the individuals only insofar as they are owners of private property themselves. Never, in any earlier period, have the productive forces taken on a form so indifferent to the intercourse of individuals *as* individuals, because their intercourse itself was formerly a restricted one. On the other hand, standing over against these productive forces, we have the majority of the individuals from whom these forces have been wrested away,

8. Marginal note by Engels: "Sismondi."

and who, robbed thus of all real life-content, have become abstract individuals, but who are, however, only by this fact put into a position to enter into relation with one another *as individuals.*

The only connection which still links them with the productive forces and with their own existence—labour—has lost all semblance of self-activity and only sustains their life by stunting it. While in the earlier periods self-activity and the production of material life were separated, in that they devolved on different persons, and while, on account of the narrowness of the individuals themselves, the production of material life was considered as a subordinate mode of self-activity, they now diverge to such an extent that altogether material life appears as the end, and what produces this material life, labour (which is now the only possible but, as we see, negative form of self-activity), as the means.

Thus things have now come to such a pass, that the individuals must appropriate the existing totality of productive forces, not only to achieve self-activity, but, also, merely to safeguard their very existence. This appropriation is first determined by the object to be appropriated, the productive forces, which have been developed to a totality and which only exist within a universal intercourse. From this aspect alone, therefore, this appropriation must have a universal character corresponding to the productive forces and the intercourse. The appropriation of these forces is itself nothing more than the development of the individual capacities corresponding to the material instruments of production. The appropriation of a totality of instruments of production is, for this very reason, the development of a totality of capacities in the individuals themselves. This appropriation is further determined by the persons appropriating. Only the proletarians of the present day, who are completely shut off from all self-activity, are in a position to achieve a complete and no longer restricted self-activity, which consists in the appropriation of a totality of productive forces and in the thus postulated development of a totality of capacities. All earlier revolutionary appropriations were restricted; individuals, whose self-activity was restricted by a crude instrument of production and a limited intercourse, appropriated this crude instrument of production, and hence merely achieved a new state of limitation. Their instrument of production became their property, but they themselves remained subordinate to the division of labour and their own instrument of production. In all expropriations up to now, a mass of individuals remained subservient to a single instrument of production; in the appropriation by the proletarians, a mass of instruments of production must be made subject to each individual, and property to all. Modern universal intercourse can be controlled by individuals, therefore, only when controlled by all.

This appropriation is further determined by the manner in which it must be effected. It can only be effected through a union, which by the character of the proletariat itself can again only be a universal one, and through a revolution, in which, on the one hand, the power of the earlier mode of production and intercourse and social organisation is overthrown, and, on the other hand, there develops the universal character and the energy of the proletariat, without which the revolution cannot be accomplished; and in which, further, the proletariat rids itself of everything that still clings to it from its previous position in society.

Only at this stage does self-activity coincide with material life, which corresponds to the development of individuals into complete individuals and the casting-off of all natural limitations. The transformation of labour into self-activity corresponds to the transformation of the earlier limited intercourse into the intercourse of individuals as such. With the appropriation of the total productive forces through united individuals, private property comes to an end. Whilst previously in history a particular condition always appeared as accidental, now the isolation of individuals and the particular private gain of each man have themselves become accidental.

The individuals, who are no longer subject to the division of labour, have been conceived by the philosophers as an ideal, under the name "Man." They have conceived the whole process which we have outlined as the evolutionary process of "Man," so that at every historical stage "Man" was substituted for the individuals and shown as the motive force of history. The whole process was thus conceived as a process of the self-estrangement of "Man," and this was essentially due to the fact that the average individual of the later stage was always foisted on to the earlier stage, and the consciousness of a later age on to the individuals of an earlier. Through this inversion, which from the first is an abstract image of the actual conditions, it was possible to transform the whole of history into an evolutionary process of consciousness.

Finally, from the conception of history we have sketched we obtain these further conclusions: (1) In the development of productive forces there comes a stage when productive forces and means of intercourse are brought into being, which, under the existing relationships, only cause mischief, and are no longer productive but destructive forces (machinery and money); and connected with this a class is called forth, which has to bear all the burdens of society without enjoying its advantages, which, ousted from society, is forced into the most decided antagonism to all other classes; a class which forms the majority of all members of society, and from which emanates the consciousness of the necessity of a fundamental revolution, the communist consciousness, which may, of course, arise among the other classes too through the contemplation of the situation of this class. (2) The conditions under which definite productive forces can be applied, are the conditions of the rule of a definite class of society, whose social power, deriving from its property, has its *practical*-idealistic expression in each case in the form of the State; and, therefore, every revolutionary struggle is directed against a class, which till then has been in power.[9] (3) In all revolutions up till now the mode of activity always remained unscathed and it was only a question of a different distribution of this activity, a new distribution of labour to other persons, whilst the communist revolution is directed against the preceding *mode* of activity, does away with *labour*, and abolishes the rule of all classes with the classes themselves, because it is carried through by the class which no longer counts as a class in society, is not recognised as a class, and is in itself the expression of the dissolution of all classes, nationalities, etc., within present society; and (4) Both for the production on a mass scale of this communist consciousness, and for the success of the cause itself, the alteration of men on a mass scale is necessary, an alteration which can only take place in a practical movement, a *revolution*; this revolution is necessary, therefore, not only because the *ruling* class cannot be overthrown in any other way, but also because the class *overthrowing* it can only in a revolution succeed in ridding itself of all the muck of ages and become fitted to found society anew.

C. COMMUNISM. THE PRODUCTION OF THE FORM OF INTERCOURSE ITSELF

Communism differs from all previous movements in that it overturns the basis of all earlier relations of production and intercourse, and for the first time consciously treats all natural premises as the creatures of hitherto existing men, strips them of their natural character and subjugates them to the power of the united individuals. Its organisation is, therefore, essentially economic, the material production of the conditions of this unity; it turns existing conditions into conditions of unity. The reality, which communism is creating, is precisely the true basis for rendering it impossible that anything should exist independently of individuals, insofar as reality is only a product of the preceding intercourse of individuals themselves. Thus the communists in practice treat the conditions created up to now by production and intercourse as inorganic con-

9. Marginal note by Marx: 'The people are interested in maintaining the present state of production."

ditions, without, however, imagining that it was the plan or the destiny of previous generations to give them material, and without believing that these conditions were inorganic for the individuals creating them. The difference between the individual as a person and what is accidental to him is not a conceptual difference but a historical fact. This distinction has a different significance at different times—e.g., the estate as something accidental to the individual in the eighteenth century, the family more or less too. It is not a distinction that we have to make for each age, but one which each age makes itself from among the different elements which it finds in existence, and indeed not according to any theory, but compelled by material collisions in life. What appears accidental to the later age as opposed to the earlier—and this applies also to the elements handed down by an earlier age—is a form of intercourse which corresponded to a definite stage of development of the productive forces. The relation of the productive forces to the form of intercourse is the relation of the form of intercourse to the occupation or activity of the individuals. (The fundamental form of this activity is, of course, material, on which depend all other forms—mental, political, religious, etc. The various shaping of material life is, of course, in every case dependent on the needs which are already developed, and the production, as well as the satisfaction, of these needs is an historical process, which is not found in the case of a sheep or a dog. (Stirner's refractory principal argument *adversus hominem*), although sheep and dogs in their present form certainly, but *malgré eux*, are products of an historical process.) The conditions under which individuals have intercourse with each other, so long as the above-mentioned contradiction is absent, are conditions appertaining to their individuality, in no way external to them; conditions under which these definite individuals, living under definite relations, can alone produce their material life and what is connected with it, are thus the conditions of their self-activity and are produced by this self-activity.[1] The definite condition under which they produce, thus corresponds, as long as the contradiction has not yet appeared, to the reality of their conditioned nature, their one-sided existence, the one-sidedness of which only becomes evident when the contradiction enters on the scene and thus exists for the later individuals. Then this condition appears as an accidental fetter, and the consciousness that it is a fetter is imputed to the earlier age as well.

These various conditions, which appear first as conditions of self-activity, later as fetters upon it, form in the whole evolution of history a coherent series of forms of intercourse, the coherence of which consists in this: in the place of an earlier form of inter-

1. Marginal note by Marx: "Production of the form of intercourse itself."

course, which has become a fetter, a new one is put, corresponding to the more developed productive forces and, hence, to the advanced mode of the self-activity of individuals—a form which in its turn becomes a fetter and is then replaced by another. Since these conditions correspond at every stage to the simultaneous development of the productive forces, their history is at the same time the history of the evolving productive forces taken over by each new generation, and is, therefore, the history of the development of the forces of the individuals themselves.

Since this evolution takes place naturally, i.e., is not subordinated to a general plan of freely combined individuals, it proceeds from various localities, tribes, nations, branches of labour, etc., each of which to start with develops independently of the others and only gradually enters into relation with the others. Furthermore, it takes place only very slowly; the various stages and interests are never completely overcome, but only subordinated to the prevailing interest and trail along beside the latter for centuries afterwards. It follows from this that within a nation itself the individuals, even apart from their pecuniary circumstances, have quite different developments, and that an earlier interest, the peculiar form of intercourse of which has already been ousted by that belonging to a later interest, remains for a long time afterwards in possession of a traditional power in the illusory community (State, law), which has won an existence independent of the individuals; a power which in the last resort can only be broken by a revolution. This explains why, with reference to individual points which allow of a more general summing-up, consciousness can sometimes appear further advanced than the contemporary empirical relationships, so that in the struggles of a latter epoch one can refer to earlier theoreticians as authorities.

On the other hand, in countries which, like North America, begin in an already advanced historical epoch, the development proceeds very rapidly. Such countries have no other natural premises than the individuals, who settled there and were led to do so because the forms of intercourse of the old countries did not correspond to their wants. Thus they begin with the most advanced individuals of the old countries, and, therefore, with the correspondingly most advanced form of intercourse, before this form of intercourse has been able to establish itself in the old countries.[2] This is the case with all colonies, insofar as they are not mere military or trading stations. Carthage, the Greek colonies, and Iceland in the

2. Personal energy of the individuals of various nations—Germans and Americans—energy even through cross-breeding—hence the cretinism of the Germans; in France and England, etc., foreign peoples transplanted to an already developed soil, in America to an entirely new soil; in Germany the natural population quietly stayed where it was. [*Marx*]

eleventh and twelfth centuries, provide examples of this. A similar relationship issues from conquest, when a form of intercourse which has evolved on another soil is brought over complete to the conquered country: whereas in its home it was still encumbered with interests and relationships left over from earlier periods, here it can and must be established completely and without hindrance, if only to assure the conquerors' lasting power. (England and Naples after the Norman conquest, when they received the most perfect form of feudal organisation.)

Nothing is more common than the notion that in history up till now it has only been a question of *taking*. The barbarians *take* the Roman Empire, and this fact of taking is made to explain the transition from the old world to the feudal system. In this taking by barbarians, however, the question is, whether the nation which is conquered has evolved industrial productive forces, as is the case with modern peoples, or whether their productive forces are based for the most part merely on their association and on the community. Taking is further determined by the object taken. A banker's fortune, consisting of paper, cannot be taken at all, without the taker's submitting to the conditions of production and intercourse of the country taken. Similarly the total industrial capital of a modern industrial country. And finally, everywhere there is very soon an end to taking, and when there is nothing more to take, you have to set about producing. From this necessity of producing, which very soon asserts itself, it follows that the form of community adopted by the settling conquerors must correspond to the stage of development of the productive forces they find in existence; or, if this is not the case from the start, it must change according to the productive forces. By this, too, is explained the fact, which people profess to have noticed everywhere in the period following the migration of the peoples, namely, that the servant was master, and that the conquerors very soon took over language, culture and manners from the conquered. The feudal system was by no means brought complete from Germany, but had its origin, as far as the conquerors were concerned, in the martial organisation of the army during the actual conquest, and this only evolved after the conquest into the feudal system proper through the action of the productive forces found in the conquered countries. To what an extent this form was determined by the productive forces is shown by the abortive attempts to realise other forms derived from reminiscences of ancient Rome (Charlemagne, etc.).

Thus all collisions in history have their origin, according to our view, in the contradiction between the productive forces and the form of intercourse. Incidentally, to lead to collisions in a country, this contradiction need not necessarily have reached its extreme limit in this particular country. The competition with industrially more advanced countries, brought about by the expansion of international intercourse, is sufficient to produce a similar contradiction in countries with a backward industry (e.g., the latent proletariat in Germany brought into view by the competition of English industry).

This contradiction between the productive forces and the form of intercourse, which, as we saw, has occurred several times in past history, without, however, endangering the basis, necessarily on each occasion burst out in a revolution, taking on at the same time various subsidiary forms, such as all-embracing collisions, collisions of various classes, contradiction of consciousness, battle of ideas, etc., political conflict, etc. From a narrow point of view one may isolate one of these subsidiary forms and consider it as the basis of these revolutions; and this is all the more easy as the individuals who started the revolutions had illusions about their own activity according to their degree of culture and the stage of historical development.

The transformation, through the division of labour, of personal powers (relationships) into material powers, cannot be dispelled by dismissing the general idea of it from one's mind, but can only be abolished by the individuals again subjecting these material powers to themselves and abolishing the division of labour.[3] This is not possible without the community. Only in community [with others has each] individual the means of cultivating his gifts in all directions; only in the community, therefore, is personal freedom possible. In the previous substitutes for the community, in the State, etc., personal freedom has existed only for the individuals who developed within the relationships of the ruling class, and only insofar as they were individuals of this class. The illusory community, in which individuals have up till now combined, always took on an independent existence in relation to them, and was at the same time, since it was the combination of one class over against another, not only a completely illusory community, but a new fetter as well. In the real community the individuals obtain their freedom in and through their association.

It follows from all we have been saying up till now that the communal relationship into which the individuals of a class entered, and which was determined by their common interests over against a third party, was always a community to which these individuals belonged only as average individuals, only insofar as they lived within the conditions of existence of their class—a relationship in which they participated not as individuals but as members of a class. With the community of revolutionary proletarians, on the

3. Marginal note by Engels: '(Feuerbach: being and essence.)"

other hand, who take their conditions of existence and those of all members of society under their control, it is just the reverse; it is as individuals that the individuals participate in it. It is just this combination of individuals (assuming the advanced stage of modern productive forces, of course) which puts the conditions of the free development and movement of individuals under their control— conditions which were previously abandoned to chance and had won an independent existence over against the separate individuals just because of their separation as individuals, and because of the necessity of their combination which had been determined by the division of labour, and through their separation had become a bond alien to them. Combination up till now (by no means an arbitrary one, such as is expounded for example in the *Contrat social*, but a necessary one) was an agreement upon these conditions, within which the individuals were free to enjoy the freaks of fortune (compare, e.g., the formation of the North American State and the South American republics). This right to the undisturbed enjoyment, within certain conditions, of fortuity and chance has up till now been called personal freedom. These conditions of existence are, of course, only the productive forces and forms of intercourse at any particular time.

If from a *philosophical* point of view one considers this evolution of individuals in the common conditions of existence of estates and classes, which followed on one another, and in the accompanying general conceptions forced upon them, it is certainly very easy to imagine that in these individuals the species, or "Man," has evolved, or that they evolved "Man"—and in this way one can give history some hard clouts on the ear.[4] One can conceive these various estates and classes to be specific terms of the general expression, subordinate varieties of the species, or evolutionary phases of "Man."

This subsuming of individuals under definite classes cannot be abolished until a class has taken shape, which has no longer any particular class interest to assert against the ruling class.

Individuals have always built on themselves, but naturally on themselves within their given historical conditions and relationships, not on the "pure" individual in the sense of the ideologists. But in the course of historical evolution, and precisely through the inevitable fact that within the division of labour social relationships take on an independent existence, there appears a division within the life of each individual, insofar as it is personal and insofar as it

4. The statement which frequently occurs with Saint Max that each is all that he is through the State is fundamentally the same as the statement that bourgeois is only a specimen of the bourgeois species; a statement which presupposes that the *class* of bourgeois existed before the individuals constituting it. [*Marx*]
  Marginal note by Marx to this sentence: "With the philosophers *pre-existence* of the class."

is determined by some branch of labour and the conditions pertaining to it (We do not mean it to be understood from this that, for example, the rentier, the capitalist, etc., cease to be persons; but their personality is conditioned and determined by quite definite class relationships, and the division appears only in their opposition to another class and, for themselves, only when they go bankrupt.) In the estate (and even more in the tribe) this is as yet concealed: for instance, a nobleman always remains a nobleman, a commoner always a commoner, apart from his other relationships, a quality inseparable from his individuality. The division between the personal and the class individual, the accidental nature of the conditions of life for the individual, appears only with the emergence of the class, which is itself a product of the bourgeoisie. This accidental character is only engendered and developed by competition and the struggle of individuals among themselves. Thus, in imagination, individuals seem freer under the dominance of the bourgeoisie than before, because their conditions of life seem accidental; in reality, of course, they are less free, because they are more subjected to the violence of things. The difference from the estate comes out particularly in the antagonism between the bourgeoisie and the proletariat. When the estate of the urban burghers, the corporations, etc., emerged in opposition to the landed nobility, their condition of existence—movable property and craft labour, which had already existed latently before their separation from the feudal ties— appeared as something positive, which was asserted against feudal landed property, and, therefore, in its own way at first took on a feudal form. Certainly the refugee serfs treated their previous servitude as something accidental to their personality. But here they only were doing what every class that is freeing itself from a fetter does; and they did not free themselves as a class but separately. Moreover, they did not rise above the system of estates, but only formed a new estate, retaining their previous mode of labour even in their new situation, and developing it further by freeing it from its earlier fetters, which no longer corresponded to the development already attained.[5]

For the proletarians, on the other hand, the condition of their existence, labour, and with it all the conditions of existence governing modern society, have become something accidental, something

5. N.B. It must not be forgotten that the serfs' very need of existing and the impossibility of a large-scale economy, which involved the distribution of the allotments among the serfs, very soon reduced the services of the serfs to their lord to an average of payments in kind and statute-labour. This made it possible for the serf to accumulate movable property and hence facilitated his escape out of possession of his lord and gave him the prospect of making his way as an urban citizen; it also created gradations among the serfs, so that the runaway serfs were already half burghers. It is likewise obvious that the serfs who were masters of a craft had the best chance of acquiring movable property. [*Marx*]

over which they, as separate individuals, have no control, and over which no *social* organisation can give them control. The contradiction between the individuality of each separate proletarian and labour, the condition of life forced upon him, becomes evident to him himself, for he is sacrificed from youth upwards and, within his own class, has no chance of arriving at the conditions which would place him in the other class.

Thus, while the refugee serfs only wished to be free to develop and assert those conditions of existence which were already there, and hence, in the end, only arrived at free labour, the proletarians, if they are to assert themselves as individuals, will have to abolish the very condition of their existence hitherto (which has, moreover, been that of all society up to the present), namely, labour. Thus they find themselves directly opposed to the form in which, hitherto, the individuals, of which society consists, have given themselves collective expression, that is, the State. In order, therefore, to assert themselves as individuals, they must overthrow the State.

PART II

The Critique of Capitalism

Wage Labour and Capital

KARL MARX

Shortly after adumbrating the materialist conception of history in the 1844 manuscripts and formulating it comprehensively in Part I of *The German Ideology*, Marx turned to the economic studies that were going to preoccupy him in the ensuing years. This did not signify any change of interests or outlook but was the logical outgrowth of the position taken in his earlier writings. If the thesis on "alienated labor" was to be made scientifically cogent and if the expectation of coming proletarian revolution was to be based upon it, he needed to show the capital-labor relationship, which he took to be the core of the bourgeois socio-economic system, to be dialectically self-destructive, i.e., transitory by virtue of its inner dynamics of development. The first work in which he attempted this analysis was *Wage Labour and Capital*.

Having first presented it in lectures to a German workers' society in Brussels in December, 1847, Marx printed the work in April, 1849, in the *Neue Rheinische Zeitung*, of which he was editor-in-chief. Several pamphlet editions appeared in later years. In editing it for the German edition of 1891 (the version that appears here), Engels made some changes in the text, mainly centering in the substitution of the phrase "labour power" for the term "labour" in contexts in which Marx had originally spoken of the worker's sale of his labour to the capitalist. This, as Engels explained in his preface to the 1891 edition, brought the reasoning of the pamphlet into line with the analysis of the capital-labor relationship as Marx had refined it by 1859, when he published *A Contribution to the Critique of Political Economy*.

Despite this, it may be said that what Marx produced in the lectures of late 1847 was the future argument of *Capital* in embryo. The work appears here in condensed form.

I

From various quarters we have been reproached with not having presented the *economic relations* which constitute the material foundation of the present class struggles and national struggles. We have designedly touched upon these relations only where they directly forced themselves to the front in political conflicts.

* * *

Now, after our readers have seen the class struggle develop in colossal political forms in 1848, the time has come to deal more closely with the economic relations themselves on which the existence of the bourgeoisie and its class rule, as well as the slavery of the workers, are founded.

* * *

Now, therefore, for the first question: *What are wages? How are they determined?*

If workers were asked: "How much are your wages?" one would reply: "I get a mark a day from my employer"; another, "I get two marks," and so on. According to the different trades to which they belong, they would mention different sums of money which they receive from their respective employers for the performance of a particular piece of work, for example, weaving a yard of linen or type-setting a printed sheet. In spite of the variety of their statements, they would all agree on one point: wages are the sum of money paid by the capitalist for a particular labour time or for a particular output of labour.

The capitalist, it seems, therefore, *buys* their labour with money. They *sell* him their labour for money. But this is merely the appearance. In reality what they sell to the capitalist for money is their labour *power*. The capitalist buys this labour power for a day, a week, a month, etc. And after he has bought it, he uses it by having the workers work for the stipulated time. For the same sum with which the capitalist has bought their labour power, for example, two marks, he could have bought two pounds of sugar or a definite amount of any other commodity. The two marks, with which he bought two pounds of sugar, are the *price* of the two pounds of sugar. The two marks, with which he bought twelve hours' use of labour power, are the price of twelve hours' labour. Labour power, therefore, is a commodity, neither more nor less than sugar. The former is measured by the clock, the latter by the scales.

* * *

Labour power is, therefore, a commodity which its possessor, the wage-worker, sells to capital. Why does he sell it? In order to live.

But the exercise of labour power, labour, is the worker's own life-activity, the manifestation of his own life. And this *life-activity* he sells to another person in order to secure the necessary *means of subsistence*. Thus his life-activity is for him only a means to enable him to exist. He works in order to live. He does not even reckon labour as part of his life, it is rather a sacrifice of his life. It is a commodity which he has made over to another. Hence, also, the product of his activity is not the object of his activity. What he produces for himself is not the silk that he weaves, not the gold that he draws from the mine, not the palace that he builds. What he produces for himself is *wages*, and silk, gold, palace resolve themselves for him into a definite quantity of the means of subsistence, perhaps into a cotton jacket, some copper coins and a lodging in a cellar. And the worker, who for twelve hours weaves, spins, drills, turns, builds, shovels, breaks stones, carries loads, etc.—does he consider this twelve hours' weaving, spinning, drilling, turning, building, shovelling, stone breaking as a manifestation of his life, as life? On the contrary, life begins for him where this activity ceases, at table, in the public house, in bed. The twelve hours' labour, on the other hand, has no meaning for him as weaving, spinning, drilling, etc., but as *earnings*, which bring him to the table, to the public house, into bed. If the silk worm were to spin in order to continue its existence as a caterpillar, it would be a complete wage-worker. Labour power was not always a *commodity*. Labour was not always wage labour, that is, *free labour*. The *slave* did not sell his labour power to the slave owner, any more than the ox sells its services to the peasant. The slave, together with his labour power, is sold once and for all to his owner. He is a commodity which can pass from the hand of one owner to that of another. He is *himself* a commodity, but the labour power is not *his* commodity. The *serf* sells only a part of his labour power. He does not receive a wage from the owner of the land; rather the owner of the land receives a tribute from him.

The serf belongs to the land and turns over to the owner of the land the fruits thereof. The *free labourer*, on the other hand, sells himself and, indeed, sells himself piecemeal. He sells at auction eight, ten, twelve, fifteen hours of his life, day after day, to the highest bidder, to the owner of the raw materials, instruments of labour and means of subsistence, that is, to the capitalist. The worker belongs neither to an owner nor to the land, but eight, ten, twelve, fifteen hours of his daily life belong to him who buys them. The worker leaves the capitalist to whom he hires himself whenever he likes, and the capitalist discharges him whenever he thinks fit, as soon as he no longer gets any profit out of him, or not the anticipated profit. But the worker, whose sole source of livelihood is the sale of his labour power, cannot leave the *whole class of purchasers, that is, the capitalist class*, without renouncing his existence. He belongs not to this or that capitalist but to the *capitalist class*, and, moreover, it is his business to dispose of himself, that is, to find a purchaser within this capitalist class.

* * *

Wages will rise and fall according to the relation of supply and demand, according to the turn taken by the competition between the buyers of labour power, the capitalists, and the sellers of labour power, the workers. The fluctuations in wages correspond in general to the fluctuations in prices of commodities. *Within these fluctuations, however, the price of labour will be determined by the cost of production, by the labour time necessary to produce this commodity—labour power.*

What, then, is the cost of production of labour power?

It is the cost required for maintaining the worker as a worker and of developing him into a worker.

The less the period of training, therefore, that any work requires the smaller is the cost of production of the worker and the lower is the price of his labour, his wages. In those branches of industry in which hardly any period of apprenticeship is required and where the mere bodily existence of the worker suffices, the cost necessary for his production is almost confined to the commodities necessary for keeping him alive and capable of working. The *price of his labour* will, therefore, be determined by the *price of the necessary means of subsistence.*

Another consideration, however, also comes in. The manufacturer in calculating his cost of production and, accordingly, the price of the products takes into account the wear and tear of the instruments of labour. If, for example, a machine costs him 1,000 marks and wears out in ten years, he adds 100 marks annually to the price of the commodities so as to be able to replace the worn-out machine by a new one at the end of ten years. In the same way, in calculating the cost of production of simple labour power, there must be included the cost of reproduction, whereby the race of workers is enabled to multiply and to replace worn-out workers by new ones. Thus the depreciation of the worker is taken into account in the same way as the depreciation of the machine.

The cost of production of simple labour power, therefore, amounts to the *cost of existence and reproduction of the worker.* The price of this cost of existence and reproduction constitutes wages. Wages so determined are called the *wage minimum.* This wage minimum, like the determination of the price of commodities by the cost of production in general, does not hold good for the *single individual* but for the *species.* Individual workers, millions of workers, do not get enough to be able to exist and reproduce themselves; *but the wages of the whole working class* level down, within their fluctuations, to this minimum.

Now that we have arrived at an understanding of the most general laws which regulate wages like the price of any other commodity, we can go into our subject more specifically.

III

Capital consists of raw materials, instruments of labour and means of subsistence of all kinds, which are utilised in order to produce new raw materials, new instruments of labour and new means of subsistence. All these component parts of capital are creations of labour, products of labour, *accumulated labour*. Accumulated labour which serves as a means of new production is capital.

So say the economists.

What is a Negro slave? A man of the black race. The one explanation is as good as the other.

A Negro is a Negro. He only becomes a slave in certain relations. A cotton-spinning jenny is a machine for spinning cotton. It becomes *capital* only in certain relations. Torn from these relationships it is no more capital than gold in itself is *money* or sugar the price of sugar.

In production, men not only act on nature but also on one another. They produce only by co-operating in a certain way and mutually exchanging their activities. In order to produce, they enter into definite connections and relations with one another and only within these social connections and relations does their action on nature, does production, take place.

These social relations into which the producers enter with one another, the conditions under which they exchange their activities and participate in the whole act of production, will naturally vary according to the character of the means of production. With the invention of a new instrument of warfare, firearms, the whole internal organisation of the army necessarily changed; the relationships within which individuals can constitute an army and act as an army were transformed and the relations of different armies to one another also changed.

Thus the social relations within which individuals produce, *the social relations of production, change, are transformed, with the change and development of the material means of production, the productive forces. The relations of production in their totality constitute what are called the social relations, society, and, specifically, a society at a definite stage of historical development*, a society with a peculiar, distinctive character. *Ancient* society, *feudal* society, *bourgeois* society are such totalities of production relations, each of which at the same time denotes a special stage of development in the history of mankind.

Capital, also, is a social relation of production. *It is a bourgeois production relation*, a production relation of bourgeois society. Are not the means of subsistence, the instruments of labour, the raw materials of which capital consists, produced and accumulated under given social conditions, in definite social relations? Are they not utilised for new production under given social conditions, in definite social relations? And is it not just this definite social character which turns the products serving for new production into *capital?*

Capital consists not only of means of subsistence, instruments of labour and raw materials, not only of material products; it consists just as much of *exchange values.* All the products of which it consists are *commodities.* Capital is, therefore, not only a sum of material products; it is a sum of commodities, of exchange values, *of social magnitudes.*

Capital remains the same, whether we put cotton in place of wool, rice in place of wheat or steamships in place of railways, provided only that the cotton, the rice, the steamships—the body of capital—have the same exchange value, the same price as the wool, the wheat, the railways in which it was previously incorporated. The body of capital can change continually without the capital suffering the slightest alteration.

But while all capital is a sum of commodities, that is, of exchange values, not every sum of commodities, of exchange values, is capital.

Every sum of exchange values is an exchange value. Every separate exchange value is a sum of exchange values. For instance, a house that is worth 1,000 marks is an exchange value of 1,000 marks. A piece of paper worth a pfennig is a sum of exchange values of one-hundred hundredths of a pfennig. Products which are exchangeable for others are commodities. The particular ratio in which they are exchangeable constitutes their *exchange value* or, expressed in money, their *price.* The quantity of these products can change nothing in their quality of being *commodities* or representing an *exchange value* or having a definite price. Whether a tree is large or small it is a tree. Whether we exchange iron for other products in ounces or in hundred-weights, does this make any difference in its character as commodity, as exchange value? It is a commodity of greater or lesser value, of higher or lower price, depending upon the quantity.

How, then, does any amount of commodities, of exchange value, become capital?

By maintaining and multiplying itself as an independent social *power,* that is, as the power *of a portion of society,* by means of its *exchange for direct, living labour power.* The existence of a class which possesses nothing but its capacity to labour is a necessary prerequisite of capital.

It is only the domination of accumulated, past, materialised labour over direct, living labour that turns accumulated labour into capital.

Capital does not consist in accumulated labour serving living labour as a means for new production. It consists in living labour serving accumulated labour as a means of maintaining and multiplying the exchange value of the latter.

What takes place in the exchange between capitalist and wage-worker?

The worker receives means of subsistence in exchange for his labour power, but the capitalist receives in exchange for his means of subsistence labour, the productive activity of the worker, the creative power whereby the worker not only replaces what he consumes but *gives to the accumulated labour a greater value than it previously possessed*. The worker receives a part of the available means of subsistence from the capitalist. For what purpose do these means of subsistence serve him? For immediate consumption. As soon, however, as I consume the means of subsistence, they are irretrievably lost to me unless I use the time during which I am kept alive by them in order to produce new means of subsistence, in order during consumption to create by my labour new values in place of the values which perish in being consumed. But it is just this noble reproductive power that the worker surrenders to the capitalist in exchange for means of subsistence received. He has, therefore, lost it for himself.

Let us take an example: a tenant farmer gives his day labourer five silver groschen a day. For these five silver groschen the labourer works all day on the farmer's field and thus secures him a return of ten silver groschen. The farmer not only gets the value replaced that he has to give to the day labourer; he doubles it. He has therefore employed, consumed, the five silver groschen that he gave to the labourer in a fruitful, productive manner. He has bought with the five silver groschen just that labour and power of the labourer which produces agricultural products of double value and makes ten silver groschen out of five. The day labourer, on the other hand, receives in place of his productive power, the effect of which he has bargained away to the farmer, five silver groschen, which he exchanges for means of subsistence, and these he consumes with greater or less rapidity. The five silver groschen have, therefore, been consumed in a double way, *reproductively* for capital, for they have been exchanged for labour power which produced ten silver groschen, *unproductively* for the worker, for they have been exchanged for means of subsistence which have disappeared forever and the value of which he can only recover by repeating the same exchange with the farmer. *Thus capital presupposes wage labour; wage labour presupposes capital. They reciprocally condition the existence of each other; they reciprocally bring forth each other.*

Does a worker in a cotton factory produce merely cotton textiles? No, he produces capital. He produces values which serve afresh to command his labour and by means of it to create new values.

Capital can only increase by exchanging itself for labour power, by calling wage labour to life. The labour power of the wage-worker can only be exchanged for capital by increasing capital, by strengthening the power whose slave it is. *Hence, increase of capital is increase of the proletariat, that is, of the working class.*

The interests of the capitalist and those of the worker are, therefore, *one and the same*, assert the bourgeois and their economists. Indeed! The worker perishes if capital does not employ him. Capital perishes if it does not exploit labour power, and in order to exploit it, it must buy it. The faster capital intended for production, productive capital, increases, the more, therefore, industry prospers, the more the bourgeoisie enriches itself and the better business is, the more workers does the capitalist need, the more dearly does the worker sell himself.

The indispensable condition for a tolerable situation of the worker is, *therefore, the fastest possible growth of productive capital.*

But what is the growth of productive capital? Growth of the power of accumulated labour over living labour. Growth of the domination of the bourgeoisie over the working class. If wage labour produces the wealth of others that rules over it, the power that is hostile to it, capital, then the means of employment, the means of subsistence, flow back to it from this hostile power, on condition that it makes itself afresh into a part of capital, into the lever which hurls capital anew into an accelerated movement of growth.

To say that·the interests of capital and those of the workers are one and the same is only to say that capital and wage labour are two sides of one and the same relation. The one conditions the other, just as usurer and squanderer condition each other.

As long as the wage-worker is a wage-worker his lot depends upon capital. That is the much-vaunted community of interests between worker and capitalist.

IV

If capital grows, the mass of wage labour grows, the number of wage-workers grows; in a word, the domination of capital extends over a greater number of individuals. * * *

* * *

To say that the worker has an interest in the rapid growth of capital is only to say that the more rapidly the worker increases the wealth of others, the richer will be the crumbs that fall to him, the greater is the number of workers that can be employed and called into existence, the more can the mass of slaves dependent on capital be increased.

We have thus seen that:

Even the *most favourable situation* for the working class, the *most rapid possible growth of capital,* however much it may improve the material existence of the worker, does not remove the antagonism between his interests and the interests of the bourgeoisie, the interests of the capitalists. *Profit and wages* remain as before in *inverse porportion.*

If capital is growing rapidly, wages may rise; the profit of capital rises incomparably more rapidly. The material position of the worker has improved, but at the cost of his social position. The social gulf that divides him from the capitalist has widened.

Finally:

To say that the most favourable condition for wage labour is the most rapid possible growth of productive capital is only to say that the more rapidly the working class increases and enlarges the power that is hostile to it, the wealth that does not belong to it and that rules over it, the more favourable will be the conditions under which it is allowed to labour anew at increasing bourgeois wealth, at enlarging the power of capital, content with forging for itself the golden chains by which the bourgeoisie drags it in its train.

V

Are *growth of productive capital and rise of wages* really so inseparably connected as the bourgeois economists maintain? We must not take their word for it. We must not even believe them when they say that the fatter capital is, the better will its slave be fed. The bourgeoisie is too enlightened, it calculates too well, to share the prejudices of the feudal lord who makes a display by the brilliance of his retinue. The conditions of existence of the bourgeoisie compel it to calculate.

We must, therefore, examine more closely:

How does the growth of productive capital affect wages?

If, on the whole, the productive capital of bourgeois society grows, a *more manifold* accumulation of labour takes place. The capitals increase in number and extent. The *numerical increase* of the capitals increases the *competition between the capitalists.* The *increasing extent* of the capitals provides the means for *bringing more powerful labour armies with more gigantic instruments of war into the industrial battlefield.*

One capitalist can drive another from the field and capture his capital only by selling more cheaply. In order to be able to sell more cheaply without ruining himself, he must produce more cheaply, that is, raise the productive power of labour as much as possible. But the productive power of labour is raised, above all, by a *greater division of labour*, by a more universal introduction and continual improvement of *machinery*. The greater the labour army among whom labour is divided, the more gigantic the scale on which machinery is introduced, the more does the cost of production proportionately decrease, the more fruitful is labour. Hence, a general rivalry arises among the capitalists to increase the division of labour and machinery and to exploit them on the greatest possible scale.

If, now, by a greater division of labour, by the utilisation of new machines and their improvement, by more profitable and extensive exploitation of natural forces, one capitalist has found the means of producing with the same amount of labour or of accumulated labour a greater amount of products, of commodities, than his competitors, if he can, for example, produce a whole yard of linen in the same labour time in which his competitors weave half a yard, how will this capitalist operate?

He could continue to sell half a yard of linen at the old market price; this would, however, be no means of driving his opponents from the field and of enlarging his own sales. But in the same measure in which his production has expanded, his need to sell has also increased. The more powerful and costly means of production that he has called into life enable him, indeed, to sell his commodities more cheaply, they *compel* him, however, at the same time *to sell more commodities*, to conquer a much *larger* market for his commodities; consequently, our capitalist will sell his half yard of linen more cheaply than his competitors.

The capitalist will not, however, sell a whole yard as cheaply as his competitors sell half a yard, although the production of the whole yard does not cost him more than the half yard costs the others. Otherwise he would not gain anything extra but only get back the cost of production by the exchange. His possibly greater income would be derived from the fact of having set a larger capital into motion, but not from having made more of his capital than the others. Moreover, he attains the object he wishes to attain, if he puts the price of his goods only a small percentage lower than that of his competitors. He drives them from the field, he wrests from them at least a part of their sales, by *underselling* them. And, finally, it will be remembered that the current price always stands *above or below the cost of production*, according to whether the sale of the commodity occurs in a favourable or unfavourable industrial season. The percentage at which the capitalist who has employed new and more fruitful means of production sells above his real cost of production will vary, depending upon whether the market price of a yard of linen stands below or above its hitherto customary cost of production.

However, the *privileged position* of our capitalist is not of long duration; other competing capitalists introduce the same machines, the same division of labour, introduce them on the same or on a larger scale, and this introduction will become so general that the price of linen *is reduced* not only *below its old*, but *below its new cost of production*.

The capitalists find themselves, therefore, in the same position relative to one another as *before* the introduction of the new means of production, and if they are able to supply by these means double the production at the same price, they are *now* forced to supply the double product *below* the old price. On the basis of this new cost of production, the same game begins again. More division of labour, more machinery, enlarged scale of exploitation of machinery and division of labour. And again competition brings the same counteraction against this result.

We see how in this way the mode of production and the means of production are continually transformed, revolutionised, *how the division of labour is necessarily followed by greater division of labour, the application of machinery by still greater application of machinery, work on a large scale by work on a still larger scale.*

That is the law which again and again throws bourgeois production out of its old course and which compels capital to intensify the productive forces of labour, *because* it has intensified them, it, the law which gives capital no rest and continually whispers in its ear: "Go on! Go on!"

This law is none other than that which, within the fluctuations of trade periods, necessarily *levels out* the price of a commodity to its *cost of production*.

However powerful the means of production which a capitalist brings into the field, competition will make these means of production universal and from the moment when it has made them universal, the only result of the greater fruitfulness of his capital is that he must now supply *for the same price* ten, twenty, a hundred times as much as before. But, as he must sell perhaps a thousand times as much as before in order to outweigh the lower selling price by the greater amount of the product sold, because a more extensive sale is now necessary, not only in order to make more profit but in order to replace the cost of production—the instrument of production itself, as we have seen, becomes more and more expensive—and because this mass sale becomes a question of life and death not only for him but also for his rivals, the old struggle begins again *all the more violently the more fruitful the already dis-*

covered means of production are. The division of labour and the application of machinery, therefore, will go on anew on an incomparably greater scale.

Whatever the power of the means of production employed may be, competition seeks to rob capital of the golden fruits of this power by bringing the price of the commodities back to the cost of production, by thus making cheaper production—the supply of ever greater amounts of products for the same total price—an imperative law to the same extent as production can be cheapened, that is, as more can be produced with the same amount of labour. Thus the capitalist would have won nothing by his own exertions but the obligation to supply more in the same labour time, in a word, *more difficult conditions for the augmentation of the value of his capital.* While, therefore, competition continually pursues him with its law of the cost of production and every weapon that he forges against his rivals recoils against himself, the capitalist continually tries to get the better of competition by incessantly introducing new machines, more expensive, it is true, but producing more cheaply, and new division of labour in place of the old, and by not waiting until competition has rendered the new ones obsolete.

If now we picture to ourselves this feverish simultaneous agitation on the *whole world market*, it will be comprehensible how the growth, accumulation and concentration of capital results in an uninterrupted division of labour, and in the application of new and the perfecting of old machinery precipitately and on an ever more gigantic scale.

But how do these circumstances, which are inseparable from the growth of productive capital, affect the determination of wages?

The greater *division of labour* enables *one* worker to do the work of five, ten or twenty; it therefore multiplies competition among the workers fivefold, tenfold and twentyfold. The workers do not only compete by one selling himself cheaper than another; they compete by *one* doing the work of five, ten, twenty; and the *division of labour*, introduced by capital and continually increased, compels the workers to compete among themselves in this way.

Further, as the *division of labour* increases, labour *is simplified*. The special skill of the worker becomes worthless. He becomes transformed into a simple, monotonous productive force that does not have to use intense bodily or intellectual faculties. His labour becomes a labour that anyone can perform. Hence, competitors crowd upon him on all sides, and besides we remind the reader that the more simple and easily learned the labour is, the lower the cost of production needed to master it, the lower do wages sink, for, like the price of every other commodity, they are determined by the cost of production.

Therefore, as labour becomes more unsatisfying, more repulsive, competition increases and wages decrease. The worker tries to keep up the amount of his wages by working more, whether by working longer hours or by producing more in one hour. Driven by want, therefore, he still further increases the evil effects of the division of labour. The result is that *the more he works the less wages he receives,* and for the simple reason that he competes to that extent with his fellow workers, hence makes them into so many competitors who offer themselves on just the same bad terms as he does himself, and that, therefore, in the last resort he *competes with himself, with himself as a member of the working class.*

Machinery brings about the same results on a much greater scale, by replacing skilled workers by unskilled, men by women, adults by children. It brings about the same results, where it is newly introduced, by throwing the hand workers on to the streets in masses, and, where it is developed, improved and replaced by more productive machinery, by discharging workers in smaller batches. We have portrayed above, in a hasty sketch, the industrial war of the capitalists among themselves; *this war has the peculiarity that its battles are won less by recruiting than by discharging the army of labour. The generals, the capitalists, compete with one another as to who can discharge most soldiers of industry.*

The economists tell us, it is true, that the workers rendered superfluous by machinery find *new* branches of employment.

They dare not assert directly that the same workers who are discharged find places in the new branches of labour. The facts cry out too loudly against this lie. They really only assert that new means of employment will open up for *other component sections of the working class,* for instance, for the portion of the young generation of workers that was ready to enter the branch of industry which has gone under. That is, of course, a great consolation for the disinherited workers. The worshipful capitalists will never want for fresh exploitable flesh and blood, and will let the dead bury their dead. This is a consolation which the bourgeois give themselves rather than one which they give the workers. If the whole class of wage-workers were to be abolished owing to machinery, how dreadful that would be for capital which, without wage labour, ceases to be capital!

Let us suppose, however, that those directly driven out of their jobs by machinery, and the entire section of the new generation that was already on the watch for this employment, *find a new occupation.* Does any one imagine that it will be as highly paid as that which has been lost? *That would contradict all the laws of economics.* We have seen how modern industry always brings with it the substitution of a more simple, subordinate occupation for the more complex and higher one.

How, then, could a mass of workers who have been thrown out

of one branch of industry owing to machinery find refuge in another, unless the latter *is lower, worse paid?*

The workers who work in the manufacture of machinery itself have been cited as an exception. As soon as more machinery is demanded and used in industry, it is said, there must necessarily be an increase of machines, consequently of the manufacture of machines, and consequently of the employment of workers in the manufacture of machines; and the workers engaged in this branch of industry are claimed to be skilled, even educated workers.

Since the year 1840 this assertion, which even before was only half true, has lost all semblance of truth because ever more versatile machines have been employed in the manufacture of machinery, no more and no less than in the manufacture of cotton yarn, and the workers employed in the machine factories, confronted by highly elaborate machines, can only play the part of highly unelaborate machines.

But in place of the man who has been discharged owing to the machine, the factory employs maybe *three* children and *one* woman. And did not the man's wages have to suffice for the three children and a woman? Did not the minimum of wages have to suffice to maintain and to propagate the race? What, then, does this favourite bourgeois phrase prove? Nothing more than that now four times as many workers' lives are used up in order to gain a livelihood for *one* worker's family.

Let us sum up: *The more productive capital grows, the more the division of labour and the application of machinery expands. The more the division of labour and the application of machinery expands, the more competition among the workers expands and the more their wages contract.*

In addition, the working class gains recruits from the *higher strata of society* also; a mass of petty industrialists and small rentiers are hurled down into its ranks and have nothing better to do than urgently stretch out their arms alongside those of the workers. Thus the forest of uplifted arms demanding work becomes ever thicker, while the arms themselves become ever thinner.

That the small industrialist cannot survive in a contest one of the first conditions of which is to produce on an ever greater scale, that is, precisely to be a large and not a small industrialist, is self-evident.

That the interest on capital decreases in the same measure as the mass and number of capitals increase, as capital grows; that, therefore, the small rentier can no longer live on his interest but must throw himself into industry, and, consequently, help to swell the ranks of the small industrialists and thereby of candidates for the proletariat—all this surely requires no further explanation.

Finally, as the capitalists are compelled, by the movement described above, to exploit the already existing gigantic means of production on a larger scale and to set in motion all the mainsprings of credit to this end, there is a corresponding increase in industrial earthquakes, in which the trading world can only maintain itself by sacrificing a part of wealth, of products and even of productive forces to the gods of the nether world—in a word, *crises* increase. They become more frequent and more violent, if only because, as the mass of production, and consequently the need for extended markets, grows, the world market becomes more and more contracted, fewer and fewer new markets remain available for exploitation, since every preceding crisis has subjected to world trade a market hitherto unconquered or only superficially exploited. But capital does not *live* only on labour. A lord, at once aristocratic and barbarous, it drags with it into the grave the corpses of its slaves, whole hecatombs of workers who perish in the crises. Thus we see: *if capital grows rapidly, competition among the workers grows incomparably more rapidly, that is, the means of employment, the means of subsistence, of the working class decrease proportionately so much the more, and, nevertheless, the rapid growth of capital is the most favourable condition for wage labour.*

The Coming Upheaval

KARL MARX

This concluding passage from Marx's anti-Proudhon tract *The Poverty of Philosophy* (1847) closes a discussion which takes England as the representative case of a revolution-bent country. It gives a vivid preview of the revolutionary upheaval towards which Marx believed that the class struggle in all capitalist countries was irresistibly moving. It was, in a way, *Capital*'s conclusion stated in advance. Note the Hegelian terminology in Marx's depiction of the proletariat becoming, in and through the warfare of labor and capital, a class not only in itself but also "for itself," i.e., collectively conscious of itself and its revolutionary aims as a class.

* * *

Economic conditions first transformed the mass of the people of the country into workers. The combination of capital has created for this mass a common situation, common interests. This mass is thus already a class as against capital, but not yet for itself. In the struggle, of which we have noted only a few phases, this mass becomes united, and constitutes itself as a class for itself. The interests it defends become class interests. But the struggle of class against class is a political struggle.

An oppressed class is the vital condition for every society founded on the antagonism of classes. The emancipation of the oppressed class thus implies necessarily the creation of a new society. For the oppressed class to be able to emancipate itself it is necessary that the productive powers already acquired and the existing social reltions should no longer be capable of existing side by side. Of all the instruments of production, the greatest productive power is the revolutionary class itself. The organization of revolutionary elements as a class supposes the existence of all the productive forces which could be engendered in the bosom of the old society.

Does this mean that after the fall of the old society there will be a new class domination culminating in a new political power? No.

The condition for the emancipation of the working class is the abolition of every class, just as the condition for the liberation of the third estate, of the bourgeois order, was the abolition of all estates and all orders.

The working class, in the course of its development, will substitute for the old civil society an association which will exclude classes and their antagonism, and there will be no more political power properly so called, since political power is precisely the official expression of antagonism in civil society.

Meanwhile the antagonism between the proletariat and the bourgeoisie is a struggle of class against class, a struggle which carried to its highest expression is a total revolution. Indeed, is it at all surprising that a society founded on the opposition of classes should culminate in brutal "contradiction," the shock of body against body, as its final *dénouement*?

Do not say that social movement excludes political movement. There is never a political movement which is not at the same time social.

It is only in an order of things in which there are no more classes and class antagonisms that *"social evolutions"* will cease to be *"political revolutions."* Till then, on the eve of every general reshuffling of society, the last word of social science will always be:

Combat or death: bloody struggle or extinction. It is thus that the question is inexorably put.[1]

1. George Sand, *Jean Ziska. A Historical Novel.*

Class Struggle and Mode of Production

KARL MARX

A brief but notable statement by Marx of what he considered most innovative in his analysis of the human historical process occurs in a letter of March 5, 1852, to his friend Joseph Weydemeyer, then living in New York.

---

* * * And now as to myself, no credit is due to me for discovering the existence of classes in modern society or the struggle between them. Long before me bourgeois historians had described the historical development of this class struggle and bourgeois economists the economic anatomy of the classes. What I did that was new was to prove: 1) that the *existence of classes* is only bound up with *particular historical phases in the development of production,* 2) that the class struggle necessarily leads to the *dictatorship of the proletariat,* 3) that this dictatorship itself only constitutes the transition to the *abolition of all classes* and to *a classless society.*

The *Grundrisse*

KARL MARX

Comprising seven notebooks written in 1857–58, this preparatory effort by Marx to put together the results of his economic studies was first published by the Institute of Marx-Engels-Lenin in Moscow in 1939–41 as *Foundations (Grundrisse) of the Critique of Political Economy*. In recent years it has attracted growing attention because of the intrinsic interest of various parts, because it forms an important link between the early writings and *Capital*, and because the very rawness of much of the text enhances its value as a revelation of Marx's creative mental process.* The great bulk of it consists of an Introduction, a "Chapter on Money," and a "Chapter on Capital." The Introduction, which appears here in full, and several selections from the "Chapter on Capital" have been chosen partly for what they add to the study of *Capital*. The reader not yet familiar with the basic argument of *Capital* may therefore prefer to turn first to that work, below, and then return to the *Grundrisse*.

The Introduction, besides stating Marx's view of the method of political economy, develops his thesis on production as the basic category; shows (in the final paragraph of its third section) that the work on which he was embarked, and which later came to fruition in *Capital*, was no more than one part of a more ambitious total project; and concludes with a discussion of the timeless character of great art. Section B defines "society." Section C deals with capitalism as incessant drive for surplus value and alludes to future communism as a society in which labour "appears no longer as labour, but as the full development of activity itself. . . ." Section D suplements *Capital* on primitive accumulation. Section E deals with pre-capitalist economies and the birth of capitalism. Section F summarizes Marx's views on population and Malthus. Section G contains a now-famous discussion of ever-increasing automation under capitalism.** Section H envisages capitalism's ultimate violent overthrow. Section I contrasts the alienation of labour under capitalism with the postulated ending of alienation in the future. In these and other passages of the *Grundrisse* Marx here and there uses the "alienation" terminology which had been pervasive in the 1844 manuscripts but would grow inconspicuous in *Capital*.

The translation and footnotes are by Martin Nicolaus. The capitalized letters and section headings following the Introduction have been added by the editor of this reader.

---

* This last point is made compellingly by Martin Nicolaus in his informative Foreword to Karl Marx, *Grundrisse: Foundations of the Critique of Political Economy*, translated by Martin Nicolaus (New York: Vintage, 1973), p. 7. The same point could be made with reference to the 1844 manuscripts.

** Some have interpreted these passages as heralding the end of manual labour under capitalism. Nicolaus (Foreword, p. 52) objects that "neither here nor anywhere else in Marx's work is there a prediction that manual industrial labour will be abolished in industrial society. . . ."

A. Introduction

(1) PRODUCTION

Independent Individuals. Eighteenth-Century Ideas

The object before us, to begin with, *material production*.

Individuals producing in society—hence socially determined individual production—is, of course, the point of departure. The individual and isolated hunter and fisherman, with whom Smith and Ricardo begin, belongs among the unimaginative conceits of the eighteenth-century Robinsonades,[1] which in no way express merely a reaction against over-sophistication and a return to a misunderstood natural life, as cultural historians imagine. As little as Rousseau's *contrat social*, which brings naturally independent, autonomous subjects into relation and connection by contract, rests on such naturalism. This is the semblance, the merely aesthetic semblance, of the Robinsonades, great and small. It is, rather, the anticipation of "civil society," in preparation since the sixteenth century and making giant strides towards maturity in the eighteenth. In this society of free competition, the individual appears detached from the natural bonds etc. which in earlier historical periods make him the accessory of a definite and limited human conglomerate. Smith and Ricardo still stand with both feet on the shoulders of the eighteenth-century prophets, in whose imaginations this eighteenth-century individual—the product on one side of the dissolution of the feudal forms of society, on the other side of the new forces of production developed since the sixteenth century—appears as an ideal, whose existence they project into the past. Not as a historic result but as history's point of departure. As the Natural Individual appropriate to their notion of human nature, not arising historically, but posited by nature. This illusion has been common to each new epoch to this day. Steuart[2] avoided this simple-mindedness because as an aristocrat, and in antithesis to the eighteenth century, he had in some respects a more historical footing.

The more deeply we go back into history, the more does the individual, and hence also the producing individual, appear as dependent, as belonging to a greater whole: in a still quite natural way in

1. Utopias on the lines of Defoe's *Robinson Crusoe*.
2. Sir James Steuart (1712–80), "the rational exponent of the Monetary and Mercantile System" (Marx), an adherent of the Stuart cause who went into exile in 1745 and pursued economic studies on the Continent. Author of *An Inquiry into the Principles of Political Economy* (London, 1767, 2 vols.; Dublin, 1770, 3 vols.—the edition used by Marx).

the family and in the family expanded into the clan [*Stamm*]; then later in the various forms of communal society arising out of the antitheses and fusions of the clans. Only in the eighteenth century, in "civil society," do the various forms of social connectedness confront the individual as a mere means towards his private purposes, as external necessity. But the epoch which produces this standpoint, that of the isolated individual, is also precisely that of the hitherto most developed social (from this standpoint, general) relations. The human being is in the most literal sense a ζῶον πολιτικόν,[3] not merely a gregarious animal, but an animal which can individuate itself only in the midst of society. Production by an isolated individual outside society—a rare exception which may well occur when a civilized person in whom the social forces are already dynamically present is cast by accident into the wilderness—is as much of an absurdity as is the development of language without individuals living *together* and talking to each other. There is no point in dwelling on this any longer. The point could go entirely unmentioned if this twaddle, which had sense and reason for the eighteenth-century characters, had not been earnestly pulled back into the centre of the most modern economics by Bastiat,[4] Carey,[5] Proudhon etc. Of course it is a convenience for Proudhon et al. to be able to give a historico-philosophic account of the source of an economic relation, of whose historic origins he is ignorant, by inventing the myth that Adam or Prometheus stumbled on the idea ready-made, and then it was adopted, etc. Nothing is more dry and boring than the fantasies of a *locus communis*.[6]

Eternalization of historic relations of production.—Production and distribution in general.—Property

Whenever we speak of production, then, what is meant is always production at a definite stage of social development—production by social individuals. It might seem, therefore, that in order to talk about production at all we must either pursue the process of historic development through its different phases, or declare beforehand that we are dealing with a specific historic epoch such as e.g.

3. A political animal.
4. Frédéric Bastiat (1801–50), French economist, and "modern bagman of Free Trade" (Marx). A believer in *Laissez-faire* and the natural harmony of interests between labour and capital; a fierce opponent of socialism in theory and in practice (as deputy in the Constituent and Legislative assemblies of 1848 to 1851).
5. Henry Charles Carey (1793–1879), American economist, opponent of Ricardian pessimism ("Carey, who does not understand Ricardo"—Marx), believed in state intervention to establish harmony between the interests of labour and of capital, and in the tendency of real wages to rise.
6. Of a commonplace (mind). Marx refers here to Bastiat's *Harmonies économiques* (Paris, 1851), pp. 16–19, and Carey's *Principles of Political Economy*, Pt. I (Philadelphia, 1837), pp. 7–8.

modern bourgeois production, which is indeed our particular theme. However, all epochs of production have certain common traits, common characteristics. *Production in general* is an abstraction, but a rational abstraction in so far as it really brings out and fixes the common element and thus saves us repetition. Still, this *general* category, this common element sifted out by comparison, is itself segmented many times over and splits into different determinations. Some determinations belong to all epochs, others only to a few. [Some] determinations will be shared by the most modern epoch and the most ancient. No production will be thinkable without them; however, even though the most developed languages have laws and characteristics in common with the least developed, nevertheless, just those things which determine their development, i.e. the elements which are not general and common, must be separated out from the determinations valid for production as such, so that in their unity—which arises already from the identity of the subject, humanity, and of the object, nature—their essential difference is not forgotten. The whole profundity of those modern economists who demonstrate the eternity and harmoniousness of the existing social relations lies in this forgetting. For example. No production possible without an instrument of production, even if this instrument is only the hand. No production without stored-up, past labour, even if it is only the facility gathered together and concentrated in the hand of the savage by repeated practice. Capital is, among other things, also an instrument of production, also objectified, past labour. Therefore capital is a general, eternal relation of nature; that is, if I leave out just the specific quality which alone makes "instrument of production" and "stored-up labour" into capital. The entire history of production relations thus appears to Carey, for example, as a malicious forgery perpetrated by governments.

If there is no production in general, then there is also no general production. Production is always a *particular* branch of production —e.g., agriculture, cattle-raising, manufactures etc.—or it is a *totality*. But political economy is not technology. The relation of the general characteristics of production at a given stage of social development to the particular forms of production to be developed elsewhere (later). Lastly, production also is not only a particular production. Rather, it is always a certain social body, a social subject, which is active in a greater or sparser totality of branches of production. Nor does the relationship between scientific presentation and the real movement belong here yet. Production in general. Particular branches of production. Totality of production.

It is the fashion to preface a work of economics with a general part—and precisely this part figures under the title "production" (see for example J. S. Mill)[7]—treating of the *general preconditions* of all production. This general part consists or is alleged to consist of (1) the conditions without which production is not possible. I.e., in fact, to indicate nothing more than the essential moments of all production. But, as we will see, this reduces itself in fact to a few very simple characteristics, which are hammered out into flat tautologies; (2) the conditions which promote production to a greater or lesser degree, such as e.g. Adam Smith's progressive and stagnant state of society. While this is of value in his work as an insight, to elevate it to scientific significance would require investigations into the periodization of *degrees of productivity* in the development of individual peoples—an investigation which lies outside the proper boundaries of the theme, but, in so far as it does belong there, must be brought in as part of the development of competition, accumulation etc. In the usual formulation, the answer amounts to the general statement that an industrial people reaches the peak of its production at the moment when it arrives at its historical peak generally. In fact. The industrial peak of a people when its main concern is not yet gain, but rather to gain. Thus the Yankees over the English. Or, also, that e.g. certain races, locations, climates, natural conditions such as harbours, soil fertility etc. are more advantageous to production than others. This too amounts to the tautology that wealth is more easily created where its elements are subjectively and objectively present to a greater degree.

But none of all this is the economists' real concern in this general part. The aim is, rather, to present production—see e.g. Mill—as distinct from distribution etc., as encased in eternal natural laws independent of history, at which opportunity *bourgeois* relations are then quietly smuggled in as the inviolable natural laws on which society in the abstract is founded. This is the more or less conscious purpose of the whole proceeding. In distribution, by contrast, humanity has allegedly permitted itself to be considerably more arbitrary. Quite apart from this crude tearing-apart of production and distribution and of their real relationship, it must be apparent from the outset that, no matter how differently distribution may have been arranged in different stages of social development, it must be possible here also, just as with production, to single out common characteristics, and just as possible to confound or to extinguish all historic differences under *general human* laws. For example, the slave, the serf and the wage labourer all receive a quantity of food which makes it possible for them to exist as slaves,

7. John Stuart Mill (1806–73), English political theorist and economist; radical in politics, confusedly and eclectically Ricardian in economics. His *Principles of Political Economy* (London, 1948), begin in Bk. I, Ch. 1, with the analysis of production.

as serfs, as wage labourers. The conqueror who lives from tribute, or the official who lives from taxes, or the landed proprietor and his rent, or the monk and his alms, or the Levite and his tithe, all receive a quota of social production, which is determined by other laws than that of the slave's, etc. The two main points which all economists cite under this rubric are: (1) property; (2) its protection by courts, police, etc. To this a very short answer may be given:

to 1. All production is appropriation of nature on the part of an individual within and through a specific form of society. In this sense it is a tautology to say that property (appropriation) is a precondition of production. But it is altogether ridiculous to leap from that to a specific form of property, e.g. private property. (Which further and equally presupposes an antithetical form, *non-property*.) History rather shows common property (e.g. in India, among the Slavs, the early Celts, etc.) to be the more original form, a form which long continues to play a significant role in the shape of communal property. The question whether wealth develops better in this or another form of property is still quite beside the point here. But that there can be no production and hence no society where some form of property does not exist is a tautology. An appropriation which does not make something into property is a *contradictio in subjecto*.

to 2. Protection of acquisitions etc. When these trivialities are reduced to their real content, they tell more than their preachers know. Namely that every form of production creates its own legal relations, form of government, etc. In bringing things which are organically related into an accidental relation, into a merely reflective connection, they display their crudity and lack of conceptual understanding. All the bourgeois economists are aware of is that production can be carried on better under the modern police than e.g. on the principle of might makes right. They forget only that this principle is also a legal relation, and that the right of the stronger prevails in their "constitutional republics" as well, only in another form.

When the social conditions corresponding to a specific stage of production are only just arising, or when they are already dying out, there are, naturally, disturbances in production, although to different degrees and with different effects.

To summarize: There are characteristics which all stages of production have in common, and which are established as general ones by the mind; but the so-called *general preconditions* of all production are nothing more than these abstract moments with which no real historical stage of production can be grasped.

(2) THE GENERAL RELATION OF PRODUCTION TO DISTRIBUTION, EXCHANGE, CONSUMPTION

Before going further in the analysis of production, it is necessary to focus on the various categories which the economists line up next to it.

The obvious, trite notion: in production the members of society appropriate (create, shape) the products of nature in accord with human needs; distribution determines the proportion in which the individual shares in the product; exchange delivers the particular products into which the individual desires to convert the portion which distribution has assigned to him; and finally, in consumption, the products become objects of gratification, of individual appropriation. Production creates the objects which correspond to the given needs; distribution divides them up according to social laws; exchange further parcels out the already divided shares in accord with individual needs; and finally, in consumption, the product steps outside this social movement and becomes a direct object and servant of individual need, and satisfies it in being consumed. Thus production appears as the point of departure, consumption as the conclusion, distribution and exchange as the middle, which is however itself twofold, since distribution is determined by society and exchange by individuals. The person objectifies himself in production, the thing subjectifies itself in the person; in distribution, society mediates between production and consumption in the form of general, dominant determinants; in exchange the two are mediated by the chance characteristics of the individual.

Distribution determines the relation in which products fall to individuals (the amount); exchange determines the production in which the individual demands the portion allotted to him by distribution.

Thus production, distribution, exchange and consumption form a regular syllogism; production is the generality, distribution and exchange the particularity, and consumption the singularity in which the whole is joined together. This is admittedly a coherence, but a shallow one. Production is determined by general natural laws, distribution by social accident, and the latter may therefore promote production to a greater or lesser extent; exchange stands between the two as formal social movement; and the concluding act, consumption, which is conceived not only as a terminal point but also as an end-in-itself, actually belongs outside economics except in so far as it reacts in turn upon the point of departure and initiates the whole process anew.

The opponents of the political economists—whether inside or outside its realm—who accuse them of barbarically tearing apart things which belong together, stand either on the same ground as they, or beneath them. Nothing is more common than the reproach that the political economists view production too much as an end in itself, that distribution is just as important. This accusation is based precisely on the economic notion that the spheres of distribution and of production are independent, autonomous neighbours. Or that these moments were not grasped in their unity. As if this rupture had made its way not from reality into the textbooks, but rather from the textbooks into reality, and as if the task were the dialectic balancing of concepts, and not the grasping of real relations!

Consumption and Production

(a_1) Production is also immediately consumption. Twofold consumption, subjective and objective: the individual not only develops his abilities in production, but also expends them, uses them up in the act of production, just as natural procreation is a consumption of life forces. Secondly: consumption of the means of production, which become worn out through use, and are partly (e.g. in combustion) dissolved into their elements again. Likewise, consumption of the raw material, which loses its natural form and composition by being used up. The act of production is therefore in all its moments also an act of consumption. But the economists admit this. Production as directly identical with consumption, and consumption as directly coincident with production, is termed by them *productive consumption*. This identity of production and consumption amounts to Spinoza's thesis: *determinatio est negatio*.[8]

But this definition of productive consumption is advanced only for the purpose of separating consumption as identical with production from consumption proper, which is conceived rather as the destructive antithesis to production. Let us therefore examine consumption proper.

Consumption is also immediately production, just as in nature the consumption of the elements and chemical substances is the production of the plant. It is clear that in taking in food, for example, which is a form of consumption, the human being produces his own body. But this is also true of every kind of consumption which in one way or another produces human beings in some particular aspect. Consumptive production. But, says economics, this produc-

8. "Determination is negation," i.e., given the undifferentiated self-identity of the universal world substance, to attempt to introduce particular determinations is to negate this self-identity (Spinoza, *Letters*, No. 50. to J. Jelles, 2 June 1674).

tion which is identical with consumption is secondary, it is derived from the destruction of the prior product. In the former, the producer objectified himself, in the latter, the object he created personifies itself. Hence this consumptive production—even though it is an immediate unity of production and consumption—is essentially different from production proper. The immediate unity in which production coincides with consumption and consumption with production leaves their immediate duality intact.

Production, then, is also immediately consumption, consumption is also immediately production. Each is immediately its opposite. But at the same time a mediating movement takes place between the two. Production mediates consumption; it creates the latter's material; without it, consumption would lack an object. But consumption also mediates production, in that it alone creates for the products the subject for whom they are products. The product only obtains its "last finish"[9] in consumption. A railway on which no trains run, hence which is not used up, not consumed, is a railway only $\delta \upsilon \nu \acute{\alpha} \mu \epsilon \iota$,[1] and not in reality. Without production, no consumption; but also, without consumption, no production; since production would then be purposeless. Consumption produces production in a double way, (1) because a product becomes a real product only by being consumed. For example, a garment becomes a real garment only in the act of being worn; a house where no one lives is in fact not a real house; thus the product, unlike a mere natural object, proves itself to be, *becomes*, a product only through consumption. Only by decomposing the product does consumption give the product the finishing touch; for the product is production not as[2] objectified activity, but rather only as object for the active subject; (2) because consumption creates the need for *new* production, that is it creates the ideal, internally impelling cause for production, which is its presupposition. Consumption creates the motive for production; it also creates the object which is active in production as its determinant aim. If it is clear that production offers consumption its external object, it is therefore equally clear that consumption *ideally posits* the object of production as an internal image, as a need, as drive and as purpose. It creates the objects of production in a still subjective form. No production without a need. But consumption reproduces the need.

Production, for its part, correspondingly (1) furnishes the material and the object for consumption.[3] Consumption without an object is not consumption; therefore, in this respect, production cre-

9. In English in the original.
1. "Potentially." Cf. Aristotle, *Metaphysics*, Bk. VIII, Ch. 6, p. 2.
2. The manuscript has: "for the prod-
uct is production not only as. . . ."
3. The manuscript has "for production."

ates, produces consumption. (2) But the object is not the only thing which production creates for consumption. Production also gives consumption its specificity, its character, its finish. Just as consumption gave the product its finish as product, so does production give finish to consumption. *Firstly*, the object is not an object in general, but a specific object which must be consumed in a specific manner, to be mediated in its turn by production itself. Hunger is hunger, but the hunger gratified by cooked meat eaten with a knife and fork is a different hunger from that which bolts down raw meat with the aid of hand, nail and tooth. Production thus produces not only the object but also the manner of consumption, not only objectively but also subjectively. Production thus creates the consumer. (3) Production not only supplies a material for the need, but it also supplies a need for the material. As soon as consumption emerges from its initial state of natural crudity and immediacy— and, if it remained at that stage, this would be because production itself had been arrested there—it becomes itself mediated as a drive by the object. The need which consumption feels for the object is created by the perception of it. The object of art—like every other product—creates a public which is sensitive to art and enjoys beauty. Production thus not only creates an object for the subject, but also a subject for the object. Thus production produces consumption (1) by creating the material for it; (2) by determining the manner of consumption; and (3) by creating the products, initially posited by it as objects, in the form of a need felt by the consumer. It thus produces the object of consumption, the manner of consumption and the motive of consumption. Consumption likewise produces the producer's *inclination* by beckoning to him as an aim-determining need.

The identities between consumption and production thus appear threefold:

(1) *Immediate identity:* Production is consumption, consumption is production. Consumptive production. Productive consumption. The political economists call both productive consumption. But then make a further distinction. The first figures as reproduction, the second as productive consumption. All investigations into the first concern productive or unproductive labour; investigations into the second concern productive or non-productive consumption.

(2) [In the sense] that one appears as a means for the other, is mediated by the other: this is expressed as their mutual dependence; a movement which relates them to one another, makes them appear indispensable to one another, but still leaves them external to each other. Production creates the material, as external object, for consumption; consumption creates the need, as internal object, as aim, for production. Without production no consumption; with-

out consumption no production. [This identity] figures in economics in many different forms.

(3) Not only is production immediately consumption and consumption immediately production, not only is production a means
for consumption and consumption the aim of production, i.e. each
supplies the other with its object (production supplying the external
object of consumption, consumption the conceived object of production); but also, each of them, apart from being immediately the
other, and apart from mediating the other, in addition to this creates the other in completing itself, and creates itself as the other
Consumption accomplishes the act of production only in completing the product as product by dissolving it, by consuming its independently material form, by raising the inclination developed in the
first act of production, through the need for repetition, to its
finished form; it is thus not only the concluding act in which the
product becomes product, but also that in which the producer
becomes producer. On the other side, production produces consumption by creating the specific manner of consumption; and, further, by creating the stimulus of consumption, the ability to consume, as a need. This last identity, as determined under (3), [is]
frequently cited in economics in the relation of demand and supply,
of objects and needs, of socially created and natural needs.

Thereupon, nothing simpler for a Hegelian than to posit production and consumption as identical. And this has been done not only
by socialist belletrists but by prosaic economists themselves, e.g.
Say[4]; in the form that when one looks at an entire people, its production is its consumption. Or, indeed, at humanity in the abstract.
Storch[5] demonstrated Say's error, namely that e.g. a people does
not consume its entire product, but also creates means of production, etc., fixed capital, etc. To regard society as one single subject
is, in addition, to look at it wrongly; speculatively. With a single
subject, production and consumption appear as moments of a single
act. The important thing to emphasize here is only that, whether
production and consumption are viewed as the activity of one or of
many individuals, they appear in any case as moments of one process, in which production is the real point of departure and hence
also the predominant moment. Consumption as urgency, as need, is
itself an intrinsic moment of productive activity. But the latter is
the point of departure for realization and hence also its predomi-

4. Jean-Baptiste Say (1767–1832), "the
inane Say," who "superficially condensed
political economy into a textbook"
(Marx), a businessman who popular-
ized and vulgarized the doctrines of
Adam Smith in his *Traité d'économie
politique* (Paris, 1803).
5. Henrich Friedrich Storch (1766–

1835), Professor of Political Economy
in the Russian Academy of Sciences at
St. Petersburg. Say issued Storch's work
Cours d'économie politique with critical notes in 1823; he attacked Say's
interpretation of his views in *Considér-
ations sur la nature du revenu national*
(Paris, 1824), pp. 144–59.

nant moment; it is the act through which the whole process again runs its course. The individual produces an object and, by consuming it, returns to himself, but returns as a productive and self-reproducing individual. Consumption thus appears as a moment of production.

In society, however, the producer's relation to the product, once the latter is finished, is an external one, and its return to the subject depends on his relations to other individuals. He does not come into possession of it directly. Nor is its immediate appropriation his purpose when he produces in society. *Distribution* steps between the producers and the products, hence between production and consumption, to determine in accordance with social laws what the producer's share will be in the world of products.

Now, does distribution stand at the side of and outside production as an autonomous sphere?

Distribution and Production

When one examines the usual works of economics, it is immediately striking that everything in them is posited doubly. For example, ground rent, wages, interest and profit figure under distribution, while land, labour and capital figure under production as agents of production. In the case of capital, now, it is evident from the outset that it is posited doubly, (1) as agent of production, (2) as source of income, as a determinant of specific forms of distribution. Interest and profit thus also figure as such in production, in so far as they are forms in which capital increases, grows, hence moments of its own production. Interest and profit as forms of distribution presuppose capital as agent of production. They are modes of distribution whose presupposition is capital as agent of production. They are, likewise, modes of reproduction of capital.

The category of wages, similarly, is the same as that which is examined under a different heading as wage labour: the characteristic which labour here possesses as an agent of production appears as a characteristic of distribution. If labour were not specified as wage labour, then the manner in which it shares in the products would not appear as wages; as, for example, under slavery. Finally, to take at once the most developed form of distribution, ground rent, by means of which landed property shares in the product, presupposes large-scale landed property (actually, large-scale agriculture) as agent of production, and not merely land as such, just as wages do not merely presuppose labour as such. The relations and modes of distribution thus appear merely as the obverse of the agents of production. An individual who participates in production in the form of wage labour shares in the products, in the results of production, in the form of wages. The structure [*Gliederung*] of distribution is completely determined by the structure of production. Distribution is itself a product of production, not only in its object, in that only the results of production can be distributed, but also in its form, in that the specific kind of participation in production determines the specific forms of distribution, i.e. the pattern of participation in distribution. It is altogether an illusion to posit land in production, ground rent in distribution, etc.

Thus, economists such as Ricardo, who are the most frequently accused of focusing on production alone, have defined distribution as the exclusive object of economics, because they instinctively conceived the forms of distribution as the most specific expression into which the agents of production of a given society are cast.

To the single individual, of course, distribution appears as a social law which determines his position within the system of production within which he produces, and which therefore precedes production. The individual comes into the world possessing neither capital nor land. Social distribution assigns him at birth to wage labour. But this situation of being assigned is itself a consequence of the existence of capital and landed property as independent agents of production.

As regards whole societies, distribution seems to precede production and to determine it in yet another respect, almost as if it were a pre-economic fact. A conquering people divides the land among the conquerors, thus imposes a certain distribution and form of property in land, and thus determines production. Or it enslaves the conquered and so makes slave labour the foundation of production. Or a people rises in revolution and smashes the great landed estates into small parcels, and hence, by this new distribution, gives production a new character. Or a system of laws assigns property in land to certain families in perpetuity, or distributes labour [as] a hereditary privilege and thus confines it within certain castes. In all these cases, and they are all historical, it seems that distribution is not structured and determined by production, but rather the opposite, production by distribution.

In the shallowest conception, distribution appears as the distribution of products, and hence as further removed from and quasi-independent of production. But before distribution can be the distribution of products, it is: (1) the distribution of the instruments of production, and (2), which is a further specification of the same relation, the distribution of the members of the society among the different kinds of production. (Subsumption of the individuals under specific relations of production.) The distribution of products is evidently only a result of this distribution, which is comprised within the process of production itself and determines the structure of production. To examine production while disregarding this internal distribution within it is obviously an empty abstraction; while conversely, the distribution of products follows by itself from this distribution which forms an original moment of production. Ricardo, whose concern was to grasp the specific social structure of modern production, and who is the economist of production *par excellence*, declares for precisely that reason that *not* production but distribution is the proper study of modern economics.[6] This again shows the ineptitude of those economists who portray production as an eternal truth while banishing history to the realm of distribution.

The question of the relation between this production-determining distribution, and production, belongs evidently within production itself. If it is said that, since production must begin with a certain distribution of the instruments of production, it follows that distribution at least in this sense precedes and forms the presupposition of production, then the reply must be that production does indeed have its determinants and preconditions, which form its moments. At the very beginning these may appear as spontaneous, natural. But by the process of production itself they are transformed from natural into historic determinants, and if they appear to one epoch as natural presuppositions of production, they were its historic product for another. Within production itself they are constantly being changed. The application of machinery, for example, changed the distribution of instruments of production as well as of products. Modern large-scale landed property is itself the product of modern commerce and of modern industry, as well as of the application of the latter to agriculture.

The questions raised above all reduce themselves in the last instance to the role played by general-historical relations in production, and their relation to the movement of history generally. The question evidently belongs within the treatment and investigation of production itself.

Still, in the trivial form in which they are raised above, they can be dealt with equally briefly. In all cases of conquest, three things are possible. The conquering people subjugates the conquered under its own mode of production (e.g. the English in Ireland in this century, and partly in India); or it leaves the old mode intact and contents itself with a tribute (e.g. Turks and Romans); or a reciprocal interaction takes place whereby something new, a synthesis, arises (the Germanic conquests, in part). In all cases, the mode of production, whether that of the conquering people, that of the conquered, or that emerging from the fusion of both, is decisive for the new distribution which arises. Although the latter appears as a pre-

6. David Ricardo, *On the Principles of*   ed. (London, 1821), preface, p. v.
Political Economy and Taxation, 3rd

supposition of the new period of production, it is thus itself in turn a product of production, not only of historical production generally, but of the specific historic mode of production.

The Mongols, with their devastations in Russia, e.g., were acting in accordance with their production, cattle-raising, for which vast uninhabited spaces are a chief precondition. The Germanic barbarians, who lived in isolation on the land and for whom agriculture with bondsmen was the traditional production, could impose these conditions on the Roman provinces all the more easily as the concentration of landed property which had taken place there had already entirely overthrown the earlier agricultural relations.

It is a received opinion that in certain periods people lived from pillage alone. But, for pillage to be possible, there must be something to be pillaged, hence production. And the mode of pillage is itself in turn determined by the mode of production. A stock-jobbing nation, for example, cannot be pillaged in the same manner as a nation of cow-herds.

To steal a slave is to steal the instrument of production directly. But then the production of the country for which the slave is stolen must be structured to allow of slave labour, or (as in South America etc.) a mode of production corresponding to the slave must be created.

Laws may perpetuate an instrument of production, e.g. land, in certain families. These laws achieve economic significance only when large-scale landed property is in harmony with the society's production, as e.g. in England. In France, small-scale agriculture survived despite the great landed estates, hence the latter were smashed by the revolution. But can laws perpetuate the small-scale allotment? Despite these laws, ownership is again becoming concentrated. The influence of laws in stabilizing relations of distribution, and hence their effect on production, requires to be determined in each specific instance.

Exchange, Finally, and Circulation

Exchange and Production

Circulation itself [is] merely a specific moment of exchange, or [it is] also exchange regarded in its totality.

In so far as *exchange* is merely a moment mediating between production with its production-determined distribution on one side and consumption on the other, but in so far as the latter itself appears as a moment of production, to that extent is exchange obviously also included as a moment within the latter.

It is clear, firstly, that the exchange of activities and abilities

236 · *The Critique of Capitalism*

which takes place within production itself belongs directly to production and essentially constitutes it. The same holds, secondly, for the exchange of products, in so far as that exchange is the means of finishing the product and making it fit for direct consumption. To that extent, exchange is an act comprised within production itself. Thirdly, the so-called exchange between dealers and dealers is by its very organization entirely determined by production, as well as being itself a producing activity. Exchange appears as independent of and indifferent to production only in the final phase where the product is exchanged directly for consumption. But (1) there is no exchange without division of labour, whether the latter is spontaneous, natural, or already a product of historic development; (2) private exchange presupposes private production; (3) the intensity of exchange, as well as its extension and its manner, are determined by the development and structure of production. For example. Exchange between town and country; exchange in the country, in the town etc. Exchange in all its moments thus appears as either directly comprised in production or determined by it.

The conclusion we reach is not that production, distribution, exchange and consumption are identical, but that they all form the members of a totality, distinctions within a unity. Production predominates not only over itself, in the antithetical definition of production, but over the other moments as well. The process always returns to production to begin anew. That exchange and consumption cannot be predominant is self-evident. Likewise, distribution as distribution of products; while as distribution of the agents of production it is itself a moment of production. A definite production thus determines a definite consumption, distribution and exchange as well as *definite relations between these different moments*. Admittedly, however, *in its one-sided form*, production is itself determined by the other moments. For example if the market, i.e. the sphere of exchange, expands, then production grows in quantity and the divisions between its different branches become deeper. A change in distribution changes production, e.g. concentration of capital, different distribution of the population between town and country, etc. Finally, the needs of consumption determine production. Mutual interaction takes place between the different moments. This the case with every organic whole.

(3) THE METHOD OF POLITICAL ECONOMY

When we consider a given country politico-economically, we begin with its population, its distribution among classes, town, country, the coast, the different branches of production, export and import, annual production and consumption, commodity prices etc.

It seems to be correct to begin with the real and the concrete, with the real precondition, thus to begin, in economics, with e.g. the population, which is the foundation and the subject of the entire social act of production. However, on closer examination this proves false. The population is an abstraction if I leave out, for example, the classes of which it is composed. These classes in turn are an empty phrase if I am not familiar with the elements on which they rest. E.g. wage labour, capital, etc. These latter in turn presuppose exchange, division of labour, prices, etc. For example, capital is nothing without wage labour, without value, money, price etc. Thus, if I were to begin with the population, this would be a chaotic conception [*Vorstellung*] of the whole, and I would then, by means of further determination, move analytically towards ever more simple concepts [*Begriff*], from the imagined concrete towards ever thinner abstractions until I had arrived at the simplest determinations. From there the journey would have to be retraced until I had finally arrived at the population again, but this time not as the chaotic conception of a whole, but as a rich totality of many determinations and relations. The former is the path historically followed by economics at the time of its origins. The economists of the seventeenth century, e.g., always begin with the living whole, with population, nation, state, several states, etc.; but they always conclude by discovering through analysis a small number of determinant, abstract, general relations such as division of labour, money, value, etc. As soon as these individual moments had been more or less firmly established and abstracted, there began the economic systems, which ascended from the simple relations, such as labour, division of labour, need, exchange value, to the level of the state, exchange between nations and the world market. The latter is obviously the scientifically correct method. The concrete is concrete because it is the concentration of many determinations, hence unity of the diverse. It appears in the process of thinking, therefore, as a process of concentration, as a result, not as a point of departure, even though it is the point of departure in reality and hence also the point of departure for observation [*Anschauung*] and conception. Along the first path the full conception was evaporated to yield an abstract determination; along the second, the abstract determinations lead towards a reproduction of the concrete by way of thought. In this way Hegel fell into the illusion of conceiving the real as the product of thought concentrating itself, probing its own depths, and unfolding itself out of itself, by itself, whereas the method of rising from the abstract to the concrete is only the way in which thought appropriates the concrete, reproduces it as the concrete in the mind. But this is by no means the process by which the concrete itself comes into being. For example, the simplest economic category, say e.g. exchange value, presupposes population, moreover a population producing in specific relations; as well as a certain kind of family, or commune, or state, etc. It can never exist other than as an abstract, one-sided relation within an already given, concrete, living whole. As a category, by contrast, exchange value leads an antediluvian existence. Therefore, to the kind of consciousness—and this is characteristic of the philosophical consciousness—for which conceptual thinking is the real human being, and for which the conceptual world as such is thus the only reality, the movement of the categories appears as the real act of production—which only, unfortunately, receives a jolt from the outside—whose product is the world; and—but this is again a tautology—this is correct in so far as the concrete totality is a totality of thoughts, concrete in thought, in fact a product of thinking and comprehending; but not in any way a product of the concept which thinks and generates itself outside or above observation and conception; a product, rather, of the working-up of observation and conception into concepts. The totality as it appears in the head, as a totality of thoughts, is a product of a thinking head, which appropriates the world in the only way it can, a way different from the artistic, religious, practical and mental appropriation of this world. The real subject retains its autonomous existence outside the head just as before; namely as long as the head's conduct is merely speculative, merely theoretical. Hence, in the theoretical method, too, the subject, society, must always be kept in mind as the presupposition.

But do not these simpler categories also have an independent historical or natural existence predating the more concrete ones? That depends. Hegel, for example, correctly begins the Philosophy of Right with possession, this being the subject's simplest juridical relation. But there is no possession preceding the family or master—servant relations, which are far more concrete relations. However, it would be correct to say that there are families or clan groups which still merely *possess*, but have no *property*. The simple category therefore appears in relation to property as a relation of simple families or clan groups. In the higher society it appears as the simpler relation of a developed organization. But the concrete substratum of which possession is a relation is always presupposed. One can imagine an individual savage as possessing something. But in that case possession is not a juridical relation. It is incorrect that possession develops historically into the family. Possession, rather, always presupposes this "more concrete juridical category." There would still always remain this much, however, namely that the simple categories are the expressions of relations within which the less developed concrete may have already realized itself before having posited the more many-sided connection or relation which is mentally expressed in the more concrete category; while the more developed concrete preserves the same category as a subordinate relation. Money may exist, and did exist historically, before capital existed, before banks existed, before wage labour existed, etc. Thus in this respect it may be said that the simpler category can express the dominant relations of a less developed whole, or else those subordinate relations of a more developed whole which already had a historic existence before this whole developed in the direction expressed by a more concrete category. To that extent the path of abstract thought, rising from the simple to the combined, would correspond to the real historical process.

It may be said on the other hand that there are very developed but nevertheless historically less mature forms of society, in which the highest forms of economy, e.g. cooperation, a developed division of labour, etc., are found, even though there is no kind of money, e.g. Peru. Among the Slav communities also, money and the exchange which determines it play little or no role within the individual communities, but only on their boundaries, in traffic with others; it is simply wrong to place exchange at the centre of communal society as the original, constituent element. It originally appears, rather, in the connection of the different communities with one another, not in the relations between the different members of a single community. Further, although money everywhere plays a role from very early on, it is nevertheless a predominant element, in antiquity, only within the confines of certain one-sidedly developed nations, trading nations. And even in the most advanced parts of the ancient world, among the Greeks and Romans, the full development of money, which is presupposed in modern bourgeois society, appears only in the period of their dissolution. This very simple category, then, makes a historic appearance in its full intensity only in the most developed conditions of society. By no means does it wade its way through all economic relations. For example, in the Roman Empire, at its highest point of development, the foundation remained taxes and payments in kind. The money system actually completely developed there only in the army. And it never took over the whole of labour. Thus, although the simpler category may have existed historically before the more concrete, it can achieve its full (intensive and extensive) development precisely in a combined form of society, while the more concrete category was more fully developed in a less developed form of society.

Labour seems a quite simple category. The conception of labour in this general form—as labour as such—is also immeasurably old. Nevertheless, when it is economically conceived in this simplicity, "labour" is as modern a category as are the relations which create this simple abstraction. The Monetary System,[7] for example, still locates wealth altogether objectively, as an external thing, in money. Compared with this standpoint, the commercial, or manufacture, system took a great step forward by locating the source of wealth not in the object but in a subjective activity—in commercial and manufacturing activity—even though it still always conceives this activity within narrow boundaries, as moneymaking. In contrast to this system, that of the Physiocrats posits a certain kind of labour —agriculture—as the creator of wealth, and the object itself no longer appears in a monetary disguise, but as the product in general, as the general result of labour. This product, as befits the narrowness of the activity, still always remains a naturally determined product—the product of agriculture, the product of the earth *par excellence*.

It was an immense step forward for Adam Smith to throw out every limiting specification of wealth-creating activity—not only manufacturing, or commercial or agricultural labour, but one as well as the others, labour in general. With the abstract universality of wealth-creating activity we now have the universality of the object defined as wealth, the product as such or again labour as such, but labour as past, objectified labour. How difficult and great was this transition may be seen from how Adam Smith himself from time to time still falls back into the Physiocratic system. Now, it might seem that all that had been achieved thereby was to discover the abstract expression for the simplest and most ancient relation in which human beings—in whatever form of society—play the role of producers. This is correct in one respect. Not in another. Indifference towards any specific kind of labour presupposes a very developed totality of real kinds of labour, of which no single one is any longer predominant. As a rule, the most general abstractions arise only in the midst of the richest possible concrete development, where one thing appears as common to many, to all. Then it ceases to be thinkable in a particular form alone. On the other side, this abstraction of labour as such is not merely the mental product of a concrete totality of labours. Indifference towards specific labours corresponds to a form of society in which individuals can with ease transfer from one labour to another, and where the specific kind is a matter of chance for them, hence of indifference. Not only the category, labour, but labour in reality has here become the means of

7. Marx considered that the Monetary System, as defined here, covered economists from the sixteenth century to the Physiocrats. However, within the Monetary System there arose what he calls here the "commercial, or manufacture system" but elsewhere the Mercantile System (known to economics textbooks as Mercantilism). He distinguishes between the two systems later in this work, but his normal practice is to link them together, since "the Mercantile System is merely a variant of the Monetary System" (*A Contribution to the Critique of Political Economy* [London, 1971], p. 158).

creating wealth in general, and has ceased to be organically linked
with particular individuals in any specific form. Such a state of
affairs is at its most developed in the most modern form of existence of bourgeois society—in the United States. Here, then, for the
first time, the point of departure of modern economics, namely the
abstraction of the category "labour," "labour as such," labour pure
and simple, becomes true in practice. The simplest abstraction,
then, which modern economics places at the head of its discussions,
and which expresses an immeasurably ancient relation valid in all
forms of society, nevertheless achieves practical truth as an abstraction only as a category of the most modern society. One could say
that this indifference towards particular kinds of labour, which is a
historic product in the United States, appears e.g. among the Russians as a spontaneous inclination. But there is a devil of a difference between barbarians who are fit by nature to be used for anything, and civilized people who apply themselves to everything. And
then in practice the Russian indifference to the specific character of
labour corresponds to being embedded by tradition within a very
specific kind of labour, from which only external influences can jar
them loose.

This example of labour shows strikingly how even the most
abstract categories, despite their validity—precisely because of their
abstractness—for all epochs, are nevertheless, in the specific character of this abstraction, themselves likewise a product of historic relations, and possess their full validity only for and within these relations.

Bourgeois society is the most developed and the most complex
historic organization of production. The categories which express its
relations, the comprehension of its structure, thereby also allows
insights into the structure and the relations of production of all the
vanished social formations out of whose ruins and elements it built
itself up, whose partly still unconquered remnants are carried along
within it, whose mere nuances have developed explicit significance
within it, etc. Human anatomy contains a key to the anatomy of the
ape. The intimations of higher development among the subordinate
animal species, however, can be understood only after the higher
development is already known. The bourgeois economy thus supplies the key to the ancient, etc. But not at all in the manner of
those economists who smudge over all historical differences and see
bourgeois relations in all forms of society. One can understand tribute, tithe, etc., if one is acquainted with ground rent. But one must
not identify them. Further, since bourgeois society is itself only a
contradictory form of development, relations derived from earlier
forms will often be found within it only in an entirely stunted
form, or even travestied. For example, communal property.

Although it is true, therefore, that the categories of bourgeois economics possess a truth for all other forms of society, this is to be taken only with a grain of salt. They can contain them in a developed, or stunted, or caricatured form etc., but always with an essential difference.The so-called historical presentation of development is founded, as a rule, on the fact that the latest form regards the previous ones as steps leading up to itself, and, since it is only rarely and only under quite specific conditions able to criticize itself— leaving aside, of course, the historical periods which appear to themselves as times of decadence—it always conceives them one-sidedly. The Christian religion was able to be of assistance in reaching an objective understanding of earlier mythologies only when its own self-criticism had been accomplished to a certain degree, so to speak, δυνάμει.[8] Likewise, bourgeois economics arrived at an understanding of feudal, ancient, oriental economics only after the self-criticism of bourgeois society had begun. In so far as the bourgeois economy did not mythologically identify itself altogether with the past, its critique of the previous economics, notably of feudalism, with which it was still engaged in direct struggle, resembled the critique which Christianity levelled against paganism, or also that of Protestantism against Catholicism.

In the succession of the economic categories, as in any other historical, social science, it must not be forgotten that their subject— here, modern bourgeois society—is always what is given, in the head as well as in reality, and that these categories therefore express the forms of being, the characteristics of existence, and often only individual sides of this specific society, this subject, and that therefore this society by no means begins only at the point where one can speak of it *as such*; this hold *for science as well*. This is to be kept in mind because it will shortly be decisive for the order and sequence of the categories. For example, nothing seems more natural than to begin with ground rent, with landed property, since this is bound up with the earth, the source of all production and of all being, and with the first form of production of all more or less settled societies—agriculture. But nothing would be more erroneous. In all forms of society there is one specific kind of production which predominates over the rest, whose relations thus assign rank and influence to the others. It is a general illumination which bathes all the other colours and modifies their particularity. It is a particular ether which determines the specific gravity of every being which has materialized within it. For example, with pastoral peoples (mere hunting and fishing peoples lie outside the point where real development begins). Certain forms of tillage occur among them, sporadic ones. Landed property is determined by this. It is held in

8. See p. 229, note 1.

common, and retains this form to a greater or lesser degree according to the greater or lesser degree of attachment displayed by these
peoples to their tradition, e.g. the communal property of the Slavs.
Among peoples with a settled agriculture—this settling already a
great step—where this predominates, as in antiquity and in the
feudal order, even industry, together with its organization and the
forms of property corresponding to it, has a more or less landed-proprietary character; is either completely dependent on it, as among
the earlier Romans, or, as in the Middle Ages, imitates, within the
city and its relations, the organization of the land. In the Middle
Ages, capital itself—apart from pure money-capital—in the form of
the traditional artisans' tools etc., has this landed-proprietary character. In bourgeois society it is the opposite. Agriculture more and
more becomes merely a branch of industry, and is entirely dominated by capital. Ground rent likewise. In all forms where landed
property rules, the natural relation still predominant. In those
where capital rules, the social, historically created element. Ground
rent cannot be understood without capital. But capital can certainly
be understood without ground rent. Capital is the all-dominating
economic power of bourgeois society. It must form the starting-
point as well as the finishing-point, and must be dealt with before
landed property. After both have been examined in particular, their
interrelation must be examined.

It would therefore be unfeasible and wrong to let the economic
categories follow one another in the same sequence as that in which
they were historically decisive. Their sequence is determined, rather,
by their relation to one another in modern bourgeois society, which
is precisely the opposite of that which seems to be their natural
order or which corresponds to historical development. The point is
not the historic position of the economic relations in the succession
of different forms of society. Even less is it their sequence "in the
idea" (Proudhon)[9] (a muddy notion of historic movement).
Rather, their order within modern bourgeois society.

The purity (abstract specificity) in which the trading peoples—
Phoenicians, Carthaginians—appear in the old world is determined
precisely by the predominance of the agricultural peoples. Capital,
as trading-capital or as money-capital, appears in this abstraction
precisely where capital is not yet the predominant element of
societies. Lombards, Jews take up the same position towards the
agricultural societies of the Middle Ages.

As a further example of the divergent positions which the same
category can occupy in different social stages: one of the latest
forms of bourgeois society, *joint-stock companies*. These also appear,

9. Pierre-Joseph Proudhon, *Système des contradictions économiques ou philoso-* *phie de la misère* (Paris, 1846), Vol. I, p. 146.

however, at its beginning, in the great, privileged monopoly trading companies.

The concept of national wealth creeps into the work of the economists of the seventeenth century—continuing partly with those of the eighteenth—in the form of the notion that wealth is created only to enrich the state, and that its power is proportionate to this wealth. This was the still unconsciously hypocritical form in which wealth and the production of wealth proclaimed themselves as the purpose of modern states, and regarded these states henceforth only as means for the production of wealth.

The order obviously has to be (1) the general, abstract determinants which obtain in more or less all forms of society, but in the above-explained sense. (2) The categories which make up the inner structure of bourgeois society and on which the fundamental classes rest. Capital, wage labour, landed property. Their interrelation. Town and country. The three great social classes. Exchange between them. Circulation. Credit system (private). (3) Concentration of bourgeois society in the form of the state. Viewed in relation to itself. The "unproductive" classes. Taxes. State debt. Public credit. The population. The colonies. Emigration. (4) The international relation of production. International division of labour. International exchange. Export and import. Rate of exchange. (5) The world market and crises.

(4) PRODUCTION. MEANS OF PRODUCTION AND RELATIONS OF PRODUCTION. RELATIONS OF PRODUCTION AND RELATIONS OF CIRCULATION. FORMS OF THE STATE AND FORMS OF CONSCIOUSNESS IN RELATION TO RELATIONS OF PRODUCTION AND CIRCULATION. LEGAL RELATIONS. FAMILY RELATIONS.

Notabene in regard to points to be mentioned here and not to be forgotten:

(1) *War* developed earlier than peace; the way in which certain economic relations such as wage labour, machinery etc. develop earlier, owing to war and in the armies etc., than in the interior of bourgeois society. The relation of productive force and relations of exchange also especially vivid in the army.

(2) *Relation of previous ideal historiography to the real. Namely of the so-called cultural histories,* which are only histories of religions and of state. (On that occasion something can also be said about the various kinds of previous historiography. The so-called objective. Subjective (moral among others). The philosophical.)

(3) *Secondary and tertiary* matters; in general, *derivative, inher-*

ited, not original relations of production. Influence here of international relations.

(4) *Accusations about the materialism of this conception. Relation to naturalistic materialism.*

(5) *Dialectic of the concepts productive force (means of production) and relation of production*, a dialectic whose boundaries are to be determined, and which does not suspend the real difference.

(6) *The uneven development of material production relative to e.g. artistic development.* In general, the concept of progress not to be conceived in the usual abstractness. Modern art etc. This disproportion not as important or so difficult to grasp as within practical-social relations themselves. E.g. the relation of education. Relation of the *United States* to Europe. But the really difficult point to discuss here is how relations of production develop unevenly as legal relations. Thus e.g. the relation of Roman private law (this less the case with criminal and public law) to modern production.

(7) *This conception appears as necessary development.* But legitimation of chance. How. (Of freedom also, among other things.) (Influence of means of communication. World history has not always existed; history as world history a result.)

(8) *The point of departure obviously from the natural characteristic*; subjectively and objectively. Tribes, races etc.

(1) In the case of the arts, it is well known that certain periods of their flowering are out of all proportion to the general development of society, hence also to the material foundation, the skeletal structure as it were, of its organization. For example, the Greeks compared to the moderns or also Shakespeare. It is even recognized that certain forms of art, e.g. the epic, can no longer be produced in their world epoch-making, classical stature as soon as the production of art, as such, begins; that is, that certain significant forms within the realm of the arts are possible only at an undeveloped stage of artistic development. If this is the case with the relation between different kinds of art within the realm of the arts, it is already less puzzling that it is the case in the relation of the entire realm to the general development of society. The difficulty consists only in the general formulation of these contradictions. As soon as they have been specified, they are already clarified.

Let us take e.g. the relation of Greek art and then of Shakespeare to the present time. It is well known that Greek mythology is not only the arsenal of Greek art but also its foundation. Is the view of nature and of social relations on which the Greek imagination and hence Greek [mythology] is based possible with self-acting mule spindles and railways and locomotives and electrical telegraphs? What chance has Vulcan against Roberts & Co., Jupiter against the lightning-rod and Hermes against the Credit Mobilier? All mythology overcomes and dominates and shapes the forces of nature in the imagination and by the imagination; it therefore vanishes with the advent of real mastery over them. What becomes of Fama alongside Printing House Square? Greek art presupposes Greek mythology, i.e. nature and the social forms already reworked in an unconsciously artistic way by the popular imagination. This is its material. Not any mythology whatever, i.e. not an arbitrarily chosen unconsciously artistic reworking of nature (here meaning everything objective, hence including society). Egyptian mythology could never have been the foundation or the womb of Greek art. But, in any case, a *mythology*. Hence, in no way a social development which excludes all mythological, all mythologizing relations to nature; which therefore demands of the artist an imagination not dependent on mythology.

From another side, is Achilles possible with powder and lead? Or the *Iliad* with the printing press, not to mention the printing machine? Do not the song and the saga and the muse necessarily come to an end with the printer's bar, hence do not the necessary conditions of epic poetry vanish?

But the difficulty lies not in understanding that the Greek arts and epic are bound up with certain forms of social development. The difficulty is that they still afford us artistic pleasure and that in a certain respect they count as a norm and as an unattainable model.

A man cannot become a child again, or he becomes childish. But does he not find joy in the child's naiveté, and must he himself not strive to reproduce its truth at a higher stage? Does not the true character of each epoch come alive in the nature of its children? Why should not the historic childhood of humanity, its most beautiful unfolding, as a stage never to return, exercise an eternal charm? There are unruly children and precocious children. Many of the old peoples belong in this category. The Greeks were normal children. The charm of their art for us is not in contradiction to the undeveloped stage of society on which it grew. [It] is its result, rather, and is inextricably bound up, rather, with the fact that the unripe social conditions under which it arose, and could alone arise, can never return.

B. Society and the Individual

Product and capital. Value and capital. Proudhon

(Nothing is more erroneous than the manner in which economists as well as socialists regard *society* in relation to economic conditions. Proudhon, for example, replies to Bastiat by saying (XVI,

29) : *"For society*, the difference between capital and product does not exist. This difference is entirely *subjective,* and related to individuals."[1] Thus he calls subjective precisely what is social; and he calls society a subjective abstraction. The difference between product and capital is exactly this, that the product expresses, as capital, a particular relation belonging to a historic form of society. This so-called contemplation from the standpoint of society means nothing more than the overlooking of the *differences* which express the *social relation* (relation of bourgeois society). Society does not consist of individuals, but expresses the sum of interrelations, the relations within which these individuals stand. As if someone were to say: Seen from the perspective of society, there are no slaves and no citizens: both are human beings. Rather, they are that outside society. To be a slave, to be a citizen, are social characteristics, relations between human beings A and B. Human being A, as such, is not a slave. He is a slave in and through society. What Mr Proudhon here says about capital and product means, for him, that from the viewpoint of society there is no difference between capitalists and workers; a difference which exists precisely only from the standpoint of society.)

* * *

C. The Dynamics of Capitalism

Surplus value. Surplus labour time.—Bastiat on wages. Value of labour. How determined?—Self-realization is self-preservation of capital. Capitalist may not live merely from his labour etc. Conditions for the self-realization of capital. Surplus labour time etc.—To the extent that capital is productive (as creator of surplus labour etc.), this only historic-transistory.—The free blacks in Jamaica.— Wealth which has gained autonomy requires slave labour or wage labour (forced labour in both cases).

* * *

What the worker exchanges with capital is his labour itself (the capacity of disposing over it); he *divests himself of it* [*entäussert sie*]. What he obtains as price is the *value* of this divestiture [*Entäusserung*]. He exchanges value-positing activity for a pre-determined value, regardless of the result of his activity. Now how is its value determined? By the objectified labour contained in his commodity. This commodity exists in his vitality. In order to maintain this from one day to the next—we are not yet dealing with the working class, i.e. the replacement for wear and tear so that it can maintain itself as a class, since the worker here confronts capital as a worker, i.e. as a presupposed perennial subject [*Subjekt*], and

1. Bastiat et Proudhon, *Gratuité du crédit* (Paris, 1850), p. 250.

not yet as a mortal individual of the working species—he has to consume a certain quantity of food, to replace his used-up blood etc. He receives no more than an equivalent. Thus tomorrow, after the completed exchange—and only after he has formally completed the exchange does he execute it in the process of production—his labouring capacity exists in the same mode as before: he has received an exact equivalent, because the price which he has obtained leaves him in possession of the same exchange value he had before. Capital has paid him the amount of objectified labour contained in his vital forces. Capital has consumed it, and because it did not exist as a thing, but as the capacity of a living being, the worker can, owing to the *specific* nature of his commodity—the specific nature of the life process—resume the exchange anew. Since we are dealing here not with any *particularly* qualified labour but with labour in general, simple labour, we are here not yet concerned with the fact that there is more labour objectified in his immediate existence than is contained in his mere vitality—i.e. the labour time necessary to pay for the products necessary to maintain his vitality —namely the values he has consumed in order to produce a specific *labouring capacity*, a special *skill*—and the value of these shows itself in the costs necessary to produce a similar labouring skill.

If one day's work were necessary in order to keep one worker alive for one day, then capital would not exist, because the working day would then exchange for its own product, so that capital could not realize itself and hence could not maintain itself as capital. The self-preservation of capital is its self-realization. If capital also had to work in order to live, then it would not maintain itself as capital but as labour. Property in raw materials and instruments of labour would be merely *nominal*; economically they would belong to the worker as much as to the capitalist, since they would create *value* for the capitalist only in so far as he himself were a worker. He would relate to them therefore not as capital, but as simple material and means of labour, like the worker himself does in the production process. If, however, only half a working day is necessary in order to keep one worker alive one whole day, then the surplus value of the product is self-evident, because the capitalist has paid the price of only half a working day but has obtained a whole day objectified in the product; thus has exchanged *nothing* for the second half of the work day. The only thing which can make him into a capitalist is not exchange, but rather a process through which he obtains *objectified labour time*, i.e. *value*, without exchange. Half the working day costs capital *nothing*; it thus obtains a value for which it has given no equivalent. And the multiplication of values can take place only if a value in excess of the equivalent has been obtained, hence *created*.

Surplus value in general is value in excess of the equivalent. The equivalent, by definition, is only the identity of value with itself. Hence surplus value can never sprout out of the equivalent; nor can it do so originally out of circulation; it has to arise from the production process of capital itself. The matter can also be expressed in this way: if the worker needs only half a working day in order to live a whole day, then, in order to keep alive as a worker, he needs to work only half a day. The second half of the labour day is forced labour; surplus-labour. What appears as surplus value on capital's side appears identically on the worker's side as surplus labour in excess of his requirements as worker, hence in excess of his immediate requirements for keeping himself alive. The great historic quality of capital is to *create* this *surplus labour*, superfluous labour from the standpoint of mere use value, mere subsistence; and its historic destiny [*Bestimmung*] is fulfilled as soon as, on one side, there has been such a development of needs that surplus labour above and beyond necessity has itself become a general need arising out of individual needs themselves—and, on the other side, when the severe discipline of capital, acting on succeeding generations [*Geschlechter*], has developed general industriousness as the general property of the new species [*Geschlecht*]—and, finally, when the development of the productive powers of labour, which capital incessantly whips onward with its unlimited mania for wealth, and of the sole conditions in which this mania can be realized, have flourished to the stage where the possession and preservation of general wealth require a lesser labour time of society as a whole, and where the labouring society relates scientifically to the process of its progressive reproduction, its reproduction in a constantly greater abundance; hence where labour in which a human being does what a thing could do has ceased. Accordingly, capital and labour relate to each other here like money and commodity; the former is the general form of wealth, the other only the substance destined for immediate consumption. Capital's ceaseless striving towards the general form of wealth drives labour beyond the limits of its natural paltriness [*Naturbedürftigkeit*], and thus creates the material elements for the development of the rich individuality which is as all-sided in its production as in its consumption, and whose labour also therefore appears no longer as labour, but as the full development of activity itself, in which natural necessity in its direct form has disappeared; because a historically created need has taken the place of the natural one. This is why *capital is productive; i.e. an essential relation for the development of the social productive forces*. It ceases to exist as such only where the development of these productive forces themselves encounters its barrier in capital itself.

The Times of November 1857 contains an utterly delightful cry of outrage on the part of a West-Indian plantation owner. This advocate analyses with great moral indignation—as a plea for the re-introduction of Negro slavery—how the *Quashees* (the free blacks of Jamaica) content themselves with producing only what is strictly necessary for their own consumption, and, alongside this "use value," regard loafing (indulgence and idleness) as the real luxury good; how they do not care a damn for the sugar and the fixed capital invested in the plantations, but rather observe the planters' impending bankruptcy with an ironic grin of malicious pleasure, and even exploit their acquired Christianity as an embellishment for this mood of malicious glee and indolence.[2] They have ceased to be slaves, but not in order to become wage labourers, but, instead, self-sustaining peasants working for their own consumption. As far as they are concerned, capital does not exist as capital, because autonomous wealth as such can exist only either on the basis of *direct* forced labour, slavery, or *indirect* forced labour, *wage labour*. Wealth confronts direct forced labour not as capital, but rather as *relation of domination* [*Herrschaftsverhältnis*]; thus, the relation of domination is the only thing which is reproduced on this basis, for which wealth itself has value only as gratification, not as wealth itself, and which can therefore never create *general industriousness*. (We shall return to this relation of slavery and wage labour.)

D. The Development of Exchange and of Capital

Original accumulation of capital. (The real accumulation).—Once developed historically, capital itself creates the conditions of its existence (not as conditions for its arising, but as results of its being).—(Performance of personal services, as opposed to wage labour.)—Inversion of the law of appropriation. Real alien relation [Fremdheit] of the worker to his product. Division of labour. Machinery etc.

Once production founded on capital is presupposed—money has become transformed into capital actually only at the *end of the first production* process, which resulted in its reproduction and in the new production of surplus capital I; surplus capital I, however, is itself *posited*, realized as surplus capital, only when it has produced surplus capital II, i.e. as soon as those presuppositions of money, while it is in the process of passing over into capital, which still lie outside the movement of *real* capital have vanished, and when capi-

---

2. *The Times*, London, Saturday, 21 November 1857, No. 22,844, p. 9. "Negroes and the Slave Trade. To the Editor of *The Times*. By Expertus."

Marx's English in this sentence has been changed to conform to modern usage.

tal has therefore itself posited, and posited in accordance with its immanent essence, the conditions which form its point of departure in production—[then] the condition that the capitalist, in order to posit himself as capital, must bring values into circulation which he created with his own labour—or by some other means, excepting only already available, previous wage labour—belongs among the antediluvian conditions of capital, belongs to its *historic presuppositions*, which, precisely as such *historic* presuppositions, are past and gone, and hence belong to the *history of its formation*, but in no way to its *contemporary* history, i.e. not to the real system of the mode of production ruled by it. While e.g. the flight of serfs to the cities is one of the *historic* conditions and presuppositions of urbanism, it is not a *condition*, not a moment of the reality of developed cities, but belongs rather to their past presuppositions, to the presuppositions of their becoming which are suspended in their being. The conditions and presuppositions of the *becoming*, of the *arising*, of capital presuppose precisely that it is not yet in being but merely in *becoming*; they therefore disappear as real capital arises, capital which itself, on the basis of its own reality, posits the conditions for its realization. Thus e.g. while the process in which money or value for-itself originally becomes capital presupposes on the part of the capitalist an accumulation—perhaps by means of savings garnered from products and values created by his own labour etc., which he has undertaken as a *not-capitalist*, i.e. while the presuppositions under which money becomes capital appear as given, external *presuppositions* for the arising of capital—[nevertheless,] as soon as capital has become capital as such, it creates its own presuppositions, i.e. the possession of the real conditions of the creation of new values *without exchange*—by means of its own production process. These presuppositions, which originally appeared as conditions of its becoming—and hence could not spring from its *action as capital*—now appear as results of its own realization, reality, as *posited by it—not as conditions of its arising, but as results of its presence*. It no longer proceeds from presuppositions in order to become, but rather it is itself presupposed, and proceeds from itself to create the conditions of its maintenance and growth. Therefore, the conditions which preceded the creation of surplus capital I, or which express the becoming of capital, do not fall into the sphere of that mode of production for which capital serves as the presupposition; as the historic preludes of its becoming, they lie behind it, just as the processes by means of which the earth made the transition from a liquid sea of fire and vapour to its present form now lie beyond its life as finished earth. That is, individual capitals can continue to arise e.g. by means of hoarding. But the hoard is transformed into capital only by means of the exploitation of labour.

252 · *The Critique of Capitalism*

The bourgeois economists who regard capital as an eternal and *natural* (not historical) form of production then attempt at the same time to legitimize it again by formulating the conditions of its becoming as the conditions of its contemporary realization; i.e. presenting the moments in which the capitalist still appropriates as not-capitalist—because he is still becoming—as the very conditions in which he appropriates *as capitalist*. These attempts at apologetics demonstrate a guilty conscience, as well as the inability to bring the mode of appropriation of capital as capital into harmony with the *general laws of property* proclaimed by capitalist society itself. On the other side, much more important for us is that our method indicates the points where historical investigation must enter in, or where bourgeois economy as a merely historical form of the production process points beyond itself to earlier historical modes of production. In order to develop the laws of bourgeois economy, therefore, it is not necessary to write the *real history of the relations of production*. But the correct observation and deduction of these laws, as having themselves become[3] in history, always leads to primary equations—like the empirical numbers e.g. in natural science—which point towards a past lying behind this system. These indications [*Andeutung*], together with a correct grasp of the present, then also offer the key to the understanding of the past—a work in its own right which, it is to be hoped, we shall be able to undertake as well.[4] This correct view likewise leads to the same time to the points at which the suspension of the present form of production relations gives signs of its becoming—foreshadowings of the future. Just as, on one side the prebourgeois phases appear as *merely historical*, i.e. suspended presuppositions, so do the contemporary conditions of production likewise appear as engaged in *suspending themselves* and hence in positing the *historic presuppositions* for a new state of society.

Now, if we initially examine the relation such as it has become, value having become capital, and living labour confronting it as mere use value, so that living labour appears as a mere means to realize objectified, dead labour, to penetrate it with an animating soul while losing its own soul to it—and having produced, as the end-product, alien wealth on one side and [, on the other,] the penury which is living labour capacity's sole possession—then the matter is simply this, that the process itself, in and by itself, posits

3. Having themselves become = having themselves undergone the process of becoming, as indicated above.
4. On 22 February 1858, Marx wrote to Lassalle that he was planning three works: (1) a critique of the economic categories or the system of bourgeois economy critically presented, (2) a critique and history of political economy and socialism, and (3) a short historical sketch of the development of economic relations or categories (*Marx-Engels Selected Correspondence*, Moscow, n.d., p. 125). Marx referred here to the third work, which he never produced in a completed form.

the real objective conditions of living labour (namely, material in which to realize itself, instrument with which to realize itself, and necessaries with which to stoke the flame of living labour capacity, to protect it from being extinguished, to supply its vital processes with the necessary fuels) and posits them as alien, independent existences — or as the mode of existence of an *alien person*, as self-sufficient values for-themselves, and hence as values which form wealth alien to an isolated and subjective labour capacity, wealth of and for the capitalist. The objective conditions of living labour appear as *separated, independent* [*verselbstandigte*] values opposite living labour capacity as subjective being, which therefore appears to them only as a value of *another kind* (not as value, but different from them, as use value). Once this separation is given, the production process can only produce it anew, reproduce it, and reproduce it on an expanded scale. How it does this, we have seen. The objective conditions of living labour capacity are presupposed as having an existence independent of it, as the objectivity of a subject distinct from living labour capacity and standing independently over against it; the reproduction and *realization* [*Verwertung*], i.e. the expansion of these *objective conditions*, is therefore at the same time their own reproduction and new production as the wealth of an alien subject indifferently and independently standing over against labour capacity. What is reproduced and produced anew [*neuproduziert*] is not only the presence of these objective conditions of living labour, *but also their presence as independent values, i.e. values belonging to an alien subject, confronting this living labour capacity*. The objective conditions of labour attain a subjective existence *vis-à-vis* living labour capacity—capital turns into capitalist; on the other side, the merely subjective presence of the labour capacity confronted by its own conditions gives it a merely indifferent, objective form as against them—it is merely a *value* of a particular use value *alongside* the conditions of its own realization [*Verwertung*] as *values* of another use value. Instead of their being realized [*realisiert*] in the production process as the conditions of its realization [*Verwirklichung*], what happens is quite the opposite: it comes out of the process as mere condition for *their* realization [*Verwertung*] and preservation as values for-themselves opposite living labour capacity. The material on which it works is *alien* material; the instrument is likewise an *alien* instrument; its labour appears as a mere accessory to their substance and hence objectifies itself in things not *belonging to it*. Indeed, living labour itself appears as *alien vis-à-vis* living labour capacity, whose labour it is, whose own life's expression [*Lebensäusserung*] it is, for it has been surrendered to capital in exchange for objectified labour, for the product of labour itself. Labour capacity relates to its labour as to an alien, and if capital were willing to pay it *without* making it labour it would enter the bargain with pleasure. Thus labour capacity's own labour is as alien to it—and it really is, as regards its direction etc.—as are material and instrument. Which is why the product then appears to it as a combination of alien material, alien instrument and alien labour—as *alien property*, and why, after production, it has become poorer by the life forces expended, but otherwise begins the drudgery anew, existing as a mere subjective labour capacity separated from the conditions of its life. The recognition [*Erkennung*] of the products as its own, and the judgement that its separation from the conditions of its realization is improper —forcibly imposed—is an enormous [advance in] awareness [*Bewusstsein*], itself the product of the mode of production resting on capital, and as much the knell to its doom as, with the slave's awareness that he *cannot be the property of another*, with his consciousness of himself as a person, the existence of slavery becomes a merely artificial, vegetative existence, and ceases to be able to prevail as the basis of production.

However, if we consider the original relation, before the entry of money into the self-realization process, then various conditions appear which have to have arisen, or been given historically, for money to become capital and labour to become capital-positing, capital-creating labour, wage labour. (*Wage labour*, here, in the strict economic sense in which we use it here, and no other—and we will later have to distinguish it from other forms of labour for day-wages etc.—is capital-positing, capital-producing labour, i.e. living labour which produces both the objective conditions of its realization as an activity, as well as the objective moments of its being as labour *capacity*, and produces them as alien powers opposite itself, as *values for-themselves, independent of it*.) The essential conditions are themselves posited in the relation as it appears originally: (1) on the one side the presence of living labour capacity as a merely *subjective* existence, separated from the *conditions* of living labour as well as from the *means of existence, the necessary goods*, the means of self-preservation of living *labour capacity*; the living possibility of labour, on the one side, in this complete abstraction; (2) the value, or objectified labour, found on the other side, must be an accumulation of use values sufficiently large to furnish the objective conditions not only for the production of the products or values required to reproduce or maintain living labour capacity, but also for the absorption of surplus labour—to supply the objective material for the latter; (3) a free exchange relation— money circulation—between both sides; between the extremes a relation founded on exchange values—not on the master-servant relation—i.e., hence, production which does not directly furnish the producer with his necessaries, but which is mediated through exchange, and which cannot therefore usurp alien labour directly, but must buy it, exchange it, from the worker himself; finally (4) one side—the side representing the objective conditions of labour in the form of independent values for-themselves—must present itself as *value*, and must regard the positing of value, self-realization, money-making, as the ultimate purpose—not direct consumption of the creation of use value.

So long as *both* sides exchange their laboour with one another in the form of *objectified* labour, the relation is impossible; it is likewise impossible if *living labour capacity* itself appears as the property of the other side, hence as not engaged in exchange. (The fact that slavery is possible at individual points within the bourgeois system of production does not contradict this. However, slavery is then possible there only because it does not exist at other points; and appears as an anomaly opposite the bourgeois system itself.)

The conditions under which the relation appears at the origin, or which appear as the historic presuppositions of its becoming, reveal at first glance a two-sided character—on one side, dissolution of lower forms of living labour; on the other, dissolution of happier forms of the same.

The first presupposition, to begin with, is that the relation of slavery or serfdom has been suspended. Living labour capacity belongs to itself, and has disposition over the expenditure of its forces, through exchange. Both sides confront each other as persons. *Formally*, their relation has the equality and freedom of exchange as such. As far as concerns the legal relation, the fact that this form is a mere *semblance*, and a *deceptive semblance*, appears as an *external matter*. What the free worker sells is always nothing more than a specific, particular measure of force-expenditure [*Kraftäusserung*]; labour capacity as a totality is greater than every particular expenditure. He sells the particular expenditure of force to a particular capitalist, whom he confronts as an independent *individual*. It is clear that this is not his relation to the existence of capital as capital, i.e. to the capitalist class. Nevertheless, in this way everything touching on the individual, real person leaves him a wide field of choice, of arbitrary will, and hence of formal freedom. In the slave relation, he belongs to the *individual, particular owner*, and is his labouring machine. As a totality of force-expenditure, as labour capacity, he is a thing [*Sache*] belonging to another, and hence does not relate as subject to his particular expenditure of force, nor to the act of living labour. In the serf relation he appears as a moment of property in land itself, is an appendage of the soil, exactly like draught-cattle. In the slave relation the worker is nothing but a living labour-machine, which therefore has a value for others, or rather is a value. The totality of the free worker's labour capacity appears to him as his property, as one of his moments, over which he, as subject, exercises domination, and which he maintains by expending it. This is to be developed later under wage labour.

The exchange of objectified labour for living labour does not yet constitute either capital on one side or wage labour on the other. The entire class of so-called *services* from the bootblack up to the king falls into this category. Likewise the free day-labourer, whom we encounter sporadically in all places where either the oriental community [*Gemeinwesen*] or the western commune [*Gemeinde*] consisting of free landowners dissolves into individual elements—as a consequence of increase of population, release of prisoners of war, accidents by which the individual is impoverished and loses the objective conditions of his self-sustaining labour, owing to division of labour etc. If A exchanges a value or money, i.e. objectified labour, in order to obtain a service from B, i.e. living labour, then this can belong:

(1) *within the relation of simple circulation*. Both in fact exchange only use values with one another; one exchanges necessaries, the other labour, a service which the other wants to consume, either directly—personal service—or he furnishes him the material etc. from which, with his labour, with the objectification of his labour, he makes a use value, a use value designed for A's consumption. For example, when the peasant takes a wandering tailor, of the kind that existed in times past, into his house, and gives him the material to make clothes with. Or if I give money to a doctor to patch up my health. What is important in these cases is the service which both do for one another. *Do ut facias* here appears on quite the same level as *facio ut des*, or *do ut des*.[5] The man who takes the cloth I supplied to him and makes me an article of clothing out of it gives me a use value. But instead of giving it directly in objective form, he gives it in the form of activity. I give him a completed use value; he completes another for me. The difference between previous, objectified labour and living, present labour here appears as a merely formal difference between the different tenses of labour, at one time in the perfect and at another in the present. It appears in fact as a merely formal difference, a difference mediated by division of labour and by exchange, whether B himself produces the necessaries on which he has to subsist, or whether he obtains them from A and, instead of producing the necessaries himself, produces an article of clothing, in exchange for which he obtains them from A. In both cases he can take possession of the use value possessed by A only by giving him an equivalent for it; which, in the last analysis,

5. *Do ut facias*: I give you that you may do; *facio ut des*: I do that you may give; *do ut des*: I give that you may give (Roman law).

always resolves itself into his own living labour, regardless of the
objective form it may adopt, whether before the exchange is concluded, or as a consequence of it. Now, the article of clothing not
only contains a specific, form-giving labour—a specific form of usefulness imparted to the cloth by the movement of labour—but it
contains also a certain quantity of labour—hence not only use
value, but *value* generally, *value* as such. But this value does not
exist for A, since he consumes the article, and is not a clothesdealer.
He has therefore bought the labour not as *value-positing* labour, but
as an activity which creates utility, use value. In the case of personal
services, this use value is consumed as such without making the
transition from the form of movement [*Bewegung*] into the form
of the object [*Sache*]. If, as is frequently the case in simple relations, the performer of the service does not obtain *money*, but
direct use values themselves, then it no longer even seems as if
value were being dealt in on one or the other side; merely use
values. But even given that A pays money for the service, this is not
a transformation of his money into capital, but rather the positing
of his money as mere medium of circulation, in order to obtain an
object for consumption, a specific use value. This act is for that
reason not an act which produces wealth, but the opposite, one
which consumes wealth. The point for A is not the objectification
in the cloth of labour as such, of a certain amount of labour time,
hence *value*, but rather the satisfaction of a certain need. Here A
sees his money not *realized* but *devalued* in its transposition from
the form of value into that of use value. Labour is here exchanged
not as use value for value, but as itself a particular use value, as
value for use. The more frequently A repeats the exchange, the
poorer does he become. This exchange is not an *act of wealth-get-
ting* for him, not an act of *value creation,* but of *devaluation* of the
values he has in hand, in his possession. The money which A here
exchanges for living labour—service in kind, or service objectified in
a thing—is not *capital* but revenue, money as a medium of circulation in order to obtain use value, money in which the form of value
is posited as merely vanishing, not money which will preserve and
realize itself as such through the acquisition of labour. Exchange of
money as revenue, as a mere medium of circulation, for living
labour, can never posit money as capital, nor, therefore, labour as
wage labour in the economic sense. A lengthy disquisition is not
required to show that to consume (spend) money is not the same
as to produce money. In situations in which the greatest part of surplus labour appears as agricultural labour, and where the owner of
the land therefore appears as owner both of surplus labour and of
the surplus product, it is the revenue of the owner of the land
which forms the labour fund for the free worker, for the worker in

manufactures (here, hand crafts) as opposed to the agricultural labourers. The exchange with them[6] is a form of the consumption of the owner of the land—he divides another part of his revenue directly—for personal services, often only the illusion of services, with a heap of retainers. In Asiatic societies, where the monarch appears as the exclusive proprietor of the agricultural surplus product, whole cities arise, which are at bottom nothing more than wandering encampments, from the exchange of his revenue with the "free hands," as Steuart calls them.[7] There is nothing of wage labour in this relation, but it *can* stand in opposition to slavery and serfdom, though *need* not do so, for it always repeats itself under various forms of the overall organization of labour. To the extent that *money* mediates this exchange the determination of prices will become important on both sides, but it will do so for A only in so far as he does not want to pay too much for the *use value* of the labour; not in so far as he is concerned with its *value*. The essence of the relation remains unchanged even if this price, which begins as conventional and traditional, is thereafter increasingly determined economically, first by the relation of demand and supply, finally by the production costs at which the vendors themselves of these living services can be produced; nothing is essentially changed thereby, because the determination of prices remains a merely formal moment for the exchange of mere use values, as before. This determination itself, however, is created by other relations, by the general laws and the self-determination of the ruling mode of production, acting, as it were, behind the back of this particular act of exchange. One of the forms in which this kind of pay [*Besoldung*] first appears in the old communities is where an *army* is maintained. The pay [*Sold*] of the common soldier is also reduced to a minimum—determined purely by the production costs necessary to procure him. But he exchanges the performance of his services not for *capital*, but for the revenue of the state.

In the bourgeois society itself, all exchange of personal services for revenue—including labour for personal consumption, cooking, sewing etc., garden work etc., up to and including all of the unproductive classes, civil servants, physicians, lawyers, scholars etc.—belongs under this rubric, within this category. All menial servants etc. By means of their services—often coerced—all these workers, from the least to the highest, obtain for themselves a share of the surplus product, of the capitalist's *revenue*. But it does not occur to anyone to think that by means of the exchange of his revenue for such services, i.e. through private consumption, the capitalist posits himself as capitalist. Rather, he thereby spends the fruits of his capital. It

6. That is, with the free workers in manufactures (hand crafts).   7. Steuart, *An Inquiry*, Vol. I, p. 40.

does not change the nature of the relation that the proportions in which revenue is exchanged for this kind of living labour are themselves determined by the general laws of production.

As we have already mentioned in the section on *money*,[8] it is here rather the performer of the service who actually posits *value*; who transposes a use value—a certain kind of labour, service etc.—into *value, money*. Hence in the Middle Ages, those who are oriented towards the production and accumulation of money proceed partly not from the side of the consuming landed nobility, but quite the opposite, from the side of living labour; they accumulate and thus become capitalists, δυνάμει, for a later period. The emancipated serf becomes, in part, the capitalist.

It thus does not depend on the general relation, but rather on the natural, particular quality of the service performed, whether the recipient of payment receives it as day-wages, or as an honorarium, or as a sinecure—and whether he appears as superior or inferior in rank to the person paying for the service. However, with the presupposition of capital as the dominant power, all these relations become more or less *dishonoured*. But this does not belong here yet —this *demystification* [*Entgötterung*] of personal services, regardless of the lofty character with which tradition may have poetically endowed them.

It is not, then, simply the exchange of *objectified labour* for *living* labour—which appear, from this standpoint, as two different aspects, as use values in different forms, the one objective, the other subjective—which constitutes capital and hence wage labour, but rather, the exchange of objectified labour as *value*, as self-sufficient value, for living labour as *its* use value, as use value not for a specific, particular use or consumption, but as use value for *value*.

In the exchange of money for labour or service, with the aim of direct consumption, a real exchange always takes place; the fact that *amounts of labour* are exchanged on both sides is of merely formal interest for measuring the *particular* forms of the utility of labour by comparing them with each other. This concerns only the *form* of the exchange; but does not form its *content*. In the exchange of capital for labour, *value* is not a measure for the exchange of two use values, but is rather the *content of the exchange* itself.

(2) In periods of the dissolution of *pre-bourgeois* relations, there sporadically occur free workers whose services are bought for purposes not of consumption, but of *production*; but, *firstly*, even if on a large scale, for the production only of *direct* use values, not of *values*; and *secondly*, if a nobleman e.g. brings the free worker together with his serfs, even if he re-sells a part of the worker's

8. Marx did not in fact mention this in the Chapter on Money but rather in the Chapter on Capital.

product, and the free worker thus creates *value* for him, then this exchange takes place only for the superfluous [product] and only for the sake of superfluity, for *luxury consumption*; is thus at bottom only a veiled purchase of alien labour for immediate consumption or as use value. Incidentally, wherever these free workers increase in number, and where this relation grows, there the old mode of production—commune, patriarchal, feudal etc.—is in the process of dissolution, and the elements of real wage labour are in preparation. But these free servants [*Knechte*] can also emerge, as e.g. in Poland etc., and vanish again, without a change in the mode of production taking place.

In order to express the relations into which capital and wage labour enter as *property relations* or *laws*, we need do no more than express the conduct of both sides in the *realization process* as an *appropriation process*. For example, the fact that surplus labour is posited as surplus value of capital means that the worker does not appropriate the product of his own labour; that it appears to him as *alien property*; inversely, that *alien labour* appears as the property of capital. This second law of bourgeois property, the inversion of the first—which, through laws of inheritance etc., attains an existence independent of the accidental transitoriness of individual capitalists —becomes just as established in law as the first. The first is the identity of labour with property; the second, labour as negated property, or property as negation of the alien quality of alien labour. In fact, in the production process of capital, as will be seen more closely in its further development, labour is a totality—a combination of labours—whose individual component parts are alien to one another, so that the overall process as a totality is *not* the *work* of the individual worker, and is furthermore the work of the different workers together only to the extent that they are [forcibly] combined, and do not [voluntarily] enter into combination with one another. The combination of this labour appears just as subservient to and led by an alien will and an alien intelligence—having its *animating unity* elsewhere—as its material unity appears subordinate to the *objective unity* of the *machinery*, of fixed capital, which, as *animated monster*, objectifies the scientific idea, and is in fact the coordinator, does not in any way relate to the individual worker as his instrument; but rather he himself exists as an animated individual punctuation mark, as its living isolated accessory. Thus, combined labour is combination *in-itself,* in a double way; not combination as a mutual relation among the individuals working together, nor as their predominance either over their particular or individual function or over the instrument of labour. Hence, just as the worker relates to the product of his labour as an alien thing, so does he relate to the combination of labour as an alien combination, as well as to his own labour as an expression of his life, which, although it belongs to him, is alien to him and coerced from him, and which A. Smith etc. therefore conceives as a *burden, sacrifice* etc.[9] Labour itself, like its product, is *negated as the labour of the particular, isolated worker*. This isolated labour, negated, is now indeed communal or combined labour, posited. The *communal or combined labour* posited in this way—as activity and in the passive, objective form—is however at the same time posited as an other towards the really existing individual labour—as an *alien objectivity* (alien property) as well as an *alien subjectivity* (of capital). Capital thus represents both labour and its product as negated individualized labour and hence as the negated property of the individualized worker. Capital therefore is the existence of social labour—the combination of labour as subject as well as object—but this existence as itself existing independently opposite its real moments—hence itself a *particular* existence apart from them. For its part, capital therefore appears as the predominant subject and owner of *alien labour*, and its relation is itself as complete a contradiction as is that of wage labour.⟩

* * *

E. Pre-Capitalist Property and Production

The original unity between a particular form of community (clan) and the corresponding property in nature, or relation to the objective conditions of production as a natural being, as an objective being of the individual mediated by the commune—this unity, which appears in one respect as the particular form of property—has its living reality in a specific *mode of production* itself, a mode which appears both as a relation between the individuals, and as their specific active relation to inorganic nature, a specific mode of working (which is always family labour, often communal labour). The community itself appears as the first great force of production; particular kinds of production conditions (e.g. stock-breeding, agriculture), develop particular modes of production and particular forces of production, subjective, appearing as qualities of individuals, as well as objective [ones].

In the last anaysis, their community, as well as the property based on it, resolves itself into a specific stage in the development of the productive forces of working subjects—to which correspond their specific relations amongst one another and towards nature. Until a certain point, reproduction. Then turns into dissolution.

Property, then, originally means—in its Asiatic, Slavonic, ancient

9. Adam Smith, *Wealth of Nations*, Vol. I, pp. 104–5.

classical, Germanic form—the relation of the working (producing or self-reproducing) subject to the conditions of his production or reproduction as his own. It will therefore have different forms depending on the conditions of this production. Production itself aims at the reproduction of the producer within and together with these, his objective conditions of existence. This relation as proprietor—not as a result but as a presupposition of labour, i.e. of production—presupposes the individual defined as a member of a clan or community (whose property the individual himself is, up to a certain point). Slavery, bondage etc., where the worker himself appears among the natural conditions of production for a third individual or community (this is *not* the case e.g. with the general slavery of the Orient, *only* from the European point of view)—i.e. property no longer the relation of the working individual to the objective conditions of labour—is always secondary, derived, never original, although [it is] a necessary and logical result of property founded on the community and labour in the community. It is of course very simple to imagine that some powerful, physically dominant individual, after first having caught the animal, then catches humans in order to have them catch animals; in a word, uses human beings as another naturally occurring condition for his reproduction (whereby his own labour reduces itself to ruling) like any other natural creature. But such a notion is stupid—correct as it may be from the standpoint of some particular given clan or commune—because it proceeds from the development of *isolated individuals*. But human beings become individuals only through the process of history. He appears originally as a *species-being* [*Gattungswesen*], *clan being, herd animal*—although in no way whatever as a ζῶον πολιτικόν[1] in the political sense. Exchange itself is a chief means of this individuation [*Vereinzelung*]. It makes the herd-like existence superfluous and dissolves it. Soon the matter [has] turned in such a way that as an individual he relates himself only to himself, while the means with which he posits himself as individuals have become the making of his generality and commonness. In this community, the objective being of the individual as proprietor, say proprietor of land, is presupposed, and presupposed moreover under certain conditions which chain him to the community, or rather form a link in his chain. In bourgeois society, the worker e.g. stands there purely without objectivity, subjectively; but the thing which *stands opposite* him has now become the *true community* [*Gemeinwesen*], which he tries to make a meal of, and which makes a meal of him.

All forms (more or less naturally arisen, spontaneous, all at the same time however results of a historic process) in which the community presupposes its subjects in a specific objective unity with

1. Political animal; literally, city-dweller.

their conditions of production, or in which a specific subjective mode of being presupposes the communities themselves as conditions of production, necessarily correspond to a development of the forces of production which is only limited, and indeed limited in principle. The development of the forces of production dissolves these forms, and their dissolution is itself a development of the human productive forces. Labour begins with a certain foundation —naturally arisen, spontaneous, at first—then historic presupposition. Then, however, this foundation or presupposition is itself suspended, or posited as a vanishing presupposition which has become too confining for the unfolding of the progressing human pack.

In so far as classical landed property reappears in modern small-parcel landownership, it itself belongs to political economy and we shall come to it in the section on landed property.

(All this is to be returned to at greater depth and length.)

What we are here concerned with is this: the relation of labour to capital, or to the objective conditions of labour as capital, presupposes a process of history which dissolves the various forms in which the worker is a proprietor, or in which the proprietor works. Thus above all (1) *Dissolution* of the relation to the earth—land and soil —as natural condition of production—to which he relates as to his own inorganic being; the workshop of his forces, and the domain of his will. All forms in which this property appears presuppose a *community*, whose members, although there may be formal distinctions between them, are, as members of it, *proprietors*. The original form of this property is therefore itself *direct common property* (*oriental form*, modified in the Slavonic; developed to the point of antithesis, but still as the secret, if antithetical, foundation in classical and Germanic property). (2) *Dissolution of the relations* in which he appears as *proprietor of the instrument*. Just as the above form of landed property presupposes a *real community*, so does this property of the worker in the instrument presuppose a particular form of the development of manufactures, namely *craft*, *artisan work*; bound up with it, the guild, corporation system etc. (The manufacture system of the ancient Orient can be examined under (1) already.) Here labour itself still half artistic, half end-in-itself etc. Mastery. Capitalist himself still master-journeyman. Attainment of particular skill in the work also secures possession of instrument etc. etc. Inheritability then to a certain extent of the mode of work together with the organization of work and the instrument of work. Medieval cities. Labour still as his own; definite self-sufficient development of one-sided abilities etc. (3) Included in both is the fact that he has the means of consumption in his possession before production, which are necessary for him to live as producer—i.e. during production, *before* its completion. As proprietor of land he appears as directly provided with the necessary consumption fund. As master in a craft he has inherited it, earned it, saved it up, and as a young he is first an *apprentice*, where he does not appear as an actual independent worker at all, but shares the master's fare in a patriarchal way. As journeyman (a genuine one) there is a certain communality in the consumption fund possessed by the master. While it is not the journeyman's *property* either, still, through the laws of the guild, tradition etc., at least co-possession etc. (To be gone into further.) (4) *Dissolution* likewise at the same time of the relations in which the *workers themselves*, the *living labour capacities* themselves, still belong *directly among the objective conditions of production*, and are appropriated as such—i.e. are slaves or serfs. For capital, the worker is not a condition of production, only work is. If it can make machines do it, or even water, air, so much the better. And it does not appropriate the worker, but his labour—not directly, but mediated through exchange.

These are, now, on one side, historic presuppositions needed before the worker can be found as a free worker, as objectless, purely subjective labour capacity confronting the objective conditions of production as his *not-property*, as *alien property*, as *value* for-itself, as capital. But the question arises, on the other side, which conditions are required so that he finds himself up against a *capital*?

⟨The formula of capital, where living labour relates to the raw material as well as to the instrument and to the means of subsistence required during labour, as negatives, as not-property, *includes*, first of all, *not-land-ownership*, or, the negation of the situation in which the working individual relates to land and soil, to the earth, as his own, i.e. in which he works, produces, as proprietor of the land and soil. In the best case he relates not only as worker to the land and soil, but also as proprietor of the land and soil to himself as working subject. Ownership of land and soil potentially also includes ownership of the raw material, as well as of the primordial instrument, the earth itself, and of its spontaneous fruits. Posited in the most original form, it means relating to the earth as proprietor, and finding raw material and instrument on hand, as well as the necessaries of life created not by labour but by the earth itself. Once this relation is reproduced, secondary instruments and fruits of the earth created through labour itself appear as included with landed property in its primitive forms. This historic situation is thus first of all negated as a full property relation, in the worker's relation to the conditions of labour as capital. This is historic state No. I, which is negated in this relation or presupposed as historically dissolved. Secondly, however, where there is *ownership of the instrument* on the part of the worker, i.e. the worker relates to the instrument as his own, where the worker works as owner of the instrument (which at the same time presupposes the subsumption of the instrument under his individual work, i.e. a particular, limited developmental stage of the productive force of labour), where this form of the *worker as owner* or of the *working owner* is already posited as an independent form beside and apart from *landed property*—the artisan-like and urban development of labour—not, as in the first case, as accidental to landed property and subsumed under it—hence where the raw material and the necessaries of life are also *mediated* as the craftsman's property, mediated through his craft work, through his property in the instrument—there a second historical stage is already presupposed beside and apart from the first, which must itself already appear significantly modified, through the *achievement of independence by this second sort of property* or *by working owners*. Since the instrument itself is already the product of labour, thus the element which constitutes property already exists as posited by labour, the community can no longer appear here in a naturally arisen, spontaneous form as in the first case—the community on which this form of property founded—but rather as itself already a produced, made, derived and secondary community, produced by the worker himself. It is clear that wherever ownership of the instrument is the relation to the conditions of production as property, there, in the real labour process, the instrument appears *only as a means* of individual labour; the art of really appropriating the instrument, of handling it as an instrument of labour, appears as the worker's particular skill, which posits him as the owner of the instrument. In short, the essential character of the guild-corporation system, of craft work as its subject, constituted by owners—can be resolved into the relation to the instrument of production—the instrument of labour as property—as distinct from the relation to the earth, to land and soil (to the raw material as such) as one's own. That the relation to this one moment of the conditions of production constitutes the working subject as owner, makes him into a working owner, this [is] historic situation No. II, which by its nature can exist only as antithesis to or, if one will, at the same time as complement of a modified form of the first—likewise negated in the first formula of capital. The third *possible form*, in which the worker relates as owner only to the necessaries of life, finding them on hand as the natural condition of the working subject, without relating to the land and soil, or to the instrument, or even (therefore) to labour itself as his own, is at bottom the formula of slavery and bondage, which is likewise negated, posited as a historically dissolved condition, in the relation of the worker to the conditions of production as capital. The original forms of property necessarily dissolve into the relation to the different objective moments which condition production, as one's own; they form the economic foundation of different forms of community, just as they for their part have specific forms of the community as presupposition. These forms are essentially modified by the inclusion of labour itself among the *objective conditions of production* (serfdom and slavery), through which the simply affirmative character of all forms of property included under No. 1 is lost and modified. They all contain, within themselves, slavery as possibility and hence as their own suspension. As regards No. II, where the particular kind of work—mastery of it, and, consequent upon that, an identity between property in the instrument and property in the conditions of production—while it excludes slavery and bondage, can take on an analogous negative development in the form of the caste system.> <The third form, ownership of the necessaries of life— if it does not reduce itself to slavery and serfdom—cannot contain a relation by the *working* individual to the conditions of production and hence of existence; it can therefore only be the relation of a member of the original community based on land ownership who has lost his landed property and not yet proceeded to variety No. II of property, such as the Roman *plebs* at the time of the bread and circuses.> <The relation of personal servitude, or of the retainers to their lord, is essentially different. For it forms, at bottom, only a mode of existence of the land-proprietor himself, who no longer works, but whose property includes, among the other conditions of production, the workers themselves as bondsmen etc. Here the *master–servant relation* [*Herrschaftsverhältnis*] as essential element of appropriation. Basically the appropriation of animals, land etc. cannot take place in a master–servant relation, although the animal provides service. The presupposition of the master–servant relation is the appropriation of an alien *will*. Whatever has no will, e.g. the animal, may well provide a service, but does not thereby make its owner into a *master*. This much can be seen here, however, that the *master–servant relation* likewise belongs in this formula of the appropriation of the instruments of production; and it forms a necessary ferment for the development and the decline and fall of all original relations of property and of production, just as it also expresses their limited nature. Still, it is reproduced—in mediated form—in capital, and thus likewise forms a ferment of its dissolution and is an emblem of its limitation.>

* * *

On one side, historic processes are presupposed which place a mass of individuals in a nation etc. in the position, if not at first of real free workers, nevertheless of such who are so δυνάμει, whose only property is their labour capacity and the possibility of exchanging it for values then present; individuals who confront all objective conditions of production as *alien property*, as their own *not-property*, but at the same time as *values*, as exchangeable, hence appropriable to a certain degree through living labour. Such historic processes of dissolution are also the dissolution of the bondage relations which fetter the worker to land and soil and to the lord of land and soil; but which factually presuppose his ownership of the necessaries of life—this is in truth the process of his release from the earth; dissolution of the landed property relations, which constituted him as a yeoman, as a free, working small landowner or tenant (*colonus*), a free peasant;[2] dissolution of the guild relations which presuppose his ownership of the instrument of labour, and which presuppose labour itself as a craftsmanlike, specific skill, as property (not merely as the source of property); likewise dissolution of the client-relations in the various forms in which *not-proprietors* appear in the retinue of their lord as co-consumers of the surplus product and wear the livery of their master as an equivalent, participate in his feuds, perform personal services, imaginery or real etc. It will be seen on closer inspection that all these processes of dissolution mean the dissolution of relations of production in which: use value predominates, production for direct consumption; in which exchange value and its production presupposes the predominance of the other form; and hence that, in all these relations, payments in kind and services in kind predominate over payment in money and money-services. But this only by the way. It will likewise be found on closer observation that all the dissolved relations were possible only with a definite degree of development of the material (and hence also the intellectual) forces of production.

What concerns us here for the moment is this: the process of dissolution, which transforms a mass of individuals of a nation etc. into free wage labourers δυνάμει—individuals forced solely by their lack of property to labour and to sell their labour—presupposes on the other side *not* that these individuals' previous sources of income and in part conditions of property have *disappeared*, but the reverse, that *only* their utilization has become different, that their mode of existence has changed, has gone over into other hands as a *free fund* or has even in part remained *in the same* hands. But this much is clear: the same process which divorced a mass of individuals from their previous relations to the *objective conditions of labour*, relations which were, in one way or another, affirmative, negated these relations, and thereby transformed these individuals into *free workers*, this same process freed—δυνάμει—these *objective conditions of labour*—land and soil, raw material, necessaries of life, instruments of labour, money or all of these—from their *previous state of attachment* to the individuals now separated from them. They are

2. The dissolution of the still earlier forms of communal property and real community goes without saying. [*Marx*]

still *there on hand*, but in another form; as a *free fund*, in which all political etc. relations are obliterated. The objective conditions of labour now confront these unbound, propertyless individuals only in the form of *values*, self-sufficient values. The same process which placed the mass face to face with the *objective conditions of labour* as free workers also placed these conditions, as *capital*, face to face with the free workers. The historic process was the divorce of elements which up until then were bound together; its result is therefore not that one of the elements disappears, but that each of them appears in a negative relation to the other—the (potentially) free worker on the one side, capital (potentially) on the other. The separation of the objective conditions from the classes which have become transformed into free workers necessarily also appears at the same time as the achievement of independence by these same conditions at the opposite pole.

If the relation of capital and wage labour is regarded not as already commanding and predominant over the whole of production,[3] but as arising historically—i.e. if we regard the original transformation of money into capital, the process of exchange between capital, still only existing δυνάμει on one side and the free workers existing δυνάμει on the other—then of course one cannot help making the simple observation, out of which the economists make a great show, that the side which appears as capital has to possess raw materials, instruments of labour and necessaries of life so that the worker can live during production, before production is completed. This further takes the form that there must have taken place on the part of the capitalist an accumulation—an accumulation prior to labour and not sprung out of it—which enables him to put the worker to work and to maintain his effectiveness, to maintain him as living labour capacity.[4] This act by capital which is independent of labour, not posited by labour, is then shifted from the prehistory of capital into the present, into a moment of its reality and of its present activity, of its self-formation. From this is ultimately derived the eternal right of capital to the fruits of alien

3. For in that case the capital presupposed as condition of wage labour is wage labour's own product, and is presupposed by it as its own presupposition, created by it as its own presupposition. [*Marx*]
4. Once capital and wage labour are posited as their own presupposition, as the basis presupposed to production itself, then what appears initially is that the capitalist possesses, in addition to the fund of raw materials and necessaries required for the labourer to reproduce himself, to create the required means of subsistence, i.e. to realize *necessary labour*, a fund of raw material and means of labour in which the worker realizes his surplus labour, i.e. the capitalist's profit. On further analysis this takes the form that the worker constantly creates a double fund for the capitalist, or in the form of capital. One part of this fund constantly fulfils the conditions of his own existence and the other part fulfils the conditions for the existence of capital. As we have seen, in the case of the surplus capital—and surplus capital in relation to its antediluvian relation to labour—all *real, present capital* and each of its elements has equally been *appropriated* without exchange, without an equivalent, as objectified, appropriated *alien labour*. [*Marx*]

labour, or rather its mode of appropriation is developed out of the simple and 'just' laws of equivalent exchange.

Wealth present in the form of money can be exchanged for the objective conditions of labour only because and if these are separated from labour itself. We saw that money can be piled up in part by way of the sheer exchange of equivalents; but this forms so insignificant a source that it is not worth mentioning historically—if it is presupposed that this money is gained through the exchange of one's own labour. The monetary wealth which becomes transformed into capital in the proper sense, into industrial capital, is rather the mobile wealth piled up through usury—especially that practised against landed property—and through mercantile profits. We shall have occasion below to speak further of both of these forms—in so far as they appear not as themselves forms of capital, but as earlier forms of wealth, as presuppositions for capital.

It is inherent in the concept of capital, as we have seen—in its origin—that it begins with *money* and hence with wealth existing in the form of money. It is likewise inherent in it that it appears as coming out of circulation, as the *product* of circulation. The formation of capital thus does not emerge from landed property (here at most from the *tenant* [*Pächter*] in so far as he is a dealer in agricultural products); or from the guild (although there is a possibility at the last point); but rather from merchant's and usurer's wealth. But the latter encounter the conditions where free labour can be purchased only when this labour has been released from its objective conditions of existence through the process of history. Only then does it also encounter the possibility of buying these *conditions* themselves. Under guild conditions, e.g., mere money, if it is not itself guild money, masters' money, cannot buy the looms to make people work with them; how many an individual may operate etc. is prescribed. In short, the instrument itself is still so intertwined with living labour, whose domain it appears, that it does not truly circulate. What enables moneywealth to become capital is the encounter, on one side, with free workers; and on the other side, with the necessaries and materials etc., which previously were in one way or another the *property* of the masses who have now become object-less, and are also *free* and purchasable. The other condition of labour, however—a certain level of skill, instrument as means of labour etc.—is already *available* to it in this preliminary or first period of capital, partly as a result of the urban guild system, partly as a result of domestic industry, or industry which is attached to agriculture as an accessory. This historic process is not the product of capital, but the presupposition for it. And it is through this process that the capitalist inserts himself as (historic) middle-man between landed property, or property generally, and labour. History knows nothing of the congenial fantasies according to which the capitalist and the workers form an association etc., nor is there a trace of them in the conceptual development of capital. *Manufactures* may develop sporadically, locally, in a framework which still belongs to a quite different period, as e.g. in the Italian cities *alongside* the guilds. But as the sole predominant forms of an epoch, the conditions for capital have to be developed not only locally but on a grand scale. (Nothwithstanding this, individual guild masters may develop into capitalists with the dissolution of the guilds; but the case is rare, in the nature of the thing as well. As a rule, the whole guild system declines and falls, both master and journeyman, where the capitalist and the worker arise.)

It goes without saying—and shows itself if we go more deeply into the historic epoch under discussion here—that in truth the *period of the dissolution* of their earlier modes of production and modes of the worker's relation to the objective conditions of labour is *at the same time a period* in which *monetary wealth* on the one side *has* already developed to a certain extent, and on the other side grows and expands rapidly through the same circumstances as accelerate the above dissolution. It is itself one of the agencies of that dissolution, while at the same time that dissolution is the condition of its transformation into capital. But the *mere presence of monetary wealth*, and even the achievement of a kind of supremacy on its part, is in no way sufficient for this *dissolution into capital* to happen. Or else ancient Rome, Byzantium etc. would have ended their history with free labour and capital, or rather begun a new history. There, too, the dissolution of the old property relations was bound up with development of monetary wealth—of trade etc. But instead of leading to industry, this dissolution led in fact to the supremacy of the countryside over the city.—The *original formation* of capital does not happen, as is sometimes imagined, with capital *heaping up* necessaries of life and instruments of labour and raw materials, in short, the *objective* conditions of labour which have already been unbound from the soil and animated by human labour.[5] Capital does not create the objective conditions of labour. Rather, its *original formation* is that, through the historic process of the dissolution of the old mode of production, value existing as money-wealth is enabled, on one side, *to buy* the objective conditions of labour; on the other side, to exchange money for the *living*

5. The first glance shows what a nonsensical circle it would be if on the one hand the *workers* whom capital has to put to work in order to posit itself as capital had first to be *created*, to be brought to life through its *stockpiling* if they waited for its command, *Let There Be Workers!*; while at the same time it were itself incapable of *stockpiling* without alien labour, could at most stockpile *its own labour*, i.e. could itself exist in the form of *not-capital* and *not-money*; since labour, before the existence of capital, can only realize itself in forms such as craft labour, petty agriculture etc., in short, all forms which can *not stockpile*, or only sparingly; in forms which allow of only a small surplus product and *eat up* most of it. We shall have to examine this notion of *stockpiling* [*Aufhäufung*] still more closely later on. [*Marx*]

labour of the workers who have been set free. All these moments are present; their divorce is itself a historic process, a process of dissolution, and it is *the latter* which enables money to transform itself into *capital.* Money itself, to the extent that it also plays an active role, does so only in so far as it intervenes in this process as itself a highly energetic solvent, and to that extent assists in the creation of the *plucked* object-less *free workers*; but certainly not by *creating* the objective conditions of their existence; rather by helping to speed up their separation from them—their propertylessness. When e.g. the great English landowners dismissed their retainers, who had, together with them, consumed the surplus product of the land; when further their tenants chased off the smaller cottagers etc., then, firstly, a mass of living labour powers was thereby thrown onto the *labour market*, a mass which was free in a double sense, free from the old relations of clientship, bondage and servitude, and secondly free of all belongings and possessions, and of every objective, material form of being, *free of all property*; dependent on the sale of its labour capacity or on begging, vagabondage and robbery as its only source of income. It is a matter of historic record that they tried the latter first, but were driven off this road by gallows, stocks and whippings, onto the narrow path to the labour market; owing to this fact, the *governments*, e.g. of Henry VII, VIII etc. appear as conditions of the historic dissolution process and as makers of the conditions for the existence of capital. On the other side, the necessaries of life etc., which the landowners previously ate up together with their retainers, now stood at the disposal of any money which might wish to buy them in order to buy labour through their instrumentality. Money neither *created* nor *stockpiled* these necessaries; they were there and were consumed and reproduced before they were consumed and reproduced through its mediation. What had changed was simply this, that these necessaries were now thrown on to the *exchange market*—were separated from their direct connection with the mouths of the retainers etc. and transformed from use values into exchange values, and thus fell into the domain and under the supremacy of money wealth. Likewise with the instruments of labour. Money wealth neither invented nor fabricated the spinning wheel and the loom. But, once unbound from their land and soil, spinner and weaver with their stools and wheels came under the command of money wealth. *Capital proper does nothing but bring together the mass of hands and instruments which it finds on hand. It agglomerates them under its command.* That is its *real stockpiling*; the stockpiling of workers, along with their instruments, at particular points. This will have to be dealt with more closely in the so-called *stockpiling* of capital. Monetary wealth—as merchant wealth—had admittedly helped to speed up and to dissolve the old relations of production, and made it possible for the proprietor of land for example, as A. Smith already nicely develops,[6] to exchange his grain and cattle etc. for use values brought from afar, instead of squandering the use values he himself produced, along with his retainers, and to locate his wealth in great part in the mass of his co-consuming retainers. It gave the *exchange value* of his revenue a higher significance for him. The same thing took place in regard to his tenants, who were already semi-capitalists, but still very hemmed-in ones. The development of exchange value —favoured by *money* existing in the form of the merchant estate— dissolves production which is more oriented towards direct use value and its corresponding forms of property—the relations of labour to its objective conditions—and thus pushes forward towards the making of the *labour market* (certainly to be distinguished from the slave market). However, even this action of money is only possible given the presupposition of an *urban artisanate* resting *not* on capital, but on the organization of labour in guilds etc. Urban labour itself had created means of production for which the guilds became just as confining as were the old relations of landownership to an improved agriculture, which was in part itself a consequence of the larger market for agricultural products in the cities etc. The other circumstances which e.g. in the sixteenth century increased the mass of circulating commodities as well as that of money, which created new needs and thereby raised the exchange value of indigenous products etc., raised prices etc., all of these promoted on one side the dissolution of the old relations of production, sped up the separation of the worker or non-worker but able-bodied individual from the objective conditions of his reproduction, and thus promoted the transformation of money into capital. There can therefore be nothing more ridiculous than to conceive this *original formation* of capital as if capital had stockpiled and created the *objective conditions of production*—necessaries, raw materials, instrument—and then offered them to the worker, who was *bare* of these possessions. Rather, monetary wealth in part helped to *strip* the labour powers of able-bodied individuals from these conditions; and in part this process of divorce proceeded without it. When the formation of capital had reached a certain level, monetary wealth could place itself as mediator between the objective conditions of life, thus liberated, and the liberated but also *homeless* and *emptyhanded* labour powers, and buy the latter with the former. But now, as far as the *formation of money-wealth* itself is concerned, this belongs to the prehistory of the bourgeois economy. Usury, trade, urbanization and the treasury rising with it play the main roles here. So, too, *hoarding* by tenants, peasants etc.; although to a lesser degree.— This shows at the same time that the development of exchange and of exchange value, which is everywhere mediated through trade, or

6. Adam Smith, *Wealth of Nations*, Vol. III, Bk. III, Ch. 4.

whose mediation may be termed trade—money achieves an independent existence in the merchant estate, as does circulation in trade—brings with it both the dissolution of *labour's relations of property in its* conditions of existence, in one respect, and at the same time the dissolution of *labour* which is itself *classed as one of the objective conditions of production;* all these are relations which express a predominance of use value and of production directed towards use value, as well as of a real community which is itself still directly present as a presupposition of production. Production based on exchange value and the community based on the exchange of these exchange values—even though they seem, as we saw in the previous chapter on money, to posit property as the outcome of *labour* alone, and to posit private property over the product of one's own labour as condition—and labour as general condition of wealth, all presuppose and produce the separation of labour from its objective conditions. This exchange of equivalents proceeds; it is only the surface layer of a production which rests on the appropriation of alien labour *without exchange,* but with the *semblance of exchange.* This system of exchange rests on *capital* as its foundation, and, when it is regarded in isolation from capital, as it appears on the surface, as an *independent* system, then it is a mere *illusion,* but a *necessary illusion.* Thus there is no longer any ground for astonishment that the system of exchange values—exchange of equivalents measured through labour— turns into, or rather reveals as its hidden background, the *appropriation of alien labour without* exchange, complete separation of labour and property. For the domination of exchange value itself, and of exchange-value-producing production, *presupposes* alien labour capacity itself as an exchange value—i.e. the separation of living labour capacity from its objective conditions; a relation to them—or to its own objectivity—as alien property; a relation to them, in a word, as *capital.* Only in the period of the decline and fall of the feudal system, but where it still struggles internally—as in England in the fourteenth and first half of the fifteenth centuries—is there a golden age for labour in the process of becoming emancipated. In order for labour to relate to its objective conditions as its property again, another system must take the place of the system of private exchange, which, as we saw, posits the exchange of objectified labour for labour capacity, and therefore the appropriation of living labour without exchange.—The way in which money transforms itself into capital often shows itself quite tangibly in history; e.g. when the merchant induces a number of weavers and spinners, who until then wove and spun as a rural, secondary occupation, to work for him, making their secondary into their chief occupation; but then has them in his power and has brought them under his command as wage labourers. To draw them away from their home towns and to concentrate them in a place of work is a further step. In this simple process it is clear that the capitalist has prepared neither the raw material, nor the instrument, nor the means of subsistence for the weaver and the spinner. All that he has done is to restrict them little by little to one kind of work in which they become dependent on selling, on the *buyer*, the *merchant*, and ultimately produce only *for* and *through* him. He bought their labour originally only by buying their product; as soon as they restrict themselves to the production of this exchange value and thus must directly produce *exchange values*, must exchange their labour entirely for money in order to survive, then they come under his command, and at the end even the illusion that they *sold* him products disappears. He buys their labour and takes their property first in the form of the product, and soon after that the instrument as well, or he leaves it to them as *sham property* in order to reduce his own production costs.—The original historic forms in which capital appears at first sporadically or *locally, alongside* the old modes of production, while exploding them little by little everywhere, is on one side *manufacture* proper (not yet the factory); this springs up where mass quantities are produced for export, for the external market—i.e. on the *basis of large-scale overland and maritime commerce*, in its emporiums like the Italian cities, Constantinople, in the Flemish, Dutch cities, a few Spanish ones, such as Barcelona etc. Manufacture seizes hold initially not of the so-called *urban trades*, but of the *rural secondary occupations*, spinning and weaving, the two which least requires guild-level skills, technical training. Apart from these great emporiums, where the external market is its basis, where production is thus, so to speak, *naturally* oriented towards exchange value—i.e. manufactures directly connected with shipping, shipbuilding itself etc.—it takes up its first residence not in the cities, but on the land, in villages lacking guilds etc. The rural subsidiary occupations have the broad basis [characteristic] of manufactures, while the urban trades demand great progress in production before they can be conducted in factory style. Likewise certain branches of production—such as glassworks, metal works, sawmills etc., which demand a higher concentration of labour powers from the outset, apply more natural energy from the outset, demand mass production, likewise concentration of the means of labour etc. Likewise paper mills. On the other side the rise of the tenant and the transformation of the agricultural population into free day-labourers. Although this transformation in the countryside is the last to push on towards its ultimate consequences and its purest form, its beginnings there are among the earliest. Classical antiquity, which could never get beyond the urban artisanate proper, could therefore never get to large industry. The first presupposition of the latter is to draw the land in all its expanse into the production not of use values but of exchange values. Glass fac-

tories, paper mills, iron works etc. cannot be operated on guild principles. They demand mass production; sales to a general market;
monetary wealth on the part of their entrepreneur—not that he creates the conditions, neither the subjective nor the objective ones;
but under the old relations of property and of production these conditions cannot be brought together.—The dissolution of relations of
serfdom, like the rise of manufacture, then little by little transforms
all branches of work into branches operated by capital.—The cities
themselves, it is true, also contain an element for the formation of
wage labour proper, in the non-guild day-labourers, unskilled labourers etc.

While, as we have seen, the transformation of money into capital
presupposes a historic process which divorces the objective conditions of labour from the worker and makes them independent of
him, it is at the same time the effect of capital and of its process,
once arisen, to conquer all of production and to develop and complete the divorce between labour and property, between labour and
the objective conditions of labour, everywhere. It will be seen in the
course of the further development how capital destroys craft and
artisan labour, working small-landownership etc., together with
itself in forms in which it does *not* appear in opposition to labour
—in *small capital* and in the intermediate species, the species
between the old modes of production (or their renewal on the foundation of capital) and the classical, adequate mode of production of
capital itself.

The only stockpiling presupposed at the origin of capital is that
of *monetary wealth*, which, regarded in and for itself, is altogether
unproductive, as it only springs up out of circulation and belongs
exclusively to it. Capital rapidly forms an internal market for itself
by destroying all rural secondary occupations, so that it spins,
weaves for everyone, clothes everyone etc., in short, brings the commodities previously created as direct use values into the form of
exchange values, a process which comes about by itself through the
separation of the workers from land and soil and from property
(even in the form of serf property) in the conditions of production.

With the urban crafts, although they rest essentially on exchange
and on the creation of exchange values, the direct and chief aim of
this production is *subsistence as craftsmen*, as *master-journeymen*,
hence use value; not *wealth*, not *exchange value as exchange value*.
Production is therefore always subordinated to a given consumption, supply to demand, and expands only slowly.

The *production of capitalists and wage labourers is thus a chief
product of capital's realization process*. Ordinary economics, which
looks only at the things produced, forgets this completely. When
objectified labour is, in this process, at the same time posited as the
worker's *non-objectivity*, as the objectivity of a subjectivity antitheti-

cal to the worker, as *property* of a will alien to him, then capital is necessarily at the same time the *capitalist*, and the idea held by some socialists that we need capital but not the capitalists is altogether wrong. It is posited within the concept of capital that the objective conditions of labour—and these are its own product—take on a *personality* towards it, or, what is the same, that they are posited as the property of a personality alien to the worker. The concept of capital contains the capitalist. * * *

* * *

F. Population, Overpopulation, and Malthus

* * *

Malthus's theory, which incidentally was not his invention, but whose fame he appropriated through the clerical fanaticism with which he propounded it—actually only through the weight he placed on it—is significant in two respects: (1) because he gives brutal expression to the brutal viewpoint of capital; (2) because he *asserted* the fact of overpopulation in all forms of society. Proved it he has not, for there is nothing more uncritical than his motley compilations from historians and travellers' descriptions. His conception is altogether false and childish (1) because he regards *overpopulation* as being *of the same kind* in all the different historic phases of economic development; does not understand their specific difference, and hence stupidly reduces these very complicated and varying relations to a single relation, two equations, in which the natural reproduction of humanity appears on the one side, and the natural reproduction of edible plants (or means of subsistence) on the other, as two natural series, the former geometric and the latter arithmetic in progression. In this way he transforms the historically distinct relations into an abstract numerical relation, which he has fished purely out of thin air, and which rests neither on natural nor on historical laws. There is allegedly a natural difference between the reproduction of mankind and e.g. grain. This baboon thereby implies that the *increase of humanity* is a purely natural process, which requires *external restraints, checks*, to prevent it from proceeding in geometrical progression. This *geometrical reproduction* is the natural reproduction process of mankind. He would find in history that population proceeds in very different relations, and that overpopulation is likewise a historically determined relation, in no way determined by abstract numbers or by the absolute limit of the productivity of the necessaries of life, but by limits posited rather by *specific conditions of production*. As well as restricted numerically. How small do the numbers which meant overpopulation for the Athenians appear to us! Secondly, restricted according to character. An overpopulation of

free Athenians who become transformed into colonists is significantly different from an overpopulation of workers who become
transformed into workhouse inmates. Similarly the begging overpopulation which consumes the surplus produce of a monastery is different from that which forms in a factory. It is Malthus who
abstracts from these specific historic laws of the movement of population, which are indeed the history of the nature of humanity, the
natural laws, but natural laws of humanity only at a specific historic
development, with a development of the forces of production determined by humanity's own process of history. Malthusian man,
abstracted from historically determined man, exists only in his
brain; hence also the geometric method of reproduction corresponding to this natural Malthusian man. Real history thus appears to
him in such a way that the reproduction of his natural humanity is
not an abstraction from the historic process of real reproduction,
but just the contrary, that real reproduction is an application of the
Malthusian theory. Hence the inherent conditions of population as
well as of overpopulation at every stage of history appear to him as
a series of *external checks* which has *prevented* the population
from developing in the Malthusian form. The conditions in which
mankind historically produces and reproduces itself appear as *barriers* to the reproduction of the Malthusian natural man, who is a
Malthusian creature. On the other hand, the production of the necessaries of life—as it is checked, determined by human action—appears as a *check* which it posits to itself. The ferns would cover the
entire earth. Their reproduction would stop only where space for
them ceased. They would obey no arithmetic proportion. It is hard
to say where Malthus has discovered that the reproduction of voluntary natural products would stop for intrinsic reasons, without *external checks*. He transforms the immanent, historically changing
limits of the human reproduction process into *outer barriers*; and
the *outer barriers* to natural reproduction into *immanent limits* or
natural laws of reproduction.

(2) He stupidly relates a specific quantity of people to a specific
quantity of necessaries.[7] Ricardo immediately and correctly confronted him with the fact that the quantity of grain available is
completely irrelevant to the worker if he has no *employment*; that it
is therefore the means of employment and not of subsistence which
put him into the category of surplus population.[8] But this should
be conceived more generally, and relates to the *social mediation* as
such, through which the individual gains access to the means of his
reproduction and creates them; hence it relates to the *conditions of
production* and his relation to them. There was no barrier to the
reproduction of the Athenian slave other than the producible neces-

7. T. R. Malthus, *An Inquiry into the Nature and Progress of Rent*, London, 1815, p. 7.

8. Ricardo, *On the Principles of Political Economy*, p. 493.

saries. And we never hear that there were *surplus slaves* in antiquity. The call for them increased, rather. There was, however, a surplus population of non-workers (in the immediate sense), who were not too many in relation to the necessaries available, but who had lost the conditions under which they could appropriate them. The invention of surplus labourers, i.e. of propertyless people who work, belongs to the period of capital. The beggars who fastened themselves to the monasteries and helped them eat up their surplus product are in the same class as the feudal retainers, and this shows that the surplus produce could not be eaten up by the small number of its owners. It is only another form of the retainers of old, or of the menial servants of today. The overpopulation e.g. among hunting peoples, which shows itself in the warfare between the tribes, proves not that the earth could not support their small numbers, but rather that the condition of their reproduction required a great amount of territory for few people. Never a relation to a *non-existent* absolute mass of means of subsistence, but rather relation to the conditions of reproduction, of the production of these means, including likewise the *conditions of reproduction of human beings*, of the total population, of relative surplus population. This surplus purely relative: in no way related to the *means of subsistence as* such, but rather to the mode of producing them. Hence also only a *surplus* at this state of development.

* * *

G. Capitalism, Machinery and Automation

The labour process.—Fixed capital. Means of labour. Machine.— Fixed capital. Transposition of powers of labour into powers of capital both in fixed and in circulating capital.—To what extent fixed capital (machine) *creates* value.—*Lauderdale. Machine presupposes a mass of workers.*

* * *

As long as the means of labour remains a means of labour in the proper sense of the term, such as it is directly, historically, adopted by capital and included in its realization process, it undergoes a merely formal modification, by appearing now as a means of labour not only in regard to its material side, but also at the same time as a particular mode of the presence of capital, determined by its total process—as *fixed capital*. But, once adopted into the production process of capital, the means of labour passes through different metamorphoses, whose culmination is the *machine*, or rather, an *automatic system of machinery* (system of machinery: the *automatic* one is merely its most complete, most adequate form, and alone transforms machinery into a system), set in motion by an

automaton, a moving power that moves itself; this automaton consisting of numerous mechanical and intellectual organs, so that the
workers themselves are cast merely as its conscious linkages. In the
machine, and even more in machinery as an automatic system, the
use value, i.e. the material quality of the means of labour, is transformed into an existence adequate to fixed capital and to capital as
such; and the form in which it was adopted into the production
process of capital, the direct means of labour, is superseded by a
form posited by capital itself and corresponding to it. In no way
does the machine appear as the individual worker's means of labour.
Its distinguishing characteristic is not in the least, as with the
means of labour, to transmit the worker's activity to the object; this
activity, rather, is posited in such a way that it merely transmits the
machine's work, the machine's action, on to the raw material—su-
pervises it and guards against interruptions. Not as with the instrument, which the worker animates and makes into his organ with his
skill and strength, and whose handling therefore depends on his vir-
tuosity. Rather, it is the machine which possesses skill and strength
in place of the worker, is itself the virtuoso, with a soul of its own
in the mechanical laws acting through it; and it consumes coal, oil
etc. (*matières instrumentales*), just as the worker consumes food, to
keep up its perpetual motion. The worker's activity, reduced to a
mere abstraction of activity, is determined and regulated on all sides
by the movement of the machinery, and not the opposite. The science which compels the inanimate limbs of the machinery, by their
construction, to act purposefully, as an automaton, does not exist in
the worker's consciousness, but rather acts upon him through the
machine as an alien power, as the power of the machine itself. The
appropriation of living labour by objectified labour—of the power
or activity which creates value by value existing for-itself—which
lies in the concept of capital, is posited, in production resting on
machinery, as the character of the production process itself, including its material elements and its material motion. The production
process has ceased to be a labour process in the sense of a process
dominated by labour as its governing unity. Labour appears, rather,
merely as a conscious organ, scattered among the individual living
workers at numerous points of the mechanical system; subsumed
under the total process of the machinery itself, as itself only a link
of the system, whose unity exists not in the living workers, but
rather in the living (active) machinery, which confronts his individual, insignificant doings as a mighty organism. In machinery, objectified labour confronts living labour within the labour process itself
as the power which rules it; a power which, as the appropriation of
living labour, is the form of capital. The transformation of the
means of labour into machinery, and of living labour into a mere
living accessory of this machinery, as the means of its action, also

posits the absorption of the labour process in its material character as a mere moment of the realization process of capital. The increase of the productive force of labour and the greatest possible negation of necessary labour is the necessary tendency of capital, as we have seen. The transformation of the means of labour into machinery is the realization of this tendency. In machinery, objectified labour materially confronts living labour as a ruling power and as an active subsumption of the latter under itself, not only by appropriating it, but in the real production process itself; the relation of capital as value which appropriates value-creating activity is, in fixed capital existing as machinery, posited at the same time as the relation of the use value of capital to the use value of labour capacity; further, the value objectified in machinery appears as a presupposition against which the value-creating power of the individual labour capacity is an infinitesimal, vanishing magnitude; the production in enormous mass quantities which is posited with machinery destroys every connection of the product with the direct need of the producer, and hence with direct use value; it is already posited in the form of the product's production and in the relations in which it is produced that it is produced only as a conveyor of value, and its use value only as condition to that end. In machinery, objectified labour itself appears not only in the form of product or of the product employed as means of labour, but in the form of the force of production itself. The development of the means of labour into machinery is not an accidental moment of capital, but is rather the historical reshaping of the traditional, inherited means of labour into a form adequate to capital. The accumulation of knowledge and of skill, of the general productive forces of the social brain, is thus absorbed into capital, as opposed to labour, and hence appears as an attribute of capital, and more specifically of *fixed capital*, in so far as it enters into the production process as a means of production proper. *Machinery* appears, then, as the most adequate form of *fixed capital*, and fixed capital, in so far as capital's relations with itself are concerned, appears as *the most adequate form of capital* as such. In another respect, however, in so far as fixed capital is condemned to an existence within the confines of a specific use value, it does not correspond to the concept of capital, which, as value, is indifferent to every specific form of use value, and can adopt or shed any of them as equivalent incarnations. In this respect, as regards capital's external relations, it is *circulating capital* which appears as the adequate form of capital, and not fixed capital.

Further, in so far as machinery develops with the accumulation of society's science, of productive force generally, general social labour presents itself not in labour but in capital. The productive force of society is measured in *fixed capital*, exists there in its objective form; and, inversely, the productive force of capital grows with this general progress, which capital appropriates free of charge. This is not the place to go into the development of machinery in detail; rather only in its general aspect; in so far as the *means of labour*, as a physical thing, loses its direct form, becomes *fixed capital*, and confronts the worker physically as *capital*. In machinery, knowledge appears as alien, external to him; and living labour [as] subsumed under self-activating objectified labour. The worker appears as superfluous to the extent that his action is not determined by [capital's] requirements.

The full development of capital, therefore, takes place—or capital has posited the mode of production corresponding to it—only when the means of labour has not only taken the economic form of *fixed capital*, but has also been suspended in its immediate form, and when *fixed capital* appears as a machine within the production process, opposite labour; and the entire production process appears as not subsumed under the direct skilfulness of the worker, but rather as the technological application of science. [It is,] hence, the tendency of capital to give production a scientific character; direct labour [is] reduced to a mere moment of this process. As with the transformation of value into capital, so does it appear in the further development of capital, that it presupposes a certain given historical development of the productive forces on one side—science too [is] among these productive forces—and, on the other, drives and forces them further onwards.

Thus the quantitative extent and the effectiveness (intensity) to which capital is developed as fixed capital indicate the general degree to which capital is developed as capital, as power over living labour, and to which it has conquered the production process as such. Also, in the sense that it expresses the accumulation of objectified productive forces, and likewise of objectified labour. However, while capital gives itself its adequate form as use value within the production process only in the form of machinery and other material manifestations of fixed capital, such as railways etc. (to which we shall return later), this in no way means that this use value—machinery as such—is capital, or that its existence as machinery is identical with its existence as capital; any more than gold would cease to have use value as gold if it were no longer *money*. Machinery does not lose its use value as soon as it ceases to be capital. While machinery is the most appropriate form of the use value of fixed capital, it does not at all follow that therefore subsumption under the social relation of capital is the most appropriate and ultimate social relation of production for the application of machinery.

To the degree that labour time—the mere quantity of labour—is posited by capital as the sole determinant element, to that degree does direct labour and its quantity disappear as the determinant principle of production—of the creation of use values—and is reduced both quantitatively, to a smaller proportion, and qualitatively, as an, of course, indispensable but subordinate moment, compared to general scientific labour, technological application of natural sciences, on one side, and to the general productive force arising from social combination [*Gliederung*] in total production on the other side—a combination which appears as a natural fruit of social labour (although it is a historic product). Capital thus works towards its own dissolution as the form dominating production.

* * *

Fixed capital and circulating capital *as two particular kinds of capital. Fixed capital and continuity of the production process.— Machinery and living labour. (Business of inventing)*

While, up to now, fixed capital and circulating capital appeared merely as different passing aspects of capital, they have now hardened into two particular modes of its existence, and fixed capital appears separately alongside circulating capital. They are now two particular kinds of capital. In so far as a capital is examined in a particular branch of production, it appears as divided into these two portions, or splits into these two kinds of capital in certain p[rop]ortions.

The division within the production process, originally between means of labour and material of labour, and finally product of labour, now appears as circulating capital (the last two) and fixed capital [the first.][9] The split within capital as regards its merely physical aspect has now entered into its form itself, and appears as differentiating it.

From a viewpoint such as Lauderdale's etc., who would like to have capital as such, separately from labour, create *value* and hence also *surplus value* (or profit), fixed capital—namely that whose physical presence or use value is machinery—is the form which gives their superficial fallacies still the greatest semblance of validity. The answer to them, e.g. in *Labour Defended*, [is] that the road-builder may share [profits] with the road-user, but the "road" itself cannot do so.[1]

Circulating capital—presupposing that it really passes through its different phases—brings about the decrease or increase, the brevity or length of circulation time, the easier or more troublesome completion of the different stages of circulation, a decrease of the surplus value which could be created in a given period of time without these interruptions—either *because the number of reproductions grows smaller*, or because the quantity of *capital continuously engaged in the production process* is reduced. In both cases this is not a reduction of the initial value, but rather a reduction of the rate of growth. From the moment, however, when fixed capital has

9. The manuscript has: ". . . now appears as circulating capital (the first two) and fixed capital."
1. Hodgskin, *Labour Defended*, p. 16.

developed to a certain extent—and this extent, as we indicated, is the measure of the development of large industry generally—hence fixed capital increases in proportion to the development of large industry's productive forces—it is itself the objectification of these productive forces, as presupposed product—from this instant on, every interruption of the production process acts as a direct reduction of capital itself, of its initial value. The value of fixed capital is reproduced only in so far as it is used up in the production process. Through disuse it loses its use value without its value passing on to the product. Hence, the greater the scale on which fixed capital develops, in the sense in which we regard it here, the more does the *continuity of the production process* or the constant flow of reproduction become an externally compelling condition for the mode of production founded on capital.

In machinery, the appropriation of living labour by capital achieves a direct reality in this respect as well: It is, firstly, the analysis and application of mechanical and chemical laws, arising directly out of science, which enables the machine to perform the same labour as that previously performed by the worker. However, the development of machinery along this path occurs only when large industry has already reached a higher stage, and all the sciences have been pressed into the service of capital; and when, secondly, the available machinery itself already provides great capabilities. Invention then becomes a business, and the application of science to direct production itself becomes a prospect which determines and solicits it. But this is not the road along which machinery, by and large, arose, and even less the road on which it progresses in detail. This road is, rather, dissection [*Analyse*]—through the division of labour, which gradually transforms the workers' operations into more and more mechanical ones, so that at a certain point a mechanism can step into their places. *(See under economy of power.)* Thus, the specific mode of working here appears directly as becoming transferred from the worker to capital in the form of the machine, and his own labour capacity devalued thereby. Hence the workers' struggle against machinery. What was the living worker's activity becomes the activity of the machine. Thus the appropriation of labour by capital confronts the worker in a coarsely sensous form; capital absorbs labour into itself—"as though its body were by love possessed."[2]

Contradiction between the foundation of bourgeois production (value as measure) and its development. Machines etc.

The exchange of living labour for objectified labour—i.e. the positing of social labour in the form of the contradiction of capital and wage labour—is the ultimate development of the *value-relation* and

2. *"Als hätt' es Lieb im Leibe,"* Goethe, *Faust*, Part I, Act 5, Auerbach's Cellar in Leipzig.

of production resting on value. Its presupposition is—and remains —the mass of direct labour time, the quantity of labour employed, as the determinant factor in the production of wealth. But to the degree that large industry develops, the creation of real wealth comes to depend less on labour time and on the amount of labour employed than on the power of the agencies set in motion during labour time, whose "powerful effectiveness" is itself in turn out of all proportion to the direct labour time spent on their production, but depends rather on the general state of science and on the progress of technology, or the application of this science to production. (The development of this science, especially natural science, and all others with the latter, is itself in turn related to the development of material production.) Agriculture, e.g., becomes merely the application of the science of material metabolism, its regulation for the greatest advantage of the entire body of society. Real wealth manifests itself, rather—and large industry reveals this—in the monstrous disproportion between the labour time applied, and its product, as well as in the qualitative imbalance between labour, reduced to a pure abstraction, and the power of the production process it superintends. Labour no longer appears so much to be included within the production process; rather, the human being comes to relate more as watchman and regulator to the production process itself. (What holds for machinery holds likewise for the combination of human activities and the development of human intercourse.) No longer does the worker insert a modified natural thing [*Naturgegenstand*] as middle link between the object [*Objekt*] and himself; rather, he inserts the process of nature, transformed into an industrial process, as a means between himself and inorganic nature, mastering it. He steps to the side of the production process instead of being its chief actor. In this transformation, it is neither the direct human labour he himself performs, nor the time during which he works, but rather the appropriation of his own general productive power, his understanding of nature and his mastery over it by virtue of his presence as a social body—it is, in a word, the development of the social individual which appears as the great foundation-stone of production and of wealth. The theft of alien labour time, on which the present wealth is based, appears a miserable foundation in face of this new one, created by large-scale industry itself. As soon as labour in the direct form has ceased to be the great well-spring of wealth, labour time ceases and must cease to be its measure, and hence exchange value [must cease to be the measure] of use value. The *surplus labour of the mass* has ceased to be the condition for the development of general wealth, just as the *non-labour of the few*, for the development of the general powers of human head. With that, production based on exchange value breaks down, and the direct, material production process is stripped of the form of penury and antithesis. The free development of individualities, and hence not the reduction of necessary labour time so as to posit surplus labour, but rather the general reduction of the necessary labour of society to a minimum, which then corresponds to the artistic, scientific etc. development of the individuals in the time set free, and with the means created, for all of them. Capital itself is the moving contradiction, [in] that it presses to reduce labour time to a minimum, while it posits labour time, on the other side, as sole measure and source of wealth. Hence it diminishes labour time in the necessary form so as to increase it in the superfluous form; hence posits the superfluous in growing measure as a condition—question of life or death—for the necessary. On the one side, then, it calls to life all the powers of science and of nature, as of social combination and of social intercourse, in order to make the creation of wealth independent (relatively) of the labour time employed on it. On the other side, it wants to use labour time as the measuring rod for the giant social forces thereby created, and to confine them within the limits required to maintain the already created value as value. Forces of production and social relations—two different sides of the development of the social individual—appear to capital as mere means, and are merely means for it to produce on its limited foundation. In fact, however, they are the material conditions to blow this foundation sky-high. "Truly wealthy a nation, when the working day is 6 rather than 12 hours. *Wealth* is not command over surplus labour time" (real wealth), "but rather, *disposable time* outside that needed in direct production, for *every individual* and the whole society." (*The Source and Remedy etc.*, 1821, p. 6)

Nature builds no machines, no locomotives, railways, electric telegraphs, self-acting mules etc. These are products of human industry; natural material transformed into organs of the human will over nature, or of human participation in nature. They are *organs of the human brain, created by the human hand*; the power of knowledge, objectified. The development of fixed capital indicates to what degree general social knowledge has become a *direct force of production*, and to what degree, hence, the conditions of the process of social life itself have come under the control of the general intellect and been transformed in accordance with it. To what degree the powers of social production have been produced, not only in the form of knowledge, but also as immediate organs of social practice, of the real life process.

Significance of the development of fixed capital (*for the development of capital generally*). *Relation between the creation of fixed capital and circulating capital. Disposable time. To create it, chief role of capital. Contradictory form of the same in capital.—Produc-*

tivity of labour and production of fixed capital. (The Source and Remedy.)—*Use and consume:* Economist. *Durability of fixed capital*

The development of fixed capital indicates in still another respect the degree of development of wealth generally, or of capital. The aim of production oriented directly towards use value, as well as of that directly oriented towards exchange value, is the product itself, destined for consumption. The part of production which is oriented towards the production of fixed capital does not produce direct objects of individual gratification, nor direct exchange values; at least not directly realizable exchange values. *Hence, only when a certain degree of productivity has already been reached—so that a part of production time is sufficient for immediate production—can an increasingly large part be applied to the production of the means of production.* This requires that society be able to wait; that a large part of the wealth already created can be withdrawn both from immediate consumption and from production for immediate consumption, in order to employ this part for labour which is *not immediately productive* (within the material production process itself). This requires a certain level of productivity and of relative overabundance, and, more specifically, a level directly related to the transformation of circulating capital into fixed capital. As the *magnitude of relative surplus labour depends on the productivity of necessary labour, so does the magnitude of labour time*—living as well as objectified— *employed on the production of fixed capital depend on the productivity of the labour time spent in the direct production of products. Surplus population* (from this standpoint), as well as *surplus production*, is a condition for this. That is, the output of the time employed in direct production must be larger, relatively, than is directly required for the reproduction of the capital employed in these branches of industry. The *smaller* the direct fruits borne by *fixed capital*, the less it intervenes in the *direct production process*, the greater must be this relative *surplus population and surplus production*; thus, more to build railways, canals, aqueducts, telegraphs etc. than to build the machinery directly active in the direct production process. Hence—a subject to which we will return later—in the constant under-and over-production of modern industry—constant fluctuations and convulsions arise from the disproportion, when sometimes too little, then again too much circulating capital is transformed into fixed capital.

⟨*The creation of a large quantity of disposable time* apart from necessary labour time for society generally and each of its members (i.e. room for the development of the individuals' full productive forces, hence those of society also), this creation of not-labour time appears in the stage of capital, as of all earlier ones, as not-labour time, free time, for a few. What capital adds is that it increases the surplus labour time of the mass by all means of art and science, because its wealth consists directly in the appropriation of surplus labour time; since *value directly its purpose*, not use value. It is thus, despite itself, instrumental in creating the means of social disposable time, in order to reduce labour time for the whole society to a diminishing minimum, and thus to free everyone's time for their own development. But its tendency always, on the one side, *to create disposable time, on the other, to convert it into surplus labour*. If it succeeds too well at the first, then it suffers from surplus production, and then necessary labour is interrupted, because *no surplus labour can be realized by capital*. The more this contradiction develops, the more does it become evident that the growth of the forces of production can no longer be bound up with the appropria tion of alien labour, but that the mass of workers must themselves appropriate their own surplus labour. Once they have done so—and *disposable time* thereby ceases to have an *antithetical* existence— then, on one side, necessary labour time will be measured by the needs of the social individual, and, on the other, the development of the power of social production will grow so rapidly that, even though production is now calculated for the wealth of all, *disposable time* will grow for all. For real wealth is the developed productive power of all individuals. The measure of wealth is then not any longer, in any way, labour time, but rather disposable time. *Labour time as the measure of value* posits wealth itself as founded on poverty, and disposable time as existing *in and because of the antithesis to surplus labour time*; or, the positing of an individual's entire time as labour time, and his degradation therefore to mere worker, subsumption under labour. *The most developed machinery thus forces the worker to work longer than the savage does, or than he himself did with the simplest, crudest tools.*>

"If the entire labour of a country were sufficient only to raise the support of the whole population, there would be no *surplus labour*, consequently nothing that could be allowed to accumulate as capi tal. If in one year the people raises enough for the support of two years, one year's consumption must perish, or for one year men must cease from productive labour. But the *possessors of* [the] *surplus produce or capital* . . . employ people upon *something not directly and immediately productive*, e.g. in the erection of machinery. So it goes on." (*The Source and Remedy of the National Difficulties*, p.4)

<As the basis on which large industry rests, the appropriation of alien labour time, ceases, with its development, to make up or to create wealth, so does *direct labour* as such cease to be the basis of production, since, in one respect, it is transformed more into a supervisory and regulatory activity; but then also because the prod-

uct ceases to be the product of isolated direct labour, and the *combination* of social activity appears, rather, as the producer. "As soon as the division of labour is developed, almost every piece of work done by a single individual is a part of a whole, *having no value or utility of itself. There is nothing on which the labourer can seize: this is my produce, this I will keep to myself.*" (*Labour Defended*, p. 25, 1, 2, xi.) In direct exchange, individual direct labour appears as realized in a particular product or part of the product, and its communal, social character—its character as objectification of general labour and satisfaction of the general need—as posited through exchange alone. In the production process of large-scale industry, by contrast, just as the conquest of the forces of nature by the social intellect is the precondition of the productive power of the means of labour as developed into the automatic process, on one side, so, on the other, is *the labour of the individual in its direct presence posited as suspended individual, i.e. as social, labour. Thus the other basis of this mode of production falls away.*>

The labour time employed in the production of fixed capital relates to that employed in the production of circulating capital, within the production process of capital itself, as does *surplus labour time to necessary* labour time. To the degree that production aimed at the satisfaction of immediate need becomes more productive, a greater part of production can be directed towards the need of production itself, or the production of means of production. In so far as the production of *fixed capital*, even in its physical aspect, is directed immediately not towards the production of direct use values, or towards the production of values required for the direct reproduction of capital—i.e. those which themselves in turn represent use value in the value-creation process—but rather towards the production of the means of value creation, that is, not towards value as an immediate object, but rather towards value creation, towards the means of realization, as an immediate object of production—the production of value posited physically in the object of production itself, as the aim of production, the objectification of productive force, the value producing power of capital—to that extent, it is in the production of *fixed capital that capital posits itself as end-in-itself* and appears active as capital, *to a higher power than it does in the production of circulating capital*. Hence, in this respect as well, the dimension already possessed by fixed capital, which its production occupies within total production, is the measuring rod *of the development* of wealth founded on the mode of production of capital.

"The number of workers depends as much on *circulating capital* as it depends on the quantity *of products of co-existing labour*, which labourers are allowed to consume." (*Labour Defended*, p. 20.)

In all the excerpts cited above from various economists fixed capital is regarded as the part of capital which is locked into the production process. "Floating capital is consumed; fixed capital is merely used in the great process of production." (*Economist*, VI, 1.) This wrong, and holds only for the part of circulating capital which is itself consumed by the fixed capital, the *matières instrumentales*. The only thing consumed "in the great process of production," if this means the immediate production process, is *fixed capital*. Consumption within the production process is, however, in fact *use*, *wearing-out*. Furthermore, the *greater durability of fixed capital* must not be conceived as a purely physical quality. The iron and the wood which make up the bed I sleep in, or the stones making up the house I live in, or the marble statue which decorates a palace, are just as durable as iron and wood etc. used for machinery. But *durability* is a condition for the instrument, the means of production, not only on the technical ground that metals etc. are the chief material of all machinery, but rather because the instrument is destined to play the same role constantly in repeated processes of production. Its durability as means of production is a required quality of its use value. The more often it must be replaced, the costlier it is; the larger the part of capital which would have to be spent on it uselessly. Its durability is its existence as means of production. Its duration is an increase of its productive force. With circulating capital, by contrast, in so far as it is not transformed into fixed capital, durability is in no way connected with the act of production itself and is therefore not a conceptually posited moment. The fact that among the articles thrown into the consumption fund there are some which are in turn characterized as *fixed capital* because they are consumed slowly, and can be consumed by many individuals in series, is connected with further determinations (renting rather than buying, interest etc.) with which we are not yet here concerned.

"Since the general introduction of soulless mechanism in British manufactures, people have with rare exceptions been treated as a secondary and subordinate machine, and far more attention has been given to the perfection of the raw materials of wood and metals than to those of body and spirit." (p. 31. Robert Owen: *Essays on the Formation of the Human Character*, 1840, London.)

Real saving—economy— = saving of labour time = development of productive force. Suspension of the contradiction between free time and labour time.—True conception of the process of social production.

<Real economy—saving—consists of the saving of labour time (minimum (and minimization) of production costs); but this saving identical with development of the productive force. Hence in no way *abstinence from consumption*, but rather the development

of power, of capabilities of production, and hence both of the capabilities as well as the means of consumption. The capability to consume is a condition of consumption, hence its primary means, and this capability is the development of an individual potential, a force of production. The saving of labour time [is] equal to an increase of free time, i.e. time for the full development of the individual, which in turn reacts back upon the productive power of labour as itself the greatest productive power. From the standpoint of the direct production process it can be regarded as the production of *fixed capital*, this fixed capital being man himself. It goes without saying, by the way, that direct labour time itself cannot remain in the abstract antithesis to free time in which it appears from the perspective of bourgeois economy. Labour cannot become play, as Fourier would like,[3] although it remains his great contribution to have expressed the suspension not of distribution, but of the mode of production itself, in a higher form, as the ultimate object. Free time—which is both idle time and time for higher activity—has naturally transformed its possessor into a different subject, and he then enters into the direct production process as this different subject. This process is then both discipline, as regards the human being in the process of becoming; and, at the same time, practice [*Ausübung*], experimental science, materially creative and objectifying science, as regards the human being who has become, in whose head exists the accumulated knowledge of society. For both, in so far as labour requires practical use of the hands and free bodily movement, as in agriculture, at the same time exercise.

As the system of bourgeois economy has developed for us only by degrees, so too its negation, which is its ultimate result. We are still concerned now with the direct production process. When we consider bourgeois society in the long view and as a whole, then the final result of the process of social production always appears as the society itself, i.e. the human being itself in its social relations. Everything that has a fixed form, such as the product etc., appears as merely a moment, a vanishing moment, in this movement. The direct production process itself here appears only as a moment. The conditions and objectifications of the process are themselves equally moments of it, and its only subjects are the individuals, but individuals in mutual relationships, which they equally reproduce and produce anew. The constant process of their own movement, in which they renew themselves even as they renew the world of wealth they create.>

3. Fourier, *Le Nouveau Monde industriel et sociétaire*, Vol. VI, pp. 242–52.

H. The End of Capitalism

* * * Beyond a certain point, the development of the powers of production becomes a barrier for capital; hence the capital relation a barrier for the development of the productive powers of labour. When it has reached this point, capital, i.e. wage labour, enters into the same relation towards the development of social wealth and of the forces of production as the guild system, serfdom, slavery, and is necessarily stripped off as a fetter. The last form of servitude assumed by human activity, that of wage labour on one side, capital on the other, is thereby cast off like a skin, and this casting-off itself is the result of the mode of production corresponding to capital; the material and mental conditions of the negation of wage labour and of capital, themselves already the negation of earlier forms of unfree social production, are themselves results of its production process. The growing incompatibility between the productive development of society and its hitherto existing relations of production expresses itself in bitter contradictions, crises, spasms. The violent destruction of capital not by relations external to it, but rather as a condition of its self-preservation, is the most striking form in which advice is given it to be gone and to give room to a higher state of social production. It is not only the growth of scientific power, but the measure in which it is already posited as fixed capital, the scope and width in which it is realized and has conquered the totality of production. It is, likewise, the development of the population etc., in short, of all moments of production; in that the productive power of labour, like the application of machinery, is related to the population; whose growth in and for itself already the presupposition as well as the result of the growth of the use values to be reproduced and hence also to be consumed. Since this decline of profit signifies the same as the decrease of immediate labour relative to the size of the objectified labour which it reproduces and newly posits, capital will attempt every means of checking the smallness of the relation of living labour to the size of the capital generally, hence also of the surplus value, if expressed as profit, relative to the presupposed capital, by reducing the allotment made to necessary labour and by still more expanding the quantity of surplus labour with regard to the whole labour employed. Hence the highest development of productive power together with the greatest expansion of existing wealth will coincide with depreciation of capital, degradation of the labourer, and a most straitened exhaustion of his vital powers. These contradictions lead to explosions, cataclysms, crises, in which by momentaneous suspension of labour and annihilation of a great portion of capital the latter is violently reduced to the point where it can go on. These contradictions, of course, lead to explosions, crises, in which momentary suspension of all labour and annihilation of a great part of the capital violently lead it back to the point where it is enabled [to go on] fully employing its productive powers without committing suicide.[4] Yet, these regularly recurring catastrophes lead to their repetition on a higher scale, and finally to its violent overthrow. * * *

I. Capitalism, Alienation, and Communism

Alienation of the conditions of labour with the development of capital. (Inversion). The inversion is the foundation of the capitalist mode of production, not only of its distribution.

The fact that in the development of the productive powers of labour the objective conditions of labour, objectified labour, must grow relative to living labour—this is actually a tautological statement, for what else does growing productive power of labour mean than that less immediate labour is required to create a greater product, and that therefore social wealth expresses itself more and more in the conditions of labour created by labour itself?—this fact appears from the standpoint of capital not in such a way that one of the moments of social activity—objective labour—becomes the ever more powerful body of the other moment, of subjective, living labour, but rather—and this is important for wage labour—that the objective conditions of labour assume an ever more colossal independence, represented by its very extent, opposite living labour, and that social wealth confront labour in more powerful portions as an alien and dominant power. The emphasis comes to be placed not on the state of being *objectified*, but on the state of being *alienated*, dispossessed, sold [Der Ton wird gelegt nicht auf das *Vergegenständlichtsein*, sondern das *Entfremdet-*, Entässert-, Veräussertsein]; on the condition that the monstrous objective power which social labour itself erected opposite itself as one of its moments belongs not to the worker, but to the personified conditions of production, i.e. to capital. To the extent that, from the standpoint of capital and wage labour, the creation of the objective body of activity happens in antithesis to the immediate labour capacity— that this process of objectification in fact appears as a process of dispossession from the standpoint of labour or as appropriation of alien labour from the standpoint of capital—to that extent, this twisting and inversion [*Verdrehung und Verkehrung*] is a *real* [*phenomenon*], not a merely *supposed one* existing merely in the imagination of the workers and the capitalists. But obviously this process of inversion is a merely *historical* necessity, a necessity for the development of the forces of production solely

4. The sentence preceding this one was inserted by Marx, above the line, *in English*; thus the apparent virtual repetition. (The sentence following also appears in English in the original.)

from a specific historic point of departure, or basis, but in no way an *absolute* necessity of production; rather, a vanishing one, and the result and the inherent purpose of this process is to suspend this basis itself, together with this form of the process. The bourgeois economists are so much cooped up within the notions belonging to a specific historic stage of social development that the necessity of the *objectification* of the powers of social labour appears to them as inseparable from the necessity of their *alienation vis-à-vis* living labour. But with the suspension of the *immediate* character of living labour, as merely *individual*, or as general merely internally or merely externally, with the positing of the activity of individuals as immediately general or *social* activity, the objective moments of production are stripped of this form of alienation; they are thereby posited as property, as the organic social body within which the individuals reproduce themselves as individuals, but as social individuals. The conditions which allow them to exist in this way in the reproduction of their life, in their productive life's process, have been posited only by the historic economic process itself; both the objective and the subjective conditions, which are only the two distinct forms of the same conditions.

The worker's propertylessness, and the ownership of living labour by objectified labour, or the appropriation of alien labour by capital —both merely expressions of the same relation from opposite poles —are fundamental conditions of the bourgeois mode of production, in no way accidents irrelevant to it. These modes of distribution are the relations of production themselves, but *sub specie distributionis*. It is therefore highly absurd when e.g. J. S. Mill says (*Principles of Political Economy*, 2nd ed., London, 1849, Vol. I, p. 240): "The laws and conditions of the production of wealth partake of the character of physical truths . . . It is not so with the distribution of wealth. That is a matter of human institutions solely." (p. 239, 240.) The "laws and conditions" of the production of wealth and the laws of the 'distribution of wealth' are the same laws under different forms, and both change, undergo the same historic process; are as such only moments of a historic process.

It requires no great penetration to grasp that, where e.g. free labour or wage labour arising out of the dissolution of bondage is the point of departure, there machines can only *arise* in antithesis to living labour, as property alien to it, and as power hostile to it; i.e. that they must confront it as capital. But it is just as easy to perceive that machines will not cease to be agencies of social production when they become e.g. property of the associated workers. In the first case, however, their distribution, i.e. that they *do not belong* to the worker, is just as much a condition of the mode of production founded on wage labour. In the second case the changed distribution would start from a *changed* foundation of production, a new foundation first created by the process of history.

Capital, Volume One

KARL MARX

Capital (*Das Kapital*) was Marx's magnum opus. Volume One, published in 1867, is the book generally referred to simply as *Capital* and is relatively complete in itself.

The following selections from it, together with Marx's Preface to the first German edition, Afterword to the second, and Preface to the French edition, are taken from the text of the English edition of 1887, as translated from the third German edition by Samuel Moore and Edward Aveling and edited by Engels. An attempt has been made here to provide those sections of the book that collectively convey the basic argument and the most characteristic themes. In some instances Marx's footnotes have been deleted in the interest of saving space.

Preface to the First German Edition

The work, the first volume of which I now submit to the public, forms the continuation of my "Zur Kritik der Politischen Oekonomie" (*A Contribution to the Critique of Political Economy*) published in 1859. The long pause between the first part and the continuation is due to an illness of many years' duration that again and again interrupted my work.

The substance of that earlier work is summarised in the first three chapters of this volume. This is done not merely for the sake of connexion and completeness. The presentation of the subject-matter is improved. As far as circumstances in any way permit, many points only hinted at in the earlier book are here worked out more fully, whilst, conversely, points worked out fully there are only touched upon in this volume. The sections on the history of the theories of value and of money are now, of course, left out altogether. The reader of the earlier work will find, however, in the notes to the first chapter additional sources of reference relative to the history of those theories.

That every beginning is difficult holds in all sciences. To understand the first chapter, especially the section that contains the analysis of commodities, will, therefore, present the greatest difficulty. That which concerns more especially the analysis of the substance of value and the magnitude of value, I have, as much as it was possible, popularised.[1] The value-form, whose fully developed shape is the money-form, is very elementary and simple. Nevertheless, the human mind has for more than 2,000 years sought in vain to get to the bottom of it, whilst on the other hand, to the successful analysis of much more composite and complex forms, there has been at least an approximation. Why? Because the body, as an organic whole, is more easy of study than are the cells of that body. In the analysis of economic forms, moreover, neither microscopes nor chemical reagents are of use. The force of abstraction must replace both. But in bourgeois society the commodity-form of the product of labour—or the value-form of the commodity—is the economic cell-form. To the superficial observer, the analysis of these forms seems to turn upon minutiæ. It does in fact deal with minutiæ, but they are of the same order as those dealt with in microscopic anatomy.

With the exception of the section on value-form, therefore, this volume cannot stand accused on the score of difficulty. I presuppose, of course, a reader who is willing to learn something new and therefore to think for himself.

The physicist either observes physical phenomena where they occur in their most typical form and most free from disturbing influence, or, wherever possible, he makes experiments under conditions that assure the occurrence of the phenomenon in its normality. In this work I have to examine the capitalist mode of production, and the conditions of production and exchange corresponding to that mode. Up to the present time, their classic ground is England. That is the reason why England is used as the chief illustration in the development of my theoretical ideas. If, however, the German reader shrugs his shoulders at the condition of the English industrial and agricultural labourers, or in optimist fashion comforts himself with the thought that in Germany things are not

1. This is the more necessary, as even the section of Ferdinand Lassalle's work against Schulze-Delitzsch, in which he professes to give "the intellectual quintessence" of my explanations on these subjects, contains important mistakes. If Ferdinand Lassalle has borrowed almost literally from my writings, and without any acknowledgement, all the general theoretical propositions in his economic works, *e.g.*, those on the historical character of capital, on the connexion between the conditions of production and the mode of production, &c., &c., even to the terminology created by me, this may perhaps be due to purposes of propaganda. I am here, of course, not speaking of his detailed working out and application of these propositions, with which I have nothing to do. [*Marx*]

nearly so bad; I must plainly tell him, *"De te fabula narratur!"*[2]

Intrinsically, it is not a question of the higher or lower degree of development of the social antagonisms that result from the natural laws of capitalist production. It is a question of these laws themselves, of these tendencies working with iron necessity towards inevitable results. The country that is more developed industrially only shows, to the less developed, the image of its own future.

But apart from this. Where capitalist production is fully naturalised among the Germans (for instance, in the factories proper) the condition of things is much worse than in England, because the counterpoise of the Factory Acts is wanting. In all other spheres, we, like all the rest of Continental Western Europe, suffer not only from the development of capitalist production, but also from the incompleteness of that development. Alongside of modern evils, a whole series of inherited evils oppress us, arising from the passive survival of antiquated modes of production, with their inevitable train of social and political anachronisms. We suffer not only from the living, but from the dead. *Le mort saisit le vif!*[3]

The social statistics of Germany and the rest of Continental Western Europe are, in comparison with those of England, wretchedly compiled. But they raise the veil just enough to let us catch a glimpse of the Medusa head behind it. We should be appalled at the state of things at *home*, if, as in England, our governments and parliaments appointed periodically commissions of inquiry into economic conditions; if these commissions were armed with the same plenary powers to get at the truth; if it was possible to find for this purpose men as competent, as free from partisanship and respect of persons as are the English factory-inspectors, her medical reporters on public health, her commissioners of inquiry into the exploitation of women and children, into housing and food. Perseus wore a magic cap that the monsters he hunted down might not see him. We draw the magic cap down over eyes and ears as a make-believe that there are no monsters.

Let us not deceive ourselves on this. As in the 18th century, the American war of independence sounded the tocsin for the European middle-class, so in the 19th century, the American Civil War sounded it for the European working-class. In England the progress of social disintegration is palpable. When it has reached a certain point, it must re-act on the Continent. There it will take a form more brutal or more humane, according to the degree of development of the working-class itself. Apart from higher motives, therefore, their own most important interests dictate to the classes that

2. This story is about you.   3. The dead man seizes the living one.

are for the nonce the ruling ones, the removal of all legally removable hindrances to the free development of the working-class. For this reason, as well as others, I have given so large a space in this volume to the history, the details, and the results of English factory legislation. One nation can and should learn from others. And even when a society has got upon the right track for the discovery of the natural laws of its movement—and it is the ultimate aim of this work, to lay bare the economic law of motion of modern society—it can neither clear by bold leaps, nor remove by legal enactments, the obstacles offered by the successive phases of its normal development. But it can shorten and lessen the birth-pangs.

To prevent possible misunderstanding, a word. I paint the capitalist and the landlord in no sense *couleur de rose*. But here individuals are dealt with only in so far as they are the personifications of economic categories, embodiments of particular class-relations and class-interests. My standpoint, from which the evolution of the economic formation of society is viewed as a process of natural history, can less than any other make the individual responsible for relations whose creature he socially remains, however much he may subjectively raise himself above them.

In the domain of Political Economy, free scientific inquiry meets not merely the same enemies as in all other domains. The peculiar nature of the material it deals with, summons as foes into the field of battle the most violent, mean and malignant passions of the human breast, the Furies of private interest. The English Established Church, *e.g.*, will more readily pardon an attack on 38 of its 39 articles than on 1/39 of its income. Now-a-days atheism itself is *culpa levis*, as compared with criticism of existing property relations. Nevertheless, there is an unmistakable advance. I refer, *e.g.*, to the Blue book published within the last few weeks: "Correspondence with Her Majesty's Missions Abroad, regarding Industrial Questions and Trades' Unions." The representatives of the English Crown in foreign countries there declare in so many words that in Germany, in France, to be brief, in all the civilised states of the European Continent, a radical change in the existing relations between capital and labour is as evident and inevitable as in England. At the same time, on the other side of the Atlantic Ocean, Mr. Wade, vice-president of the United States,[4] declared in public

---

4. Marx was inaccurate here, although for an easily understandable reason. The vice presidency became vacant when Vice President Andrew Johnson succeeded to the presidency upon Lincoln's assassination in 1865. In 1867 Senator Benjamin F. Wade of Ohio was elected president *pro tem* of the Senate. He thereby became first in line of succession to the presidency during the Johnson administration and in this sense was the equivalent of a vice president although he did not in fact occupy that office. [*R. T.*]

meetings that, after the abolition of slavery, a radical change of the relations of capital and of property in land is next upon the order of the day. These are signs of the times, not to be hidden by purple mantles or black cassocks. They do not signify that tomorrow a miracle will happen. They show that, within the ruling-classes themselves, a foreboding is dawning, that the present society is no solid crystal, but an organism capable of change, and is constantly changing.

The second volume of this work will treat of the process of the circulation of capital (Book II.), and of the varied forms assumed by capital in the course of its development (Book III.), the third and last volume (Book IV.), the history of the theory.

Every opinion based on scientific criticism I welcome. As to the prejudices of so-called public opinion, to which I have never made concessions, now as aforetime the maxim of the great Florentine is mine:

"*Segui il tuo corso, e lascia dir le genti.*"[5]

London, July 25, 1867   *Karl Marx*

Preface to the French Edition

To the citizen Maurice Lachâtre

Dear Citizen,

I applaud your idea of publishing the translation of "Das Kapital" as a serial. In this form the book will be more accessible to the working-class, a consideration which to me outweighs everything else.

That is the good side of your suggestion, but here is the reverse of the medal: the method of analysis which I have employed, and which had not previously been applied to economic subjects, makes the reading of the first chapters rather arduous, and it is to be feared that the French public, always impatient to come to a conclusion, eager to know the connexion between general principles and the immediate questions that have aroused their passions, may be disheartened because they will be unable to move on at once.

That is a disadvantage I am powerless to overcome, unless it be by forewarning and forearming those readers who zealously seek the

5. "Follow your own course, no matter what people say."

truth. There is no royal road to science, and only those who do not dread the fatiguing climb of its steep paths have a chance of gaining its luminous summits.

> Believe me,
> > dear citizen
> > > Your devoted,

London, March 18, 1872   *Karl Marx*

From the Afterword to the Second German Edition

That the method employed in "Das Kapital" has been little understood, is shown by the various conceptions, contradictory one to another, that have been formed of it.

Thus the Paris *Revue Positiviste* reproaches me in that, on the one hand, I treat economics metaphysically, and on the other hand—imagine!—confine myself to the mere critical analysis of actual facts, instead of writing receipts (Comtist ones?) for the cook-shops of the future. In answer to the reproach *in re* metaphysics, Professor Sieber has it: "In so far as it deals with actual theory, the method of Marx is the deductive method of the whole English school, a school whose failings and virtues are common to the best theoretic economists." M. Block—"Les Théoriciens du Socialisme en Allemagne. Extrait du Journal des Economistes, Juillet et Août 1872"—makes the discovery that my method is analytic and says: "Par cet ouvrage M. Marx se classe parmi les esprits analytiques les plus éminents."[6] German reviews, of course, shriek out at "Hegelian sophistics." The *European Messenger* of St. Petersburg in an article dealing exclusively with the method of "Das Kapital" (May number, 1872, pp. 427–436), finds my method of inquiry severely realistic, but my method of presentation, unfortunately, German-dialectical. It says: "At first sight, if the judgment is based on the external form of the presentation of the subject, Marx is the most ideal of ideal philosophers, always in the German, *i.e.*, the bad sense of the word. But in point of fact he is infinitely more realistic than all his fore-runners in the work of economic criticism. He can in no sense be called an idealist." I cannot answer the writer better than by aid of a few extracts from his own criticism, which may interest some of my readers to whom the Russian original is inaccessible.

6. "With this work Marx takes his place among the most eminent analytic minds."

After a quotation from the preface to my "Criticism of Political Economy," Berlin, 1859, pp. IV–VII, where I discuss the materialistic basis of my method, the writer goes on: "The one thing which is of moment to Marx, is to find the law of the phenomena with whose investigation he is concerned; and not only is that law of moment to him, which governs these phenomena, in so far as they have a definite form and mutual connexion within a given historical period. Of still greater moment to him is the law of their variation, of their development, *i.e.*, of their transition from one form into another, from one series of connexions into a different one. This law once discovered, he investigates in detail the effects in which it manifests itself in social life. Consequently, Marx only troubles himself about one thing: to show, by rigid scientific investigation, the necessity of successive determinate orders of social conditions, and to establish, as impartially as possible, the facts that serve him for fundamental starting-points. For this it is quite enough, if he proves, at the same time, both the necessity of the present order of things, and the necessity of another order into which the first must inevitably pass over, and this all the same, whether men believe or do not believe it, whether they are conscious or unconscious of it. Marx treats the social movement as a process of natural history, governed by laws not only independent of human will, consciousness and intelligence, but rather, on the contrary, determining that will, consciousness and intelligence. . . . If in the history of civilisation the conscious element plays a part so subordinate, then it is self-evident that a critical inquiry whose subject-matter is civilisation, can, less than anything else, have for its basis any form of, or any result of, consciousness. That is to say, that not the idea, but the material phenomenon alone can serve as its starting-point. Such an inquiry will confine itself to the confrontation and the comparison of a fact, not with ideas, but with another fact. For this inquiry, the one thing of moment is, that both facts be investigated as accurately as possible, and that they actually form, each with respect to the other, different momenta of an evolution; but most important of all is the rigid analysis of the series of successions, of the sequences and concatenations in which the different stages of such an evolution present themselves. But it will be said, the general laws of economic life are one and the same, no matter whether they are applied to the present or the past. This Marx directly denies. According to him, such abstract laws do not exist. On the contrary, in his opinion every historical period has laws of its own. . . . As soon as society has outlived a given period of development, and is passing over from one given stage to another, it begins to be subject also to other laws. In a word, economic life offers us a phenomenon analogous to the history of evolution in other branches of biology. The old economists misunderstood the nature of economic laws when they likened them to the laws of physics and chemistry. A more thorough analysis of phenomena shows that social organisms differ among themselves as fundamentally as plants or animals. Nay, one and the same phenomenon falls under quite different laws in consequence of the different structure of those organisms as a whole, of the variations of their individual organs, of the different conditions in which those organs function, &c. Marx, *e.g.*, denies that the law of population is the same at all times and in all places. He asserts, on the contrary, that every stage of development has its own law of population.... With the varying degree of development of productive power, social conditions and the laws governing them vary too. Whilst Marx sets himself the task of following and explaining from this point of view the economic system established by the sway of capital, he is only formulating, in a strictly scientific manner, the aim that every accurate investigation into economic life must have. The scientific value of such an inquiry lies in the disclosing of the special laws that regulate the origin, existence, development, death of a given social organism and its replacement by another and higher one. And it is this value that, in point of fact, Marx's book has."

Whilst the writer pictures what he takes to be actually my method, in this striking and [as far as concerns my own application of it] generous way, what else is he picturing but the dialectic method?

Of course the method of presentation must differ in form from that of inquiry. The latter has to appropriate the material in detail, to analyse its different forms of development, to trace out their inner connexion. Only after this work is done, can the actual movement be adequately described. If this is done successfully, if the life of the subject-matter is ideally reflected as in a mirror, then it may appear as if we had before us a mere a priori construction.

My dialectic method is not only different from the Hegelian, but is its direct opposite. To Hegel, the life-process of the human brain, *i.e.*, the process of thinking, which, under the name of "the Idea," he even transforms into an independent subject, is the demiurgos of the real world, and the real world is only the external, phenomenal form of "the Idea." With me, on the contrary, the ideal is nothing else than the material world reflected by the human mind, and translated into forms of thought.

The mystifying side of Hegelian dialectic I criticised nearly thirty years ago, at a time when it was still the fashion. But just as I was working at the first volume of "Das Kapital," it was the good pleasure of the peevish, arrogant, mediocre epigones who now talk large in cultured Germany, to treat Hegel in the same way as the brave Moses Mendelssohn in Lessing's time treated Spinoza, *i.e.*, as a "dead dog." I therefore openly avowed myself the pupil of that mighty thinker, and even here and there, in the chapter on the theory of value, coquetted with the modes of expression peculiar to him. The mystification which dialectic suffers in Hegel's hands, by no means prevents him from being the first to present its general form of working in a comprehensive and conscious manner. With him it is standing on its head. It must be turned right side up again, if you would discover the rational kernel within the mystical shell.

In its mystified form, dialectic became the fashion in Germany, because it seemed to transfigure and to glorify the existing state of things. In its rational form it is a scandal and abomination to bourgeoisdom and its doctrinaire professors, because it includes in its comprehension an affirmative recognition of the existing state of things, at the same time also, the recognition of the negation of that state, of its inevitable breaking up; because it regards every historically developed social form as in fluid movement, and therefore takes into account its transient nature not less than its momentary existence; because it lets nothing impose upon it, and is in its essence critical and revolutionary.

The contradictions inherent in the movement of capitalist society impress themselves upon the practical bourgeois most strikingly in the changes of the periodic cycle, through which modern industry runs, and whose crowning point is the universal crisis. That crisis is once again approaching, although as yet but in its preliminary stage; and by the universality of its theatre and the intensity of its action it will drum dialectics even into the heads of the mushroom-upstarts of the new, holy Prusso-German empire.

London, January 24, 1873   *Karl Marx*

Part I. Commodities and Money

CHAPTER I. COMMODITIES

Section 1. The Two Factors of a Commodity: Use-Value and Value (The Substance of Value and the Magnitude of Value)

The wealth of those societies in which the capitalist mode of production prevails, presents itself as "an immense accumulation of commodities,"[1] its unit being a single commodity. Our investigation must therefore begin with the analysis of a commodity.

A commodity is, in the first place, an object outside us, a thing that by its properties satisfies human wants of some sort or another. The nature of such wants, whether, for instance, they spring from the stomach or from fancy, makes no difference.[2] Neither are we here concerned to know how the object satisfies these wants, whether directly as means of subsistence, or indirectly as means of production.

Every useful thing, as iron, paper, &c., may be looked at from the two points of view of quality and quantity. It is an assemblage of many properties, and may therefore be of use in various ways. To discover the various uses of things is the work of history.[3] So also is the establishment of socially-recognised standards of measure for the quantities of these useful objects. The diversity of these measures has its origin partly in the diverse nature of the objects to be measured, partly in convention.

The utility of a thing makes it a use-value.[4] But this utility is not a thing of air. Being limited by the physical properties of the commodity, it has no existence apart from that commodity. A commodity, such as iron, corn, or a diamond, is therefore, so far as it is a material thing, a use-value, something useful. This property of a commodity is independent of the amount of labour required to appropriate its useful qualities. When treating of use-value, we always assume to be dealing with definite quantities, such as dozens of watches, yards of linen, or tons of iron. The use-values of commodities furnish the material for a special study, that of the commercial knowledge of commodities.[5] Use-values become a reality only by use or consumption: they also constitute the substance of all wealth, whatever may be the social form of that wealth. In the

1. Karl Marx, "Zur Kritik der Politischen Oekonomie." Berlin, 1859, p. 3. [*Marx*]

2. "Desire implies want; it is the appetite of the mind, and as natural as hunger to the body. . . . The greatest number (of things) have their value from supplying the wants of the mind." Nicholas Barbon: "A Discourse Concerning Coining the New Money Lighter. In Answer to Mr. Locke's Considerations," &c., London, 1696, pp. 2, 3. [*Marx*]

3. "Things have an intrinsick vertue" (this is Barbon's special term for value in use) "which in all places have the same vertue; as the loadstone to attract iron" (l. c., p. 6). The property which the magnet possesses of attracting iron, became of use only after by means of that property the polarity of the magnet had been discovered. [*Marx*]

4. "The natural worth of anything consists in its fitness to supply the necessities, or serve the conveniences of human life." (John Locke, "Some Considerations on the Consequences of the Lowering of Interest, 1691," in Works Edit. Lond., 1777, Vol. II., p. 28.) In English writers of the 17th century we frequently find "worth" in the sense of value in use, and "value" in the sense of exchange-value. This is quite in accordance with the spirit of a language that likes to use a Teutonic word for the actual thing, and a Romance word for its reflexion. [*Marx*]

5. In bourgeois societies the economic fictio juris prevails, that every one, as a buyer, possesses an encyclopaedic knowledge of commodities. [*Marx*]

form of society we are about to consider, they are, in addition, the material depositories of exchange-value.

Exchange-value, at first sight, presents itself as a quantitative relation, as the proportion in which values in use of one sort are exchanged for those of another sort,[6] a relation constantly changing with time and place. Hence exchange-value appears to be something accidental and purely relative, and consequently an intrinsic value, *i.e.*, an exchange-value that is inseparably connected with, inherent in commodities, seems a contradiction in terms.[7] Let us consider the matter a little more closely.

A given commodity, *e.g.*, a quarter of wheat is exchanged for x blacking, y silk, or z gold, &c.—in short, for other commodities in the most different proportions. Instead of one exchange-value, the wheat has, therefore, a great many. But since x blacking, y silk, or z gold, &c., each represent the exchange-value of one quarter of wheat, x blacking, y silk, z gold, &c., must, as exchange-values, be replaceable by each other, or equal to each other. Therefore, first: the valid exchange-values of a given commodity express something equal; secondly, exchange-value, generally, is only the mode of expression, the phenomenal form, of something contained in it, yet distinguishable from it.

Let us take two commodities, *e.g.*, corn and iron. The proportions in which they are exchangeable, whatever those proportions may be, can always be represented by an equation in which a given quantity of corn is equated to some quantity of iron: *e.g.*, 1 quarter corn $=$ x cwt. iron. What does this equation tell us? It tells us that in two different things—in 1 quarter of corn and x cwt. of iron, there exists in equal quantities something common to both. The two things must therefore be equal to a third, which in itself is neither the one nor the other. Each of them, so far as it is exchange-value, must therefore be reducible to this third.

A simple geometrical illustration will make this clear. In order to calculate and compare the areas of rectilinear figures, we decompose them into triangles. But the area of the triangle itself is expressed by something totally different from its visible figure, namely, by half the product of the base into the altitude. In the same way the exchange-values of commodities must be capable of being expressed in terms of something common to them all, of which thing they represent a greater or less quantity.

This common "something" cannot be either a geometrical, a chemical, or any other natural property of commodities. Such prop-

---

6. "La valeur consiste dans le rapport d'échange qui se trouve entre telle chose et telle autre, entre telle mesure d'une production, et telle mesure d'une autre." (Le Trosne: "De l'Intérêt Social." Physiocrates, Ed. Daire. Paris, 1846. P. 889.) [*Marx*]

7. "Nothing can have an intrinsick value." (N. Barbon, 1. c., p. 6); or as Butler says—
"The value of a thing
is just as much as it will bring."
[*Marx*]

erties claim our attention only in so far as they affect the utility of those commodities, make them use-values. But the exchange of commodities is evidently an act characterised by a total abstraction from use-value. Then one use-value is just as good as another, provided only it be present in sufficient quantity. Or, as old Barbon says, "one sort of wares are as good as another, if the values be equal. There is no difference or distinction in things of equal value. ... An hundred pounds' worth of lead or iron, is of as great value as one hundred pounds' worth of silver or gold." As use-values, commodities are, above all, of different qualities, but as exchange values they are merely different quantities, and consequently do not contain an atom of use-value.

If then we leave out of consideration the use-value of commodities, they have only one common property left, that of being products of labour. But even the product of labour itself has undergone a change in our hands. If we make abstraction from its use-value, we make abstraction at the same time from the material elements and shapes that make the product a use-value; we see in it no longer a table, a house, yarn, or any other useful thing. Its existence as a material thing is put out of sight. Neither can it any longer be regarded as the product of the labour of the joiner, the mason, the spinner, or of any other definite kind of productive labour. Along with the useful qualities of the products themselves, we put out of sight both the useful character of the various kinds of labour embodied in them, and the concrete forms of that labour; there is nothing left but what is common to them all; all are reduced to one and the same sort of labour, human labour in the abstract.

Let us now consider the residue of each of these products; it consists of the same unsubstantial reality in each, a mere congelation of homogeneous human labour, of labour-power expended without regard to the mode of its expenditure. All that these things now tell us is, that human labour-power has been expended in their production, that human labour is embodied in them. When looked at as crystals of this social substance, common to them all, they are —Values.

We have seen that when commodities are exchanged, their exchange-value manifests itself as something totally independent of their use-value. But if we abstract from their use-value, there remains their Value as defined above. Therefore, the common substance that manifests itself in the exchange-value of commodities, whenever they are exchanged, is their value. The progress of our investigation will show that exchange-value is the only form in which the value of commodities can manifest itself or be expressed. For the present, however, we have to consider the nature of value independently of this, its form.

A use-value, or useful article, therefore, has value only because human labour in the abstract has been embodied or materialised in it. How, then, is the magnitude of this value to be measured? Plainly, by the quantity of the value-creating substance, the labour, contained in the article. The quantity of labour, however, is measured by its duration, and labour-time in its turn finds its standard in weeks, days, and hours.

Some people might think that if the value of a commodity is determined by the quantity of labour spent on it, the more idle and unskillful the labourer, the more valuable would his commodity be, because more time would be required in its production. The labour, however, that forms the substance of value, is homogeneous human labour, expenditure of one uniform labour-power. The total labour-power of society, which is embodied in the sum total of the values of all commodities produced by that society, counts here as one homogeneous mass of human labour-power, composed though it be of innumerable individual units. Each of these units is the same as any other, so far as it has the character of the average labour-power of society, and takes effect as such; that is, so far as it requires for producing a commodity, no more time than is needed on an average, no more than is socially necessary. The labour-time socially necessary is that required to produce an article under the normal conditions of production, and with the average degree of skill and intensity prevalent at the time. The introduction of power-looms into England probably reduced by one-half the labour required to weave a given quantity of yarn into cloth. The hand-loom weavers, as a matter of fact, continued to require the same time as before; but for all that, the product of one hour of their labour represented after the change only half an hour's social labour, and consequently fell to one-half its former value.

We see then that that which determines the magnitude of the value of any article is the amount of labour socially necessary, or the labour-time socially necessary for its production.[8] Each individual commodity, in this connexion, is to be considered as an average sample of its class.[9] Commodities, therefore, in which equal quantities of labour are embodied, or which can be produced in the same time, have the same value. The value of one commodity is to the value of any other, as the labour-time necessary for the production of the one is to that necessary for the production of the other.

8. "The value of them (the necessaries of life), when they are exchanged the one for another, is regulated by the quantity of labour necessarily required and commonly taken in producing them." ("Some Thoughts on the Interest of Money in General, and Particularly in the Publick Funds, &c." Lond., p. 36.) This remarkable anonymous work, written in the last century, bears no date. It is clear, however, from internal evidence, that it appeared in the reign of George II. about 1739 or 1740. [*Marx*]

9. "Toutes les productions d'un même genre ne forment proprement qu'une masse, dont le prix se détermine en général et sans égard aux circonstances particulières." (Le Trosne, l. c., p. 893.) [*Marx*]

"As values, all commodities are only definite masses of congealed labour-time."

The value of a commodity would therefore remain constant, if the labour-time required for its production also remained constant. But the latter changes with every variation in the productiveness of labour. This productiveness is determined by various cicumstances, amongst others, by the average amount of skill of the workmen, the state of science, and the degree of its practical application, the social organisation of production, the extent and capabilities of the means of production, and by physical conditions. For example, the same amount of labour in favourable seasons is embodied in 8 bushels of corn, and in unfavourable, only in four. The same labour extracts from rich mines more metal than from poor mines. Diamonds are of very rare occurrence on the earth's surface, and hence their discovery costs, on an average, a great deal of labour-time. Consequently much labour is represented in a small compass. Jacob doubts whether gold has ever been paid for at its full value. This applies still more to diamonds. According to Eschwege, the total produce of the Brazilian diamond mines for the eighty years, ending in 1823, had not realised the price of one-and-a-half years' average produce of the sugar and coffee plantations of the same country, although the diamonds cost much more labour, and therefore represented more value. With richer mines, the same quantity of labour would embody itself in more diamonds, and their value would fall. If we could succeed at a small expenditure of labour, in converting carbon into diamonds, their value might fall below that of bricks. In general, the greater the productiveness of labour, the less is the labour-time required for the production of an article, the less is the amount of labour crystallised in that article, and the less is its value; and *vice versa*, the less the productiveness of labour, the greater is the labour-time required for the production of an article, and the greater is its value. The value of a commodity, therefore, varies directly as the quantity, and inversely as the productiveness, of the labour incorporated in it.

A thing can be a use-value, without having value. This is the case whenever its utility to man is not due to labour. Such are air, virgin soil, natural meadows, &c. A thing can be useful, and the product of human labour, without being a commodity. Whoever directly satisfies his wants with the produce of his own labour, creates, indeed, use-values, but no commodities. In order to produce the latter, he must not only produce use-values, but use-values for others, social use-values. (And not only for others, without more. The mediæval peasant produced quit-rent-corn for his feudal lord and tithe-corn for his parson. But neither the quit-rent-corn nor the tithe-corn became commodities by reason of the fact that they had been produced for others. To become a commodity a product must be transferred to another, whom it will serve as a use-value, by means of an exchange.)[1] Lastly nothing can have value, without being an object of utility. If the thing is useless, so is the labour contained in it; the labour does not count as labour, and therefore creates no value.

Section 2. The Two-fold Character of the Labour Embodied in Commodities

At first sight a commodity presented itself to us as a complex of two things—use-value and exchange-value. Later on, we saw also that labour, too, possesses the same two-fold nature; for, so far as it finds expression in value, it does not possess the same characteristics that belong to it as a creator of use-values. I was the first to point out and to examine critically this two-fold nature of the labour contained in commodities. As this point is the pivot on which a clear comprehension of Political Economy turns, we must go more into detail.

Let us take two commodities such as a coat and 10 yards of linen, and let the former be double the value of the latter, so that, if 10 yards of linen = W, the coat = 2W.

The coat is a use-value that satisfies a particular want. Its existence is the result of a special sort of productive activity, the nature of which is determined by its aim, mode of operation, subject, means, and result. The labour, whose utility is thus represented by the value in use of its product, or which manifests itself by making its product a use-value, we call useful labour. In this connexion we consider only its useful effect.

As the coat and the linen are two qualitatively different use-values, so also are the two forms of labour that produce them, tailoring and weaving. Were these two objects not qualitatively different, not produced respectively by labour of different quality, they could not stand to each other in the relation of commodities. Coats are not exchanged for coats, one use-value is not exchanged for another of the same kind.

To all the different varieties of values in use there correspond as many different kinds of useful labour, classified according to the order, genus, species, and variety to which they belong in the social division of labour. This division of labour is a necessary condition for the production of commodities, but it does not follow, conversely, that the production of commodities is a necessary condition for the division of labour. In the primitive Indian community there

1. I am inserting the parenthesis because its omission has often given rise to the misunderstanding that every product that is consumed by some one other than its producer is considered in Marx a commodity. [*Engels, 4th German edition*]

is social division of labour, without production of commodities. Or, to take an example nearer home, in every factory the labour is divided according to a system, but this division is not brought about by the operatives mutually exchanging their individual products. Only such products can become commodities with regard to each other, as result from different kinds of labour, each kind being carried on independently and for the account of private individuals.

To resume, then: In the use-value of each commodity there is contained useful labour, *i.e.*, productive activity of a definite kind and exercised with a definite aim. Use-values cannot confront each other as commodities, unless the useful labour embodied in them is qualitatively different in each of them. In a community, the produce of which in general takes the form of commodities, *i.e.*, in a community of commodity producers, this qualitative difference between the useful forms of labour that are carried on independently by individual producers, each on their own account, develops into a complex system, a social division of labour.

Anyhow, whether the coat be worn by the tailor or by his customer, in either case it operates as a use-value. Nor is the relation between the coat and the labour that produced it altered by the circumstance that tailoring may have become a special trade, an independent branch of the social division of labour. Wherever the want of clothing forced them to it, the human race made clothes for thousands of years, without a single man becoming a tailor. But coats and linen, like every other element of material wealth that is not the spontaneous produce of Nature, must invariably owe their existence to a special productive activity, exercised with a definite aim, an activity that appropriates particular nature-given materials to particular human wants. So far therefore as labour is a creator of use-value, is useful labour, it is a necessary condition, independent of all forms of society, for the existence of the human race; it is an eternal nature-imposed necessity, without which there can be no material exchanges between man and Nature, and therefore no life.

The use-values, coat, linen, &c., *i.e.*, the bodies of commodities, are combinations of two elements—matter and labour. If we take away the useful labour expended upon them, a material substratum is always left, which is furnished by Nature without the help of man. The latter can work only as Nature does, that is by changing the form of matter. Nay more, in this work of changing the form he is constantly helped by natural forces. We see, then, that labour is not the only source of material wealth, of use-values produced by labour. As William Petty puts it, labour is its father and the earth its mother.

Let us now pass from the commodity considered as a use-value to the value of commodities.

By our assumption, the coat is worth twice as much as the linen.

But this is a mere quantitative difference, which for the present does not concern us. We bear in mind, however, that if the value of the coat is double that of 10 yds. of linen, 20 yds. of linen must have the same value as one coat. So far as they are values, the coat and the linen are things of a like substance, objective expressions of essentially identical labour. But tailoring and weaving are, qualitatively, different kinds of labour. There are, however, states of society in which one and the same man does tailoring and weaving alternately, in which case these two forms of labour are mere modifications of the labour of the same individual, and no special and fixed functions of different persons; just as the coat which our tailor makes one day, and the trousers which he makes another day, imply only a variation in the labour of one and the same individual. Moreover, we see at a glance that, in our capitalist society, a given portion of human labour is, in accordance with the varying demand, at one time supplied in the form of tailoring, at another in the form of weaving. This change may possibly not take place without friction, but take place it must.

Productive activity, if we leave out of sight its special form, viz., the useful character of the labour, is nothing but the expenditure of human labour-power. Tailoring and weaving, though qualitatively different productive activities, are each a productive expenditure of human brains, nerves, and muscles, and in this sense are human labour. They are but two different modes of expending human labour-power. Of course, this labour-power, which remains the same under all its modifications, must have attained a certain pitch of development before it can be expended in a multiplicity of modes. But the value of a commodity represents human labour in the abstract, the expenditure of human labour in general. And just as in society, a general or a banker plays a great part, but mere man, on the other hand, a very shabby part,[2] so here with human labour. It is the expenditure of simple labour-power, *i.e.*, of the labour-power which, on an average, apart from any special development, exists in the organism of every ordinary individual. Simple average labour, it is true, varies in character in different countries and at different times, but in a particular society it is given. Skilled labour counts only as simple labour intensified, or rather, as multiplied simple labour, a given quantity of skilled being considered equal to a greater quantity of simple labour. Experience shows that this reduction is constantly being made. A commodity may be the product of the most skilled labour, but its value, by equating it to the product of simple unskilled labour, represents a definite quantity of the latter labour alone.[3] The different proportions in which

2. Comp. Hegel, "Philosophie des Rechts." Berlin, 1840. P. 250, § 190. [*Marx*]

different sorts of labour are reduced to unskilled labour as their standard, are established by a social process that goes on behind the backs of the producers, and, consequently, appear to be fixed by custom. For simplicity's sake we shall henceforth account every kind of labour to be unskilled, simple labour; by this we do no more than save ourselves the trouble of making the reduction.

Just as, therefore, in viewing the coat and linen as values, we abstract from their different use-values, so it is with the labour represented by those values: we disregard the difference between its useful forms, weaving and tailoring. As the use-values, coat and linen, are combinations of special productive activities with cloth and yarn, while the values, coat and linen, are, on the other hand, mere homogeneous congelations of undifferentiated labour, so the labour embodied in these latter values does not count by virtue of its productive relation to cloth and yarn, but only as being expenditure of human labour-power. Tailoring and weaving are necessary factors in the creation of the use-values, coat and linen, precisely because these two kinds of labour are of different qualities; but only in so far as abstraction is made from their special qualities, only in so far as both possess the same quality of being human labour, do tailoring and weaving form the substance of the values of the same article.

Coats and linen, however, are not merely values, but values of definite magnitude, and according to our assumption, the coat is worth twice as much as the ten yards of linen. Whence this difference in their values? It is owing to the fact that the linen contains only half as much labour as the coat, and consequently, that in the production of the latter, labour-power must have been expended during twice the time necessary for the production of the former.

While, therefore, with reference to use-value, the labour contained in a commodity counts only qualitatively, with reference to value it counts only quantitatively, and must first be reduced to human labour pure and simple. In the former case, it is a question of How and What, in the latter of How much? How long a time? Since the magnitude of the value of a commodity represents only the quantity of labour embodied in it, it follows that all commodities, when taken in certain proportions, must be equal in value.

If the productive power of all the different sorts of useful labour required for the production of a coat remains unchanged, the sum of the values of the coats produced increases with their number. If one coat represents x days' labour, two coats represent 2x days'

3. The reader must note that we are not speaking here of the wages or value that the labourer gets for a given labour-time, but of the value of the commodity in which that labour-time is materialised. Wages is a category that, as yet, has no existence at the present stage of our investigation. [*Marx*]

labour, and so on. But assume that the duration of the labour necessary for the production of a coat becomes doubled or halved. In the first case, one coat is worth as much as two coats were before; in the second case, two coats are only worth as much as one was before, although in both cases one coat renders the same service as before, and the useful labour embodied in it remains of the same quality. But the quantity of labour spent on its production has altered.

An increase in the quantity of use-values is an increase of material wealth. With two coats two men can be clothed, with one coat only one man. Nevertheless, an increased quantity of material wealth may correspond to a simultaneous fall in the magnitude of its value. This antagonistic movement has its origin in the two-fold character of labour. Productive power has reference, of course, only to labour of some useful concrete form, the efficacy of any special productive activity during a given time being dependent on its productiveness. Useful labour becomes, therefore, a more or less abundant source of products, in proportion to the rise or fall of its productiveness. On the other hand, no change in this productiveness affects the labour represented by value. Since productive power is an attribute of the concrete useful forms of labour, of course it can no longer have any bearing on that labour, so soon as we make abstraction from those concrete useful forms. However then productive power may vary, the same labour, exercised during equal periods of time, always yields equal amounts of value. But it will yield, during equal periods of time, different quantities of values in use; more, if the productive power rise, fewer, if it fall. The same change in productive power, which increases the fruitfulness of labour, and, in consequence, the quantity of use-values produced by that labour, will diminish the total value of this increased quality of use-values, provided such change shorten the total labour-time necessary for their production; and *vice versa*.

On the one hand all labour is, speaking physiologically, an expenditure of human labour-power, and in its character of identical abstract human labour, it creates and forms the value of commodities. On the other hand, all labour is the expenditure of human labour-power in a special form and with a definite aim, and in this, its character of concrete useful labour, it produces use-values.

Section 3. *The Form of Value or Exchange-Value*

Commodities come into the world in the shape of use-values, articles, or goods, such as iron, linen, corn, &c. This is their plain, homely, bodily form. They are, however, commodities, only because they are something two-fold, both objects of utility, and, at the same time, depositories of value. They manifest themselves therefore as commodities, or have the form of commodities, only in so far as they have two forms, a physical or natural form and a value-form.

The reality of the value of commodities differs in this respect from Dame Quickly, that we don't know "where to have it." The value of commodities is the very opposite of the coarse materiality of their substance, not an atom of matter enters into its composition. Turn and examine a single commodity, by itself, as we will, yet in so far as it remains an object of value, it seems impossible to grasp it. If, however, we bear in mind that the value of commodities has a purely social reality, and that they acquire this reality only in so far as they are expressions or embodiments of one identical social substance, viz., human labour, it follows as a matter of course, that value can only manifest itself in the social relation of commodity to commodity. In fact we started from exchange-value, or the exchange relation of commodities, in order to get at the value that lies hidden behind it. We must now return to this form under which value first appeared to us.

Every one knows, if he knows nothing else, that commodities have a value-form common to them all, and presenting a marked contrast with the varied bodily forms of their use-values. I mean their money-form. Here, however, a task is set us, the performance of which has never yet even been attempted by *bourgeois* economy, the task of tracing the genesis of this money-form, of developing the expression of value implied in the value-relation of commodities, from its simplest, almost imperceptible outline, to the dazzling money-form. By doing this we shall, at the same time, solve the riddle presented by money.

The simplest value-relation is evidently that of one commodity to some one other commodity of a different kind. Hence the relation between the values of two commodities supplies us with the simplest expression of the value of a single commodity.

A. ELEMENTARY OR ACCIDENTAL FORM OF VALUE

x commodity A = y commodity B, or
x commodity A is worth y commodity B.
20 yards of linen = 1 coat, or
20 yards of linen are worth 1 coat.

1. *The Two Poles of the Expression of Value: Relative Form and Equivalent Form*

The whole mystery of the form of value lies hidden in this elementary form. Its analysis, therefore, is our real difficulty.

Here two different kinds of commodities (in our example the linen and the coat), evidently play two different parts. The linen expresses its value in the coat; the coat serves as the material in which that value is expressed. The former plays an active, the latter a passive, part. The value of the linen is represented as relative value, or appears in relative form. The coat officiates as equivalent, or appears in equivalent form.

The relative form and the equivalent form are two intimately connected, mutually dependent and inseparable elements of the expression of value; but, at the same time, are mutually exclusive, antagonistic extremes—*i.e.*, poles of the same expression. They are allotted respectively to the two different commodities brought into relation by that expression. It is not possible to express the value of linen in linen. 20 yards of linen = 20 yards of linen is no expression of value. On the contrary, such an equation merely says that 20 yards of linen are nothing else than 20 yards of linen, a definite quantity of the use-value linen. The value of the linen can therefore be expressed only relatively—*i.e.*, in some other commodity. The relative form of the value of the linen pre-supposes, therefore, the presence of some other commodity—here the coat—under the form of an equivalent. On the other hand, the commodity that figures as the equivalent cannot at the same time assume the relative form. That second commodity is not the one whose value is expressed. Its function is merely to serve as the material in which the value of the first commodity is expressed.

No doubt, the expression 20 yards of linen = 1 coat, or 20 yards of linen are worth 1 coat, implies the opposite relation: 1 coat = 20 yards of linen, or 1 coat is worth 20 yards of linen. But, in that case, I must reverse the equation, in order to express the value of the coat relatively; and, so soon as I do that, the linen becomes the equivalent instead of the coat. A single commodity cannot, therefore, simultaneously assume, in the same expression of value, both forms. The very polarity of these forms makes them mutually exclusive.

Whether, then, a commodity assumes the relative form, or the opposite equivalent form, depends entirely upon its accidental position in the expression of value—that is, upon whether it is the commodity whose value is being expressed or the commodity in which value is being expressed.

2. *The Relative Form of Value*

a. *The Nature and Import of This Form*

In order to discover how the elementary expression of the value of a commodity lies hidden in the value-relation of two commodities, we must, in the first place, consider the latter entirely apart from its quantitative aspect. The usual mode of procedure is generally the reverse, and in the value-relation nothing is seen but the proportion between definite quantities of two different sorts of commodities that are considered equal to each other. It is apt to be forgotten that the magnitudes of different things can be compared quantitatively, only when those magnitudes are expressed in terms of the same unit. It is only as expressions of such a unit that they are of the same denomination, and therefore commensurable.

Whether 20 yards of linen = 1 coat or = 20 coats or = x coats—that is, whether a given quantity of linen is worth few or many coats, every such statement implies that the linen and coats, as magnitudes of value, are expressions of the same unit, things of the same kind. Linen = coat is the basis of the equation.

But the two commodities whose identity of quality is thus assumed, do not play the same part. It is only the value of the linen that is expressed. And how? By its reference to the coat as its equivalent, as something that can be exchanged for it. In this relation the coat is the mode of existence of value, is value embodied, for only as such is it the same as the linen. On the other hand, the linen's own value comes to the front, receives independent expression, for it is only as being value that it is comparable with the coat as a thing of equal value, or exchangeable with the coat. To borrow an illustration from chemistry, butyric acid is a different substance from propyl formate. Yet both are made up of the same chemical substances, carbon (C), hydrogen (H), and oxygen (O), and that, too, in like proportions—namely $C_4H_8O_2$. If now we equate butyric acid to propyl formate, then, in the first place, propyl formate would be, in this relation, merely a form of existence of $C_4H_8O_2$; and in the second place, we should be stating that butyric acid also consists of $C_4H_8O_2$. Therefore, by thus equating the two substances, expression would be given to their chemical composition., while their different physical forms would be neglected.

If we say that, as values, commodities are mere congelations of human labour, we reduce them by our analysis, it is true, to the abstraction, value; but we ascribe to this value no form apart from their bodily form. It is otherwise in the value-relation of one commodity to another. Here, the one stands forth in its character of value by reason of its relation to the other.

By making the coat the equivalent of the linen, we equate the labour embodied in the former to that in the latter. Now, it is true that the tailoring, which makes the coat, is concrete labour of a different sort from the weaving which makes the linen. But the act of equating it to the weaving, reduces the tailoring to that which is really equal in the two kinds of labour, to their common character of human labour. In this roundabout way, then, the fact is expressed, that weaving also, in so far as it weaves value, has nothing to distinguish it from tailoring, and, consequently, is ʹabstract human labour. It is the expression of equivalence between different sorts of commodities that alone brings into relief the specific character of value-creating labour, and this it does by actually reducing the different varieties of labour embodied in the different kinds of commodities to their common quality of human labour in the abstract.[4]

There is, however, something else required beyond the expression of the specific character of the labour of which the value of the linen consists. Human labour-power in motion, or human labour, creates value, but is not itself value. It becomes value only in its congealed state, when embodied in the form of some object. In order to express the value of the linen as a congelation of human labour, that value must be expressed as having objective existence, as being a something materially different from the linen itself, and yet a something common to the linen and all other commodities. The problem is already solved.

When occupying the position of equivalent in the equation of value, the coat ranks qualitatively as the equal of the linen, as something of the same kind, because it is value. In this position it is a thing in which we see nothing but value, or whose palpable bodily form represents value. Yet the coat itself, the body of the commodity, coat, is a mere use-value. A coat as such no more tells us it is value, than does the first piece of linen we take hold of. This shows that when placed in value-relation to the linen, the coat signifies more than when out of that relation, just as many a man strutting about in a gorgeous uniform counts for more than when in mufti.

In the production of the coat, human labour-power, in the shape of tailoring, must have been actually expended. Human labour is therefore accumulated in it. In this aspect the coat is a depository of value, but though worn to a thread, it does not let this fact show through. And as equivalent of the linen in the value equation, it exists under this aspect alone, counts therefore as embodied value, as a body that is value. A, for instance, cannot be "your majesty" to B, unless at the same time majesty in B's eyes assumes the

4. The celebrated Franklin, one of the first economists, after Wm. Petty, who saw through the nature of value, says: "Trade in general being nothing else but the exchange of labour for labour, the value of all things is . . . most justly measured by labour." ("The works of B. Franklin, &c.," edited by Sparks. Boston, 1836, Vol. II., p. 267.) Franklin is unconscious that by estimating the value of everything in labour, he makes abstraction from any difference in the sorts of labour exchanged, and thus reduces them all to equal human labour. But although ignorant of this, yet he says it. He speaks first of "the one labour," then of "the other labour," and finally of "labour," without further qualification, as the substance of the value of everything. [*Marx*]

bodily form of A, and, what is more, with every new father of the people, changes its features, hair, and many other things besides.

Hence, in the value equation, in which the coat is the equivalent of the linen, the coat officiates as the form of value. The value of the commodity linen is expressed by the bodily form of the commodity coat, the value of one by the use-value of the other. As a use-value, the linen is something palpably different from the coat; as value, it is the same as the coat, and now has the appearance of a coat. Thus the linen acquires a value-form different from its physical form. The fact that it is value, is made manifest by its equality with the coat, just as the sheep's nature of a Christian is shown in his resemblance to the Lamb of God.

We see, then, all that our analysis of the value of commodities has already told us, is told us by the linen itself, so soon as it comes into communication with another commodity, the coat. Only it betrays its thoughts in that language with which alone it is familiar, the language of commodities. In order to tell us that its own value is created by labour in its abstract character of human labour, it says that the coat, in so far as it is worth as much as the linen, and therefore is value, consists of the same labour as the linen. In order to inform us that its sublime reality as value is not the same as its buckram body, it says that value has the appearance of a coat, and consequently that so far as the linen is value, it and the coat are as like as two peas. We may here remark, that the language of commodities has, besides Hebrew, many other more or less correct dialects. The German "Wertsein," to be worth, for instance, expresses in a less striking manner than the Romance verbs "valere," "valer," "valoir," that the equating of commodity B to commodity A, is commodity A's own mode of expressing its value. Paris vaut bien une messe.

By means, therefore, of the value-relation expressed in our equation, the bodily form of commodity B becomes the value-form of commodity A, or the body of commodity B acts as a mirror to the value of commodity A.[5] By putting itself in relation with commodity B, as value *in propria persona,* as the matter of which human labour is made up, the commodity A converts the value in use, B, into the substance in which to express its, A's, own value. The value of A, thus expressed in the use-value of B, has taken the form of relative value.

5. In a sort of way, it is with man as with commodities. Since he comes into the world neither with a looking glass in his hand, nor as a Fichtian philosopher, to whom "I am I" is sufficient, man first sees and recognises himself in other men. Peter only establishes his own identity as a man by first comparing himself with Paul as being of like kind. And thereby Paul, just as he stands in his Pauline personality, becomes to Peter the type of the genus homo. [*Marx*]

b. Quantitative Determination of Relative Value

Every commodity, whose value it is intended to express, is a useful object of given quantity, as 15 bushels of corn, or 100 lbs. of coffee. And a given quantity of any commodity contains a definite quantity of human labour. The value-form must therefore not only express value generally, but also value in definite quantity. Therefore, in the value-relation of commodity A to commodity B, of the linen to the coat, not only is the latter, as value in general, made the equal in quality of the linen, but a definite quantity of coat (1 coat) is made the equivalent of a definite quantity (20 yards) of linen.

The equation, 20 yards of linen=1 coat, or 20 yards of linen are worth one coat, implies that the same quantity of value-substance (congealed labour) is embodied in both; that the two commodities have each cost the same amount of labour of the same quantity of labour-time. But the labour-time necessary for the production of 20 yards of linen or 1 coat varies with every change in the productiveness of weaving or tailoring. We have now to consider the influence of such changes on the quantitative aspect of the relative expression of value.

I. Let the value of the linen vary,[6] that of the coat remaining constant. If, say in consequence of the exhaustion of flax-growing soil, the labour-time necessary for the production of the linen be doubled, the value of the linen will also be doubled. Instead of the equation, 20 yards of linen=1 coat, we should have 20 yards of linen=2 coats, since 1 coat would now contain only half the labour-time embodied in 20 yards of linen. If, on the other hand, in consequence, say, of improved looms, this labour-time be reduced by one-half, the value of the linen would fall by one-half. Consequently, we should have 20 yards of linen=½ coat. The relative value of commodity A, *i.e.*, its value expressed in commodity B, rises and falls directly as the value of A, the value of B being supposed constant.

II. Let the value of the linen remain constant, while the value of the coat varies. If, under these circumstances, in consequence, for instance, of a poor crop of wool, the labour-time necessary for the production of a coat becomes doubled, we have instead of 20 yards of linen=1 coat, 20 yards of linen=½ coat. If, on the other hand, the value of the coat sinks by one-half, then 20 yards of linen=2 coats. Hence, if the value of commodity A remain constant, its relative value expressed in commodity B rises and falls inversely as the value of B.

6. Value is here, as occasionally in the preceding pages, used in sense of value determined as to quantity, or of magnitude of value. [*Marx*]

If we compare the different cases in I. and II., we see that the same change of magnitude in relative value may arise from totally opposite causes. Thus, the equation, 20 yards of linen=1 coat, becomes 20 yards of linen=2 coats, either, because the value of the linen has doubled, or because the value of the coat has fallen by one-half; and it becomes 20 yards of linen=½ coat, either, because the value of the linen has fallen by one-half, or because the value of the coat has doubled.

III. Let the quantities of labour-time respectively necessary for the production of the linen and the coat vary simultaneously in the same direction and in the same proportion. In this case 20 yards of linen continue equal to 1 coat, however much their values may have altered. Their change of value is seen as soon as they are compared with a third commodity, whose value has remained constant. If the values of all commodities rose or fell simultaneously, and in the same proportion, their relative values would remain unaltered. Their real change of value would appear from the diminished or increased quantity of commodities produced in a given time.

IV. The labour-time respectively necessary for the production of the linen and the coat, and therefore the value of these commodities may simultaneously vary in the same direction, but at unequal rates, or in opposite directions, or in other ways. The effect of all these possible different variations, on the relative value of a commodity, may be deduced from the results of I., II., and III.

Thus real changes in the magnitude of value are neither unequivocally nor exhaustively reflected in their relative expression, that is, in the equation expressing the magnitude of relative value. The relative value of a commodity may vary, although its value remains constant. Its relative value may remain constant, although its value varies; and finally, simultaneous variations in the magnitude of value and in that of its relative expression by no means necessarily correspond in amount. * * *

Section 4. The Fetishism of Commodities and the Secret Thereof

A commodity appears, at first sight, a very trivial thing, and easily understood. Its analysis shows that it is, in reality, a very queer thing, abounding in metaphysical subtleties and theological niceties. So far as it is a value in use, there is nothing mysterious about it, whether we consider it from the point of view that by its properties it is capable of satisfying human wants, or from the point that those properties are the product of human labour. It is as clear as noon-day, that man, by his industry, changes the forms of the materials furnished by Nature, in such a way as to make them useful to him. The form of wood, for instance, is altered, by making a table out of it. Yet, for all that, the table continues to be that common, every-day thing, wood. But, so soon as it steps forth as a commodity, it is changed into something transcendent. It not only stands with its feet on the ground, but, in relation to all other commodities, it stands on its head, and evolves out of its wooden brain grotesque ideas, far more wonderful than "table-turning" ever was.

The mystical character of commodities does not originate, therefore, in their use-value. Just as little does it proceed from the nature of the determining factors of value. For, in the first place, however varied the useful kinds of labour, or productive activities, may be, it is a physiological fact, that they are functions of the human organism, and that each such function, whatever may be its nature or form, is essentially the expenditure of human brain, nerves, muscles, &c. Secondly, with regard to that which forms the ground-work for the quantitative determination of value, namely, the duration of that expenditure, or the quantity of labour, it is quite clear that there is a palpable difference between its quantity and quality. In all states of society, the labour-time that it costs to produce the means of subsistence, must necessarily be an object of interest to mankind, though not of equal interest in different stages of development.[7] And lastly, from the moment that men in any way work for one another, their labour assumes a social form.

Whence, then, arises the enigmatical character of the product of labour, so soon as it assumes the form of commodities? Clearly from this form itself. The equality of all sorts of human labour is expressed objectively by their products all being equally values; the measure of the expenditure of labour-power by the duration of that expenditure, takes the form of the quantity of value of the products of labour; and finally, the mutual relations of the producers, within which the social character of their labour affirms itself, take the form of a social relation between the products.

A commodity is therefore a mysterious thing, simply because in it the social character of men's labour appears to them as an objective character stamped upon the product of that labour; because the relation of the producers to the sum total of their own labour is presented to them as a social relation, existing not between themselves, but between the products of their labour. This is the reason why the products of labour become commodities, social things whose qualities are at the same time perceptible and imperceptible

7. Among the ancient Germans the unit for measuring land was what could be harvested in a day, and was called Tagwerk, Tagwanne (jurnale, or terra jurnalis, or diornalis), Mannsmaad, &c. (See G. L. von Maurer. "Einleitung zur Geschichte der Mark—, &c. Verfassung," München, 1854, p. 129 sq.) [*Marx*]

by the senses. In the same way the light from an object is perceived by us not as the subjective excitation of our optic nerve, but as the objective form of something outside the eye itself. But, in the act of seeing, there is at all events, an actual passage of light from one thing to another, from the external object to the eye. There is a physical relation between physical things. But it is different with commodities. There, the existence of the things *quâ* commodities, and the value-relation between the products of labour which stamps them as commodities, have absolutely no connexion with their physical properties and with the material relations arising therefrom. There it is a definite social relation between men, that assumes, in their eyes, the fantastic form of a relation between things. In order, therefore, to find an analogy, we must have recourse to the mist-enveloped regions of the religious world. In that world the productions of the human brain appear as independent beings endowed with life, and entering into relation both with one another and the human race. So it is in the world of commodities with the products of men's hands. This I call the Fetishism which attaches itself to the products of labour, so soon as they are produced as commodities, and which is therefore inseparable from the production of commodities.

This Fetishism of commodities has its origin, as the foregoing analysis has already shown, in the peculiar social character of the labour that produces them.

As a general rule, articles of utility become commodities, only because they are products of the labour of private individuals or groups of individuals who carry on their work independently of each other. The sum total of the labour of all these private individuals forms the aggregate labour of society. Since the producers do not come into social contact with each other until they exchange their products, the specific social character of each producer's labour does not show itself except in the act of exchange. In other words, the labour of the individual asserts itself as a part of the labour of society, only by means of the relations which the act of exchange establishes directly between the products, and indirectly, through them, between the producers. To the latter, therefore, the relations connecting the labour of one individual with that of the rest appear, not as direct social relations between individuals at work, but as what they really are, material relations between persons and social relations between things. It is only by being exchanged that the products of labour acquire, as values, one uniform social status, distinct from their varied forms of existence as objects of utility. This division of a product into a useful thing and a value becomes practically important, only when exchange has acquired such an extension that useful articles are produced for the purpose of being exchanged, and their character as values has therefore to be taken into account, beforehand, during production. From this moment the labour of the individual producer acquires socially a two-fold character. On the one hand, it must, as a definite useful kind of labour, satisfy a definite social want, and thus hold its place as part and parcel of the collective labour of all, as a branch of a social division of labour that has sprung up spontaneously. On the other hand, it can satisfy the manifold wants of the individual producer himself, only in so far as the mutual exchangeability of all kinds of useful private labour is an established social fact, and therefore the private useful labour of each producer ranks on an equality with that of all others. The equalisation of the most different kinds of labour can be the result only of an abstraction from their inequalities, or of reducing them to their common denominator, viz., expenditure of human labour-power or human labour in the abstract. The two-fold social character of the labour of the individual appears to him, when reflected in his brain, only under those forms which are impressed upon that labour in every-day practice by the exchange of products. In this way, the character that his own labour possesses of being socially useful takes the form of the condition, that the product must be not only useful, but useful for others, and the social character that his particular labour has of being the equal of all other particular kinds of labour, takes the form that all the physically different articles that are the products of labour, have one common quality, viz., that of having value.

Hence, when we bring the products of our labour into relation with each other as values, it is not because we see in these articles the material receptacles of homogeneous human labour. Quite the contrary: whenever, by an exchange, we equate as values our different products, by that very act, we also equate, as human labour, the different kinds of labour expended upon them. We are not aware of this, nevertheless we do it. Value, therefore, does not stalk about with a label describing what it is. It is value, rather, that converts every product into a social hieroglyphic. Later on, we try to decipher the hieroglyphic, to get behind the secret of our own social products; for to stamp an object of utility as a value, is just as much a social product as language. The recent scientific discovery, that the products of labour, so far as they are values, are but material expressions of the human labour spent in their production, marks, indeed, an epoch in the history of the development of the human race, but, by no means, dissipates the mist through which the social character of labour appears to us to be an objective character of the products themselves. The fact, that in the particular form of production with which we are dealing, viz., the production of commodities, the specific social character of private labour carried on independently, consists in the equality of every kind of that labour, by virtue of its being human labour, which character, therefore, assumes in the product the form of value—this fact appears to the producers, notwithstanding the discovery above referred to, to be just as real and final, as the fact, that, after the discovery by science of the component gases of air, the atmosphere itself remained unaltered.

What, first of all, practically concerns producers when they make an exchange, is the question, how much of some other product they get for their own? in what proportions the products are exchangeable? When these proportions have, by custom, attained a certain stability, they appear to result from the nature of the products, so that, for instance, one ton of iron and two ounces of gold appear as naturally to be of equal value as a pound of gold and a pound of iron in spite of their different physical and chemical qualities appear to be of equal weight. The character of having value, when once impressed upon products, obtains fixity only by reason of their acting and re-acting upon each other as quantities of value. These quantities vary continually, independently of the will, foresight and action of the producers. To them, their own social action takes the form of the action of objects, which rule the producers instead of being ruled by them. It requires a fully developed production of commodities before, from accumulated experience alone, the scientific conviction springs up, that all the different kinds of private labour, which are carried on independently of each other, and yet as spontaneously developed branches of the social division of labour, are continually being reduced to the quantitative proportions in which society requires them. And why? Because, in the midst of all the accidental and ever fluctuating exchange-relations between the products, the labour-time socially necessary for their production forcibly asserts itself like an over-riding law of Nature. The law of gravity thus asserts itself when a house falls about our ears.[8] The determination of the magnitude of value by labour-time is therefore a secret, hidden under the apparent fluctuations in the relative values of commodities. Its discovery, while removing all appearance of mere accidentality from the determination of the magnitude of the values of products, yet in no way alters the mode in which that determination takes place.

Man's reflections on the forms of social life, and consequently, also, his scientific analysis of those forms, take a course directly

---

8. "What are we to think of a law that asserts itself only by periodical revolutions? It is just nothing but a law of Nature, founded on the want of knowledge of those whose action is the subject of it." (Friedrich Engels: "Umrisse zu einer Kritik de Nationalökonomie," in the "Deutsch-Französische Jahrbücher," edited by Arnold Ruge and Karl Marx. Paris, 1844.) [*Marx*]

opposite to that of their actual historical development. He begins, post festum, with the results of the process of development ready to hand before him. The characters that stamp products as commodities, and whose establishment is a necessary preliminary to the circulation of commodities, have already acquired the stability of natural, self-understood forms of social life, before man seeks to decipher, not their historical character, for in his eyes they are immutable, but their meaning. Consequently it was the analysis of the prices of commodities that alone led to the determination of the magnitude of value, and it was the common expression of all commodities in money that alone led to the establishment of their characters as values. It is, however, just this ultimate money-form of the world of commodities that actually conceals, instead of disclosing, the social character of private labour, and the social relations between the individual producers. When I state that coats or boots stand in a relation to linen, because it is the universal incarnation of abstract human labour, the absurdity of the statement is self-evident. Nevertheless, when the producers of coats and boots compare those articles with linen, or, what is the same thing, with gold or silver, as the universal equivalent, they express the relation between their own private labour and the collective labour of society in the same absurd form.

The categories of bourgeois economy consist of such like forms. They are forms of thought expressing with social validity the conditions and relations of a definite, historically determined mode of production, viz., the production of commodities. The whole mystery of commodities, all the magic and necromancy that surrounds the products of labour as long as they take the form of commodities, vanishes therefore, so soon as we come to other forms of production.

Since Robinson Crusoe's experiences are a favourite theme with political economists, let us take a look at him on his island. Moderate though he be, yet some few wants he has to satisfy, and must therefore do a little useful work of various sorts, such as making tools and furniture, taming goats, fishing and hunting. Of his prayers and the like we take no account, since they are a source of pleasure to him, and he looks upon them as so much recreation. In spite of the variety of his work, he knows that his labour, whatever its form, is but the activity of one and the same Robinson, and consequently, that it consists of nothing but different modes of human labour. Necessity itself compels him to apportion his time accurately between his different kinds of work. Whether one kind occupies a greater space in his general activity than another, depends on the difficulties, greater or less as the case may be, to be overcome in attaining the useful effect aimed at. This our friend

Robinson soon learns by experience, and having rescued a watch, ledger, and pen and ink from the wreck, commences, like a true-born Briton, to keep a set of books. His stock-book contains a list of the objects of utility that belong to him, of the operations necessary for their production; and lastly, of the labour-time that definite quantities of those objects have, on an average, cost him. All the relations between Robinson and the objects that form this wealth of his own creation, are here so simple and clear as to be intelligible without exertion, even to Mr. Sedley Taylor. And yet those relations contain all that is essential to the determination of value.

Let us now transport ourselves from Robinson's island bathed in light to the European middle ages shrouded in darkness. Here, instead of the independent man, we find everyone dependent, serfs and lords, vassals and suzerains, laymen and clergy. Personal dependence here characterises the social relations of production just as much as it does the other spheres of life organised on the basis of that production. But for the very reason that personal dependence forms the ground-work of society, there is no necessity for labour and its products to assume a fantastic form different from their reality. They take the shape, in the transactions of society, of services in kind and payments in kind. Here the particular and natural form of labour, and not, as in a society based on production of commodities, its general abstract form is the immediate social form of labour. Compulsory labour is just as properly measured by time, as commodity-producing labour, but every serf knows that what he expends in the service of his lord, is a definite quantity of his own personal labour-power. The tithe to be rendered to the priest is more matter of fact than his blessing. No matter, then, what we may think of the parts played by the different classes of people themselves in this society, the social relations between individuals in the performance of their labour, appear at all events as their own mutual personal relations, and are not disguised under the shape of social relations between the products of labour.

For an example of labour in common or directly associated labour, we have no occasion to go back to that spontaneously developed form which we find on the threshold of the history of all civilised races. We have one close at hand in the patriarchal industries of a peasant family, that produces corn, cattle, yarn, linen, and clothing for home use. These different articles are, as regards the family, so many products of its labour, but as between themselves, they are not commodities. The different kinds of labour, such as tillage, cattle tending, spinning, weaving and making clothes, which result in the various products, are in themselves, and such as they are, direct social functions, because functions of the family, which, just as much as a society based on the production of commodities,

taneously developed system of division of labour.
ion of the work within the family, and the regulation
our-time of the several members, depend as well upon
nces of age and sex as upon natural conditions varying with
seasons. The labour-power of each individual, by its very
nature, operates in this case merely as a definite portion of the
whole labour-power of the family, and therefore, the measure of the
expenditure of individual labour-power by its duration, appears here
by its very nature as a social character of their labour.

Let us now picture to ourselves, by way of change, a community
of free individuals, carrying on their work with the means of production in common, in which the labour-power of all the different
individuals is consciously applied as the combined labour-power of
the community. All the characteristics of Robinson's labour are
here repeated, but with this difference, that they are social, instead
of individual. Everything produced by him was exclusively the
result of his own personal labour, and therefore simply an object of
use for himself. The total product of our community is a social
product. One portion serves as fresh means of production and
remains social. But another portion is consumed by the members
as means of subsistence. A distribution of this portion amongst
them is consequently necessary. The mode of this distribution will
vary with the productive organisation of the community, and the
degree of historical development attained by the producers. We
will assume, but merely for the sake of a parallel with the production of commodities, that the share of each individual producer in
the means of subsistence is determined by his labour-time.
Labour-time would, in that case, play a double part. Its apportionment in accordance with a definite social plan maintains the proper
proportion between the different kinds of work to be done and the
various wants of the community. On the other hand, it also serves
as a measure of the portion of the common labour borne by each
individual, and of his share in the part of the total product destined for individual consumption. The social relations of the individual producers, with regard both to their labour and to its products, are in this case perfectly simple and intelligible, and that with
regard not only to production but also to distribution.

The religious world is but the reflex of the real world. And for a
society based upon the production of commodities, in which the
producers in general enter into social relations with one another by
treating their products as commodities and values, whereby they
reduce their individual private labour to the standard of homogeneous human labour—for such a society, Christianity with its
cultus of abstract man, more especially in its bourgeois developments, Protestantism, Deism, &c., is the most fitting form of reli-

gion. In the ancient Asiatic and other ancient modes of production we find that the conversion of products into commodities, and therefore the conversion of men into producers of commodities, holds a subordinate place, which, however, increases in importance as the primitive communities approach nearer and nearer to their dissolution. Trading nations, properly so called, exist in the ancient world only in its interstices, like the gods of Epicurus in the Intermundia, or like Jews in the pores of Polish society. Those ancient social organisms of production are, as compared with bourgeois society, extremely simple and transparent. But they are founded either on the immature development of man individually, who has not yet severed the umbilical cord that unites him with his fellowmen in a primitive tribal community, or upon direct relations of subjection. They can arise and exist only when the development of the productive power of labour has not risen beyond a low stage, and when, therefore, the social relations within the sphere of material life, between man and man, and between man and Nature, are correspondingly narrow. This narrowness is reflected in the ancient worship of Nature, and in the other elements of the popular religions. The religious reflex of the real world can, in any case, only then finally vanish, when the practical relations of every-day life offer to man none but perfectly intelligible and reasonable relations with regard to his fellowmen and to Nature.

The life-process of society, which is based on the process of material production, does not strip off its mystical veil until it is treated as production by freely associated men, and is consciously regulated by them in accordance with a settled plan. This, however, demands for society a certain material ground-work or set of conditions of existence which in their turn are the spontaneous product of a long and painful process of development.

Political Economy has indeed analysed, however incompletely, value and its magnitude, and has discovered what lies beneath these forms. But it has never once asked the question why labour is represented by the value of its product and labour-time by the magnitude of that value. These formulæ, which bear it stamped upon them in unmistakeable letters that they belong to a state of society, in which the process of production has the mastery over man, instead of being controlled by him, such formulæ appear to the bourgeois intellect to be as much a self-evident necessity imposed by Nature as productive labour itself. Hence forms of social production that preceded the bourgeois form, are treated by the bourgeoisie in much the same way as the Fathers of the Church treated pre-Christian religions.

To what extent some economists are misled by the Fetishism inherent in commodities, or by the objective appearance of the

tics of labour, is shown, amongst other ways, by
edious quarrel over the part played by Nature in the
of exchange-value. Since exchange-value is a definite
anner of expressing the amount of labour bestowed upon
t, Nature has no more to do with it, than it has in fixing the
ourse of exchange.

The mode of production in which the product takes the form of
a commodity, or is produced directly for exchange, is the most general and most embryonic form of bourgeois production. It therefore
makes its appearance at an early date in history, though not in the
same predominating and characteristic manner as now-a-days. Hence
its Fetish character is comparatively easy to be seen through. But
when we come to more concrete forms, even this appearance of simplicity vanishes. Whence arose the illusions of the monetary
system? To it gold and silver, when serving as money, did not represent a social relation between producers but were natural objects
with strange social properties. And modern economy, which looks
down with such disdain on the monetary system, does not its
superstition come out as clear as noon-day, whenever it treats of
capital? How long is it since economy discarded the physiocratic
illusion, that rents grow out of the soil and not out of society?

But not to anticipate, we will content ourselves with yet another
example relating to the commodity-form. Could commodities themselves speak, they would say: Our use-value may be a thing that
interests men. It is no part of us as objects. What, however, does
belong to us as objects, is our value. Our natural intercourse as
commodities proves it. In the eyes of each other we are nothing but
exchange-values. Now listen how those commodities speak through
the mouth of the economist. "Value"—(*i.e.*, exchange-value) "is a
property of things, riches"—(*i.e.*, use-value) "of man. Value, in
this sense, necessarily implies exchanges, riches do not." "Riches"
(use-value) "are the attribute of men, value is the attribute of commodities. A man or a community is rich, a pearl or a diamond is
valuable. . . . A pearl or a diamond is valuable" as a pearl or diamond. So far no chemist has ever discovered exchange-value either
in a pearl or a diamond. The economic discoverers of this chemical
element, who by-the-by lay special claim to critical acumen, find
however that the use-value of objects belongs to them independently of their material properties, while their value, on the other
hand, forms a part of them as objects. What confirms them in this
view, is the peculiar circumstance that the use-value of objects is
realised without exchange, by means of a direct relation between
the objects and man, while, on the other hand, their value is realised only by exchange, that is, by means of a social process. Who
fails here to call to mind our good friend, Dogberry, who informs

neighbour Seacoal, that, "To be a well-favoured man is the gift fortune; but reading and writing comes by Nature."

Part II. The Transformation of Money into Capital

CHAPTER IV. THE GENERAL FORMULA FOR CAPITAL

The circulation of commodities is the starting-point of capital. The production of commodities, their circulation, and that more developed form of their circulation called commerce, these form the historical ground-work from which it rises. The modern history of capital dates from the creation in the 16th century of a world-embracing commerce and a world-embracing market.

If we abstract from the material substance of the circulation of commodities, that is, from the exchange of the various use-values, and consider only the economic forms produced by this process of circulation, we find its final result to be money: this final product of the circulation of commodities is the first form in which capital appears.

As a matter of history, capital, as opposed to landed property, invariably takes the form at first of money; it appears as moneyed wealth, as the capital of the merchant and of the usurer. But we have no need to refer to the origin of capital in order to discover that the first form of appearance of capital is money. We can see it daily under our very eyes. All new capital, to commence with, comes on the stage, that is, on the market, whether of commodities, labour, or money, even in our days, in the shape of money that by a definite process has to be transformed into capital.

The first distinction we notice between money that is money only, and money that is capital, is nothing more than a difference in their form of circulation.

The simplest form of the circulation of commodities is C—M—C, the transformation of commodities into money, and the change of the money back again into commodities; or selling in order to buy. But alongside of this form we find another specifically different form: M—C—M, the transformation of money into commodities, and the change of commodities back again into money; or buying in order to sell. Money that circulates in the latter manner is thereby transformed into, becomes capital, and is already potentially capital.

Now let us examine the circuit M—C—M a little closer. It consists, like the other, of two antithetical phases. In the first phase, M—C, or the purchase, the money is changed into a commodity.

...e, C—M, or the sale, the commodity is changed ... money. The combination of these two phases con- ...single movement whereby money is exchanged for a ...y, and the same commodity is again exchanged for ...; whereby a commodity is bought in order to be sold, or, neg- ...ing the distinction in form between buying and selling, whereby a commodity is bought with a commodity. The result, in which the phases of the process vanish, is the exchange of money for money, M—M. If I purchase 2,000 lbs. of cotton for £100, and resell the 2,000 lbs. of cotton for £110, I have, in fact, exchanged £100 for £110, money for money.

Now it is evident that the circuit M—C—M would be absurd and without meaning if the intention were to exchange by this means two equal sums of money, £100 for £100. The miser's plan would be far simpler and surer; he sticks to his £100 instead of exposing it to the dangers of circulation. And yet, whether the merchant who has paid £100 for his cotton sells it for £110, or lets it go for £100, or even £50, his money has, at all events, gone through a characteristic and original movement, quite different in kind from that which it goes through in the hands of the peasant who sells corn, and with the money thus set free buys clothes. We have therefore to examine first the distinguishing characteristics of the forms of the circuits M—C—M and C—M—C, and in doing this the real difference that underlies the mere difference of form will reveal itself.

Let us see, in the first place, what the two forms have in common.

Both circuits are resolvable into the same two antithetical phases, C—M, a sale, and M—C, a purchase. In each of these phases the same material elements—a commodity, and money, and the same economic dramatis personæ, a buyer and a seller—confront one another. Each circuit is the unity of the same two antithetical phases, and in each case this unity is brought about by the intervention of three contracting parties, of whom one only sells, another only buys, while the third both buys and sells.

What, however, first and foremost distinguishes the circuit C—M—C from the circuit M—C—M, is the inverted order of succession of the two phases. The simple circulation of commodities begins with a sale and ends with a purchase, while the circulation of money as capital begins with a purchase and ends with a sale. In the one case both the starting-point and the goal are commodities, in the other they are money. In the first form the movement is brought about by the intervention of money, in the second by that of a commodity.

In the circulation C—M—C, the money is in the end converted into a commodity, that serves as a use-value; it is spent once for all.

In the inverted form, M—C—M, on the contrary, the buyer lays out money in order that, as a seller, he may recover money. By the purchase of his commodity he throws money into circulation, in order to withdraw it again by the sale of the same commodity. He lets the money go, but only with the sly intention of getting it back again. The money, therefore, is not spent, it is merely advanced.

In the circuit C—M—C, the same piece of money changes its place twice. The seller gets it from the buyer and pays it away to another seller. The complete circulation, which begins with the receipt, concludes with the payment, of money for commodities. It is the very contrary in the circuit M—C—M. Here it is not the piece of money that changes its place twice, but the commodity. The buyer takes it from the hands of the seller and passes it into the hands of another buyer. Just as in the simple circulation of commodities the double change of place of the same piece of money effects its passage from one hand into another, so here the double change of place of the same commodity brings about the reflux of the money to its point of departure.

Such reflux is not dependent on the commodity being sold for more than was paid for it. This circumstance influences only the amount of the money that comes back. The reflux itself takes place, so soon as the purchased commodity is resold, in other words, so soon as the circuit M—C—M is completed. We have here, therefore, a palpable difference between the circulation of money as capital, and its circulation as mere money.

The circuit C—M—C comes completely to an end, so soon as the money brought in by the sale of one commodity is abstracted again by the purchase of another.

If, nevertheless, there follows a reflux of money to its starting-point, this can only happen through a renewal or repetition of the operation. If I sell a quarter of corn of £3, and with this £3 buy clothes, the money, so far as I am concerned, is spent and done with. It belongs to the clothes merchant. If I now sell a second quarter of corn, money indeed flows back to me, not however as a sequel to the first transaction, but in consequence of its repetition. The money again leaves me, so soon as I complete this second transaction by a fresh purchase. Therefore, in the circuit C—M—C, the expenditure of money has nothing to do with its reflux. On the other hand, in M—C—M, the reflux of the money is conditioned by the very mode of its expenditure. Without this reflux, the operation fails, or the process is interrupted and incomplete, owing to the absence of its complementary and final phase, the sale.

The circuit C—M—C starts with one commodity, and finishes with another, which falls out of circulation and into consumption. Consumption, the satisfaction of wants, in one word, use-value, is its end and aim. The circuit M—C—M, on the contrary, commences with money and ends with money. Its leading motive, and the goal that attracts it, is therefore mere exchange-value.

In the simple circulation of commodities, the two extremes of the circuit have the same economic form. They are both commodities, and commodities of equal value. But they are also use-values differing in their qualities, as, for example, corn and clothes. The exchange of products, of the different materials in which the labour of society is embodied, forms here the basis of the movement. It is otherwise in the circulation M—C—M, which at first sight appears purposeless, because tautological. Both extremes have the same economic form. They are both money, and therefore are not qualitatively different use-values; for money is but the converted form of commodities, in which their particular use-values vanish. To exchange £100 for cotton, and then this same cotton again for £110, is merely a roundabout way of exchanging money for money, the same for the same, and appears to be an operation just as purposeless as it is absurd. One sum of money is distinguishable from another only by its amount. The character and tendency of the process M—C—M, is therefore not due to any qualitative difference between its extremes, both being money, but solely to their quantitative difference. More money is withdrawn from circulation at the finish than was thrown into it at the start. The cotton that was bought for £100 is perhaps resold for £100+£10 or £110. The exact form of this process is therefore M—C—M′, where M′ = M+△M = the original sum advanced, plus an increment. This increment or excess over the original value I call "surplus-value." The value originally advanced, therefore, not only remains intact while in circulation, but adds to itself a surplus-value or expands itself. It is this movement that converts it into capital.

Of course, it is also possible, that in C—M—C, the two extremes C—C, say corn and clothes, may represent different quantities of value. The farmer may sell his corn above its value, or may buy the clothes at less than their value. He may, on the other hand, "be done" by the clothes merchant. Yet, in the form of circulation now under consideration, such differences in value are purely accidental. The fact that the corn and the clothes are equivalents, does not deprive the process of all meaning, as it does in M—C—M. The equivalence of their values is rather a necessary condition to its normal course.

The repetition or renewal of the act of selling in order to buy, is kept within bounds by the very object it aims at, namely, consumption or the satisfaction of definite wants, an aim that lies altogether outside the sphere of circulation. But when we buy in order to sell, we, on the contrary, begin and end with the same thing, money, exchange-value; and thereby the movement becomes interminable. No doubt, M becomes M+△M, £100 become £110. But when viewed in their qualitative aspect alone, £110 are the same as £100, namely money; and considered quantitatively, £110 is, like £100, a sum of definite and limited value. If now, the £110 be spent as money, they cease to play their part. They are no longer capital. Withdrawn from circulation, they become petrified into a hoard, and though they remained in that state till doomsday, not a single farthing would accrue to them. If, then, the expansion of value is once aimed at, there is just the same inducement to augment the value of the £110 as that of the £100; for both are but limited expressions for exchange-value, and therefore both have the same vocation to approach, by quantitative increase, as near as possible to absolute wealth. Momentarily, indeed, the value originally advanced, the £100, is distinguishable from the surplus-value of £10 that is annexed to it during circulation; but the distinction vanishes immediately. At the end of the process, we do not receive with one hand the original £100, and with the other, the surplus-value of £10. We simply get a value of £110, which is in exactly the same condition and fitness for commencing the expanding process, as the original £100 was. Money ends the movement only to begin it again.[9] Therefore, the final result of every separate circuit, in which a purchase and consequent sale are completed, forms of itself the starting-point of a new circuit. The simple circulation of commodities—selling in order to buy—is a means of carrying out a purpose unconnected with circulation, namely, the appropriation of use-values, the satisfaction of wants. The circulation of money as capital is, on the contrary, an end in itself, for the expansion of value takes place only within this constantly renewed movement. The circulation of capital has therefore no limits.[1]

9. "Capital is divisible ... into the original capital and the profit, the increment to the capital ... although in practice this profit is immediately turned into capital, and set in motion with the original." (F. Engels, "Umrisse zu einer Kritik der Nationalökonomie, in the "Deutsch-Französische Jahrbücher," edited by Arnold Ruge and Karl Marx." Paris, 1844, p. 99.) [*Marx*]

1. Aristotle opposes Oeconomic to Chrematistic. He starts from the former. So far as it is the art of gaining a livelihood, it is limited to procuring those articles that are necessary to existence, and useful either to a household or the state. "True wealth consists of such values in use; for the quantity of possessions of this kind, capable of making life pleasant, is not unlimited. There is, however, a second mode of acquiring things, to which we may by preference and with correctness give the name of Chrematistic, and in this case there appear to be no limits to riches and possessions. Trade (literally retail trade, and Aristotle takes this kind because in it values in use predominate) does not in its nature belong to Chrematistic, for here the exchange has reference only to what is necessary to themselves (the buyer or seller)." Therefore, as he goes on to show, the original form of trade was barter, but with the extension of the latter, there arose the necessity for money. On the discovery of money, barter of necessity developed into trading in commodities, and this again, in opposition to its original tendency, grew into Chrematistic, into the art of making money. Now Chrematistic is distinguishable from Oeconomic in this way, that "in the case of Chrematistic circulation is the source of riches. And it appears to revolve about money, for money is the beginning and end of this kind of exchange. Therefore also riches, such as Chrematistic strives for, are unlimited. Just as every art that is not a means to an end, but an end in itself, has no limit to its aims, because it seeks constantly to approach nearer and nearer to that end, while those arts that

As the conscious representative of this movement, the possessor of money becomes a capitalist. His person, or rather his pocket, is the point from which the money starts and to which it returns. The expansion of value, which is the objective basis or main-spring of the circulation M—C—M, becomes his subjective aim, and it is only in so far as the appropriation of ever more and more wealth in the abstract becomes the sole motive of his operations, that he functions as a capitalist, that is, as capital personified and endowed with consciousness and a will. Use-values must therefore never be looked upon as the real aim of the capitalist; neither must the profit on any single transaction. The restless never-ending process of profit-making alone is what he aims at. This boundless greed after riches, this passionate chase after exchange-value, is common to the capitalist and the miser; but while the miser is merely a capitalist gone mad, the capitalist is a rational miser. The never-ending augmentation of exchange-value, which the miser strives after, by seeking to save his money from circulation, is attained by the more acute capitalist, by constantly throwing it afresh into circulation.

The independent form, *i.e.*, the money-form, which the value of commodities assumes in the case of simple circulation, serves only one purpose, namely, their exchange, and vanishes in the final result of the movement. On the other hand, in the circulation M—C—M, both the money and the commodity represent only different modes of existence of value itself, the money its general mode, and the commodity its particular, or, so to say, disguised mode. It is constantly changing from one form to the other without thereby becoming lost, and thus assumes an automatically active character. If now we take in turn each of the two different forms which self-expanding value successively assumes in the course of its life, we then arrive at these two propositions: Capital is money: Capital is commodities. In truth, however, value is here the active factor in a process, in which, while constantly assuming the form in turn of money and commodities, it at the same time changes in magnitude, differentiates itself by throwing off surplus-value from itself; the original value, in other words, expands spontaneously. For the movement, in the course of which it adds surplus-value, is its own movement, its expansion, therefore, is automatic expansion. Because it is value, it has acquired the occult quality of being able

---

pursue means to an end, are not boundless, since the goal itself imposes a limit upon them, so with Chrematistic, there are no bounds to its aims, these aims being absolute wealth. Oeconomic not Chrematistic has a limit . . . the object of the former is something different from money, of the latter the augmentation of money. . . . By confounding these two forms, which overlap each other, some people have been led to look upon the preservation and increase of money ad infinitum as the end and aim of Oeconomic." (Aristoteles, "De-Rep." edit. Bekker. lib. I. c. 8, 9. passim.) [*Marx*]

to add value to itself. It brings forth living offspring, or, at the least, lays golden eggs.

Value, therefore, being the active factor in such a process, and assuming at one time the form of money, at another that of commodities, but through all these changes preserving itself and expanding, it requires some independent form, by means of which its identity may at any time be established. And this form it possesses only in the shape of money. It is under the form of money that value begins and ends, and begins again, every act of its own spontaneous generation. It began by being £100, it is now £110, and so on. But the money itself is only one of the two forms of value. Unless it takes the form of some commodity, it does not become capital. There is here no antagonism, as in the case of hoarding, between the money and commodities. The capitalist knows that all commodities, however scurvy they may look, or however badly they may smell, are in faith and in truth money, inwardly circumcised Jews, and what is more, a wonderful means whereby out of money to make more money.

In simple circulation, C—M—C, the value of commodities attained at the most a form independent of their use-values, *i.e.*, the form of money; but that same value now in the circulation M—C—M, or the circulation of capital, suddenly presents itself as an independent substance, endowed with a motion of its own, passing through a life-process of its own, in which money and commodities are mere forms which it assumes and casts off in turn. Nay, more: instead of simply representing the relations of commodities, it enters now, so to say, into private relations with itself. It differentiates itself as original value from itself as surplus-value; as the father differentiates himself from himself quâ the son, yet both are one and of one age: for only by the surplus-value of £10 does the £100 originally advanced become capital, and so soon as this takes place, so soon as the son, and by the son, the father, is begotten, so soon does their difference vanish, and they again become one, £110.

Value therefore now becomes value in process, money in process, and, as such, capital. It comes out of circulation, enters into it again, preserves and multiplies itself within its circuit, comes back out of it with expanded bulk, and begins the same round ever afresh. M—M', money which begets money, such is the description of Capital from the mouths of its first interpreters, the Mercantilists.

Buying in order to sell, or, more accurately, buying in order to sell dearer, M—C—M', appears certainly to be a form peculiar to one kind of capital alone, namely merchants' capital. But industrial capital too is money, that is changed into commodities, and by the sale of these commodities, is re-converted into more money.

The events that take place outside the sphere of circulation, in the interval between the buying and selling, do not affect the form of this movement. Lastly, in the case of interest-bearing capital, the circulation M—C—M′ appears abridged. We have its result without the intermediate stage, in the form M—M′, "en style lapidaire" so to say, money that is worth more money, value that is greater than itself.

M—C—M′ is therefore in reality the general formula of capital as it appears prima facie within the sphere of circulation. * * *

CHAPTER VI. THE BUYING AND SELLING OF LABOUR-POWER

The change of value that occurs in the case of money intended to be converted into capital, cannot take place in the money itself, since in its function of means of purchase and of payment, it does no more than realise the price of the commodity it buys or pays for; and, as hard cash, it is value petrified, never varying. Just as little can it originate in the second act of circulation, the re-sale of the commodity, which does no more than transform the article from its bodily form back again into its money-form. The change must, therefore, take place in the commodity bought by the first act, M —C, but not in its value, for equivalents are exchanged, and the commodity is paid for at its full value. We are, therefore, forced to the conclusion that the change originates in the use-value, as such, of the commodity, *i.e.*, in its consumption. In order to be able to extract value from the consumption of a commodity, our friend, Moneybags, must be so lucky as to find, within the sphere of circulation, in the market, a commodity, whose use-value possesses the peculiar property of being a source of value, whose actual consumption, therefore, is itself an embodiment of labour, and consequently, a creation of value. The possessor of money does find on the market such a special commodity in capacity for labour or labour-power.

By labour-power or capacity for labour is to be understood the aggregate of those mental and physical capabilities existing in a human being, which he exercises whenever he produces a use-value of any description.

But in order that our owner of money may be able to find labour-power offered for sale as a commodity, various conditions must first be fulfilled. The exchange of commodities of itself implies no other relations of dependence than those which result from its own nature. On this assumption, labour-power can appear upon the market as a commodity, only if, and so far as, its possessor, the individual whose labour-power it is, offers it for sale, or sells it, as a commodity. In order that he may be able to do this, he must have it at his disposal, must be the untrammelled owner of his capacity for labour, *i.e.*, of his person.[2] He and the owner of money meet in the market, and deal with each other as on the basis of equal rights, with this difference alone, that one is buyer, the other seller; both, therefore, equal in the eyes of the law. The continuance of this relation demands that the owner of the labour-power should sell it only for a definite period, for it he were to sell it rump and stump, once for all, he would be selling himself, converting himself from a free man into a slave, from an owner of a commodity into a commodity. He must constantly look upon his labour-power as his own property, his own commodity, and this he can only do by placing it at the disposal of the buyer temporarily, for a definite period of time. By this means alone can he avoid renouncing his rights of ownership over it.[3]

The second essential condition to the owner of money finding labour-power in the market as a commodity is this—that the labourer instead of being in the position to sell commodities in which his labour is incorporated, must be obliged to offer for sale as a commodity that very labour-power, which exists only in his living self.

In order that a man may be able to sell commodities other than labour-power, he must of course have the means of production, as raw material, implements, &c. No boots can be made without leather. He requires also the means of subsistence. Nobody—not even "a musician of the future"—can live upon future products, or upon use-values in an unfinished state; and ever since the first

2. In encyclopaedias of classical antiquities we find such nonsense as this—that in the ancient world capital was fully developed, "except that the free labourer and a system of credit was wanting." Mommsen also, in his "History of Rome," commits, in this respect, one blunder after another. [*Marx*]
3. Hence legislation in various countries fixes a maximum for labour-contracts. Wherever free labour is the rule, the laws regulate the mode of terminating this contract. In some States, particularly in Mexico (before the American Civil War, also in the territories taken from Mexico, and also, as a matter of fact, in the Danubian provinces till the revolution effected by Kusa), slavery is hidden under the form of *peonage*. By means of advances, repayable in labour, which are handed down from generation to generation, not only the individual labour-

er, but his family, become, *de facto*, the property of other persons and their families. Juarez abolished peonage. The so-called Emperor Maximilian re-established it by a decree, which, in the House of Representatives at Washington, was aptly denounced as a decree for the re-introduction of slavery into Mexico. "I may make over to another the use, for a limited time, of my particular bodily and mental aptitudes and capabilities; because, in consequence of this restriction, they are impressed with a character of alienation with regard to me as a whole. But by the alienation of all my labour-time and the whole of my work, I should be converting the substance itself, in other words, my general activity and reality, my person, into the property of another." (Hegel, *Philosophie des Rechts*, Berlin, 1840, p. 104, § 67.) [*Marx*]

moment of his appearance on the world's stage, man always has been, and must still be a consumer, both before and while he is producing. In a society where all products assume the form of commodities, these commodities must be sold after they have been produced, it is only after their sale that they can serve in satisfying the requirements of their producer. The time necessary for their sale is superadded to that necessary for their production.

For the conversion of his money into capital, therefore, the owner of money must meet in the market with the free labourer, free in the double sense, that as a free man he can dispose of his labour-power as his own commodity, and that on the other hand he has no other commodity for sale, is short of everything necessary for the realisation of his labour-power.

The question why this free labourer confronts him in the market, has no interest for the owner of money, who regards the labour-market as a branch of the general market for commodities. And for the present it interests us just as little. We cling to the fact theoretically, as he does practically. One thing, however, is clear—Nature does not produce on the one side owners of money or commodities, and on the other men possessing nothing but their own labour-power. This relation has no natural basis, neither is its social basis one that is common to all historical periods. It is clearly the result of a past historical development, the product of many economic revolutions, of the extinction of a whole series of older forms of social production.

So, too, the economic categories, already discussed by us, bear the stamp of history. Definite historical conditions are necessary that a product may become a commodity. It must not be produced as the immediate means of subsistence of the producer himself. Had we gone further, and inquired under what circumstances all, or even the majority of products take the form of commodities, we should have found that this can only happen with production of a very specific kind, capitalist production. Such an inquiry, however, would have been foreign to the analysis of commodities. Production and circulation of commodities can take place, although the great mass of the objects produced are intended for the immediate requirements of their producers, are not turned into commodities, and consequently social production is not yet by a long way dominated in its length and breadth by exchange-value. The appearance of products as commodities pre-supposes such a development of the social division of labour, that the separation of use-value from exchange-value, a separation which first begins with barter, must already have been completed. But such a degree of development is common to many forms of society, which in other respects present the most varying historical features. On the other hand, if we consider money, its existence implies a definite stage in the exchange of commodities. The particular functions of money which it performs, either as the mere equivalent of commodities, or as means of circulation, or means of payment, as hoard or as universal money, point, according to the extent and relative preponderance of the one function or the other, to very different stages in the process of social production. Yet we know by experience that a circulation of commodities relatively primitive, suffices for the production of all these forms. Otherwise with capital. The historical conditions of its existence are by no means given with the mere circulation of money and commodities. It can spring into life, only when the owner of the means of production and subsistence meets in the market with the free labourer selling his labour-power. And this one historical condition comprises a world's history. Capital, therefore, announces from its first appearance a new epoch in the process of social production.[4]

We must now examine more closely this peculiar commodity, labour-power. Like all others it has a value.[5] How is that value determined?

The value of labour-power is determined, as in the case of every other commodity, by the labour-time necessary for the production, and consequently also the reproduction, of this special article. So far as it has value, it represents no more than a definite quantity of the average labour of society incorporated in it. Labour-power exists only as a capacity, or power of the living individual. Its production consequently pre-supposes his existence. Given the individual, the production of labour-power consists in his reproduction of himself or his maintenance. For his maintenance he requires a given quantity of the means of subsistence. Therefore the labour-time requisite for the production of labour-power reduces itself to that necessary for the production of those means of subsistence; in other words, the value of labour-power is the value of the means of subsistence necessary for the maintenance of the labourer. Labour-power, however, becomes a reality only by its exercise; it sets itself in action only by working. But thereby a definite quantity of human muscle, nerve, brain, &c., is wasted, and these require to be restored. This increased expenditure demands a larger income.[6] If the owner

---

4. The capitalist epoch is therefore characterised by this, that labour power takes in the eyes of the labourer himself the form of a commodity which is his property; his labour consequently becomes wage-labour. On the other hand, it is only from this moment that the produce of labour universally becomes a commodity. [*Marx*]
5. "The value or worth of a man, is as of all other things his price—that is to say, so much as would be given for the use of his power." (Thomas Hobbes, *Leviathan*, in *Works*, ed. Molesworth, London, 1839–44, Vol. III, p. 76.) [*Marx*]
6. Hence the Roman Villicus, as overlooker of the agricultural slaves, received "more meagre fare than working slaves, because his work was lighter." (Theodor Mommsen, *Römisches Geschichte*, 1856, p. 810.) [*Marx*]

of labour-power works to-day, to-morrow he must again be able to repeat the same process in the same conditions as regards health and strength. His means of subsistence must therefore be sufficient to maintain him in his normal state as a labouring individual. His natural wants, such as food, clothing, fuel, and housing, vary according to the climatic and other physical conditions of his country. On the other hand, the number and extent of his so-called necessary wants, as also the modes of satisfying them, are themselves the product of historical development, and depend therefore to a great extent on the degree of civilization of a country, more particularly on the conditions under which, and consequently on the habits and degree of comfort in which, the class of free labourers has been formed.[7] In contradistinction therefore to the case of other commodities, there enters into the determination of the value of labour-power a historical and moral element. Nevertheless, in a given country, at a given period, the average quantity of the means of subsistence necessary for the labourer is practically known.

The owner of labour-power is mortal. If then his appearance in the market is to be continuous, and the continuous conversion of money into capital assumes this, the seller of labour-power must pepetuate himself, "in the way that every living individual perpetuates himself, by procreation."[8] The labour-power withdrawn from the market by wear and tear and death, must be continually replaced by, at the very least, an equal amount of fresh labour-power. Hence the sum of the means of subsistence necessary for the production of labour-power must include the means necessary for the labourer's substitutes, *i.e.*, his children, in order that this race of peculiar commodity-owners may perpetuate its appearance in the market.[9]

In order to modify the human organism, so that it may acquire skill and handiness in a given branch of industry, and become labour-power of a special kind, a special education or training is requisite, and this, on its part, costs an equivalent in commodities of a greater or less amount. This amount varies according to the more or less complicated character of the labour-power. The expenses of this education (excessively small in the case of ordinary labour-power), enter pro tanto into the total value spent in its production.

The value of labour-power resolves itself into the value of a

---

7. Compare W. T. Thornton, *Over-Population and Its Remedy*, London, 1846. [*Marx*]
8. Petty. [*Marx*]
9. "Its [labour's] natural price . . . consists in such a quantity of necessaries and conforts of life, as, from the nature of the climate, and the habits of the country, are necessary to support the labourer, and to enable him to rear such a family as may preserve, in the market, an undiminished supply of labour." (R. Torrens, *An Essay on the External Corn Trade*, London, 1815, p. 62.) The word *labour* is here wrongly used for *labour-power*. [*Marx*]

definite quantity of the means of subsistence. It therefore varies with the value of these means or with the quantity of labour requisite for their production.

Some of the means of subsistence, such as food and fuel, are consumed daily, and a fresh supply must be provided daily. Other such as clothes and furniture last for longer periods and require to be replaced only at longer intervals. One article must be bought or paid for daily, another weekly, another quarterly, and so on. But in whatever way the sum total of these outlays may be spread over the year, they must be covered by the average income, taking one day with another. If the total of the commodities required daily for the production of labour-power—A, and those required weekly=B, and those required quarterly=C, and so on, the daily average of these commodities= $\dfrac{365A+52B+4C+\&c.}{365}$ Suppose that in this mass of commodities requisite for the average day there are embodied six hours of social labour, then there is incorporated daily in labour-power half a day's average social labour, in other words, half a day's labour is requisite for the daily production of labour-power. This quantity of labour forms the value of a day's labour-power or the value of the labour-power daily reproduced. If half a day's average social labour is incorporated in three shillings, then three shillings is the price corresponding to the value of a day's labour-power. If its owner therefore offers it for sale at three shillings a day, its selling price is equal to its value, and according to our supposition, our friend Moneybags, who is intent upon converting his three shillings into capital, pays this value.

The minimum limit of the value of labour-power is determined by the value of the commodities, without the daily supply of which the labourer cannot renew his vital energy, consequently by the value of those means of subsistence that are physically indispensable. If the price of labour-power fall to this minimum, it falls below its value, since under such circumstances it can be maintained and developed only in a crippled state. But the value of every commodity is determined by the labour-time requisite to turn it out so as to be normal quality.

It is a very cheap sort of sentimentality which declares this method of determining the value of labour-power, a method prescribed by the very nature of the case, to be a brutal method, and which wails with Rossi that, "To comprehend capacity for labour (*puissance de travail*) at the same time that we make abstraction from the means of subsistence of the labourers during the process of production, is to comprehend a phantom (*être de raison*). When we speak of labour, or capacity for labour, we speak at the same time of the labourer and his means of subsistence, of labourer and wages."[1] When we speak of capacity for labour, we do not speak of labour, any more than when we speak of capacity for digestion, we speak of digestion. The latter process requires something more than a good stomach. When we speak of capacity for labour, we do not abstract from the necessary means of subsistence. On the contrary, their value is expressed in its value. If his capacity for labour remains unsold, the labourer derives no benefit from it, but rather he will feel it to be a cruel nature-imposed necessity that this capacity has cost for its production a definite amount of the means of subsistence and that it will continue to do so for its reproduction. He will then agree with Sismondi: "that capacity for labour . . . is nothing unless it is sold."[2]

One consequence of the peculiar nature of labour-power as a commodity is, that its use-value does not, on the conclusion of the contract between the buyer and seller, immediately pass into the hands of the former. Its value, like that of every other commodity, is already fixed before it goes into circulation, since a definite quantity of social labour has been spent upon it; but its use-value consists in the subsequent exercise of its force. The alienation of labour-power and its actual appropriation by the buyer, its employment as a use-value, are separated by an interval of time. But in those cases in which the formal alienation by sale of the use-value of a commodity, is not simultaneous with its actual delivery to the buyer, the money of the latter usually functions as means of payment. In every country in which the capitalist mode of production reigns, it is the custom not to pay for labour-power before it has been exercised for the period fixed by the contract, as for example, the end of each week. In all cases, therefore, the use-value of the labour-power is advanced to the capitalist: the labourer allows the buyer to consume it before he receives payment of the price; he everywhere gives credit to the capitalist. That this credit is no mere fiction, is shown not only by the occasional loss of wages on the bankruptcy of the capitalist, but also by a series of more enduring consequences. Nevertheless, whether money serves as means of purchase or as a means of payment, this makes no alteration in the nature of the exchange of commodities. The price of the labour-power is fixed by the contract, although it is not realised till later, like the rent of a house. The labour-power is sold, although it is only paid for at a later period. It will, therefore, be useful, for a clear comprehension of the relation of the parties, to assume provisionally, that the possessor of labour-power, on the occasion of each sale, immediately receives the price stipulated to be paid for it.

We now know how the value paid by the purchaser to the posses-

1. Rossi, *Cours d'Econ. Polit.*, Bruxelles, 1842, p. 370. [*Marx*]

2. Sismondi, *Nouv. Princ. etc.*, Vol. I, p. 112. [*Marx*]

sor of the peculiar commodity, labour-power, is determined. The use-value which the former gets in exchange, manifests itself only in the actual usufruct, in the consumption of the labour-power. The money-owner buys everything necessary for this purpose, such as raw material, in the market, and pays for it at its full value. The consumption of labour-power is at one and the same time the production of commodities and of surplus-value. The consumption of labour-power is completed, as in the case of every other commodity, outside the limits of the market or of the sphere of circulation. Accompanied by Mr. Moneybags and by the possessor of labour-power, we therefore take leave for a time of this noisy sphere, where everything takes place on the surface and in view of all men, and follow them both into the hidden abode of production, on whose threshold there stares us in the face "No admittance except on business." Here we shall see, not only how capital produces, but how capital is produced. We shall at last force the secret of profit making.

This sphere that we are deserting, within whose boundaries the sale and purchase of labour-power goes on, is in fact a very Eden of the innate rights of man. There alone rule Freedom, Equality, Property and Bentham. Freedom, because both buyer and seller of a commodity, say of labour-power, are constrained only by their own free will. They contract as free agents, and the agreement they come to, is but the form in which they give legal expression to their common will. Equality, because each enters into relation with the other, as with a simple owner of commodities, and they exchange equivalent for equivalent. Property, because each disposes only of what is his own. And Bentham, because because each looks only to himself. The only force that brings them together and puts them in relation with each other, is the selfishness, the gain and the private interests of each. Each looks to himself only, and no one troubles himself about the rest, and just because they do so, do they all, in accordance with the preestablished harmony of things, or under the auspices of an all-shrewd providence, work together to their mutual advantage, for the common weal and in the interest of all.

On leaving this sphere of simple circulation or of exchange of commodities, which furnishes the "Free-trader Vulgaris" with his views and ideas, and with the standard by which he judges a society based on capital and wages, we think we can perceive a change in the physiognomy of our dramatis personæ. He, who before was the money-owner, now strides in front as capitalist; the possessor of labour-power follows as his labourer. The one with an air of importance, smirking, intent on business; the other, timid and holding back, like one who is bringing his own hide to market and has nothing to expect but—a hiding.

Part III. The Production of Absolute Surplus-Value

CHAPTER VII. THE LABOUR-PROCESS AND THE PROCESS OF PRODUCING SURPLUS-VALUE

Section 1. The Labour-Process or the Production of Use-Values

The capitalist buys labour-power in order to use it; and labour-power in use is labour itself. The purchaser of labour-power consumes it by setting the seller of it to work. By working, the latter becomes actually, what before he only was potentially, labour-power in action, a labourer. In order that his labour may re-appear in a commodity, he must, before all things, expend it on something useful, on something capable of satisfying a want of some sort. Hence, what the capitalist sets the labourer to produce, is a particular use-value, a specified article. The fact that the production of use-values or goods, is carried on under the control of a capitalist and on his behalf, does not alter the general character of that production. We shall, therefore, in the first place, have to consider the labour-process independently of the particular form it assumes under given social conditions.

Labour is, in the first place, a process in which both man and Nature participate, and in which man of his own accord starts, regulates, and controls the material re-actions between himself and Nature. He opposes himself to Nature as one of her own forces, setting in motion arms and legs, head and hands, the natural forces of his body, in order to appropriate Nature's productions in a form adapted to his own wants. By thus acting on the external world and changing it, he at the same time changes his own nature. He develops his slumbering powers and compels them to act in obedience to his sway. We are not now dealing with those primitive instinctive forms of labour that remind us of the mere animal. An immeasurable interval of time separates the state of things in which a man brings his labour-power to market for sale as a commodity, from that state in which human labour was still in its first instinctive stage. We pre-suppose labour in a form that stamps it as exclusively human. A spider conducts operations that resemble those of a weaver, and a bee puts to shame many an architect in the construction of her cells. But what distinguishes the worst architect from the best of bees is this, that the architect raises his structure in imagination before he erects it in reality. At the end of every labour-process, we get a result that already existed in the imagination of the labourer at its commencement. He not only effects a change of form in the material on which he works, but he also realises a purpose of his own that gives the law to his modus operandi, and to which he must subordinate his will. And this subordination is no mere momentary act. Besides the exertion of the bodily organs, the process demands that, during the whole operation, the workman's will be steadily in consonance with his purpose. This means close attention. The less he is attracted by the nature of the work, and the mode in which it is carried on, and the less, therefore, he enjoys it as something which gives play to his bodily and mental powers, the more close his attention is forced to be.

The elementary factors of the labour-process are (1), the personal activity of man, *i.e.*, work itself, (2), the subject of that work, and (3), its instruments.

The soil (and this, economically speaking, includes water) in the virgin state in which it supplies man with necessaries or the means of subsistence ready to hand, exists independently of him, and is the universal subject of human labour. All those things which labour merely separates from immediate connexion with their environment, are subjects of labour spontaneously provided by Nature. Such are fish which we catch and take from their element, water, timber which we fell in the virgin forest, and ores which we extract from their veins. If, on the other hand, the subject of labour has, so to say, been filtered through previous labour, we call it raw material; such is ore already extracted and ready for washing. All raw material is the subject of labour, but not every subject of labour is raw material: it can only become so, after it has undergone some alteration by means of labour.

An instrument of labour is a thing, or a complex of things, which the labourer interposes between himself and the subject of his labour, and which serves as the conductor of his activity. He makes use of the mechanical, physical, and chemical properties of some substances in order to make other substances subservient to his aims.[3] Leaving out of consideration such ready-made means of subsistence as fruits, in gathering which a man's own limbs serve as the instruments of his labour, the first thing of which the labourer possesses himself is not the subject of labour but its instrument. Thus Nature becomes one of the organs of his activity, one that he annexes to his own bodily organs, adding stature to himself in spite

3. "Reason is just as cunning as she is powerful. Her cunning consists principally in her mediating activity, which, by causing objects to act and re-act on each other in accordance with their own nature, in this way, without any direct interference in the process, carries out reason's intentions." (Hegel: "Enzyklopädie, Erster Theil, Die Logik," Berlin, 1840, p. 382.) [*Marx*]

of the Bible. As the earth is his original larder, so too it is his original tool house. It supplies him, for instance, with stones for throwing, grinding, pressing, cutting, &c. The earth itself is an instrument of labour, but when used as such in agriculture implies a whole series of other instruments and a comparatively high development of labour. No sooner does labour undergo the least development, than it requires specially prepared instruments. Thus in the oldest caves we find stone implements and weapons. In the earliest period of human history domesticated annimals, *i.e.*, animals which have been bred for the purpose, and have undergone modifications by means of labour, play the chief part as instruments of labour along with specially prepared stones, wood, bones, and shells. The use and fabrication of instruments of labour, although existing in the germ among certain species of animals, is specifically characteristic of the human labour-process, and Franklin therefore defines man as a tool-making animal. Relics of bygone instruments of labour possess the same importance for the investigation of extinct economic forms of society, as do fossil bones for the determination of extinct species of animals. It is not the articles made, but how they are made, and by what instruments, that enables us to distinguish different economic epochs. Instruments of labour not only supply a standard of the degree of development to which human labour has attained, but they are also indicators of the social conditions under which that labour is carried on. Among the instruments of labour, those of a mechanical nature, which, taken as a whole, we may call the bone and muscles of production, offer much more decided characteristics of a given epoch of production, than those which, like pipes, tubs, baskets, jars, &c., serve only to hold the materials for labour, which latter class, we may in a general way, call the vascular system of production. The latter first begins to play an important part in the chemical industries.

In a wider sense we may include among the instruments of labour, in addition to those things that are used for directly transferring labour to its subject, and which therefore, in one way or another, serve as conductors of activity, all such objects as are necessary for carrying on the labour-process. These do not enter directly into the process, but without them it is either impossible for it to take place at all, or possible only to a partial extent. Once more we find the earth to be a universal instrument of this sort, for it furnishes a locus standi to the labourer and a field of employment for his activity. Among instruments that are the result of previous labour and also belong to this class, we find workshops, canals, roads, and so forth.

In the labour-process, therefore, man's activity, with the help of the instruments of labour, effects an alteration, designed from the commencement, in the material worked upon. The process disappears in the product; the latter is a use-value, Nature's material adapted by a change of form to the wants of man. Labour has incorporated itself with its subject: the former is materialised, the latter transformed. That which in the labourer appeared as movement, now appears in the product as a fixed quality without motion. The blacksmith forges and the product is a forging.

If we examine the whole process from the point of view of its result, the product, it is plain that both the instruments and the subject of labour, are means of production, and that the labour itself is productive labour.

Though a use-value, in the form of a product, issues from the labour-process, yet other use-values, products of previous labour, enter into it as means of production. The same use-value is both the product of a previous process, and a means of production in a later process. Products are therefore not only results, but also essential conditions of labour.

With the exception of the extractive industries, in which the material for labour is provided immediately by Nature, such as mining, hunting, fishing, and agriculture (so far as the latter is confined to breaking up virgin soil), all branches of industry manipulate raw material, objects already filtered through labour, already products of labour. Such is seed in agriculture. Animals and plants, which we are accustomed to consider as products of Nature, are in their present form, not only products of, say last year's labour, but the result of a gradual transformation, continued through many generations, under man's superintendence, and by means of his labour. But in the great majority of cases, instruments of labour show even to the most superficial observer, traces of the labour of past ages.

Raw material may either form the principal substance of a product, or it may enter into its formation only as an accessory. An accessory may be consumed by the instruments of labour, as coal under a boiler, oil by a wheel, hay by draft-horses, or it may be mixed with the raw material in order to produce some modification thereof, as chlorine into unbleached linen, coal with iron, dye-stuff with wool, or again, it may help to carry on the work itself, as in the case of the materials used for heating and lighting workshops. The distinction between principal substance and accessory vanishes in the true chemical industries, because there none of the raw material re-appears, in its original composition, in the substance of the product.

Every object possesses various properties, and is thus capable of being applied to different uses. One and the same product may therefore serve as raw material in very different processes. Corn, for example, is a raw material for millers, starch-manufacturers, distillers, and cattle-breeders. It also enters as raw material into its own production in the shape of seed; coal, too, is at the same time the product of, and a means of production in, coal-mining.

Again, a particular product may be used in one and the same process, both as an instrument of labour and as raw material. Take, for instance, the fattening of cattle, where the animal is the raw material, and at the same time an instrument for the production of manure.

A product, though ready for immediate consumption, may yet serve as raw material for a further product, as grapes when they become the raw material for wine. On the other hand, labour may give us its product in such a form, that we can use it only as raw material, as is the case with cotton, thread, and yarn. Such a raw material, though itself a product, may have to go through a whole series of different processes: in each of these in turn, it serves, with constantly varying form, as raw material, until the last process of the series leaves it a perfect product, ready for individual consumption, or for use as an instrument of labour.

Hence we see, that whether a use-value is to be regarded as raw material, as instrument of labour, or as product, this is determined entirely by its function in the labour-process, by the position it there occupies: as this varies, so does its character.

Whenever therefore a product enters as a means of production into a new labour-process, it thereby loses its character of product, and becomes a mere factor in the process. A spinner treats spindles only as implements for spinning, and flax only as the material that he spins. Of course it is impossible to spin without material and spindles; and therefore the existence of these things as products, at the commencement of the spinning operation, must be presumed: but in the process itself, the fact that they are products of previous labour, is a matter of utter indifference; just as in the digestive process, it is of no importance whatever, that bread is the produce of the previous labour of the farmer, the miller, and the baker. On the contrary, it is generally by their imperfections as products, that the means of production in any process assert themselves in their character of products. A blunt knife or weak thread forcibly remind us of Mr. A., the cutler, or Mr. B., the spinner. In the finished product the labour by means of which it has acquired its useful qualities is not palpable, has apparently vanished.

A machine which does not serve the purposes of labour, is useless. In addition, it falls a prey to the destructive influence of

natural forces. Iron rusts and wood rots. Yarn with which we neither weave nor knit, is cotton wasted. Living labour must seize
upon these things and rouse them from their death-sleep, change
them from mere possible use-values into real and effective ones.
Bathed in the fire of labour, appropriated as part and parcel of
labour's organism, and, as it were, made alive for the performance
of their functions in the process, they are in truth consumed, but
consumed with a purpose, as elementary constituents of new use-
values, of new products, ever ready as means of subsistence for individual consumption, or as means of production for some new
labour-process.

If then, on the one hand, finished products are not only results,
but also necessary conditions, of the labour-process, on the other
hand, their assumption into that process, their contact with living
labour, is the sole means by which they can be made to retain their
character of use-values, and be utilised.

Labour uses up its material factors, its subject and its instruments, consumes them, and is therefore a process of consumption.
Such productive consumption is distinguished from individual consumption by this, that the latter uses up products, as means of subsistence for the living individual; the former, as means whereby
alone, labour, the labour-power of the living individual, is enabled
to act. The product, therefore, of individual consumption, is the
consumer himself; the result of productive consumption, is a product distinct from the consumer.

In so far then, as its instruments and subjects are themselves
products, labour consumes products in order to create products, or
in other words, consumes one set of products by turning them into
means of production for another set. But, just as in the beginning,
the only participators in the labour-process were man and the earth,
which latter exists independently of man, so even now we still
employ in the process many means of production, provided directly
by Nature, that do not represent any combination of natural substances with human labour.

The labour-process, resolved as above into its simple elementary
factors, is human action with a view to the production of use-
values, appropriation of natural substances to human requirements;
it is the necessary condition for effecting exchange of matter
between man and Nature; it is the everlasting Nature-imposed condition of human existence, and therefore is independent of every
social phase of that existence, or rather, is common to every such
phase. It was, therefore, not necessary to represent our labourer in
connexion with other labourers; man and his labour on one side,
Nature and its materials on the other, sufficed. As the taste of the

porridge does not tell you who grew the oats, no more does this simple process tell you of itself what are the social conditions under which it is taking place, whether under the slave-owner's brutal lash, or the anxious eye of the capitalist, whether Cincinnatus carries it on in tilling his modest farm or a savage in killing wild animals with stones.

Let us now return to our would-be capitalist. We left him just after he had purchased, in the open market, all the necessary factors of the labour-process; its objective factors, the means of production, as well as its subjective factor, labour-power. With the keen eye of an expert, he has selected the means of production and the kind of labour-power best adapted to his particular trade, be it spinning, bootmaking, or any other kind. He then proceeds to consume the commodity, the labour-power that he has just bought, by causing the labourer, the impersonation of that labour-power, to consume the means of production by his labour. The general character of the labour-process is evidently not changed by the fact, that the labourer works for the capitalist instead of for himself; moreover, the particular methods and operations employed in bootmaking or spinning are not immediately changed by the intervention of the capitalist. He must begin by taking the labour-power as he finds it in the market, and consequently be satisfied with labour of such a kind as would be found in the period immediately preceding the rise of capitalists. Changes in the methods of production by the subordination of labour to capital, can take place only at a later period, and therefore will have to be treated of in a later chapter.

The labour-process, turned into the process by which the capitalist consumes labour-power, exhibits two characteristic phenomena. First, the labourer works under the control of the capitalist to whom his labour belongs; the capitalist taking good care that the work is done in a proper manner, and that the means of production are used with intelligence, so that there is no unnecessary waste of raw material, and no wear and tear of the implements beyond what is necessarily caused by the work.

Secondly, the product is the property of the capitalist and not that of the labourer, its immediate producer. Suppose that a capitalist pays for a day's labour-power at its value; then the right to use that power for a day belongs to him, just as much as the right to use any other commodity, such as a horse that he has hired for the day. To the purchaser of a commodity belongs its use, and the seller of labour-power, by giving his labour, does no more, in reality, than part with the use-value that he has sold. From the instant he steps into the workshop, the use-value of his labour-power, and therefore also its use, which is labour, belongs to the capitalist. By the purchase of labour-power, the capitalist incorporates labour, as a living ferment, with the lifeless constituents of the product. From his point of view, the labour-process is nothing more than the consumption of the commodity purchased, *i.e.*, of labour-power; but this consumption cannot be effected except by supplying the labour-power with the means of production. The labour-process is a process between things that the capitalist has purchased, things that have become his property. The product of this process belongs, therefore, to him, just as much as does the wine which is the product of a process of fermentation completed in his cellar.

Section 2. The Production of Surplus-Value

The product appropriated by the capitalist is a use-value, as yarn, for example, or boots. But, although boots are, in one sense, the basis of all social progress, and our capitalist is a decided "progressist," yet he does not manufacture boots for their own sake. Use-value is, by no means, the thing "qu'on aime pour lui-même" in the production of commodities. Use-values are only produced by capitalists, because, and in so far as, they are the material substratum, the depositories of exchange-value. Our capitalist has two objects in view: in the first place, he wants to produce a use-value that has a value in exchange, that is to say, an article destined to be sold, a commodity; and secondly, he desires to produce a commodity whose value shall be greater than the sum of the values of the commodities used in its production, that is, of the means of production and the labour-power, that he purchased with his good money in the open market. His aim is to produce not only a use-value, but a commodity also; not only use-value, but value; not only value, but at the same time surplus-value.

It must be borne in mind, that we are now dealing with the production of commodities, and that, up to this point, we have only considered one aspect of the process. Just as commodities are, at the same time, use-values and values, so the process of producing them must be a labour-process, and at the same time, a process of creating value.

Let us now examine production as a creation of value.

We know that the value of each commodity is determined by the quantity of labour expended on and materialised in it, by the working-time necessary, under given social conditions, for its production. This rule also holds good in the case of the product that accrued to our capitalist, as the result of the labour-process carried on for him. Assuming this product to be 10 lbs. of yarn, our first step is to calculate the quantity of labour realised in it.

For spinning the yarn, raw material is required; suppose in this case 10 lbs. of cotton. We have no need at present to investigate the value of this cotton, for our capitalist has, we will assume, bought it at its full value, say of ten shillings. In this price the labour required for the production of the cotton is already expressed in terms of the average labour of society. We will further assume that the wear and tear of the spindle, which, for our present purpose, may represent all other instruments of labour employed, amounts to the value of 2s. If, then, twenty-four hours' labour, or two working-days are required to produce the quantity of gold represented by twelve shillings, we have here, to begin with, two days' labour already incorporated in the yarn.

We must not let ourselves be misled by the circumstance that the cotton has taken a new shape while the substance of the spindle has to a certain extent been used up. By the general law of value, if the value of 40 lbs. of yarn = the value of 40 lbs. of cotton + the value of a whole spindle, *i.e.*, if the same working-time is required to produce the commodities on either side of this equation, then 10 lbs. of yarn are an equivalent for 10 lbs. of cotton, together with one-fourth of a spindle. In the case we are considering the same working-time is materialised in the 10 lbs. of yarn on the one hand, and in the 10 lbs. of cotton and the fraction of a spindle on the other. Therefore, whether value appears in cotton, in a spindle, or in yarn, makes no difference in the amount of that value. The spindle and cotton, instead of resting quietly side by side, join together in the process, their forms are altered, and they are turned into yarn; but their value is no more affected by this fact than it would be if they had been simply exchanged for their equivalent in yarn.

The labour required for the production of the cotton, the raw material of the yarn, is part of the labour necessary to produce the yarn, and is therefore contained in the yarn. The same applies to the labour embodied in the spindle, without whose wear and tear the cotton could not be spun.

Hence, in determining the value of the yarn, or the labour-time required for its production, all the special processes carried on at various times and in different places, which were necessary, first to produce the cotton and the wasted portion of the spindle, and then with the cotton and spindle to spin the yarn, may together be looked on as different and successive phases of one and the same process. The whole of the labour in the yarn is past labour; and it is a matter of no importance that the operations necessary for the production of its constituent elements were carried on at times which, referred to the present, are more remote than the final operation of spinning. If a definite quantity of labour, say thirty days, is requisite to build a house, the total amount of labour incorporated in it is not altered by the fact that the work of the last day is done twenty-nine days later than that of the first. Therefore the labour contained in the raw material and the instruments of labour can be treated just as if it were labour expended in an earlier stage of the spinning process, before the labour of actual spinning commenced.

The values of the means of production, *i.e.*, the cotton and the spindle, which values are expressed in the price of twelve shillings, are therefore constituent parts of the value of the yarn, or, in other words, of the value of the product.

Two conditions must nevertheless be fulfilled. First, the cotton and spindle must concur in the production of a use value; they must in the present case become yarn. Value is independent of the particular use-value by which it is borne, but it must be embodied in a use-value of some kind. Secondly, the time occupied in the labour of production must not exceed the time really necessary under the given social conditions of the case. Therefore, if no more than 1 lb. of cotton be requisite to spin 1 lb. of yarn, care must be taken that no more than this weight of cotton is consumed in the production of 1 lb. of yarn; and similarly with regard to the spindle. Though the capitalist have a hobby, and use a gold instead of a steel spindle, yet the only labour that counts for anything in the value of the yarn is that which would be required to produce a steel spindle, because no more is necessary under the given social conditions.

We now know what portion of the value of the yarn is owing to the cotton and the spindle. It amounts to twelve shillings or the value of two days' work. The next point for our consideration is, what portion of the value of the yarn is added to the cotton by the labour of the spinner.

We have now to consider this labour under a very different aspect from that which it had during the labour-process; there, we viewed it solely as that particular kind of human activity which changes cotton into yarn; there, the more the labour was suited to the work, the better the yarn, other circumstances remaining the same. The labour of the spinner was then viewed as specifically different from other kinds of productive labour, different on the one hand in its special aim, viz., spinning, different, on the other hand, in the special character of its operations, in the special nature of its means of production and in the special use value of its product. For the operation of spinning, cotton and spindles are a necessity, but for making rifled cannon they would be of no use whatever. Here, on the contrary, where we consider the labour of the spinner only so far as it is value-creating, *i.e.*, a source of value, his labour differs in no respect from the labour of the man who bores cannon, or (what here more nearly concerns us), from the labour of the cotton-planter and spindle-maker incorporated in the means of production. It is solely by reason of this identity, that cotton planting, spindle making and spinning, are capable of forming the component parts, differing only quantitatively from each other, of one whole, namely, the value of the yarn. Here, we have nothing more to do with the quality, the nature and the specific character of the labour, but merely with its quantity. And this simply requires to be calculated. We proceed upon the assumption that spinning is simple, unskilled labour, the average labour of a given state of society. Hereafter we shall see that the contrary assumption would make no difference.

While the labourer is at work, his labour constantly undergoes a transformation: from being motion, it becomes an object without motion; from being the labourer working, it becomes the thing produced. At the end of one hour's spinning, that act is represented by a definite quantity of yarn; in other words, a definite quantity of labour, namely that of one hour, has become embodied in the cotton. We say labour, *i.e.*, the expenditure of his vital force by the spinner, and not spinning labour, because the special work of spinning counts here, only so far as it is the expenditure of labour-power in general, and not in so far as it is the specific work of the spinner.

In the process we are now considering it is of extreme importance, that no more time be consumed in the work of transforming the cotton into yarn than is necessary under the given social conditions. If under normal, *i.e.*, average social conditions of production, a pounds of cotton ought to be made into b pounds of yarn by one hour's labour, then a day's labour does not count as 12 hours' labour unless 12 a pounds of cotton have been made into 12 b pounds of yarn; for in the creation of value, the time that is socially necessary alone counts.

Not only the labour, but also the raw material and the product now appear in quite a new light, very different from that in which we viewed them in the labour-process pure and simple. The raw material serves now merely as an absorbent of a definite quantity of labour. By this absorption it is in fact changed into yarn, because it is spun, because labour-power in the form of spinning is added to it; but the product, the yarn, is now nothing more than a measure of the labour absorbed by the cotton. If in one hour $1\frac{2}{3}$ lbs. of cotton can be spun into $1\frac{2}{3}$ lbs. of yarn, then 10 lbs. of yarn indicate the absorption of 6 hours' labour. Definite quantities of product, these quantities being determined by experience, now represent nothing but definite quantities of labour, definite masses of crystallised labour-time. They are nothing more than the materialisation of so many hours or so many days of social labour.

We are here no more concerned about the facts, that the labour is the specific work of spinning, that its subject is cotton and its product yarn, than we are about the fact that the subject itself is already a product and therefore raw material. If the spinner, instead of spinning, were working in a coal mine, the subject of his labour, the coal, would be supplied by Nature; nevertheless, a definite quantity of extracted coal, a hundredweight for example, would represent a definite quantity of absorbed labour.

We assumed, on the occasion of its sale, that the value of a day's labour-power is three shillings, and that six hours' labour is incorporated in that sum; and consequently that this amount of labour is requisite to produce the necessaries of life daily required on an average by the labourer. If now our spinner by working for one hour, can convert 1⅔ lbs. of cotton into 1⅔ lbs. of yarn,[4] it follows that in six hours he will convert 10 lbs. of cotton into 10 lbs. of yarn. Hence, during the spinning process, the cotton absorbs six hours' labour. The same quantity of labour is also embodied in a piece of gold of the value of three shillings. Consequently by the mere labour of spinning, a value of three shillings is added to the cotton.

Let us now consider the total value of the product, the 10 lbs. of yarn. Two and a half days' labour has been embodied in it, of which two days were contained in the cotton and in the substance of the spindle worn away, and half a day was absorbed during the process of spinning. This two and a half days' labour is also represented by a piece of gold of the value of fifteen shillings. Hence, fifteen shillings is an adequate price for the 10 lbs. of yarn, or the price of one pound is eighteenpence.

Our capitalist stares in astonishment. The value of the product is exactly equal to the value of the capital advanced. The value so advanced has not expanded, no surplus-value has been created, and consequently money has not been converted into capital. The price of the yarn is fifteen shillings, and fifteen shillings were spent in the open market upon the constituent elements of the product, or, what amounts to the same thing, upon the factors of the labour-process; ten shillings were paid for the cotton, two shillings for the substance of the spindle worn away, and three shillings for the labour-power. The swollen value of the yarn is of no avail, for it is merely the sum of the values formerly existing in the cotton, the spindle, and the labour-power: out of such a simple addition of existing values, no surplus-value can possibly arise. These separate values are now all concentrated in one thing; but so they were also in the sum of fifteen shillings, before it was split up into three parts, by the purchase of the commodities.

There is in reality nothing very strange in this result. The value

---

4. These figures are quite arbitrary. [*Marx*]

of one pound of yarn being eighteenpence, if our capitalist buys 10 lbs. of yarn in the market, he must pay fifteen shillings for them. It is clear that, whether a man buys his house ready built, or gets it built for him, in neither case will the mode of acquisition increase the amount of money laid out on the house.

Our capitalist, who is at home in his vulgar economy, exclaims: "Oh! but I advanced my money for the express purpose of making more money." The way to Hell is paved with good intentions, and he might just as easily have intended to make money, without producing at all. He threatens all sorts of things. He won't be caught napping again. In future he will buy the commodities in the market, instead of manufacturing them himself. But if all his brother capitalists were to do the same, where would he find his commodities in the market? And his money he cannot eat. He tries persuasion. "Consider my abstinence; I might have played ducks and drakes with the 15 shillings; but instead of that I consumed it productively, and made yarn with it." Very well, and by way of reward he is now in possession of good yarn instead of a bad conscience; and as for playing the part of the miser; it would never do for him to relapse into such bad ways as that; we have seen before to what results such asceticism leads. Besides, where nothing is, the king has lost his rights; whatever may be the merit of his abstinence, there is nothing wherewith specially to remunerate it, because the value of the product is merely the sum of the values of the commodities that were thrown into the process of production. Let him therefore console himself with the reflection that virtue is its own reward. But no, he becomes importunate. He says: "The yarn is of no use to me: I produced it for sale." In that case let him sell it, or, still better, let him for the future produce only things for satisfying his personal wants, a remedy that his physician MacCulloch has already prescribed as infallible against an epidemic of over-production. He now gets obstinate. "Can the labourer," he asks, "merely with his arms and legs, produce commodities out of nothing? Did I not supply him with the materials, by means of which, and in which alone, his labour could be embodied? And as the greater part of society consists of such ne'er-do-wells, have I not rendered society incalculable service by my instruments of production, my cotton and my spindle, and not only society, but the labourer also, whom in addition I have provided with the necessaries of life? And am I to be allowed nothing in return for all this service?" Well, but has not the labourer rendered him the equivalent service of changing his cotton and spindle into yarn? Moreover, there is here no question of service. A service is nothing more than the useful effect of a use-value, be it of a commodity, or be it of labour. But here we are dealing with exchange-value. The capitalist paid to the labourer a value of 3 shillings, and the labourer gave him back an exact equivalent in the value of 3 shillings, added by him to the cotton: he gave him value for value. Our friend, up to this time so purse-proud, suddenly assumes the modest demeanour of his own workman, and exclaims: "Have I myself not worked? Have I not performed the labour of superintendence and of overlooking the spinner? And does not this labour, too, create value?" His overlooker and his manager try to hide their smiles. Meanwhile, after a hearty laugh, he re-assumes his usual mien. Though he chanted to us the whole creed of the economists, in reality, he says, he would not give a brass farthing for it. He leaves this and all such like subterfuges and juggling tricks to the professors of Political Economy, who are paid for it. He himself is a practical man; and though he does not always consider what he says outside his business, yet in his business he knows what he is about.

Let us examine the matter more closely. The value of a day's labour-power amounts to 3 shillings, because on our assumption half a day's labour is embodied in that quantity of labour-power, *i.e.*, because the means of subsistence that are daily required for the production of labour-power, cost half a day's labour. But the past labour that is embodied in the labour-power, and the living labour that it can call into action; the daily cost of maintaining it, and its daily expenditure in work, are two totally different things. The former determines the exchange value of the labour-power, the latter is its use-value. The fact that half a day's labour is necessary to keep the labourer alive during 24 hours, does not in any way prevent him from working a whole day. Therefore, the value of labour-power, and the value which that labour-power creates in the labour-process, are two entirely different magnitudes; and this difference of the two values was what the capitalist had in view, when he was purchasing the labour-power. The useful qualities that labour-power possesses, and by virtue of which it makes yarn or boots, were to him nothing more than a conditio sine qua non; for in order to create value, labour must be expended in a useful manner. What really influenced him was the specific use-value which this commodity possesses of being *a source not only of value, but of more value than it has itself*. This is the special service that the capitalist expects from labour-power, and in this transaction he acts in accordance with the "eternal laws" of the exchange of commodities. The seller of labour-power, like the seller of any other commodity, realises its exchange-value, and parts with its use-value. He cannot take the one without giving the other. The use-value of labour-power, or in other words, labour, belongs just as little to its seller, as the use-value of oil after it has been sold belongs to the dealer who has sold it. The owner of the money has paid the value of a day's labour-power; his, therefore, is the use of it for a day; a day's labour belongs to him. The circumstance, that on the one hand the daily sustenance of labour-power costs only half a day's labour, while on the other hand the very same labour-power can work during a whole day, that consequently the value which its use during one day creates, is double what he pays for that use, this circumstance is, without doubt, a piece of good luck for the buyer, but by no means an injury to the seller.

Our capitalist foresaw this state of things, and that was the cause of his laughter. The labourer therefore finds, in the workshop, the means of production necessary for working, not only during six, but during twelve hours. Just as during the six hours' process our 10 lbs. of cotton absorbed six hours' labour, and became 10 lbs. of yarn, so now, 20 lbs. of cotton will absorb 12 hours' labour and be changed into 20 lbs. of yarn. Let us now examine the product of this prolonged process. There is now materialised in this 20 lbs. of yarn the labour of five days, of which four days are due to the cotton and the lost steel of the spindle, the remaining day having been absorbed by the cotton during the spinning process. Expressed in gold, the labour of five days is thirty shillings. This is therefore the price of the 20 lbs. of yarn, giving, as before, eighteenpence as the price of a pound. But the sum of the values of the commodities that entered into the process amounts to 27 shillings. The value of the yarn is 30 shillings. Therefore the value of the product is 1/9 greater than the value advanced for its production; 27 shillings have been transformed into 30 shillings; a surplus-value of 3 shillings has been created. The trick has at last succeeded; money has been converted into capital.

Every condition of the problem is satisfied, while the laws that regulate the exchange of commodities, have been in no way violated. Equivalent has been exchanged for equivalent. For the capitalist as buyer paid for each commodity, for the cotton, the spindle and the labour-power, its full value. He then did what is done by every purchaser of commodities; he consumed their use-value. The consumption of the labour-power, which was also the process of producing commodities, resulted in 20 lbs. of yarn, having a value of 30 shillings. The capitalist, formerly a buyer, now returns to market as a seller, of commodities. He sells his yarn at eighteenpence a pound, which is its exact value. Yet for all that he withdraws 3 shillings more from circulation than he originally threw into it. This metamorphosis, this conversion of money into capital, takes place both within the sphere of circulation and also outside it; within the circulation, because conditioned by the purchase of the labour-power in the market; outside the circulation, because what is done within it is only a stepping-stone to the production of surplus-value, a process which is entirely confined to the sphere of production. Thus "tout est pour le mieux dans le meilleur des mondes possibles."

By turning his money into commodities that serve as the material elements of a new product, and as factors in the labour-process, by incorporating living labour with their dead substance, the capitalist at the same time converts value, *i.e.*, past, materialised, and dead labour into capital, into value big with value, a live monster that is fruitful and multiplies.

If we now compare the two processes of producing value and of creating surplus-value, we see that the latter is nothing but the continuation of the former beyond a definite point. If on the one hand the process be not carried beyond the point, where the value paid by the capitalist for the labour-power is replaced by an exact equivalent, it is simply a process of producing value; if, on the other hand, it be continued beyond that point, it becomes a process of creating surplus-value.

If we proceed further, and compare the process of producing value with the labour-process, pure and simple, we find that the latter consists of the useful labour, the work, that produces use-values. Here we contemplate the labour as producing a particular article; we view it under its qualitative aspect alone, with regard to its end and aim. But viewed as a value-creating process, the same labour-process presents itself under its quantitative aspect alone. Here it is a question merely of the time occupied by the labourer in doing the work; of the period during which the labour-power is usefully expended. Here, the commodities that take part in the process, do not count any longer as necessary adjuncts of labour-power in the production of a definite, useful object. They count merely as depositories of so much absorbed or materialised labour; that labour, whether previously embodied in the means of production, or incorporated in them for the first time during the process of the action of labour-power, counts in either case only according to its duration; it amounts to so many hours or days as the case may be.

Moreover, only so much of the time spent in the production of any article is counted, as, under the given social conditions, is necessary. The consequences of this are various. In the first place, it becomes necessary that the labour should be carried on under normal conditions. If a self-acting mule is the implement in general use for spinning, it would be absurd to supply the spinner with a distaff and spinning wheel. The cotton too must not be such rubbish as to cause extra waste in being worked, but must be of suitable quality. Otherwise the spinner would be found to spend more time in producing a pound of yarn than is socially necessary, in which case the excess of time would create neither value nor money. But whether the material factors of the process are of normal quality or not, depends not upon the labourer, but entirely upon the capitalist. Then again, the labour-power itself must be of average efficacy. In the trade in which it is being employed, it must possess the average skill, handiness and quickness prevalent in that trade, and our capitalist took good care to buy labour-power of such normal goodness. This power must be applied with the average amount of exertion and with the usual degree of intensity; and the capitalist is as careful to see that this is done, as that his workmen are not idle for a single moment. He has bought the use of the labour-power for a definite period, and he insists upon his rights. He has no intention of being robbed. Lastly, and for this purpose our friend has a penal code of his own, all wasteful consumption of raw material or instruments of labour is strictly forbidden, because what is so wasted, represents labour superfluously expended, labour that does not count in the product or enter into its value.

We now see, that the difference between labour, considered on the one hand as producing utilities, and on the other hand, as creating value, a difference which we discovered by our analysis of a commodity, resolves itself into a distinction between two aspects of the process of production.

The process of production, considered on the one hand as the unity of the labour-process and the process of creating value, is production of commodities; considered on the other hand as the unity of the labour-process and the process of producing surplus-value, it is the capitalist process of production, or capitalist production of commodities.

We stated, on a previous page, that in the creation of surplus-value it does not in the least matter, whether the labour appropriated by the capitalist be simple unskilled labour of average quality or more complicated unskilled labour. All labour of a higher or more complicated character than average labour is expenditure of labour-power of a more costly kind, labour-power whose production has cost more time and labour, and which therefore has a higher value, than unskilled or simple labour-power. This power being of higher value, its consumption is labour of a higher class, labour that creates in equal times proportionally higher values than unskilled labour does. Whatever difference in skill there may be between the labour of a spinner and that of a jeweller, the portion of his labour by which the jeweller merely replaces the value of his own labour-power, does not in any way differ in quality from the additional portion by which he creates surplus-value. In the making of jewellery, just as in spinning, the surplus-value results only from a quan-

titative excess of labour, from a lengthening-out of one and the
same labour-process, in the one case, of the process of making
jewels, in the other of the process of making yarn.

But on the other hand, in every process of creating value, the
reduction of skilled labour to average social labour, *e.g.*, one day of
skilled to six days of unskilled labour, is unavoidable. We therefore
save ourselves a superfluous operation, and simplify our analysis, by
the assumption, that the labour of the workman employed by the
capitalist is unskilled average labour. * * *

CHAPTER X. THE WORKING-DAY

Section 1. The Limits of the Working-Day

We started with the supposition that labour-power is bought and
sold at its value. Its value, like that of all other commodities, is
determined by the working-time necessary to its production. If the
production of the average daily means of subsistence of the
labourer takes up 6 hours, he must work, on the average, 6 hours
every day, to produce his daily labour-power, or to reproduce the
value received as the result of its sale. The necessary part of his
working-day amounts to 6 hours, and is, therefore, *caeteris paribus*, a
given quantity. But with this, the extent of the working-day itself is
not yet given.

Let us assume that the line A B represents the length of the
necessary working-time, say 6 hours. If the labour be prolonged 1, 3,
or 6 hours beyond A B, we have 3 other lines:

Working-day I.   Working-day II.   Working-day III.
A —— B — C.   A —— B —— C.   A—— B ——C.

representing 3 different working-days of 7, 9, and 12 hours. The
extension B C of the line A B represents the length of the
surplus-labour. As the working-day is A B+B or A C, it varies
with the variable quantity B C. Since A B is constant, the ratio of
B C to A B can always be calculated. In working-day I, it is 1/6, in
working-day II, 3/6, in working-day III, 6/6 of A B. Since, further,
the ratio $\frac{\text{surplus working-time,}}{\text{necessary working-time,}}$ determines the rate of the surplus value, the latter is given by the ratio of B C to A B. It
amounts in the 3 different working-days respectively to 16 2/3, 50
and 100 per cent. On the other hand, the rate of surplus-value
alone would not give us the extent of the working-day. If this rate,
e.g., were 100 per cent, the working-day might be of 8, 10, 12, or
more hours. It would indicate that the 2 constituent parts of the
working-day, necessary-labour and surplus-labour time, were equal

in extent, but not how long each of these two constituent parts was.

The working-day is thus not a constant, but a variable quantity. One of its parts, certainly, is determined by the working-time required for the reproduction of the labour-power of the labourer himself. But its total amount varies with the duration of the surplus-labour. The working-day is, therefore, determinable, but is, *per se*, indeterminate.

Although the working-day is not a fixed, but a fluent quantity, it can, on the other hand, only vary within certain limits. The minimum limit is, however, not determinable; of course, if we make the extension line B C or the surplus-labour = 0, we have a minimum limit, *i.e.*, the part of the day which the labourer must necessarily work for his own maintenance. On the basis of capitalist production, however, this necessary labour can form a part only of the working-day; the working-day itself can never be reduced to this minimum. On the other hand, the working-day has a maximum limit. It cannot be prolonged beyond a certain point. This maximum limit is conditioned by two things. First, by the physical bounds of labour-power. Within the 24 hours of the natural day a man can expend only a definite quantity of his vital force. A horse, in like manner, can only work from day to day, 8 hours. During part of the day this force must rest, sleep; during another part the man has to satisfy other physical needs, to feed, wash, and clothe himself. Besides these purely physical limitations, the extension of the working-day encounters moral ones. The labourer needs time for satisfying his intellectual and social wants, the extent and number of which are conditioned by the general state of social advancement. The variation of the working-day fluctuates, therefore, within physical and social bounds. But both these limiting conditions are of a very elastic nature, and allow the greatest latitude. So we find working-days of 8, 10, 12, 14, 16, 18 hours, *i.e.*, of the most different lengths.

The capitalist has bought the labour-power at its day-rate. To him its use-value belongs during one working-day. He has thus acquired the right to make the labourer work for him during one day. But, what is a working-day?

At all events, less than a natural day. By how much? The capitalist has his own views of this *ultima Thule*, the necessary limit of the working-day. As capitalist, he is only capital personified. His soul is the soul of capital. But capital has one single life impulse, the tendency to create value and surplus-value, to make its constant factor, the means of production, absorb the greatest possible amount of surplus-labour.

Capital is dead labour, that, vampire-like, only lives by sucking living labour, and lives the more, the more labour it sucks. The time during which the labourer works, is the time during which the capitalist consumes the labour-power he has purchased of him.

If the labourer consumes his disposable time for himself, he robs the capitalist.

The capitalist then takes his stand on the law of the exchange of commodities. He, like all other buyers, seeks to get the greatest possible benefit out of the use-value of his commodity. Suddenly the voice of the labourer, which had been stifled in the storm and stress of the process of production, rises:

The commodity that I have sold to you differs from the crowd of other commodities, in that its use creates value, and a value greater than its own. That is why you bought it. That which on your side appears a spontaneous expansion of capital, is on mine extra expenditure of labour-power. You and I know on the market only one law, that of the exchange of commodities. And the consumption of the commodity belongs not to the seller who parts with it, but to the buyer, who acquires it. To you, therefore, belongs the use of my daily labour-power. But by means of the price that you pay for it each day, I must be able to reproduce it daily, and to sell it again. Apart from natural exhaustion through age, &c., I must be able on the morrow to work with the same normal amount of force, health and freshness as to-day. You preach to me constantly the gospel of "saving" and "abstinence." Good! I will, like a sensible saving owner, husband my sole wealth, labour-power, and abstain from all foolish waste of it. I will each day spend, set in motion, put into action only as much of it as is compatible with its normal duration, and healthy development. By an unlimited extension of the working-day, you may in one day use up a quantity of labour-power greater than I can restore in three. What you gain in labour I lose in substance. The use of my labour-power and the spoliation of it are quite different things. If the average time that (doing a reasonable amount of work) an average labourer can live, is 30 years, the value of my labour-power, which you pay me from day to day is $\frac{1}{365 \times 30}$ or $\frac{1}{10950}$ of its total value. But if you consume it in 10 years, you pay me daily $\frac{1}{10950}$ instead of $\frac{1}{3650}$ of its total value, *i.e.*, only 1/3 of its daily value, and you rob me, therefore, every day of 2/3 of the value of my commodity. You pay me for one day's labour-power, whilst you use that of 3 days. That is against our contract and the law of exchanges. I demand, therefore, a working-day of normal length, and I demand it without any appeal to your heart, for in money matters sentiment is out of place. You may be a model citizen, perhaps a member of the Society for the

Prevention of Cruelty to Animals, and in the odour of sanctity to boot; but the thing that you represent face to face with me has no heart in its breast. That which seems to throb there is my own heart-beating. I demand the normal working-day because I, like every other seller, demand the value of my commodity.

We see then, that, apart from extremely elastic bounds, the nature of the exchange of commodities itself imposes no limit to the working-day, no limit to surplus-labour. The capitalist maintains his rights as a purchaser when he tries to make the working-day as long as possible, and to make, whenever possible, two working-days out of one. On the other hand, the peculiar nature of the commodity sold implies a limit to its consumption by the purchaser, and the labourer maintains his right as seller when he wishes to reduce the working-day to one of definite normal duration. There is here, therefore, an antinomy, right against right, both equally bearing the seal of the law of exchanges. Between equal rights force decides. Hence is it that in the history of capitalist production, the determination of what is a working-day, presents itself as the result of a struggle, a struggle between collective capital, *i.e.*, the class of capitalists, and collective labour, *i.e.*, the working-class.

Section 2. The Greed for Surplus-Labour. Manufacturer and Boyard

Capital has not invented surplus-labour. Wherever a part of society possesses the monopoly of the means of production, the labourer, free or not free, must add to the working-time necessary for his own maintenance an extra working-time in order to produce the means of subsistence for the owners of the means of production, whether this proprietor be the Athenian nobleman, Etruscan theocrat, civis Romanus, Norman baron, American slave-owner, Wallachian Boyard, modern landlord or capitalist. It is, however, clear that in any given economic formation of society, where not the exchange-value but the use-value of the product predominates, surplus-labour will be limited by a given set of wants which may be greater or less, and that here no boundless thirst for surplus-labour arises from the nature of the production itself. Hence in antiquity over-work becomes horrible only when the object is to obtain exchange-value in its specific independent money-form; in the production of gold and silver. Compulsory working to death is here the recognised form of over-work. Only read Diodorus Siculus. Still these are exceptions in antiquity. But as soon as people, whose production still moves within the lower forms of slave-labour, corvée-labour, &c., are drawn into the whirlpool of an international market dominated by the capitalistic mode of production, the sale of their products for export becoming their principal interest, the civilised horrors of over-work are grafted on the barbaric horrors of slavery, serfdom, &c. Hence the negro labour in the Southern States of the American Union preserved something of a patriarchal character, so long as production was chiefly directed to immediate local consumption. But in proportion, as the export of cotton became of vital interest to these states, the over-working of the negro and sometimes the using up of his life in 7 years of labour became a factor in a calculated and calculating system. It was no longer a question of obtaining from him a certain quantity of useful products. It was now a question of production of surplus-labour itself. So was it also with the corvée, *e.g.*, in the Danubian Principalities (now Roumania).

The comparison of the greed for surplus-labour in the Danubian Principalities with the same greed in English factories has a special interest, because surplus-labour in the corvée has an independent and palpable form.

Suppose the working-day consists of 6 hours of necessary labour, and 6 hours of surplus-labour. Then the free labourer gives the capitalist every week 6×6 or 36 hours of surplus-labour. It is the same as if he worked 3 days in the week for himself, and 3 days in the week gratis for the capitalist. But this is not evident on the surface. Surplus-labour and necessary labour glide one into the other. I can, therefore, express the same relationship by saying, *e.g.*, that the labourer in every minute works 30 seconds for himself, and 30 for the capitalist, etc. It is otherwise with the corvée. The necessary labour which the Wallachian peasant does for his own maintenance is distinctly marked off from his surplus-labour on behalf of the Boyard. The one he does on his own field, the other on the seignorial estate. Both parts of the labour-time exist, therefore, independently, side by side one with the other. In the corvée the surplus-labour is accurately marked off from the necessary labour. This, however, can make no difference with regard to the quantitative relation of surplus-labour to necessary labour. Three days' surplus-labour in the week remain three days that yield no equivalent to the labourer himself, whether it be called corvée or wage-labour. But in the capitalist the greed for surplus labour appears in the straining after an unlimited extension of the working-day, in the Boyard more simply in a direct hunting after days of corvée. * * *

The Factory Act of 1850 now in force (1867) allows for the average working-day 10 hours, *i.e.*, for the first 5 days 12 hours from 6 a.m. to 6 p.m., including ½ an hour for breakfast, and an hour for dinner, and thus leaving 10½ working-hours, and 8 hours for Saturday, from 6 a.m. to 2 p.m., of which ½ an hour is subtracted for breakfast. 60 working-hours are left, 10½ for each of the first 5 days, 7½ for the last. Certain guardians of these laws are appointed, Factory Inspectors, directly under the Home Secretary, whose reports are published half-yearly, by order of Parliament. They give regular and official statistics of the capitalistic greed for surplus-labour.

Let us listen, for a moment, to the Factory Inspectors. "The fraudulent mill-owner begins work a quarter of an hour (sometimes more, sometimes less) before 6 a.m., and leaves off a quarter of an hour (sometimes more, sometimes less) after 6 p.m. He takes 5 minutes from the beginning and from the end of the half hour nominally allowed for breakfast, and 10 minutes at the beginning and end of the hour nominally allowed for dinner. He works for a quarter of an hour (sometimes more, sometimes less) after 2 p.m. on Saturday. Thus his gain is—

Before 6 a.m.,	15 minutes.
After 6 p.m.,	15 minutes.
At breakfast time,	10 minutes.
At dinner time,	20 minutes.
Five days—300 minutes,	60 minutes.
On Saturday before 6 a.m.,	15 minutes.
At breakfast time,	10 minutes.
After 2 p.m.,	15 minutes.
	40 minutes.
Total weekly,	340 minutes.

Or 5 hours and 40 minutes weekly, which multiplied by 50 working weeks in the year (allowing two for holidays and occasional stoppages) is equal to 27 working-days."

"Five minutes a day's increased work, multiplied by weeks, are equal to two and a half days of produce in the year."

"An additional hour a day gained by small instalments before 6 a.m., after 6 p.m., and at the beginning and end of the times nominally fixed for meals, is nearly equivalent to working 13 months in the year." * * *

These "small thefts" of capital from the labourer's meal and recreation time, the factory inspectors also designate as "petty pilferings of minutes," "snatching a few minutes," or, as the labourers technically called them, "nibbling and cribbling at meal-times."

It is evident that in this atmosphere the formation of surplus-value by surplus-labour, is no secret. "If you allow me," said a highly respectable master to me, "to work only ten minutes in the day over-time, you put one thousand a year in my *pocket*." "Moments are the elements of profit."

Nothing is from this point of view more characteristic than the designation of the workers who work full time as "full-timers," and the children under 13 who are only allowed to work 6 hours as "half-timers." The worker is here nothing more than personified labour-time. All individual distinctions are merged in those of "full-timers" and "half-timers."

Section 3. *Branches of English Industry Without Legal Limits to Exploitation*

We have hitherto considered the tendency to the extension of the working-day, the were-wolf's hunger for surplus-labour in a department where the monstrous exactions, not surpassed, says an English bourgeois economist, by the cruelties of the Spaniards to the American red-skins, caused capital at last to be bound by the chains of legal regulations. Now, let us cast a glance at certain branches of production in which the exploitation of labour is either free from fetters to this day, or was so yesterday.

Mr. Broughton Charlton, county magistrate, declared, as chairman of a meeting held at the Assembly Rooms, Nottingham, on the 14th of January, 1860, "that there was an amount of privation and suffering among that portion of the population connected with the lace trade, unknown in other parts of the kingdom, indeed, in the civilised world. . . . Children of nine or ten years are dragged from their squalid beds at two, three, or four o'clock in the morning and compelled to work for a bare subsistence until ten, eleven, or twelve at night, their limbs wearing away, their frames dwindling, their faces whitening, and their humanity absolutely sinking into a stone-like torpor, utterly horrible to contemplate. . . . We are not surprised that Mr. Mallett, or any other manufacturer, should stand forward and protest against discussion. . . . The system, as the Rev. Montagu Valpy describes it, is one of unmitigated slavery, socially, physically, morally, and spiritually. . . . What can be thought of a town which holds a public meeting to petition that the period of labour for men shall be diminished to eighteen hours a day? . . . We declaim against the Virginian and Carolinian cotton-planters. Is their black-market, their lash, and their barter of human flesh more detestable than this slow sacrifice of humanity which takes place in order that veils and collars may be fabricated for the benefit of capitalists?" * * *

The manufacture of lucifer matches dates from 1833, from the discovery of the method of applying phosphorus to the match itself. Since 1845 this manufacture has rapidly developed in England, and has extended especially amongst the thickly populated parts of London as well as in Manchester, Birmingham, Liverpool, Bristol, Norwich, Newcastle and Glasgow. With it has spread the form of lockjaw, which a Vienna physician in 1845 discovered to be a disease peculiar to lucifer-matchmakers. Half the workers are children under thirteen, and young persons under eighteen. The manufacture is on account of its unhealthiness and unpleasantness in such bad odour that only the most miserable part of the labouring class, half-starved widows and so forth, deliver up their children to it, "the ragged, half-starved, untaught children."

Of the witnesses that Commissioner White examined (1863), 270 were under 18, 50 under 10, 10 only 8, and 5 only 6 years old. A range of the working-day from 12 to 14 or 15 hours, night-labour, irregular meal-times, meals for the most part taken in the very workrooms that are pestilent with phosphorus. Dante would have found the worst horrors of his Inferno surpassed in this manufacture. * * *

No branch of industry in England (we do not take into account the making of bread by machinery recently introduced) has preserved up to the present day a method of production so archaic, so—as we see from the poets of the Roman Empire—pre-christian, as baking. But capital, as was said earlier, is at first indifferent as to the technical character of the labour-process; it begins by taking it just as it finds it.

The incredible adulteration of bread, especially in London, was first revealed by the House of Commons Committee "on the adulteration of articles of food" (1855–56), and Dr. Hassall's work, "Adulterations detected." The consequence of these revelations was the Act of August 6th, 1860, "for preventing the adulteration of articles of food and drink," an inoperative law, as it naturally shows the tenderest consideration for every Free-trader who determines by the buying or selling of adulterated commodities "to turn an honest penny." The Committee itself formulated more or less naïvely its conviction that Free-trade meant essentially trade with adulterated, or as the English ingeniously put it, "sophisticated" goods. In fact this kind of sophistry knows better than Protagoras how to make white black, and black white, and better than the Eleatics how to demonstrate *ad oculos* that everything is only appearance.

At all events the Committee had directed the attention of the public to its "daily bread," and therefore to the baking trade. At the same time in public meetings and in petitions to Parliament rose the cry of the London journeymen bakers against their overwork, &c. The cry was so urgent that Mr. H. S. Tremenheere, also a member of the Commission of 1863 several times mentioned, was appointed Royal Commissioner of Inquiry. His report, together with the evidence given, roused not the heart of the public but its stomach. Englishmen, always well up in the Bible, knew well enough that man, unless by elective grace a capitalist, or landlord, or sinecurist, is commanded to eat his bread in the sweat of his brow, but they did not know that he had to eat daily in his bread a certain quantity of human perspiration mixed with the discharge of abscesses, cobwebs, dead black-beetles, and putrid German yeast, without counting alum, sand, and other agreeable mineral ingredients. Without any regard to his holiness, Free-trade, the free baking-trade was therefore placed under the supervision of the State inspectors (Close of the Parliamentary session of 1863), and by the same Act of Parliament, work from 9 in the evening to 5 in the morning was forbidden for journeymen bakers under 18. The last clause speaks volumes as to the over-work in this old-fashioned, homely line of business.

"The work of a London journeyman baker begins, as a rule, at about eleven at night. At that hour he 'makes the dough,'—a laborious process, which lasts from half an hour to three quarters of an hour, according to the size of the batch or the labour bestowed upon it. He then lies down upon the kneading-board, which is also the covering of the trough in which the dough is 'made'; and with a sack under him, and another rolled up as a pillow, he sleeps for about a couple of hours. He is then engaged in a rapid and continuous labour for about five hours—throwing out the dough, 'scaling it off,' moulding it, putting it into the oven, preparing and baking rolls and fancy bread, taking the batch bread out of the oven, and up into the shop, &c., &c. The temperature of a bakehouse ranges from about 75 to upwards of 90 degrees, and in the smaller bakehouses approximates usually to the higher rather than to the lower degree of heat. When the business of making the bread, rolls, &c., is over, that of its distribution begins, and a considerable proportion of the journeymen in the trade, after working hard in the manner described during the night, are upon their legs for many hours during the day, carrying baskets, or wheeling hand-carts, and sometimes again in the bakehouse, leaving off work at various hours between 1 and 6 p.m. according to the season of the year, or the amount and nature of their master's business; while others are again engaged in the bakehouse in 'bringing out' more batches until late in the afternoon. . . . During what is called 'the London season,' the operatives belonging to the 'full-priced' bakers at the West End of the town, generally begin work at 11 p.m., and are engaged in making the bread, with one or two short (sometimes very short) intervals of rest, up to 8 o'clock the next morning. They are then engaged all day long, up to 4, 5, 6, and as late as 7 o'clock in the evening carrying out bread, or sometimes in the afternoon in the bakehouse again, assisting in the biscuit-baking. They may have, after they have done their work, sometimes five or six, sometimes only four or five hours' sleep before they begin again. On Fridays they always begin sooner, some about ten o'clock, and continue in some cases, at work, either in making or delivering the bread up to 8 p.m. on Saturday night, but more generally up to 4 or 5 o'clock, Sunday morning. On Sundays the men must attend twice or three times during the day for an hour or two to make preparations for the next day's bread. . . . The men employed by the underselling masters (who sell their bread under the 'full price,' and who, as already pointed out, comprise three-fourths of the London bakers) have not only to work on the average longer hours, but their work is almost entirely confined to the bakehouse. The underselling masters generally sell their bread. . . . in the shop. If they send it out, which is not common, except as supplying chandler's shops, they usually employ other hands for that purpose. It is not their practice to deliver bread from house to house. Towards the end of the week . . . the men begin on Thursday night at 10 o'clock, and continue on with only slight intermission until late on Saturday evening."

Even the bourgeois intellect understands the position of the "underselling" masters. "The unpaid labour of the men was made the source whereby the competition was carried on." And the "full-priced" baker denounces his underselling competitors to the Commission of Inquiry as thieves of foreign labour and adulterators. "They only exist now by first defrauding the public, and next getting 18 hours' work out of their men for 12 hours' wages."

The adulteration of bread and the formation of a class of bakers that sells the bread below the full price, date from the beginning of the 18th century, from the time when the corporate character of the trade was lost, and the capitalist in the form of the miller or flour-factor, rises behind the nominal master baker. Thus was laid the foundation of capitalistic production in this trade, of the unlimited extension of the working-day and of night-labour, although the latter only since 1824 gained a serious footing, even in London.

After what has just been said, it will be understood that the Report of the Commission classes journeymen bakers among the short-lived labourers, who, having by good luck escaped the normal decimation of the children of the working-class, rarely reach the age of 42. Nevertheless, the baking trade is always overwhelmed with applicants. The sources of the supply of these labour-powers to London are Scotland, the western agricultural districts of England, and Germany. * * *

From the motley crowd of labourers of all callings, ages, sexes, that press on us more busily than the souls of the slain on Ulysses, on whom without referring to the Blue books under their arms—we see at a glance the mark of over-work, let us take two more figures whose striking contrast proves that before capital all men are alike—a milliner and a blacksmith.

In the last week of June, 1863, all the London daily papers published a paragraph with the "sensational" heading, "Death from simple over-work." It dealt with the death of the milliner, Mary Anne Walkley, 20 years of age, employed in a highly-respectable dressmaking establishment, exploited by a lady with the pleasant name of Elise. The old, often-told story, was once more recounted. This girl worked, on an average, 16½ hours, during the season often 30 hours, without a break, whilst her failing labour-power was revived by occasional supplies of sherry, port, or coffee. It was just now the height of the season. It was necessary to conjure up in the twinkling of an eye the gorgeous dresses for the noble ladies bidden to the ball in honour of the newly-imported Princess of Wales. Mary Anne Walkley had worked without intermission for 26½ hours, with 60 other girls, 30 in one room, that only afforded ⅓ of the cubic feet of air required for them. At night, they slept in pairs in one of the stifling holes into which the bedroom was divided by partitions of board. And this was one of the best millinery establishments in London. Mary Anne Walkley fell ill on the Friday, died on Sunday, without, to the astonishment of Madame Elise, having previously completed the work in hand. The doctor, Mr. Keys, called too late to the death-bed, duly bore witness before the coroner's jury that "Mary Anne Walkley had died from long hours of work in an over-crowded workroom, and a too small and badly-ventilated bedroom." In order to give the doctor a lesson in good manners, the coroner's jury thereupon brought in a verdict that "the deceased had died of apoplexy, but there was reason to fear that her death had been accelerated by over-work in an over-crowded workroom, &c." "Our white slaves," cried the *Morning Star*, the organ of the Free-traders, Cobden and Bright, "our white slaves, who are toiled into the grave, for the most part silently pine and die."

"It is not in dressmakers' rooms that working to death is the order of the day, but in a thousand other places, in every place I had almost said, where 'a thriving business' has to be done. . . . We will take the blacksmith as a type. If the poets were true, there is no man so hearty, so merry, as the blacksmith; he rises early and strikes his sparks before the sun; he eats and drinks and sleeps as no other man. Working in moderation, he is, in fact, in one of the best of human positions, physically speaking. But we follow him into the city or town, and we see the stress of work on that strong man, and what then is his position in the death-rate of his country. In Marylebone, blacksmiths die at the rate of 31 per thousand per annum, or 11 above the mean of the male adults of the country in its entirety. The occupation, instinctive almost as a portion of human art, unobjectionable as a branch of human industry, is made by mere excess of work, the destroyer of the man. He can strike so many blows per day, walk so many steps, breathe so many breaths, produce so much work, and live an average, say of fifty years; he is made to strike so many more blows, to walk so many more steps, to breathe so many more breaths per day, and to increase altogether a fourth of his life. He meets the effort; the result is, that producing for a limited time a fourth more work, he dies at 37 for 50."

Section 4. Day and Night Work. The Relay System

Constant capital, the means of production, considered from the standpoint of the creation of surplus-value, only exist to absorb labour, and with every drop of labour a proportional quantity of surplus-labour. While they fail to do this, their mere existence causes a relative loss to the capitalist, for they represent during the time they lie fallow, a useless advance of capital. And this loss becomes positive and absolute as soon as the intermission of their employment necessitates additional outlay at the recommencement of work. The prolongation of the working-day beyond the limits of the natural day, into the night, only acts as a palliative. It quenches only in a slight degree the vampire thirst for the living blood of labour. To appropriate labour during all the 24 hours of the day is, therefore, the inherent tendency of capitalist production. But as it is physically impossible to exploit the same individual labour-power constantly during the night as well as the day, to overcome this physical hindrance, an alternation becomes necessary between the workpeople whose powers are exhausted by day, and those who are used up by night. This alternation may be effected in various ways; *e.g.*, it may be so arranged that part of the workers are one week employed on day-work, the next week on night-work. It is well known that this relay system, this alternation of two sets of workers, held full sway in the full-blooded youth-time of the English cotton manufacture, and that at the present time it still flourishes, among others, in the cotton spinning of the Moscow district. This 24 hours' process of production exists to-day as a system in many of the branches of industry of Great Britain that are still "free," in the blast-furnaces, forges, plate-rolling mills, and other metallurgical establishments in England, Wales, and Scotland. The working-time here includes, besides the 24 hours of the 6 working-days, a great part also of the 24 hours of Sunday. The workers consist of men and women, adults and children of both sexes. The ages of the children and young persons run through all intermediate grades, from 8 (in some cases from 6) to 18.

In some branches of industry, the girls and women work through the night together with the males. * * *

Section 5. The Struggle for a Normal Working-Day. Compulsory Laws for the Extension of the Working-Day from the Middle of the 14th to the End of the 17th Century

"What is a working-day? What is the length of time during which capital may consume the labour-power whose daily value it buys? How far may the working-day be extended beyond the working-time necessary for the reproduction of labour-power itself?" It has been seen that to these questions capital replies: the working-day contains the full 24 hours, with the deduction of the few hours of repose without which labour-power absolutely refuses its services again. Hence it is self-evident that the labourer is nothing else, his whole life through, than labour-power, that therefore all his disposable time is by nature and law labour-time, to be devoted to the self-expansion of capital. Time for education, for intellectual development, for the fulfilling of social functions and for social intercourse, for the free-play of his bodily and mental activity, even the rest time of Sunday (and that in a country of Sabbatarians!)—moonshine! But in its blind unrestrainable passion, its were-wolf hunger for surplus-labour, capital oversteps not only the moral, but even the merely physical maximum bounds of the working-day. It usurps the time for growth, development, and healthy maintenance of the body. It steals the time required for the consumption of fresh air and sunlight. It higgles over a meal-time, incorporating it where possible with the process of production itself, so that food is given to the labourer as to a mere means of production, as coal is supplied to the boiler, grease and oil to the machinery. It reduces the sound sleep needed for the restoration, reparation, refreshment of the bodily powers to just so many hours of torpor as the revival of an organism, absolutely exhausted, renders essential. It is not the normal maintenance of the labour-power which is to determine the limits of the working-day; it is the greatest possible daily expenditure of labour-power, no matter how diseased, compulsory, and painful it may be, which is to determine the limits of the labourers' period of repose. Capital cares nothing for the length of life of labour-power. All that concerns it is simply and solely the maximum of labour-power, that can be rendered fluent in a working-day. It attains this end by shortening the extent of the labourer's life, as a greedy farmer snatches increased produce from the soil by robbing it of its fertility.

The capitalistic mode of production (essentially the production of surplus-value, the absorption of surplus-labour), produces thus, with the extension of the working-day, not only the deterioration of human labour-power by robbing it of its normal, moral and physical, conditions of development and function. It produces also the premature exhaustion and death of this labour-power itself. It extends the labourer's time of production during a given period by shortening his actual life-time.

But the value of the labour-power includes the value of the commodities necessary for the reproduction of the worker, or for the keeping up of the working-class. If then the unnatural extension of the working-day, that capital necessarily strives after in its unmeasured passion for self-expansion, shortens the length of life of the individual labourer, and therefore the duration of his labour-power, the forces used up have to be replaced at a more rapid rate and the sum of the expenses for the reproduction of labour-power will be greater; just as in a machine the part of its value to be reproduced every day is greater the more rapidly the machine is worn out. It would seem therefore that the interest of capital itself points in the direction of a normal working-day.

The slave-owner buys his labourer as he buys his horse. If he loses his slave, he loses capital that can only be restored by new outlay in the slave-mart. But "the rice-grounds of Georgia, or the swamps of the Mississippi may be fatally injurious to the human constitution; but the waste of human life which the cultivation of these districts necessitates, is not so great that it cannot be repaired from the teeming preserves of Virginia and Kentucky. Considerations of economy, moreover, which, under a natural system, afford some security for human treatment by identifying the master's interest with the slave's preservation, when once trading in slaves is practised, become reasons for racking to the uttermost the toil of the slave; for, when his place can at once be supplied from foreign preserves, the duration of his life becomes a matter of less moment than its productiveness while it lasts. It is accordingly a maxim of slave management, in slave-importing countries, that the most effective economy is that which takes out of the human chattel in the shortest space of time the utmost amount of exertion it is capable of putting forth. It is in tropical culture, where annual profits often equal the whole capital of plantations, that negro life is most recklessly sacrificed. It is the agriculture of the West Indies, which has been for centuries prolific of fabulous wealth, that has engulfed millions of the African race. It is in Cuba, at this day, whose revenues are reckoned by millions, and whose planters are princes, that we see in the servile class, the coarsest fare, the most exhausting and unremitting toil, and even the absolute destruction of a portion of its numbers every year."

Mutato nomine de te fabula narratur.[5] For slave-trade read labour-market, for Kentucky and Virginia, Ireland and the agricultural districts of England, Scotland, and Wales, for Africa, Germany. We heard how over-work thinned the ranks of the bakers in London. Nevertheless, the London labour-market is always overstocked with German and other candidates for death in the bakeries. Pottery, as we saw, is one of the shortest-lived industries. Is there any want therefore of potters? Josiah Wedgwood, the inventor of modern pottery, himself originally a common workman, said in 1785 before the House of Commons that the whole trade employed from 15,000 to 20,000 people. In the year 1861 the population alone of the town centres of this industry in Great Britain numbered 101,302. "The cotton trade has existed for ninety years. . . . It has existed for three generations of the English race, and I believe I may safely say that during that period it has destroyed nine generations of factory operatives." * * *

What experience shows to the capitalist generally is a constant excess of population, *i.e.*, an excess in relation to the momentary requirements of surplus-labour-absorbing capital, although this excess is made up of generations of human beings stunted, shortlived, swiftly replacing each other, plucked, so to say, before maturity. And, indeed, experience shows to the intelligent observer with what swiftness and grip the capitalist mode of production, dating, historically speaking, only from yesterday, has seized the vital power of the people by the very root—shows how the degeneration of the industrial population is only retarded by the constant absorption of primitive and physically uncorrupted elements from the country—shows how even the country labourers, in spite of fresh air and the principle of natural selection, that works so powerfully amongst them, and only permits the survival of the strongest, are already beginning to die off. Capital that has such good reasons for denying the sufferings of the legions of workers that surround it, is in practice moved as much and as little by the sight of the coming degradation and final depopulation of the human race, as by the probable fall of the earth into the sun. In every stock-jobbing swindle every one knows that some time or other the crash must come, but every one hopes that it may fall on the head of his neighbour, after he himself has caught the shower of gold and placed it in safety. *Après moi le déluge!* is the watchword of every capitalist and of every capitalist nation. Hence Capital is reckless of the health or length of life of the labourer, unless under compulsion from

5. "The name being changed, this story is about you" (Horace, *Satires*, I, i, 69–70). [R. T.]

society. To the out-cry as to the physical and mental degradation, the premature death, the torture of over-work, it answers: Ought these to trouble us since they increase our profits? But looking at things as a whole, all this does not, indeed, depend on the good or ill will of the individual capitalist. Free competition brings out the inherent laws of capitalist production, in the shape of external coercive laws having power over every individual capitalist.

The establishment of a normal working-day is the result of centuries of struggle between capitalist and labourer. The history of this struggle shows two opposed tendencies. Compare, *e.g.*, the English factory legislation of our time with the English Labour Statutes from the 14th century to well into the middle of the 18th. Whilst the modern Factory Acts compulsorily shortened the working-day, the earlier statutes tried to lengthen it by compulsion. Of course the pretensions of capital in embryo—when, beginning to grow, it secures the right of absorbing a *quantum sufficit* of surplus-labour, not merely by the force of economic relations, but by the help of the State—appear very modest when put face to face with the concessions that, growling and struggling, it has to make in its adult condition. It takes centuries ere the "free" labourer, thanks to the development of capitalistic production, agrees, *i.e.*, is compelled by social conditions, to sell the whole of his active life, his very capacity for work, for the price of the necessaries of life, his birthright for a mess of pottage. Hence it is natural that the lengthening of the work-day, which capital, from the middle of the 14th to the end of the 17th century, tries to impose by State-measures on adult labourers, approximately coincides with the shortening of the working-day which, in the second half of the 19th century, has here and there been effected by the State to prevent the coining of children's blood into capital. That which to-day, *e.g.*, in the State of Massachusetts, until recently the freest State of the North-American Republic, has been proclaimed as the statutory limit of the labour of children under 12, was in England, even in the middle of the 17th century, the normal working-day of able-bodied artisans, robust labourers, athletic blacksmiths. * * *

Part IV. Production of Relative Surplus-Value

CHAPTER XII. THE CONCEPT OF RELATIVE SURPLUS-VALUE

That portion of the working-day which merely produces an equivalent for the value paid by the capitalist for his labour-power, has, up to this point, been treated by us as a constant magnitude, and such in fact it is, under given conditions of production and at a given stage in the economic development of society. Beyond this, his necessary labour-time, the labourer, we saw, could continue to work for 2, 3, 4, 6, &c., hours. The rate of surplus-value and the length of the working-day depended on the magnitude of this prolongation. Though the necessary labour-time was constant, we saw, on the other hand, that the total working-day was variable. Now suppose we have a working-day whose length, and whose apportionment between necessary labour and surplus-labour, are given. Let the whole line a c, a————b—c represent, for example, a working-day of 12 hours; the portion of a b 10 hours of necessary labour, and the portion b c 2 hours of surplus-labour. How now can the production of surplus value be increased, *i.e.*, how can the surplus-labour be prolonged, without, or independently of, any prolongation of a c?

Although the length of a c is given, b c appears to be capable of prolongation, if not by extension beyond its end c, which is also the end of the working-day a c, yet, at all events, by pushing back its starting-point b in the direction of a. Assume that b′—b in the line a b′ b c is equal to half of b c

a————————————b′—b——c

or to one hour's labour-time. If now, in a c, the working-day of 12 hours, we move the point b to b′, b c becomes b′ c; the surplus-labour increases by one half, from 2 hours to 3 hours, although the working-day remains as before at 12 hours. This extension of the surplus labour-time from b c to b′ c, from 2 hours to 3 hours, is, however, evidently impossible, without a simultaneous contraction of the necessary labour-time from a b into a b′, from 10 hours to 9 hours. The prolongation of the surplus-labour would correspond to a shortening of the necessary labour; or a portion of the labour-time previously consumed, in reality, for the labourer's own benefit, would be converted into labour-time for the benefit of the capitalist. There would be an alteration, not in the length of the working-day, but in its division into necessary labour-time and surplus labour-time.

On the other hand, it is evident that the duration of the surplus-labour is given, when the length of the working-day, and the value of labour-power, are given. The value of labour-power, *i.e.*, the labour-time requisite to produce labour-power, determines the labour-time necessary for the reproduction of that value. If one working-hour be embodied in sixpence, and the value of a day's labour-power be five shillings, the labourer must work 10 hours a day, in order to replace the value paid by capital for his labour-power, or to produce an equivalent for the value of his daily necessary means of subsistence. Given the value of these means of subsistence, the value of his labour-power is given; and given the value of his labour-power, the duration of his necessary labour-time is given. The duration of the surplus-labour, however, is arrived at, by subtracting the necessary labour-time from the total working-day. Ten hours subtracted from twelve, leave two, and it is not easy to see, how, under the given conditions, the surplus-labour can possibly be prolonged beyond two hours. No doubt, the capitalist can, instead of five shillings, pay the labourer four shillings and sixpence or even less. For the reproduction of this value of four shillings and sixpence, nine hours' labour-time would suffice; and consequently three hours of surplus-labour, instead of two, would accrue to the capitalist, and the surplus-value would rise from one shilling to eighteenpence. This result, however, would be obtained only by lowering the wages of the labourer below the value of his labour-power. With the four shillings and sixpence which he produces in nine hours, he commands one-tenth less of the necessaries of life than before, and consequently the proper reproduction of his labour-power is crippled. The surplus-labour would in this case be prolonged only by an overstepping of its normal limits; its domain would be extended only by a usurpation of part of the domain of necessary labour-time. Despite the important part which this method plays in actual practice, we are excluded from considering it in this place, by our assumption, that all commodities, including labour-power, are bought and sold at their full value. Granted this, it follows that the labour-time necessary for the production of labour-power, or for the reproduction of its value, cannot be lessened by a fall in the labourer's wages below the value of his labour-power, but only by a fall in this value itself. Given the length of the working-day, the prolongation of the surplus-labour must of necessity originate in the curtailment of the necessary labour-time; the latter cannot arise from the former. In the example we have taken, it is necessary that the value of labour-power should actually fall by one-tenth, in order that the necessary labour-time may be diminished by one-tenth, *i.e.*, from ten hours to nine, and in order that the surplus-labour may consequently be prolonged from two hours to three.

Such a fall in the value of labour-power implies, however, that the same necessaries of life which were formerly produced in ten hours, can now be produced in nine hours. But this is impossible without an increase in the productiveness of labour. For example, suppose a shoemaker, with given tools, makes in one working-day of twelve hours, one pair of boots. If he must make two pairs in the same time, the productiveness of his labour must be doubled; and this cannot be done, except by an alteration in his tools or in his mode of working, or in both. Hence, the conditions of production, *i.e.*, his mode of production, and the labour-process itself, must be revolutionised. By increase in the productiveness of labour, we mean, generally, an alteration in the labour-process, of such a kind as to shorten the labour-time socially necessary for the production of a commodity, and to endow a given quantity of labour with the power of producing a greater quantity of use-value. Hitherto in treating of surplus-value, arising from a simple prolongation of the working-day, we have assumed the mode of production to be given and invariable. But when surplus-value has to be produced by the conversion of necessary labour into surplus-labour, it by no means suffices for capital to take over the labour-process in the form under which it has been historically handed down, and then simply to prolong the duration of that process. The technical and social conditions of the process, and consequently the very mode of production must be revolutionised, before the productiveness of labour can be increased. By that means alone can the value of labour-power be made to sink, and the portion of the working-day necessary for the reproduction of that value, be shortened.

The surplus-value produced by prolongation of the working-day, I call *absolute surplus-value*. On the other hand, the surplus-value arising from the curtailment of the necessary labour-time, and from the corresponding alteration in the respective lengths of the two components of the working-day, I call *relative surplus-value*.

In order to effect a fall in the value of labour-power, the increase in the productiveness of labour must seize upon those branches of industry, whose products determine the value of labour-power, and consequently either belong to the class of customary means of subsistence, or are capable of supplying the place of those means. But the value of a commodity is determined, not only by the quantity of labour which the labourer directly bestows upon that commodity, but also by the labour contained in the means of production. For instance, the value of a pair of boots depends, not only on the cobbler's labour, but also on the value of the leather, wax, thread, &c. Hence, a fall in the value of labour-power is also brought about by an increase in the productiveness of labour, and by a corresponding cheapening of commodities in those industries which supply the instruments of labour and the raw material, that form the material elements of the constant capital required for producing the necessaries of life. But an increase in the productiveness of labour in those branches of industry which supply neither the necessaries of life, nor the means of production for such necessaries, leaves the value of labour-power undisturbed.

The cheapened commodity, of course, causes only a pro tanto fall in the value of labour-power, a fall proportional to the extent of that commodity's employment in the reproduction of labour-power. Shirts, for instance, are a necessary means of subsistence, but are only one out of many. The totality of the necessaries of life consists, however, of various commodities, each the product of a distinct industry; and the value of each of those commodities enters as a component part into the value of labour-power. This latter value decreases with the decrease of the labour-time necessary for its reproduction; the total decrease being the sum of all the different curtailments of labour-time effected in those various and distinct industries. This general result is treated, here, as if it were the immediate result directly aimed at in each individual case. Whenever an individual capitalist cheapens shirts, for instance, by increasing the productiveness of labour, he by no means necessarily aims at reducing the value of labour-power and shortening, pro tanto, the necessary labour-time. But it is only in so far as he ultimately contributes to this result, that he assists in raising the general rate of surplus-value. The general and necessary tendencies of capital must be distinguished from their forms of manifestation.

It is not our intention to consider, here, the way in which the laws, immanent in capitalist production, manifest themselves in the movements of individual masses of capital, where they assert themselves as coercive laws of competition, and are brought home to the mind and consciousness of the individual capitalist as the directing motives of his operations. But this much is clear; a scientific analysis of competition is not possible, before we have a conception of the inner nature of capital, just as the apparent motions of the heavenly bodies are not intelligible to any but him, who is acquainted with their real motions, motions which are not directly perceptible by the senses. Nevertheless, for the better comprehension of the production of relative surplus-value, we may add the following remarks, in which we assume nothing more than the results we have already obtained.

If one hour's labour is embodied in sixpence, a value of six shillings will be produced in a working-day of 12 hours. Suppose, that with the prevailing productiveness of labour, 12 articles are produced in these 12 hours. Let the value of the means of production used up in each article be sixpence. Under these circumstances, each article costs one shilling: sixpence for the value of the means of production, and sixpence for the value newly added in working with those means. Now let some one capitalist contrive to double the productiveness of labour, and to produce in the working-day of 12 hours, 24 instead of 12 such articles. The value of the means of production remaining the same, the value of each article will fall to ninepence, made up of sixpence for the value of the means of production and threepence for the value newly added by the labour. Despite the doubled productiveness of labour, the day's labour creates, as before, a new value of six shillings and no more, which, however, is now spread over twice as many articles. Of this value each article now has embodied in it 1/24th, instead of 1/12th, three-pence instead of sixpence; or, what amounts to the same thing, only half an hour's instead of a whole hour's labour-time, is now added to the means of production while they are being transformed into each article. The individual value of these articles is now below their social value; in other words, they have cost less labour-time than the great bulk of the same article produced under the average social conditions. Each article costs, on an average, one shilling, and represents 2 hours of social labour; but under the altered mode of production it costs only ninepence, or contains only 1½ hours' labour. The real value of a commodity is, however, not its individual value, but its social value; that is to say, the real value is not measured by the labour-time that the article in each individual case costs the producer, but by the labour-time socially required for its production. If therefore, the capitalist who applies the new method, sells his commodity at its social value of one shilling, he sells it for threepence above its individual value, and thus realises an extra surplus-value of threepence. On the other hand, the working-day of 12 hours is, as regards him, now represented by 24 articles instead of 12. Hence, in order to get rid of the product of one working-day, the demand must be double what it was, *i.e.*, the market must become twice as extensive. Other things being equal, his commodities can command a more extended market only by a diminution of their prices. He will therefore sell them above their individual but under their social value, say at tenpence each. By this means he still squeezes an extra surplus-value of one penny out of each. This augmentation of surplus-value is pocketed by him, whether his commodities belong or not to the class of necessary means of subsistence that participate in determining the general value of labour-power. Hence, independently of this latter circumstance, there is a motive for each individual capitalist to cheapen his commodities, by increasing the productiveness of labour.

Nevertheless, even in this case, the increased production of surplus-value arises from the curtailment of the necessary labour-time, and from the corresponding prolongation of the surplus-labour. Let the necessary labour-time amount to 10 hours, the value of a day's labour power to five shillings, the surplus labour-time to 2 hours, and the daily surplus-value to one shilling. But the capitalist now produces 24 articles, which he sells at tenpence a-piece, making twenty shillings in all. Since the value of the means of production is twelve shillings, 14 2/5 of these articles merely replace the constant capital advanced. The labour of the 12 hours' working-day is represented by the remaining 9 3/5 articles. Since the price of the labour-power is five shillings, 6 articles represent the necessary labour-time, and 3 3/5 articles the surplus-labour. The ratio of the necessary labour to the surplus-labour, which under average social conditions was 5:1, is now only 5:3. The same result may be arrived at in the following way. The value of the product of the working-day of 12 hours is twenty shillings. Of this sum, twelve shillings belong to the value of the means of production, a value that merely re-appears. There remain eight shillings, which are the expression in money, of the value newly created during the working-day. This sum is greater than the sum in which average social labour of the same kind is expressed: twelve hours of the latter labour are expressed by six shillings only. The exceptionally productive labour operates as intensified labour; it creates in equal periods of time greater values than average social labour of the same kind. But our capitalist still continues to pay as before only five shillings as the value of a day's labour-power. Hence, instead of 10 hours, the labourer need now work only 7 4/5 hours, in order to reproduce this value. His surplus-labour is, therefore, increased by 2 4/5 hours, and the surplus-value he produces grows from one, into three shillings. Hence, the capitalist who applies the improved method of production, appropriates to surplus-labour a greater portion of the working-day, than the other capitalists in the same trade. He does individually, what the whole body of capitalists engaged in producing relative surplus-value, do collectively. On the other hand, however, this extra surplus-value vanishes, so soon as the new method of production has become general, and has consequently caused the difference between the individual value of the cheapened commodity and its social value to vanish. The law of the determination of value by labour-time, a law which brings under its sway the individual capitalist who applies the new method of production, by compelling him to sell his goods under their social value, this same law, acting as a coercive law of competition, forces his competitors to adopt the new method. The general rate of surplus-value is, therefore, ultimately affected by the whole process, only when the increase in the productiveness of labour, has seized upon those branches of production that are connected with, and has cheapened those commodities that form part of, the necessary means of subsistence, and are therefore elements of the value of labour-power.

The value of commodities is in inverse ratio to the productiveness of labour. And so, too, is the value of labour-power, because it depends on the values of commodities. Relative surplus-value is, on the contrary, directly proportional to that productiveness. It rises with rising and falls with falling productiveness. The value of money being assumed to be constant, an average social working-day of 12 hours always produces the same new value, six shillings, no matter how this sum may be apportioned between surplus-value and wages. But if, in consequence of increased productiveness, the value of the necessaries of life fall, and the value of a day's labour-power be thereby reduced from five shillings to three, the surplus-value increases from one shilling to three. Ten hours were necessary for the reproduction of the value of the labour-power; now only six are required. Four hours have been set free, and can be annexed to the domain of surplus-labour. Hence there is immanent in capital an inclination and constant tendency, to heighten the productiveness of labour, in order to cheapen commodities, and by such cheapening to cheapen the labourer himself.

The value of a commodity is, in itself, of no interest to the capitalist. What alone interests him, is the surplus-value that dwells in it, and is realisable by sale. Realisation of the surplus-value necessarily carries with it the refunding of the value that was advanced. Now, since relative surplus-value increases in direct proportion to the development of the productiveness of labour, while, on the other hand, the value of commodities diminishes in the same proportion; since one and the same process cheapens commodities, and augments the surplus-value contained in them; we have here the solution of the riddle: why does the capitalist, whose sole concern is the production of exchange-value, continually strive to depress the exchange-value of commodities? A riddle with which Quesnay, one of the founders of Political Economy, tormented his opponents, and to which they could give him no answer. "You acknowledge," he says, "that the more expenses and the cost of labour can, in the manufacture of industrial products, be reduced without injury to production, the more advantageous is such reduction, because it diminishes the price of the finished article. And yet, you believe that the production of wealth, which arises from the labour of the workpeople, consists in the augmentation of the exchange-value of their products."

The shortening of the working-day is, therefore, by no means what is aimed at, in capitalist production, when labour is economised by increasing its productiveness. It is only the shortening of the labour-time, necessary for the production of a definite quantity of commodities, that is aimed at. The fact that the workman, when the productiveness of his labour has been increased, produces, say 10 times as many commodities as before, and thus spends one-tenth as much labour-time on each, by no means prevents him from continuing to work 12 hours as before, nor from producing in those 12 hours 1,200 articles instead of 120. Nay, more, his working-day may be prolonged at the same time, so as to make him produce, say 1,400 articles in 14 hours. In the treatises, therefore, of economists of the stamp of MacCulloch, Ure, Senior, and tutti quanti, we may read upon one page, that the labourer owes a debt of gratitude to capital for developing his productiveness, because the necessary labour-time is thereby shortened, and on the next page, that he must prove his gratitude by working in future for 15 hours instead of 10. The object of all development of the productiveness of labour, within the limits of capitalist production, is to shorten that part of the working-day, during which the workman must labour for his own benefit, and by that very shortening, to lengthen the other part of the day, during which he is at liberty to work gratis for the capitalist. How far this result is also attainable, without cheapening commodities, will appear from an examination of the particular modes of producing relative surplus-value, to which examination we now proceed.

CHAPTER XIII. CO-OPERATION

Capitalist production only then really begins, as we have already seen, when each individual capital employs simultaneously a comparatively large number of labourers; when consequently the labour-process is carried on on an extensive scale and yields, relatively, large quantities of products. A greater number of labourers working together, at the same time, in one place (or, if you will, in the same field of labour), in order to produce the same sort of commodity under the mastership of one capitalist, constitutes, both historically and logically, the starting-point of capitalist production. With regard to the mode of production itself, manufacture, in its strict meaning, is hardly to be distinguished, in its earliest stages, from the handicraft trades of the guilds, otherwise than by the greater number of workmen simultaneously employed by one and the same individual capital. The workshop of the mediæval master handicraftsman is simply enlarged. * * *

We saw in a former chapter, that a certain minimum amount of capital was necessary, in order that the number of labourers simultaneously employed, and consequently, the amount of surplus-value produced, might suffice to liberate the employer himself from manual labour, to convert him from a small master into a capitalist, and thus formally to establish capitalist production. We now see that a certain minimum amount is a necessary condition for the conversion of numerous isolated and independent processes into one combined social process.

We also saw that at first, the subjection of labour to capital was only a formal result of the fact, that the labourer, instead of working for himself, works for and consequently under the capitalist. By the co-operation of numerous wage-labourers, the sway of capital develops into a requisite for carrying on the labour-process itself, into a real requisite of production. That a capitalist should command on the field of production, is now as indispensable as that a general should command on the field of battle.

All combined labour on a large scale requires, more or less, a directing authority, in order to secure the harmonious working of the individual activities, and to perform the general functions that have their origin in the action of the combined organism, as distinguished from the action of its separate organs. A single violin player is his own conductor; an orchestra requires a separate one. The work of directing, superintending, and adjusting, becomes one of the functions of capital, from the moment that the labour under the control of capital, becomes co-operative. Once a function of capital, it acquires special characteristics.

The directing motive, the end and aim of capitalist production, is to extract the greatest possible amount of surplus-value, and consequently to exploit labour-power to the greatest possible extent. As the number of the co-operating labourers increases, so too does their resistance to the domination of capital, and with it, the necessity for capital to overcome this resistance by counter-pressure. The control exercised by the capitalist is not only a special function, due to the nature of the social labour-process, and peculiar to that process, but it is, at the same time, a function of the exploitation of a social labour-process, and is consequently rooted in the unavoidable antagonism between the exploiter and the living and labouring raw material he exploits.

Again, in proportion to the increasing mass of the means of production, now no longer the property of the labourer, but of the capitalist, the necessity increases for some effective control over the proper application of those means. Moreover, the co-operation of wage-labourers is entirely brought about by the capital that employs them. Their union into one single productive body and the establishment of a connexion between their individual functions, are matters foreign and external to them, are not their own act, but the act of the capital that brings and keeps them together. Hence the connexion existing between their various labours appears to them, ideally, in the shape of a preconceived plan of the capitalist, and practically in the shape of the authority of the same capitalist, in the shape of the powerful will of another, who subjects their activity to his aims. If, then, the control of the capitalist is in substance two-fold by reason of the two-fold nature of the process of production itself,—which, on the one hand, is a social process for producing use-values, on the other, a process for creating surplus-value—in form that control is despotic. As co-operation extends its scale, this despotism takes forms peculiar to itself. Just as at first the capitalist is relieved from actual labour so soon as his capital has reached that minimum amount with which capitalist production, as such, begins, so now, he hands over the work of direct and constant supervision of the individual workmen, and groups of workmen, to a special kind of wage-labourer. An industrial army of workmen, under the command of a capitalist, requires, like a real army, officers (managers), and sergeants (foremen, overlookers), who, while the work is being done, command in the name of the capitalist. The work of supervision becomes their established and exclusive function. When comparing the mode of production of isolated peasants and artisans with production by slave-labour, the political economist counts this labour of superintendence among the *faux frais* of production. But, when considering the capitalist mode of production, he, on the contrary, treats the work of control made necessary by the co-operative character of the labour-process as identical with the different work of control, necessitated by the capitalist character of that process and the antagonism of interests between capitalist and labourer. It is not because he is a leader of industry that a man is a capitalist; on the contrary, he is a leader of industry because he is a capitalist. The leadership of industry is an attribute of capital, just as in feudal times the functions of general and judge, were attributes of landed property.

The labourer is the owner of his labour-power until he has done bargaining for its sale with the capitalist; and he can sell no more than what he has—*i.e.*, his individual, isolated labour-power. This state of things is in no way altered by the fact that the capitalist, instead of buying the labour-power of one man, buys that of 100, and enters into separate contracts with 100 unconnected men instead of with one. He is at liberty to set the 100 men to work, without letting them co-operate. He pays them the value of 100 independent labour-powers, but he does not pay for the combined labour-power of the hundred. Being independent of each other, the labourers are isolated persons, who enter into relations with the capitalist, but not with one another. This co-operation begins only with the labour-process, but they have then ceased to belong to themselves. On entering that process, they become incorporated with capital. As co-operators, as members of a working organism they are but special modes of existence of capital. Hence, the productive power developed by the labourer when working in co-operation, is the productive power of capital. This power is developed gratuitously, whenever the workmen are placed under given conditions, and it is capital that places them under such conditions. Because this power costs capital nothing, and because, on the other hand, the labourer himself does not develop it before his labour belongs to capital, it appears as a power with which capital is endowed by Nature—a productive power that is immanent in capital.

The colossal effects of simple co-operation are to be seen in the gigantic structures of the ancient Asiatics, Egyptians, Etruscans, &c.

"It has happened in times past that these Oriental States, after supplying the expenses of their civil and military establishments, have
found themselves in possession of a surplus which they could apply
to works of magnificence or utility and in the construction of these
their command over the hands and arms of almost the entire non-
agricultural population has produced stupendous monuments which
still indicate their power. The teeming valley of the Nile . . . produced food for a swarming non-agricultural population, and this
food, belonging to the monarch and the priesthood, afforded the
means of erecting the mighty monuments which filled the land. . . .
In moving the colossal statues and vast masses of which the transport creates wonder, human labour almost alone, was prodigally
used. . . . The number of the labourers and the concentration of
their efforts sufficed. We see mighty coral reefs rising from the
depths of the ocean into islands and firm land, yet each individual
depositor is puny, weak, and contemptible. The non-agricultural
labourers of an Asiatic monarchy have little but their individual
bodily exertions to bring to the task, but their number is their
strength, and the power of directing these masses gave rise to the
palaces and temples, the pyramids, and the armies of gigantic
statues of which the remains astonish and perplex us. It is that con-
finement of the revenues which feed them, to one or a few hands,
which makes such undertakings possible." This power of Asiatic
and Egyptian kings, Etruscan theocrats, &c., has in modern society
been transferred to the capitalist, whether he be an isolated, or as
in joint-stock companies, a collective capitalist.

Co-operation, such as we find it at the dawn of human development, among races who live by the chase, or, say, in the agriculture
of Indian communities, is based, on the one hand, on ownership in
common of the means of production, and on the other hand, on
the fact, that in those cases, each individual has no more torn himself off from the navel-string of his tribe or community, than each
bee has freed itself from connexion with the hive. Such
co-operation is distinguished from capitalistic co-operation by both
of the above characteristics. The sporadic application of
co-operation on a large scale in ancient times, in the middle ages,
and in modern colonies, reposes on relations of dominion and servitude, principally on slavery. The capitalistic form, on the contrary,
pre-supposes from first to last, the free wage-labourer, who sells his
labour power to capital. Historically, however, this form is developed in opposition to peasant agriculture and to the carrying on of
independent handicrafts whether in guilds or not. From the standpoint of these, capitalistic co-operation does not manifest itself as a
particular historical form of co-operation, but co-operation itself
appears to be a historical form peculiar to, and specifically distinguishing, the capitalist process of production.

Just as the social productive power of labour that is developed by co-operation, appears to be the productive power of capital, so co-operation itself, contrasted with the process of production carried on by isolated independent labourers, or even by small employers, appears to be a specific form of the capitalist process of production. It is the first change experienced by the actual labour-process, when subjected to capital. This change takes place spontaneously. The simultaneous employment of a large number of wage-labourers, in one and the same process, which is a necessary condition of this change, also forms the starting-point of capitalist production. This point coincides with the birth of capital itself. If then, on the one hand, the capitalist mode of production presents itself to us historically, as a necessary condition to the transformation of the labour-process into a social process, so, on the other hand, this social form of the labour-process presents itself, as a method employed by capital for the more profitable exploitation of labour, by increasing that labour's productiveness.

In the elementary form, under which we have hitherto viewed it, co-operation is a necessary concomitant of all production on a large scale, but it does not, in itself, represent a fixed form characteristic of a particular epoch in the development of the capitalist mode of production. At the most it appears to do so, and that only approximately, in the handicraft-like beginnings of manufacture, and in that kind of agriculture on a large scale, which corresponds to the epoch of manufacture, and is distinguished from peasant agriculture, mainly by the number of the labourers simultaneously employed, and by the mass of the means of production concentrated for their use. Simple co-operation is always the prevailing form, in those branches of production in which capital operates on a large scale, and division of labour and machinery play but a subordinate part.

Co-operation ever constitutes the fundamental form of the capitalist mode of production; nevertheless the elementary form of co-operation continues to subsist as a particular form of capitalist production side by side with the more developed forms of that mode of production.

CHAPTER XIV. DIVISION OF LABOUR AND MANUFACTURE

Section 1. Two-fold Origin of Manufacture

That co-operation which is based on division of labour, assumes its typical form in manufacture, and is the prevalent characteristic form of the capitalist process of production throughout the manufacturing period properly so called. That period, roughly speaking, extends from the middle of the 16th to the last third of the 18th century.

Manufacture takes its rise in two ways:—

(1) By the assemblage, in one workshop under the control of a single capitalist, of labourers belonging to various independent handicrafts, but through whose hands a given article must pass on its way to completion. A carriage, for example, was formerly the product of the labour of a great number of independent artificers, such as wheelwrights, harness-makers, tailors, locksmiths, upholsterers, turners, fringe-makers, glaziers, painters, polishers, gilders, &c. In the manufacture of carriages, however, all these different artificers are assembled in one building where they work into one another's hands. * * *

(2) Manufacture also arises in a way exactly the reverse of this—namely, by one capitalist employing simultaneously in one workshop a number of artificers, who all do the same, or the same kind of work, such as making paper, type, or needles. This is co-operation in its most elementary form. Each of these artificers (with the help, perhaps, of one or two apprentices), makes the entire commodity, and he consequently performs in succession all the operations necessary for its production. He still works in his old handicraft-like way. But very soon external circumstances cause a different use to be made of the concentration of the workmen on one spot, and of the simultaneousness of their work. An increased quantity of the article has perhaps to be delivered within a given time. The work is therefore re-distributed. Instead of each man being allowed to perform all the various operations in succession, these operations are changed into disconnected, isolated ones, carried on side by side; each is assigned to a different artificer, and the whole of them together are performed simultaneously by the co-operating workmen. * * *

The mode in which manufacture arises, its growth out of handicrafts, is therefore two-fold. On the one hand, it arises from the union of various independent handicrafts, which become stripped of their independence and specialised to such an extent as to be reduced to mere supplementary partial processes in the production of one particular commodity. On the other hand, it arises from the co-operation of artificers of one handicraft; it splits up that particular handicraft into its various detail operations, isolating, and making these operations independent of one another up to the point where each becomes the exclusive function of a particular labourer. On the one hand, therefore, manufacture either introduces division of labour into a process of production, or further develops that division; on the other hand, it unites together handicrafts that were formerly separate. But whatever may have been its particular starting-point, its final form is invariably the same—a productive mechanism whose parts are human beings. * * *

Section 2. *The Detail Labourer and His Implements*

If we now go more into detail, it is, in the first place, clear that a labourer who all his life performs one and the same simple operation, converts his whole body into the automatic, specialised implement of that operation. Consequently, he takes less time in doing it, than the artificer who performs a whole series of operations in succession. But the collective labourer, who constitutes the living mechanism of manufacture, is made up solely of such specialised detail labourers. Hence, in comparison with the independent handicraft, more is produced in a given time, or the productive power of labour is increased. Moreover, when once this fractional work is established as the exclusive function of one person, the methods it employs become perfected. The workman's continued repetition of the same simple act, and the concentration of his attention on it, teach him by experience how to attain the desired effects with the minimum of exertion. But since there are always several generations of labourers living at one time, and working together at the manufacture of a given article, the technical skill, the tricks of the trade thus acquired, become established, and are accumulated and handed down. Manufacture, in fact, produces the skill of the detail labourer, by reproducing, and systematically driving to an extreme within the workshop, the naturally developed differentiation of trades, which it found ready to hand in society at large. On the other hand, the conversion of fractional work into the life-calling of one man, corresponds to the tendency shown by earlier societies, to make trades hereditary; either to petrify them into castes, or whenever definite historical conditions beget in the individual a tendency to vary in a manner incompatible with the nature of castes, to ossify them into guilds. * * *

An artificer, who performs one after another the various fractional operations in the production of a finished article, must at one time change his place, at another his tools. The transition from one operation to another interrupts the flow of his labour, and creates, so to say, gaps in his working-day. These gaps close up so soon as he is tied to one and the same operation all day long; they vanish in proportion as the changes in his work diminish. The resulting increased productive power is owing either to an increased expenditure of labour-power in a given time—*i.e.*, to increased intensity of labour—or to a decrease in the amount of labour-power unproductively consumed. The extra expenditure of power, demanded by every transition from rest to motion, is made up for by prolonging the duration of the normal velocity when once acquired. On the other hand, constant labour of one uniform kind disturbs the intensity and flow of a man's animal spirits, which find recreation and delight in mere change of activity. * * *

Early in the manufacturing period, the principle of lessening the necessary labour-time in the production of commodities, was accepted and formulated: and the use of machines, especially for certain simple first processes that have to be conducted on a very large scale, and with the application of great force, sprang up here and there. Thus, at an early period in paper manufacture, the tearing up of the rags was done by paper-mills; and in metal works, the pounding of the ores was effected by stamping mills. The Roman Empire had handed down the elementary form of all machinery in the water-wheel.

The handicraft period bequeathed to us the great inventions of the compass, of gunpowder, of type-printing, and of the automatic clock. But, on the whole, machinery played that subordinate part which Adam Smith assigns to it in comparison with division of labour. The sporadic use of machinery in the 17th century was of the greatest importance, because it supplied the great mathematicians of that time with a practical basis and stimulant to the creation of the science of mechanics.

The collective labourer, formed by the combination of a number of detail labourers, is the machinery specially characteristic of the manufacturing period. The various operations that are performed in turns by the producer of a commodity, and coalesce one with another during the progress of production, lay claim to him in various ways. In one operation he must exert more strength, in another more skill, in another more attention; and the same individual does not possess all these qualities in an equal degree. After Manufacture has once separated, made independent, and isolated the various operations, the labourers are divided, classified, and grouped according to their predominating qualities. If their natural endowments are, on the one hand, the foundation on which the division of labour is built up, on the other hand, Manufacture, once introduced, develops in them new powers that are by nature fitted only for limited and special functions. The collective labourer now possesses, in an equal degree of excellence, all the qualities requisite for production, and expends them in the most economical manner, by exclusively employing all his organs, consisting of particular labourers, or groups of labourers, in performing their special functions. The one-sidedness and the deficiencies of the detail labourer become perfections when he is a part of the collective labourer. The habit of doing only one thing converts him into a never failing instrument, while his connexion with the whole mechanism compels him to work with the regularity of the parts of a machine.

Since the collective labourer has functions, both simple and complex, both high and low, his members, the individual labour-powers, require different degrees of training, and must therefore have different values. Manufacture, therefore, develops a hierarchy of labour-powers, to which there corresponds a scale of wages. If, on the one hand, the individual labourers are appropriated and annexed for life by a limited function; on the other hand, the various operations of the hierarchy are parcelled out among the labourers according to both their natural and their acquired capabilities. Every process of production, however, requires certain simple manipulations, which every man is capable of doing. They too are now severed from their connexion with the more pregnant moments of activity, and ossified into exclusive functions of specially appointed labourers. Hence, Manufacture begets, in every handicraft that it seizes upon, a class of so-called unskilled labourers, a class which handicraft industry strictly excluded. * * *

Section 4. Division of Labour in Manufacture, and Division of Labour in Society

We first considered the origin of Manufacture, then its simple elements, then the detail labourer and his implements, and finally, the totality of the mechanism. We shall now lightly touch upon the relation between the division of labour in manufacture, and the social division of labour, which forms the foundation of all production of commodities.

If we keep labour alone in view, we may designate the separation of social production into its main divisions or *genera*—viz., agriculture, industries, &c., as division of labour in general, and the splitting up of these families into species and sub-species, as division of labour in particular, and the division of labour within the workshop as division of labour in singular or in detail.

Division of labour in a society, and the corresponding tying down of individuals to a particular calling, develops itself, just as does the division of labour in manufacture, from opposite starting-points. Within a family, and after further development with a tribe, there springs up naturally a division of labour, caused by differences of sex and age, a division that is consequently based on a purely physiological foundation, which division enlarges its materials by the expansion of the community, by the increase of population, and more especially, by the conflicts between different tribes, and the subjugation of one tribe by another. On the other hand, as I have before remarked, the exchange of products springs up at the points where different families, tribes, communities, come in contact; for, in the beginning of civilisation, it is not private individuals but families, tribes, &c., that meet on an independent footing. Different communities find different means of production, and different means of subsistence in their natural environment. Hence, their modes of production, and of living, and their products are different. It is this spontaneously developed difference which, when different communities come in contact, calls forth the mutual exchange of products, and the consequent gradual conversion of those products into commodities. * * *

The foundation of every division of labour that is well developed, and brought about by the exchange of commodities, is the separation between town and country. It may be said, that the whole economic history of society is summed up in the movement of this antithesis. We pass it over, however, for the present.

Just as a certain number of simultaneously employed labourers are the material pre-requisites for division of labour in manufacture, so are the number and density of the populations, which here correspond to the agglomeration in one workshop, a necessary condition for the division of labour in society. Nevertheless, this density is more or less relative. A relatively thinly populated country, with well-developed means of communication, has a denser population than a more numerously populated country, with badly-developed means of communication; and in this sense the Northern States of the American Union, for instance, are more thickly populated than India.

Since the production and the circulation of commodities are the general pre-requisites of the capitalist mode of production, division of labour in manufacture demands, that division of labour in society at large should previously have attained a certain degree of development. Inversely, the former division reacts upon and develops and multiplies the latter. Simultaneously, with the differentiation of the instruments of labour, the industries that produce these instruments, become more and more differentiated. If the manufacturing system seize upon an industry, which, previously, was carried on in connexion with others, either as a chief or as a subordinate industry, and by one producer, these industries immediately separate their connexion, and become independent. If it seize upon a particular stage in the production of a commodity, the other stages of its production become converted into so many independent industries. It has already been stated, that where the finished article consists merely of a number of parts fitted together, the detail operations may re-establish themselves as genuine and separate handicrafts. In order to carry out more perfectly the division of labour in manufacture, a single branch of production is, according to the varieties of its raw material, or the various forms that one and the same raw material may assume, split up into numerous, and to some extent, entirely new manufactures. Accordingly, in France alone, in the first half of the 18th century, over 100 different kinds of silk stuffs were woven, and, in Avignon, it was law, that "every apprentice should devote himself to only one sort of fabrication, and should not learn the preparation of several kinds of stuff at once." The territorial division of labour, which confines special branches of production to special districts of a country, acquires fresh stimulus from the manufacturing system, which exploits every special advantage. The Colonial system and the opening out of the markets of the world, both of which are included in the general conditions of existence of the manufacturing period, furnish rich material for developing the division of labour in society. It is not the place, here, to go on to show how division of labour seizes upon, not only the economic, but every other sphere of society, and everywhere lays the foundation of that all engrossing system of specialising and sorting men, that development in a man of one single faculty at the expense of all other faculties, which caused A. Ferguson, the master of Adam Smith, to exclaim: "We make a nation of Helots, and have no free citizens."

But, in spite of the numerous analogies and links connecting them, division of labour in the interior of a society, and that in the interior of a workshop, differ not only in degree, but also in kind. The analogy appears most indisputable where there is an invisible bond uniting the various branches of trade. For instance the cattle-breeder produces hides, the tanner makes the hides into leather, and the shoemaker, the leather into boots. Here the thing produced by each of them is but a step towards the final form, which is the product of all their labours combined. There are, besides, all the various industries that supply the cattle-breeder, the tanner, and the shoemaker with the means of production. Now it is quite possible to imagine, with Adam Smith, that the difference between the above social division of labour, and the division in manufacture, is merely subjective, exists merely for the observer, who, in a manufacture, can see with one glance, all the numerous operations being performed on one spot, while in the instance given above, the spreading out of the work over great areas, and the great number of people employed in each branch of labour, obscure the connexion. But what is it that forms the bond between the independent labours of the cattle-breeder, the tanner, and the shoemaker? It is the fact that their respective products are commodities. What, on the other hand, characterises division of labour in manufactures? The fact that the detail labourer produces no commodities. It is only the common product of all the detail labourers that

becomes a commodity. Division of labour in society is brought
about by the purchase and sale of the products of different
branches of industry, while the connexion between the detail operations in a workshop, is due to the sale of the labour-power of several workmen to one capitalist, who applies it as combined
labour-power. The division of labour in the workshop implies concentration of the means of production in the hands of one capitalist; the division of labour in society implies their dispersion among
many independent producers of commodities. While within the
workshop, the iron law of proportionality subjects definite numbers
of workmen to definite functions, in the society outside the workshop, chance and caprice have full play in distributing the producers and their means of production among the various branches of
industry. The different spheres of production, it is true, constantly
tend to an equilibrium: for, on the one hand, while each producer
of a commodity is bound to produce a use-value, to satisfy a particular social want, and while the extent of these wants differs quantitatively, still there exists an inner relation which settles their proportions into a regular system, and that system one of spontaneous
growth; and, on the other hand, the law of the value of commodities ultimately determines how much of its disposable working-
time society can expend on each particular class of commodities.
But this constant tendency to equilibrium, of the various spheres of
production, is exercised, only in the shape of a reaction against the
constant upsetting of this equilibrium. The *a priori* system on
which the division of labour, within the workshop, is regularly carried out, becomes in the division of labour within the society, an *a
posteriori*, nature-imposed necessity, controlling the lawless caprice
of the producers, and perceptible in the barometrical fluctuations of
the market-prices. Division of labour within the workshop implies
the undisputed authority of the capitalist over men, that are but
parts of a mechanism that belongs to him. The division of labour
within the society brings into contact independent commodity-
producers, who acknowledge no other authority but that of competition, of the coercion exerted by the pressure of their mutual interests; just as in the animal kingdom, the *bellum omnium contra
omnes* more or less preserves the conditions of existence of every
species. The same bourgeois mind which praises division of labour
in the workshop, life-long annexation of the labourer to a partial
operation, and his complete subjection to capital, as being an organisation of labour that increases its productiveness—that same
bourgeois mind denounces with equal vigour every conscious
attempt to socially control and regulate the process of production,
as an inroad upon such sacred things as the rights of property, freedom and unrestricted play for the bent of the individual capitalist.

It is very characteristic that the enthusiastic apologists of the factory system have nothing more damning to urge against a general organisation of the labour of society, than that it would turn all society into one immense factory.

If, in a society with capitalist production, anarchy in the social division of labour and despotism in that of the workshop are mutual conditions the one of the other, we find, on the contrary, in those earlier forms of society in which the separation of trades has been spontaneously developed, then crystallised, and finally made permanent by law, on the one hand, a specimen of the organisation of the labour of society, in accordance with an approved and authoritative plan, and on the other, the entire exclusion of division of labour in the workshop, or at all events a mere dwarf-like or sporadic and accidental development of the same.

Those small and extremely ancient Indian communities, some of which have continued down to this day, are based on possession in common of the land, on the blending of agriculture and handicrafts, and on an unalterable division of labour, which serves, whenever a new community is started, as a plan and scheme ready cut and dried. * * * The law that regulates the division of labour in the community acts with the irresistible authority of a law of Nature, at the same time that each individual artificer, the smith, the carpenter, and so on, conducts in his workshop all the operations of his handicraft in the traditional way, but independently, and without recognising any authority over him. The simplicity of the organisation for production in these self-sufficing communities that constantly reproduce themselves in the same form, and when accidentally destroyed, spring up again on the spot and with the same name—this simplicity supplies the key to the secret of the unchangeableness of Asiatic societies, an unchangeableness in such striking contrast with the constant dissolution and refounding of Asiatic States, and the never-ceasing changes of dynasty. The structure of the economic elements of society remains untouched by the storm-clouds of the political sky.

The rules of the guilds, as I have said before, by limiting most strictly the number of apprentices and journeymen that a single master could employ, prevented him from becoming a capitalist. Moreover, he could not employ his journeymen in many other handicrafts than the one in which he was a master. The guilds zealously repelled every encroachment by the capital of merchants, the only form of free capital with which they came in contact. A merchant could buy every kind of commodity, but labour as a commodity he could not buy. He existed only on sufferance, as a dealer in the products of the handicrafts. If circumstances called for a further division of labour, the existing guilds split themselves up into varieties, or founded new guilds by the side of the old ones; all this, however, without concentrating various handicrafts in a single workshop. Hence, the guild organisation, however much it may have contributed by separating, isolating, and perfecting the handicrafts, to create the material conditions for the existence of manufacture, excluded division of labour in the workshop. On the whole, the labourer and his means of production remained closely united, like the snail with its shell, and thus there was wanting the principal basis of manufacture, the separation of the labourer from his means of production, and the conversion of these means into capital.

While division of labour in society at large, whether such division be brought about or not by exchange of commodities, is common to economic formations of society the most diverse, division of labour in the workshop, as practised by manufacture, is a special creation of the capitalist mode of production alone.

Section 5. The Capitalistic Character of Manufacture

An increased number of labourers under the control of one capitalist is the natural starting-point, as well of co-operation generally, as of manufacture in particular. But the division of labour in manufacture makes this increase in the number of workmen a technical necessity. The minimum number that any given capitalist is bound to employ is here prescribed by the previously established division of labour. On the other hand, the advantages of further division are obtainable only by adding to the number of workmen, and this can be done only by adding multiples of the various detail groups. But an increase in the variable component of the capital employed necessitates an increase in its constant component, too, in the workshops, implements, &c., and, in particular, in the raw material, the call for which grows quicker than the number of workmen. The quantity of it consumed in a given time, by a given amount of labour, increases in the same ratio as does the productive power of that labour in consequence of its division. Hence, it is a law, based on the very nature of manufacture, that the minimum amount of capital, which is bound to be in the hands of each capitalist, must keep increasing; in other words, that the transformation into capital of the social means of production and subsistence must keep extending.

In manufacture, as well as in simple co-operation, the collective working organism is a form of existence of capital. The mechanism that is made up of numerous individual detail labourers belongs to the capitalist. Hence, the productive power resulting from a combination of labours appears to be the productive power of capital. Manufacture proper not only subjects the previously independent workman to the discipline and command of capital, but, in addition, creates a hierarchic gradation of the workmen themselves.

While simple co-operation leaves the mode of working by the individual for the most part unchanged, manufacture thoroughly revolutionises it, and seizes labour-power by its very roots. It converts the labourer into a crippled monstrosity, by forcing his detail dexterity at the expense of a world of productive capabilities and instincts; just as in the States of La Plata they butcher a whole beast for the sake of his hide or his tallow. Not only is the detail work distributed to the different individuals, but the individual himself is made the automatic motor of a fractional operation, and the absurd fable of Menenius Agrippa, which makes man a mere fragment of his own body, becomes realised. If, at first, the workman sells his labour-power to capital, because the material means of producing a commodity fail him, now his very labour-power refuses its services unless it has been sold to capital. Its functions can be exercised only in an environment that exists in the workshop of the capitalist after the sale. By nature unfitted to make anything independently, the manufacturing labourer develops productive activity as a mere appendage of the capitalist's workshop. As the chosen people bore in their features the sign manual of Jehovah, so division of labour brands the manufacturing workman as the property of capital.

The knowledge, the judgment, and the will, which, though in ever so small a degree, are practised by the independent peasant or handicraftsman, in the same way as the savage makes the whole art of war consist in the exercise of his personal cunning—these faculties are now required only for the workshop as a whole. Intelligence in production expands in one direction, because it vanishes in many others. What is lost by the detail labourers, is concentrated in the capital that employs them. It is a result of the division of labour in manufactures, that the labourer is brought face to face with the intellectual potencies of the material process of production, as the property of another, and as a ruling power. This separation begins in simple co-operation, where the capitalist represents to the single workman, the oneness and the will of the associated labour. It is developed in manufacture which cuts down the labourer into a detail labourer. It is completed in modern industry, which makes science a productive force distinct from labour and presses it into the service of capital.

In manufacture, in order to make the collective labourer, and through him capital, rich in social productive power, each labourer must be made poor in individual productive powers. "Ignorance is the mother of industry as well as of superstition. Reflection and fancy are subject to err; but a habit of moving the hand or the foot is independent of either. Manufactures, accordingly, prosper most where the mind is least consulted, and where the workshop may . . . be considered as an engine, the parts of which are men." As a matter of fact, some few manufacturers in the middle of the 18th century preferred for certain operations that were trade secrets, to employ half-idiotic persons.

"The understandings of the greater part of men," says Adam Smith, "are necessarily formed by their ordinary employments. The man whose whole life is spent in performing a few simple operations . . . has no occasion to exert his understanding. . . . He generally becomes as stupid and ignorant as it is possible for a human creature to become." After describing the stupidity of the detail labourer he goes on: "The uniformity of his stationary life naturally corrupts the courage of his mind. . . . It corrupts even the activity of his body and renders him incapable of exerting his strength with vigour and perseverance in any other employments than that to which he has been bred. His dexterity at his own particular trade seems in this manner to be acquired at the expense of his intellectual, social, and martial virtues. But in every improved and civilised society, this is the state into which the labouring poor, that is, the great body of the people, must necessarily fall." For preventing the complete deterioration of the great mass of the people by division of labour, A. Smith recommends education of the people by the State, but prudently, and in homœopathic doses. G. Garnier, his French translator and commentator, who, under the first French Empire, quite naturally developed into a senator, quite as naturally opposes him on this point. Education of the masses, he urges, violates the first law of the division of labour, and with it "our whole social system would be proscribed." "Like all other divisions of labour," he says, "that between hand labour and head labour is more pronounced and decided in proportion as society (he rightly uses this word, for capital, landed property and their State) becomes richer. This division of labour, like every other, is an effect of past, and a cause of future progress . . . ought the government then to work in opposition to this division of labour, and to hinder its natural course? Ought it to expend a part of the public money in the attempt to confound and blend together two classes of labour, which are striving after division and separation?"[6]

Some crippling of body and mind is inseparable even from division of labour in society as a whole. Since, however, manufacture carries this social separation of branches of labour much further, and also, by its peculiar division, attacks the individual at the very roots of his life, it is the first to afford the materials for, and to give a start to, industrial pathology.

"To subdivide a man is to execute him, if he deserves the sentence, to assassinate him if he does not. . . . The subdivision of labour is the assassination of a people."

6. G. Garnier, Vol. V of his translation of A. Smith, pp. 4–5. [*Marx*]

Co-operation based on division of labour, in other words, manufacture, commences as a spontaneous formation. So soon as it attains some consistence and extension, it becomes the recognised methodical and systematic form of capitalist production. History shows how the division of labour peculiar to manufacture, strictly so called, acquires the best adapted form at first by experience, as it were behind the backs of the actors, and then, like the guild handicrafts, strives to hold fast that form when once found, and here and there succeeds in keeping it for centuries. Any alteration in this form, except in trivial matters, is solely owing to a revolution in the instruments of labour. Modern manufacture wherever it arises—I do not here allude to modern industry based on machinery—either finds the disjecta membra poetæ ready to hand, and only waiting to be collected together, as is the case in the manufacture of clothes in large towns, or it can easily apply the principle of division, simply by exclusively assigning the various operations of a handicraft (such as book-binding) to particular men. In such cases, a week's experience is enough to determine the proportion between the numbers of the hands necessary for the various functions.[7]

By decomposition of handicrafts, by specialisation of the instruments of labour, by the formation of detail labourers, and by grouping and combining the latter into a single mechanism, division of labour in manufacture creates a qualitative gradation, and a quantitative proportion in the social process of production; it consequently creates a definite organisation of the labour of society, and thereby develops at the same time new productive forces in the society. In its specific capitalist form—and under the given conditions, it could take no other form than a capitalistic one—manufacture is but a particular method of begetting relative surplus-value, or of augmenting at the expense of the labourer the self-expansion of capital—usually called social wealth, "Wealth of Nations," &c. It increases the social productive power of labour, not only for the benefit of the capitalist instead of for that of the labourer, but it does this by crippling the individual labourers. It creates new conditions for the lordship of capital over labour. If, therefore, on the one hand, it presents itself historically as a progress and as a necessary phase in the economic development of society, on the other hand, it is a refined and civilised method of exploitation.

7. The simple belief in the inventive genius exercised a priori by the individual capitalist in division of labour, exists now-a-days only among German professors, of the stamp of Herr Roscher, who, to recompense the capitalist from whose Jovian head division of labour sprang ready formed, dedicates to him "various wages" (diverse Arbeitslöhne). The more or less extensive application of division of labour depends on length of purse, not on greatness of genius. [*Marx*]

Political Economy, which as an independent science, first sprang into being during the period of manufacture, views the social division of labour only from the standpoint of manufacture, and sees in it only the means of producing more commodities with a given quantity of labour, and, consequently, of cheapening commodities and hurrying on the accumulation of capital. In most striking contrast with this accentuation of quantity and exchange-value, is the attitude of the writers of classical antiquity, who hold exclusively by quality and use-value. In consequence of the separation of the social branches of production, commodities are better made, the various bents and talents of men select a suitable field, and without some restraint no important results can be obtained anywhere. Hence both product and producer are improved by division of labour. If the growth of the quantity produced is occasionally mentioned, this is only done with reference to the greater abundance of use-values. There is not a word alluding to exchange-value or to the cheapening of commodities. This aspect, from the standpoint of use-value alone, is taken as well by Plato,[8] who treats division of labour as the foundation on which the division of society into classes is based, as by Xenophon, who with characteristic bourgeois instinct, approaches more nearly to division of labour within the workshop. Plato's Republic, in so far as division of labour is treated in it, as the formative principle of the State, is merely the Athenian idealisation of the Egyptian system of castes, Egypt having served as the model of an industrial country to many of his contemporaries also, amongst others to Isocrates, and it continued to have this importance to the Greeks of the Roman Empire.

During the manufacturing period proper, *i.e.*, the period during which manufacture is the predominant form taken by capitalist production, many obstacles are opposed to the full development of the peculiar tendencies of manufacture. Although manufacture creates, as we have already seen, a simple separation of the labourers

8. With Plato, division of labour within the community is a development from the multifarious requirements, and the limited capacities of individuals. The main point with him is, that the labourer must adapt himself to the work, not the work to the labourer; which latter is unavoidable, if he carries on several trades at once, thus making one or the other of them subordinate. So in Thucydides: "Seafaring is an art like any other, and cannot, as circumstances require, be carried on as a subsidiary occupation; nay, other subsidiary occupations cannot be carried on alongside of this one." If the work, says Plato, has to wait for the labourer, the critical point in the process is missed and the article spoiled. The same Platonic idea is found recurring in the protest of the English bleachers against the clause in the Factory Act that provides fixed meal-times for all operatives. Their business cannot wait the convenience of the workmen, for "in the various operations of singeing, washing, bleaching, mangling, calendering, and dyeing, none of them can be stopped at a given moment without risk of damage . . . to enforce the same dinner hour for all the workpeople might occasionally subject valuable goods to the risk of danger by incomplete operations." Le platonisme où va-t-il se nicher! [*Marx*]

into skilled and unskilled, simultaneously with their hierarchic arrangement in classes, yet the number of the unskilled labourers, owing to the preponderating influence of the skilled, remains very limited. Although it adapts the detail operations to the various degrees of maturity, strength, and development of the living instruments of labour, thus conducing to exploitation of women and children, yet this tendency as a whole is wrecked on the habits and the resistance of the male labourers. Although the splitting up of handicrafts lowers the cost of forming the workman, and thereby lowers his value, yet for the more difficult detail work, a longer apprenticeship is necessary, and, even where it would be superfluous, is jealously insisted upon by the workmen. In England, for instance, we find the laws of apprenticeship, with their seven years' probation, in full force down to the end of the manufacturing period; and they are not thrown on one side till the advent of Modern Industry. Since handicraft skill is the foundation of manufacture, and since the mechanism of manufacture as a whole possesses no framework, apart from the labourers themselves, capital is constantly compelled to wrestle with the insubordination of the workmen. "By the infirmity of human nature," says friend Ure, "it happens that the more skilful the workman, the more self-willed and intractable he is apt to become, and of course the less fit a component of a mechanical system in which . . . he may do great damage to the whole." Hence throughout the whole manufacturing period there runs the complaint of want of discipline among the workmen. And had we not the testimony of contemporary writers, the simple facts, that during the period between the 16th century and the epoch of Modern Industry, capital failed to become the master of the whole disposable working-time of the manufacturing labourers, that manufacturers are short-lived, and change their locality from one country to another with the emigrating or immigrating workmen, these facts would speak volumes. "Order must in one way or another be established," exclaims in 1770 the oft-cited author of the "Essay on Trade and Commerce." "Order," re-echoes Dr. Andrew Ure 66 years later, "Order" was wanting in manufacture based on "the scholastic dogma of division of labour," and "Arkwright created order."

At the same time manufacture was unable, either to seize upon the production of society to its full extent, or to revolutionise that production to its very core. It towered up as an economic work of art, on the broad foundation of the town handicrafts, and of the rural domestic industries. At a given stage in its development, the narrow technical basis on which manufacture rested, came into conflict with requirements of production that were created by manufacture itself.

One of its most finished creations was the workshop for the

production of the instruments of labour themselves, including especially the complicated mechanical apparatus then already employed. A machine-factory, says Ure, "displayed the division of labour in manifold gradations—the file, the drill, the lathe, having each its different workman in the order of skill." (P. 21.) This workshop, the product of the division of labour in manufacture, produced in its turn—machines. It is they that swept away the handicraftsman's work as the regulating principle of social production. Thus, on the one hand, the technical reason for the life-long annexation of the workman to a detail function is removed. On the other hand, the fetters that this same principle laid on the dominion of capital, fall away.

Part IV. (Continued). Production of Relative Surplus-Value

CHAPTER XV. MACHINERY AND MODERN INDUSTRY

Section 1. The Development of Machinery

John Stuart Mill says in his "Principles of Political Economy": "It is questionable if all the mechanical inventions yet made have lightened the day's toil of any human being."[9] That is, however, by no means the aim of the capitalistic application of machinery. Like every other increase in the productiveness of labour, machinery is intended to cheapen commodities, and, by shortening that portion of the working-day, in which the labourer works for himself, to lengthen the other portion that he gives, without an equivalent, to the capitalist. In short, it is a means for producing surplus-value.

In manufacture, the revolution in the mode of production begins with the labour-power, in modern industry it begins with the instruments of labour. Our first inquiry then is, how the instruments of labour are converted from tools into machines, or what is the difference between a machine and the implements of handicraft? We are only concerned here with striking and general characteristics; for epochs in the history of society are no more separated from each other by hard and fast lines of demarcation, than are geological epochs. * * *

Section 3. The Proximate Effects of Machinery on the Workman

The starting-point of Modern Industry is, as we have shown, the revolution in the instruments of labour, and this revolution attains its most highly developed form in the organised system of machin-

9. Mill should have said, "of any human being not fed by other people's labour," for, without doubt, machinery has greatly increased the number of well-to-do idlers. [*Marx*]

ery in a factory. Before we inquire how human material is incorporated with this objective organism, let us consider some general effects of this revolution on the labourer himself.

A. APPROPRIATION OF SUPPLEMENTARY LABOUR-POWER BY CAPITAL. THE EMPLOYMENT OF WOMEN AND CHILDREN

In so far as machinery dispenses with muscular power, it becomes a means of employing labourers of slight muscular strength, and those whose bodily development is incomplete, but whose limbs are all the more supple. The labour of women and children was, therefore, the first thing sought for by capitalists who used machinery. That mighty substitute for labour and labourers was forthwith changed into a means for increasing the number of wage-labourers by enrolling, under the direct sway of capital, every member of the workman's family, without distinction of age or sex. Compulsory work for the capitalist usurped the place, not only of the children's play, but also of free labour at home within moderate limits for the support of the family.

The value of labour-power was determined, not only by the labour-time necessary to maintain the individual adult labourer, but also by that necessary to maintain his family. Machinery, by throwing every member of that family on to the labour-market, spreads the value of the man's labour-power over his whole family. It thus depreciates his labour-power. To purchase the labour-power of a family of four workers may, perhaps, cost more than it formerly did to purchase the labour-power of the head of the family, but, in return, four days' labour takes the place of one, and their price falls in proportion to the excess of the surplus-labour of four over the surplus-labour of one. In order that the family may live, four people must now, not only labour, but expend surplus-labour for the capitalist. Thus we see, that machinery, while augmenting the human material that forms the principal object of capital's exploiting power, at the same time raises the degree of exploitation. * * *

B. PROLONGATION OF THE WORKING-DAY

If machinery be the most powerful means for increasing the productiveness of labour—*i.e.*, for shortening the working-time required in the production of a commodity, it becomes in the hands of capital the most powerful means, in those industries first invaded by it, for lengthening the working-day beyond all bounds set by human nature. It creates, on the one hand, new conditions by which capital is enabled to give free scope to this its constant tendency, and on the other hand, new motives with which to whet capital's appetite for the labour of others.

In the first place, in the form of machinery, the implements of labour become automatic, things moving and working independent of the workman. They are thenceforth an industrial *perpetuum mobile*, that would go on producing forever, did it not meet with certain natural obstructions in the weak bodies and the strong wills of its human attendants. The automaton, as capital, and because it is capital, is endowed, in the person of the capitalist, with intelligence and will; it is therefore animated by the longing to reduce to a minimum the resistance offered by that repellent yet elastic natural barrier, man. This resistance is moreover lessened by the apparent lightness of machine work, and by the more pliant and docile character of the women and children employed on it. * * *

Machinery produces relative surplus value; not only by directly depreciating the value of labour-power, and by indirectly cheapening the same through cheapening the commodities that enter into its reproduction, but also, when it is first introduced sporadically into an industry, by converting the labour employed by the owner of that machinery, into labour of a higher degree and greater efficacy, by raising the social value of the article produced above its individual value, and thus enabling the capitalist to replace the value of a day's labour-power by a smaller portion of the value of a day's product. During this transition period, when the use of machinery is a sort of monopoly, the profits are therefore exceptional, and the capitalist endeavours to exploit thoroughly "the sunny time of this his first love," by prolonging the working-day as much as possible. The magnitude of the profit whets his appetite for more profit.

As the use of machinery becomes more general in a particular industry, the social value of the product sinks down to its individual value, and the law that surplus-value does not arise from the labour-power that has been replaced by the machinery, but from the labour-power actually employed in working with the machinery, asserts itself. Surplus-value arises from variable capital alone, and we saw that the amount of surplus-value depends on two factors, viz., the rate of surplus-value and the number of the workmen simultaneously employed. Given the length of the working-day, the rate of surplus-value is determined by the relative duration of the necessary labour and of the surplus-labour in a day. The number of the labourers simultaneously employed depends, on its side, on the ratio of the variable to the constant capital. Now, however much the use of machinery may increase the surplus-labour at the expense of the necessary labour by heightening the productiveness of labour, it is clear that it attains this result, only by diminishing the number of workmen employed by a given amount of capital. It converts what was formerly variable capital, invested in labour-power, into machinery which, being constant capital, does not produce surplus-value. It is impossible, for instance, to squeeze as much surplus-value out of 2 as out of 24 labourers. If each of these 24 men gives only one hour of surplus-labour in 12, the 24 men give together 24 hours of surplus-labour, while 24 hours is the total labour of the two men. Hence, the application of machinery to the production of surplus-value implies a contradiction which is immanent in it, since of the two factors of the surplus-value created by a given amount of capital, one, the rate of surplus-value, cannot be increased, except by diminishing the other, the number of workmen. This contradiction comes to light, as soon as by the general employment of machinery in a given industry, the value of the machine-produced commodity regulates the value of all commodities of the same sort; and it is this contradiction, that in its turn, drives the capitalist, without his being conscious of the fact, to excessive lengthening of the working-day, in order that he may compensate the decrease in the relative number of labourers exploited, by an increase not only of the relative, but of the absolute surplus-labour.

If, then, the capitalistic employment of machinery, on the one hand, supplies new and powerful motives to an excessive lengthening of the working-day, and radically changes, as well the methods of labour, as also the character of the social working organism, in such a manner as to break down all opposition to this tendency, on the other hand it produces, partly by opening out to the capitalist new strata of the working-class, previously inaccessible to him, partly by setting free the labourers it supplants, a surplus working population, which is compelled to submit to the dictation of capital. Hence that remarkable phenomenon in the history of Modern Industry, that machinery sweeps away every moral and natural restriction on the length of the working-day. Hence, too, the economic paradox, that the most powerful instrument for shortening labour-time, becomes the most unfailing means for placing every moment of the labourer's time and that of his family, at the disposal of the capitalist for the purpose of expanding the value of his capital. "If," dreamed Aristotle, the greatest thinker of antiquity, "if every tool, when summoned, or even of its own accord, could do the work that befits it, just as the creations of Dædalus moved of themselves, or the tripods of Hephæstos went of their own accord to their sacred work, if the weavers' shuttles were to weave of themselves, then there would be no need either of apprentices for the master workers, or of slaves for the lords." And Antipatros, a Greek poet of the time of Cicero, hailed the invention of the water-wheel for grinding corn, an invention that is the elementary form of all machinery, as the giver of freedom to female slaves, and the bringer back of the golden age. Oh! those heathens! They understood, as the learned Bastiat, and before him the still wiser MacCulloch have discovered, nothing of Political Economy and Christianity. They did not, for example, comprehend that machinery is the surest means of lengthening the working-day. They perhaps excused the slavery of one on the ground that it was a means to the full development of another. But to preach slavery of the masses, in order that a few crude and half-educated parvenus, might become "eminent spinners," "extensive sausage makers," and "influential shoeblack dealers," to do this, they lacked the bump[1] of Christianity.

C. INTENSIFICATION OF LABOUR

The immoderate lengthening of the working-day, produced by machinery in the hands of capital, leads to a reaction on the part of society, the very sources of whose life are menaced; and, thence, to a normal working day whose length is fixed by law. Thenceforth a phenomenon that we have already met with, namely, the intensification of labour, develops into great importance. Our analysis of absolute surplus-value had reference primarily to the extension or duration of the labour, its intensity being assumed as given. We now proceed to consider the substitution of a more intensified labour for labour of more extensive duration, and the degree of the former. * * *

Section IV. The Factory

At the commencement of this chapter we considered that which we may call the body of the factory, *i.e.*, machinery organised into a system. We there saw how machinery, by annexing the labour of women and children, augments the number of human beings who form the material for capitalistic exploitation, how it confiscates the whole of the workman's disposable time, by immoderate extension of the hours of labour, and how finally its progress, which allows of enormous increase of production in shorter and shorter periods, serves as a means of systematically getting more work done in a shorter time, or of exploiting labour-power more intensely. We now turn to the factory as a whole, and that in its most perfect form. * * *

So far as division of labour re-appears in the factory, it is primarily a distribution of the workmen among the specialised machines; and of masses of workmen, not however organised into groups, among the various departments of the factory, in each of which they work at a number of similar machines placed together; their co-operation, therefore, is only simple. The organised group, peculiar to manufacture, is replaced by the connexion between the head workman and his few assistants. The essential division is, into work-

---

1. A reference to the pseudo-science of phrenology, in which the "bumps" on a person's skull were thought to represent particular character traits. [*R. T.*]

men who are actually employed on the machines (among whom
are included a few who look after the engine), and into mere
attendants (almost exclusively children) of these workmen. Among
the attendants are reckoned more or less all "Feeders" who supply
the machines with the material to be worked. In addition to these
two principal classes, there is a numerically unimportant class of
persons, whose occupation it is to look after the whole of the machinery and repair it from time to time; such as engineers, mechanics, joiners, &c. This is a superior class of workmen, some of them
scientifically educated, others brought up to a trade; it is distinct
from the factory operative class, and merely aggregated to it. This
division of labour is purely technical.

To work at a machine, the workman should be taught from
childhood, in order that he may learn to adapt his own movements
to the uniform and unceasing motion of an automaton. When the
machinery, as a whole, forms a system of manifold machines, working simultaneously and in concert, the co-operation based upon it,
requires the distribution of various groups of workmen among the
different kinds of machines. But the employment of machinery does
away with the necessity of crystallising this distribution after the
manner of Manufacture, by the constant annexation of a particular
man to a particular function. Since the motion of the whole system
does not proceed from the workman, but from the machinery, a
change of persons can take place at any time without an interruption of the work. The most striking proof of this is afforded by the
relays system, put into operation by the manufacturers during their
revolt from 1848 to 1850. Lastly, the quickness with which machine
work is learnt by young people, does away with the necessity of
bringing up for exclusive employment by machinery, a special class
of operatives. With regard to the work of the mere attendants, it
can, to some extent, be replaced in the mill by machines, and
owing to its extreme simplicity, it allows of a rapid and constant
change of the individuals burdened with this drudgery.

Although then, technically speaking, the old system of division
of labour is thrown overboard by machinery, it hangs on in the factory, as a traditional habit handed down from Manufacture, and is
afterwards systematically re-moulded and established in a more
hideous form by capital, as a means of exploiting labour-power.
The life-long speciality of handling one and the same tool, now
becomes the life-long speciality of serving one and the same
machine. Machinery is put to a wrong use, with the object of transforming the workman, from his very childhood, into a part of a
detail-machine. In this way, not only are the expenses of his reproduction considerably lessened, but at the same time his helpless
dependence upon the factory as a whole, and therefore upon the

capitalist, is rendered complete. Here as everywhere else, we must distinguish between the increased productiveness due to the development of the social process of production, and that due to the capitalist exploitation of that process. In handicrafts and manufacture, the workman makes use of a tool, in the factory, the machine makes use of him. There the movements of the instrument of labour proceed from him, here it is the movements of the machine that he must follow. In manufacture the workmen are parts of a living mechanism. In the factory we have a lifeless mechanism independent of the workman, who becomes its mere living appendage. "The miserable routine of endless drudgery and toil in which the same mechanical process is gone through over and over again, is like the labour of Sisyphus. The burden of labour, like the rock, keeps ever falling back on the worn-out labourer."[2] At the same time that factory work exhausts the nervous system to the uttermost, it does away with the many-sided play of the muscles, and confiscates every atom of freedom, both in bodily and intellectual activity. The lightening of the labour, even, becomes a sort of torture, since the machine does not free the labourer from work, but deprives the work of all interest. Every kind of capitalist production, in so far as it is not only a labour-process, but also a process of creating surplus-value, has this in common, that it is not the workman that employs the instruments of labour, but the instruments of labour that employ the workman. But it is only in the factory system that this inversion for the first time acquires technical and palpable reality. By means of its conversion into an automaton, the instrument of labour confronts the labourer, during the labour-process, in the shape of capital, of dead labour, that dominates, and pumps dry, living labour-power. The separation of the intellectual powers of production from the manual labour, and the conversion of those powers into the might of capital over labour, is, as we have already shown, finally completed by modern industry erected on the foundation of machinery. The special skill of each individual insignificant factory operative vanishes as an infinitesimal quantity before the science, the gigantic physical forces, and the mass of labour that are embodied in the factory mechanism and, together with that mechanism, constitute the power of the "master." This "master," therefore, in whose brain the machinery and his monopoly of it are inseparably united, whenever he falls out with his

2. F. Engels, *The Condition of the Working Class in England in 1844*, p. 217.—Even an ordinary optimistic freetrader like Mr. Molinari goes so far as to say: "A man will become exhausted sooner if he watches over the uniform motion of a mechanism fifteen hours day than if he exercises his physical force over the same interval of time. This work of watching over something, which could be useful perhaps as mental gymnastics provided it were not too prolonged, will, in the long run, destroy both body and mind through excess."—G. de Molinari, *Études économiques*, Paris, 1846.

"hands," contemptuously tells them: "The factory operatives should keep in wholesome remembrance the fact that theirs is really a low species of skilled labour; and that there is none which is more easily acquired, or of its quality more amply remunerated, or which by a short training of the least expert can be more quickly, as well as abundantly, acquired. ... The master's machinery really plays a far more important part in the business of production than the labour and the skill of the operative, which six months' education can teach, and a common labourer can learn." The technical subordination of the workman to the uniform motion of the instruments of labour, and the peculiar composition of the body of workpeople, consisting as it does of individuals of both sexes and of all ages, give rise to a barrack discipline, which is elaborated into a complete system in the factory, and which fully develops the before mentioned labour of overlooking, thereby dividing the workpeople into operatives and overlookers, into private soldiers and sergeants of an industrial army. "The main difficulty [in the automatic factory] ... lay ... above all in training human beings to renounce their desultory habits of work, and to identify themselves with the unvarying regularity of the complex automaton. To devise and administer a successful code of factory discipline, suited to the necessities of factory diligence, was the Herculean enterprise, the noble achievement of Arkwright! Even at the present day, when the system is perfectly organised and its labour lightened to the utmost, it is found nearly impossible to convert persons past the age of puberty, into useful factory hands." The factory code in which capital formulates, like a private legislator, and at his own good will, his autocracy over his workpeople, unaccompanied by that division of responsibility, in other matters so much approved of by the bourgeoisie, and unaccompanied by the still more approved representative system, this code is but the capitalistic caricature of that social regulation of the labour-process which becomes requisite in co-operation on a great scale, and in the employment in common, of instruments of labour and especially of machinery. The place of the slave-driver's lash is taken by the overlooker's book of penalties. All punishments naturally resolve themselves into fines and deductions from wages, and the law-giving talent of the factory Lycurgus so arranges matters, that a violation of his laws is, if possible, more profitable to him than the keeping of them.

We shall here merely allude to the material conditions under which factory labour is carried on. Every organ of sense is injured in an equal degree by artificial elevation of the temperature, by the dust-laden atmosphere, by the deafening noise, not to mention danger to life and limb among the thickly crowded machinery, which, with the regularity of the seasons, issues its list of the killed and wounded in the industrial battle. Economy of the social means of production, matured and forced as in a hothouse by the factory system, is turned, in the hands of capital, into systematic robbery of what is necessary for the life of the workman while he is at work, robbery of space, light, air, and of protection to his person against the dangerous and unwholesome accompaniments of the productive process, not to mention the robbery of appliances for the comfort of the workman. Is Fourier wrong when he calls factories "tempered bagnos"?

Section 5. The Strife Between Workman and Machine

The contest between the capitalist and the wage-labourer dates back to the very origin of capital. It raged on throughout the whole manufacturing period. But only since the introduction of machinery has the workman fought against the instrument of labour itself, the material embodiment of capital. He revolts against this particular form of the means of production, as being the material basis of the capitalist mode of production. * * *

Section 9. The Factory Acts. Sanitary and Educational Clauses of the Same. Their General Extension in England

Factory legislation, that first conscious and methodical reaction of society against the spontaneously developed form of the process of production, is, as we have seen, just as much the necessary product of modern industry as cotton yarn, self-actors, and the electric telegraph. Before passing to the consideration of the extension of that legislation in England, we shall shortly notice certain clauses contained in the Factory Acts, and not relating to the hours of work.

Apart from their wording, which makes it easy for the capitalist to evade them, the sanitary clauses are extremely meagre, and, in fact, limited to provisions for whitewashing the walls, for insuring cleanliness in some other matters, for ventilation, and for protection against dangerous machinery. In the third book we shall return again to the fanatical opposition of the masters to those clauses which imposed upon them a slight expenditure on appliances for protecting the limbs of their workpeople, an opposition that throws a fresh and glaring light on the Free-trade dogma, according to which, in a society with conflicting interests, each individual necessarily furthers the common weal by seeking nothing but his own personal advantage! * * *

Paltry as the education clauses of the Act appear on the whole, yet they proclaim elementary education to be an indispensable condition to the employment of children. The success of those clauses proved for the first time the possibility of combining education and gymnastics with manual labour, and, consequently, of combining manual labour with education and gymnastics. The factory inspectors soon found out by questioning the schoolmasters, that the factory children, although receiving only one half the education of the regular day scholars, yet learnt quite as much and often more. "This can be accounted for by the simple fact that, with only being at school for one half of the day, they are always fresh, and nearly always ready and willing to receive instruction. The system on which they work, half manual labour, and half school, renders each employment a rest and a relief to the other; consequently, both are far more congenial to the child, than would be the case were he kept constantly at one. It is quite clear that a boy who has been at school all the morning, cannot (in hot weather particularly) cope with one who comes fresh and bright from his work." Further information on this point will be found in Senior's speech at the Social Science Congress at Edinburgh in 1863. He there shows, amongst other things, how the monotonous and uselessly long school hours of the children of the upper and middle classes, uselessly add to the labour of the teacher, "while he not only fruitlessly but absolutely injuriously, wastes the time, health, and energy of the children." From the Factory system budded, as Robert Owen has shown us in detail, the germ of the education of the future, an education that will, in the case of every child over a given age, combine productive labour with instruction and gymnastics, not only as one of the methods of adding to the efficiency of production, but as the only method of producing fully developed human beings.

Modern Industry, as we have seen, sweeps away by technical means the manufacturing division of labour, under which each man is bound hand and foot for life to a single detail-operation. At the same time, the capitalistic form of that industry reproduces this same division of labour in a still more monstrous shape; in the factory proper, by converting the workman into a living appendage of the machine; and everywhere outside the Factory, partly by the sporadic use of machinery and machine workers, partly by re-establishing the division of labour on a fresh basis by the general introduction of the labour of women and children, and of cheap unskilled labour.

The antagonism between the manufacturing division of labour and the methods of Modern Industry makes itself forcibly felt. It manifests itself, amongst other ways, in the frightful fact that a great part of the children employed in modern factories and manufactures, are from their earliest years riveted to the most simple manipulations, and exploited for years, without being taught a single sort of work that would afterwards make them of use, even in the same manufactory or factory.

Modern Industry never looks upon and treats the existing form of a process as final. The technical basis of that industry is therefore revolutionary, while all earlier modes of production were essentially conservative. By means of machinery, chemical processes and other methods, it is continually causing changes not only in the technical basis of production, but also in the functions of the labourer, and in the social combinations of the labour-process. At the same time, it thereby also revolutionises the division of labour within the society, and incessantly launches masses of capital and of workpeople from one branch of production to another. But if Modern Industry, by its very nature, therefore necessitates variation of labour, fluency of function, universal mobility of the labourer, on the other hand, in its capitalistic form, it reproduces the old division of labour with its ossified particularisations. We have seen how this absolute contradiction between the technical necessities of Modern Industry, and the social character inherent in its capitalistic form, dispels all fixity and security in the situation of the labourer; how it constantly threatens, by taking away the instruments of labour, to snatch from his hands his means of subsistence, and, by suppressing his detail-function, to make him superfluous. We have seen, too, how this antagonism vents its rage in the creation of that monstrosity, an industrial reserve army, kept in misery in order to be always at the disposal of capital; in the incessant human sacrifices from among the working-class, in the most reckless squandering of labour-power, and in the devastation caused by a social anarchy which turns every economic progress into a social calamity. This is the negative side. But if, on the one hand, variation of work at present imposes itself after the manner of an overpowering natural law, and with the blindly destructive action of a natural law that meets with resistance at all points, Modern Industry, on the other hand, through its catastrophes imposes the necessity of recognising, as a fundamental law of production, variation of work, consequently fitness of the labourer for varied work, consequently the greatest possible development of his varied aptitudes. It becomes a question of life and death for society to adapt the mode of production to the normal functioning of this law. Modern Industry, indeed, compels society, under penalty of death, to replace the detail-worker of to-day, crippled by life-long repetition of one and the same trivial operation, and thus reduced to the mere fragment of a man, by the fully developed individual, fit for a variety of labours, ready to face any change of production, and to whom the different social functions he performs, are but so many modes of giving free scope to his own natural and acquired powers.

One step already spontaneously taken towards effecting this revolution is the establishment of technical and agricultural schools, and of "écoles d'enseignement professionnel," in which the children of the working-men receive some little instruction in technology and in the practical handling of the various implements of labour. Though the Factory Act, that first and meagre concession wrung from capital, is limited to combining elementary education with work in the factory, there can be no doubt that when the working-class comes into power, as inevitably it must, technical instruction, both theoretical and practical, will take its proper place in the working-class schools. There is also no doubt that such revolutionary ferments, the final result of which is the abolition of the old division of labour, are diametrically opposed to the capitalistic form of production, and to the economic status of the labourer corresponding to that form. But the historical development of the antagonisms, immanent in a given form of production, is the only way in which that form of production can be dissolved and a new form established. "Ne sutor ultra crepidam"—this ne plus ultra of handicraft wisdom became sheer nonsense, from the moment the watchmaker Watt invented the steam-engine, the barber Arkwright, the throstle, and the working-jeweller, Fulton, the steamship.

So long as Factory legislation is confined to regulating the labour in factories, manufactories, &c., it is regarded as a mere interference with the exploiting rights of capital. But when it comes to regulating the so-called "home-labour," it is immediately viewed as a direct attack on the patria potestas, on parental authority. The tender-hearted English Parliament long affected to shrink from taking this step. The force of facts, however, compelled it at last to acknowledge that modern industry, in overturning the economic foundation on which was based the traditional family, and the family labour corresponding to it, had also unloosened all traditional family ties. The rights of the children had to be proclaimed. The final report of the Ch. Empl. Comm. of 1866, states: "It is unhappily, to a painful degree, apparent throughout the whole of the evidence, that against no persons do the children of both sexes so much require protection as against their parents." The system of unlimited exploitation of children's labour in general and the so-called home-labour in particular is "maintained only because the parents are able, without check or control, to exercise this arbitrary and mischievous power over their young and tender offspring. . . . Parents must not possess the absolute power of making their children mere 'machines to earn so much weekly wage.' . . . The children and young persons, therefore, in all such cases may justifiably claim from the legislature, as a natural right, that an exemption should be secured to them, from what destroys prematurely their physical strength, and lowers them in the scale of intellectual and moral beings." It was not, however, the misuse of parental authority that created the capitalistic exploitation, whether direct or indirect, of children's labour; but, on the contrary, it was the capitalistic mode of exploitation which, by sweeping away the economic basis of parental authority, made its exercise degenerate into a mischievous misuse of power. However terrible and disgusting the dissolution, under the capitalist system, of the old family ties may appear, nevertheless, modern industry, by assigning as it does an important part in the process of production, outside the domestic sphere, to women, to young persons, and to children of both sexes, creates a new economic foundation for a higher form of the family and of the relations between the sexes. It is, of course, just as absurd to hold the Teutonic-Christian form of the family to be absolute and final as it would be to apply that character to the ancient Roman, the ancient Greek, or the Eastern forms which, moreover, taken together form a series in historical development. Moreover, it is obvious that the fact of the collective working group being composed of individuals of both sexes and all ages, must necessarily, under suitable conditions, become a source of humane development; although in its spontaneously developed, brutal, capitalistic form, where the labourer exists for the process of production, and not the process of production for the labourer, that fact is a pestiferous source of corruption and slavery. * * *

Section 10. Modern Industry and Agriculture

The revolution called forth by modern industry in agriculture, and in the social relations of agricultural producers, will be investigated later on. In this place we shall merely indicate a few results by way of anticipation. If the use of machinery in agriculture is for the most part free from the injurious physical effect it has on the factory operative, its action in superseding the labourers is more intense, and finds less resistance, as we shall see later in detail. In the counties of Cambridge and Suffolk, for example, the area of cultivated land has extended very much within the last twenty years (up to 1868), while in the same period the rural population has diminished, not only relatively, but absolutely. In the United States it is as yet only virtually that agricultural machines replace labourers; in other words, they allow of the cultivation by the farmer of a larger surface, but do not actually expel the labourers employed. In 1861 the number of persons occupied in England and Wales in the manufacture of agricultural machines was 1,034, whilst the number of agricultural labourers employed in the use of agricultural machines and steam-engines did not exceed 1,205.

In the sphere of agriculture, modern industry has a more revolutionary effect than elsewhere, for this reason, that it annihilates the peasant, that bulwark of the old society, and replaces him by the wage-labourer. Thus the desire for social changes, and the class antagonisms are brought to the same level in the country as in the towns. The irrational, old-fashioned methods of agriculture are replaced by scientific ones. Capitalist production completely tears asunder the old bond of union which held together agriculture and manufacture in their infancy. But at the same time it creates the material conditions for a higher synthesis in the future, viz., the union of agriculture and industry on the basis of the more perfected forms they have each acquired during their temporary separation. Capitalist production, by collecting the population in great centres, and causing an ever-increasing preponderance of town population, on the one hand concentrates the historical motive power of society; on the other hand, it disturbs the circulation of matter between man and the soil, i.e., prevents the return to the soil of its elements consumed by man in the form of food and clothing; it therefore violates the conditions necessary to lasting fertility of the soil. By this action it destroys at the same time the health of the town labourer and the intellectual life of the rural labourer. But while upsetting the naturally grown conditions for the maintenance of that circulation of matter, it imperiously calls for its restoration as a system, as a regulating law of social production, and under a form appropriate to the full development of the human race. In agriculture as in manufacture, the transformation of production under the sway of capital, means, at the same time, the martyrdom of the producer; the instrument of labour becomes the means of enslaving, exploiting, and impoverishing the labourer; the social combination and organisation of labour-processes is turned into an organised mode of crushing out the workman's individual vitality, freedom, and independence. The dispersion of the rural labourers over larger areas breaks their power of resistance while concentration increases that of the town operatives. In modern agriculture, as in the urban industries, the increased productiveness and quantity of the labour set in motion are bought at the cost of laying waste and consuming by disease labour-power itself. Moreover, all progress in capitalistic agriculture is a progress in the art, not only of robbing the labourer, but of robbing the soil; all progress in increasing the fertility of the soil for a given time, is a progress towards ruining the lasting sources of that fertility. The more a country starts its development on the foundation of modern industry, like the United States, for example, the more rapid is this process of destruction. Capitalist production, therefore, develops technology, and the combining together of various processes into a social whole, only by sapping the original sources of all wealth—the soil and the labourer.

Part V. The Production of Absolute and of Relative Surplus-Value

CHAPTER XVI. ABSOLUTE AND RELATIVE SURPLUS-VALUE

In considering the labour-process, we began by treating it in the abstract, apart from its historical forms, as a process between man and Nature. We stated: "If we examine the whole labour-process, from the point of view of its result, it is plain that both the instruments and the subjects of labour are means of production, and that the labour itself is productive labour." And we further added: "This method of determining, from the standpoint of the labour-process alone, what is productive labour, is by no means directly applicable to the case of the capitalist process of production." We now proceed to the further development of this subject.

So far as the labour-process is purely individual, one and the same labourer unites in himself all the functions, that later on become separated. When an individual appropriates natural objects for his livelihood, no one controls him but himself. Afterwards he is controlled by others. A single man cannot operate upon Nature without calling his own muscles into play under the control of his own brain. As in the natural body head and hand wait upon each other, so the labour-process unites the labour of the hand with that of the head. Later on they part company and even become deadly foes. The product ceases to be the direct product of the individual, and becomes a social product, produced in common by a collective labourer, *i.e.*, by a combination of workmen, each of whom takes only a part, greater or less, in the manipulation of the subject of their labour. As the co-operative character of the labour-process becomes more and more marked, so, as a necessary consequence, does our notion of productive labour, and of its agent the productive labourer, become extended. In order to labour productively, it is no longer necessary for you to do manual work yourself; enough, if you are an organ of the collective labourer, and perform one of its subordinate functions. The first definition given above of productive labour, a definition deduced from the very nature of the production of material objects, still remains correct for the collective labourer, considered as a whole. But it no longer holds good for each member taken individually.

On the other hand, however, our notion of productive labour becomes narrowed. Capitalist production is not merely the production of commodities, it is essentially the production of surplus-value. The labourer produces, not for himself, but for capital. It no longer suffices, therefore, that he should simply produce. He must produce surplus-value. That labourer alone is productive, who produces surplus-value for the capitalist, and thus works for the self-expansion of capital. If we may take an example from outside the sphere of production of material objects, a schoolmaster is a productive labourer, when, in addition to belabouring the heads of his scholars, he works like a horse to enrich the school proprietor. That the latter has laid out his capital in a teaching factory, instead of in a sausage factory, does not alter the relation. Hence the notion of a productive labourer implies not merely a relation between work and useful effect, between labourer and product of labour, but also a specific, social relation of production, a relation that has sprung up historically and stamps the labourer as the direct means of creating surplus-value. To be a productive labourer is, therefore, not a piece of luck, but a misfortune. * * *

The prolongation of the working-day beyond the point at which the labourer would have produced just an equivalent for the value of his labour-power, and the appropriation of that surplus-labour by capital, this is production of absolute surplus-value. It forms the general groundwork of the capitalist system, and the starting-point for the production of relative surplus-value. The latter pre-supposes that the working-day is already divided into two parts, necessary labour, and surplus-labour. In order to prolong the surplus-labour, the necessary labour is shortened by methods whereby the equivalent for the wages is produced in less time. The production of absolute surplus-value turns exclusively upon the length of the working-day; the production of relative surplus-value, revolutionises out and out the technical processes of labour, and the composition of society. It therefore pre-supposes a specific mode, the capitalist mode of production, a mode which, along with its methods, means, and conditions, arises and develops itself spontaneously on the foundation afforded by the formal subjection of labour to capital. In the course of this development, the formal subjection is replaced by the real subjection of labour to capital. * * *

From one standpoint, any distinction between absolute and relative surplus-value appears illusory. Relative surplus-value is absolute, since it compels the absolute prolongation of the working-day beyond the labour-time necessary to the existence of the labourer himself. Absolute surplus-value is relative, since it makes necessary such a development of the productiveness of labour, as will allow of the necessary labour-time being confined to a portion of the working-day. But if we keep in mind the behaviour of surplus-value, this appearance of identity vanishes. Once the capitalist mode of production established and become general, the difference between absolute and relative surplus-value makes itself felt, whenever there is a question of raising the rate of surplus-value. Assuming that labour-power is paid for at its value, we are confronted by this alternative: given the productiveness of labour and its normal intensity, the rate of surplus-value can be raised only by the actual prolongation of the working-day; on the other hand, given the length of the working-day, that rise can be effected only by a change in the relative magnitudes of the components of the working-day, viz., necessary labour and surplus-labour; a change which, if the wages are not to fall below the value of labour-power, pre-supposes a change either in the productiveness or in the intensity of the labour.

If the labourer wants all his time to produce the necessary means of subsistence for himself and his race, he has no time left in which to work gratis for others. Without a certain degree of productiveness in his labour, he has no such superfluous time at his disposal; without such superfluous time, no surplus-labour, and therefore no capitalists, no slave-powers, no feudal lords, in one word, no class of large proprietors. * * *

CHAPTER XXV. THE GENERAL LAW OF CAPITALIST ACCUMULATION

Section 1. The Increased Demand for Labour-Power That Accompanies Accumulation, the Composition of Capital Remaining the Same

In this chapter we consider the influence of the growth of capital on the lot of the labouring class. The most important factor in this inquiry, is the composition of capital and the changes it undergoes in the course of the process of accumulation.

The composition of capital is to be understood in a two-fold sense. On the side of value, it is determined by the proportion in which it is divided into constant capital or value of the means of production, and variable capital or value of labour-power, the sum total of wages. On the side of material, as it functions in the process of production, all capital is divided into means of production and living labour-power. This latter composition is determined by the relation between the mass of the means of production employed, on the one hand, and the mass of labour necessary for their employment on the other. I call the former the *value-composition*, the latter the *technical composition* of capital. Between the two there is a strict correlation. To express this, I call the value-composition of capital, in so far as it is determined by its technical composition and mirrors the changes of the latter, the *organic composition* of capital. Wherever I refer to the composition of capital, without further qualification, its organic composition is always understood.

The many individual capitals invested in a particular branch of production have, one with another, more or less different compositions. The average of the individual compositions gives us the composition of the total capital in this branch of production. Lastly, the average of these averages, in all branches of production, gives us the composition of the total social capital of a country, and with this alone are we, in the last resort, concerned in the following investigation.

Growth of capital involves growth of its variable constituent or of the part invested in labour-power. A part of the surplus-value turned into additional capital must always be re-transformed into variable capital, or additional labour-fund. If we suppose that, all other circumstances remaining the same, the composition of capital also remains constant (*i.e.*, that a definite mass of means of production constantly needs the same mass of labour-power to set it in motion), then the demands for labour and the subsistence-fund of the labourers clearly increase in the same proportion as the capital, and the more rapidly, the more rapidly the capital increases. Since the capital produces yearly a surplus-value, of which one part is yearly added to the original capital; since this increment itself grows yearly along with the augmentation of the capital already functioning; since lastly, under special stimulus to enrichment, such as the opening of new markets, or of new spheres for the outlay of capital in consequence of newly developed social wants, &c., the scale of accumulation may be suddenly extended, merely by a change in the division of the surplus-value or surplus-product into capital and revenue, the requirements of accumulating capital may exceed the increase of labour-power or of the number of labourers; the demand for labourers may exceed the supply, and, therefore, wages may rise. This must, indeed, ultimately be the case if the conditions supposed above continue. For since in each year more labourers are employed than in its predecessor, sooner or later a point must be reached, at which the requirements of accumulation begin to surpass the customary supply of labour, and, therefore, a rise of wages takes place. A lamentation on this score was heard in England during the whole of the fifteenth, and the first half of the eighteenth centuries. The more or less favourable circumstances in which the wage-working class supports and multiplies itself, in no way alter the fundamental character of capitalist production. As simple reproduction constantly reproduces the capital-relation itself, *i.e.*, the relation of capitalists on the one hand, and wage-workers on the other, so reproduction on a progressive scale, *i.e.*, accumulation, reproduces the capital-relation on a progressive scale, more capitalists or larger capitalists at this pole, more wage-workers at that. The reproduction of a mass of labour-power, which must incessantly re-incorporate itself with capital for that capital's self-expansion, which cannot get free from capital, and whose enslavement to capital is only concealed by the variety of individual capitalists to whom it sells itself, this reproduction of labour-power forms, in fact, an essential of the reproduction of capital itself. Accumulation of capital is, therefore, increase of the proletariat. * * *

The law of capitalist production, that is at the bottom of the pretended "natural law of population," reduces itself simply to this: The correlation between accumulation of capital and rate of wages is nothing else than the correlation between the unpaid labour transformed into capital, and the additional paid labour necessary for the setting in motion of this additional capital. It is therefore in no way a relation between two magnitudes, independent one of the other: on the one hand, the magnitude of the capital; on the other, the number of the labouring population; it is rather, at bottom, only the relation between the unpaid and the paid labour of the same labouring population. If the quantity of unpaid labour supplied by the working-class, and accumulated by the capitalist class, increases so rapidly that its conversion into capital requires an extraordinary addition of paid labour, then wages rise, and, all other circumstances remaining equal, the unpaid labour diminishes in proportion. But as soon as this diminution touches the point at which the surplus-labour that nourishes capital is no longer supplied in normal quantity, a reaction sets in: a smaller part of revenue is capitalised, accumulation lags, and the movement of rise in wages receives a check. The rise of wages therefore is confined within limits that not only leave intact the foundations of the capitalistic system, but also secure its reproduction on a progressive scale. The law of capitalistic accumulation, metamorphosed by economists into a pretended law of Nature, in reality merely states that the very nature of accumulation excludes every diminution in the degree of exploitation of labour, and every rise in the price of labour, which could seriously imperil the continual reproduction, on an ever-enlarging scale, of the capitalistic relation. It cannot be otherwise in a mode of production in which the labourer exists to satisfy the needs of self-expansion of existing values, instead of, on the contrary, material wealth existing to satisfy the needs of development on the part of the labourer. As, in religion, man is governed by the products of his own brain, so in capitalistic production, he is governed by the products of his own hand.

Section 3. Progressive Production of a Relative Surplus-Population or Industrial Reserve Army

The accumulation of capital, though originally appearing as its quantitative extension only, is effected, as we have seen, under a progressive qualitative change in its composition, under a constant increase of its constant, at the expense of its variable constituent.

* * *

* * * With the growth of the total capital, its variable constituent or the labour incorporated in it, also does increase, but in a constantly diminishing proportion. The intermediate pauses are shortened, in which accumulation works as simple extension of production, on a given technical basis. It is not merely that an accelerated accumulation of total capital, accelerated in a constantly growing progression, is needed to absorb an additional number of labourers, or even, on account of the constant metamorphosis of old capital, to keep employed those already functioning. In its turn, this increasing accumulation and centralisation becomes a source of new changes in the composition of capital, of a more accelerated diminution of its variable, as compared with its constant constituent. This accelerated relative diminution of the variable constituent, that goes along with the accelerated increase of the total capital, and moves more rapidly than this increase, takes the inverse form, at the other pole, of an apparently absolute increase of the labouring population, an increase always moving more rapidly than that of the variable capital or the means of employment. But in fact, it is capitalistic accumulation itself that constantly produces, and produces in the direct ratio of its own energy and extent, a relatively redundant population of labourers, i.e., a population of greater extent than suffices for the average needs of the self-expansion of capital, and therefore a surplus-population.

* * *

* * * The labouring population therefore produces, along with the accumulation of capital produced by it, the means by which itself is made relatively superfluous, is turned into a relative surplus-population; and it does this to an always increasing extent. This is a law of population peculiar to the capitalist mode of production; and in fact every special historic mode of production has its own special laws of population, historically valid within its limits alone. An abstract law of population exists for plants and animals only, and only in so far as man has not interfered with them.

But if a surplus labouring population is a necessary product of accumulation or of the development of wealth on a capitalist basis, this surplus-population becomes, conversely, the lever of capitalistic accumulation, nay, a condition of existence of the capitalist mode of production. It forms a disposable industrial reserve army, that belongs to capital quite as absolutely as if the latter had bred it at its own cost. Independently of the limits of the actual increase of population, it creates, for the changing needs of the self-expansion of capital, a mass of human material always ready for exploitation. With accumulation, and the development of the productiveness of labour that accompanies it, the power of sudden expansion of capital grows also; it grows, not merely because the elasticity of the capital already functioning increases, not merely because the absolute wealth of society expands, of which capital only forms an elastic part, not merely because credit, under every special stimulus, at once places an unusual part of this wealth at the disposal of production in the form of additional capital; it grows, also, because the technical conditions of the process of production themselves— machinery, means of transport, &c.—now admit of the rapidest transformation of masses of surplus-product into additional means of production. The mass of social wealth, overflowing with the advance of accumulation, and transformable into additional capital, thrusts itself frantically into old branches of production, whose market suddenly expands, or into newly formed branches, such as railways, &c., the need for which grows out of the development of the old ones. In all such cases, there must be the possibility of throwing great masses of men suddenly on the decisive points without injury to the scale of production in other spheres. Overpopulation supplies these masses. The course characteristic of modern industry, viz., a decennial cycle (interrupted by smaller oscillations), of periods of average activity, production at high pressure, crisis and stagnation, depends on the constant formation, the greater or less absorption, and the re-formation of the industrial reserve army or surplus-population. In their turn, the varying phases of the industrial cycle recruit the surplus-population, and become one of the most energetic agents of its reproduction. This peculiar course of modern industry, which occurs in no earlier period of human history, was also impossible in the childhood of capitalist production. The composition of capital changed but very slowly. With its accumulation, therefore, there kept pace, on the whole, a corresponding growth in the demand for labour. Slow as was the advance of accumulation compared with that of more modern times, it found a check in the natural limits of the exploitable labouring population, limits which could only be got rid of by forcible means to be mentioned later. The expansion by fits and starts of the scale of production is the preliminary to its equally sudden contraction; the latter again evokes the former, but the former is impossible without disposable human material, without an increase in the number of labourers independently of the absolute growth of the population. This increase is effected by the simple process that constantly "sets free" a part of the labourers; by methods which lessen the number of labourers employed in proportion to the increased production. The whole form of the movement of modern industry depends, therefore, upon the constant transformation of a part of the labouring population into unemployed or half-employed hands.

* * *

* * * Even Malthus recognises over-population as a necessity of modern industry, though, after his narrow fashion, he explains it by the absolute over-growth of the labouring population, not by their becoming relatively supernumerary. He says: "Prudential habits with regard to marriage, carried to a considerable extent among the labouring class of a country mainly depending upon manufactures and commerce, might injure it. . . . From the nature of a population, an increase of labourers cannot be brought into market in consequence of a particular demand till after the lapse of sixteen or eighteen years, and the conversion of revenue into capital, by saving, may take place much more rapidly; a country is always liable to an increase in the quantity of the funds for the maintenance of labour faster than the increase of population."[3] After Political Economy has thus demonstrated the constant production of a relative surplus-population of labourers to be a necessity of capitalistic accumulation, she very aptly, in the guise of an old maid, puts in the mouth of her *beau ideal* of a capitalist the following words addressed to those supernumeraries thrown on the streets by their own creation of additional capital:—"We manufacturers do what we can for you, whilst we are increasing that capital on which you must subsist, and you must do the rest by accommodating your numbers to the means of subsistence."[4]

Capitalist production can by no means content itself with the quantity of disposable labour-power which the natural increase of population yields. It requires for its free play an industrial reserve army independent of these natural limits.

Up to this point it has been assumed that the increase or diminution of the variable capital corresponds rigidly with the increase or diminution of the number of labourers employed.

3. Malthus, *Principles of Political Economy*, pp. 215, 319, 320. In this work, Malthus finally discovers, with the help of Sismondi, the beautiful Trinity of capitalistic production: over-production, over-population, over-consumption—three very delicate monsters, indeed. [*Marx*]
4. Harriet Martineau, *A Manchester Strike*, 1832, p. 101. [*Marx*]

The number of labourers commanded by capital may remain the same, or even fall, while the variable capital increases. This is the case if the individual labourer yields more labour, and therefore his wages increase, and this although the price of labour remains the same or even falls, only more slowly than the mass of labour rises. Increase of variable capital, in this case, becomes an index of more labour, but not of more labourers employed. It is the absolute interest of every capitalist to press a given quantity of labour out of a smaller, rather than a greater number of labourers, if the cost is about the same. In the latter case, the outlay of constant capital increases in proportion to the mass of labour set in action; in the former that increase is much smaller. The more extended the scale of production, the stronger this motive. Its force increases with the accumulation of capital.

We have seen that the development of the capitalist mode of production and of the productive power of labour—at once the cause and effect of accumulation—enables the capitalist, with the same outlay of variable capital, to set in action more labour by greater exploitation (extensive or intensive) of each individual labour-power. We have further seen that the capitalist buys with the same capital a greater mass of labour-power, as he progressively replaces skilled labourers by less skilled, mature labour-power by immature, male by female, that of adults by that of young persons or children.

On the one hand, therefore, with the progress of accumulation, a larger variable capital sets more labour in action without enlisting more labourers; on the other, a variable capital of the same magnitude sets in action more labour with the same mass of labour-power; and finally, a greater number of inferior labour-powers by displacement of higher.

The production of a relative surplus-population, or the setting free of labourers, goes on therefore yet more rapidly than the technical revolution of the process of production that accompanies, and is accelerated by, the advance of accumulation; and more rapidly than the corresponding diminution of the variable part of capital as compared with the constant. If the means of production, as they increase in extent and effective power, become to a less extent means of employment of labourers, this state of things is again modified by the fact that in proportion as the productiveness of labour increases, capital increases its supply of labour more quickly than its demand for labourers. The overwork of the employed part of the working-class swells the ranks of the reserve, whilst conversely the greater pressure that the latter by its competition exerts on the former, forces these to submit to over-work and to subjugation under the dictates of capital. The condemnation of one part of the working-class to enforced idleness by the over-work of the other part; and the converse, becomes a means of enriching the individual capitalists,[5] and accelerates at the same time the production of the industrial reserve army on a scale corresponding with the advance of social accumulation. How important is this element in the formation of the relative surplus-population, is shown by the example of England. Her technical means for saving labour are colossal. Nevertheless, if to-morrow morning labour generally were reduced to a rational amount, and proportioned to the different sections of the working-class according to age and sex, the working population to hand would be absolutely insufficient for the carrying on of national production on its present scale. The great majority of the labourers now "unproductive" would have to be turned into "productive" ones.

Taking them as a whole, the general movements of wages are exclusively regulated by the expansion and contraction of the industrial reserve army, and these again correspond to the periodic changes of the industrial cycle. They are, therefore, not determined by the variations of the absolute number of the working population, but by the varying proportions in which the working-class is divided into active and reserve army, by the increase or diminution in the relative amount of the surplus-population, by the extent to which it is now absorbed, now set free. For Modern Industry with its decennial cycles and periodic phases, which, moreover, as accumulation advances, are complicated by irregular oscillations following each other more and more quickly, that would indeed be a beautiful law, which pretends to make the action of capital dependent on the absolute variation of the population, instead of regulating the demand and supply of labour by the alternate expansion and con-

5. Even in the cotton famine of 1863 we find, in a pamphlet of the operative cotton-spinners of Blackburn, fierce denunciations of over-work, which, in consequence of the Factory Acts, of course only affected adult male labourers. "The adult operatives at this mill have been asked to work from twelve to thirteen hours per day, while there are hundreds who are compelled to be idle who would willingly work partial time, in order to maintain their families and save their brethren from a premature grave through being over-worked. . . . We," it goes on to say, "would ask if the practice of working overtime by a number of hands is likely to create a good feeling between masters and servants. Those who are worked over-time feel the injustice equally with those who are condemned to forced idleness. There is in the district almost sufficient work to give to all partial employment if fairly distributed. We are only asking what is right in requesting the masters generally to pursue a system of short hours, particularly until a better state of things begins to dawn upon us, rather than to work a portion of the hands over-time, while others, for want of work, are compelled to exist upon charity." ("Reports of Insp. of Fact., Oct. 31, 1863," p. 8.) The author of the "Essay on Trade and Commerce" grasps the effect of a relative surplus-population on the employed labourers with his usual unerring bourgeois instinct. "Another cause of idleness in this kingdom is the want of a sufficient number of labouring hands. . . . Whenever from extraordinary demand for manufactures, labour grows scarce, the labourers feel their own consequence, and will make their masters feel it likewise—it is amazing; but so depraved are the dispositions of these people, that in such cases a set of workmen have combined to distress the employer by idling a whole day together." ("Essay, &c.," pp. 27, 28.) The fellows in fact were hankering after a rise in wages. [*Marx*]

traction of capital, the labour-market now appearing relatively under-full, because capital is expanding, now again over-full, because it is contracting. Yet this is the dogma of the economists. According to them, wages rise in consequence of accumulation of capital. The higher wages stimulate the working population to more rapid multiplication, and this goes on until the labour-market becomes too full, and therefore capital, relatively to the supply of labour, becomes insufficient. Wages fall, and now we have the reverse of the medal. The working population is little by little decimated as the result of the fall in wages, so that capital is again in excess relatively to them, or, as others explain it, falling wages and the corresponding increase in the exploitation of the labourer again accelerates accumulation, whilst, at the same time, the lower wages hold the increase of the working-class in check. Then comes again the time, when the supply of labour is less than the demand, wages rise, and so on. A beautiful mode of motion this for developed capitalist production! Before, in consequence of the rise of wages, any positive increase of the population really fit for work could occur, the time would have been passed again and again, during which the industrial campaign must have been carried through, the battle fought and won.

* * *

The industrial reserve army, during the periods of stagnation and average prosperity, weighs down the active labour-army; during the periods of over-production and paroxysm, it holds its pretensions in check. Relative surplus-population is therefore the pivot upon which the law of demand and supply of labour works. It confines the field of action of this law within the limits absolutely convenient to the activity of exploitation and to the domination of capital.

This is the place to return to one of the grand exploits of economic apologetics. It will be remembered that if through the introduction of new, or the extension of old, machinery, a portion of variable capital is transformed into constant, the economic apologist interprets this operation which "fixes" capital and by that very act sets labourers "free," in exactly the opposite way, pretending that it sets free capital for the labourers. Only now can one fully understand the effrontery of these apologists. What are set free are not only the labourers immediately turned out by the machines, but also their future substitutes in the rising generation, and the additional contingent, that with the usual extension of trade on the old basis would be regularly absorbed. They are now all "set free," and every new bit of capital looking out for employment can dispose of them. Whether it attracts them or others, the effect on the general labour demand will be nil, if this capital is just sufficient to take out of the market as many labourers as the machines threw upon it. If it employs a smaller number, that of the supernumeraries increases; if it employs a greater, the general demand for labour only increases to the extent of the excess of the employed over those "set free." The impulse that additional capital, seeking an outlet, would otherwise have given to the general demand for labour, is therefore in every case neutralised to the extent of the labourers thrown out of employment by the machine. That is to say, the mechanism of capitalistic production so manages matters that the absolute increase of capital is accompanied by no corresponding rise in the general demand for labour. And this the apologist calls a compensation for the misery, the sufferings, the possible death of the displaced labourers during the transition period that banishes them into the industrial reserve army! The demand for labour is not identical with increase of capital, nor supply of labour with increase of the working-class. It is not a case of two independent forces working on one another. Les dés sont pipés. Capital works on both sides at the same time. If its accumulation, on the one hand, increases the demand for labour, it increases on the other the supply of labourers by the "setting free" of them, whilst at the same time the pressure of the unemployed compels those that are employed to furnish more labour, and therefore makes the supply of labour, to a certain extent, independent of the supply of labourers. The action of the law of supply and demand of labour on this basis completes the despotism of capital. As soon, therefore, as the labourers learn the secret, how it comes to pass that in the same measure as they work more, as they produce more wealth for others, and as the productive power of their labour increases, so in the same measure even their function as a means of the self-expansion of capital becomes more and more precarious for them; as soon as they discover that the degree of intensity of the competition among themselves depends wholly on the pressure of the relative surplus-population; as soon as, by Trades' Unions, &c., they try to organize a regular co-operation between employed and unemployed in order to destroy or to weaken the ruinous effects of this natural law of capitalistic production on their class, so soon capital and its sycophant, Political Economy, cry out at the infringement of the "eternal" and so to say "sacred" law of supply and demand. Every combination of employed and enemployed disturbs the "harmonious" action of this law. But, on the other hand, as soon as (in the colonies, e.g.) adverse circumstances prevent the creation of an industrial reserve army and, with it, the absolute dependence of the working-class upon the capitalist class, capital, along with its commonplace Sancho Panza, rebels against the "sacred" law of supply and demand, and tries to check its inconvenient action by forcible means and State interference.

Section 4. Different Forms of the Relative Surplus-Population. The General Law of Capitalistic Accumulation

The relative surplus-population exists in every possible form. Every labourer belongs to it during the time when he is only partially employed or wholly unemployed. Not taking into account the great periodically recurring forms that the changing phases of the industrial cycle impress on it, now an acute form during the crisis, then again a chronic form during dull times—it has always three forms, the floating, the latent, the stagnant. * * *

The lowest sediment of the relative surplus-population finally dwells in the sphere of pauperism. Exclusive of vagabonds, criminals, prostitutes, in a word, the "dangerous" classes, this layer of society consists of three categories. First, those able to work. One need only glance superficially at the statistics of English pauperism to find that the quantity of paupers increases with every crisis, and diminishes with every revival of trade. Second, orphans and pauper children. These are candidates for the industrial reserve army, and are, in times of great prosperity, as 1860, *e.g.*, speedily and in large numbers enrolled in the active army of labourers. Third, the demoralised and ragged, and those unable to work, chiefly people who succumb to their incapacity for adaptation, due to the division of labour; people who have passed the normal age of the labourer; the victims of industry, whose number increases with the increase of dangerous machinery, of mines, chemical works, &c., the mutilated, the sickly, the widows, &c. Pauperism is the hospital of the active labour-army and the dead weight of the industrial reserve army. Its production is included in that of the relative surplus-population, its necessity in theirs; along with the surplus-population, pauperism forms a condition of capitalist production, and of the capitalist development of wealth. It enters into the *faux frais* of capitalist production; but capital knows how to throw these, for the most part, from its own shoulders on to those of the working-class and the lower middle class.

The greater the social wealth, the functioning capital, the extent and energy of its growth, and, therefore, also the absolute mass of the proletariat and the productiveness of its labour, the greater is the industrial reserve army. The same causes which develop the expansive power of capital, develop also the labour-power at its disposal. The relative mass of the industrial reserve army increases therefore with the potential energy of wealth. But the greater this reserve army in proportion to the active labour-army, the greater is the mass of a consolidated surplus-population, whose misery is in inverse ratio to its torment of labour. The more extensive, finally, the lazarus-layers of the working-class, and the industrial reserve army, the greater is official pauperism. *This is the absolute general law of capitalist accumulation.* Like all other laws it is modified in its working by many circumstances, the analysis of which does not concern us here.

The folly is now patent of the economic wisdom that preaches to the labourers the accommodation of their number to the requirements of capital. The mechanism of capitalist production and accumulation constantly effects this adjustment. The first word of this adaptation is the creation of a relative surplus-population, or industrial reserve army. Its last word is the misery of constantly extending strata of the active army of labour, and the dead weight of pauperism.

The law by which a constantly increasing quantity of means of production, thanks to the advance in the productiveness of social labour, may be set in movement by a progressively diminishing expenditure of human power, this law, in a capitalist society—where the labourer does not employ the means of production, but the means of production employ the labourer—undergoes a complete inversion and is expressed thus: the higher the productiveness of labour, the greater is the pressure of the labourers on the means of employment, the more precarious, therefore, becomes their condition of existence, viz., the sale of their own labour-power for the increasing of another's wealth, or for the self-expansion of capital. The fact that the means of production, and the productiveness of labour, increase more rapidly than the productive population, expresses itself, therefore, capitalistically in the inverse form that the labouring population always increases more rapidly than the conditions under which capital can employ this increase for its own self-expansion.

We saw in Part IV., when analysing the production of relative surplus-value: within the capitalist system all methods for raising the social productiveness of labour are brought about at the cost of the individual labourer; all means for the development of production transform themselves into means of domination over, and exploitation of, the producers; they mutilate the labourer into a fragment of a man, degrade him to the level of an appendage of a machine, destroy every remnant of charm in his work and turn it into a hated toil; they estrange from him the intellectual potentialities of the labour-process in the same proportion as science is incorporated in it as an independent power; they distort the conditions under which he works, subject him during the labour-process to a despotism the more hateful for its meanness; they transform his life-time into working-time, and drag his wife and child beneath the wheels of the Juggernaut of capital. But all methods for the production of surplus-value are at the same time methods of accumulation; and every extension of accumulation becomes again a means for the development of those methods. It follows therefore that in proportion as capital accumulates, the lot of the labourer, be his payment high or low, must grow worse. The law, finally, that always equilibrates the relative surplus-population, or industrial reserve army, to the extent and energy of accumulation, this law rivets the labourer to capital more firmly than the wedges of Vulcan did Prometheus to the rock. It establishes an accumulation of misery, corresponding with accumulation of capital. Accumulation of wealth at one pole is, therefore, at the same time accumulation of misery, agony of toil, slavery, ignorance, brutality, mental degradation, at the opposite pole, *i.e.*, on the side of the class that produces its own product in the form of capital. * * *

Part VIII. The So-Called Primitive Accumulation

CHAPTER XXVI. THE SECRET OF PRIMITIVE ACCUMULATION

We have seen how money is changed into capital; how through capital surplus-value is made, and from surplus-value more capital. But the accumulation of capital pre-supposes surplus-value; surplus-value pre-supposes capitalistic production; capitalistic production pre-supposes the pre-existence of considerable masses of capital and of labour-power in the hands of producers of commodities. The whole movement, therefore, seems to turn in a vicious circle, out of which we can only get by supposing a primitive accumulation (previous accumulation of Adam Smith) preceding capitalistic accumulation; an accumulation not the result of the capitalist mode of production but its starting point.

This primitive accumulation plays in Political Economy about the same part as original sin in theology. Adam bit the apple, and thereupon sin fell on the human race. Its origin is supposed to be explained when it is told as an anecdote of the past. In times long gone by there were two sorts of people; one, the diligent, intelligent, and above all, frugal élite; the other, lazy rascals, spending their substance, and more, in riotous living. The legend of theological original sin tells us certainly how man came to be condemned to eat his bread in the sweat of his brow; but the history of economic original sin reveals to us that there are people to whom this is by no means essential. Never mind! Thus it came to pass that the former sort accumulated wealth, and the latter sort had at last nothing to sell except their own skins. And from this original sin dates the poverty of the great majority that, despite all its labour, has up to now nothing to sell but itself, and the wealth of the few that increases constantly although they have long ceased to work. Such insipid childishness is every day preached to us in the defence of property. M. Thiers, *e.g.*, had the assurance to repeat it with all the solemnity of a statesman, to the French people, once so *spirituel*. But as soon as the question of property crops up, it becomes a sacred duty to proclaim the intellectual food of the infant as the one thing fit for all ages and for all stages of development. In actual history it is notorious that conquest, enslavement, robbery, murder, briefly force, play the great part. In the tender annals of Political Economy, the idyllic reigns from time immemorial. Right and "labour" were from all time the sole means of enrichment, the present year of course always excepted. As a matter of fact, the methods of primitive accumulation are anything but idyllic.

In themselves money and commodities are no more capital than are the means of production and of subsistence. They want transforming into capital. But this transformation itself can only take place under certain circumstances that centre in this, viz., that two very different kinds of commodity-possessors must come face to face and into contact; on the one hand, the owners of money, means of production, means of subsistence, who are eager to increase the sum of values they possess, by buying other people's labour-power; on the other hand, free labourers, the sellers of their own labour-power, and therefore the sellers of labour. Free labourers, in the double sense that neither they themselves form part and parcel of the means of production, as in the case of slaves, bondsmen, &c., nor do the means of production belong to them, as in the case of peasant-proprietors; they are, therefore, free from, unencumbered by, any means of production of their own. With this polarisation of the market for commodities, the fundamental conditions of capitalist production are given. The capitalist system presupposes the complete separation of the labourers from all property in the means by which they can realise their labour. As soon as capitalist production is once on its own legs, it not only maintains this separation, but reproduces it on a continually extending scale. The process, therefore, that clears the way for the capitalist system, can be none other than the process which takes away from the labourer the possession of his means of production; a process that transforms, on the one hand, the social means of subsistence and of production into capital, on the other, the immediate producers into wage-labourers. The so-called primitive accumulation, therefore, is nothing else than the historical process of divorcing the producer from the means of production. It appears as primitive, because it forms the pre-historic stage of capital and of the mode of production corresponding with it.

The economic structure of capitalistic society has grown out of the economic structure of feudal society. The dissolution of the latter set free the elements of the former.

The immediate producer, the labourer, could only dispose of his own person after he had ceased to be attached to the soil and ceased to be the slave, serf, or bondman of another. To become a free seller of labour-power, who carries his commodity wherever he finds a market, he must further have escaped from the regime of the guilds, their rules for apprentices and journeymen, and the impediments of their labour regulations. Hence, the historical movement which changes the producers into wage-workers, appears, on the one hand, as their emancipation from serfdom and from the fetters of the guilds, and this side alone exists for our bourgeois historians. But, on the other hand, these new freedmen became sellers of themselves only after they had been robbed of all their own means of production, and of all the guarantees of existence afforded by the old feudal arrangements. And the history of this, their expropriation, is written in the annals of mankind in letters of blood and fire.

The industrial capitalists, these new potentates, had on their part not only to displace the guild masters of handicrafts, but also the feudal lords, the possessors of the sources of wealth. In this respect their conquest of social power appears as the fruit of a victorious struggle both against feudal lordship and its revolting prerogatives, and against the guilds and the fetters they laid on the free development of production and the free exploitation of man by man. The chevaliers d'industrie, however, only succeeded in supplanting the chevaliers of the sword by making use of events of which they themselves were wholly innocent. They have risen by means as vile as those by which the Roman freedman once on a time made himself the master of his *patronus*.

The starting-point of the development that gave rise to the wage-labourer as well as to the capitalist, was the servitude of the labourer. The advance consisted in a change of form of this servitude, in the transformation of feudal exploitation into capitalist exploitation. To understand its march, we need not go back very far. Although we come across the first beginnings of capitalist production as early as the 14th or 15th century, sporadically, in certain towns of the Mediterranean, the capitalistic era dates from the 16th century. Wherever it appears, the abolition of serfdom has been long effected, and the highest development of the middle ages, the existence of sovereign towns, has been long on the wane.

In the history of primitive accumulation, all revolutions are epoch-making that act as levers for the capitalist class in course of formation; but, above all, those moments when great masses of men are suddenly and forcibly torn from their means of subsistence, and hurled as free and "unattached" proletarians on the labour-market. The expropriation of the agricultural producer, of the peasant, from the soil, is the basis of the whole process. The history of this expropriation, in different countries, assumes different aspects, and runs through its various phases in different orders of succession, and at different periods. In England alone, which we take as our example, has it the classic form.

CHAPTER XXVII. EXPROPRIATION OF THE AGRICULTURAL POPULATION FROM THE LAND

In England, serfdom had practically disappeared in the last part of the 14th century. The immense majority of the population consisted then, and to a still larger extent, in the 15th century, of free peasant proprietors, whatever was the feudal title under which their right of property was hidden. * * *

The prelude of the revolution that laid the foundation of the capitalist mode of production, was played in the last third of the 15th, and the first decade of the 16th century. A mass of free proletarians was hurled on the labour-market by the breaking-up of the bands of feudal retainers, who, as Sir James Steuart well says, "everywhere uselessly filled house and castle." Although the royal power, itself a product of bourgeois development, in its strife after absolute sovereignty forcibly hastened on the dissolution of these bands of retainers, it was by no means the sole cause of it. In insolent conflict with king and parliament, the great feudal lords created an incomparably larger proletariat by the forcible driving of the peasantry from the land, to which the latter had the same feudal right as the lord himself, and by the usurpation of the common lands. The rapid rise of the Flemish wool manufactures, and the corresponding rise in the price of wool in England, gave the direct impulse to these evictions. The old nobility had been devoured by the great feudal wars. The new nobility was the child of its time, for which money was the power of all powers. Transformation of arable land into sheep-walks was, therefore, its cry. * * *

With the development of capitalist production during the manufacturing period, the public opinion of Europe had lost the last remnant of shame and conscience. The nations bragged cynically of every infamy that served them as a means to capitalistic accumulation. Read, *e.g.*, the naïve Annals of Commerce of the worthy A. Anderson. Here it is trumpeted forth as a triumph of English statecraft that at the Peace of Utrecht, England extorted from the Spaniards by the Asiento Treaty the privilege of being allowed to ply the negro-trade, until then only carried on between Africa and the English West Indies, between Africa and Spanish America as well. England thereby acquired the right of supplying Spanish America until 1743 with 4,800 negroes yearly. This threw, at the same time, an official cloak over British smuggling. Liverpool waxed fat on the slave-trade. This was its method of primitive accumulation. And, even to the present day, Liverpool "respectability" is the Pindar of the slave-trade which—compare the work of Aikin [1795] already quoted—"has coincided with that spirit of bold adventure which has characterised the trade of Liverpool and rapidly carried it to its present state of prosperity; has occasioned vast employment for shipping and sailors, and greatly augmented the demand for the manufactures of the country" (p. 339). Liverpool employed in the slave-trade, in 1730, 15 ships; in 1751, 53; in 1760, 74; in 1770, 96; and in 1792, 132.

Whilst the cotton industry introduced child-slavery in England, it gave in the United States a stimulus to the transformation of the earlier, more or less patriarchal slavery, into a system of commercial exploitation. In fact, the veiled slavery of the wage-workers in Europe needed, for its pedestal, slavery pure and simple in the new world.

Tantæ molis erat, to establish the "eternal laws of Nature" of the capitalist mode of production, to complete the process of separation between labourers and conditions of labour, to transform, at one pole, the social means of production and subsistence into capital, at the opposite pole, the mass of the population into wage-labourers, into "free labouring poor," that artificial product of modern society. If money, according to Augier, "comes into the world with a congenital blood-stain on one cheek," capital comes dripping from head to foot, from every pore, with blood and dirt.

CHAPTER XXXI. GENESIS OF THE INDUSTRIAL CAPITALIST

The genesis of the industrial capitalist did not proceed in such a gradual way as that of the farmer. Doubtless many small guild-masters, and yet more independent small artisans, or even wage-labourers, transformed themselves into small capitalists, and (by gradually extending exploitation of wage-labour and corresponding accumulation) into full-blown capitalists. In the infancy of capitalist production, things often happened as in the infancy of mediaeval towns, where the question which of the escaped serfs should be master and which servant, was in great part decided by the earlier or later date of their flight. * * *

* * *

The discovery of gold and silver in America, the extirpation, enslavement and entombment in mines of the aboriginal population, the beginning of the conquest and looting of the East Indies, the turning of Africa into a warren for the commercial hunting of black-skins, signalised the rosy dawn of the era of capitalist production.

These idyllic proceedings are the chief momenta of primitive accumulation. On their heels treads the commercial war of the European nations, with the globe for a theatre. It begins with the revolt of the Netherlands from Spain, assumes giant dimensions in England's Anti-Jacobin War, and is still going on in the opium wars against China, &c.

The different momenta of primitive accumulation distribute themselves now, more or less in chronological order, particularly over Spain, Portugal, Holland, France, and England. In England at the end of the 17th century, they arrive at a systematical combination, embracing the colonies, the national debt, the modern mode of taxation, and the protectionist system. These methods depend in part on brute force, *e.g.*, the colonial system. But they all employ the power of the State, the concentrated and organised force of society, to hasten, hothouse fashion, the process of transformation of the feudal mode of production into the capitalist mode, and to shorten the transition. Force is the midwife of every old society pregnant with a new one. It is itself an economic power.

* * *

CHAPTER XXXII. HISTORICAL TENDENCY OF CAPITALIST ACCUMULATION

What does the primitive accumulation of capital, *i.e.*, its historical genesis, resolve itself into? In so far as it is not immediate transformation of slaves and serfs into wage-labourers, and therefore a mere change of form, it only means the expropriation of the immediate producers, *i.e.*, the dissolution of private property based on the labour of its owner. Private property, as the antithesis to social, collective property, exists only where the means of labour and the external conditions of labour belong to private individuals. But according as these private individuals are labourers or not labourers, private property has a different character. The numberless shades, that it at first sight presents, correspond to the intermediate stages lying between these two extremes. The private property of the labourer in his means of production is the foundation of petty industry, whether agricultural, manufacturing, or both; petty industry, again, is an essential condition for the development of social production and of the free individuality of the labourer himself. Of course, this petty mode of production exists also under slavery, serfdom, and other states of dependence. But it flourishes, it lets loose its whole energy, it attains its adequate classical form, only where the labourer is the private owner of his own means of labour set in action by himself: the peasant of the land which he cultivates, the artisan of the tool which he handles as a virtuoso. This mode of production pre-supposes parcelling of the soil, and scattering of the other means of production. As it excludes the concentration of these means of production, so also it excludes co-operation, division of labour within each separate process of production, the control over, and the productive application of the forces of Nature by society, and the free development of the social productive powers. It is compatible only with a system of production, and a society, moving within narrow and more or less primitive bounds. To perpetuate it would be, as Pecqueur rightly says, "to decree universal mediocrity." At a certain stage of development it brings forth the material agencies for its own dissolution. From that moment new forces and new passions spring up in the bosom of society; but the old social organisation fetters them and keeps them down. It must be annihilated; it is annihilated. Its annihilation, the transformation of the individualised and scattered means of production into socially concentrated ones, of the pigmy property of the many into the huge property of the few, the expropriation of the great mass of the people from the soil, from the means of subsistence, and from the means of labour, this fearful and painful expropriation of the mass of the people forms the prelude to the history of capital. It comprises a series of forcible methods, of which we have passed in review only those that have been epoch-making as methods of the primitive accumulation of capital. The expropriation of the immediate producers was accomplished with merciless Vandalism, and under the stimulus of passions the most infamous, the most sordid, the pettiest, the most meanly odious. Self-earned private property, that is based, so to say, on the fusing together of the isolated, independent labouring-individual with the conditions of his labour, is supplanted by capitalistic private property, which rests on exploitation of the nominally free labour of others, *i.e.*, on wage-labour.

As soon as this process of transformation has sufficiently decomposed the old society from top to bottom, as soon as the labourers are turned into proletarians, their means of labour into capital, as soon as the capitalist mode of production stands on its own feet, then the further socialisation of labour and further transformation of the land and other means of production into socially exploited and, therefore, common means of production, as well as the further expropriation of private proprietors, takes a new form. That which is now to be expropriated is no longer the labourer working for himself, but the capitalist exploiting many labourers. This expropriation is accomplished by the action of the immanent laws of capitalistic production itself, by the centralisation of capital. One capitalist always kills many. Hand in hand with this centralisation, or this expropriation of many capitalists by a few, develop, on an ever-extending scale, the co-operative form of the labour-process, the conscious technical application of science, the methodical cultivation of the soil, the transformation of the instruments of labour into instruments of labour only usable in common, the economising of all means of production by their use as the means of production of combined, socialised labour, the entanglement of all peoples in the net of the world-market, and with this, the international character of the capitalistic régime. Along with the constantly diminishing number of the magnates of capital, who usurp and monopolise all advantages of this process of transformation, grows the mass of misery, oppression, slavery, degradation, exploitation; but with this too grows the revolt of the working-class, a class always increasing in numbers, and disciplined, united, organised by the very mechanism of the process of capitalist production itself. The monopoly of capital becomes a fetter upon the mode of production, which has sprung up and flourished along with, and under it. Centralisation of the means of production and socialisation of labour at last reach a point where they become incompatible with their capitalist integument. This integument is burst asunder. The knell of capitalist private property sounds. The expropriators are expropriated.

The capitalist mode of appropriation, the result of the capitalist mode of production, produces capitalist private property. This is the first negation of individual private property, as founded on the labour of the proprietor. But capitalist production begets, with the inexorability of a law of Nature, its own negation. It is the negation of negation. This does not re-establish private property for the producer, but gives him individual property based on the acquisitions of the capitalist era: i.e., on co-operation and the possession in common of the land and of the means of production.

The transformation of scattered private property, arising from individual labour, into capitalist private property is, naturally, a process, incomparably more protracted, violent, and difficult, than the transformation of capitalistic private property, already practically resting on socialised production, into socialised property. In the former case, we had the expropriation of the mass of the people by a few usurpers; in the latter, we have the expropriation of a few usurpers by the mass of the people.

Capital, Volume Three

KARL MARX

Volumes Two and Three of *Capital*, left in incomplete manuscript by Marx, were later edited and brought out by Engels. Two excerpts from Volume Three are presented here.

The first (whose title has been given by the editor of this reader) gives Marx's vision of man in a future condition of freedom—creative leisure—made possible by machine industry and the worldwide proletarian revolution that, as he saw it, was destined to liberate man's productive activity from the fetters of capitalist acquisitiveness. But there would remain, in this realm of freedom, a residual realm of necessity: the labour time required to produce needed goods under even the most advanced technology.

The second selection is the famous last chapter of Volume Three, entitled "Classes," in which the manuscript breaks off after Marx has asked: "What constitutes a class?" In fact, there is no mystery about his answer. A class, in Marx's view, is a special form of the division of labor in society.*

On the Realm of Necessity and the Realm of Freedom

We have seen that the capitalist process of production is a historically determined form of the social process of production in general. The latter is as much a production process of material conditions of human life as a process taking place under specific historical and economic production relations, producing and reproducing these production relations themselves, and thereby also the bearers of this process, their material conditions of existence and their mutual relations, i.e., their particular socio-economic form. For the aggregate of these relations, in which the agents of this production stand with respect to Nature and to one another, and in which they produce, is precisely society, considered from the standpoint of its economic structure. Like all its predecessors, the capitalist process of production proceeds under definite material conditions, which are, however, simultaneously the bearers of definite social relations entered into by individuals in the process of reproducing

---

* See, for example, his statement in *The Eighteenth Brumaire of Louis Bonaparte* (p. 608, below): "In so far as millions of families live under economic conditions of existence that divide their mode of life, their interests and their culture from those of the other classes, and put them in hostile contrast to the latter, they form a class."

439

their life. Those conditions, like these relations, are on the one hand prerequisites, on the other hand results and creations of the capitalist process of production; they are produced and reproduced by it. We saw also that capital—and the capitalist is merely capital personified and functions in the process of production solely as the agent of capital—in its corresponding social process of production, pumps a definite quantity of surplus labour out of the direct producers, or labourers; capital obtains this surplus labour without an equivalent, and in essence it always remains forced labour—no matter how much it may seem to result from free contractual agreement. This surplus labour appears as surplus value, and this surplus value exists as a surplus product. Surplus labour in general, as labour performed over and above the given requirements, must always remain. In the capitalist as well as in the slave system, etc., it merely assumes an antagonistic form and is supplemented by complete idleness of a stratum of society. A definite quantity of surplus labour is required as insurance against accidents, and by the necessary and progressive expansion of the process of reproduction in keeping with the development of the needs and the growth of population, which is called accumulation from the viewpoint of the capitalist. It is one of the civilizing aspects of capital that it enforces this surplus labour in a manner and under conditions which are more advantageous to the development of the productive forces, social relations, and the creation of the elements for a new and higher form than under the preceding forms of slavery, serfdom, etc. Thus it gives rise to a stage, on the one hand, in which coercion and monopolization of social development (including its material and intellectual advantages) by one portion of society at the expense of the other are eliminated; on the other hand, it creates the material means and embryonic conditions, making it possible in a higher form of society to combine this surplus labour with a greater reduction of time devoted to material labour in general. For, depending on the development of labour productivity, surplus labour may be large in a small total working day, and relatively small in a large total working day. If the necessary labour time $=$ 3 and the surplus labour $= 3$, then the total working day $= 6$ and the rate of surplus labour $= 100\%$. If the necessary labour $= 9$ and the surplus labour $= 3$, then the total working day $= 12$ and the rate of surplus labour only $33\frac{1}{3}\%$. In that case, it depends upon the labour productivity how much use value shall be produced in a definite time, hence also in a definite surplus labour time. The actual wealth of society, and the possibility of constantly expanding its reproduction process, therefore, do not depend upon the duration of surplus labour, but upon its productivity and the more or less copious conditions of production under which it is performed. In fact, the realm of freedom actually begins only where labour which is determined by necessity and mundane considerations ceases; thus in the very nature of things it lies beyond the sphere of actual material production. Just as the savage must wrestle with Nature to satisfy his wants, to maintain and reproduce life, so must civilized man, and he must do so in all social formations and under all possible modes of production. With his development this realm of physical necessity expands as a result of his wants; but, at the same time, the forces of production which satisfy these wants also increase. Freedom in this field can only consist in socialized man, the associated producers, rationally regulating their interchange with Nature, bringing it under their common control, instead of being ruled by it as by the blind forces of Nature; and achieving this with the least expenditure of energy and under conditions most favourable to, and worthy of, their human nature. But it nonetheless still remains a realm of necessity. Beyond it begins that development of human energy which is an end in itself, the true realm of freedom, which, however, can blossom forth only with the realm of necessity as its basis. The shortening of the working day is its basic prerequisite.

Classes

The owners merely of labour-power, owners of capital, and landowners, whose respective sources of income are wages, profit and ground-rent, in other words, wage-labourers, capitalists and landowners, constitute then three big classes of modern society based upon the capitalist mode of production.

In England, modern society is indisputably most highly and classically developed in economic structure. Nevertheless, even here the stratification of classes does not appear in its pure form. Middle and intermediate strata even here obliterate lines of demarcation everywhere (although incomparably less in rural districts than in the cities). However, this is immaterial for our analysis. We have seen that the continual tendency and law of development of the capitalist mode of production is more and more to divorce the means of production from labour and more and more to concentrate the scattered means of production into large groups, thereby transforming labour into wage-labour and the means of production into capital. And to this tendency, on the other hand, corresponds the independent separation of landed property from capital and labour, or the transformation of all landed property into the form of landed property corresponding to the capitalist mode of production.

The first question to be answered is this: What constitutes a class?—and the reply to this follows naturally from the reply to another question, namely: What makes wage-labourers, capitalists and landlords constitute the three great social classes?

At first glance—the identity of revenues and sources of revenue. There are three great social groups whose members, the individuals forming them, live on wages, profit and ground-rent respectively, on the realisation of their labour-power, their capital, and their landed property.

However, from this standpoint, physicians and officials, e.g., would also constitute two classes, for they belong to two distinct social groups, the members of each of these groups receiving their revenue from one and the same source. The same would also be true of the infinite fragmentation of interest and rank into which the division of social labour splits labourers as well as capitalists and landlords—the latter, e.g., into owners of vineyards, farm owners, owners of forests, mine owners and owners of fisheries.[1]

1. Here the manuscript breaks off.

Crisis Theory

KARL MARX

Business cycles and the related though not identical topic of economic crises fascinated Marx. He invested much time in their study and often indicated how important he considered their impact on society and political systems. Yet he left no developed account of his views on crises. The selection presented here comes from one of Marx's most underappreciated works, *Theories of Surplus Value*, a three-volume work which has sometimes been described as Volume Four of *Capital*.

It is Chapter XVII of this work, and not *Capital* proper, that contains the best and most systematic discussion by Marx of economic crises. The discussion takes the form of an attack on Say's Law of Markets. This was an argument, put forward by Jean-Baptiste Say (1767–1832) and James Mill (1773–1836) and accepted by David Ricardo (1772–1823), for the impossibility of a sustained general glut (of "overproduced" commodities). It is interesting that Marx's attack, like modern criticism of Say, centers on the potentially grave consequences for economic equilibrium of the generalization of the money economy.*

Ricardo's Denial of General Over-Production. Possibility of a Crisis Inherent in the Inner Contradictions of Commodity and Money

* * *

So far as crises are concerned, all those writers who describe the real movement of prices, or all experts, who write in the actual situation of a crisis, have been right in ignoring the allegedly theoretical twaddle and in contenting themselves with the idea that what may be true in abstract theory—namely, that no gluts of the market and so forth are possible—is, nevertheless, wrong in practice. The constant recurrence of crises has in fact reduced the rigmarole of Say and others to a phraseology which is now only used in times of prosperity but is cast aside in times of crises.

In the crises of the world market, the contradictions and antagonisms of bourgeois production are strikingly revealed. Instead of investigating the nature of the conflicting elements which erupt in the catastrophe, the apologists content themselves with denying the catastrophe itself and insisting, in the face of their regular and periodic recurrence, that if production were carried on according to the

* The above headnote was prepared by Thomas Ferguson. [R. T.]

textbooks, crises would never occur. Thus the apologetics consist in the falsification of the simplest economic relations, and particularly in clinging to the concept of unity in the face of contradiction.

If, for example, purchase and sale—or the metamorphosis of commodities—represent the unity of two processes, or rather the movement of one process through two opposite phases, and thus essentially the unity of the two phases, the movement is essentially just as much the separation of these two phases and their becoming independent of each other. Since, however, they belong together, the independence of the two correlated aspects can only *show itself* forcibly, as a destructive process. It is just the *crises* in which they assert their unity, the unity of the different aspects. The independence which these two linked and complementary phases assume in relation to each other is forcibly destroyed. Thus the crisis manifests the unity of the two phases that have become independent of each other. There would be no crisis without this inner unity of factors that are apparently indifferent to each other. But no, says the apologetic economist. Because there is this unity, there can be *no* crises. Which in turn means nothing but that the unity of contradictory factors excludes contradiction.

In order to prove that capitalist production cannot lead to general crises, all its conditions and distinct forms, all its principles and specific features—in short *capitalist production* itself—are denied. In fact it is demonstrated that if the capitalist mode of production had not developed in a specific way and become a unique form of social production, but were a mode of production dating back to the most rudimentary stages, then its peculiar contradictions and conflicts and hence also their eruption in crises would not exist.

Following Say, Ricardo writes: "Productions are always bought by productions, or by services; money is only the medium by which the exchange is effected" (341). Here, therefore, firstly *commodity*, in which the contradiction between exchange-value and use-value exists, becomes mere product (use-value) and therefore the exchange of commodities is transformed into mere barter of products, of simple use-values. This is a return not only to the time before capitalist production, but even to the time before there was simple commodity production; and the most complicated phenomenon of capitalist production—the world market crises—is flatly denied, by denying the first condition of capitalist production, namely, that the product must be a commodity and therefore express itself as money and undergo the process of metamorphosis. Instead of speaking of wage-labour, the term "services" is used. This word again omits the specific characteristic of wage-labour and of its use—namely, that it increases the value of the commodities against which it is exchanged, that it creates surplus-value—and in doing so, it disregards the specific relationship through which money and commodities are transformed into capital. *"Service"* is labour seen only as *use-value* (which is a side issue in capitalist production) just as the term *"productions"* fails to express the essence of *commodity* and its inherent contradiction. It is quite consistent that *money* is then regarded merely as an intermediary in the exchange of products, and not as an essential and necessary form of existence of the commodity which must manifest itself as exchange-value, as general social labour. Since the transformation of the commodity into mere use-value (product) obliterates the essence of exchange-value, it is just as easy to deny, or rather it is necessary to deny, that *money* is an essential aspect of the commodity and that in the process of metamorphosis it is *independent* of the original form of the commodity.

Crises are thus reasoned out of existence here by forgetting or denying the first elements of capitalist production: the existence of the product as a commodity, the duplication of the commodity in commodity and money, the consequent separation which takes place in the exchange of commodities and finally the relation of money or commodities to wage-labour.

Incidentally, those economists are no better, who (like John Stuart Mill) want to explain the crises by these simple *possibilities* of crisis contained in the metamorphosis of commodities—such as the separation between purchase and sale. These factors which explain the possibility of crises, by no means explain their actual occurrence. They do not explain *why* the phases of the process come into such conflict that their inner unity can only assert itself through a crisis, through a violent process. This *separation* appears in the crisis; it is the elementary form of the crisis. To *explain* the crisis on the basis of this, its elementary form, is to explain the existence of the crisis by describing its most abstract form, that is to say, to explain the crisis by the crisis. Ricardo says:

> No man produces, but with a view to consume or *sell*, and he never sells, but with an intention to *purchase* some other commodity, which may be immediately useful to him, or which may contribute to *future production*. By producing, then, he necessarily becomes either the consumer of his own goods, or the purchaser and consumer of the goods of some person. It is not to be supposed that he should, *for any length of time*, be ill-informed of the commodities which he can most advantageously produce, to attain the object which he has in view, namely, the *possession of other goods*; and, *therefore*, it is not probable that he will *continually* produce a commodity for which there is no demand. [Pp. 339–40.]

This is the childish babble of a Say, but it is not worthy of Ricardo. In the first place, no capitalist produces in order to consume his product. And when speaking of capitalist production, it is right to say that: "no man produces with a view to consume his own product," even if he uses portions of his product for industrial consumption. But here the point in question is private consumption. Previously it was forgotten that the product is a commodity. Now even the social division of labour is forgotten. In a situation where men produce for themselves, there are indeed no crises, but neither is there capitalist production. Nor have we ever heard that the ancients, with their slave production ever knew crises, although individual producers among the ancients too, did go bankrupt. The first part of the alternative is nonsense. The second as well. A man who has produced does not have the choice of selling or not selling. He must *sell*. In the crisis there arises the very situation in which he cannot sell or can only sell below the cost-price or must even sell at a positive loss. What difference does it make, therefore, to him or to us that he has produced in order to sell? The very question we want to solve is what has thwarted this good intention of his?

Further: he "never *sells*, but with an intention to *purchase* some other commodity, which may be immediately useful to him, or which may contribute to future production" (p. 339).

What a cosy description of bourgeois conditions! Ricardo even forgets that a person may *sell* in order to *pay*, and that these forced sales play a very significant role in the crises. The capitalist's immediate object in selling, is to turn his commodity, or rather his commodity capital, back into *money capital*, and thereby to *realise* his profit. Consumption—revenue—is by no means the guiding motive in this process, although it is for the person who only sells *commodities* in order to transform them into means of subsistence. But this is not capitalist production, in which revenue appears as the result and not as the determining purpose. Everyone *sells* first of all in order to sell, that is to say, in order to transform commodities into money.

During the crisis, a man may be very pleased, if he has *sold* his commodities without immediately thinking of a purchase. On the other hand, if the value that has been realised is again to be used as capital, it must go through the process of reproduction, that is, it must be exchanged for labour and commodities. But the crisis is precisely the phase of disturbance and interruption of the process of reproduction. And this disturbance cannot be explained by the fact that it does not occur in those times when there is no crisis. There is no doubt that no one "will continually produce a commodity for which there is no demand" (p. 340), but no one is talking about such an absurd hypothesis. Nor has it anything to do with the problem. The immediate purpose of capitalist production is not "the possession of other goods," but the appropriation of value, of money, of abstract wealth.

Ricardo's statements here are also based on James Mill's proposition on the "metaphysical equilibirum of purchases and sales," which I examined previously—an equilibrium which sees *only* the unity, but not the separation in the processes of purchase and sale. Hence also Ricardo's assertion (following James Mill): "Too much of a *particular* commodity may be produced, of which there may be such a glut in the market, as not to repay the capital expended on it; but this cannot be the case with respect to *all* commodities" (pp. 341–42).

Money is not only "the medium by which the exchange is effected" (p. 341), but at the same time the medium by which the exchange of product with product is divided into two acts, which are independent of each other, and separate in time and space. With Ricardo, however, this false conception of money is due to the fact that he concentrates exclusively on the *quantitative determination* of exchange-value, namely, that it is equal to a definite quantity of labour-time, forgetting on the other hand the *qualitative* characteristic, that individual labour must present itself as *abstract, general social* labour only through its alienation.[1]

That only *particular* commodities, and not *all* kinds of commodities, can form "a glut in the market" and that therefore over-production can always only be partial, is a poor way out. In the first place, if we consider only the nature of the commodity, there is nothing to prevent *all commodities* from being super-abundant on the market, and therefore all falling below their price. We are here only concerned with the factor of crisis. That is all commodities, apart from money [may be super-abundant]. [The proposition] *the* commodity must be converted into money, only means that: *all* commodities must do so. And just as the difficulty of undergoing this metamorphosis exists for an individual commodity, so it can exist for all commodities. The general nature of the metamorphosis of commodities—which includes the separation of purchase and sale just as it does their unity—instead of excluding the *possibility* of a general glut, on the contrary, contains the possibility of a general glut.

Ricardo's and similar types of reasoning are moreover based not only on the relation of *purchase and sale*, but also on that of *demand and supply*, which we have to examine only when considering the competition of capitals. As Mill says, purchase is sale etc., therefore demand is supply and supply demand. But they also fall apart and can become independent of each other. At a given

1. That Ricardo [regards] money merely as *means of circulation* is synonymous with his regarding *exchange-value* as a merely transient form, and altogether as something purely formal in bourgeois or capitalist production, which is consequently for him not a specific definite mode of production, but simply *the* mode of production. [*Marx*]

moment, the supply of all commodities can be greater than the demand for all commodities, since the demand for the *general commodity*, money, exchange-value, is greater than the demand for all particular commodities, in other words the motive to turn the commodity into money, to realise its exchange-value, prevails over the motive to transform the commodity again into use-value.

If relation of demand and supply is taken in a wider and more concrete sense, then it comprises the relation of *production* and *consumption* as well. Here again the *unity* of these two phases, which does exist and which forcibly asserts itself during the crisis, must be seen as opposed to the *separation* and *antagonism* of these two phases, separation and antagonism which exist just as much, and are moreover typical of bourgeois production.

With regard to the contradiction between partial and universal over-production, in so far as the existence of the former is affirmed in order to evade the latter, the following observation may be made:

Firstly: Crises are usually preceded by a general inflation in prices of all articles of capitalist production. All of them therefore participate in the subsequent crash and at their former prices they cause a glut in the market. The market can absorb a larger volume of commodities at falling prices, at prices which have fallen below their cost-prices, than it could absorb at their former prices. The excess of commodities is always relative; in other words it is an excess at particular prices. The prices at which the commodities are then absorbed are ruinous for the producer or merchant.

Secondly: For a crisis (and therefore also for over-production) to be general, it suffices for it to affect the principal commercial goods.

Ricardo's Wrong Conception of the Relation Between Production and Consumption Under the Conditions of Capitalism

Let us take a closer look at how Ricardo seeks to deny the possibility of a general glut in the market:

Too much of a particular commodity may be produced, of which there may be such a glut in the market, as not to repay the capital expended on it; but this cannot be the case with respect to all commodities; the demand for corn is limited by the mouths which are to eat it, for shoes and coats by the persons who are to wear them; but through a community, or a part of a community, may have as much corn, and as many hats and shoes, as it is able or may wish to consume, *the same cannot be said of every commodity produced by nature or by art*. Some would consume more wine, if they had the ability to procure it. Others having enough of wine, would to increase the quantity or improve the quality of their furniture. Others might wish to ornament their grounds, or to enlarge their houses. The wish to do all or some of these is implanted in every man's breast; *nothing is required but the means, and nothing can afford the means, but an increase of production.* [Pp. 341–42.]

Could there be a more childish argument? It runs like this: more of a particular commodity may be produced than can be consumed of it; but this cannot apply to *all* commodities at the same time. Because the needs, which the commodities satisfy, have no limits and all these needs are not satisfied at the same time. On the contrary. The fulfillment of one need makes another, so to speak, latent. Thus nothing is required, but the means to satisfy these wants, and these means can only be provided through an increase in production. Hence no general overproduction is possible.

What is the purpose of all this? In periods of over-production, a large part of the nation (especially the working class) is less well provided than ever with corn, shoes etc., not to speak of wine and furniture. If over-production could only occur when all the members of a nation had satisfied even their most urgent needs, there could never, in the history of bourgeois society up to now, have been a state of general over-production or even of partial over-production. When, for instance, the market is glutted by shoes or calicoes or wines or colonial products, does this perhaps mean that four-sixths of the nation have more than satisfied their needs in shoes, calicoes etc.? What after all has over-production to do with absolute needs? It is only concerned with demand that is backed by ability to pay. It is not a question of absolute over-production—over-production as such in relation to the absolute need or the desire to possess commodities. In this sense there is neither partial nor general over-production; and the one is not opposed to the other.

But—Ricardo will say—when there are a lot of people who want shoes and calicoes, why do they not obtain the means to acquire them, by producing something which will enable them to buy shoes and calicoes? Would it not be even simpler to say: Why do they not produce shoes and calicoes for themselves? An even stranger aspect of over-production is that the workers, the actual producers of the very commodities which glut the market, are in need of these commodities. It cannot be said here that they should produce things in order to obtain them, for they have produced them and yet they have not got them. Nor can it be said that a particular commodity gluts the market, because no one is in want of it. If, therefore, it is even impossible to explain that *partial* over-production arises because the demand for the commodities that glut the market has been more than satisfied, it is quite impossible to explain away *universal* over-production by declaring that needs, unsatisfied needs, exist for many of the commodities which are on the market.

Let us keep to the example of the weaver of calico. So long as reproduction continued uninterruptedly—and therefore also the phase of this reproduction in which the product existing as a saleable commodity, the calico, was reconverted into money, at its value—so long, shall we say, the workers who produced the calico, also consumed a part of it, and with the expansion of reproduction, that is to say, with accumulation, they were consuming more of it, or also more workers were employed in the production of calico, who also consumed part of it.

Crisis, Which Was a Contingency, Becomes a Certainty. The Crisis as the Manifestation of All the Contradictions of Bourgeois Economy.

Now before we proceed further, the following must be said:

The *possibility* of crisis, which became apparent in the *simple metamorphosis* of the commodity, is once more demonstrated, and further developed, by the disjunction between the (direct) process of production and the process of circulation. As soon as these processes do not merge smoothly into one another but become independent of one another, the crisis is there.

The possibility of crisis is indicated in the metamorphosis of the commodity like this:

Firstly, the commodity which actually exists as use-value, and nominally, in its price, as exchange-value, must be transformed into money. C—M. If this difficulty, the sale, is solved then the purchase, M—C, presents no difficulty, since money is directly exchangeable for everything else. The use-value of the commodity, the usefulness of the labour contained in it, must be assumed from the start, otherwise it is no commodity at all. It is further assumed that the individual value of the commodity is equal to its social value, that is to say, that the labour-time materialised in it is equal to the socially *necessary* labour-time for the production of this commodity. The possibility of a crisis, in so far as it shows itself in the simple form of metamorphosis, thus only arises from the fact that the differences in form—the phases—which it passes through in the course of its progress, are in the first place necessarily complementary and secondly, despite this intrinsic and necessary correlation, they are distinct parts and forms of the process, independent of each other, diverging in time and space, separable and separated from each other. The possibility of crisis therefore lies solely in the separation of sale from purchase. It is thus only in the form of commodity that the commodity has to pass through this difficulty here.

As soon as it assumes the form of money it has got over this difficulty. Subsequently however this too resolves into the separation of sale and purchase. If the commodity could not be withdrawn from circulation in the form of money or its retransformation into commodity could not be postponed—as with direct barter—if purchase and sale coincided, then the *possibility* of crisis would, under the assumptions made, disappear. For it is assumed that the commodity represents *use-value* for other owners of commodities. In the form of direct barter, the commodity is not exchangeable only if it has no use-value or when there are no other use-values on the other side which can be exchanged for it; therefore, only under these two conditions: either if one side has produced *useless* things or if the other side has nothing *useful* to exchange as an equivalent for the first use-value. In both cases, however, no exchange whatsoever would take place. *But in so far as exchange did take place,* its phases would not be separated. The buyer would be seller and the seller buyer. The *critical* stage, which arises from the form of the exchange—in so far as it is circulation—would therefore cease to exist, and if we say that the simple form of metamorphosis comprises the possibility of crisis, we only say that in this form itself lies the possibility of the rupture and separation of essentially complimentary phases.

But this applies also to the content. In direct barter, the bulk of production is intended by the producer to satisfy his own needs, or, where the division of labour is more developed, to satisfy the needs of his fellow producers, needs that are known to him. What is exchanged as a commodity is the surplus and it is unimportant whether this surplus is exchanged or not. In *commodity production* the conversion of the product into money, the sale, is a *conditio sine qua non.* Direct production for personal needs does not take place. Crisis results from the impossibility to sell. The difficulty of transforming the *commodity*—the particular product of individual labour—into its opposite, money, i.e., abstract general social labour, lies in the fact that *money* is not the particular product of individual labour, and that the person who has effected a sale, who therefore has commodities in the form of money, is not compelled to buy again at once, to transform the money again into a particular product of individual labour. In barter this contradiction does not exist: no one can be a seller without being a buyer or a buyer without being a seller. The difficulty of the seller—on the assumption that his commodity has use-value—only stems from the ease with which the buyer can defer the retransformation of money into commodity. The difficulty of converting the commodity into money, of selling it, only arises from the fact that the commodity must be turned into money but the money need not be immediately turned into commodity, and therefore *sale* and *purchase* can be separated. We have said that this *form* contains the *possibility of crisis*, that is to say, the possibility that elements which are correlated, which are inseparable, are separated and consequently are forcibly reunited, their coherence is violently asserted against their mutual independence. *Crisis* is nothing but the forcible assertion of the unity of phases of the production process which have become independent of each other.

The general, abstract possibility of crisis denotes no more than the *most abstract form* of crisis, without content, without a compelling motivating factor. Sale and purchase may fall apart. They thus represent potential *crisis* and their coincidence always remains a critical factor for the commodity. The transition from one to the other may, however, proceed smoothly. The *most abstract form of crisis* (and therefore the formal possibility of crisis) is thus the *metamorphosis of the commodity* itself; the contradiction of exchange-value and use-value, and furthermore of money and commodity, comprised within the unity of the commodity, exists in metamorphosis only as an involved movement. The factors which turn this possibility of crisis into [an actual] crisis are not contained in this form itself; it only implies that *the framework* for a crisis exists.

And in a consideration of the bourgeois economy, that is the important thing. The world trade crises must be regarded as the real concentration and forcible adjustment of all the contradictions of bourgeois economy. The individual factors, which are condensed in these crises, must therefore emerge and must be described in each sphere of the bourgeois economy, and the further we advance in our examination of the latter, the more aspects of this conflict must be traced on the one hand, and on the other hand it must be shown that its more abstract forms are recurring and are contained in the more concrete forms.

It can therefore be said that the crisis in its first form is the metamorphosis of the commodity itself, the falling asunder of purchase and sale.

The crisis in its second form is the function of money as a means of payment, in which money has two different functions and figures in two different phases, divided from each other in time. Both these forms are as yet quite abstract, although the second is more concrete than the first.

To begin with therefore, in considering the *reproduction process* of capital (which coincides with its circulation) it is necessary to prove that the above forms are simply repeated, or rather, that only here they receive a content, a basis on which to manifest themselves.

Let us look at the movement of capital from the moment in which it leaves the production process as a commodity in order once again to emerge from it as a commodity. If we abstract here from all the other factors determining its content, then the total commodity capital and each individual commodity of which it is made up, must go through the process C—M—C, the metamorphosis of the commodity. The general possibility of crisis, which is contained in this form—the falling apart of purchase and sale—is thus contained in the movement of capital, in so far as the latter is *also* commodity and nothing but commodity. From the interconnection of the metamorphoses of commodities it follows, moreover, that one commodity is transformed into money because another is retransformed from the form of money into commodity. Furthermore, the separation of purchase and sale appears here in such a way that the transformation of one capital from the form commodity into the form money, must correspond to the retransformation of the other capital from the form money into the form commodity. The first metamorphosis of one capital must correspond to the second metamorphosis of the other; one capital leaves the production process as the other capital returns into the production process. This intertwining and coalescence of the processes of reproduction or circulation of different capitals is on the one hand necessitated by the division of labour, on the other hand it is accidental; and thus the definition of the content of crisis is already fuller.

Secondly, however, with regard to the possibility of crisis arising from the form of money as *means of payment*, it appears that capital may provide a much more concrete basis for turning this possibility into reality. For example, the weaver must pay for the whole of the constant capital whose elements have been produced by the spinner, the flax-grower, the machine-builder, the iron and timber manufacturer, the producer of coal, etc. In so far as these latter produce constant capital that only enters into the production of constant capital, without entering into the cloth, the final commodity, they replace each other's means of production through the exchange of capital. Supposing the weaver now sells the cloth for £ 1,000 to the *merchant* but in return for a bill of exchange so that money figures as *means of payment*. The weaver for his part hands over the bill of exchange to the *banker*, to whom he may thus be repaying a debt or, on the other hand, the banker may negotiate the bill for him. The flax-grower has sold to the spinner in return for a bill of exchange, the spinner to the weaver, ditto the machine manufacturer to the weaver, ditto the iron and timber manufacturer to the machine manufacturer, ditto the coal producer to the spinner, weaver, machine manufacturer, iron and timber supplier. Besides, the iron, coal, timber and flax producers have paid one another with bills of exchange. Now if the merchant does not pay, then the weaver cannot pay his bill of exchange to the banker.

The flax-grower has drawn on the spinner, the machine manufacturer on the weaver and the spinner. The spinner cannot pay because the weaver cannot pay, neither of them pay the machine manufacturer, and the latter does not pay the iron, timber or coal supplier. And all of these in turn, as they cannot realise the value of their commodities, cannot replace that portion of value which is to replace their constant capital. Thus the general crisis comes into being. This is nothing other than the *possibility of crisis* described when dealing with money as a means of payment; but here—in capitalist production—we can already see the connection between the mutual claims and obligations, the sales and purchases, through which the possibility can develop into actuality.

In any case: If purchase and sale do not get bogged down, and therefore do not require forcible adjustment—and, on the other hand, money as means of payment functions in such a way that claims are mutually settled, and thus the contradiction inherent in money as a means of payment is not realised—if therefore neither of these two abstract forms of crisis become real, no crisis exists. No crisis can exist unless sale and purchase are separated from one another and come into conflict, or the contradictions contained in money as a means of payment actually come into play; crisis, therefore, cannot exist without manifesting itself at the same time in its simple form, as the contradiction between sale and purchase and the contradiction of money as a means of payment. But these are merely *forms*, general possibilities of crisis, and hence also forms, abstract forms, of actual crisis. In them, the nature of crisis appears in its simplest forms, and, in so far as this form is itself the simplest content of crisis, in its simplest content. But the content is not yet *substantiated*. Simple circulation of money and even the circulation of money as a means of payment—and both come into being long *before* capitalist production, while there are no crises—are possible and actually take place without crises. These forms alone, therefore, do not explain why their crucial aspect becomes prominent and why the potential contradiction contained in them becomes a real contradiction.

This shows how insipid the economists are who, when they are no longer able to explain away the phenomenon of over-production and crises, are content to say that these forms contain the possibility of *crises*, that it is therefore *accidental* whether or not crises occur and consequently their occurrence is itself merely a *matter of chance*.

The contradictions inherent in the circulation of commodities, which are further developed in the circulation of money—and thus, also, the possibilities of crisis—reproduce themselves, automatically, in capital, since developed circulation of commodities and of money, in fact, only take place on the basis of capital.

But now the further development of the potential crisis has to be traced—the real crisis can only be educed from the real movement of capitalist production, competition and credit—in so far as crisis arises out of the special aspects of capital which are *peculiar* to it as capital, and not merely comprised in its existence as commodity and money.

The mere (direct) *production process* of capital in itself, cannot add anything new in this context. In order to exist at all, its conditions are presupposed. The first section dealing with capital—the *direct* process of production—does not contribute any new element of crisis. Although it *does* contain such an element, because the production process implies appropriation and hence production of surplus-value. But this cannot be shown when dealing with the production process itself, for the latter is not concerned with the *realisation* either of the reproduced value or of the surplus-value.

This can only emerge in the *circulation process* which is in itself also a *process of reproduction*.

Furthermore it is necessary to describe the circulation or reproduction process before dealing with the already existing capital—*capital and profit*—since we have to explain, not only how capital produces, but also how capital is produced. But the actual movement starts from the existing capital—i.e., the actual movement denotes developed capitalist production, which starts from and presupposes its own basis. The process of reproduction and the predisposition to crisis which is further developed in it, are therefore only partially described under this heading and require further elaboration in the chapter on "*Capital and Profit.*"

The circulation process as a whole or the reproduction process of capital as a whole is the unity of its production phase and its circulation phase, so that it comprises both these processes or phases. Therein lies a further developed possibility or abstract form of crisis. The economists who deny crises consequently assert only the unity of these two phases. If they were only separate, without being a unity, then their unity could not be established by force and there could be no crisis. If they were only a unity without being separate, then no violent separation would be possible implying a crisis. Crisis is the forcible establishment of unity between elements that have become independent and the enforced separation from one another of elements which are essentially one.

On the Forms of Crisis

Therefore:

1. The general *possibility* of crisis is given in the process of *metamorphosis of capital* itself, and in two ways: in so far as money functions as *means of circulation*, [the possibility of crisis lies in] the separation of *purchase and sale*; and in so far as money func-

tions as *means of payment*, it has two different aspects, it acts as *measure of value* and *as realisation of value*. These two aspects [may] become separated. If *in the interval* between them the value has changed, if the commodity at the moment of its sale is not *worth* what it was *worth* at the moment when money was acting as a measure of value and therefore as a measure of the reciprocal obligations, then the obligation cannot be met from the *proceeds of the sale of the commodity*, and therefore the whole series of transactions which retrogressively depend on this one transaction, cannot be settled. If even for only *a limited period of time* the commodity cannot be sold then, although its value has not altered, *money* cannot function as *means of payment*, since it must function as such in a *definite given period of time*. But as the same sum of money acts for a whole series of reciprocal transactions and obligations here, *inability to pay* occurs not only at one, but at many points, hence a *crisis* arises.

These are the *formal possibilities* of crisis. The form mentioned first is possible without the latter—that is to say, crises are possible without credit, without money functioning as a means of payment. But the second form is not possible *without the first*—that is to say, without the separation between purchase and sale. But in the latter case, the crisis occurs not only because the commodity is unsaleable, but because it is not saleable within a *particular period of time*, and the crisis arises and derives its character not only from the *unsaleability* of the commodity, but from the *non-fulfilment of a whole series of payments* which depend on the sale of this particular commodity within this particular period of time. This is the *characteristic form of money crises*.

If the *crisis* appears, therefore, because purchase and sale become separated, it becomes a *money crisis*, as soon as money has developed as *means of payment*, and this *second form* of crisis follows as a matter of course, when the *first occurs*. In investigating why the general *possibility of crisis* turns into a *real* crisis, in investigating the *conditions* of crisis, it is therefore quite superfluous to concern oneself with the *forms* of crisis which arise out of the development of money as *means of payment*. This is precisely why economists like to suggest that this *obvious* form is the *cause* of crises. (In so far as the development of money as means of payment is linked with the development of credit and of *excess credit* the causes of the latter have to be examined, but this is not yet the place to do it.)

2. In so far as crises arise from *changes in prices and revolutions in prices*, which do not coincide with *changes in the values* of commodities, they naturally cannot be investigated during the examination of capital in general, in which the prices of commodities are assumed to be *identical* with the *values* of commodities.

3. The *general possibility* of crisis is the formal *metamorphosis* of capital itself, the separation, in time and space, of purchase and sale. But this is never the *cause* of the crisis. For it is nothing but the *most general form of crisis*, i.e., the crisis itself in *its most generalised expression*. But it cannot be said that the *abstract form of crisis* is the *cause of crisis*. If one asks what its cause is, one wants to know why *its abstract form*, the form of its possibility, turns from possibility into *actuality*.

4. The *general conditions* of crisis, in so far as they are independent of *price fluctuations* (whether these are linked with the credit system or not) as distinct from fluctuations in value, must be explicable from the general conditions of capitalist production.

(A *crisis* can arise: 1. in the course of the *reconversion* [of money] *into productive capital*; 2. through *changes in the value* of the elements of productive capital, particularly of *raw material*, for example when there is a decrease in the quantity of cotton harvested. Its *value* will thus rise. We are not as yet concerned with prices here but with *values*.)

First Phase. The *reconversion of money into capital*. A definite level of *production or reproduction* is assumed. Fixed capital can be regarded here as given, as remaining unchanged and not entering into the *process of the creation of value*. Since the reproduction of raw material is not dependent solely on the labour employed on it, but on the productivity of this labour which is bound up with *natural conditions*, it is possible for the volume, the *amount* of the product of the *same* quantity of labour, to fall (as a result of bad *harvests*). The *value of the raw material therefore rises*; its *volume* decreases, in other words the *proportions* in which the money has to be reconverted into the *various component parts of capital* in order to continue production on the former scale, are upset. More must be expended on *raw material*, less remains for *labour*, and it is not possible to absorb the same quantity of labour as before. Firstly this is *physically impossible*, because of the deficiency in raw material. *Secondly*, it is impossible because a greater *portion of the value of the product* has to be converted into raw material, thus leaving less for conversion into *variable capital*. Reproduction cannot be *repeated* on the same scale. A part of *fixed capital* stands idle and a part of the workers is thrown out on the streets. The *rate of profit* falls because the value of constant capital has risen as against that of variable capital and less variable capital is employed. The fixed charges—interests, rent—which were based on the anticipation of a *constant* rate of profit and exploitation of labour, remain the same and in part *cannot be paid*. Hence *crisis*. Crisis of labour and crisis of capital. This is therefore a *disturbance in the reproduction process* due to the increase in the value of that part of constant capital which has to be replaced out of the value of the product. Moreover, although the *rate of profit* is decreasing, there is a *rise in the price of the product*. If this product enters into other spheres of production as a means of production, the rise in its price will result in the same disturbance in *reproduction* in these spheres. If it enters into general consumption as a means of subsistence, it either enters also into *the consumption of the workers* or *not*. If it does so, then its effects will be the same as those of a disturbance in *variable capital*, of which we shall speak later. But in so far as it enters into *general consumption* it may result (if its consumption is not reduced) in a diminished *demand* for other products and consequently *prevent their reconversion* into money at their value, thus disturbing the *other aspect* of their reproduction—not the *reconversion of money* into productive capital but the *reconversion* of commodities into money. In any case, the *volume of profits* and the *volume of wages* is reduced in this branch of production thereby reducing a *part of the necessary returns* from the sale of commodities from other branches of production.

Such a *shortage* of *raw material* may, however, occur not only because of the *influence of harvests* or of the *natural productivity* of the labour which supplies the raw material. For if an *excessive portion of the surplus-value, of the additional capital,* is laid out in machinery etc. in a particular branch of production, then, although the raw material would have been sufficient for the *old level of production*, it will be insufficient for the *new*. This therefore arises from the *disproportionate* conversion of additional capital into its various elements. It is a case of *over-production of fixed capital* and gives rise to exactly the same phenomena as occur in the first case. (See the previous page.) [2]

Or they [the crises] are due to an *over-production of fixed capital* and therefore a relative under-production of circulating capital.

Since fixed capital, like circulating, consists of commodities, it is quite ridiculous that the same economists who admit the *over-production of fixed capital*, deny the *over-production of commodities*.

2. In the manuscript, the upper left-hand corner of the next page has been torn away. Consequently, out of the first nine lines of the text, only the right ends of six lines have been preserved. This does not make it possible to reproduce the complete text here, but it does permit us to surmise that Marx speaks here of crises which arise "out of [the] *revolution in the value* of the variable capital." The "increased price of the *necessary means of subsistence*" caused, for example, by a poor harvest, leads to a rise in costs for those workers who "are set in motion by variable capital." "At the same time, this rise" causes a fall in the demand for "*all other commodities* that do not enter into the consumption" of the workers. It is therefore impossible "to sell the commodities at their value; the first *phase* in their reproduction," the transformation of the commodity into money, is interrupted. The increased price of the means of subsistence thus leads to "crisis in other branches" of production.

The two last lines of the demaged part of the page seem to summarize this train of thought, by saying that crises can arise as a result of increased prices of raw materials, "whether these raw materials enter as raw materials into constant capital or as means of subsistence" into the consumption of the workers.

5. *Crises arising from disturbances in the first phase of reproduction:* that is to say, interrupted conversion of commodities into money or *interruption of sale.* In the case of crises of the first sort [which result from the rise in the price of raw materials] the crisis arises from interruptions in the *flowing back* of the elements of productive capital.

The Contradiction Between the Impetuous Development of the Productive Powers and the Limitations of Consumption Leads to Over-Production. The Theory of the Impossibility of General Over-Production Is Essentially Apologetic in Tendency.

The word *over-production* in itself leads to error. So long as the most urgent needs of a large part of society are not satisfied, or *only* the most immediate needs are satisfied, there can of course be absolutely no talk of an *over-production of products*— in the sense that the amount of products is excessive in relation to the need for them. On the contrary, it must be said that on the basis of capitalist production, there is constant *under-production* in this sense. The limits to production are set by the profit of the capitalist and in no way by the needs of the producers. But over-production of products and over-production of *commodities* are two entirely different things. If Ricardo thinks that the *commodity* form makes no difference to the product, and furthermore, that *commodity circulation* differs only formally from barter, that in this context the exchange-value is only a fleeting form of the exchange of things, and that money is therefore merely a formal means of circulation—then this in fact is in line with his presupposition that the bourgeois mode of production is the absolute mode of production, hence it is a mode of production without any definite specific characteristics, its distinctive traits are merely formal. He cannot therefore admit that the bourgeois mode of production contains within itself a barrier to the free development of the productive forces, a barrier which comes to the surface in crises and, in particular, in *over-production*—the basic phenomenon in crises.

Ricardo saw from the passages of Adam Smith, which he quotes, approves, and therefore also repeats, that the limitless "desire" for all kinds of use-values is always satisfied on the basis of a state of affairs in which the mass of producers remains more or less restricted to necessities—"food" and other "necessaries"—that consequently this great majority of producers remains more or less excluded from the consumption of wealth—in so far as wealth goes beyond the bounds of the necessary means of subsistence.

This was indeed also the case, and to an even higher degree, in the ancient mode of production which depended on slavery. But the ancients never thought of transforming the surplus-product into capital. Or at least only to a very limited extent. (The fact that the hoarding of treasure in the narrow sense was widespread among them shows how much surplus-product lay completely idle.) They used a large part of the surplus-product for unproductive expenditure on art, religious works and public works. Still less was their production directed to the release and development of the material productive forces—division of labour, machinery, the application of the powers of nature and science to private production. In fact, by and large, they never went beyond handicraft labour. The wealth which they produced for private consumption was therefore relatively small and only appears great because it was amassed in the hands of a few persons, who, incidentally, did not know what to do with it. Although, therefore, there was no *over-production* among the ancients, there was *over-consumption* by the rich, which in the final periods of Rome and Greece turned into mad extravagance. The few trading peoples among them lived partly at the expense of all these essentially poor nations. It is the unconditional development of the productive forces and therefore mass production on the basis of a mass of producers who are confined within the bounds of the necessary means of subsistence on the one hand and on the other, the barrier set up by the capitalists' profits, which [forms] the basis of modern over-production.

All the objections which Ricardo and others raise against over-production etc. rest on the fact that they regard bourgeois production either as a mode of production in which no distinction exists between purchase and sale—direct barter—or as *social* production, implying that society, as if according to a plan, distributes its means of production and productive forces in the degree and measure which is required for the fulfilment of the various social needs, so that each sphere of production receives the *quota* of social capital required to satisfy the corresponding need. This fiction arises entirely from the inability to grasp the specific form of bourgeois production and this inability in turn arises from the obsession that bourgeois production is production as such, just like a man who believes in a particular religion and sees it as *the* religion, and everything outside of it only as *false* religions.

On the contrary, the question that has to be answered is: since, on the basis of capitalist production, everyone works for himself and a particular labour must at the same time appear as its opposite, as abstract general labour and in this form as social labour—how is it possible to achieve the necessary balance and interdependence of the various spheres of production, their dimensions and the proportions between them, except through the constant neutralisation of a constant disharmony? This is admitted by those who speak of adjustments through competition, for these adjustments always presuppose that there is something to adjust, and therefore that harmony is always only a result of the movement which neutralises the existing disharmony.

That is why Ricardo admits that a glut of certain commodities is possible. What is supposed to be *impossible* is only a simultaneous general glut of the market. The possibility of over-production in any particular sphere of production is therefore not denied. It is the *simultaneity* of this phenomenon for *all* spheres of production which is said to be impossible and therefore makes impossible [general] over-production and thus a general glut of the market. (This expression must always be taken *cum grano salis,* since in times of general over-production, the over-production in some spheres is always only the *result,* the *consequence,* of over-production in the leading articles of commerce; [it is] always only *relative,* i.e., over-production because over-production exists in other spheres.)

Apologetics turns this into its very opposite. [There is only] over-production in the leading articles of commerce, in which alone, active over-production shows itself—these are on the whole articles which can only be produced on a mass scale and by factory methods (also in agriculture), because over-production exists in those articles in which relative or passive over-production manifests itself. According to this, over-production only exists because over-production is not universal. The *relativity* of over-production—that actual over-production in a few spheres calls forth over-production in others—is expressed in this way: There is no *universal* over-production, because if over-production were universal, all spheres of production would retain the same relation to one another; therefore *universal* over-production is proportional production which excludes over-production. And this is supposed to be an argument against universal over-production. For, since *universal over-production* in the absolute sense would not be over-production but only a greater than usual development of the productive forces in all spheres of production, it is alleged that *actual over-production,* which is precisely not this non-existent, self-abrogating over production, does *not* exist—although it only exists because it is not this.

If this miserable sophistry is more closely examined, it amounts to this: Suppose, that there is over-production in iron, cotton goods, linen, silk, woollen cloth etc.; then it cannot be said, for example, that too little coal has been produced and that this is the reason for the above over-production. For that over-production of iron etc. involves an exactly similar over-production of coal, as, say, the over-production of woven cloth does of yarn. (Over-production of yarn as compared with cloth, iron as compared with machinery, etc., could occur. This would always be a relative over-production of constant capital.) There cannot, therefore, be any question of the under-production of those articles whose over-production is implied because they enter as an element, raw material, auxiliary material or means of production, into those articles (the "particular commodity of which too much may be produced, of which there may be such a glut in the market, as not to repay the capital expended on it" (pp. 341–42), whose positive over-production is precisely the fact to be explained. Rather, it is a question of other articles which belong directly to [other] spheres of production and [can] neither [be] subsumed under the leading articles of commerce which, according to the assumption, have been over-produced, nor be attributed to spheres in which, because they supply the *intermediate product* for the leading articles of commerce, production must have reached at least the same level as in the final phases of the product—although there is nothing to prevent production in those spheres from having gone even further ahead thus causing an over-production within the over-production. For example, although sufficient coal must have been produced in order to keep going all those industries into which coal enters as necessary condition of production, and therefore the *over-production* of coal is implied in the *over-production* of iron, yarn etc. (even if coal was produced only in proportion to the production of iron and yarn [etc.]), it is *also* possible that more coal was produced than was required even for the over-production of iron, yarn etc. This is not only possible, but very probable. For *the production of coal and yarn* and of all other spheres of production which produce only the conditions or earlier phases of a product to be completed in another sphere, is governed not by the immediate demand, by the immediate production or reproduction, but by the *degree, measure, proportion* in which these are expanding. And it is self-evident that in this calculation, the target may well be overshot. Thus not enough has been produced of other articles such as, for example, pianos, precious stones, etc., they have been *under-produced*. (There are, however, also cases where the over-production of non-leading articles is not the result of over-production, but where, on the contrary, *under-production* is the cause of over-production, as for instance when there has been a failure in the grain crop or the cotton crop.)

The absurdity of this statement becomes particularly marked if it is applied to the international scene, as it has been by Say and others after him. For instance, that England has not *over-produced* but Italy has *under-produced*. There would have been no over-production, if in the first place Italy had enough capital to replace the

English capital exported to Italy in the form of commodities; and secondly if Italy had invested this capital in such a way that it produced those particular articles which are required by English capital —partly in order to replace itself and partly in order to replace the revenue yielded by it. Thus the fact of the actually existing *over-production in England*—in relation to the *actual* production in Italy —would not have existed, but only the fact of *imaginary under-production* in *Italy*; imaginary only because it presupposes a capital in Italy and a development of the productive forces that do not exist there, and secondly because it makes the equally utopian assumption, that this capital which does *not* exist in Italy, has been employed in exactly the way required to make English supply and Italian demand, English and Italian production, complementary to each other. In other words, this means nothing but: there would be no over-production, if demand and supply corresponded to each other, if the capital were distributed in such proportions in all spheres of production, that the production of one article involved the consumption of the other, and thus its own consumption. There would be no over-production, if there were no over-production. Since, however, capitalist production can allow itself free rein only in certain spheres, under certain conditions, there could be no capitalist production at all if it had to develop *simultaneously* and *evenly* in all spheres. Because absolute over-production takes place in certain spheres, relative over-production occurs also in the spheres where there has been no over-production.

This explanation of over-production in one field by under-production in another field therefore means merely that if production were proportionate, there would be no over-production. The same could be said if demand and supply corresponded to each other, or if all spheres provided equal opportunities for capitalist production and its expansion—division of labor, machinery, export to distant markets etc., mass production, i.e., if all countries which traded with one another possessed the same capacity for production (and indeed for different and complementary production). Thus over-production takes place because all these pious wishes are not fulfilled. Or, in even more abstract form: There would be no over-production in one place, if over-production took place to the same extent everywhere. But there is not enough capital to over-produce so universally, and therefore there is partial over-production.

Let us examine this fantasy more closely:

It is admitted that there can be over-production in *each particular* industry. The only circumstance which could prevent over-production in *all* industries simultaneously is, according to the assertions made, the fact that commodity exchanges against commodity —i.e., recourse is taken to the supposed conditions of barter. But this loop-hole is blocked by the very fact that trade [under capitalist conditions] is not barter, and that therefore the seller of a commodity is not necessarily at the same time the buyer of another. This whole subterfuge then rests on abstracting from *money* and from the fact that we are not concerned with the exchange of products, but with the circulation of commodities, an essential part of which is the separation of purchase and sale.

The circulation of capital contains within itself the *possibilities* of interruptions. In the reconversion of money into its conditions of production, for example, it is not only a question of transforming money into the same use-values (in kind), but for the repetition of the reproduction process [it is] essential that these use-values can again be obtained at their old value (at a lower value would of course be even better). A very significant part of these elements of reproduction, which consists of raw materials, can however rise in price for two reasons. *Firstly*, if the instruments of production increase more rapidly than the amount of raw materials that can be provided at the given time. *Secondly*, as a result of the variable character of the harvests. That is why weather conditions, as Tooke rightly observes, play such an important part in modern industry. (The same applies to the means of subsistence in relation to wages.) The reconversion of money into commodity can thus come up against difficulties and can create the possibilities of crisis, just as well as can the conversion of commodity into money. When one examines simple circulation—not the circulation of capital—these difficulties do not arise. (There are, besides, a large number of other factors, conditions, possibilities of crises, which can only be examined when considering the concrete conditions, particularly the competition of capitals and credit.)

The over-production of commodities is denied but the *over-pro-luction of capital* is admitted. Capital itself however consists of ₋ommodities or, in so far as it consists of money, it must be reconverted into commodities of one kind or another, in order to be able to function as capital. What then does *over-production of capital* mean? Over-production of value destined to produce surplus-value or, if one considers the material content, over-production of commodities destined for reproduction—that is, *reproduction on too large a scale*, which is the same as over-production pure and simple.

Defined more closely, this means nothing more than that too much has been produced for the purpose of *enrichment*, or that too great a part of the product is intended not for consumption as revenue, but *for making more money* (for accumulation): not to satisfy the personal needs of its owner, but to give him money, abstract social riches and capital, more power over the labour of others, i.e., to increase this power. This is what one side says. (Ricardo denies it.) And the other side, how does it explain the over-production of commodities? By saying that production is not sufficiently diversified, that certain articles of consumption have not been produced in sufficiently large quantities. That it is not a matter of industrial consumption is obvious, for the manufacturer who over-produces linen, thereby necessarily increases his demand for yarn, machinery, labour etc. It is therefore a question of personal consumption. Too much linen has been produced, but perhaps too few oranges. Previously the existence of money was denied, in order to show [that there was no] separation between sale and purchase. Here the existence of capital is denied, in order to transform the capitalists into people who carry out the simple operation C—M—C and who produce for individual consumption and not *as* capitalists with the aim of enrichment, i.e., the reconversion of part of the surplus-value into capital. But the statement that there is *too much capital*, after all means merely that too little is consumed as *revenue*, and that more cannot be consumed in the given conditions. (*Sismondi.*) Why does the producer of linen demand from the producer of corn, that he should consume more linen, or the latter demand that the linen manufacturer should consume more corn? Why does the man who produces linen not himself convert a larger part of his revenue (surplus-value) into linen and the farmer into corn? So far as each individual is concerned, it will be admitted that his desire for capitalisation (apart from the limits of his needs) prevents him from doing this. But for all of them collectively, this is not admitted.

(We are entirely leaving out of account here that element of crises which arises from the fact that commodities are reproduced more cheaply than they were produced. Hence the depreciation of the commodities on the market.)

In world market crises, all the contradictions of bourgeois production erupt collectively; in particular crises (*particular* in their content and in extent) the eruptions are only sporadical, isolated and one-sided.

Over-production is specifically conditioned by the general law of the production of capital: to produce to the limit set by the productive forces, that is to say, to exploit the maximum amount of labour with the given amount of capital, without any consideration for the actual limits of the market or the needs backed by the ability to pay; and this is carried out through continuous expansion of reproduction and accumulation, and therefore constant reconversion of revenue into capital, while on the other hand, the mass of the producers remain tied to the average level of needs, and must remain tied to it according to the nature of capitalist production.

PART III

Revolutionary Program and Strategy

Manifesto of the Communist Party

MARX AND ENGELS

In 1836 German radical workers living in Paris formed a secret association called "League of the Just." At congresses in London in 1847 it changed its name to "Communist League" and commissioned Marx and Engels, who had recently become members, to draw up a manifesto on its behalf. Both men prepared first drafts. Engels' draft, preserved under the title "The Principles of Communism," was in the form of a catechism with twenty-five questions and answers. Marx is believed to have had the greater hand in giving the *Communist Manifesto* its final form as both a programmatic statement and a compressed summary of the Marxian theory of history. It was originally published in London in February, 1848, and brought out in a French translation in Paris shortly before the insurrection of June, 1848, there. It has become the most widely read and influential single document of modern socialism. The text given here is that of the English edition of 1888, edited by Engels.

Preface to the German Edition of 1872

The Communist League, an international association of workers, which could of course be only a secret one under the conditions obtaining at the time, commissioned the undersigned, at the Congress held in London in November 1847, to draw up for publication a detailed theoretical and practical programme of the Party. Such was the origin of the following Manifesto, the manuscript of which travelled to London, to be printed, a few weeks before the February Revolution.[1] First published in German, it has been republished in that language in at least twelve different editions in Germany, England and America. It was published in English for the first time in 1850 in the *Red Republican*, London, translated by Miss Helen Macfarlane, and in 1871 in at least three different translations in America. A French version first appeared in Paris shortly before the June insurrection of 1848 and recently in *Le Soci-*

1. The February Revolution in France, 1848.

aliste of New York. A new translation is in the course of preparation. A Polish version appeared in London shortly after it was first published in German. A Russian translation was published in Geneva in the sixties. Into Danish, too, it was translated shortly after its first appearance.

However much the state of things may have altered during the last twenty-five years, the general principles laid down in this Manifesto are, on the whole, as correct today as ever. Here and there some detail might be improved. The practical application of the principles will depend, as the Manifesto itself states, everywhere and at all times, on the historical conditions for the time being existing, and, for that reason, no special stress is laid on the revolutionary measures proposed at the end of Section II. That passage would, in many respects, be very differently worded today. In view of the gigantic strides of Modern Industry in the last twenty-five years, and of the accompanying improved and extended party organisation of the working class, in view of the practical experience gained, first in the February Revolution, and then, still more, in the Paris Commune, where the proletariat for the first time held political power for two whole months, this programme has in some details become antiquated. One thing especially was proved by the Commune, *viz.*, that "the working class cannot simply lay hold of the ready-made State machinery, and wield it for its own purposes." (See *The Civil War in France; Address of the General Council of the International Working Men's Association,* London, Trulove, 1871, p. 15, where this point is further developed.)[2] Further, it is self-evident that the criticism of socialist literature is deficient in relation to the present time, because it comes down only to 1847; also, that the remarks on the relation of the Communists to the various opposition parties (Section IV), although in principle still correct, yet in practice are antiquated, because the political situation has been entirely changed, and the progress of history has swept from off the earth the greater portion of the political parties there enumerated.

But, then, the Manifesto has become a historical document which we have no longer any right to alter. A subsequent edition may perhaps appear with an introduction bridging the gap from 1847 to the present day; this reprint was too unexpected to leave us time for that.

London, June 24, 1872   *Karl Marx*   *Friedrich Engels*

2. See Engels' comment, p. 627, below. [R. T.]

Preface to the Russian Edition of 1882

The first Russian edition of the *Manifesto of the Communist Party*, translated by Bakunin, was published early in the sixties[3] by the printing office of the *Kolokol*. Then the West could see in it (the *Russian* edition of the Manifesto) only a literary curiosity. Such a view would be impossible today.

What a limited field the proletarian movement still occupied at that time (December 1847) is most clearly shown by the last section of the Manifesto: the position of the Communists in relation to the various opposition parties in the various countries. Precisely Russia and the United States are missing here. It was the time when Russia constituted the last great reserve of all European reaction, when the United States absorbed the surplus proletarian forces of Europe through immigration. Both countries provided Europe with raw materials and were at the same time markets for the sale of its industrial products. At that time both were, therefore, in one way or another, pillars of the existing European order.

How very different today! Precisely European immigration fitted North America for a gigantic agricultural production, whose competition is shaking the very foundations of European landed property—large and small. In addition it enabled the United States to exploit its tremendous industrial resources with an energy and on a scale that must shortly break the industrial monopoly of Western Europe, and especially of England, existing up to now. Both circumstances react in revolutionary manner upon America itself. Step by step the small and middle landownership of the farmers, the basis of the whole political constitution, is succumbing to the competition of giant farms; simultaneously, a mass proletariat and a fabulous concentration of capitals are developing for the first time in the industrial regions.

And now Russia! During the Revolution of 1848-49 not only the European princes, but the European bourgeois as well, found their only salvation from the proletariat, just beginning to awaken, in Russian intervention. The tsar was proclaimed the chief of European reaction. Today he is a prisoner of war of the revolution, in Gatchina, and Russia forms the vanguard of revolutionary action in Europe.

The Communist Manifesto had as its object the proclamation of the inevitably impending dissolution of modern bourgeois property. But in Russia we find, face to face with the rapidly developing capitalist swindle and bourgeois landed property, just beginning to

3. The date is not correct; the edition referred to appeared in 1869.

develop, more than half the land owned in common by the peasants. Now the question is: Can the Russian *obshchina*,[4] though greatly undermined, yet a form of the primeval common ownership of land, pass directly to the higher form of communist common ownership? Or, on the contrary, must it first pass through the same process of dissolution as constitutes the historical evolution of the West?

The only answer to that possible today is this: If the Russian Revolution becomes the signal for a proletarian revolution in the West, so that both complement each other, the present Russian common ownership of land may serve as the starting-point for a communist development.

London, January 21, 1882   *Karl Marx   Friedrich Engels*

Preface to the German Edition of 1883

The preface to the present edition I must, alas, sign alone. Marx, the man to whom the whole working class of Europe and America owes more than to anyone else, rests at Highgate Cemetery and over his grave the first grass is already growing. Since his death, there can be even less thought of revising or supplementing the Manifesto. All the more do I consider it necessary again to state here the following expressly:

The basic thought running through the Manifesto—that economic production and the structure of society of every historical epoch necessarily arising therefrom constitute the foundation for the political and intellectual history of that epoch; that consequently (ever since the dissolution of the primeval communal ownership of land) all history has been a history of class struggles, of struggles between exploited and exploiting, between dominated and dominating classes at various stages of social development; that this struggle, however, has now reached a stage where the exploited and oppressed class (the proletariat) can no longer emancipate itself from the class which exploits and oppresses it (the bourgeoisie), without at the same time forever freeing the whole of society from exploitation, oppression and class struggles—this basic thought belongs solely and exclusively to Marx.

I have already stated this many times; but precisely now it is necessary that it also stand in front of the Manifesto itself.

London, June 28, 1883   *Friedrich Engels*

4. Village community.

MANIFESTO
OF THE COMMUNIST PARTY

A spectre is haunting Europe—the spectre of Communism. All the Powers of old Europe have entered into a holy alliance to exorcise this spectre: Pope and Czar, Metternich and Guizot, French Radicals and German police-spies.

Where is the party in opposition that has not been decried as Communistic by its opponents in power? Where the Opposition that has not hurled back the branding reproach of Communism, against the more advanced opposition parties, as well as against its reactionary adversaries?

Two things result from this fact.

I. Communism is already acknowledged by all European Powers to be itself a Power.

II. It is high time that Communists should openly, in the face of the whole world, publish their views, their aims, their tendencies, and meet this nursery tale of the Spectre of Communism with a Manifesto of the party itself.

To this end, Communists of various nationalities have assembled in London, and sketched the following Manifesto, to be published in the English, French, German, Italian, Flemish and Danish languages.

I. Bourgeois and Proletarians[5]

The history of all hitherto existing society[6] is the history of class struggles.

Freeman and slave, patrician and plebeian, lord and serf,

5. By bourgeoisie is meant the class of modern Capitalists, owners of the means of social production and employers of wage-labour. By proletariat, the class of modern wage-labourers who, having no means of production of their own, are reduced to selling their labour-power in order to live. [*Engels, English edition of 1888*]

6. That is, all *written* history. In 1847, the pre-history of society, the social organisation existing previous to recorded history, was all but unknown. Since then, Haxthausen discovered common ownership of land in Russia, Maurer proved it to be the social foundation from which all Teutonic races started in history, and by and by village communities were found to be, or to have been the primitive form of society everywhere from India to Ireland. The inner organisation of this primitive Communistic society was laid bare, in its typical form, by Morgan's crowning discovery of the true nature of the *gens* and its relation to the *tribe*. With the dissolution of these primaeval communities society begins to be differentiated into separate and finally antagonistic classes. I have attempted to retrace this process of dissolution in: "Der Ursprung der Familie, des Privateigenthums und des Staats" [*The Origin of the Family, Private Property and the State*], 2nd edition, Stuttgart 1886. [*Engels, English edition of 1888*]

guild-master[7] and journeyman, in a word, oppressor and oppressed, stood in constant opposition to one another, carried on an uninterrupted, now hidden, now open fight, a fight that each time ended, either in a revolutionary re-constitution of society at large, or in the common ruin of the contending classes.

In the earlier epochs of history, we find almost everywhere a complicated arrangement of society into various orders, a manifold gradation of social rank. In ancient Rome we have patricians, knights, plebeians, slaves; in the Middle Ages, feudal lords, vassals, guild-masters, journeymen, apprentices, serfs; in almost all of these classes, again, subordinate gradations.

The modern bourgeois society that has sprouted from the ruins of feudal society has not done away with clash antagonisms. It has but established new classes, new conditions of oppression, new forms of struggle in place of the old ones.

Our epoch, the epoch of the bourgeoisie, possesses, however, this distinctive feature: it has simplified the class antagonisms: Society as a whole is more and more splitting up into two great hostile camps, into two great classes directly facing each other: Bourgeoisie and Proletariat.

From the serfs of the Middle Ages sprang the chartered burghers of the earliest towns. From these burgesses the first elements of the bourgeoisie were developed.

The discovery of America, the rounding of the Cape, opened up fresh ground for the rising bourgeoisie. The East-Indian and Chinese markets, the colonisation of America, trade with the colonies, the increase in the means of exchange and in commodities generally, gave to commerce, to navigation, to industry, an impulse never before known, and thereby, to the revolutionary element in the tottering feudal society, a rapid development.

The feudal system of industry, under which industrial production was monopolised by closed guilds, now no longer sufficed for the growing wants of the new markets. The manufacturing system took its place. The guild-masters were pushed on one side by the manufacturing middle class; division of labour between the different corporate guilds vanished in the face of division of labour in each single workshop.

Meantime the markets kept ever growing, the demand ever rising. Even manufacture no longer sufficed. Thereupon, steam and machinery revolutionised industrial production. The place of manufacture was taken by the giant, Modern Industry, the place of the industrial middle class, by industrial millionaires, the leaders of whole industrial armies, the modern bourgeois.

7. Guild-master, that is, a full member of a guild, a master within, not a head of a guild. [*Engels, English edition of 1888*]

Modern industry has established the world-market, for which the discovery of America paved the way. This market has given an immense development to commerce, to navigation, to communication by land. This development has, in its turn, reacted on the extension of industry; and in proportion as industry, commerce, navigation, railways extended, in the same proportion the bourgeoisie developed, increased its capital, and pushed into the background every class handed down from the Middle Ages.

We see, therefore, how the modern bourgeoisie is itself the product of a long course of development, of a series of revolutions in the modes of production and of exchange.

Each step in the development of the bourgeoisie was accompanied by a corresponding political advance of that class. An oppressed class under the sway of the feudal nobility, an armed and self-governing association in the mediaeval commune;[8] here independent urban republic (as in Italy and Germany), there taxable "third estate" of the monarchy (as in France), afterwards, in the period of manufacture proper, serving either the semi-feudal or the absolute monarchy as a counterpoise against the nobility, and, in fact, corner-stone of the great monarchies in general, the bourgeoisie has at last, since the establishment of Modern Industry and of the world-market, conquered for itself, in the modern representative State, exclusive political sway. The executive of the modern State is but a committee for managing the common affairs of the whole bourgeoisie.

The bourgeoisie, historically, has played a most revolutionary part.

The bourgeoisie, wherever it has got the upper hand, has put an end to all feudal, patriarchal, idyllic relations. It has pitilessly torn asunder the motley feudal ties that bound man to his "natural superiors," and has left remaining no other nexus between man and man than naked self-interest, than callous "cash payment." It has drowned the most heavenly ecstasies of religious fervour, of chivalrous enthusiasm, of philistine sentimentalism, in the icy water of egotistical calculation. It has resolved personal worth into exchange value, and in place of the numberless indefeasible chartered freedoms, has set up that single, unconscionable freedom—Free Trade. In one word, for exploitation, veiled by religious and political illusions, it has substituted naked, shameless, direct, brutal exploitation.

8. "Commune" was the name taken, in France, by the nascent towns even before they had conquered from their feudal lords and masters local self-government and political rights as the "Third Estate." Generally speaking, for the economical development of the bourgeoisie, England is here taken as the typical country; for its political development, France. [*Engels, English edition of 1888*]

This was the name given their urban communities by the townsmen of Italy and France, after they had purchased or wrested their initial rights of self-government from their feudal lords. [*Engels, German edition of 1890*]

The bourgeoisie has stripped of its halo every occupation hitherto honoured and looked up to with reverent awe. It has converted the physician, the lawyer, the priest, the poet, the man of science, into its paid wage-labourers.

The bourgeoisie has torn away from the family its sentimental veil, and has reduced the family relation to a mere money relation.

The bourgeoisie has disclosed how it came to pass that the brutal display of vigour in the Middle Ages, which Reactionists so much admire, found its fitting complement in the most slothful indolence. It has been the first to show what man's activity can bring about. It has accomplished wonders far surpassing Egyptian pyramids, Roman aqueducts, and Gothic cathedrals; it has conducted expeditions that put in the shade all former Exoduses of nations and crusades.

The bourgeoisie cannot exist without constantly revolutionising the instruments of production, and thereby the relations of production, and with them the whole relations of society. Conservation of the old modes of production in unaltered form, was, on the contrary, the first condition of existence for all earlier industrial classes. Constant revolutionising of production, uninterrupted disturbance of all social conditions, everlasting uncertainty and agitation distinguish the bourgeois epoch from all earlier ones. All fixed, fast-frozen relations, with their train of ancient and venerable prejudices and opinions, are swept away, all new-formed ones become antiquated before they can ossify. All that is solid melts into air, all that is holy is profaned, and man is at last compelled to face with sober senses, his real conditions of life, and his relations with his kind.

The need of a constantly expanding market for its products chases the bourgeoisie over the whole surface of the globe. It must nestle everywhere, settle everywhere, establish connexions everywhere.

The bourgeoisie has through its exploitation of the world-market given a cosmopolitan character to production and consumption in every country. To the great chagrin of Reactionists, it has drawn from under the feet of industry the national ground on which it stood. All old-established national industries have been destroyed or are daily being destroyed. They are dislodged by new industries, whose introduction becomes a life and death question for all civilised nations, by industries that no longer work up indigenous raw material, but raw material drawn from the remotest zones; industries whose products are consumed, not only at home, but in every quarter of the globe. In place of the old wants, satisfied by the productions of the country, we find new wants, requiring for their satisfaction the products of distant lands and climes. In place of the old local and national seclusion and self-sufficiency, we have intercourse in every direction, universal inter-dependence of nations. And as in material, so also in intellectual production. The intellectual creations of individual nations become common property. National one-sidedness and narrow-mindedness become more and more impossible, and from the numerous national and local literatures, there arises a world literature.

The bourgeoisie, by the rapid improvement of all instruments of production, by the immensely facilitated means of communication, draws all, even the most barbarian, nations into civilisation. The cheap prices of its commodities are the heavy artillery with which it batters down all Chinese walls, with which it forces the barbarians' intensely obstinate hatred of foreigners to capitulate. It compels all nations, on pain of extinction, to adopt the bourgeois mode of production; it compels them to introduce what it calls civilisation into their midst, *i.e.*, to become bourgeois themselves. In one word, it creates a world after its own image.

The bourgeoisie has subjected the country to the rule of the towns. It has created enormous cities, has greatly increased the urban population as compared with the rural, and has thus rescued a considerable part of the population from the idiocy of rural life. Just as it has made the country dependent on the towns, so it has made barbarian and semi-barbarian countries dependent on the civilised ones, nations of peasants on nations of bourgeois, the East on the West.

The bourgeoisie keeps more and more doing away with the scattered state of the population, of the means of production, and of property. It has agglomerated population, centralised means of production, and has concentrated property in a few hands. The necessary consequence of this was political centralisation. Independent, or but loosely connected provinces, with separate interests, laws, governments and systems of taxation, became lumped together into one nation, with one government, one code of laws, one national class-interest, one frontier and one customs-tariff.

The bourgeoisie, during its rule of scarce one hundred years, has created more massive and more colossal productive forces than have all preceding generations together. Subjection of Nature's forces to man, machinery, application of chemistry to industry and agriculture, steam-navigation, railways, electric telegraphs, clearing of whole continents for cultivation, canalisation of rivers, whole populations conjured out of the ground—what earlier century had even a presentiment that such productive forces slumbered in the lap of social labour?

We see then: the means of production and of exchange, on whose foundation the bourgeoisie built itself up, were generated in feudal society. At a certain stage in the development of these means of production and of exchange, the conditions under which feudal society produced and exchanged, the feudal organisation of agriculture and manufacturing industry, in one word, the feudal relations of property became no longer compatible with the already developed productive forces; they became so many fetters. They had to be burst asunder; they were burst asunder.

Into their place stepped free competition, accompanied by a social and political constitution adapted to it, and by the economical and political sway of the bourgeois class.

A similar movement is going on before our own eyes. Modern bourgeois society with its relations of production, of exchange and of property, a society that has conjured up such gigantic means of production and of exchange, is like the sorcerer, who is no longer able to control the powers of the nether world whom he has called up by his spells. For many a decade past the history of industry and commerce is but the history of the revolt of modern productive forces against modern conditions of production, against the property relations that are the conditions for the existence of the bourgeoisie and of its rule. It is enough to mention the commercial crises that by their periodical return put on its trial, each time more threateningly, the existence of the entire bourgeois society. In these crises a great part not only of the existing products, but also of the previously created productive forces, are periodically destroyed. In these crises there breaks out an epidemic that, in all earlier epochs, would have seemed an absurdity—the epidemic of over-production. Society suddenly finds itself put back into a state of momentary barbarism; it appears as if a famine, a universal war of devastation had cut off the supply of every means of subsistence; industry and commerce seem to be destroyed; and why? Because there is too much civilisation, too much means of subsistence, too much industry, too much commerce. The productive forces at the disposal of society no longer tend to further the development of the conditions of bourgeois property; on the contrary, they have become too powerful for these conditions, by which they are fettered, and so soon as they overcome these fetters, they bring disorder into the whole of bourgeois society, endanger the existence of bourgeois property. The conditions of bourgeois society are too narrow to comprise the wealth created by them. And how does the bourgeoisie get over these crises? On the one hand by enforced destruction of a mass of productive forces; on the other, by the conquest of new markets, and by the more thorough exploitation of the old ones. That is to say, by paving the way for more extensive and more destructive crises, and by diminishing the means whereby crises are prevented.

The weapons with which the bourgeoisie felled feudalism to the ground are now turned against the bourgeoisie itself.

But not only has the bourgeoisie forged the weapons that bring death to itself; it has also called into existence the men who are to wield those weapons—the modern working class—the proletarians.

In proportion as the bourgeoisie, *i.e.*, capital, is developed, in the same proportion is the proletariat, the modern working class, developed—a class of labourers, who live only so long as they find work, and who find work only so long as their labour increases capital. These labourers, who must sell themselves piece-meal, are a commodity, like every other article of commerce, and are consequently exposed to all the vicissitudes of competition, to all the fluctuations of the market.

Owing to the extensive use of machinery and to division of labour, the work of the proletarians has lost all individual character, and consequently, all charm for the workman. He becomes an appendage of the machine, and it is only the most simple, most monotonous, and most easily acquired knack, that is required of him. Hence, the cost of production of a workman is restricted, almost entirely, to the means of subsistence that he requires for his maintenance, and for the propagation of his race. But the price of a commodity, and therefore also of labour,[9] is equal to its cost of production. In proportion, therefore, as the repulsiveness of the work increases, the wage decreases. Nay more, in proportion as the use of machinery and division of labour increases, in the same proportion the burden of toil also increases, whether by prolongation of the working hours, by increase of the work exacted in a given time or by increased speed of the machinery, etc.

Modern industry has converted the little workshop of the patriarchal master into the great factory of the industrial capitalist. Masses of labourers, crowded into the factory, are organised like soldiers. As privates of the industrial army they are placed under the command of a perfect hierarchy of officers and sergeants. Not only are they slaves of the bourgeois class, and of the bourgeois State; they are daily and hourly enslaved by the machine, by the over-looker, and, above all, by the individual bourgeois manufacturer himself. The more openly this despotism proclaims gain to be its end and aim, the more petty, the more hateful and the more embittering it is.

The less the skill and exertion of strength implied in manual labour, in other words, the more modern industry becomes developed, the more is the labour of men superseded by that of women. Differences of age and sex have no longer any distinctive social validity for the working class. All are instruments of labour, more or less expensive to use, according to their age and sex.

No sooner is the exploitation of the labourer by the manufacturer, so far, at an end, that he receives his wages in cash, than he is set upon by the other portions of the bourgeoisie, the landlord, the shopkeeper, the pawnbroker, etc.

The lower strata of the middle class—the small tradespeople, shopkeepers, and retired tradesmen generally, the handicraftsmen

9. Subsequently Marx pointed out that the worker sells not his labour but his labour power.

and peasants—all these sink gradually into the proletariat, partly because their diminutive capital does not suffice for the scale on which Modern Industry is carried on, and is swamped in the competition with the large capitalists, partly because their specialised skill is rendered worthless by new methods of production. Thus the proletariat is recruited from all classes of the population.

The proletariat goes through various stages of development. With its birth begins its struggle with the bourgeoisie. At first the contest is carried on by individual labourers, then by the workpeople of a factory, then by the operatives of one trade, in one locality, against the individual bourgeois who directly exploits them. They direct their attacks not against the bourgeois conditions of production, but against the instruments of production themselves; they destroy imported wares that compete with their labour, they smash to pieces machinery, they set factories ablaze, they seek to restore by force the vanished status of the workman of the Middle Ages.

At this stage the labourers still form an incoherent mass scattered over the whole country, and broken up by their mutual competition. If anywhere they unite to form more compact bodies, this is not yet the consequence of their own active union, but of the union of the bourgeoisie, which class, in order to attain its own political ends, is compelled to set the whole proletariat in motion, and is moreover yet, for a time, able to do so. At this stage, therefore, the proletarians do not fight their enemies, but the enemies of their enemies, the remnants of absolute monarchy, the landowners, the non-industrial bourgeois, the petty bourgeoisie. Thus the whole historical movement is concentrated in the hands of the bourgeoisie; every victory so obtained is a victory for the bourgeoisie.

But with the development of industry the proletariat not only increases in number; it becomes concentrated in greater masses, its strength grows, and it feels that strength more. The various interests and conditions of life within the ranks of the proletariat are more and more equalised, in proportion as machinery obliterates all distinctions of labour, and nearly everywhere reduces wages to the same low level. The growing competition among the bourgeois, and the resulting commercial crises, make the wages of the workers ever more fluctuating. The unceasing improvement of machinery, ever more rapidly developing, makes their livelihood more and more precarious; the collisions between individual workmen and individual bourgeois take more and more the character of collisions between two classes. Thereupon the workers begin to form combinations (Trades Unions) against the bourgeois; they club together in order to keep up the rate of wages; they found permanent associations in order to make provision beforehand for these occasional revolts. Here and there the contest breaks out into riots.

Now and then the workers are victorious, but only for a time. The real fruit of their battles lies, not in the immediate result, but in the ever-expanding union of the workers. This union is helped on by the improved means of communication that are created by modern industry and that place the workers of different localities in contact with one another. It was just this contact that was needed to centralise the numerous local struggles, all of the same character, into one national struggle between classes. But every class struggle is a political struggle. And that union, to attain which the burghers of the Middle Ages, with their miserable highways, required centuries, the modern proletarians, thanks to railways, achieve in a few years.

This organisation of the proletarians into a class, and consequently into a political party, is continually being upset again by the competition between the workers themselves. But it ever rises up again, stronger, firmer, mightier. It compels legislative recognition of particular interests of the workers, by taking advantage of the divisions among the bourgeoisie itself. Thus the ten-hours' bill in England was carried.

Altogether collisions between the classes of the old society further, in many ways, the course of development of the proletariat. The bourgeoisie finds itself involved in a constant battle. At first with the aristocracy; later on, with those portions of the bourgeoisie itself, whose interests have become antagonistic to the progress of industry; at all times, with the bourgeoisie of foreign countries. In all these battles it sees itself compelled to appeal to the proletariat, to ask for its help, and thus, to drag it into the political arena. The bourgeoisie itself, therefore, supplies the proletariat with its own elements of political and general education, in other words, it furnishes the proletariat with weapons for fighting the bourgeoisie.

Further, as we have already seen, entire sections of the ruling classes are, by the advance of industry, precipitated into the proletariat, or are at least threatened in their conditions of existence. These also supply the proletariat with fresh elements of enlightenment and progress.

Finally, in times when the class struggle nears the decisive hour, the process of dissolution going on within the ruling class, in fact within the whole range of society, assumes such a violent, glaring character, that a small section of the ruling class cuts itself adrift, and joins the revolutionary class, the class that holds the future in its hands. Just as, therefore, at an earlier period, a section of the nobility went over to the bourgeoisie, so now a portion of the bourgeoisie goes over to the proletariat, and in particular, a portion of the bourgeois ideologists, who have raised themselves to the level of comprehending theoretically the historical movement as a whole.

Of all the classes that stand face to face with the bourgeoisie today, the proletariat alone is a really revolutionary class. The other classes decay and finally disappear in the face of Modern Industry; the proletariat is its special and essential product.

The lower middle class, the small manufacturer, the shopkeeper, the artisan, the peasant, all these fight against the bourgeoisie, to save from extinction their existence as fractions of the middle class. They are therefore not revolutionary, but conservative. Nay more, they are reactionary, for they try to roll back the wheel of history. If by chance they are revolutionary, they are so only in view of their impending transfer into the proletariat, they thus defend not their present, but their future interests, they desert their own standpoint to place themselves at that of the proletariat.

The "dangerous class," the social scum, that passively rotting mass thrown off by the lowest layers of old society, may, here and there, be swept into the movement by a proletarian revolution; its conditions of life, however, prepare it far more for the part of a bribed tool of reactionary intrigue.

In the conditions of the proletariat, those of old society at large are already virtually swamped. The proletarian is without property; his relation to his wife and children has no longer anything in common with the bourgeois family-relations; modern industrial labour, modern subjection to capital, the same in England as in France, in America as in Germany, has stripped him of every trace of national character. Law, morality, religion, are to him so many bourgeois prejudices, behind which lurk in ambush just as many bourgeois interests.

All the preceding classes that got the upper hand, sought to fortify their already acquired status by subjecting society at large to their conditions of appropriation. The proletarians cannot become masters of the productive forces of society, except by abolishing their own previous mode of appropriation, and thereby also every other previous mode of appropriation. They have nothing of their own to secure and to fortify; their mission is to destroy all previous securities for, and insurances of, individual property.

All previous historical movements were movements of minorities, or in the interests of minorities. The proletarian movement is the self-conscious, independent movement of the immense majority, in the interests of the immense majority. The proletariat, the lowest stratum of our present society, cannot stir, cannot raise itself up, without the whole superincumbent strata of official society being sprung into the air.

Though not in substance, yet in form, the struggle of the proletariat with the bourgeoisie is at first a national struggle. The proletariat of each country must, of course, first of all settle matters with its own bourgeoisie.

In depicting the most general phases of the development of the proletariat, we traced the more or less veiled civil war, raging within existing society, up to the point where that war breaks out into open revolution, and where the violent overthrow of the bourgeoisie lays the foundation for the sway of the proletariat.

Hitherto, every form of society has been based, as we have already seen, on the antagonism of oppressing and oppressed classes. But in order to oppress a class, certain conditions must be assured to it under which it can, at least, continue its slavish existence. The serf, in the period of serfdom, raised himself to membership in the commune, just as the petty bourgeois, under the yoke of feudal absolutism, managed to develop into a bourgeois. The modern labourer, on the contrary, instead of rising with the progress of industry, sinks deeper and deeper below the conditions of existence of his own class. He becomes a pauper, and pauperism develops more rapidly than population and wealth. And here it becomes evident, that the bourgeoisie is unfit any longer to be the ruling class in society, and to impose its conditions of existence upon society as an over-riding law. It is unfit to rule because it is incompetent to assure an existence to its slave within his slavery, because it cannot help letting him sink into such a state, that it has to feed him, instead of being fed by him. Society can no longer live under this bourgeoisie, in other words, its existence is no longer compatible with society.

The essential condition for the existence, and for the sway of the bourgeois class, is the formation and augmentation of capital; the condition for capital is wage-labour. Wage-labour rests exclusively on competition between the labourers. The advance of industry, whose involuntary promoter is the bourgeoisie, replaces the isolation of the labourers, due to competition, by their revolutionary combination, due to association. The development of Modern Industry, therefore, cuts from under its feet the very foundation on which the bourgeoisie produces and appropriates products. What the bourgeoisie, therefore, produces, above all, is its own grave-diggers. Its fall and the victory of the proletariat are equally inevitable.

II. Proletarians and Communists

In what relation do the Communists stand to the proletarians as a whole?

The Communists do not form a separate party opposed to other working class parties.

They have no interests separate and apart from those of the proletariat as a whole.

They do not set up any sectarian principles of their own, by which to shape and mould the proletarian movement.

The Communists are distinguished from the other working-class parties by this only: (1) In the national struggles of the proletarians of the different countries, they point out and bring to the front the common interests of the entire proletariat, independently of all nationality. (2) In the various stages of development which the struggle of the working class against the bourgoisie has to pass through, they always and everywhere represent the interests of the movement as a whole.

The Communists, therefore, are on the one hand, practically, the most advanced and resolute section of the working-class parties of every country, that section which pushes forward all others; on the other hand, theoretically, they have over the great mass of the proletariat the advantage of clearly understanding the line of march, the conditions, and the ultimate general results of the proletarian movement.

The immediate aim of the Communists is the same as that of all the other proletarian parties: formation of the proletariat into a class, overthrow of the bourgeois supremacy, conquest of political power by the proletariat.

The theoretical conclusions of the Communists are in no way based on ideas or principles that have been invented, or discovered, by this or that would-be universal reformer.

They merely express, in general terms, actual relations springing from an existing class struggle, from a historical movement going on under our very eyes. The abolition of existing property relations is not at all a distinctive feature of Communism.

All property relations in the past have continually been subject to historical change consequent upon the change in historical conditions.

The French Revolution, for example, abolished feudal property in favour of bourgeois property.

The distinguishing feature of Communism is not the abolition of property generally, but the abolition of bourgeois property. But modern bourgeois private property is the final and most complete expression of the system of producing and appropriating products, that is based on class antagonisms, on the exploitation of the many by the few.

In this sense, the theory of the Communists may be summed up in the single sentence: Abolition of private property.

We Communists have been reproached with the desire of abolishing the right of personally acquiring property as the fruit of a man's own labour, which property is alleged to be the groundwork of all personal freedom, activity and independence.

Hard-won, self-acquired, self-earned property! Do you mean the property of the petty artisan and of the small peasant, a form of property that preceded the bourgeois form? There is no need to abolish that; the development of industry has to a great extent already destroyed it, and is still destroying it daily.

Or do you mean modern bourgeois private property?

But does wage-labour create any property for the labourer? Not a bit. It creates capital, *i.e.*, that kind of property which exploits wage-labour, and which cannot increase except upon condition of begetting a new supply of wage-labour for fresh exploitation. Property, in its present form, is based on the antagonism of capital and wage-labour. Let us examine both sides of this antagonism.

To be a capitalist, is to have not only a purely personal, but a social *status* in production. Capital is a collective product, and only by the united action of many members, nay, in the last resort, only by the united action of all members of society, can it be set in motion.

Capital is, therefore, not a personal, it is a social power.

When, therefore, capital is converted into common property, into the property of all members of society, personal property is not thereby transformed into social property. It is only the social character of the property that is changed. It loses its class character.

Let us now take wage-labour.

The average price of wage-labour is the minimum wage, *i.e.*, that quantum of the means of subsistence, which is absolutely requisite to keep the labourer in bare existence as a labourer. What, therefore, the wage-labourer appropriates by means of his labour, merely suffices to prolong and reproduce a bare existence. We by no means intend to abolish this personal appropriation of the products of labour, an appropriation that is made for the maintenance and reproduction of human life, and that leaves no surplus wherewith to command the labour of others. All that we want to do away with, is the miserable character of this appropriation, under which the labourer lives merely to increase capital, and is allowed to live only in so far as the interest of the ruling class requires it.

In bourgeois society, living labour is but a means to increase accumulated labour. In Communist society, accumulated labour is but a means to widen, to enrich, to promote the existence of the labourer.

In bourgeois society, therefore, the past dominates the present; in Communist society, the present dominates the past. In bourgeois society capital is independent and has individuality, while the living person is dependent and has no individuality.

And the abolition of this state of things is called by the bourgeois, abolition of individuality and freedom! And rightly so. The abolition of bourgeois individuality, bourgeois independence, and bourgeois freedom is undoubtedly aimed at.

By freedom is meant, under the present bourgeois conditions of production, free trade, free selling and buying.

But if selling and buying disappears, free selling and buying disappears also. This talk about free selling and buying, and all the other "brave words" of our bourgeoisie about freedom in general, have a meaning, if any, only in contrast with restricted selling and buying, with the fettered traders of the Middle Ages, but have no meaning when opposed to the Communistic abolition of buying and selling, of the bourgeois conditions of production, and of the bourgeoisie itself.

You are horrified at our intending to do away with private property. But in your existing society, private property is already done away with for nine-tenths of the population; its existence for the few is solely due to its non-existence in the hands of those nine-tenths. You reproach us, therefore, with intending to do away with a form of property, the necessary condition for whose existence is the non-existence of any property for the immense majority of society.

In one word, you reproach us with intending to do away with your property. Precisely so; that is just what we intend.

From the moment when labour can no longer be converted into capital, money, or rent, into a social power capable of being monopolised, *i.e.*, from the moment when individual property can no longer be transformed into bourgeois property, into capital, from that moment, you say, individuality vanishes.

You must, therefore, confess that by "individual" you mean no other person than the bourgeois, than the middle-class owner of property. This person must, indeed, be swept out of the way, and made impossible.

Communism deprives no man of the power to appropriate the products of society; all that it does is to deprive him of the power to subjugate the labour of others by means of such appropriation.

It has been objected that upon the abolition of private property all work will cease, and universal laziness will overtake us.

According to this, bourgeois society ought long ago to have gone to the dogs through sheer idleness; for those of its members who work, acquire nothing, and those who acquire anything, do not work. The whole of this objection is but another expression of the tautology: that there can no longer be any wage-labour when there is no longer any capital.

All objections urged against the Communistic mode of producing and appropriating material products, have, in the same way, been urged against the Communistic modes of producing and appropriating intellectual products. Just as, to the bourgeois, the disappearance of class property is the disappearance of production itself, so the disappearance of class culture is to him identical with the disappearance of all culture.

That culture, the loss of which he laments, is, for the enormous majority, a mere training to act as a machine.

But don't wrangle with us so long as you apply, to our intended abolition of bourgeois property, the standard of your bourgeois notions of freedom, culture, law, &c. Your very ideas are but the outgrowth of the conditions of your bourgeois production and bourgeois property, just as your jurisprudence is but the will of your class made into a law for all, a will, whose essential character and direction are determined by the economical conditions of existence of your class.

The selfish misconception that induces you to transform into eternal laws of nature and of reason, the social forms springing from your present mode of production and form of property—historical relations that rise and disappear in the progress of production—this misconception you share with every ruling class that has preceded you. What you see clearly in the case of ancient property, what you admit in the case of feudal property, you are of course forbidden to admit in the case of your own bourgeois form of property.

Abolition of the family! Even the most radical flare up at this infamous proposal of the Communists.

On what foundation is the present family, the bourgeois family, based? On capital, on private gain. In its completely developed form this family exists only among the bourgeoisie. But this state of things finds its complement in the practical absence of the family among the proletarians, and in public prostitution.

The bourgeois family will vanish as a matter of course when its complement vanishes, and both will vanish with the vanishing of capital.

Do you charge us with wanting to stop the exploitation of children by their parents? To this crime we plead guilty.

But, you will say, we destroy the most hallowed of relations, when we replace home education by social.

And your education! Is not that also social, and determined by the social conditions under which you educate, by the intervention, direct or indirect, of society, by means of schools, &c.? The Communists have not invented the intervention of society in education; they do but seek to alter the character of that intervention, and to rescue education from the influence of the ruling class.

The bourgeois clap-trap about the family and education, about the hallowed co-relation of parent and child, becomes all the more disgusting, the more, by the action of Modern Industry, all family ties among the proletarians are torn asunder, and their children transformed into simple articles of commerce and instruments of labour.

But you Communists would introduce community of women, screams the whole bourgeoisie in chorus.

The bourgeois sees in his wife a mere instrument of production. He hears that the instruments of production are to be exploited in common, and, naturally, can come to no other conclusion than that the lot of being common to all will likewise fall to the women.

He has not even a suspicion that the real point aimed at is to do away with the status of women as mere instruments of production.

For the rest, nothing is more ridiculous than the virtuous indignation of our bourgeois at the community of women which, they pretend, is to be openly and officially established by the Communists. The Communists have no need to introduce community of women; it has existed almost from time immemorial.

Our bourgeois, not content with having the wives and daughters of their proletarians at their disposal, not to speak of common prostitutes, take the greatest pleasure in seducing each other's wives.

Bourgeois marriage is in reality a system of wives in common and thus, at the most, what the Communists might possibly be reproached with, is that they desire to introduce, in substitution for a hypocritically concealed, an openly legalised community of women. For the rest, it is self-evident that the abolition of the present system of production must bring with it the abolition of the community of women springing from that system, *i.e.*, of prostitution both public and private.

The Communists are further reproached with desiring to abolish countries and nationality.

The working men have no country. We cannot take from them what they have not got. Since the proletariat must first of all acquire political supremacy, must rise to be the leading class of the nation, must constitute itself *the* nation, it is, so far, itself national, though not in the bourgeois sense of the word.

National differences and antagonisms between peoples are daily more and more vanishing, owing to the development of the bourgeoisie, to freedom of commerce, to the world-market, to uniformity in the mode of production and in the conditions of life corresponding thereto.

The supremacy of the proletariat will cause them to vanish still faster. United action, of the leading civilised countries at least, is one of the first conditions for the emancipation of the proletariat.

In proportion as the exploitation of one individual by another is put an end to, the exploitation of one nation by another will also be put an end to. In proportion as the antagonism between classes within the nation vanishes, the hostility of one nation to another will come to an end.

The charges against Communism made from a religious, a philosophical, and, generally, from an ideological standpoint, are not deserving of serious examination.

Does it require deep intuition to comprehend that man's ideas, views and conceptions, in one word, man's consciousness, changes with every change in the conditions of his material existence, in his social relations and in his social life?

What else does the history of ideas prove, than that intellectual production changes its character in proportion as material production is changed? The ruling ideas of each age have ever been the ideas of its ruling class.

When people speak of ideas that revolutionise society, they do but express the fact, that within the old society, the elements of a new one have been created, and that the dissolution of the old ideas keeps even pace with the dissolution of the old conditions of existence.

When the ancient world was in its last throes, the ancient religions were overcome by Christianity. When Christian ideas succumbed in the 18th century to rationalist ideas, feudal society fought its death battle with the then revolutionary bourgeoisie. The ideas of religious liberty and freedom of conscience merely gave expression to the sway of free competition within the domain of knowledge.

"Undoubtedly," it will be said, "religious, moral, philosophical and juridical ideas have been modified in the course of historical development. But religion, morality, philosophy, political science, and law, constantly survived this change."

"There are, besides, eternal truths, such as Freedom, Justice, etc., that are common to all states of society. But Communism abolishes eternal truths, it abolishes all religion, and all morality, instead of constituting them on a new basis; it therefore acts in contradiction to all past historical experience."

What does this accusation reduce itself to? The history of all past society has consisted in the development of class antagonisms, antagonisms that assumed different forms at different epochs.

But whatever form they may have taken, one fact is common to all past ages, viz., the exploitation of one part of society by the other. No wonder, then, that the social consciousness of past ages, despite all the multiplicity and variety it displays, moves within certain common forms, or general ideas, which cannot completely vanish except with the total disappearance of class antagonisms.

The Communist revolution is the most radical rupture with traditional property relations; no wonder that its development involves the most radical rupture with traditional ideas.

But let us have done with the bourgeois objections to Communism.

We have seen above, that the first step in the revolution by the working class, is to raise the proletariat to the position of ruling class, to win the battle of democracy.

The proletariat will use its political supremacy to wrest, by degrees, all capital from the bourgeoisie, to centralise all instruments of production in the hands of the State, *i.e.*, of the proletariat organised as the ruling class; and to increase the total of productive forces as rapidly as possible.

Of course, in the beginning, this cannot be effected except by means of despotic inroads on the rights of property, and on the conditions of bourgeois production; by means of measures, therefore, which appear economically insufficient and untenable, but which, in the course of the movement, outstrip themselves, necessitate further inroads upon the old social order, and are unavoidable as a means of entirely revolutionising the mode of production.

These measures will of course be different in different countries.

Nevertheless in the most advanced countries, the following will be pretty generally applicable.

1. Abolition of property in land and application of all rents of land to public purposes.

2. A heavy progressive or graduated income tax.

3. Abolition of all right of inheritance.

4. Confiscation of the property of all emigrants and rebels.

5. Centralisation of credit in the hands of the State, by means of a national bank with State capital and an exclusive monopoly.

6. Centralisation of the means of communication and transport in the hands of the State.

7. Extension of factories and instruments of production owned by the State; the bringing into cultivation of waste-lands, and the improvement of the soil generally in accordance with a common plan.

8. Equal liability of all to labour. Establishment of industrial armies, especially for agriculture.

9. Combination of agriculture with manufacturing industries; gradual abolition of the distinction between town and country, by a more equable distribution of the population over the country.

10. Free education for all children in public schools. Abolition of children's factory labour in its present form. Combination of education with industrial production, &c., &c.

When, in the course of development, class distinctions have disappeared, and all production has been concentrated in the hands of a vast association of the whole nation, the public power will lose its political character. Political power, properly so called, is merely the organised power of one class for oppressing another. If the proletariat during its contest with the bourgeoisie is compelled, by the force of circumstances, to organise itself as a class, if, by means of a revolution, it makes itself the ruling class, and, as such, sweeps away by force the old conditions of production, then it will, along with these conditions, have swept away the conditions for the existence of class antagonisms and of classes generally, and will thereby have abolished its own supremacy as a class.

In place of the old bourgeois society, with its classes and class antagonisms, we shall have an association, in which the free development of each is the condition for the free development of all.

III. Socialist and Communist Literature

1. REACTIONARY SOCIALISM

A. *Feudal Socialism*

Owing to their historical position, it became the vocation of the aristocracies of France and England to write pamphlets against modern bourgeois society. In the French revolution of July 1830, and in the English reform agitation, these aristocracies again succumbed to the hateful upstart. Thenceforth, a serious political contest was altogether out of the question. A literary battle alone remained possible. But even in the domain of literature the old cries of the restoration period[1] had become impossible.

In order to arouse sympathy, the aristocracy were obliged to lose sight, apparently, of their own interests, and to formulate their indictment against the bourgeoisie in the interest of the exploited working class alone. Thus the aristocracy took their revenge by singing lampoons on their new master, and whispering in his ears sinister prophecies of coming catastrophe.

In this way arose Feudal Socialism: half lamentation, half lampoon; half echo of the past, half menace of the future; at times, by its bitter, witty and incisive criticism, striking the bourgeoisie to the very heart's core; but always ludicrous in its effect, through total incapacity to comprehend the march of modern history.

The aristocracy, in order to rally the people to them, waved the proletarian alms-bag in front for a banner. But the people, so often as it joined them, saw on their hindquarters the old feudal coats of arms, and deserted with loud and irreverent laughter.

One section of the French Legitimists[2] and "Young England"[3] exhibited this spectacle.

1. Not the English Restoration 1660 to 1689, but the French Restoration 1814 to 1830. [*Engels, English edition of 1888*]
2. The party of the noble landowners, who advocated the restoration of the Bourbon dynasty.
3. A group of British Conservatives—aristocrats and men of politics and literature—formed about 1842. Prominent among them were Disraeli, Thomas Carlyle, and others.

In pointing out that their mode of exploitation was different to that of the bourgeoisie, the feudalists forget that they exploited under circumstances and conditions that were quite different, and that are now antiquated. In showing that, under their rule, the modern proletariat never existed, they forget that the modern bourgeoisie is the necessary offspring of their own form of society.

For the rest, so little do they conceal the reactionary character of their criticism that their chief accusation against the bourgeoisie amounts to this, that under the bourgeois *régime* a class is being developed, which is destined to cut up root and branch the old order of society.

What they upbraid the bourgeoisie with is not so much that it creates a proletariat, as that it creates a *revolutionary* proletariat.

In political practice, therefore, they join in all coercive measures against the working class; and in ordinary life, despite their high falutin phrases, they stoop to pick up the golden apples dropped from the tree of industry, and to barter truth, love, and honour for traffic in wool, beetroot-sugar, and potato spirits.[4]

As the parson has ever gone hand in hand with the landlord, so has Clerical Socialism with Feudal Socialism.

Nothing is easier than to give Christian asceticism a Socialist tinge. Has not Christianity declaimed against private property, against marriage, against the State? Has it not preached in the place of these, charity and poverty, celibacy and mortification of the flesh, monastic life and Mother Church? Christian Socialism is but the holy water with which the priest consecrates the heart-burnings of the aristocrat.

B. Petty-Bourgeois Socialism

The feudal aristocracy was not the only class that was ruined by the bourgeoisie, not the only class whose conditions of existence pined and perished in the atmosphere of modern bourgeois society. The mediaeval burgesses and the small peasant proprietors were the precursors of the modern bourgeoisie. In those countries which are but little developed, industrially and commercially, these two classes still vegetate side by side with the rising bourgeoisie.

In countries where modern civilisation has become fully developed, a new class of petty bourgeois has been formed, fluctuating between proletariat and bourgeoisie and ever renewing itself as a

---

4. This applies chiefly to Germany where the landed aristocracy and squirearchy have large portions of their estates cultivated for their own account by stewards, and are, moreover, extensive beetroot-sugar manufacturers and distillers of potato spirits. The wealthier British aristocracy are, as yet, rather above that; but they, too, know how to make up for declining rents by lending their names to floaters of more or less shady joint-stock companies. [*Engels, English edition of 1888*]

supplementary part of bourgeois society. The individual members of this class, however, are being constantly hurled down into the proletariat by the action of competition, and, as modern industry develops, they even see the moment approaching when they will completely disappear as an independent section of modern society, to be replaced, in manufactures, agriculture and commerce, by overlookers, bailiffs and shopmen.

In countries like France, where the peasants constitute far more than half of the population, it was natural that writers who sided with the proletariat against the bourgeoisie, should use, in their criticism of the bourgeois *régime*, the standard of the peasant and petty bourgeois, and from the standpoint of these intermediate classes should take up the cudgels for the working class. Thus arose petty-bourgeois Socialism. Sismondi was the head of this school, not only in France but also in England.

This school of Socialism dissected with great acuteness the contradictions in the conditions of modern production. It laid bare the hypocritical apologies of economists. It proved, incontrovertibly, the disastrous effects of machinery and division of labour; the concentration of capital and land in a few hands; overproduction and crises; it pointed out the inevitable ruin of the petty bourgeois and peasant, the misery of the proletariat, the anarchy in production, the crying inequalities in the distribution of wealth, the industrial war of extermination between nations, the dissolution of old moral bonds, of the old family relations, of the old nationalities.

In its positive aims, however, this form of Socialism aspires either to restoring the old means of production and of exchange, and with them the old property relations, and the old society, or to cramping the modern means of production and of exchange, within the framework of the old property relations that have been, and were bound to be, exploded by those means. In either case, it is both reactionary and Utopian.

Its last words are: corporate guilds for manufacture, patriarchal relations in agriculture.

Ultimately, when stubborn historical facts had dispersed all intoxicating effects of self-deception, this form of Socialism ended in a miserable fit of the blues.

C. German, or "True," Socialism

The Socialist and Communist literature of France, a literature that originated under the pressure of a bourgeoisie in power, and that was the expression of the struggle against this power, was introduced into Germany at a time when the bourgeoisie, in that country, had just begun its contest with feudal absolutism.

German philosophers, would-be philosophers, and *beaux esprits*, eagerly seized on this literature, only forgetting, that when these writings immigrated from France into Germany, French social conditions had not immigrated along with them. In contact with German social conditions, this French literature lost all its immediate practical significance, and assumed a purely literary aspect. Thus, to the German philosophers of the eighteenth century, the demands of the first French Revolution were nothing more than the demands of "Practical Reason" in general, and the utterance of the will of the revolutionary French bourgeoisie signified in their eyes the law of pure Will, of Will as it was bound to be, of true human Will generally.

The work of the German *literati* consisted solely in bringing the new French ideas into harmony with their ancient philosophical conscience, or rather, in annexing the French ideas without deserting their own philosophic point of view.

This annexation took place in the same way in which a foreign language is appropriated, namely, by translation.

It is well known how the monks wrote silly lives of Catholic Saints *over* the manuscripts on which the classical works·of ancient heathendom had been written. The German *literati* reversed this process with the profane French literature. They wrote their philosophical nonsense beneath the French original. For instance, beneath the French criticism of the economic functions of money, they wrote "Alienation of Humanity," and beneath the French criticism of the bourgeois State they wrote "dethronement of the Category of the General," and so forth.

The introduction of these philosophical phrases at the back of the French historical criticisms they dubbed "Philosophy of Action," "True Socialism," "German Science of Socialism," "Philosophical Foundation of Socialism," and so on.

The French Socialist and Communist literature was thus completely emasculated. And, since it ceased in the hands of the German to express the struggle of one class with the other, he felt conscious of having overcome "French one-sidedness" and of representing, not true requirements, but the requirements of truth; not the interests of the proletariat, but the interests of Human Nature, of Man in general, who belongs to no class, has no reality, who exists only in the misty realm of philosophical fantasy.

This German Socialism, which took its schoolboy task so seriously and solemnly, and extolled its poor stock-in-trade in such mountebank fashion, meanwhile gradually lost its pedantic innocence.

The fight of the German, and especially, of the Prussian bourgeoisie, against feudal aristocracy and absolute monarchy, in other words, the liberal movement, became more earnest.

By this, the long wished-for opportunity was offered to "True" Socialism of confronting the political movement with the Socialist demands, of hurling the traditional anathemas against liberalism, against representative government, against bourgeois competition, bourgeois freedom of the press, bourgeois legislation, bourgeois liberty and equality, and of preaching to the masses that they had nothing to gain, and everything to lose, by this bourgeois movement. German Socialism forgot, in the nick of time, that the French criticism, whose silly echo it was, presupposed the existence of modern bourgeois society, with its corresponding economic conditions of existence, and the political constitution adapted thereto, the very things whose attainment was the object of the pending struggle in Germany.

To the absolute governments, with their following of parsons, professors, country squires and officials, it served as a welcome scarecrow against the threatening bourgeoisie.

It was a sweet finish after the bitter pills of floggings and bullets with which these same governments, just at that time, dosed the German working-class risings.

While this "True" Socialism thus served the governments as a weapon for fighting the German bourgeoisie, it, at the same time, directly represented a reactionary interest, the interest of the German Philistines. In Germany the *petty-bourgeois* class, a relic of the sixteenth century, and since then constantly cropping up again under various forms, is the real social basis of the existing state of things.

To preserve this class is to preserve the existing state of things in Germany. The industrial and political supremacy of the bourgeoisie threatens it with certain destruction; on the one hand, from the concentration of capital; on the other, from the rise of a revolutionary proletariat. "True" Socialism appeared to kill these two birds with one stone. It spread like an epidemic.

The robe of speculative cobwebs, embroidered with flowers of rhetoric, steeped in the dew of sickly sentiment, this transcendental robe in which the German Socialists wrapped their sorry "eternal truths," all skin and bone, served to wonderfully increase the sale of their goods amongst such a public.

And on its part, German Socialism recognised, more and more, its own calling as the bombastic representative of the petty-bourgeois Philistine.

It proclaimed the German nation to be the model nation, and the German petty Philistine to be the typical man. To every villainous meanness of this model man it gave a hidden, higher, Socialistic interpretation, the exact contrary of its real character. It went to the extreme length of directly opposing the "brutally destructive" tendency of Communism, and of proclaiming its supreme and impartial contempt of all class struggles. With very few exceptions, all the so-called Socialist and Communist publications that now (1847) circulate in Germany belong to the domain of this foul and enervating literature.[5]

2. CONSERVATIVE, OR BOURGEOIS, SOCIALISM

A part of the bourgeoisie is desirous of redressing social grievances, in order to secure the continued existence of bourgeois society.

To this section belong economists, philanthropists, humanitarians, improvers of the condition of the working class, organisers of charity, members of societies for the prevention of cruelty to animals, temperance fanatics, hole-and-corner reformers of every imaginable kind. This form of Socialism has, moreover, been worked out into complete systems.

We may site Proudhon's *Philosophie de la Misère* as an example of this form.

The Socialistic bourgeois want all the advantages of modern social conditions without the struggles and dangers necessarily resulting therefrom. They desire the existing state of society minus its revolutionary and disintegrating elements. They wish for a bourgeoisie without a proletariat. The bourgeoisie naturally conceives the world in which it is supreme to be the best; and bourgeois Socialism develops this comfortable conception into various more or less complete systems. In requiring the proletariat to carry out such a system, and thereby to march straightway into the social New Jerusalem, it but requires in reality, that the proletariat should remain within the bounds of existing society, but should cast away all its hateful ideas concerning the bourgeoisie.

A second and more practical, but less systematic, form of this Socialism sought to depreciate every revolutionary movement in the eyes of the working class, by showing that no mere political reform, but only a change in the material conditions of existence, in economical relations, could be of any advantage to them. By changes in the material conditions of existence, this form of Socialism, however, by no means understands abolition of the bourgeois relations of production, an abolition that can be effected only by a revolution, but administrative reforms, based on the continued existence of these relations; reforms, therefore, that in no respect affect the

5. The revolutionary storm of 1848 swept away this whole shabby tendency and cured its protagonists of the desire to dabble further in Socialism. The chief representative and classical type of this tendency is Herr Karl Grün. [*Engels, German edition of 1890*]

relations between capital and labour, but, at the best, lessen the cost, and simplify the administrative work, of bourgeois government.

Bourgeois Socialism attains adequate expression, when, and only when, it becomes a mere figure of speech.

Free trade: for the benefit of the working class. Protective duties: for the benefit of the working class. Prison Reform: for the benefit of the working class. This is the last word and the only seriously meant word of bourgeois Socialism.

It is summed up in the phrase: the bourgeois is a bourgeois—for the benefit of the working class.

3. CRITICAL-UTOPIAN SOCIALISM AND COMMUNISM

We do not here refer to that literature which, in every great modern revolution, has always given voice to the demands of the proletariat, such as the writings of Babeuf and others.

The first direct attempts of the proletariat to attain its own ends, made in times of universal excitement, when feudal society was being overthrown, these attempts necessarily failed, owing to the then undeveloped state of the proletariat, as well as to the absence of the economic conditions for its emancipation, conditions that had yet to be produced, and could be produced by the impending bourgeois epoch alone. The revolutionary literature that accompanied these first movements of the proletariat had necessarily a reactionary character. It inculcated universal asceticism and social levelling in its crudest form.

The Socialist and Communist systems properly so called, those of Saint-Simon, Fourier, Owen and others, spring into existence in the early undeveloped period, described above, of the struggle between proletariat and bourgeoisie (see Section I. Bourgeois and Proletarians).

The founders of these systems see, indeed, the class antagonisms, as well as the action of the decomposing elements, in the prevailing form of society. But the proletariat, as yet in its infancy, offers to them the spectacle of a class without any historical initiative or any independent political movement.

Since the development of class antagonism keeps even pace with the development of industry, the economic situation, as they find it, does not as yet offer to them the material conditions for the emancipation of the proletariat. They therefore search after a new social science, after new social laws, that are to create these conditions.

Historical action is to yield to their personal inventive action, historically created conditions of emancipation to fantastic ones, and the gradual, spontaneous class-organisation of the proletariat to the organisation of society specially contrived by these inventors. Future history resolves itself, in their eyes, into the propaganda and the practical carrying out of their social plans.

In the formation of their plans they are conscious of caring chiefly for the interests of the working class, as being the most suffering class. Only from the point of view of being the most suffering class does the proletariat exist for them.

The undeveloped state of the class struggle, as well as their own surroundings, causes Socialists of this kind to consider themselves far superior to all class antagonisms. They want to improve the condition of every member of society, even that of the most favoured. Hence, they habitually appeal to society at large, without distinction of class; nay, by preference, to the ruling class. For how can people, when once they understand their system, fail to see in it the best possible plan of the best possible state of society?

Hence, they reject all political, and especially all revolutionary, action; they wish to attain their ends by peaceful means, and endeavour, by small experiments, necessarily doomed to failure, and by the force of example, to pave the way for the new social Gospel.

Such fantastic pictures of future society, painted at a time when the proletariat is still in a very undeveloped state and has but a fantastic conception of its own position correspond with the first instinctive yearnings of that class for a general reconstruction of society.

But these Socialist and Communist publications contain also a critical element. They attack every principle of existing society. Hence they are full of the most valuable materials for the enlightenment of the working class. The practical measures proposed in them —such as the abolition of the distinction between town and country, of the family, of the carrying on of industries for the account of private individuals, and of the wage system, the proclamation of social harmony, the conversion of the functions of the State into a mere superintendence of production, all these proposals, point solely to the disappearance of class antagonisms which were, at that time, only just cropping up, and which, in these publications, are recognised in their earliest, indistinct and undefined forms only. These proposals, therefore, are of a purely Utopian character.

The significance of Critical-Utopian Socialism and Communism bears an inverse relation to historical development. In proportion as the modern class struggle develops and takes definite shape, this fantastic standing apart from the contest, these fantastic attacks on it, lose all practical value and all theoretical justification. Therefore, although the originators of these systems were, in many respects, revolutionary, their disciples have, in every case, formed mere reactionary sects. They hold fast by the original views of their masters, in opposition to the progressive historical development of the proletariat. They, therefore, endeavour, and that consistently, to deaden the class struggle and to reconcile the class antagonisms. They still dream of experimental realisation of their social Utopias, of founding isolated *"phalanstères,"* of establishing "Home Colonies," of setting up a "Little Icaria"[6]—duodecimo editions of the New Jerusalem—and to realise all these castles in the air, they are compelled to appeal to the feelings and purses of the bourgeois. By degrees they sink into the category of the reactionary conservative Socialists depicted above, differing from these only by more systematic pedantry, and by their fanatical and superstitious belief in the miraculous effects of their social science.

They, therefore, violently oppose all political action on the part of the working class; such action, according to them, can only result from blind unbelief in the new Gospel.

The Owenites in England, and the Fourierists in France, respectively, oppose the Chartists and the *Réformistes*.[7]

IV. Position of the Communists in Relation to the Various Existing Opposition Parties

Section II has made clear the relations of the Communists to the existing working-class parties, such as the Chartists in England and the Agrarian Reformers in America.

The Communists fight for the attainment of the immediate aims, for the enforcement of the momentary interests of the working class; but in the movement of the present, they also represent and take care of the future of that movement. In France the Communists ally themselves with the Social-Democrats,[8] against the conservative and radical bourgeoisie, reserving, however, the right to

6. *Phalanstères* were Socialist colonies on the plan of Charles Fourier; *Icaria* was the name given by Cabet to his Utopia and, later on, to his American Communist colony. [*Engels, English edition of 1888*]
"Home colonies" were what Owen called his Communist model societies. *Phalanstères* was the name of the public palaces planned by Fourier. *Icaria* was the name given to the Utopian land of fancy, whose Communist institutions Cabet portrayed. [*Engels, German edition of 1890*]
7. This refers to the adherents of the newspaper *La Réforme*, which was published in Paris from 1843 to 1850.

8. The party then represented in Parliament by Ledru-Rollin, in literature by Louis Blanc, in the daily press by the *Réforme*. The name of Social-Democracy signified, with these its inventors, a section of the Democratic or Republican party more or less tinged with Socialism. [*Engels, English edition of 1888*]
The party in France which at that time called itself Socialist-Democratic was represented in political life by Ledru-Rollin and in literature by Louis Blanc; thus it differed immeasurably from present-day German Social-Democracy. [*Engels, German edition of 1890*]

take up a critical position in regard to phrases and illusions traditionally handed down from the great Revolution.

In Switzerland they support the Radicals, without losing sight of the fact that this party consists of antagonistic elements, partly of Democratic Socialists, in the French sense, partly of radical bourgeois.

In Poland they support the party that insists on an agrarian revolution as the prime condition for national emancipation, that party which fomented the insurrection of Cracow in 1846.

In Germany they fight with the bourgeoisie whenever it acts in a revolutionary way, against the absolute monarchy, the feudal squirearchy, and the petty bourgeoisie.[9]

But they never cease, for a single instant, to instil into the working class the clearest possible recognition of the hostile antagonism between bourgeoisie and proletariat, in order that the German workers may straightway use, as so many weapons against the bourgeoisie, the social and political conditions that the bourgeoisie must necessarily introduce along with its supremacy, and in order that, after the fall of the reactionary classes in Germany, the fight against the bourgeoisie itself may immediately begin.

The Communists turn their attention chiefly to Germany, because that country is on the eve of a bourgeois revolution that is bound to be carried out under more advanced conditions of European civilisation, and with a much more developed proletariat, than that of England was in the seventeenth, and of France in the eighteenth century, and because the bourgeois revolution in Germany will be but the prelude to an immediately following proletarian revolution.

In short, the Communists everywhere support every revolutionary movement against the existing social and political order of things.

In all these movements they bring to the front, as the leading question in each, the property question, no matter what its degree of development at the time.

Finally, they labour everywhere for the union and agreement of the democratic parties of all countries.

The Communists disdain to conceal their views and aims. They openly declare that their ends can be attained only by the forcible overthrow of all existing social conditions. Let the ruling classes tremble at a Communistic revolution. The proletarians have nothing to lose but their chains. They have a world to win.

WORKING MEN OF ALL COUNTRIES, UNITE!

9. *Kleinbürgerei* in the German original. Marx and Engels used this term to describe the reactionary elements of the urban petty bourgeoisie.

Address of the Central Committee
to the Communist League

MARX AND ENGELS

In 1848 most of the German workers in the Communist League returned
to their homeland, and some played prominent parts in the revolutionary
events there. In early 1850, when the wave of revolution had subsided but
hope still existed for a new wave, Marx and Engels wrote this Address and
dispatched it with an emissary to Germany for circulation among League
members. In it they presented a radical political strategy for use in event of
a resurgence of revolution in Germany, a strategy aimed at "making the revolution permanent." This meant preventing the "petty bourgeois democracy," which would inevitably lead the initial phase of a new revolutionary
wave, from consolidating its ascendancy and keeping the movement in
purely reformist channels. Looking back in 1885, in his essay "On the History of the Communist League," Engels wrote that the Address "is still of
interest today, because petty-bourgeois democracy is even now the party
which must certainly be the first to come to power in Germany as the sav-
ior of society from the communist workers on the occasion of the next European upheaval now soon due (the European revolutions, 1815, 1830,
1848–52, 1870, have occurred at intervals of fifteen to eighteen years in
our century)."

Brothers! In the two revolutionary years 1848–49 the League
proved itself in double fashion: first, in that its members energetically took part in the movement in all places, that in the press, on
the barricades and on the battlefields, they stood in the front ranks
of the only decidedly revolutionary class, the proletariat. The
League further proved itself in that its conception of the movement
as laid down in the circulars of the congresses and of the Central
Committee of 1847 as well as in the *Communist Manifesto* turned
out to be the only correct one, that the expectations expressed in
those documents were completely fulfilled and the conception of

present-day social conditions, previously propagated only in secret by the League, is now on everyone's lips and is openly preached in the market places. At the same time the former firm organisation of the League was considerably slackened. A large part of the members who directly participated in the revolutionary movement believed the time for secret societies to have gone by and public activities alone sufficient. The individual circles and communities allowed their connections with the Central Committee to become loose and gradually dormant. Consequently, while the democratic party, the party of the petty bourgeoisie, organised itself more and more in Germany, the workers' party lost its only firm foothold, remained organised at the most in separate localities for local purposes and in the general movement thus came completely under the domination and leadership of the petty-bourgeois democrats. An end must be put to this state of affairs, the independence of the workers must be restored. The Central Committee realised this necessity and therefore already in the winter of 1848–49 it sent an emissary, Josef Moll, to Germany for the reorganisation of the League. Moll's mission, however, was without lasting effect, partly because the German workers at that time had not acquired sufficient experience and partly because it was interrupted by the insurrection of the previous May. Moll himself took up the musket, entered the Baden-Palatinate army and fell on July 19 in the encounter at the Murg. The League lost in him one of its oldest, most active and most trustworthy members, one who had been active in all the congresses and Central Committees and even prior to this had carried out a series of missions with great success. After the defeat of the revolutionary parties of Germany and France in July 1849, almost all the members of the Central Committee came together again in London, replenished their numbers with new revolutionary forces and set about the reorganisation of the League with renewed zeal.

Reorganisation can only be carried out by an emissary, and the Central Committee considers it extremely important that the emissary should leave precisely at this moment when a new revolution is impending, when the workers' party, therefore, must act in the most organised, most unanimous and most independent fashion possible if it is not to be exploited and taken in tow again by the bourgeoisie as in 1848.

Brothers! We told you as early as 1848 that the German liberal bourgeois would soon come to power and would immediately turn their newly acquired power against the workers. You have seen how this has been fulfilled. In fact it was the bourgeois who, immediately after the March movement of 1848, took possession of the state power and used this power to force back at once the workers, their allies in the struggle, into their former oppressed position.

Though the bourgeoisie was not able to accomplish this without uniting with the feudal party, which had been disposed of in March, without finally even surrendering power once again to this feudal absolutist party, still it has secured conditions for itself which, in the long run, owing to the financial embarrassment of the government, would place power in its hands and would safeguard all its interests, if it were possible for the revolutionary movement to assume already now a so-called peaceful development. The bourgeoisie, in order to safeguard its rule, would not even need to make itself obnoxious by violent measures against the people, since all such violent steps have already been taken by the feudal counterrevolution. Developments, however, will not take this peaceful course. On the contrary, the revolution, which will accelerate this development, is near at hand, whether it will be called forth by an independent uprising of the French proletariat or by an invasion of the Holy Alliance against the revolutionary Babylon.[1]

And the role, this so treacherous role which the German liberal bourgeois played in 1848 against the people, will in the impending revolution be taken over by the democratic petty bourgeois, who at present occupy the same position in the opposition as the liberal bourgeois before 1848. This party, the democratic party, which is far more dangerous to the workers than the previous liberal one, consists of three elements:

I. Of the most advanced sections of the big bourgeoisie, which pursue the aim of the immediate complete overthrow of feudalism and absolutism. This faction is represented by the one-time Berlin compromisers, by the tax resisters.

II. Of the democratic-constitutional petty bourgeois, whose main aim during the previous movement was the establishment of a more or less democratic federal state as striven for by their representatives, the Lefts in the Frankfort Assembly, and later by the Stuttgart parliament, and by themselves in the campaign for the Reich Constitution.

III. Of the republican petty bourgeois, whose ideal is a German federative republic after the manner of Switzerland, and who now call themselves Red and social-democratic because they cherish the pious wish of abolishing the pressure of big capital on small capital, of the big bourgeois on the small bourgeois. The representatives of this faction were the members of the democratic congresses and committees, the leaders of the democratic associations, the editors of the democratic newspapers.

Now, after their defeat, all these factions call themselves Republicans or Reds, just as the republican petty bourgeois in France now

1. *Revolutionary Babylon:* The reference is to Paris, which ever since the French bourgeois revolution of the end of the eighteenth century was considered the hotbed of the revolution.

call themselves Socialists. Where, as in Württemberg, Bavaria, etc., they still find opportunity to pursue their aims constitutionally, they seize the occasion to retain their old phrases and to prove by deeds that they have not changed in the least. It is evident, moreover, that the altered name of this party does not make the slightest difference in its attitude to the workers, but merely proves that they are now obliged to turn against the bourgeoisie, which is united with absolutism, and to seek support in the proletariat.

The petty-bourgeois democratic party in Germany is very powerful; it comprises not only the great majority of the bourgeois inhabitants of the towns, the small people in industry and trade and the guild masters; it numbers among its followers also the peasants and the rural proletariat, in so far as the latter has not yet found a support in the independent urban proletariat.

The relation of the revolutionary workers' party to the petty-bourgeois democrats is this: it marches together with them against the faction which it aims at overthrowing, it opposes them in everything whereby they seek to consolidate their position in their own interests.

Far from desiring to revolutionise all society for the revolutionary proletarians, the democratic petty bourgeois strive for a change in social conditions by means of which existing society will be made as tolerable and comfortable as possible for them. Hence they demand above all diminution of state expenditure by a curtailment of the bureaucracy and shifting the chief taxes on to the big landowners and bourgeois. Further, they demand the abolition of the pressure of big capital on small, through public credit institutions and laws against usury, by which means it will be possible for them and the peasants to obtain advances, on favourable conditions, from the state instead of from the capitalists; they also demand the establishment of bourgeois property relations in the countryside by the complete abolition of feudalism. To accomplish all this they need a democratic state structure, either constitutional or republican, that will give them and their allies, the peasants, a majority; also a democratic communal structure that will give them direct control over communal property and over a series of functions now performed by the bureaucrats.

The domination and speedy increase of capital is further to be counteracted partly by restricting the right of inheritance and partly by transferring as many jobs of work as possible to the state. As far as the workers are concerned, it remains certain above all that they are to remain wage-workers as before; the democratic petty bourgeois only desire better wages and a more secure existence for the workers and hope to achieve this through partial employment by the state and through charity measures; in short, they hope to bribe the workers by more or less concealed alms and to break their revolutionary potency by making their position tolerable for the moment. The demands of the petty-bourgeois democracy here summarised are not put forward by all of its factions at the same time and only a very few members of them consider that these demands constitute definite aims in their entirety. The further separate individuals or factions among them go, the more of these demands will they make their own, and those few who see their own programme in what has been outlined above might believe that thereby they have put forward the utmost that can be demanded from the revolution. But these demands can in nowise suffice for the party of the proletariat. While the democratic petty bourgeois wish to bring the revolution to a conclusion as quickly as possible, and with the achievement, at most, of the above demands, it is our interest and our task to make the revolution permanent, until all more or less possessing classes have been forced out of their position of dominance, until the proletariat has conquered state power, and the association of proletarians, not only in one country but in all the dominant countries of the world, has advanced so far that competition among the proletarians of these countries has ceased and that at least the decisive productive forces are concentrated in the hands of the proletarians. For us the issue cannot be the alteration of private property but only its annihilation, not the smoothing over of class antagonisms but the abolition of classes, not the improvement of existing society but the foundation of a new one. That during the further development of the revolution, the petty-bourgeois democracy will for a moment obtain predominating influence in Germany is not open to doubt. The question, therefore, arises as to what the attitude of the proletariat and in particular of the League will be in relation to it:

1. During the continuance of the present conditions where the petty-bourgeois democrats are likewise oppressed;

2. In the next revolutionary struggle, which will give them the upper hand;

3. After this struggle, during the period of preponderance over the overthrown classes and the proletariat.

1. At the present moment, when the democratic petty bourgeois are everywhere oppressed, they preach in general unity and reconciliation to the proletariat, they offer it their hand and strive for the establishment of a large opposition party which will embrace all shades of opinion in the democratic party, that is, they strive to entangle the workers in a party organisation in which general social-democratic phrases predominate, behind which their special inter-

ests are concealed and in which the particular demands of the proletariat may not be brought forward for the sake of beloved peace. Such a union would turn out solely to their advantage and altogether to the disadvantage of the proletariat. The proletariat would lose its whole independent, laboriously achieved position and once more sink down to being an appendage of official bourgeois democracy. This union must, therefore, be most decisively rejected. Instead of once again stooping to serve as the applauding chorus of the bourgeois democrats, the workers, and above all the League, must exert themselves to establish an independent, secret and public organisation of the workers' party alongside of the official democrats and make each section the central point and nucleus of workers' societies in which the attitude and interests of the proletariat will be discussed independently of bourgeois influences. How far the bourgeois democrats are from seriously considering an alliance in which the proletarians would stand side by side with them with equal power and equal rights is shown, for example, by the Breslau democrats who, in their organ, the *Neue Oder-Zeitung*,[2] most furiously attack the independently organised workers, whom they style Socialists. In the case of a struggle against a common adversary no special union is required. As soon as such an adversary has to be fought directly, the interests of both parties, for the moment, coincide, and, as previously, so also in the future, this connection, calculated to last only for the moment, will arise of itself. It is self-evident that in the impending bloody conflicts, as in all earlier ones, it is the workers who, in the main, will have to win the victory by their courage, determination and self-sacrifice. As previously, so also in this struggle, the mass of the petty bourgeois will as long as possible remain hesitant, undecided and inactive, and then, as soon as the issue has been decided, will seize the victory for themselves, will call upon the workers to maintain tranquillity and return to their work, will guard against so-called excesses and bar the proletariat from the fruits of victory. It is not in the power of the workers to prevent the petty-bourgeois democrats from doing this, but it is in their power to make it difficult for them to gain the upper hand as against the armed proletariat, and to dictate such conditions to them that the rule of the bourgeois democrats will from the outset bear within it the seeds of their downfall, and that their subsequent extrusion by the rule of the proletariat will be considerably facilitated. Above all things, the workers must counteract, as much as is at all possible, during the conflict and immediately after the struggle, the bourgeois endeavours to allay the storm, and must

2. *Neue Oder-Zeitung* (*New Oder Gazette*): Appeared daily in Breslau in 1849–55.

compel the democrats to carry out their present terrorist phrases. Their actions must be so aimed as to prevent the direct revolutionary excitement from being suppressed again immediately after the victory. On the contrary, they must keep it alive as long as possible. Far from opposing so-called excesses, instances of popular revenge against hated individuals or public buildings that are associated only with hateful recollections, such instances must not only be tolerated but the leadership of them taken in hand. During the struggle and after the struggle, the workers must, at every opportunity, put forward their own demands alongside of the demands of the bourgeois democrats. They must demand guarantees for the workers as soon as the democratic bourgeois set about taking over the government. If necessary they must obtain these guarantees by force and in general they must see to it that the new rulers pledge themselves to all possible concessions and promises—the surest way to compromise them. In general, they must in every way restrain as far as possible the intoxication of victory and the enthusiasm for the new state of things, which make their appearance after every victorious street battle, by a calm and dispassionate estimate of the situation and by unconcealed mistrust in the new government. Alongside of the new official governments they must establish simultaneously their own revolutionary workers' governments, whether in the form of municipal committees and municipal councils or in the form of workers' clubs or workers' committees, so that the bourgeois-democratic governments not only immediately lose the support of the workers but from the outset see themselves supervised and threatened by authorities which are backed by the whole mass of the workers. In a word, from the first moment of victory, mistrust must be directed no longer against the conquered reactionary party, but against the workers' previous allies, against the party that wishes to exploit the common victory for itself alone.

2. But in order to be able energetically and threateningly to oppose this party, whose treachery to the workers will begin from the first hour of victory, the workers must be armed and organised. The arming of the whole proletariat with rifles, muskets, cannon and munitions must be put through at once, the revival of the old Citizens' Guard directed against the workers must be resisted. However, where the latter is not feasible the workers must attempt to organise themselves independently as a proletarian guard with commanders elected by themselves and with a general staff of their own choosing, and to put themselves at the command not of the state authority but of the revolutionary community councils which the workers will have managed to get adopted. Where workers are employed at the expense of the state they must see that they are

armed and organised in a separate corps with commanders of their own choosing or as part of the proletarian guard. Arms and ammunition must not be surrendered on any pretext; any attempt at disarming must be frustrated, if necessary by force. Destruction of the influence of the bourgeois democrats upon the workers, immediate independent and armed organisation of the workers and the enforcement of conditions as difficult and compromising as possible upon the inevitable momentary rule of the bourgeois democracy— these are the main points which the proletariat and hence the League must keep in view during and after the impending insurrection.

3. As soon as the new governments have consolidated their positions to some extent, their struggle against the workers will begin. Here, in order to be able to offer energetic opposition to the democratic petty bourgeois, it is above all necessary that the workers shall be independently organised and centralised in clubs. After the overthrow of the existing governments, the Central Committee will, as soon as it is at all possible, betake itself to Germany, immediately convene a congress and put before the latter the necessary proposals for the centralisation of the workers' clubs under a leadership established in the chief seat of the movement. The speedy organisation of at least a provincial interlinking of the workers' clubs is one of the most important points for the strengthening and development of the workers' party; the immediate consequence of the overthrow of the existing governments will be the election of a national representative assembly. Here the proletariat must see to it:

I. That no groups of workers are barred on any pretext or by any kind of trickery on the part of local authorities or government commissioners.

II. That everywhere workers' candidates are put up alongside of the bourgeois-democratic candidates, that they should consist as far as possible of members of the League, and that their election is promoted by all possible means. Even where there is no prospect whatsoever of their being elected, the workers must put up their own candidates in order to preserve their independence, to count their forces and to bring before the public their revolutionary attitude and party standpoint. In this connection they must not allow themselves to be seduced by such arguments of the democrats as, for example, that by so doing they are splitting the democratic party and making it possible for the reactionaries to win. The ultimate intention of all such phrases is to dupe the proletariat. The advance which the proletarian party is bound to make by such independent action is infinitely more important than the disadvantage that might be incurred by the presence of a few reactionaries in the representative body. If the democracy from the outset comes out resolutely and terroristically against the reaction, the influence of the latter in the elections will be destroyed in advance.

The first point on which the bourgeois democrats will come into conflict with the workers will be the abolition of feudalism. As in the first French Revolution, the petty bourgeois will give the feudal lands to the peasants as free property, that is to say, try to leave the rural proletariat in existence and form a petty-bourgeois peasant class which will go through the same cycle of impoverishment and indebtedness which the French peasant is now still going through.

The workers must oppose this plan in the interest of the rural proletariat and in their own interest. They must demand that the confiscated feudal property remain state property and be converted into workers' colonies cultivated by the associated rural proletariat with all the advantages of large-scale agriculture, through which the principle of common property immediately obtains a firm basis in the midst of the tottering bourgeois property relations. Just as the democrats combine with the peasants so must the workers combine with the rural proletariat. Further, the democrats will work either directly for a federative republic, or, if they cannot avoid a single and indivisible republic, they will at least attempt to cripple the central government by the utmost possible autonomy and independence for the communities[3] and provinces. The workers, in opposition to this plan, must not only strive for a single and indivisible German republic, but also within this republic for the most determined centralisation of power in the hands of the state authority. They must not allow themselves to be misguided by the democratic talk of freedom for the communities, of self-government, etc. In a country like Germany where there are still so many relics of the Middle Ages to be abolished, where there is so much local and provincial obstinacy to be broken, it must under no circumstances be permitted that every village, every town and every province should put a new obstacle in the path of revolutionary activity, which can proceed with full force only from the centre. It is not to be tolerated that the present state of affairs should be renewed, that Germans must fight separately in every town and in every province for one and the same advance. Least of all is it to be tolerated that a form of property, namely, communal property, which still lags behind modern private property and which everywhere is necessarily passing into the latter, together with the quarrels resulting from it between poor and rich communities, as well as communal civil law, with its trickery against the workers, that exists alongside of state civil law, should be perpetuated by a so-called free communal constitution. As in France in 1793 so today in Germany it is the task of

---

3. *Community* (*Gemeinde*): This term is employed here in a wide sense to embrace both urban municipalities and rural communities.

the really revolutionary party to carry through the strictest central-isation.[4]

We have seen how the democrats will come to power with the next movement, how they will be compelled to propose more or less socialistic measures. It will be asked what measures the workers ought to propose in reply. At the beginning of the movement, of course, the workers cannot yet propose any directly communistic measures. But they can:

1. Compel the democrats to interfere in as many spheres as possible of the hitherto existing social order, to disturb its regular course and to compromise themselves as well as to concentrate the utmost possible productive forces, means of transport, factories, railways, etc., in the hands of the state;

2. They must drive the proposals of the democrats, who in any case will not act in a revolutionary but in a merely reformist manner, to the extreme and transform them into direct attacks upon private property; thus, for example, if the petty bourgeois propose purchase of the railways and factories, the workers must demand that these railways and factories shall be simply confiscated by the state without compensation as being the property of reactionaries. If the democrats propose proportional taxes, the workers must demand progressive taxes; if the democrats themselves put forward a moderately progressive tax, the workers must insist on a tax with rates that rise so steeply that big capital will be ruined by it; if the democrats demand the regulation of state debts, the workers must demand state bankruptcy. Thus, the demands of the workers must everywhere be governed by the concessions and measures of the democrats.

If the German workers are not able to attain power and achieve their own class interests without completely going through a

4. It must be recalled today that this passage is based on a misunderstanding. At that time—thanks to the Bonapartist and liberal falsifiers of history—it was considered as established that the French centralised machine of administration had been introduced by the Great Revolution and in particular that it had been operated by the Convention as an indispensable and decisive weapon for defeating the royalist and federalist reaction and the external enemy. It is now, however, a well-known fact that throughout the whole revolution up to the eighteenth Brumaire the whole administration of the departments, arrondissements and communes consisted of authorities elected by the respective constituents themselves, and that these authorities acted with complete freedom within the general state laws; that precisely this provincial and local self-government, similar to the American, became the most powerful lever of the revolution and indeed to such an extent that Napoleon, immediately after his *coup d'état* of the eighteenth Brumaire, hastened to replace it by an administration by prefects, which still exists and which, therefore, was a pure instrument of reaction from the beginning. But just as little as local and provincial self-government is in contradiction to political, national centralisation, so is it to an equally small extent necessarily bound up with that narrow-minded, cantonal or communal self-seeking which strikes us as so repulsive in Switzerland, and which all the South German federal republicans wanted to make the rule in Germany in 1849. [*Engels, 1885 edition*]

lengthy revolutionary development, they at least know for a certainty this time that the first act of this approaching revolutionary drama will coincide with the direct victory of their own class in France and will be very much accelerated by it.

But they themselves must do the utmost for their final victory by clarifying their minds as to what their class interests are, by taking up their position as an independent party as soon as possible and by not allowing themselves to be seduced for a single moment by the hypocritical phrases of the democratic petty bourgeois into refraining from the independent organisation of the party of the proletariat. Their battle cry must be: The Revolution in Permanence.

Inaugural Address of the
Working Men's International Association

KARL MARX

Marx wrote the Inaugural Address in October, 1864, as a charter document
for the Working Men's International Association (otherwise known as the
First International), which was established on September 28, 1864, at a
meeting in St. Martin's Hall in London. It was both a review of the work-
ing-class movement since 1848 and a program. Despite the echo of the
Communist Manifesto in the closing words ("Proletarians of all countries,
Unite!"), some have seen the Inaugural Address, with its salute to the
English Ten Hours' Bill, as a herald of the decreasingly revolutionary
Marxist Social Democratic movement of the late nineteenth century.
Against this interpretation must be set Marx's shorthand recapitulation of
his theory of history and proletarian revolution in the statement here that
"hired labor is but a transitory and inferior form, destined to disappear before associated labour plying its toil with a willing hand, a ready mind, and
a joyous heart." Given the disparate character of the various national con-
tingents of the new association, some less radical than others, there was
also a tactical reason for restraint on revolutionary rhetoric. As Marx wrote
to Engels on November 4, 1864: "It was very difficult to frame the thing
so that our view should appear in a form acceptable from the present standpoint of the workers' movement. . . . It will take time before the reawak-
ened movement allows the old boldness of speech."

Working Men,

It is a great fact that the misery of the working masses has not
diminished from 1848 to 1864, and yet this period is unrivalled for
the development of its industry and the growth of its commerce. In
1850, a moderate organ of the British middle class, of more than
average information, predicted that if the exports and imports of
England were to rise 50 per cent, English pauperism would sink to
zero. Alas! on April 7, 1864, the Chancellor of the Exchequer
delighted his parliamentary audience by the statement that the total

import and export trade of England had grown in 1863 "to £443,955,000! that astonishing sum about three times the trade of the comparatively recent epoch of 1843!" With all that, he was eloquent upon "poverty." "Think," he exclaimed, "of those who are on the border of that region," upon "wages . . . not increased"; upon "human life . . . in nine cases out of ten but a struggle of existence!" He did not speak of the people of Ireland, gradually replaced by machinery in the north, and by sheep-walks in the south, though even the sheep in that unhappy country are decreasing, it is true, not at so rapid a rate as the men. He did not repeat what then had been just betrayed by the highest representatives of the upper ten thousand in a sudden fit of terror. When the garotte[1] panic had reached a certain height, the House of Lords caused an inquiry to be made into, and a report to be published upon, transportation and penal servitude. Out came the murder in the bulky Blue Book of 1863, and proved it was, by official facts and figures, that the worst of the convicted criminals, the penal serfs of England and Scotland, toiled much less and fared far better than the agricultural labourers of England and Scotland. But this was not all. When, consequent upon the Civil War in America, the operatives of Lancashire and Cheshire were thrown upon the streets, the same House of Lords sent to the manufacturing districts a physician commissioned to investigate into the smallest possible amount of carbon and nitrogen, to be administered in the cheapest and plainest from, which on an average might just suffice to "avert starvation diseases." Dr. Smith, the medical deputy, ascertained that 28,000 grains of carbon, and 1,330 grains of nitrogen were the weekly allowance that would keep an average adult . . . just over the level of starvation diseases, and he found furthermore that quantity pretty nearly to agree with the scanty nourishment to which the pressure of extreme distress had actually reduced the cotton operatives.[2] But now mark! The same learned Doctor was later on again deputed by the medical officer of the Privy Council to inquire into the nourishment of the poorer labouring classes. The results of his researches are embodied in the "Sixth Report on Public Health," published by order of Parliament in the course of the present year. What did the Doctor discover? That the silk weavers, the needle women, the kid glovers, the stocking weavers, and so forth, received, on an average, not even the distress pittance of the cotton

1. *Garotters*: Street robbers whose attacks increased in London in the beginning of the sixties to such an extent that Parliament was compelled to take up the matter.
2. We need hardly remind the reader that, apart from the elements of water and certain inorganic substances, carbon and nitrogen form the raw materials of human food. However, to nourish the human system, those simple chemical constituents must be supplied in the form of vegetable or animal substances. Potatoes, for instance, contain mainly carbon, while wheaten bread contains carbonaceous and nitrogenous substances in a due proportion. [*Marx*]

operatives, not even the amount of carbon and nitrogen "just sufficient to avert starvation diseases."

"Moreover," we quote from the report, "as regards the examined families of the agricultural population, it appeared that more than a fifth were with less than the estimated sufficiency of carbonaceous food, that more than one-third were with less than the estimated sufficiency of nitrogenous food, and that in three counties (Berkshire, Oxfordshire and Somersetshire) insufficiency of nitrogenous food was the average local diet." "It must be remembered," adds the official report, "that privation of food is very reluctantly borne, and that, as a rule, great poorness of diet will only come when other privations have preceded it. . . . Even cleanliness will have been found costly or difficult, and if there still be self-respectful endeavours to maintain it, every such endeavour will represent additional pangs of hunger." "These are painful reflections, especially when it is remembered that the poverty to which they advert is not the deserved poverty of idleness; in all cases it is the poverty of working populations. Indeed, the work which obtains the scanty pittance of food is for the most part excessively prolonged." The report brings out the strange, and rather unexpected fact: "That of the divisions of the United Kingdom," England, Wales, Scotland, and Ireland, "the agricultural population of England," the richest division, "is considerably the worst fed"; but that even the agricultural labourers of Berkshire, Oxfordshire, and Somersetshire, fare better than great numbers of skilled indoor operatives of the East of London.

Such are the official statements published by order of Parliament in 1864, during the millennium of free trade, at a time when the Chancellor of the Exchequer told the House of Commons that "the average condition of the British labourer has improved in a degree we know to be extraordinary and unexampled in the history of any country or any age." Upon these official congratulations jars the dry remark of the official Public Health Report: "The public health of a country means the health of its masses, and the masses will scarcely be healthy unless, to their very base, they be at least moderately prosperous."

Dazzled by the "Progress of the Nation" statistics dancing before his eyes, the Chancellor of the Exchequer exclaims in wild ecstasy: "From 1842 to 1852 the taxable income of the country increased by 6 per cent; in the eight years from 1853 to 1861, it has increased from the basis taken in 1853 20 per cent! the fact is so astonishing as to be almost incredible! . . . This intoxicating augmentation of wealth and power," adds Mr. Gladstone, "is entirely confined to classes of property!"

If you want to know under what conditions of broken health, tainted morals and mental ruin, that "intoxicating augmentation of wealth and power entirely confined to classes of property" was, and is being produced by the classes of labour, look to the picture hung up in the last "Public Health Report" of the workshops of tailors, printers and dressmakers! Compare the "Report of the Children's Employment Commission" of 1863, where it is stated, for instance, that: "The potters as a class, both men and women, represent a much degenerated population, both physically and mentally," that "the unhealthy child is an unhealthy parent in his turn," that "a progressive deterioration of the race must go on," and that "the degenerescence of the population of Staffordshire would be even greater were it not for the constant recruiting from the adjacent country, and the intermarriages with more healthy races." Glance at Mr. Tremenheere's Blue Book on the "Grievances complained of by the Journeymen Bakers"! And who has not shuddered at the paradoxical statement made by the inspectors of factories, all illustrated by the Registrar General, that the Lancashire operatives, while put upon the distress pittance of food, were actually improving in health, because of their temporary exclusion by the cotton famine from the cotton factory, and that the mortality of the children was decreasing, because their mothers were now at last allowed to give them, instead of Godfrey's cordial, their own breasts.

Again reverse the medal! The Income and Property Tax Returns laid before the House of Commons on July 20, 1864, teach us that the persons with yearly incomes, valued by the tax-gatherer at £50,000 and upwards, had, from April 5, 1862, to April 5, 1863, been joined by a dozen and one, their number having increased in that single year from 67 to 80. The same returns disclose the fact that about 3,000 persons divide amongst themselves a yearly income of about £25,000,000 sterling, rather more than the total revenue doled out annually to the whole mass of the agricultural labourers of England and Wales. Open the census of 1861, and you will find that the number of the male landed proprietors of England and Wales had decreased from 16,934 in 1851, to 15,066 in 1861, so that the concentration of land had grown in 10 years 11 per cent. If the concentration of the soil of the country in a few hands proceeds at the same rate, the land question will become singularly simplified, as it had become in the Roman empire, when Nero grinned at the discovery that half the Province of Africa was owned by six gentlemen.

We have dwelt so long upon these "facts so astonishing to be almost incredible," because England heads the Europe of commerce and industry. It will be remembered that some months ago one of the refugee sons of Louis Philippe publicly congratulated the English agricultural labourer on the superiority of his lot over that of his less florid comrade on the other side of the Channel. Indeed, with local colours changed, and on a scale somewhat contracted, the English acts reproduce themselves in all the industrious and progressive countries of the Continent. In all of them there has taken place, since 1848, an unheard-of development of industry, and an undreamed-of expansion of imports and exports. In all of them "the augmentation of wealth and power entirely confined to classes of property" was truly "intoxicating." In all of them, as in England, a minority of the working classes got their real wages somewhat advanced; while in most cases the monetary rise of wages denoted no more a real access of comforts than the inmate of the metropolitan poor-house or orphan asylum, for instance, was in the least benefited by his first necessaries costing £9 15s. 8d. in 1861 against £7 7s. 4d. in 1852. Everywhere the great mass of the working classes were sinking down to a lower depth, at the same rate at least, that those above them were rising in the social scale. In all countries of Europe it has now become a truth demonstrable to every unprejudiced mind, and only denied by those, whose interest it is to hedge other people in a fool's paradise, that no improvement of machinery, no appliance of science to production, no contrivances of communication, no new colonies, no emigration, no opening of markets, no free trade, nor all these things put together, will do away with the miseries of the industrious masses; but that, on the present false base, every fresh development of the productive powers of labour must tend to deepen social contrasts and point social antagonisms. Death of starvation rose almost to the rank of an institution, during this intoxicating epoch of economical progress, in the metropolis of the British Empire. That epoch is marked in the annals of the world by the quickened return, the widening compass, and the deadlier effects of the social pest called a commercial and industrial crisis.

After the failure of the Revolutions of 1848, all party organisations and party journals of the working classes were, on the Continent, crushed by the iron hand of force, the most advanced sons of labour fled in despair to the Transatlantic Republic, and the short-lived dreams of emancipation vanished before an epoch of industrial fever, moral marasme, and political reaction. The defeat of the Continental working classes, partly owed to the diplomacy of the English Government, acting then as now in fraternal solidarity with the Cabinet of St. Petersburg, soon spread its contagious effects to this side of the Channel. While the rout of their Continental brethren unmanned the English working classes, and broke their faith in their own cause, it restored to the landlord and the money-lord their somewhat shaken confidence. They insolently withdrew concessions already advertised. The discoveries of new goldlands led to an immense exodus, leaving an irreparable void in the ranks of the

British proletariat. Others of its formerly active members were caught by the temporary bribe of greater work and wages, and turned into "political blacks." All the efforts made at keeping up, or remodeling, the Chartist Movement, failed signally; the press organs of the working class died one by one of the apathy of the masses, and, in point of fact, never before seemed the English working class so thoroughly reconciled to a state of political nullity. If, then, there had been no solidarity of action between the British and the Continental working classes, there was, at all events, a solidarity of defeat.

And yet the period passed since the Revolutions of 1848 has not been without its compensating features. We shall here only point to two great facts.

After a thirty years' struggle, fought with most admirable perseverance, the English working classes, improving a momentaneous split between the landlords and money-lords, succeeded in carrying the Ten Hours' Bill. The immense physical, moral and intellectual benefits hence accruing to the factory operatives, half-yearly chronicled in the reports of the inspectors of factories, are now acknowledged on all sides. Most of the Continental governments had to accept the English Factory Act in more or less modified forms, and the English Parliament itself is every year compelled to enlarge its sphere of action. But besides its practical import, there was something else to exalt the marvellous success of this working men's measure. Through their most notorious organs of science, such as Dr. Ure, Professor Senior, and other sages of that stamp, the middle class had predicted, and to their heart's content proved, that any legal restriction of the hours of labour must sound the death knell of British industry, which, vampyre like, could but live by sucking blood, and children's blood, too. In olden times, child murder was a mysterious rite of the religion of Moloch, but it was practised on some very solemn occasions only, once a year perhaps, and then Moloch had no exclusive bias for the children of the poor. This struggle about the legal restriction of the hours of labour raged the more fiercely since, apart from frightened avarice, it told indeed upon the great contest between the blind rule of the supply and demand laws which form the political economy of the middle class, and social production controlled by social foresight, which forms the political economy of the working class. Hence the Ten Hours' Bill was not only a great practical success; it was the victory of a principle; it was the first time that in broad daylight the political economy of the middle class succumbed to the political economy of the working class.

But there was in store a still greater victory of the political economy of labour over the political economy of property. We speak of the co-operative movement, especially the co-operative factories raised by the unassisted efforts of a few bold "hands." The value of these great social experiments cannot be over-rated. By deed, instead of by argument, they have shown that production on a large scale, and in accord with the behests of modern science, may be carried on without the existence of a class of masters employing a class of hands; that to bear fruit, the means of labour need not be monopolised as a means of dominion over, and of extortion against, the labouring man himself; and that, like slave labour, like serf labour, hired labour is but a transitory and inferior form, destined to disappear before associated labour plying its toil with a willing hand, a ready mind, and a joyous heart. In England, the seeds of the co-operative system were sown by Robert Owen; the working men's experiments, tried on the Continent, were, in fact, the practical upshot of the theories, not invented, but loudly proclaimed, in 1848.

At the same time, the experience of the period from 1848 to 1864 has proved beyond doubt that, however excellent in principle, and however useful in practice, co-operative labour, if kept within the narrow circle of the casual efforts of private workmen, will never be able to arrest the growth in geometrical progression of monopoly, to free the masses, nor even to perceptibly lighten the burden of their miseries. It is perhaps for this very reason that plausible noblemen, philanthropic middle-class spouters, and even keen political economists, have all at once turned nauseously complimentary to the very co-operative labour system they had vainly tried to nip in the bud by deriding it as the Utopia of the dreamer, or stigmatising it as the sacrilege of the Socialist. To save the industrious masses, co-operative labour ought to be developed to national dimensions, and consequently, to be fostered by national means. Yet, the lords of land and the lords of capital will always use their political privileges for the defence and perpetuation of their economical monopolies. So far from promoting, they will continue to lay every possible impediment in the way of the emancipation of labour. Remember the sneer with which, last session, Lord Palmerston put down the advocates of the Irish Tenants' Right Bill. The House of Commons, cried he, is a house of landed proprietors. To conquer political power has therefore become the great duty of the working classes. They seem to have comprehended this, for in England, Germany, Italy, and France there have taken place simultaneous revivals, and simultaneous efforts are being made at the political reorganisation of the working men's party.

One element of success they possess—numbers; but numbers weigh only in the balance, if united by combination and led by knowledge. Past experience has shown how disregard of that bond of brotherhood which ought to exist between the workmen of different countries, and incite them to stand firmly by each other in all their struggles for emancipation, will be chastised by the common discomfiture of their incoherent efforts. This thought prompted the working men of different countries assembled on September 28, 1864, in public meeting at St. Martin's Hall, to found the International Association.

Another conviction swayed that meeting.

If the emancipation of the working classes requires their fraternal concurrence, how are they to fulfil that great mission with a foreign policy in pursuit of criminal designs, playing upon national prejudices, and squandering in piratical wars the people's blood and treasure? It was not the wisdom of the ruling classes, but the heroic resistance to their criminal folly by the working classes of England that saved the West of Europe from plunging headlong into an infamous crusade for the perpetuation and propagation of slavery on the other side of the Atlantic. The shameless approval, mock sympathy, or idiotic indifference, with which the upper classes of Europe have witnessed the mountain fortress of the Caucasus falling a prey to, and heroic Poland being assassinated by, Russia; the immense and unresisted encroachments of that barbarous power, whose head is at St. Petersburg, and whose hands are in every cabinet of Europe, have taught the working classes the duty to master themselves the mysteries of international politics; to watch the diplomatic acts of their respective Governments; to counteract them, if necessary, by all means in their power; when unable to prevent, to combine in simultaneous denunciations, and to vindicate the simple laws of morals and justice, which ought to govern the relations of private individuals, as the rules paramount of the intercourse of nations.

The fight for such a foreign policy forms part of the general struggle for the emancipation of the working classes.

Proletarians of all countries, Unite!

Economics and Politics in the Labor Movement

KARL MARX

That the trade unionist pressure for a shorter working day endorsed in the Inaugural Address did not mean to Marx the abandonment of the revolutionary politics of class struggle is shown in the following selection from his letter of November 23, 1871, to F. Bolte.

---

* * * The political movement of the working class has as its ultimate object, of course, the conquest of political power for this class, and this naturally requires a previous organisation of the working class developed up to a certain point and arising precisely from its economic struggles.

On the other hand, however, every movement in which the working class comes out as a *class* against the ruling classes and tries to coerce them by pressure from without is a political movement. For instance, the attempt in a particular factory or even in a particular trade to force a shorter working day out of individual capitalists by strikes, etc., is a purely economic movement. On the other hand, the movement to force through an eight-hour, etc., *law* is a *political* movement. And in this way out of the separate economic movements of the workers there grows up everywhere a *political* movement, that is to say, a movement of the *class*, with the object of enforcing its interests in a general form, in a form possessing general, socially coercive force. While these movements presuppose a certain degree of previous organization, they are in turn equally a means of developing this organization.

Where the working class is not yet far enough advanced in its organization to undertake a decisive campaign against the collective power, i.e., the political power of the ruling classes, it must at any rate be trained for this by continual agitation against this power and by a hostile attitude toward the policies of the ruling classes.

Against Personality Cults

KARL MARX

Marx may have been the person to coin the now commonly used term "personality cult." Moreover, this passage from his letter of November 10, 1877, to W. Blos was cited by Nikita Khrushchev in his "secret speech" before the closed session of the Soviet Twentieth Party Congress in February, 1956—to support his claim that any cult of personality, such as Stalin's, was alien to Marxism and to Communism.*

Neither of us[1] cares a straw for popularity. A proof of this is, for example, that, because of aversion to any personality cult, I have never permitted the numerous expressions of appreciation from various countries with which I was pestered during the existence of the International to reach the realm of publicity, and have never answered them, except occasionally by a rebuke. When Engels and I first joined the secret Communist Society we made it a condition that everything tending to encourage superstitious belief in authority was to be removed from the statutes. (Later on Lassalle exerted his influence in the opposite direction. * * *)

---

* For the view, and supporting evidence, that personality cults are not alien to Marxism or Communism as movements or forms of culture, see Robert C. Tucker, *Stalin as Revolutionary, 1879–1929: A Study in History and Personality* (New York: Norton, 1973), pp. 34–63, 279–288.
1. The reference is to himself and Engels. [R. T.]

The Possibility of Non-Violent Revolution

KARL MARX

Marx delivered this speech at Amsterdam on September 8, 1872, after a congress of the First International. Its restatement of revolutionary goals contained an important qualification: that in some countries the workers might attain the socialist goal "by peaceful means." For a commentary on this, see the Introduction, above, p. xxxvi.

The translation and notes are by Saul K. Padover.

In the eighteenth century the kings and the potentates were in the habit of meeting at The Hague to discuss the interests of their dynasties.

It is precisely in this place that we wanted to hold our workers' meeting, despite attempts to arouse apprehensions among us. We wanted to appear amid the most reactionary population, to reinforce the existence, propagation, and hope for the future of our great Association.[1]

When our decision became known, it was rumored that we sent emissaries to prepare the ground. Yes, we do not deny that we have such emissaries everywhere; but they are mostly unknown to us. Our emissaries in The Hague were the workers whose labor is as toilsome as that of our emissaries in Amsterdam, who are likewise workers laboring sixteen hours a day. Those are our emissaries; we have no other; and in all the countries where we recruit we find them prepared to receive us with open hearts, because they understand immediately that we strive to improve their lot.

The congress at The Hague has brought to maturity three important points:

It has proclaimed the necessity for the working class to fight the old, disintegrating society on political as well as social grounds; and we congratulate ourselves that this resolution of the London Conference will henceforth be in our Statutes.

In our midst there has been formed a group advocating the workers' abstention from political action. We have considered it our

1. The International Working Men's Association.

duty to declare how dangerous and fatal for our cause such principles appear to be.

Someday the worker must seize political power in order to build up the new organization of labor; he must overthrow the old politics which sustain the old institutions, if he is not to lose heaven on earth, like the old Christians who neglected and despised politics.

But we have not asserted that the ways to achieve that goal are everywhere the same.

You know that the institutions, mores, and traditions of various countries must be taken into consideration, and we do not deny that there are countries—such as America, England, and if I were more familiar with your institutions, I would perhaps also add Holland—where the workers can attain their goal by peaceful means. This being the case, we must also recognize the fact that in most countries on the Continent the lever of our revolution must be force; it is force to which we must someday appeal in order to erect the rule of the labor.

The Hague Congress has granted the General Council[2] new and wider authority. In fact, at the moment when the kings are assembling in Berlin, whence are to be issued new and decisive measures of oppression against us by the mighty representatives of feudalism and of the past—precisely at that moment, when persecution is being organized, the congress of The Hague considered it proper and necessary to enlarge the authority of the General Council and to centralize all action for the approaching struggle, which would otherwise be impotent in isolation. And, moreover, where else could the authorizations of the General Council arouse disquiet if not among our enemies? Does the General Council have a bureaucracy and an armed police to compel obedience? Is not its authority entirely a moral one, and does it not submit its decisions to the judgment of the various federations entrusted with their execution? Under such conditions—without an army, without police, without courts—on the day when the kings are forced to maintain their power only with moral influence and moral authority, they will form a weak obstacle to the forward march of the revolution.

Finally, the congress of The Hague has moved the headquarters of the General Council to New York. Many, even among our friends, seem to have wondered at such a decision. Do they then forget that America will be the workers' continent par excellence, that half a million men—workers—emigrate there yearly, and that on such soil, where the worker dominates, the International is bound to strike strong roots? Moreover, the decision of the congress gives the General Council the right to employ [in Europe] any mem-

2. The London-based administrative body of the International Working Men's Association.

bers whose collaboration it considers necessary and useful for the common welfare. Let us trust its prudence and hope it will succeed in selecting persons who will be capable of carrying out their task and who will understand how to hold up the banner of our Association in Europe with a firm hand.

Citizens, let us think of the basic principle of the International: Solidarity. Only when we have established this life-giving principle on a sound basis among the numerous workers of all countries will we attain the great final goal which we have set ourselves. The revolution must be carried out with solidarity; this is the great lesson of the French Commune, which fell because none of the other centers —Berlin, Madrid, etc.—developed great revolutionary movements comparable to the mighty uprising of the Paris proletariat.

So far as I am concerned, I will continue my work and constantly strive to strengthen among all workers this solidarity that is so fruitful for the future. No, I do not withdraw from the International, and all the rest of my life will be, as have been all my efforts of the past, dedicated to the triumph of the social ideas which—you may be assured!—will lead to the world domination by the proletariat.

Critique of the Gotha Program

KARL MARX

Marx's most detailed pronouncement on programmatic matters was made in this letter of early May, 1875, to the leaders of the so-called Eisenach faction of the German Social Democratic movement, with whom he and Engels were in close association. At the forthcoming party congress in the town of Gotha, the Eisenachers planned to unite with the Lassallean faction to form a unified German Social Democratic Party, and they sent the draft program for a united party to Marx and Engels for their comments. They found it fundamentally flawed by the influence of ideas of Ferdinand Lassalle, and Marx's lengthy reply to the Eisenachers, a letter in the form of marginal notes on the draft program, was vitriolic in this regard. Practical political interests were involved in the unification movement, however, and the Gotha Congress, held in late May, 1875, adopted the draft program with only minor alterations. Much later, in 1891, when the party had declared its intention of adopting a new program, Engels caused Marx's programmatic letter to be published in the party organ *Neue Zeit*, and gave it the title "Critique of the Gotha Program."

I

1. "Labour is the source of all wealth and all culture, *and since* useful labour is possible only in society and through society, the proceeds of labour belong undiminished with equal right to all members of society."

First Part of the Paragraph: "Labour is the source of all wealth and all culture."

Labour is *not the source* of all wealth. *Nature* is just as much the source of use values (and it is surely of such that material wealth consists!) as labour, which itself is only the manifestation of a force of nature, human labour power. The above phrase is to be found in all children's primers and is correct in so far as it is *implied* that labour is performed with the appurtenant subjects and instruments.

But a socialist programme cannot allow such bourgeois phrases to pass over in silence the *conditions* that alone give them meaning. And in so far as man from the beginning behaves towards nature, the primary source of all instruments and subjects of labour, as an owner, treats her as belonging to him, his labour becomes the source of use values, therefore also of wealth. The bourgeois have very good grounds for falsely ascribing *supernatural creative power* to labour; since precisely from the fact that labour depends on nature it follows that the man who posseses no other property than his labour power must, in all conditions of society and culture, be the slave of other men who have made themselves the owners of the material conditions of labour. He can work only with their permission, hence live only with their permission.

Let us now leave the sentence as it stands, or rather limps. What would one have expected in conclusion? Obviously this:

"Since labour is the source of all wealth, no one in society can appropriate wealth except as the product of labour. Therefore, if he himself does not work, he lives by the labour of others and also acquires his culture at the expense of the labour of others."

Instead of this, by means of the verbal rivet *"and since"* a second proposition is added in order to draw a conclusion from this and not from the first one.

Second Part of the Paragraph: "Useful labour is possible only in society and through society."

According to the first proposition, labour was the source of all wealth and all culture; therefore no society is possible without labour. Now we learn, conversely, that no "useful" labour is possible without society.

One could just as well have said that only in society can useless and even socially harmful labour become a branch of gainful occupation, that only in society can one live by being idle, etc., etc.—in short, one could just as well have copied the whole of Rousseau.

And what is "useful" labour? Surely only labour which produces the intended useful result. A savage—and man was a savage after he had ceased to be an ape—who kills an animal with a stone, who collects fruits, etc., performs "useful" labour.

Thirdly. The Conclusion: "And since useful labour is possible only in society and through society, the proceeds of labour belong undiminished with equal right to all members of society."

A fine conclusion! If useful labour is possible only in society and through society, the proceeds of labour belong to society—and only so much therefrom accrues to the individual worker as is not required to maintain the "condition" of labour, society.

In fact, this proposition has at all times been made use of by the champions of the *state of society prevailing at any given time*. First come the claims of the government and everything that sticks to it, since it is the social organ for the maintenance of the social order; then come the claims of the various kinds of private property, for the various kinds of private property are the foundations of society, etc. One sees that such hollow phrases can be twisted and turned as desired.

The first and second parts of the paragraph have some intelligible connection only in the following wording:

"Labour becomes the source of wealth and culture only as social labour," or, what is the same thing, "in and through society."

This proposition is incontestably correct, for although isolated labour (its material conditions presupposed) can create use values, it can create neither wealth nor culture.

But equally incontestable is this other proposition:

"In proportion as labour develops socially, and becomes thereby a source of wealth and culture, poverty and destitution develop among the workers, and wealth and culture among the non-workers."

This is the law of all history hitherto. What, therefore, had to be done here, instead of setting down general phrases about "labour" and "society," was to prove concretely how in present capitalist society the material, etc., conditions have at last been created which enable and compel the workers to lift this social curse.

In fact, however, the whole paragraph, bungled in style and content, is only there in order to inscribe the Lassallean catchword of the "undiminished proceeds of labour" as a slogan at the top of the party banner. I shall return later to the "proceeds of labour," "equal right," etc., since the same thing recurs in a somewhat different form further on.

2. "In present-day society, the instruments of labour are the monopoly of the capitalist class; the resulting dependence of the working class is the cause of misery and servitude in all its forms."

This sentence, borrowed from the Rules of the International, is incorrect in this "improved" edition.

In present-day society the instruments of labour are the monopoly of the landowners (the monopoly of property in land is even the basis of the monopoly of capital) *and* the capitalists. In the passage in question, the Rules of the International do not mention either the one or the other class of monopolists. They speak of the *"monopoliser of the means of labour, that is, the sources of life."* The addition, *"sources of life,"* makes it sufficiently clear that land is included in the instruments of labour.

The correction was introduced because Lassalle, for reasons now generally known, attacked *only* the capitalist class and not the land-

528 · *Revolutionary Program and Strategy*

owners. In England, the capitalist is usually not even the owner of the land on which his factory stands.

3. "The emancipation of labour demands the promotion of the instruments of labour to the common property of society and the co-operative regulation of the total labour with a fair distribution of the proceeds of labour."

"Promotion of the instruments of labour to the common property" ought obviously to read their "conversion into the common property"; but this only in passing.

What are "proceeds of labour"? The product of labour or its value? And in the latter case, is it the total value of the product or only that part of the value which labour has newly added to the value of the means of production consumed?

"Proceeds of labour" is a loose notion which Lassalle has put in the place of definite economic conceptions.

What is "a fair distribution"?

Do not the bourgeois assert that the present-day distribution is "fair"? And is it not, in fact, the only "fair" distribution on the basis of the present-day mode of production? Are economic relations regulated by legal conceptions or do not, on the contrary, legal relations arise from economic ones? Have not also the socialist sectarians the most varied notions about "fair" distribution?

To understand what is implied in this connection by the phrase "fair distribution," we must take the first paragraph and this one together. The latter presupposes a society wherein "the instruments of labour are common property and the total labour is cooperatively regulated," and from the first paragraph we learn that "the proceeds of labour belong undiminished with equal right to all members of society."

"To all members of society"? To those who do not work as well? What remains then of the "undiminished proceeds of labour"? Only to those members of society who work? What remains then of the "equal right" of all members of society?

But "all members of society" and "equal right" are obviously mere phrases. The kernel consists in this, that in this communist society every worker must receive the "undiminished" Lassallean "proceeds of labour."

Let us take first of all the words "proceeds of labour" in the sense of the product of labour; then the co-operative proceeds of labour are the *total social product*.

From this must now be deducted:

First, cover for replacement of the means of production used up.

Secondly, additional portion for expansion of production.

Thirdly, reserve or insurance funds to provide against accidents, dislocations caused by natural calamities, etc.

These deductions from the "undiminished proceeds of labour" are an economic necessity and their magnitude is to be determined according to available means and forces, and partly by computation of probabilities, but they are in no way calculable by equity.

There remains the other part of the total product, intended to serve as means of consumption.

Before this is divided among the individuals, there has to be deducted again, from it:

First, the general costs of administration not belonging to production

This part will, from the outset, be very considerably restricted in comparison with present-day society and it diminishes in proportion as the new society develops.

Secondly, that which is intended for the common satisfaction of needs, such as schools, health services, etc.

From the outset this part grows considerably in comparison with present-day society and it grows in proportion as the new society develops.

Thirdly, funds for those unable to work, etc., in short, for what is included under so-called official poor relief today.

Only now do we come to the "distribution" which the programme, under Lassallean influence, alone has in view in its narrow fashion, namely, to that part of the means of consumption which is divided among the individual producers of the co-operative society.

The "undiminished proceeds of labour" have already unnoticeably become converted into the "diminished" proceeds, although what the producer is deprived of in his capacity as a private individual benefits him directly or indirectly in his capacity as a member of society.

Just as the phrase of the "undiminished proceeds of labour" has disappeared, so now does the phrase of the "proceeds of labour" disappear altogether.

Within the co-operative society based on common ownership of the means of production, the producers do not exchange their products; just as little does the labour employed on the products appear here *as the value* of these products, as a material quality possessed by them, since now, in contrast to capitalist society, individual labour no longer exists in an indirect fashion but directly as a component part of the total labour. The phrase "proceeds of labour," objectionable also today on account of its ambiguity, thus loses all meaning.

What we have to deal with here is a communist society, not as it has *developed* on its own foundations, but, on the contrary, just as it *emerges* from capitalist society; which is thus in every respect, economically, morally and intellectually, still stamped with the birth marks of the old society from whose womb it emerges. Accordingly, the individual producer receives back from society—after the deductions have been made—exactly what he gives to it. What he has given to it is his individual quantum of labour. For example, the social working day consists of the sum of the individual hours of work; the individual labour time of the individual producer is the part of the social working day contributed by him, his share in it. He receives a certificate from society that he has furnished such and such an amount of labour (after deducting his labour for the common funds), and with this certificate he draws from the social stock of means of consumption as much as costs the same amount of labour. The same amount of labour which he has given to society in one form he receives back in another.

Here obviously the same principle prevails as that which regulates the exchange of commodities, as far as this is exchange of equal values. Content and form are changed, because under the altered circumstances no one can give anything except his labour, and because, on the other hand, nothing can pass to the ownership of individuals except individual means of consumption. But, as far as the distribution of the latter among the individual producers is concerned, the same principle prevails as in the exchange of commodity equivalents: a given amount of labour in one form is exchanged for an equal amount of labour in another form.

Hence, *equal right* here is still in principle—*bourgeois right*, although principle and practice are no longer at loggerheads, while the exchange of equivalents in commodity exchange only exists *on the average* and not in the individual case.

In spite of this advance, this *equal right* is still constantly stigmatised by a bourgeois limitation. The right of the producers is *proportional* to the labour they supply; the equality consists in the fact that measurement is made with an *equal standard*, labour.

But one man is superior to another physically or mentally and so supplies more labour in the same time, or can labour for a longer time; and labour, to serve as a measure, must be defined by its duration or intensity, otherwise it ceases to be a standard of measurement. This *equal* right is an unequal right for unequal labour. It recognises no class differences, because everyone is only a worker like everyone else; but it tacitly recognises unequal individual endowment and thus productive capacity as natural privileges. *It is, therefore, a right of inequality, in its content, like every right.* Right by its very nature can consist only in the application of an equal standard; but unequal individuals (and they would not be different individuals if they were not unequal) are measurable only by an equal standard in so far as they are brought under an equal point of view, are taken from one *definite* side only, for instance, in the present case, are regarded *only as workers* and nothing more is seen in them, everything else being ignored. Further, one worker is married, another not; one has more children than another, and so on and so forth. Thus, with an equal performance of labour, and hence an equal share in the social consumption fund, one will in fact receive more than another, one will be richer than another, and so on. To avoid all these defects, right instead of being equal would have to be unequal.

But these defects are inevitable in the first phase of communist society as it is when it has just emerged after prolonged birth pangs from capitalist society. Right can never be higher than the eco nomic structure of society and its cultural development conditioned thereby.

In a higher phase of communist society, after the enslaving subor-dination of the individual to the division of labour, and therewith also the antithesis between mental and physical labour, has van-ished; after labour has become not only a means of life but life's prime want; after the productive forces have also increased with the all-round development of the individual, and all the springs of co-operative wealth flow more abundantly—only then can the narrow horizon of bourgeois right be crossed in its entirety and society inscribe on its banner: From each according to his ability, to each according to his needs!

I have dealt more at length with the "undiminished proceeds of labour," on the one hand, and with "equal right" and "fair distribu-tion," on the other, in order to show what a crime it is to attempt, on the one hand, to force on our Party again, as dogmas, ideas which in a certain period had some meaning but have now become obsolete verbal rubbish, while again perverting, on the other, the realistic outlook, which it cost so much effort to instil into the Party but which has now taken root in it, by means of ideological non-sense about right and other trash so common among the democrats and French Socialists.

Quite apart from the analysis so far given, it was in general a mis-take to make a fuss about so-called *distribution* and put the princi-pal stress on it.

Any distribution whatever of the means of consumption is only a consequence of the distribution of the conditions of production themselves. The latter distribution, however, is a feature of the mode of production itself. The capitalist mode of production, for example, rests on the fact that the material conditions of produc-tion are in the hands of non-workers in the form of property in cap-ital and land, while the masses are only owners of the personal con-dition of production, of labour power. If the elements of production are so distributed, then the present-day distribution of the means of consumption results automatically. If the material conditions of production are the co-operative property of the workers themselves, then there likewise results a distribution of the means of consumption different from the present one. Vulgar socialism (and from it in turn a section of the democracy) has taken over from the bourgeois economists the consideration and treatment of distribution as independent of the mode of production and hence the presentation of socialism as turning principally on distribution. After the real relation has long been made clear, why retrogress again?

4. "The emancipation of labour must be the work of the working class, relatively to which all other classes are *only one reactionary mass*."

The first strophe is taken from the introductory words of the Rules of the International, but "improved." There it is said: "The emancipation of the working class must be the act of the workers themselves"; here, on the contrary, the "working class" has to emancipate—what? "Labour." Let him understand who can.

In compensation, the antistrophe, on the other hand, is a Lassallean quotation of the first water: "relatively to which (the working class) all other classes are *only one reactionary mass*."

In the *Communist Manifesto* it is said: "Of all the classes that stand face to face with the bourgeoisie today, the proletariat alone is a *really revolutionary class*. The other classes decay and finally disappear in the face of modern industry; the proletariat is its special and essential product."

The bourgeoisie is here conceived as a revolutionary class—as the bearer of large-scale industry—relatively to the feudal lords and the lower middle class, who desire to maintain all social positions that are the creation of obsolete modes of production. Thus they do not form *together* with the *bourgeoisie* only one reactionary mass.

On the other hand, the proletariat is revolutionary relatively to the bourgeoisie because, having itself grown up on the basis of large-scale industry, it strives to strip off from production the capitalist character that the bourgeoisie seeks to perpetuate. But the *Manifesto* adds that the "lower middle class" is becoming revolutionary "in view of [its] impending transfer into the proletariat."

From this point of view, therefore, it is again nonsense to say that it, together with the bourgeoisie, and with the feudal lords into the bargain, "form only one reactionary mass" relatively to the working class.

Has one proclaimed to the artisans, small manufacturers, etc., and *peasants* during the last elections: Relatively to us you, together with the bourgeoisie and feudal lords, form only one reactionary mass?

Lassalle knew the *Communist Manifesto* by heart, as his faithful followers know the gospels written by him. If, therefore, he has falsified it so grossly, this has occurred only to put a good colour on his alliance with absolutist and feudal opponents against the bourgeoisie.

In the above paragraph, moreover, his oracular saying is dragged in by main force without any connection with the botched quotation from the Rules of the International. Thus is it here simply an impertinence, and indeed not at all displeasing to Herr Bismarck, one of those cheap pieces of insolence in which the Marat of Berlin[1] deals.

5. "The working class strives for its emancipation first of all *within the framework of the present-day national state,* conscious that the necessary result of its efforts, which are common to the workers of all civilised countries, will be the international brotherhood of peoples."

Lassalle, in opposition to the *Communist Manifesto* and to all earlier socialism, conceived the workers' movement from the narrowest national standpoint. He is being followed in this—and that after the work of the International!

It is altogether self-evident that, to be able to fight at all, the working class must organise itself at home *as a class* and that its own country is the immediate arena of its struggle. In so far its class struggle is national, not in substance, but, as the *Communist Manifesto* says, "in form." But the "framework of the present-day national state," for instance, the German Empire, is itself in its turn economically "within the framework" of the world market, politically "within the framework" of the system of states. Every businessman knows that German trade is at the same time foreign trade, and the greatness of Herr Bismarck consists, to be sure, precisely in his pursuing a kind of *international* policy.

And to what does the German workers' party reduce its internationalism? To the consciousness that the result of its efforts will be *"the international brotherhood of peoples"*—a phrase borrowed from the bourgeois League of Peace and Freedom[2] which is intended to pass as equivalent to the international brotherhood of the working classes in the joint struggle against the ruling classes and their governments. Not a word, therefore, *about the international functions* of the German working class! And it is thus that it is to challenge its own bourgeoisie—which is already linked up in brotherhood against it with the bourgeois of all other countries—and Herr Bismarck's international policy of conspiracy!

In fact, the internationalism of the programme stands *even*

---

1. A reference to Hasselmann, the chief editor of the *Neuer Sozial-Demokrat,* the central organ of the Lassalleans.

2. The International League of Peace and Freedom was organized in Geneva in 1867 by liberals and pacifists.

infinitely below that of the Free Trade Party. The latter also asserts that the result of its efforts will be "the international brotherhood of peoples." But it also *does* something to make trade international and by no means contents itself with the consciousness—that all peoples are carrying on trade at home.

The international activity of the working classes does not in any way depend on the existence of the *International Working Men's Association*. This was only the first attempt to create a central organ for that activity; an attempt which was a lasting success on account of the impulse which it gave but which was no longer realisable in its *first historical form* after the fall of the Paris Commune.

Bismarck's *Norddeutsche* was absolutely right when it announced, to the satisfaction of its master, that the German workers' party had sworn off internationalism in the new programme.[3]

II

"Starting from these basic principles, the German workers' party strives by all legal means for the *free state—and—*socialist society: the abolition of the wage system *together with* the *iron law of wages*—and—exploitation in every form; the elimination of all social and political inequality."

I shall return to the "free" state later.

So, in future, the German workers' party has got to believe in Lassalle's "iron law of wages"! That this may not be lost, the non-sense is perpetrated of speaking of the "abolition of the wage system" (it should read: system of wage labour) "*together with* the iron law of wages." If I abolish wage labour, then naturally I abolish its laws also, whether they are of "iron" or sponge. But Lassalle's attack on wage labour turns almost solely on this so-called law. In order, therefore, to prove that Lassalle's sect has conquered, the "wage system" must be abolished "*together with*" the iron law of wages" and not without it.

It is well known that nothing of the "iron law of wages" is Lassalle's except the word "iron" borrowed from Goethe's "great eternal iron laws." The word *iron* is a label by which the true believers recognise one another. But if I take the law with Lassalle's stamp on it and, consequently, in his sense, then I must also take it with his substantiation for it. And what is that? As Lange already showed, shortly after Lassalle's death, it is the Malthusian theory of population (preached by Lange himself). But if this theory is

3. Marx refers to the editorial which appeared in No. 67 of the *Norddeutsche Allgemeine Zeitung* (*North German General Newspaper*) of March 20, 1875. It stated with regard to Article 5 of the Social-Democratic Programme that "Social-Democratic agitation had in many respects become more prudent" and that it was "repudiating the International."

correct, then again I *cannot* abolish the law even if I abolish wage labour a hundred times over, because the law then governs not only the system of wage labour but *every* social system. Basing themselves directly on this, the economists have been proving for fifty years and more that socialism cannot abolish poverty, *which has its basis in nature*, but can only make it *general*, distribute it simultaneously over the whole surface of society!

But all this is not the main thing. *Quite apart* from the *false* Lassallean formulation of the law, the truly outrageous retrogression consists in the following.

Since Lassalle's death there has asserted itself in *our* Party the scientific understanding that wages are not what they *appear* to be, namely, the *value*, or *price*, *of labour*, but only a masked form for the *value*, or *price*, *of labour power*. Thereby the whole bourgeois conception of wages hitherto, as well as all the criticism hitherto directed against this conception, was thrown overboard once for all and it was made clear that the wage-worker has permission to work for his own subsistence, that is, *to live*, only in so far as he works for a certain time gratis for the capitalist (and hence also for the latter's co-consumers of surplus value); that the whole capitalist system of production turns on the increase of this gratis labour by extending the working day or by developing the productivity, that is, increasing the intensity of labour power, etc; that, consequently, the system of wage labour is a system of slavery, and indeed of a slavery which becomes more severe in proportion as the social productive forces of labour develop, whether the worker receives better or worse payment. And after this understanding has gained more and more ground in our Party, one returns to Lassalle's dogmas, although one must have known that Lassalle *did not know* what wages were, but following in the wake of the bourgeois economists took the appearance for the essence of the matter.

It is as if, among slaves who have at last got behind the secret of slavery and broken out in rebellion, a slave still in thrall to obsolete notions were to inscribe on the programme of the rebellion: Slavery must be abolished because the feeding of slaves in the system of slavery cannot exceed a certain low maximum!

Does not the mere fact that the representatives of our Party were capable of perpetrating such a monstrous attack on the understanding that has spread among the mass of our Party prove by itself with what criminal levity and with what lack of conscience they set to work in drawing up this compromise programme!

Instead of the indefinite concluding phrase of the paragraph, "the elimination of all social and political inequality," it ought to have been said that with the abolition of class distinctions all social and political inequality arising from them would disappear of itself.

III

"The German workers' party, in order *to pave the way to the solution of the social question*, demands the establishment of producers' co-operative societies *with state aid under the democratic control of the toiling people*. The producers' co-operative societies *are to be called into being* for industry and agriculture on such a scale *that the socialist organisation of the total labour will arise from them.*"

After the Lassallean "iron law of wages," the physic of the prophet. The way to it is "paved" in worthy fashion. In place of the existing class struggle appears a newspaper scribbler's phrase: "the social *question*," to the "*solution*" of which one "paves the way." Instead of arising from the revolutionary process of transformation of society, the "socialist organisation of the total labour" "arises" from the "state aid" that the state gives to the producers' co-operative societies and which the *state*, not the worker, "*calls into being*." It is worthy of Lassalle's imagination that with state loans one can build a new society just as well as a new railway!

From the remnants of a sense of shame, "state aid" has been put —under the democratic control of the "toiling people."

In the first place, the majority of the "toiling people" in Germany consists of peasants, and not of proletarians.

Secondly, "democratic" means in German "*volksherrschaftlich*" ["by the rule of the people"]. But what does "control by the rule of the people of the toiling people" mean? And particularly in the case of a toiling people which, through these demands that it puts to the state, expresses its full consciousness that it neither rules nor is ripe for ruling!

It would be superfluous to deal here with the criticism of the recipe prescribed by Buchez in the reign of Louis Philippe in *opposition* to the French Socialists and accepted by the reactionary workers of the *Atelier*.[4] The chief offence does not lie in having inscribed this specific nostrum in the programme, but in taking, in general, a retrograde step from the standpoint of a class movement to that of a sectarian movement.

That the workers desire to establish the conditions for co-operative production on a social scale, and first of all on a national scale in their own country, only means that they are working to revolutionise the present conditions of production, and it has nothing in common with the foundation of co-operative societies with state aid. But as far as the present co-operative societies are concerned, they are of value *only* in so far as they are the independent crea-

4. *Atelier* (Workshop): A workers' monthly which appeared in Paris in 1840–50. It was under the influence of the Catholic socialism of Buchez.

tions of the workers and not protégés either of the government or of the bourgeois.

IV

I come now to the democratic section.

A. *"The free basis of the state."*

First of all, according to II, the German workers' party strives for "the free state."

Free state—what is this?

It is by no means the aim of the workers, who have got rid of the narrow mentality of humble subjects, to set the state free. In the German Empire the "state" is almost as "free" as in Russia. Freedom consists in converting the state from an organ superimposed upon society into one completely subordinate to it, and today, too, the forms of state are more free or less free to the extent that they restrict the "freedom of the state."

The German workers' party—at least if it adopts the programme —shows that its socialist ideas are not even skin-deep; in that, instead of treating existing society (and this holds good for any future one) as the *basis* of the existing state (or of the future state in the case of future society), it treats the state rather as independent entity that possesses its own *intellectual, ethical and libertarian bases*.

And what of the riotous misuse which the programme makes of the words *"present-day state," "present-day society,"* and of the still more riotous misconception it creates in regard to the state to which it addresses its demands?

"Present-day society" is capitalist society, which exists in all civilised countries, more or less free from medieval admixture, more or less modified by the special historical development of each country, more or less developed. On the other hand, the "present-day state" changes with a country's frontier. It is different in the Prusso-German Empire from what it is in Switzerland, it is different in England from what it is in the United States. The "present-day state" is, therefore, a fiction.

Nevertheless, the different states of the different civilised countries, in spite of their manifold diversity of form, all have this in common, that they are based on modern bourgeois society, only one more or less capitalistically developed. They have, therefore, also certain essential features in common. In this sense it is possible to speak of the "present-day state," in contrast with the future, in which its present root, bourgeois society, will have died off.

The question then arises: what transformation will the state undergo in communist society? In other words, what social functions will remain in existence there that are analogous to present functions of the state? This question can only be answered scientifically, and one does not get a flea-hop nearer to the problem by a thousandfold combination of the word people with the word state.

Between capitalist and communist society lies the period of the revolutionary transformation of the one into the other. There corresponds to this also a political transition period in which the state can be nothing but *the revolutionary dictatorship of the proletariat.*

Now the programme does not deal with this nor with the future state of communist society.

Its political demands contain nothing beyond the old democratic litany familiar to all: universal suffrage, direct legislation, popular rights, a people's militia, etc. They are a mere echo of the bourgeois People's Party, of the League of Peace and Freedom. They are all demands which, in so far as they are not exaggerated in fantastic presentation, have already been *realised.* Only the state to which they belong does not lie within the borders of the German Empire, but in Switzerland, the United States, etc. This sort of "state of the future" is a present-day state, although existing outside the "framework" of the German Empire.

But one thing has been forgotten. Since the German workers' party expressly declares that it acts within "the present-day national state," hence within *its own* state, the Prusso-German Empire—its demands would indeed otherwise be largely meaningless, since one only demands what one has not got—it should not have forgotten the chief thing, namely, that all those pretty little gewgaws rest on the recognition of the so-called sovereignty of the people and hence are appropriate only in a *democratic republic.*

Since one has not the courage—and wisely so, for the circumstances demand caution—to demand the democratic republic, as the French workers' programmes under Louis Philippe and under Louis Napoleon did, one should not have resorted, either, to the subterfuge, neither "honest"[5] nor decent, of demanding things which have meaning only in a democratic republic from a state which is nothing but a police-guarded military despotism, embellished with parliamentary forms, alloyed with a feudal admixture, already influenced by the bourgeoisie and bureaucratically carpentered, and then to assure this state into the bargain that one imagines one will be able to force such things upon it "by legal means."

Even vulgar democracy, which sees the millennium in the democratic republic and has no suspicion that it is precisely in this last form of state of bourgeois society that the class struggle has to be

---

5. *"Honest"* was the epithet applied to the Eisenachers. Here a play upon words.

fought out to a conclusion—even it towers mountains above this kind of democratism which keeps within the limits of what is permitted by the police and not permitted by logic.

That, in fact, by the word "state" is meant the government machine, or the state in so far as it forms a special organism separated from society through division of labour, is shown by the words "the German worker's party demands *as the economic basis of the state*: a single progressive income tax," etc. Taxes are the economic basis of the government machinery and of nothing else. In the state of the future, existing in Switzerland, this demand has been pretty well fulfilled. Income tax presupposes various sources of income of the various social classes, and hence capitalist society. It is, therefore, nothing remarkable that the Liverpool financial reformers, bourgeois headed by Gladstone's brother, are putting forward the same demand as the programme.

B. "The German workers' party demands as the intellectual and ethical basis of the state:

"1. Universal and *equal elementary education* by the state. Universal compulsory school attendance. Free instruction."

Equal elementary education? What idea lies behind these words? Is it believed that in present-day society (and it is only with this one has to deal) education can be *equal* for all classes? Or is it demanded that the upper classes also shall be compulsorily reduced to the modicum of education—the elementary school—that alone is compatible with the economic conditions not only of the wage-workers but of the peasants as well?

"Universal compulsory school attendance. Free instruction." The former exists even in Germany, the second in Switzerland and in the United States in the case of elementary schools. If in some states of the latter country higher educational institutions are also "free" that only means in fact defraying the cost of the education of the upper classes from the general tax receipts. Incidentally, the same holds good for "free administration of justice" demanded under A, 5. The administration of criminal justice is to be had free everywhere; that of civil justice is concerned almost exclusively with conflicts over property and hence affects almost exclusively the possessing classes. Are they to carry on their litigation at the expense of the national coffers?

The paragraph on the schools should at least have demanded technical schools (theoretical and practical) in combination with the elementary school.

"*Elementary education by the state*" is altogether objectionable. Defining by a general law the expenditures on the elementary schools, the qualifications of the teaching staff, the branches of instruction, etc., and, as is done in the United States, supervising the fulfilment of these legal specifications by state inspectors, is a very different thing from appointing the state as the educator of the people! Government and Church should rather be equally excluded from any influence on the school. Particularly, indeed, in the Prusso-German Empire (and one should not take refuge in the rotten subterfuge that one is speaking of a "state of the future"; we have seen how matters stand in this respect) the state has need, on the contrary, of a very stern education by the people.

But the whole programme, for all its democratic clang, is tainted through and through by the Lassallean sect's servile belief in the state, or, what is no better, by a democratic belief in miracles, or rather it is a compromise between these two kinds of belief in miracles, both equally remote from socialism.

"Freedom of science" says a paragraph of the Prussian Constitution. Why, then, here?

"Freedom of conscience"! If one desired at this time of the *Kulturkampf*[6] to remind liberalism of its old catchwords, it surely could have been done only in the following form: Everyone should be able to attend to his religious as well as his bodily needs without the police sticking their noses in. But the workers' party ought at any rate in this connection to have expressed its awareness of the fact that bourgeois "freedom of conscience" is nothing but the toleration of all possible kinds of *religious freedom of conscience*, and that for its part it endeavours rather to liberate the conscience from the witchery of religion. But one chooses not to transgress the "bourgeois" level.

I have now come to the end, for the appendix that now follows in the programme does not constitute a characteristic component part of it. Hence I can be very brief here.

2. *"Normal working day."*

In no other country has the workers' party limited itself to such an indefinite demand, but has always fixed the length of the working day that it considers normal under the given circumstances.

3. *"Restriction of female labour and prohibition of child labour."*

The standardisation of the working day must include the restriction of female labour, in so far as it relates to the duration, intermissions, etc., of the working day; otherwise it could only mean the exclusion of female labour from branches of industry that are especially unhealthy for the female body or are objectionable morally for the female sex. If that is what was meant, it should have been said so.

6. *Kulturkampf* (Struggle for culture): Bismarck's struggle in the seventies against the German Catholic Party, the Party of the "Centre," by means of police persecution of Catholicism.

"Prohibition of child labour." Here it was absolutely essential to state the age limit.

A *general prohibition* of child labour is incompatible with the existence of large-scale industry and hence an empty, pious wish. Its realisation—if it were possible—would be reactionary, since, with a strict regulation of the working time according to the different age groups and other safety measures for the protection of children, an early combination of productive labour with education is one of the most potent means for the transformation of present-day society.

4 "State supervision of factory, workshop and domestic industry."

In consideration of the Prusso-German state it should definitely have been demanded that the inspectors are to be removable only by a court of law; that any worker can have them prosecuted for neglect of duty; that they must belong to the medical profession.

5. "Regulation of prison labour."

A petty demand in a general workers' programme. In any case, it should have been clearly stated that there is no intention from fear of competition to allow ordinary criminals to be treated like beasts, and especially that there is no desire to deprive them of their sole means of betterment, productive labour. This was surely the least one might have expected from Socialists.

6. "An effective liability law."

It should have been stated what is meant by an "effective" liability law.

Be it noted, incidentally, that in speaking of the normal working day the part of factory legislation that deals with health regulations and safety measures, etc., has been overlooked. The liability law only comes into operation when these regulations are infringed.

In short, this appendix also is distinguished by slovenly editing.

Dixi et salvavi animam meam.[7]

7. "I have spoken and saved my soul."

After the Revolution: Marx Debates Bakunin

KARL MARX

After Pierre-Joseph Proudhon, the Russian revolutionary Mikhail Bakunin was perhaps the most influential representative of the anarchist current in nineteenth-century socialism. His theoretical tract *Statehood and Anarchy* was published in 1873 and became a programmatic document. Bakunin was then both a sharp critic of Marx and a rival in working-class movements. Marx read and prepared a conspectus of Bakunin's book in 1874–75, including in it the lengthy passages of rebuttal of Bakunin's criticism that are presented here (the indented material consists of passages that Marx copied out in the conspectus, often interspersing his own ironic comments parenthetically). Because Marx and Engels said rather little about the specifics of the predicted "dictatorship of the proletariat" and about how they envisaged developments in the aftermath of the proletarian revolution, Marx's comments in this obscure source are of great interest. The conspectus was first published in the journal *Letopisi marksizma* (Annals of Marxism) in 1926. It appears in Karl Marx and Friedrich Engels, *Werke*, Vol. 18 (Berlin: Dietz Verlag, 1962), pp. 599–642. This English translation is by Robert C. Tucker.

* * * We have already expressed our deep aversion to the theory of Marx and Lassalle that recommends to the workers, if not as an ultimate ideal then at any rate as the immediate main aim, the founding of a people's state which, as they explain it, will be nothing other than the proletariat "organized as the ruling class." The question arises, if the proletariat is ruling, over whom will it rule? This means that there will remain another proletariat which will be subordinated to this new domination, this new state.[1]

This means that so long as other classes continue to exist, the capitalist class in particular, the proletariat fights it (for with the

1. The term "people's state" was not Marx's but, as he indicates further on, one put into currency by the prominent German Social Democrat Wilhelm Lieb-knecht and later picked up by Ferdinand Lassalle. The phrase "organized as the ruling class" appears in the *Communist Manifesto* (see above, p. 490). [*R. T.*]

coming of the proletariat to power, its enemies will not yet have disappeared, the old organization of society will not yet have disappeared), it must use measures of *force*, hence governmental measures; if it itself still remains a class and the economic conditions on which the class struggle and the existence of classes have not yet disappeared, they must be forcibly removed or transformed, and the process of their transformation must be forcibly accelerated.

For example, the peasant rabble [*das gemeine Bauernvolk, der Bauernröbe*], which, as is well known, does not enjoy favor with the Marxists and which, being on a lower level of culture, will probably be governed by the urban and factory proletariat.

It means that where the peasant exists on a mass scale as a private land proprietor, where he even forms a more or less considerable majority as in all the countries of the West European continent, where he has not disappeared and been replaced by agricultural laborers, as in England—the following will take place: either the peasant will start to create obstacles and bring about the fall of any worker revolution, as he has done heretofore in France, or else the proletariat (for the peasant proprietor does not belong to the proletariat; even when his situation places him in it he thinks that he doesn't belong to it) must, as the government, take steps as a result of which the situation of the peasant will directly improve and which will therefore bring him over to the side of the revolution; steps which embryonically facilitate the transition from private ownership of the land to collective ownership, so that the peasant will himself come to this by economic means; but there should be no stunning of the peasant by, for example, proclaiming the abrogation of the right of inheritance or of his property; that is possible only where the capitalist *rentier* has squeezed the peasant out and the real tiller of the soil has become just as much a proletarian as the hired worker, as the urban worker, and hence has the same interests not indirectly but *directly*; still less should parcelled-out property be strengthened by increasing the parcels through outright turning over of big estates to the peasants, as in the Bakuninist approach to revolution.

Or, if one looks at this question from a national point of view, we may suppose that for the Germans, the Slavs for the same reason will enter into the same slavish subordination to the victorious German proletariat as the latter will now enjoy with respect to its own bourgeoisie.

Schoolboy drivel! A radical social revolution is connected with certain historical conditions of economic development; the latter are its presupposition. Therefore it is possible only where the industrial proletariat, together with capitalist production, occupies at least a substantial place in the mass of the people. And in order for it to have any chance at all of being victorious, it must be capable, *mutatis mutandis,* of doing at least as much directly for the peasant as the French bourgeoisie did during its revolution for the French peasant of that time. A fine idea, that the rule of the workers includes the enslavement of agricultural labor! But here appears the innermost thought of Herr Bakunin. He understands absolutely nothing about social revolution; all he knows are its political phrases. For him its economic requisites do not exist. Since all hitherto existing economic formations, developed or undeveloped, have included the enslavement of the working person (whether in the form of the wage worker, the peasant, etc.), he thinks that a *radical revolution* is possible under all these formations. Not only that! He wants a European social revolution, resting on the economic foundation of capitalist production, to take place on the level of the Russian or Slavic agricultural and pastoral peoples and not to overstep that level; although he does see that *navigation* creates a difference between the brothers, but only *navigation*, for that is a difference all politicians know about! *Will power* and not economic conditions is the basis of his social revolution.

If there exists a state, there is inevitably domination [*Herrschaft*], hence also slavery; domination is unthinkable without open or concealed slavery, that's why we're enemies of the state. What does it mean for the proletariat to be "organized as the ruling class"?

It means that the proletariat, instead of fighting against the economically privileged classes in each individual instance, has acquired sufficient power and organization to use the general means of coercion against them; however, it can use only such economic means as abolish its own character as wage worker, hence as a class; so its complete victory coincides with the end of its domination, for its class character comes to an end.

Can it really be that the entire proletariat will stand at the head of the administration?

Can it really be that in a trade union, for example, the entire union forms its executive committee? Can it be that there will disappear from the factory all division of labor and difference of functions stemming from it? And in the Bakuninist arrangement "from bottom to top," will everyone be at the "top"? In that case there will be no "bottom." Will all the members of the township in equal measure supervise the general affairs of the "district"? In that event there will be no distinction between township and district.

There are about forty million Germans. Will all forty millions really be members of the government?

Certainly, because the thing starts with self-government of the township.

The entire nation will be governors and there will be no governed ones.

When a person governs himself, then he doesn't—on this principle—govern himself; after all, he's only he himself and nobody else.

Then there will be no government, no state, but if there is a state, there will be governors and slaves.

This means only: when class domination ends, there will be no state in the present political sense of the word.

This dilemma has a simple solution in the Marxists' theory. By popular administration they [that is, Bakunin] understand administration of the people by means of a small number of representatives elected by the people.

The ass! This is democratic nonsense, political windbaggery! Elections are a political form, even in the smallest Russian township and *artel*.[2] The character of elections depends not on these designations but on the economic foundations, on the economic ties of the voters amongst one another, and from the moment these functions cease being political (1) no governmental functions any longer exist; (2) the distribution of general functions takes on a business character and involves no domination; (3) elections completely lose their present political character.

The universal right of election of people's representatives and rulers of the state by the whole people—

—such a thing as a whole people in the present sense of the word is a fantasy—

this is the Marxists' final word, as it is of the democratic school, a lie which covers up a despotism of a *governing minority*, all the more dangerous in that it is an expression of a supposed people's will.

2. A cooperative association in agriculture or handicrafts.

Under collective ownership the so-called people's will disappears to make way for the real will of the cooperative.

So, in sum: government of the great majority of popular masses by a privileged minority. But this minority will be composed of workers, say the Marxists.

Where do they say that?

Of former workers, perhaps, but just as soon as they become representatives or rulers of the people *they will cease to be workers*.

No more than a factory-owner ceases to be a capitalist nowadays because he has become a member of the town council.

And they'll start looking down on all ordinary workers from the heights of the state: they will now represent not the people but themselves and their claims to govern the people. He who doubts this simply doesn't know human nature.

If Herr Bakunin knew even one thing about the situation of the manager of a workers' cooperative factory, all his hallucinations about domination would go to the devil. He would have to ask himself what form the functions of administration can assume on the basis of such a worker state, if it pleases him to call it that.

But these chosen ones will be ardent in their conviction, and learned socialists too. The words constantly being used in the works and speeches of the Lassalleans and Marxists . . .

—the words *"learned socialism,"* never used before, and *"scientific socialism,"* used only in opposition to utopian socialism, which tries to impose new hallucinations and illusions on the people instead of confining the scope of its knowledge to the study of the social movement of the people itself; see my book against Proudhon—

by themselves prove that the so-called people's state will be nothing other than the quite despotic administration of the masses of the people by a new and very non-numerous aristocracy of real and supposed learned ones. The people is not learned, so it will be entirely freed from the cares of governing, wholly incorporated into the governed herd. A fine liberation! The Marxists sense this [!] contradiction and, realizing that the regime of the learned [*quelle reverie!*], the hardest, most offensive, and most contemptuous in the world will in fact be a dictatorship in spite of all the democratic forms, console themselves with the thought that the dictatorship will be temporary and short-lived.

Non, mon cher! The *class domination* of the workers over the resisting strata of the old world must last until the economic foundations of the existence of classes are destroyed.

They say that their only care and aim will be to shape and elevate the people [café politicians!] both economically and politically to such a degree that all government will soon be superfluous and the state, having lost all political, i.e., dominating, character, will all by itself turn into a free organization of economic interests and communes. If their state is going to be really a people's one, why should it abolish itself, but if its aboliton is necessary for the real liberation of the people, how can they dare to call it a people's state?

Leaving aside the attempt to ride on Liebknecht's *people's state*, which in general is nonsense aimed against the *Communist Manifesto* and so on, this only means: in view of the fact that during the time of struggle to destroy the old society the proletariat still acts on the foundation of the old society and therefore still gives its movement political forms that more or less belong to the old society, in this time of struggle it has not yet attained its final organization and uses means for its liberation which will fall away after the liberation; from this Herr Bakunin deduces that it's best for the proletariat not to undertake any action but to sit and await—the day of *general liquidation*, the Last Judgment.

By our polemic against them which, of course, appeared before my book against Proudhon and before the *Communist Manifesto*, even before Saint-Simon: what a fine *hysteron proteron*[3] *we* brought them to the *realization* that freedom or anarchy [Herr Bakunin has, quite simply, translated Proudhon's and Stirner's[4] anarchy into a savage Tartar dialect], i.e., the free organization of the worker masses from bottom to top [nonsense!], is the final aim of social development and that any state, not excluding their people's one, is a yoke giving rise to despotism on the one hand and slavery on the other. They say that such a state yoke, a dictatorship, is a necessary transitional means for attaining the most complete popular liberation. So, to liberate the masses of the people they first have to be enslaved. Our polemic rests and is founded on this contradiction. They maintain that only a dictatorship, their own naturally, can create the people's will; we answer: no dictatorship can have any other aim than to perpetuate itself, and it can only give rise to and instill

---

3. Reversal of the proper order. [*R. T.*]
4. Pierre-Joseph Proudhon (1809–65) and Henri de Saint-Simon (1760–1825) were early French socialist thinkers. Max Stirner (1806–56) was a German anarchist philosopher. [*R. T.*]

slavery in the people that tolerates it; freedom can only be created by freedom [Bakunin's permanent *citoyen*], i.e., by general insurrection and the free organization of the masses from bottom to top. Whereas the politico-social theory of the anti-state socialists, or anarchists, leads them steadily and directly to the fullest break with all governments, with all forms of bourgeois politics, leaving no other outcome but social revolution

and leaving of social revolution nothing but the phrase,

the contrary theory, the theory of the statist communists and scientific authority, just as steadily, under the pretext of political tactics, draws and entangles them into constant "deals" with governments and various bourgeois political parties, i.e., drives them straight into reaction.

* * *

Circular Letter to Bebel, Liebknecht, Bracke, and Others

KARL MARX

Movements in radical opposition to an existing order must often contend with voices within their midst that urge a toning down of the radical program in the interests of piecemeal reform and collaboration with liberal elements who desire only gradual and partial change of the society. The German socialist movement of the 1870's was a case in point. In this circular letter to the Social Democratic Party leaders, Marx and Engels registered their strong protest against reformist voices within the movement. They still stood firm in their radical opposition to the existing order and their commitment to class struggle as the means of overthrowing it, and they wished the party to do likewise. The "three Zurichers" referred to in the letter were Höchberg, Bernstein, and Schramm; the article attacked by Marx and Engels in the letter was published in the *Jahrbuch für Sozialwissenschaft und Sozialpolitik* (*Annual for Social Sciences and Social Policy*).

London, September 17–18, 1879

The Manifesto of the Three Zurichers

In the meantime Höchberg's *Jahrbuch* has reached us, containing an article, "The Socialist Movement in Germany in Retrospect," which, as Höchberg himself tells me, has been written by precisely the three members of the Zurich Commission. Here we have their authentic criticism of the movement up till now and with it their authentic programme for the line of the new organ in so far as this depends on them.

Right at the beginning we read:

"The movement, which Lassalle regarded as an eminently political one, to which he summoned not only the workers but all honest democrats, *at the head of which* were to march the independent representatives of science and *all men imbued with true love of humanity*, was diminished under the presidency of Johann Baptist Schweitzer to a *one-sided struggle of the industrial workers in their own interests.*"

I shall not examine whether or how far this is historically accurate. The special reproach here levelled against Schweitzer is that he *diminished* Lassalleanism, which is here taken as a bourgeois-democratic-philanthropic movement, to a one-sided struggle in the interest of the industrial workers, by *deepening* its character as a class struggle of the industrial workers against the bourgeois. He is further reproached with having "rejected bourgeois democracy." What business has bourgeois democracy within the Social-Democratic Party anyway? If it consists of "honest men" it cannot wish for admission, and if it does nevertheless wish to be admitted this can only be in order to start a row.

The Lassallean party "chose to conduct itself *in the most one-sided* way as a *workers' party.*" The gentlemen who write that are themselves members of the party which conducts itself in the most one-sided way as a workers' party, they are at present invested with offices and dignities in this party. Here there is an absolute incompatibility. If they mean what they write they must leave the party, or at least resign their offices and dignities. If they do not do so, they admit that they are proposing to utilise their official position in order to combat the proletarian character of the Party. Thus, if the Party leaves them their offices and dignities it will be betraying itself.

In the opinion of these gentlemen, then, the Social-Democratic Party should *not* be a one-sided workers' party but an all-sided party of "all men imbued with true love of humanity." It must prove this above all by laying aside coarse proletarian passions and placing itself under the guidance of educated, philanthropic bourgeois "in order to cultivate good taste" and "learn good form" (p. 85). Then the "disreputable behaviour" of some of the leaders will give way to a thoroughly respectable "bourgeois behaviour." (As if the externally disreputable appearance of those here referred to were not the least they can be reproached with!) Then, too, "*numerous adherents* from the circles of the *educated* and *propertied* classes will make their appearance. But *these* must first be won if the . . . agitation conducted is to attain *tangible successes.*" German socialism has "attached too much importance to the winning of the *masses* and in so doing has neglected energetic [!] propaganda among the so-called upper strata of society." For "the Party still lacks men fit to represent it in the Reichstag." It is, however, "desirable and necessary to entrust the mandates to men who have the time and opportunity to make themselves thoroughly acquainted with the relevant material. The simple worker and small master craftsman . . . have necessary leisure for this only in rare and exceptional cases." So elect bourgeois!

In short: the working class of itself is incapable of its own emancipation. For this purpose it must place itself under the leadership of "educated and propertied" bourgeois who alone possess the "time and opportunity" to acquaint themselves with what is good for the workers. And secondly, the bourgeoisie is on no account to be fought against but—to be *won over* by energetic propaganda.

But if one wants to win over the upper strata of society or only its well-disposed elements one must not frighten them on any account. And here the three Zurichers think they have made a reassuring discovery:

"Precisely at the present time, under the pressure of the Anti-Socialist Law, the Party is showing that it *is not inclined* to pursue the path of violent bloody revolution but is determined . . . to follow the path of legality, that is, of *reform*." So if the 500,000 to 600,000 Social-Democratic voters—between a tenth and an eighth of the whole electorate and, besides, dispersed over the length and breadth of the land—have the sense not to run their heads against a wall and to attempt a "bloody revolution" of one against ten, this proves that they for ever *renounce* taking advantage of some tremendous external event, a sudden revolutionary upsurge arising from it or even a *victory* of the people gained in a conflict resulting from it. If Berlin should ever again be so uneducated as to have another March 18[1] the Social-Democrats, instead of taking part in the fight as "riff-raff with a mania for barricades" (p. 88), must rather "follow the path of legality," put on the brakes, clear away the barricades and if necessary march with the glorious army against the one-sided, coarse, uneducated masses. Or if the gentlemen assert that this is not what they meant, what then did they mean?

But still better follows.

"Hence, the more quiet, objective and deliberate it [the Party] is in its criticism of existing conditions and in its proposals to change them, the less possible will it be to repeat the present successful move [when the Anti-Socialist Law was introduced] by which the conscious reactionaries intimidated the bourgeoisie by conjuring up the Red bogey" (p. 88).

In order to relieve the bourgeoisie of the last trace of anxiety it must be clearly and convincingly proved to it that the Red bogey is really only a bogey, and does not exist. But what is the secret of the Red bogey if not the bourgeoisie's dread of the inevitable life-and-

---

1. This refers to the revolutionary barricade fighting in Berlin on March 18–19, 1848.

death struggle between it and the proletariat? Dread of the inevitable outcome of the modern class struggle? Do away with the class struggle and the bourgeoisie and "all independent people" will "not be afraid to go hand in hand with the proletarians"! And the ones to be cheated would be precisely the proletarians.

Let the Party, therefore, prove by its humble and lowly manner that it has once and for all laid aside the "improprieties and excesses" which occasioned the Anti-Socialist Law. If it voluntarily promises that it only intends to act within the limits of this law, Bismarck and the bourgeoisie will surely have the kindness to repeal it, as it will then be superfluous!

"Let no one misunderstand us"; we do not want "to give up our Party and our programme, but think that for years hence we shall have enough to do if we concentrate our whole strength and energy upon the attainment of certain immediate aims which must in any case be achieved before the realisation of the more far-reaching aspirations can be thought of." Then those bourgeois, petty bourgeois and workers who are "at present frightened away . . . by our far-reaching demands" will join us in masses.

The programme is not to be *given up* but only *postponed*—for an indefinite period. One accepts it, though not really for oneself and one's own lifetime but posthumously, as an heirloom to be handed down to one's children and grandchildren. In the meantime one devotes one's "whole strength and energy" to all sorts of petty rubbish and the patching up of the capitalist order of society in order at least to produce the appearance of something happening without at the same time scaring the bourgeoisie. There I must really praise the "Communist" Miquel, who proves his unshakable belief in the inevitable overthrow of capitalist society in the course of the next few hundred years by swindling for all he's worth, contributing his honest best to the crash of 1873[2] and so *really* doing something to help along the collapse of the existing order.

Another offence against good form was the "exaggerated attacks on the company promoters," who were after all "only children of their time"; it would therefore "have been better to abstain . . . from abusing Strousberg and similar people." Unfortunately everyone is only a "child of his time" and if this is a sufficient excuse nobody ought ever to be attacked any more, all controversy, all struggle on our part ceases; we quietly accept all the kicks our adversaries give us because we, who are so wise, know that these adversaries are "only children of their time" and cannot act otherwise. Instead of repaying their kicks with interest we ought rather to pity these unfortunates.

2. The crash of 1873 ended the so-called *"Grunder taumel"* (the promoting frenzy), a period of furious specu-lation and stock-exchange gambling which followed on the termination of the Franco-Prussian War of 1870–71.

Then again the support of the Commune had the disadvantage, nevertheless, that "people who were otherwise well disposed to us were alienated and in general the *hatred of the bourgeoisie* against us was increased." Furthermore, the Party "is not wholly without blame for the passage of the October Law,[3] for it had increased the *hatred of the bourgeoisie* unnecessarily."

There you have the programme of the three censors of Zurich. In clarity it leaves nothing to be desired. Least of all to us, who are very familiar with the whole of this phraseology from the 1848 days. It is the representatives of the petty bourgeoisie who are here presenting themselves, full of anxiety that the proletariat, under the pressure of its revolutionary position, may "go too far." Instead of determined political opposition, general mediation; instead of struggle against the government and the bourgeoisie, an attempt to win over and persuade them; instead of defiant resistance to ill treatment from above, humble submission and confession that the punishment was deserved. Historically necessary conflicts are all interpreted as misunderstandings, and all discussion ends with the assurance that after all we are all agreed on the main point. The people who came out as bourgeois democrats in 1848 could just as well call themselves Social-Democrats now. To the former the democratic republic was as unattainably remote as the overthrow of the capitalist system is to the latter, and therefore is of absolutely no importance in present-day politics; one can mediate, compromise and philanthropise to one's heart's content. It is just the same with the class struggle because its existence can no longer be denied, but in practice it is hushed up, diluted, attenuated, The Social-Democratic Party *is not* to be a workers' party, is not to incur the odium of the bourgeoisie or of anyone else; it should above all conduct energetic propaganda among the bourgeoisie; instead of laying stress on far-reaching aims which frighten away the bourgeoisie and after all are not attainable in our generation, it should rather devote its whole strength and energy to those petty-bourgeois patchwork reforms which, by providing the old order of society with new props, may perhaps transform the ultimate catastrophe into a gradual, piecemeal and as far as possible peaceful process of dissolution. These are the same people who, ostensibly engaged in indefatigable activity, not only do nothing themselves but try to prevent anything happening at all except—chatter; the same people whose fear of every form of action in 1848 and 1849 obstructed the movement at every step and finally brought about its downfall, the same people who never see reaction and are then quite astonished to find themselves in the end in a blind alley where neither resistance nor flight is possible,

3. Exceptional Law against the Socialists, introduced by Bismarck in October 1878.

the same people who want to confine history within their narrow Philistine horizon and over whose heads history invariably proceeds to the order of the day.

As to their socialist convictions, this has been adequately criticised already in the *Manifesto*, the chapter on "German, or 'True,' Socialism." Where the class struggle is pushed aside as a disagreeable "coarse" phenomenon, nothing remains as a basis for socialism but "true love of humanity" and empty phraseology about "justice."

It is an inevitable phenomenon, rooted in the course of development, that people from what have hitherto been the ruling classes should also join the militant proletariat and supply it with educative elements. We clearly stated this in the *Manifesto*. But here two points are to be noted:

First, in order to be of use to the proletarian movement these people must bring real educative elements into it. But with the great majority of the German bourgeois converts that is not the case. Neither the *Zukunft* nor the *Neue Gesellschaft*[4] have contributed anything which could advance the movement one step further. Here there is an absolute lack of real education material, whether factual or theoretical. In its place there are attempts to bring superficially mastered socialist ideas into harmony with the exceedingly varied theoretical standpoints which these gentlemen have brought with them from the university or elsewhere and of which, owing to the process of decomposition which the remnants of German philosophy are at present undergoing, one is more confused than the other. Instead of thoroughly studying the new science themselves to begin with, each of them preferred to trim it to fit the point of view he already had brought along, made himself forthwith a private science of his own and at once came forward with the pretension of wanting to teach it. Hence, there are about as many points of view among these gentry as there are heads; instead of producing clarity in a single case they have only produced desperate confusion—fortunately almost exclusively among themselves. Educative elements whose first principle is to teach what they have not learnt can very well be dispensed with by the Party.

Secondly. If people of this kind from other classes join the proletarian movement, the first condition must be that they should not bring any remnants of bourgeois, petty-bourgeois, etc., prejudices with them but should whole-heartedly adopt the proletarian outlook. But these gentlemen, as has been proved, are chock-full of bourgeois and petty-bourgeois ideas. In such a petty-bourgeois coun-

4. *Zukunft* [*Future*] and *Neue Gesell-schaft* [*New Society*]: Social-reformist journals. The former appeared in Zu-rich in 1877–80; the latter in Berlin in 1877–78.

try as Germany these ideas certainly have their justification. But only *outside* the Social-Democratic Workers' Party. If these gentlemen constitute themselves into a Social-Democratic petty-bourgeois party they have a perfect right to do so; one could then negotiate with them, form a *bloc* according to circumstances, etc. But in a workers' party they are an adulterating element. If reasons exist for tolerating them there for the moment it is also duty *only* to tolerate them, to allow them no influence in the Party leadership and to remain aware that a break with them is only a matter of time. That time, moreover, seems to have come. How the Party can tolerate the authors of this article in its midst any longer is incomprehensible to us. But if even the leadership of the Party should fall more or less into the hands of such people, the Party would simply be castrated and there would be an end of proletarian snap.

As for ourselves, in view of our whole past there is only one path open to us. For almost forty years we have stressed the class struggle as the immediate driving power of history and in particular the class struggle between bourgeoisie and proletariat as the great lever of the modern social revolution; it is, therefore, impossible for us to co-operate with people who wish to expunge this class struggle from the movement. When the International was formed we expressly formulated the battle cry: The emancipation of the working class must be the work of the working class itself. We cannot, therefore, co-operate with people who openly state that the workers are too uneducated to emancipate themselves and must first be freed from above by philanthropic big bourgeois and petty bourgeois. If the new Party organ adopts a line corresponding to the views of these gentlemen, a line that is bourgeois and not proletarian, then nothing remains for us, much though we should regret it, but publicly to declare our opposition to it, and to dissolve the solidarity with which we have hitherto represented the German Party abroad. But it is to be hoped that things will not come to *that* pass.

The Tactics of Social Democracy

FRIEDRICH ENGELS

In 1895 Engels put out Marx's *The Class Struggles in France*, 1848–1850 as a separate pamphlet with a long Introduction, which proved to be his valedictory to the Social Democratic movement, as he died later that year. Surveying changes in the European scene over the more than forty years since Marx's pamphlet was written, Engels hailed the steady progress made by Social Democracy, particularly in Germany, through the electoral process. His endorsement of peaceful political tactics was further accentuated when, in March, 1895, *Vorwärts*, the central organ of the German Social Democratic Party, printed an abbreviated version of the Introduction featuring those portions of it which, as Engels complained in a private letter, could serve to "defend the tactics of peace at all costs and of the abhorrence of force. . . ." On April 1, 1895, Engels wrote further to Karl Kautsky: ". . . I see today in the *Vorwärts* an extract from my Introduction, printed without my prior knowledge and trimmed in such a fashion that I appear as a peaceful worshipper of legality *quand même*. So much the more would I like the Introduction to appear unabridged in the *Neue Zeit*, so that this disgraceful impression will be wiped out." Even in its unabridged form, however, as printed here, the Introduction is notable for its hearty approval of the tactics that had evolved in Social Democratic practice in the late nineteenth century. For the work by Marx for which Engels wrote this introduction, see below, pp. 586–593.

The work here republished was Marx's first attempt to explain a section of contemporary history by means of his materialist conception, on the basis of the given economic situation. In the *Communist Manifesto*, the theory was applied in broad outline to the whole of modern history; in the articles by Marx and myself in the *Neue Rheinische Zeitung*, it was constantly used to interpret political events of the day. Here, on the other hand, the question was to demonstrate the inner causal connection in the course of a development which extended over some years, a development as critical, for the whole of Europe, as it was typical; hence, in accordance with the conception of the author, to trace political events back to effects of what were, in the final analysis, economic causes.

If events and series of events are judged by current history, it will never be possible to go back to the *ultimate* economic causes. Even today, when the specialised press concerned provides such rich material, it still remains impossible even in England to follow day by day the movement of industry and trade in the world market and the changes which take place in the methods of production in such a way as to be able to draw a general conclusion, for any point of time, from these manifold, complicated and ever-changing factors, the most important of which, into the bargain, generally operate a long time in secret before they suddenly make themselves violently felt on the surface. A clear survey of the economic history of a given period can never be obtained contemporaneously, but only subsequently, after a collecting and sifting of the material has taken place. Statistics are a necessary auxiliary means here, and they always lag behind. For this reason, it is only too often necessary, in current history, to treat this, the most decisive, factor as constant, and the economic situation existing at the beginning of the period concerned as given and unalterable for the whole period, or else to take notice of only such changes in this situation as arise out of the patently manifest events themselves, and are, therefore, likewise patently manifest. Hence, the materialist method has here quite often to limit itself to tracing political conflicts back to the struggles between the interests of the existing social classes and fractions of classes created by the economic development, and to prove the particular political parties to be the more or less adequate political expression of these same classes and fractions of classes.

It is self-evident that this unavoidable neglect of contemporaneous changes in the economic situation, the very basis of all the processes to be examined, must be a source of error. But all the conditions of a comprehensive presentation of current history unavoidably include sources of error—which, however, keeps nobody from writing current history.

When Marx undertook this work, the source of error mentioned was even more unavoidable. It was simply impossible during the period of the Revolution of 1848–49 to follow up the economic transformations taking place at the same time or even to keep them it view. It was the same during the first months of exile in London, in the autumn and winter of 1849–50. But that was just the time when Marx began this work. And in spite of these unfavourable circumstances, his exact knowledge both of the economic situation in

France before, and of the political history of that country after the February Revolution made it possible for him to give a picture of events which laid bare their inner connections in a way never attained ever since, and which later brilliantly stood the double test applied by Marx himself.

The first test resulted from the fact that after the spring of 1850 Marx once again found leisure for economic studies, and first of all took up the economic history of the last ten years. Thereby what he had hitherto deduced, half *a priori*, from sketchy material, became absolutely clear to him from the facts themselves, namely, that the world trade crisis of 1847 had been the true mother of the February and March Revolutions, and that the industrial prosperity, which had been returning gradually since the middle of 1848 and attained full bloom in 1849 and 1850, was the revitalising force of the newly strengthened European reaction. That was decisive. Whereas in the first three articles (which appeared in the January, February and March issues of the *Neue Rheinische Zeitung, Politisch-ökonomische Revue*,[1] Hamburg, 1850) there was still the expectation of a early new upsurge of revolutionary energy, the historical review written by Marx and myself for the last issue, a double issue (May to October), which was published in the autumn of 1850, breaks once and for all with these illusions: "A new revolution is possible only in the wake of a new crisis. It is, however, just as certain as this crisis." But that was the only essential change which had to be made. There was absolutely nothing to alter in the interpretation of events given in the earlier chapters, or in the causal connections established therein, as the continuation of the narrative from March 10 up to the autumn of 1850 in the review in question proves. I have, therefore, included this continuation as the fourth article in the present new edition.

The second test was even more severe. Immediately after Louis Bonaparte's *coup d'état* of December 2, 1851, Marx worked out anew the history of France from February 1848 up to this event, which concluded the revolutionary period for the time being. (*The Eighteenth Brumaire of Louis Bonaparte*. Third edition, Hamburg, Meissner, 1885). In this pamphlet the period depicted in our present publication is again dealt with, although more briefly. Compare this second presentation, written in the light of the decisive event which happened over a year later, with ours and it will be found that the author had very little to change.

What, besides, gives our work quite special significance is the circumstance that it was the first to express the formula in which, by

---

1. *New Rhenish Gazette, Politico-Economic Review*, a journal published by Marx and Engels in January–October 1850.

common agreement, the workers' parties of all countries in the world briefly summarise their demand for economic transformation: the appropriation of the means of production by society. In the second chapter, in connection with the "right to work," which is characterised as "the first clumsy formula wherein the revolutionary demands of the proletariat are summarised," it is said: "But behind the right to work stands the power over capital; behind the power over capital, the *appropriation of the means of production*, their subjection to the associated working class and, therefore, the abolition of wage labour as well as of capital and of their mutual relations." Thus, here, for the first time, the proposition is formulated by which modern workers' socialism is equally sharply differentiated both from all the different shades of feudal, bourgeois, petty-bourgeois, etc., socialism and also from the confused community of goods of utopian and of spontaneous workers' communism. If, later, Marx extended the formula to include appropriation of the means of exchange, this extension, which in any case was self-evident after the *Communist Manifesto*, only expressed a corollary to the main proposition. A few wiseacres in England have of late added that the "means of distribution" should also be handed over to society. It would be difficult for these gentlemen to say what these economic means of distribution are, as distinct from the means of production and exchange; unless *political* means of distribution are meant, taxes, poor relief, including the *Sachsenwald*[2] and other endowments. But, first, these are already now means of distribution in possession of society in the aggregate, either of the state or of the community, and secondly, it is precisely the abolition of these that we desire.

When the February Revolution broke out, all of us, as far as our conceptions of the conditions and the course of revolutionary movements were concerned, were under the spell of previous historical experience, particularly that of France. It was, indeed, the latter which had dominated the whole of European history since 1789, and from which now once again the signal had gone forth for general revolutionary change. It was, therefore, natural and unavoidable that our conceptions of the nature and the course of the "social" revolution proclaimed in Paris in February 1848, of the revolution of the proletariat, should be strongly coloured by memories of the prototypes of 1789 and 1830. Moreover, when the Paris uprising found its echo in the victorious insurrections in Vienna, Milan and Berlin; when the whole of Europe right up to the Russian frontier was swept into the movement; when thereupon in Paris, in June,

2. A vast estate granted to Bismarck by William I in 1871.

the first great battle for power between the proletariat and the bourgeoisie was fought; when the very victory of its class so shook the bourgeoisie of all countries that it fled back into the arms of the monarchist-feudal reaction which had just been overthrown—there could be no doubt for us, under the circumstances then obtaining, that the great decisive combat had commenced, that it would have to be fought out in a single, long and vicissitudinous period of revolution, but that it could only end in the final victory of the proletariat.

After the defeats of 1849 we in no way shared the illusions of the vulgar democracy grouped around the future provisional governments *in partibus*.[3] This vulgar democracy reckoned on a speedy and finally decisive victory of the "people" over the "tyrants"; we looked to a long struggle, after the removal of the "tyrants," among the antagonistic elements concealed within this "people" itself. Vulgar democracy expected a renewed outbreak any day; we declared as early as autumn 1850 that at least the *first* chapter of the revolutionary period was closed and that nothing was to be expected until the outbreak of a new world economic crisis. For which reason we were excommunicated, as traitors to the revolution, by the very people who later, almost without exception, made their peace with Bismarck—so far as Bismarck found them worth the trouble.

But history has shown us too to have been wrong, has revealed our point of view of that time to have been an illusion. It has done even more: it has not merely dispelled the erroneous notions we then held; it has also completely transformed the conditions under which the proletariat has to fight. The mode of struggle of 1848 is today obsolete in every respect, and this is a point which deserves closer examination on the present occasion.

All revolutions up to the present day have resulted in the displacement of one definite class rule by another; but all ruling classes up to now have been only small minorities in relation to the ruled mass of the people. One ruling minority was thus overthrown; another minority seized the helm of state in its stead and refashioned the state institutions to suit its own interests. This was on every occasion the minority group qualified and called to rule by the given degree of economic development; and just for that reason, and only for that reason, it happened that the ruled majority either participated in the revolution for the benefit of the former or else calmly acquiesced in it. But if we disregard the concrete content in each case, the common form of all these revolutions was that they were minority revolutions. Even when the majority took part, it did

---

3. *In partibus infidelium:* literally, in the lands of the infidels, that is, beyond the frontiers of one's own country, in emigration.

so—whether wittingly or not— only in the service of a minority; but because of this, or even simply because of the passive, unresisting attitude of the majority, this minority acquired the appearance of being the representative of the whole people.

As a rule, after the first great success, the victorious minority divided; one half was satisfied with what had been gained, the other wanted to go still further, and put forward new demands, which, partly at least, were also in the real or apparent interest of the great mass of the people. In individual cases these more radical demands were actually forced through, but often only for the moment, the more moderate party would regain the upper hand, and what had last been won would wholly or partly be lost again; the vanquished would then shriek of treachery or ascribe their defeat to accident. In reality, however, the truth of the matter was largely this: the achievements of the first victory were only safeguarded by the second victory of the more radical party; this having been attained, and, with it, what was necessary for the moment, the radicals and their achievements vanished once more from the stage.

All revolutions of modern times, beginning with the great English Revolution of the seventeenth century, showed these features, which appeared inseparable from every revolutionary struggle. They appeared applicable, also, to the struggle of the proletariat for its emancipation; all the more applicable, since precisely in 1848 there were but a very few people who had any idea at all of the direction in which this emancipation was to be sought. The proletarian masses themselves, even in Paris, after the victory, were still absolutely in the dark as to the path to be taken. And yet the movement was there, instinctive, spontaneous, irrepressible. Was not this just the situation in which a revolution had to succeed, led, true, by a minority, but this time not in the interest of the minority, but in the veriest interest of the majority? If, in all the longer revolutionary periods, it was so easy to win the great masses of the people by the merely plausible false representations of the forward-thrusting minorities, why should they be less susceptible to ideas which were the truest reflection of their economic condition, which were nothing but the clear, rational expression of their needs, of needs not yet understood but merely vaguely felt by them? To be sure, this revolutionary mood of the masses had almost always, and usually very speedily, given way to lassitude or even to a revulsion of feeling as soon as illusion evaporated and disappointment set in. But here it was not a question of false representations, but of giving effect to the highest special interests of the great majority itself, interests which, true, were at that time by no means clear to this great majority, but which soon enough had to become clear to it, in the course of giving practical effect to them, by their convincing obviousness. And when, as Marx showed in this third article, in the spring of 1850, the development of the bourgeois republic that arose out of the "social" Revolution of 1848 had even concentrated real power in the hands of the big bourgeoisie—monarchistically inclined as it was into the bargain—and, on the other hand, had grouped all the other social classes, peasantry as well as petty bourgeoisie, round the proletariat, so that, during and after the common victory, not they but the proletariat grown wise by experience had to become the decisive factor—was there not every prospect then of turning the revolution of the minority into a revolution of the majority?

History has proved us, and all who thought like us, wrong. It has made it clear that the state of economic development on the Continent at that time was not, by a long way, ripe for the elimination of capitalist production; it has proved this by the economic revolution which, since 1848, has seized the whole of the Continent, and has caused big industry to take real root in France, Austria, Hungary, Poland and, recently, in Russia, while it has made Germany positively an industrial country of the first rank—all on a capitalist basis, which in the year 1848, therefore, still had great capacity for expansion. But it is just this industrial revolution which has everywhere produced clarity in class relations, has removed a number of intermediate forms handed down from the period of manufacture and in Eastern Europe even from guild handicraft, has created a genuine bourgeoisie and a genuine large-scale industrial proletariat and has pushed them into the foreground of social development. However, owing to this, the struggle between these two great classes, a struggle which, apart from England, existed in 1848 only in Paris and, at the most, in a few big industrial centres, has spread over the whole of Europe and reached an intensity still inconceivable in 1848. At that time the many obscure evangels of the sects, with their panaceas; today the *one* generally recognised, crystal-clear theory of Marx, sharply formulating the ultimate aims of the struggle. At that time the masses, sundered and differing according to locality and nationality, linked only by the feeling of common suffering, undeveloped, helplessly tossed to and fro from enthusiasm to despair; today the *one* great international army of Socialists, marching irresistibly on and growing daily in number, organisation, discipline, insight and certainty of victory. If even this mighty army of the proletariat has still not reached its goal, if, far from winning victory by one mighty stroke, it has slowly to press forward from position to position in a hard, tenacious struggle, this only proves, once and for all, how impossible it was in 1848 to win social transformation by a simple surprise attack.

A bourgeoisie split into two dynastic-monarchist sections,[4] a bourgeoisie, however, which demanded, above all, peace and security for its financial operations, faced by a proletariat vanquished, indeed, but still always a menace, a proletariat round which petty bourgeois and peasants grouped themselves more and more—the continual threat of a violent outbreak, which, nevertheless, offered absolutely no prospect of a final solution—such was the situation, as if specially created for the *coup d'état* of the third, the pseudo-democratic pretender, Louis Bonaparte. On December 2, 1851, by means of the army, he put an end to the tense situation and secured Europe domestic tranquillity in order to confer upon it the blessing of a new era of wars.[5] The period of revolutions from below was concluded for the time being; there followed a period of revolutions from above.

The reversion to the empire in 1851 gave new proof of the unripeness of the proletarian aspirations of that time. But it was itself to create the conditions under which they were bound to ripen. Internal tranquillity ensured the full development of the new industrial boom; the necessity of keeping the army occupied and of diverting the revolutionary currents outwards produced the wars in which Bonaparte, under the pretext of asserting "the principle of nationality," sought to hook annexations for France. His imitator, Bismarck, adopted the same policy for Prussia; he made his *coup d'état*, his revolution from above, in 1866, against the German Confederation and Austria, and no less against the Prussian *Konfliktskammer*.[6] But Europe was too small for two Bonapartes and the irony of history so willed it that Bismarck overthrew Bonaparte, and King William of Prussia not only established the little German empire,[7] but also the French republic. The general result, however, was that in Europe the independence and internal unity of the great nations, with the exception of Poland, had become a fact. Within relatively modest limits, it is true, but, for all that, on a scale large enough to allow the development of the working class to proceed without finding national complications any longer a serious

4. The parties referred to are the *Legitimists,* the supporters of the "legitimate," Bourbon, dynasty, who were in power in France up to 1792 and also during the epoch of the Restoration (1814–30), and the *Orleanists,* the supporters of the Orléans dynasty, who came to power during the July Revolution of 1830 and were overthrown by the Revolution of 1848.
5. During the reign of Napoleon III, France took part in the Crimean Campaign (1854–55), carried on war with Austria on account of Italy (1859), participated together with England in the wars against China (1856–58 and 1860), began the conquest of Indo-China, organised an expedition into Syria (1860–61) and Mexico (1862–67), and finally, in 1870–71, waged war against Prussia.
6. *Konfliktskammer,* that is, the Prussian Chamber then in conflict with the government.
7. This term is applied to the German Empire (without Austria) that arose in 1871 under Prussia's hegemony.

obstacle. The grave-diggers of the Revolution of 1848 had become the executors of its will. And alongside of them already rose threateningly the heir of 1848, the proletariat, in the shape of the *International*.

After the war of 1870–71, Bonaparte vanishes from the stage and Bismarck's mission is fulfilled, so that he can now sink back again into the ordinary *Junker*. The period, however, is brought to a close by the Paris Commune. An underhand attempt by Thiers to steal the cannon of the Paris National Guard called forth a victorious rising. It was shown once more that in Paris none but a proletarian revolution is any longer possible. After the victory power fell, quite of itself and quite undisputed, into the hands of the working class. And once again it was proved how impossible even then, twenty years after the time described in our work, this rule of the working class still was. On the one hand, France left Paris in the lurch, looked on while it bled profusely from the bullets of MacMahon; on the other hand, the Commune was consumed in unfruitful strife between the two parties which split it, the Blanquists (the majority) and the Proudhonists (the minority), neither of which knew what was to be done. The victory which came as a gift in 1871 remained just as unfruitful as the surprise attack of 1848.

It was believed that the militant proletariat had been finally buried with the Paris Commune. But, completely to the contrary, it dates its most powerful resurgence from the Commune and the Franco-Prussian War. The recruitment of the whole of the population able to bear arms into armies that henceforth could be counted only in millions, and the introduction of fire-arms, projectiles and explosives of hitherto undreamt-of efficacy, created a complete revolution in all warfare. This revolution, on the one hand, put a sudden end to the Bonapartist war period and ensured peaceful industrial development by making any war other than a world war of unheard-of cruelty and absolutely incalculable outcome an impossibility. On the other hand, it caused military expenditure to rise in geometrical progression and thereby forced up taxes to exorbitant levels and so drove the poorer classes of people into the arms of socialism. The annexation of Alsace-Lorraine, the immediate cause of the mad competition in armaments, was able to set the French and German bourgeoisie chauvinistically at each other's throats; for the workers of the two countries it became a new bond of unity. And the anniversary of the Paris Commune became the first universal day of celebration of the whole proletariat.

The war of 1870–71 and the defeat of the Commune transferred the centre of gravity of the European workers' movement for the time being from France to Germany, as Marx had foretold. In France it naturally took years to recover from the blood-letting of

May 1871. In Germany, on the other hand, where industry—fostered, in addition, in positively hothouse fashion by the blessing of the French milliards[8] developed more and more rapidly, Social-Democracy experienced a still more rapid and enduring growth. Thanks to the intelligent use which the German workers made of the universal suffrage introduced in 1866, the astonishing growth of the party is made plain to all the world by incontestable figures: 1871, 102,000; 1874, 352,000; 1877, 493,000 Social-Democratic votes. Then came recognition of this advance by high authority in the shape of the Anti-Socialist Law; the party was temporarily broken up, the number of votes dropped to 312,000 in 1881. But that was quickly overcome, and then, under the pressure of the Exceptional Law, without a press, without a legal organisation and without the right of combination and assembly, rapid expansion really began: 1884, 550,000; 1887, 763,000; 1890, 1,427,000 votes. Thereupon the hand of the state was paralysed. The Anti-Socialist Law disappeared; socialist votes rose to 1,787,000, over a quarter of all the votes cast. The government and the ruling classes had exhausted all their expedients—uselessly, purposelessly, unsuccessfully. The tangible proofs of their impotence, which the authorities, from night watchman to the imperial chancellor, had had to accept—and that from the despised workers!—these proofs were counted in millions. The state was at the end of its tether, the workers only at the beginning of theirs.

But, besides, the German workers rendered a second great service to their cause in addition to the first, a service performed by their mere existence as the strongest, best disciplined and most rapidly growing Socialist Party. They supplied their comrades in all countries with a new weapon, and one of the sharpest, when they showed them how to make use of universal suffrage.

There had long been universal suffrage in France, but it had fallen into disrepute through the misuse to which the Bonapartist government had put it. After the Commune there was no workers' party to make use of it. It also existed in Spain since the republic, but in Spain boycott of elections was ever the rule of all serious opposition parties. The experience of the Swiss with universal suffrage was also anything but encouraging for a workers' party. The revolutionary workers of the Latin countries had been wont to regard the suffrage as a snare, as an instrument of government trickery. It was otherwise in Germany. The *Communist Manifesto* had already proclaimed the winning of universal suffrage, of democracy, as one of the first and most important tasks of the militant proletariat, and Lassalle had again taken up this point. Now, when Bis-

8. The reference is to the payment of the five-billion-franc indemnity by France to Germany under the terms of the Frankfurt Peace Treaty of May 10, 1871.

marck found himself compelled to introduce this franchise as the only means of interesting the mass of the people in his plans, our workers immediately took it in earnest and sent August Bebel to the first, constituent Reichstag. And from that day on, they have used the franchise in a way which has paid them a thousandfold and has served as a model to the workers of all countries. The franchise has been, in the words of the French Marxist programme, *transformé, de moyen de duperie qu'il a été jusqu'ici, en instrument d'émancipation*—transformed by them from a means of deception, which it was before, into an instrument of emancipation.[9] And if universal suffrage had offered no other advantage than that it allowed us to count our numbers every three years; that by the regularly established, unexpectedly rapid rise in the number of our votes it increased in equal measure the workers' certainty of victory and the dismay of their opponents, and so became our best means of propaganda; that it accurately informed us concerning our own strength and that of all hostile parties, and thereby provided us with a measure of proportion for our actions second to none, safeguarding us from untimely timidity as much as from untimely foolhardiness—if this had been the only advantage we gained from the suffrage, it would still have been much more than enough. But it did more than this by far. In election agitation it provided us with a means, second to none, of getting in touch with the mass of the people where they still stand aloof from us; of forcing all parties to defend their views and actions against our attacks before all the people; and, further, it provided our representatives in the Reichstag with a platform from which they could speak to their opponents in parliament, and to the masses without, with quite other authority and freedom than in the press or at meetings. Of what avail was their Anti-Socialist Law to the government and the bourgeoisie when election campaigning and socialist speeches in the Reichstag continually broke through it?

With this successful utilisation of universal suffrage, however, an entirely new method of proletarian struggle came into operation, and this method quickly developed further. It was found that the state institutions, in which the rule of the bourgeoisie is organised, offer the working class still further opportunities to fight these very state institutions. The workers took part in elections to particular Diets, to municipal councils and to trades courts; they contested with the bourgeoisie every post in the occupation of which a sufficient part of the proletariat had a say. And so it happened that the bourgeoisie and the government came to be much more afraid

9. This phrase was taken from the preamble, written by Marx, of the programme of the French Workers' Party. The programme was adopted in 1880, at the Havre Congress of the Party.

of the legal than of the illegal action of the workers' party, of the results of elections than of those of rebellion.

For here, too, the conditions of the struggle had essentially changed. Rebellion in the old style, street fighting with barricades, which decided the issue everywhere up to 1848, was to a considera-

Let us have no illusions about it: a real victory of an insurrection ble extent obsolete.

over the military in street fighting, a victory as between two armies, is one of the rarest exceptions. And the insurgents counted on it just as rarely. For them it was solely a question of making the troops yield to moral influences which, in a fight between the armies of two warring countries, do not come into play at all or do so to a much smaller extent. If they succeed in this, the troops fail to respond, or the commanding officers lose their heads, and the insurrection wins. If they do not succeed in this, then, even where the military are in the minority, the superiority of better equipment and training, of single leadership, of the planned employment of the military forces and of discipline makes itself felt. The most that an insurrection can achieve in the way of actual tactical operations is the proper construction and defence of a single barricade. Mutual support, the disposition and employment of reserves—in short, concerted and co-ordinated action of the individual detachments, indispensable even for the defence of one section of a town, not to speak of the whole of a large town, will be attainable only to a very limited extent, and most of the time not at all. Concentration of the military forces at a decisive point is, of course, out of the question here. Hence passive defence is the prevailing form of fighting; the attack will rise here and there, but only by way of exception, to occasional thrusts and flank assaults; as a rule, however, it will be limited to occupation of positions abandoned by retreating troops. In addition, the military have at their disposal artillery and fully equipped corps of trained engineers, resources of war which, in nearly every case, the insurgents entirely lack. No wonder, then, that even the barricade fighting conducted with the greatest heroism—Paris, June 1848; Vienna, October 1848; Dresden, May 1849—ended in the defeat of the insurrection as soon as the leaders of the attack, unhampered by political considerations, acted from the purely military standpoint, and their soldiers remained reliable.

The numerous successes of the insurgents up to 1848 were due to a great variety of causes. In Paris, in July 1830 and February 1848, as in most of the Spanish street fighting, a citizens' guard stood between the insurgents and the military. This guard either sided directly with the insurrection, or else by its lukewarm, indecisive attitude caused the troops likewise to vacillate, and supplied the insurrection with arms into the bargain. Where this citizens' guard opposed the insurrection from the outset, as in June 1848 in Paris, the insurrection was vanquished. In Berlin in 1848, the people were victorious partly through a considerable accession of new fighting forces during the night and the morning of [March] the 19th, partly as a result of the exhaustion and bad victualling of the troops, and, finally, partly as a result of the paralysis that was seizing the command. But in all cases the fight was won because the troops failed to respond, because the commanding officers lost the faculty to decide or because their hands were tied.

Even in the classic time of street fighting, therefore, the barricade produced more of a moral than a material effect. It was a means of shaking the steadfastness of the military. If it held out until this was attained, victory was won; if not, there was defeat. This is the main point, which must be kept in view, likewise, when the chances of possible future street fighting are examined.

Already in 1849, these chances were pretty poor. Everywhere the bourgeoisie had thrown in its lot with the governments, "culture and property" had hailed and feasted the military moving against insurrection. The spell of the barricade was broken; the soldier no longer saw behind it "the people," but rebels, agitators, plunderers, levellers, the scum of society; the officer had in the course of time become versed in the tactical forms of street fighting, he no longer marched straight ahead and without cover against the improvised breastwork, but went round it through gardens, yards and houses. And this was now successful, with a little skill, in nine cases out of ten.

But since then there have been very many more changes, and all in favour of the military. If the big towns have become considerably bigger, the armies have become bigger still. Paris and Berlin have, since 1848, grown less than fourfold, but their garrisons have grown more than that. By means of the railways, these garrisons can, in twenty-four hours, be more than doubled, and in forty-eight hours they can be increased to huge armies. The arming of this enormously increased number of troops has become incomparably more effective. In 1848 the smooth-bore, muzzle-loading percussion gun, today the small-calibre, breech-loading magazine rifle, which shoots four times as far, ten times as accurately and ten times as fast as the former. At that time the relatively ineffective round shot and grapeshot of the artillery; today the percussion shells, of which one is sufficient to demolish the best barricade. At that time the pick-axe of the sapper for breaking through fire-walls; today the dynamite cartridge.

On the other hand, all the conditions of the insurgents' side have grown worse. An insurrection with which all sections of the people sympathise will hardly recur; in the class struggle all the middle strata will probably never group themselves round the proletariat so exclusively that in comparison the party of reaction gathered round the bourgeoisie will well-nigh disappear. The "people," therefore, will always appear divided, and thus a most powerful lever, so extraordinarily effective in 1848, is gone. If more soldiers who have seen service came over to the insurrectionists, the arming of them would become so much the more difficult. The hunting and fancy guns of the munitions shops—even if not previously made unusable by removal of part of the lock by order of the police—are far from being a match for the magazine rifle of the soldier, even in close fighting. Up to 1848 it was possible to make the necessary ammunition oneself out of powder and lead; today the cartridges differ for each gun, and are everywhere alike only in one point, namely, that they are a complicated product of big industry, and therefore not to be manufactured *ex tempore*, with the result that most guns are useless as long as one does not possess the ammunition specially suited to them. And, finally, since 1848 the newly built quarters of the big cities have been laid out in long, straight, broad streets, as though made to give full effect to the new cannon and rifles. The revolutionist would have to be mad who himself chose the new working-class districts in the North or East of Berlin for a barricade fight.

Does that mean that in the future street fighting will not longer play any role? Certainly not. It only means that the conditions since 1848 have become far more unfavourable for civilian fighters and far more favourable for the military. In future, street fighting can, therefore, be victorious only if this disadvantageous situation is compensated by other factors. Accordingly, it will occur more seldom in the beginning of a great revolution than in its further progress, and will have to be undertaken with greater forces. These, however, may then well prefer, as in the whole great French Revolution or on September 4 and October 31, 1870,[1] in Paris, the open attack to the passive barricade tactics.

Does the reader now understand why the powers that be positively want to get us to go where the guns shoot and the sabres slash? Why they accuse us today of cowardice, because we do not betake ourselves without more ado into the street, where we are certain of defeat in advance? Why they so earnestly implore us to play for once the part of cannon fodder?

The gentlemen pour out their prayers and their challenges for nothing, for absolutely nothing. We are not so stupid. They might just as well demand from their enemy in the next war that he

1. On September 4, 1870, the government of Louis Bonaparte was overthrown and the republic proclaimed, and on October 31 of the same year there took place the unsuccessful attempt of the Blanquists to make an insurrection against the Government of "National Defence."

should accept battle in the line formation of old Fritz,[2] or in the columns of whole divisions à la Wagram and Waterloo, and with the flint-lock in his hands at that. If conditions have changed in the case of war between nations, this is no less true in the case of the class struggle. The time of surprise attacks, of revolutions carried through by small conscious minorities at the head of unconscious masses, is past. Where it is a question of a complete transformation of the social organisation, the masses themselves must also be in it, must themselves already have grasped what is at stake, what they are going in for, body and soul. The history of the last fifty years has taught us that. But in order that the masses may understand what is to be done, long, persistent work is required, and it is just this work that we are now pursuing, and with a success which drives the enemy to despair.

In the Latin countries, also, it is being realised more and more that the old tactics must be revised. Everywhere the German example of utilising the suffrage, of winning all posts accessible to us, has been imitated; everywhere the unprepared launching of an attack has been relegated to the background. In France, where for more than a hundred years the ground has been undermined by revolution after revolution, where there is not a single party which has not done its share in conspiracies, insurrections and all other revolutionary actions; in France, where, as a result, the government is by no means sure of the army and where, in general, the conditions for an insurrectionary *coup de main* are far more favourable than in Germany—even in France the Socialists are realising more and more that no lasting victory is possible for them, unless they first win the great mass of the people, that is, in this case, the peasants. Slow propaganda work and parliamentary activity are recognised here, too, as the immediate tasks of the party. Successes were not lacking. Not only have a whole series of municipal councils been won; fifty Socialists have seats in the Chambers, and they have already overthrown three ministries and a president of the republic. In Belgium last year the workers forced the adoption of the franchise, and have been victorious in a quarter of the constituencies. In Switzerland, in Italy, in Denmark, yes, even in Bulgaria and Rumania the Socialists are represented in the parliaments. In Austria all parties agree that our admission to the *Reichsrat* can no longer be withheld. We will get in, that is certain; the only question still in dispute is: by which door? And even in Russia, when the famous *Zemsky Sobor* meets —that National Assembly to which young Nicholas offers such vain resistance—even there we can reckon with certainty on being represented in it.

Of course, our foreign comrades do not thereby in the least re-

2. Frederick II, King of Prussia (1740–86).

nounce their right to revolution. The right to revolution is, after all, the only *really* "historical right," the only right on which all modern states without exception rest, Mecklenburg included, whose aristocratic revolution was ended in 1755 by the "hereditary settlement" ["Erbvergleich"], the glorious charter of feudalism still valid today. The right to revolution is so incontestably recognised in the general consciousness that even General von Boguslawski derives the right to a *coup d'état*, which he vindicates for his Kaiser, solely from this popular right.

But whatever may happen in other countries, the German Social-Democracy occupies a special position and therewith, at least in the immediate future, has a special task. The two million voters whom it sends to the ballot box, together with the young men and women who stand behind them as non-voters, form the most numerous, most compact mass, the decisive "shock force" of the international proletarian army. This mass already supplies over a fourth of the votes cast; and as the by-elections to the *Reichstag*, the Diet elections in individual states, the municipal council and trades court elections demonstrate, it increases incessantly. Its growth proceeds as spontaneously, as steadily, as irresistibly, and at the same time as tranquilly as a natural process. All government intervention has proved powerless against it. We can count even today on two and a quarter million voters. If it continues in this fashion, by the end of the century we shall conquer the greater part of the middle strata of society, petty bourgeois and small peasants, and grow into the decisive power in the land, before which all other powers will have to bow, whether they like it or not. To keep this growth going without interruption until it of itself gets beyond the control of the prevailing governmental system, not to fritter away this daily increasing shock force in vanguard skirmishes, but to keep it intact until the decisive day, that is our main task. And there is only one means by which the steady rise of the socialist fighting forces in Germany could be temporarily halted, and even thrown back for some time: a clash on a big scale with the military, a blood-letting like that of 1871 in Paris. In the long run that would also be overcome. To shoot a party which numbers millions out of existence is too much even for all the magazine rifles of Europe and America. But the normal development would be impeded, the shock force would, perhaps, not be available at the critical moment, the decisive combat would be delayed, protracted and attended by heavier sacrifices.

The irony of world history turns everything upside down. We, the "revolutionists," the "overthrowers"—we are thriving far better on legal methods than on illegal methods and overthrow. The parties of Order, as they call themselves, are perishing under the legal conditions created by themselves. They cry despairingly with

Odilon Barrot: *la légalité nous tue,* legality is the death of us; whereas we, under this legality, get firm muscles and rosy cheeks and look like life eternal. And if *we* are not so crazy as to let ourselves be driven to street fighting in order to please them, then in the end there is nothing left for them to do but themselves break through this fatal legality.

Meanwhile they make new laws against overthrows. Again everything is turned upside down. These anti-overthrow fanatics of today, are they not themselves the overthrowers of yesterday? Have *we* perchance evoked the civil war of 1866? Have *we* driven the King of Hanover, the Elector of Hesse, and the Duke of Nassau from their hereditary lawful domains and annexed these hereditary domains? And these overthrowers of the German Confederation and three crowns by the grace of God complain of overthrow! *Quis tulerit Gracchos de seditione queretes?*[3] Who could allow the Bismarck worshippers to rail at overthrow?

Let them, nevertheless, put through their anti-overthrow bills, make them still worse, transform the whole penal law into indiarubber, they will gain nothing but new proof of their impotence. If they want to deal Social-Democracy a serious blow they will have to resort to quite other measures in addition. They can cope with the Social-Democratic overthrow, which just now is doing so well by keeping the law, only by an overthrow on the part of the parties of Order, an overthrow which cannot live without breaking the law. Herr Rössler, the Prussian bureaucrat, and Herr von Boguslawski, the Prussian general, have shown them the only way perhaps still possible of getting at the workers, who simply refuse to let themselves be lured into street fighting. Breach of the constitution, dictatorship, return to absolutism, *regis voluntas suprema lex!*[4] Therefore, take courage, gentlemen; here half measures will not do; here you must go the whole hog!

But do not forget that the German empire, like all small states and generally all modern states, is a *product of contract;* of the contract, first, of the princes with one another and, second, of the princes with the people. If one side breaks the contract, the whole contract falls to the ground; the other side is then also no longer bound, as Bismarck demonstrated to us so beautifully in 1866. If, therefore, you break the constitution of the Reich, the Social-Democracy is free, and can do as it pleases with regard to you. But it will hardly blurt out to you today what it is going to do then.

It is now, almost to the year, sixteen centuries since a dangerous party of overthrow was likewise active in the Roman empire. It undermined religion and all the foundations of the state; it flatly

3. Who would suffer the Gracchi to complain of sedition? 4. The King's will is the supreme law!

denied that Caesar's will was the supreme law; it was without a fatherland, was international; it spread over all countries of the empire, from Gaul to Asia, and beyond the frontiers of the empire. It had long carried on seditious activities in secret, underground; for a considerable time, however, it had felt itself strong enough to come out into the open. This party of overthrow, which was known by the name of Christians, was also strongly represented in the army; whole legions were Christian. When they were ordered to attend the sacrificial ceremonies of the pagan established church, in order to do the honours there, the subversive soldiers had the audacity to stick peculiar emblems—crosses—on their helmets in protest. Even the wonted barrack bullying of their superior officers was fruitless. The Emperor Diocletian could no longer quietly look on while order, obedience and discipline in his army were being undermined. He interfered energetically, while there was still time. He promulgated an anti-Socialist—beg pardon, I meant to say anti-Christian —law. The meetings of the overthrowers were forbidden, their meeting halls were closed or even pulled down, the Christian emblems, crosses, etc., were, like the red handkerchiefs in Saxony, prohibited. Christians were declared incapable of holding public office; they were not to be allowed to become even corporals. Since there were not available at that time judges so well trained in "respect of persons" as Herr von Köller's anti-overthrow bill[5] assumes, Christians were forbidden out of hand to seek justice before a court. This exceptional law was also without effect. The Christians tore it down from the walls with scorn; they are even supposed to have burnt the Emperor's palace in Nicomedia over his head. Then the latter revenged himself by the great persecution of Christians in the year 303 of our era. It was the last of its kind. And it was so effective that seventeen years later the army consisted overwhelmingly of Christians, and the succeeding autocrat of the whole Roman empire, Constantine, called the Great by the priests, proclaimed Christianity the state religion.

5. A new bill against the Socialists, introduced in the Reichstag on December 5, 1894, and rejected on May 11, 1895.

PART IV

Society and Politics in the Nineteenth Century

Speech at the Anniversary
of the *People's Paper*

KARL MARX

This speech is a vivid expression of Marx's sense of proletarian revolution as a volcanic presence in European society of the mid-nineteenth century, and also of his intensely moralistic vision of the coming revolution as capital punishment of a society that deserved to die. He gave the speech in English on April 14, 1856, and it was published a few days later in the *People's Paper*. This was a Chartist paper, published in London from 1852 to 1858, for which Marx occasionally wrote articles.

The so-called Revolutions of 1848 were but poor incidents—small fractures and fissures in the dry crust of European society. However, they denounced the abyss. Beneath the apparently solid surface, they betrayed oceans of liquid matter, only needing expansion to rend into fragments continents of hard rock. Noisily and confusedly they proclaimed the emancipation of the Proletarian, *i.e.*, the secret of the nineteenth century, and of the revolution of that century. That social revolution, it is true, was no novelty invented in 1848. Steam, electricity, and the self-acting mule were revolutionists of a rather more dangerous character than even citizens Barbès, Raspail and Blanqui. But, although the atmosphere in which we live, weighs upon every one with a 20,000 lb. force, do you feel it? No more than European society before 1848 felt the revolutionary atmosphere enveloping and pressing it from all sides. There is one great fact, characteristic of this our nineteenth century, a fact which no party dares deny. On the one hand, there have started into life industrial and scientific forces, which no epoch of the former human history had ever suspected. On the other hand, there exist symptoms of decay, far surpassing the horrors recorded of the latter times of the Roman empire. In our days everything seems pregnant with its contrary. Machinery, gifted with the wonderful power of shortening and fructifying human labour, we behold starving and overworking it. The new-fangled sources of wealth, by some strange weird spell, are turned into sources of want. The victories of art seem bought by the loss of character. At the same pace that mankind masters nature, man seems to become enslaved to other men or to his own infamy. Even the pure light of science seems unable to shine but on the dark background of ignorance. All our invention and progress seem to result in endowing material forces with intellectual life, and in stultifying human life into a material force. This antagonism between modern industry and science on the one hand, modern misery and dissolution on the other hand; this antagonism between the productive powers, and the social relations of our epoch is a fact, palpable, overwhelming, and not to be controverted. Some parties may wail over it; others may wish to get rid of modern arts, in order to get rid of modern conflicts. Or they may imagine that so signal a progress in industry wants to be completed by as signal a regress in politics. On our part, we do not mistake the shape of the shrewd spirit that continues to mark all these contradictions. We know that to work well the new-fangled forces of society, they only want to be mastered by new-fangled men—and such are the working men. They are as much the invention of modern time as machinery itself. In the signs that bewilder the middle class, the aristocracy and the poor prophets of regression, we do recognise our brave friend, Robin Goodfellow,[1] the old mole that can work in the earth so fast, that worthy pioneer —the Revolution. The English working men are the first born sons of modern industry. They will then, certainly, not be the last in aiding the social revolution produced by that industry, a revolution, which means the emancipation of their own class all over the world, which is as universal as capital-rule and wages-slavery. I know the heroic struggles the English working class have gone through since the middle of the last century—struggles no less glorious, because they are shrouded in obscurity, and buried by the middle class historian. To revenge the misdeeds of the ruling class, there existed in the middle ages, in Germany, a secret tribunal, called the "Vehmgericht." If a red cross was seen marked on a house, people knew that its owner was doomed by the "Vehm." All the houses of Europe are now marked with the mysterious red cross. History is the judge —its executioner, the proletarian.

1. A sprite who was popularly believed in England during the sixteenth and seventeenth centuries to lend people a helping hand. He is one of the chief characters in Shakespeare's comedy *A Midsummer Night's Dream*.

Working-Class Manchester

FRIEDRICH ENGELS

Engels, the son of a well-to-do German manufacturer, was sent to England in 1842, at the age of twenty-two, to learn business in the office of the Ermen and Engels paper mill in the industrial city of Manchester He remained in England for nearly two years and while there gathered material for his first book, *The Condition of the Working Class in England in 1844*, which was published in German in 1845. The extract below, from the chapter on "The Great Towns," is taken from the English translation published by the Foreign Languages Publishing House, Moscow, in 1962.

---

* * * I now proceed to describe Manchester's worker districts. First of all, there is the Old Town, which lies between the northern boundary of the commercial district and the Irk. Here the streets, even the better ones, are narrow and winding, as Todd Street, Long Millgate, Withy Grove, and Shude Hill, the houses dirty, old, and tumble down, and the construction of the side streets utterly horrible. Going from the Old Church to Long Millgate, the stroller has at once a row of old-fashioned houses at the right, of which not one has kept its original level; these are remnants of the old pre-manufacturing Manchester, whose former inhabitants have removed with their descendants into better-built districts, and have left the houses, which were not good enough for them, to a working-class population strongly mixed with Irish blood. Here one is in an almost undisguised working-men's quarter, for even the shops and beerhouses hardly take the trouble to exhibit a trifling degree of cleanliness. But all this is nothing in comparison with the courts and lanes which lie behind, to which access can be gained only through covered passages, in which no two human beings can pass at the same time. Of the irregular cramming together of dwellings in ways which defy all rational plan, of the tangle in which they are crowded literally one upon the other, it is impossible to convey an idea. And it is not the buildings surviving from the old times of Manchester which are to blame for this; the confusion has only recently reached its height when every scrap of space left by the old way of building has been filled up and patched over until not a foot of land is left to be further occupied.

To confirm my statement I have drawn here a small section of the plan of Manchester—not the worst spot and not one-tenth of the whole Old Town.

This drawing will suffice to characterise the irrational manner in which the entire district was built, particularly the part near the Irk. The south bank of the Irk is here very steep and between fifteen and thirty feet high. On this declivitous hillside there are planted three rows of houses, of which the lowest rise directly out of the river, while the front walls of the highest stand on the crest of the hill in Long Millgate. Among them are mills on the river, in short, the method of construction is as crowded and disorderly here as in the lower part of Long Millgate. Right and left a multitude of covered passages lead from the main street into numerous courts, and he who turns in thither gets into a filth and disgusting grime, the equal of which is not be found—especially in the courts which lead down to the Irk, and which contain unqualifiedly the most horrible

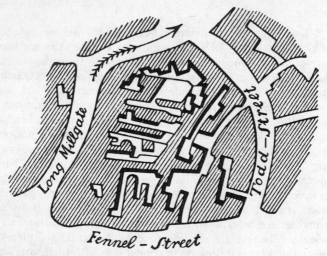

dwellings which I have yet beheld. In one of these courts there stands directly at the entrance, at the end of the covered passage, a privy without a door, so dirty that the inhabitants can pass into and out of the court only by passing through foul pools of stagnant urine and excrement. This is the first court on the Irk above Ducie Bridge—in case any one should care to look into it. Below it on the river there are several tanneries which fill the whole neighborhood with the stench of animal putrefaction. Below Ducie Bridge the only entrance to most of the houses is by means of narrow, dirty stairs and over heaps of refuse and filth. The first court below Ducie Bridge, known as Allen's Court, was in such a state at the time of the cholera that the sanitary police ordered it evacuated, swept and disinfected with chloride of lime. Dr. Kay gives a terrible description of the state of this court at that time.[1] Since then, it seems to have been partially torn away and rebuilt; at least looking down from Ducie Bridge, the passer-by sees several ruined walls and heaps of *débris* with some newer houses. The view from this bridge, mercifully concealed from mortals of small stature by a parapet as high as a man, is characteristic for the whole district. At the bottom flows, or rather stagnates, the Irk, a narrow, coal-black, foul-smelling stream, full of *débris* and refuse, which it deposits on the shallower right bank. In dry weather, a long string of the most disgusting blackish-green slime pools are left standing on this bank, from the depths of which bubbles of miasmatic gas constantly arise and give forth a stench unendurable even on the bridge forty or fifty feet above the surface of the stream. But besides this, the stream itself is checked every few paces by high weirs, behind which slime and refuse accumulate and rot in thick masses. Above the bridge are tanneries, bonemills, and gasworks, from which all drains and refuse find their way into the Irk, which receives further the contents of all the neighbouring sewers and privies. It may be easily imagined, therefore, what sort of residue the stream deposits. Below the bridge you look upon the piles of *débris*, the refuse, filth, and offal from the courts on the steep left bank; here each house is packed close behind its neighbour and a piece of each is visible, all black, smoky, crumbling, ancient, with broken panes and window-frames. The background is furnished by old barrack-like factory buildings. On the lower right bank stands a long row of houses and mills; the second house being a ruin without a roof, piled with *débris*; the third stands so low that the lowest floor is uninhabitable, and therefore without windows or doors. Here the background embraces the pauper burial-ground, the station of the Liverpool and Leeds railway, and, in the rear of this, the Workhouse, the "Poor-Law Bastille" of Manchester, which, like a citadel, looks threateningly down from behind its high walls and parapets on the hilltop, upon the working-people's quarter below.

Above Ducie Bridge, the left bank grows more flat and the right bank steeper, but the condition of the dwellings on both banks grows worse rather than better. He who turns to the left here from the main street, Long Millgate, is lost; he wanders from one court

1. "The Moral and Physical Condition of the Working-Class employed in the Cotton Manufacture in Manchester." By James Ph. Kay, M.D. 2nd Ed. 1832. Dr. Kay confuses the working-class in general with the factory workers; otherwise, an excellent pamphlet. [*Engels*]

to another, turns countless corners, passes nothing but narrow, filthy nooks and alleys, until after a few minutes he has lost all clue, and knows not whither to turn. Everywhere half or wholly ruined buildings, some of them actually uninhabited, which means a great deal here; rarely a wooden or stone floor to be seen in the houses, almost uniformly broken, ill-fitting windows and doors, and a state of filth! Everywhere heaps of *débris*, refuse, and offal; standing pools for gutters, and a stench which alone would make it impossible for a human being in any degree civilised to live in such a district. The newly-built extension of the Leeds railway, which crosses the Irk here, has swept away some of these courts and lanes, laying others completely open to view. Immediately under the railway bridge there stands a court, the filth and horrors of which surpass all the others by far, just because it was hitherto so shut off, so secluded that the way to it could not be found without a good deal of trouble. I should never have discovered it myself, without the breaks made by the railway, though I thought I knew this whole region thoroughly. Passing along a rough bank, among stakes and washing-lines, one penetrates into this chaos of small one-storied, one-roomed huts, in most of which there is no artificial floor; kitchen, living and sleeping-room all in one. In such a hole, scarcely five feet long by six broad, I found two beds—and such bedsteads and beds! —which, with a staircase and chimney-place, exactly filled the room. In several others I found absolutely nothing, while the door stood open, and the inhabitants leaned against it. Everywhere before the doors refuse and offal; that any sort of pavement lay underneath could not be seen but only felt, here and there, with the feet. This whole collection of cattle-sheds for human beings was surrounded on two sides by houses and a factory, and on the third by the river, and besides the narrow stair up the bank, a narrow doorway alone led out into another almost equally ill-built, ill-kept labyrinth of dwellings.

Enough! The whole side of the Irk is built in this way, a planless, knotted chaos of houses, more or less on the verge of uninhabitableness, whose unclean interiors fully correspond with their filthy external surroundings. And how could the people be clean with no proper opportunity for satisfying the most natural and ordinary wants? Privies are so rare here that they are either filled up every day, or are too remote for most of the inhabitants to use. How can people wash when they have only the dirty Irk water at hand, while pumps and water pipes can be found in decent parts of the city alone? In truth, it cannot be charged to the account of these helots of modern society if their dwellings are not more clean than the pig sties which are here and there to be seen among them. The landlords are not ashamed to let dwellings like the six or seven cellars on the quay directly below Scotland Bridge, the floors of which stand at least two feet below the low-water level of the Irk that flows not six feet away from them; or like the upper floor of the corner-house on the opposite shore directly above the bridge, where the ground-floor, utterly uninhabitable, stands deprived of all fittings for doors and windows, a case by no means rare in this region, when this open ground-floor is used as a privy by the whole neighbourhood for want of other facilities!

If we leave the Irk and penetrate once more on the opposite side from Long Millgate into the midst of the working-men's dwellings, we shall come into a somewhat newer quarter, which stretches from St. Michael's Church to Withy Grove and Shude Hill. Here there is somewhat better order. In place of the chaos of buildings, we find at least long straight lanes and alleys or courts, built according to a plan and usually square. But if, in the former case, every house was built according to caprice, here each lane and court is so built, without reference to the situation of the adjoining ones. The lanes run now in this direction, now in that, while every two minutes the wanderer gets into a blind alley, or on turning a corner, finds himself back where he started from; certainly no one who has not lived a considerable time in this labyrinth can find his way through it.

If I may use the word at all in speaking of this district, the ventilation of these streets and courts is, in consequence of this confusion, quite as imperfect as in the Irk region; and if this quarter may, nevertheless, be said to have some advantage over that of the Irk, the houses being newer and the streets occasionally having gutters, nearly every house has, on the other hand, a cellar dwelling, which is rarely found in the Irk district, by reason of the greater age and more careless construction of the houses. As for the rest, the filth, *débris*, and offal heaps, and the pools in the streets are common to both quarters, and in the district now under discussion, another feature most injurious to the cleanliness of the inhabitants, is the multitude of pigs walking about in all the alleys, rooting into the offal heaps, or kept imprisoned in small pens. Here, as in most of the working-men's quarters of Manchester, the pork-raisers rent the courts and build pig-pens in them. In almost every court one or even several such pens may be found, into which the inhabitants of the court throw all refuse and offal, whence the swine grow fat; and the atmosphere, confined on all four sides, is utterly corrupted by putrefying animal and vegetable substances. Through this quarter, a broad and measurably decent street has been cut, Millers Street, and the background has been pretty successfully concealed. But if any one should be led by curiosity to pass through one of the numerous passages which lead into the courts, he will find this piggery repeated at every twenty paces.

Such is the Old Town of Manchester, and on re-reading my description, I am forced to admit that instead of being exaggerated, it is far from black enough to convey a true impression of the filth, ruin, and uninhabitableness, the defiance of all considerations of cleanliness, ventilation, and health which characterise the construction of this single district, containing at least twenty to thirty thousand inhabitants. And such a district exists in the heart of the second city of England, the first manufacturing city of the world. If any one wishes to see in how little space a human being can move, how little air—and *such* air!—he can breathe, how little of civilisation he may share and yet live, it is only necessary to travel hither. True, this is the *Old* Town, and the people of Manchester emphasise the fact whenever any one mentions to them the frightful condition of this Hell upon Earth; but what does that prove? Everything which here arouses horror and indignation is of recent origin, belongs to the *industrial epoch*. The couple of hundred houses, which belong to old Manchester, have been long since abandoned by their original inhabitants; the industrial epoch alone has crammed into them the swarms of workers whom they now shelter; the industrial epoch alone has built up every spot between these old houses to win a covering for the masses whom it has conjured hither from the agricultural districts and from Ireland; the industrial epoch alone enables the owners of these cattlesheds to rent them for high prices to human beings, to plunder the poverty of the workers, to undermine the health of thousands, in order that they *alone*, the owners, may grow rich. In the industrial epoch alone has it become possible that the worker scarcely freed from feudal servitude could be used as mere material, a mere chattel; that he must let himself be crowded into a dwelling too bad for every other, which he for his hard-earned wages buys the right to let go utterly to ruin. This manufacture has achieved, which, without these workers, this poverty, this slavery could not have lived. True, the original construction of this quarter was bad, little good could have been made out of it; but, have the landowners, has the municipality done anything to improve it when rebuilding? On the contrary, wherever a nook or corner was free, a house has been run up; where a superfluous passage remained, it has been built up; the value of land rose with the blossoming out of manufacture, and the more it rose, the more madly was the work of building up carried on, without reference to the health or comfort of the inhabitants, with sole reference to the highest possible profit on the principle that *no hole is so bad but that some poor creature must take it who can pay for nothing better*. However, it is the Old Town, and with this reflection the bourgeoisie is comforted. Let us see, therefore, how much better it is in the New Town.

The New Town, known also as Irish Town, stretches up a hill of clay, beyond the Old Town, between the Irk and St. George's Road. Here all the features of a city are lost. Single rows of houses or groups of streets stand, here and there, like little villages on the naked, not even grassgrown clay soil; the houses, or rather cottages, are in bad order, never repaired, filthy, with damp, unclean, cellar dwellings; the lanes are neither paved nor supplied with sewers, but harbour numerous colonies of swine penned in small sties or yards, or wandering unrestrained through the neighbourhood. The mud in the streets is so deep that there is never a chance, except in the dryest weather, of walking without sinking into it ankle deep at every step. In the vicinity of St. George's Road, the separate groups of buildings approach each other more closely, ending in a continuation of lines, blind alleys, back lanes and courts, which grow more and more crowded and irregular the nearer they approach the heart of the town. True, they are here oftener paved or supplied with paved sidewalks and gutters; but the filth, the bad odor of the houses, and especially of the cellars, remain the same. *   *   *

The Class Struggles in France, 1848-1850

KARL MARX

France opened the round of revolutions of 1848 in Europe.* The Parisian workers figured importantly in the French revolutionary events from their opening in February, when King Louis Philippe was forced to abdicate, through the June workers' insurrection, which was suppressed with great ferocity by General Cavaignac's forces. Later, the national election of December 10, 1848, brought to the French Republic's presidency Napoleon's nephew, Louis Napoleon Bonaparte, who in 1851 made himself emperor by *coup d'état*.

In this most mordantly brilliant of his revolutionary pamphlets, first published in 1850 as a series of articles in *Neue Rheinische Zeitung*, Marx not only coined such well-known phrases as "Revolutions are the locomotives of history"; he portrayed the French workers' action as the debut of a coming Europe-wide proletarian revolution, and interspersed his narrative of France's 1848 revolution with passages of broader import that illuminate key points in his thought. These passages have been gathered together in the selection presented here.**

With the exception of only a few chapters, every more important part of the annals of the revolution from 1848 to 1849 carries the heading: *Defeat of the revolution!*

What succumbed in these defeats was not the revolution. It was the pre-revolutionary traditional appendages, results of social relationships which had not yet come to the point of sharp class antagonisms—persons, illusions, conceptions, projects from which the revolutionary party before the February Revolution was not free, from which it could be freed not by the *victory of February*, but only by a series of *defeats*.

In a word: the revolution made progress, forged ahead, not by its immediate tragicomic achievements, but on the contrary by the creation of a powerful, united counter-revolution, by the creation of an opponent in combat with whom, only, the party of overthrow ripened into a really revolutionary party.

To prove this is the task of the following pages.

* * *

* See Priscilla Robertson, *Revolutions of 1848: A Social History* (Princeton: Princeton University Press, 1952) for a general survey. The French experience is covered in chapters I–VI.
** For a summary by Marx of the events of 1848 in France, see Section I of *The Eighteenth Brumaire of Louis Bonaparte*, pp. 594–603, below.
1. A newspaper which appeared in Paris in 1830–51.

The *Provisional Government* which emerged from the February barricades necessarily mirrored in its composition the different parties which shared in the victory. It could not be anything but a *compromise between the different classes* which together had overturned the July throne, but whose interests were mutually antagonistic. The *great majority* of its members consisted of representatives of the bourgeoisie. The republican petty bourgeoisie was represented by Ledru-Rollin and Flocon, the republican bourgeoisie by the people from the *National*,[1] the dynastic opposition by Crémieux, Dupont de l'Eure, etc. The working class had only two representatives, Louis Blanc and Albert. Finally, Lamartine in the Provisional Government, this was at first no real interest, no definite class; this was the February Revolution itself, the common uprising with its illusions, its poetry, its visionary content and its phrases. For the rest, the spokesman of the February Revolution, by his position and his views, belonged to the *bourgeoisie*.

If Paris, as a result of political centralisation, rules France, the workers, in moments of revolutionary earthquakes, rule Paris. The first act in the life of the Provisional Government was an attempt to escape from this overpowering influence by an appeal from intoxicated Paris to sober France. Lamartine disputed the right of the barricade fighters to proclaim a republic on the ground that only the majority of Frenchmen had that right; they must await their votes, the Paris proletariat must not besmirch its victory by a usurpation. The bourgeoisie allows the proletariat only one usurpation—that of fighting.

* * *

Even the memory of the limited aims and motives which drove the bourgeoisie into the February Revolution was extinguished by the proclamation of the republic on the basis of universal suffrage. Instead of only a few factions of the bourgeoisie, all classes of French society were suddenly hurled into the orbit of political power, forced to leave the boxes, the stalls and the gallery and to act in person upon the revolutionary stage! With the constitutional monarchy vanished also the semblance of a state power independently confronting bourgeois society as well as the whole series of subordinate struggles which this semblance of power called forth!

By dictating the republic to the Provisional Government and through the Provisional Government to the whole of France, the proletariat stepped into the foreground forthwith as an independent party, but at the same time challenged the whole of bourgeois France to enter the lists against it. What it won was the terrain for the fight for its revolutionary emancipation, but by no means this emancipation itself.

In common with the bourgeoisie the workers had made the February Revolution, and *alongside* the bourgeoisie they sought to secure the advancement of their interest, just as they had installed a worker in the Provisional Government itself alongside the bourgeois majority. *Organise labour!* But wage labour, that is the existing, the bourgeois organisation of labour. Without it there is no capital, no bourgeoisie, no bourgeois society. A *Special Ministry of Labour!* But the Ministries of Finance, of Trade, of Public Works—are not these the *bourgeois* Ministries of Labour? And *alongside* these a *proletarian* Ministry of Labour had to be a ministry of impotence, a ministry of pious wishes, a Luxembourg Commission. Just as the workers thought they would be able to emancipate themselves side by side with the bourgeoisie, so they thought they would be able to consummate a proletarian revolution within the national walls of France, side by side with the remaining bourgeois nations. But French relations of production are conditioned by the foreign trade of France, by her position on the world market and the laws thereof; how was France to break them without a European revolutionary war, which would strike back at the despot of the world market, England?

As soon as it has risen up, a class in which the revolutionary interests of society are concentrated finds the content and the material for its revolutionary activity directly in its own situation: foes to be laid low, measures dictated by the needs of the struggle to be taken; the consequences of its own deeds drive it on. It makes no theoretical inquiries into its own task. The French working class had not attained this level; it was still incapable of accomplishing its own revolution.

The development of the industrial proletariat is, in general, conditioned by the development of the industrial bourgeoisie. Only under its rule does the proletariat gain that extensive national existence which can raise its revolution to a national one, and does it itself create the modern means of production, which become just so many means of its revolutionary emancipation. Only its rule tears up the material roots of feudal society and levels the ground on which alone a proletarian revolution is possible. French industry is more developed and the French bourgeoisie more revolutionary than that of the rest of the Continent. But was not the February Revolution levelled directly against the finance aristocracy? This fact proved that the industrial bourgeoisie did not rule France. The industrial bourgeoisie can rule only where modern industry shapes all property relations to suit itself, and industry can win this power only where it has conquered the world market, for national bounds are inadequate for its development. But French industry, to a great extent, maintains its command even of the national market only through a more or less modified system of prohibitive duties. While, therefore, the French proletariat, at the moment of a revolution, possesses in Paris actual power and influence which spur it on to a drive beyond its means, in the rest of France it is crowded into separate, scattered industrial centres, being almost lost in the superior numbers of peasants and petty bourgeois. The struggle against capital in its developed, modern form, in its decisive aspect, the struggle of the industrial wage-worker against the industrial bourgeois, is in France a partial phenomenon, which after the February days could so much the less supply the national content of the revolution, since the struggle against capital's secondary modes of exploitation, that of the peasant against usury and mortgages or of the petty bourgeois against the wholesale dealer, banker and manufacturer, in a word, against bankruptcy, was still hidden in the general uprising against the finance aristocracy.

* * *

Thus in the approaching *mêlée* between bourgeoisie and proletariat, all the advantages, all the decisive posts, all the middle strata of society were in the hands of the bourgeoisie, at the same time as the waves of the February Revolution rose high over the whole Continent and each new post brought a new bulletin of revolution, now from Italy, now from Germany, now from the remotest parts of South-Eastern Europe, and maintained the general ecstasy of the people, giving it constant testimony of a victory that it had already forfeited.

* * *

The workers were left no choice; they had to starve or let fly. They answered on June 22 with the tremendous insurrection in which the first great battle was fought between the two classes that split modern society. It was a fight for the preservation or annihilation of the *bourgeois* order. The veil that shrouded the republic was torn asunder.

It is well known how the workers, with unexampled bravery and ingenuity, without leaders, without a common plan, without means and, for the most part, lacking weapons, held in check for five days the army, the Mobile Guard, the Paris National Guard, and the National Guard that streamed in from the provinces. It is well known how the bourgeoisie compensated itself for the mortal anguish it suffered by unheard-of brutality, massacring over 3,000 prisoners.

* * *

The official representatives of French democracy were steeped in republican ideology to such an extent that it was only some weeks later that they began to have an inkling of the significance of the June fight. They were stupefied by the gunpower smoke in which their fantastic republic dissolved.

The Paris proletariat was *forced* into the June insurrection by the bourgeoisie. This sufficed to mark its doom. Its immediate, avowed needs did not drive it to engage in a light for the forcible overthrow of the bourgeoisie, nor was it equal to this task. The *Moniteur* had to inform it officially that the time was past when the republic saw any occasion to bow and scrape to its illusions, and only its defeat convinced it of the truth that the slightest improvement in its position remains a *utopia within* the bourgeois republic, a utopia that becomes a crime as soon as it wants to become a reality. In place of its demands, exuberant in form, but petty and even bourgeois still in content, the concession of which it wanted to wring from the February republic, there appeared the bold slogan of revolutionary struggle: *Overthrow of the bourgeoisie! Dictatorship of the working class!*

By making its burial place the birthplace of the *bourgeois republic,* the proletariat compelled the latter to come out forthwith in its pure form as the state whose admitted object it is to perpetuate the rule of capital, the slavery of labour. Having constantly before its eyes the scarred, irreconcilable, invincible enemy—invincible because his existence is the condition of its own life—bourgeois rule, freed from all fetters, was bound to turn immediately into *bourgeois terrorism.* With the proletariat removed for the time being from the stage and bourgeois dictatorship recognised officially, the middle strata of bourgeois society, the petty bourgeoisie and the peasant class, had to adhere more and more closely to the proletariat as their position became more unbearable and their antagonism to the bourgeoisie more acute. Just as earlier they had to find the cause of their distress in its upsurge, so now in its defeat.

If the June insurrection raised the self-assurance of the bourgeoisie all over the Continent, and caused it to league itself openly with the feudal monarchy against the people, who was the first victim of this alliance? The Continental bourgeoisie itself. The June defeat prevented it from consolidating its rule and from bringing the people, half satisfied and half out of humour, to a standstill at the lowest stage of the bourgeois revolution.

Finally, the defeat of June divulged to the despotic powers of Europe the secret that France must maintain peace abroad at any price in order to be able to wage civil war at home. Thus the peoples who had begun the fight for their national independence were abandoned to the superior power of Russia, Austria and Prussia, but, at the same time, the fate of these national revolutions was made subject to the fate of the proletarian revolution, and they were robbed of their apparent autonomy, their independence of the great social revolution. The Hungarian shall not be free, nor the Pole, nor the Italian, as long as the worker remains a slave!

Finally, with the victories of the Holy Alliance, Europe has taken on a form that makes every fresh proletarian upheaval in France directly coincide with a *world war*. The new French revolution is forced to leave its national soil forthwith and *conquer the European terrain*, on which alone the social revolution of the nineteenth century can be accomplished.

Thus only the June defeat has created all the conditions under which France can seize the *initiative* of the European revolution. Only after being dipped in the blood of the *June insurgents* did the tricolour become the flag of the European revolution—the *red flag!*

And we exclaim: *The revolution is dead! Long live the revolution!*

* * *

December 10, 1848, was the day of the *peasant insurrection.*[2] Only from this day does the February of the French peasants date. The symbol that expressed their entry into the revolutionary movement, clumsily cunning, knavishly naïve, doltishly sublime, a calculated superstition, a pathetic burlesque, a cleverly stupid anachronism, a world-historic piece of buffoonery and an undecipherable hieroglyphic for the understanding of the civilised—this symbol bore the unmistakable physiognomy of the class that represents barbarism within civilisation. The republic had announced itself to this class with the *tax collector*; it announced itself to the republic with the *emperor*. Napoleon was the only man who had exhaustively represented the interests and the imagination of the peasant class, newly created in 1789. By writing his name on the frontispiece of the republic, it declared war abroad and the enforcing of its class interests at home. Napoleon was to the peasants not a person but a programme. With banners, with beat of drums and blare of trumpets, they marched to the polling booths shouting: *plus d'impôts, à bas les riches, à bas la république, vive l'Empereur!* No more taxes, down with the rich, down with the republic, long live the emperor! Behind the emperor was hidden the peasant war. The republic that they voted down was the *republic of the rich*.

December 10 was the *coup d'état* of the peasants, which overthrew the existing government. And from that day on, when they had taken a government from France and given a government to her, their eyes were fixed steadily on Paris. For a moment active heroes of the revolutionary drama, they could no longer be forced back into the inactive and spineless role of the chorus.

* * *

In France, the petty bourgeois does what normally the industrial bourgeois would have to do; the worker does what normally would be the task of the petty bourgeois; and the task of the worker, who

2. Marx refers to the election of Louis Napoleon, for whom the peasants voted en masse. [*R. T.*]

accomplishes that? No one. In France it is not accomplished; in France it is proclaimed. It is not accomplished anywhere within the national walls; the class war within French society turns into a world war, in which the nations confront one another. Accomplishment begins only at the moment when, through the world war, the proletariat is pushed to the van of the people that dominates the world market, to the van of England. The revolution, which finds here not its end, but its organisational beginning is no short-lived revolution. The present generation is like the Jews whom Moses led through the wilderness. It has not only a new world to conquer, it must go under in order to make room for the men who are able to cope with a new world.

* * *

So swiftly had the march of the revolution ripened conditions that the friends of reform of all shades, the most moderate claims of the middle classes, were compelled to group themselves round the banner of the most extreme party of revolution, round the *red flag*.

* * *

* * * Since it[3] dreams of the peaceful achievement of its socialism—allowing, perhaps, for a second February Revolution lasting a brief day or so—the coming historical process naturally appears to it as an *application of systems*, which the thinkers of society, whether in companies or as individual inventors, devise or have devised. Thus they become the eclectics or adepts of the existing socialist *systems*, *of doctrinaire socialism*, which was the theoretical expression of the proletariat only as long as it had not yet developed further into a free historical movement of its own.

While this *utopia, doctrinaire socialism*, which subordinates the total movement to one of its moments, which puts in place of common, social production the brainwork of individual pedants and, above all, in fantasy does away with the revolutionary struggle of the classes and its requirements by small conjurers' tricks or great sentimentality; while this doctrinaire socialism, which at bottom only idealises present society, takes a picture of it without shadows and wants to achieve its ideal athwart the realities of present society; while the proletariat surrenders this socialism to the petty bourgeoisie; while the struggle of the different socialist leaders among themselves sets forth each of the so-called systems as a pretentious adherence to one of the transit points of the social revolution as against another—the *proletariat* rallies more and more round *revolutionary socialism*, round *communism*, for which the bourgeoisie has itself invented the name of *Blanqui*. This socialism is the *declaration of the permanence of the revolution*, the *class dictator-*

3. Marx is referring to such moderate forms of socialism as that of Louis Blanc, who figured prominently in the French 1848 events with his scheme of "social workshops." [R. T.]

ship of the proletariat as the necessary transit point to the *abolition of class distinctions generally*, to the abolition of all the relations of production on which they rest, to the abolition of all the social relations that correspond to these relations of production, to the revolutionising of all the ideas that result from these social relations.

The scope of this exposition does not permit of developing the subject further.

* * *

Just as the period of crisis occurs later on the Continent than in England, so does that of prosperity. The original process always takes place in England; it is the demiurge of the bourgeois cosmos. On the Continent, the different phases of the cycle through which bourgeois society is ever speeding anew occur in secondary and tertiary form. First, the Continent exported incomparably more to England than to any other country. This export to England, however, in turn depends on the position of England, particularly with regard to the overseas market. Then England exports to the overseas lands incomparably more than the entire Continent, so that the quantity of Continental exports to these lands is always dependent on England's overseas exports at the time. While, therefore, the crises first produce revolutions on the Continent, the foundation for these is, nevertheless, always laid in England. Violent outbreaks must naturally occur rather in the extremities of the bourgeois body than in its heart, since the possibility of adjustment is greater here than there. On the other hand, the degree to which the Continental revolutions react on England is at the same time the barometer which indicates how far these revolutions really call in question the bourgeois conditions of life, or how far they only hit their political formations.

With this general prosperity, in which the productive forces of bourgeois society develop as luxuriantly as is at all possible within bourgeois relationships, there can be no talk of a real revolution. Such a revolution is only possible in the periods when *both* these *factors*, the *modern* productive *forces* and the *bourgeois productive forms* come *in collision* with each other. The various quarrels in which the representatives of the individual factions of the Continental party of Order now indulge and mutually compromise themselves, far from providing the occasion for new revolutions are, on the contrary, possible only because the basis of the relationships is momentarily so secure and, what the reaction does not know, so *bourgeois*. From it all attempts of the reaction to hold up bourgeois development will rebound just as certainly as all moral indignation and all enthusiastic proclamations of the democrats. A *new revolution is possible only in consequence of a new crisis. It is, however, just as certain as this crisis.*

* * *

The Eighteenth Brumaire
of Louis Bonaparte

KARL MARX

This pamphlet, a stylistic masterpiece, shows Marx in his most brilliant form as a social and political historian, treating actual historical events—those leading up to Louis Bonaparte's *coup d'état* of December 2, 1851—from the viewpoint of the materialist conception of history. In a preface to the second edition, he himself said it was the intention of the work to "demonstrate how the *class struggle* in France created circumstances and relationships that made it possible for a grotesque mediocrity to play a hero's part." Since Louis Bonaparte's rise and rule have been seen as a forerunner of the phenomenon that was to become known in the twentieth century as fascism, Marx's interpretation of it is of interest, among other ways, as a sort of prologue to later Marxist thought on the nature and meaning of fascism.

The Eighteenth Brumaire was written by Marx in late 1851 and early 1852, and originally appeared in 1852 in a magazine entitled *Die Revolution,* published in New York. The most important sections—the first and the last—appear here.

I

Hegel remarks somewhere that all great, world-historical facts and personages occur, as it were, twice. He has forgotten to add: the first time as tragedy, the second as farce. Caussidière for Danton, Louis Blanc for Robespierre, the Mountain of 1848 to 1851 for the Mountain of 1793 to 1795, the Nephew for the Uncle. And the same caricature occurs in the circumstances in which the second edition of the Eighteenth Brumaire is taking place.[1]

1. On the Eighteenth Brumaire (according to the calendar introduced in the period of the first French bourgeois revolution), or November 9, 1799, Napoleon I carried out the *coup d'état* whereby as First Consul he concentrated supreme power in his hands; in 1804 he declared himself emperor. By "the second edition of the Eighteenth Brumaire," Marx means the *coup d'état* accomplished by Louis Bonaparte, the nephew of Napoleon I, on December 2, 1851. The "Mountain" refers to the Social Democratic bloc in the National Assembly. [*R. T.*]

Men make their own history, but they do not make it just as they please; they do not make it under circumstances chosen by themselves, but under circumstances directly found, given and transmitted from the past. The tradition of all the dead generations weighs like a nightmare on the brain of the living. And just when they seem engaged in revolutionising themselves and things, in creating something entirely new, precisely in such epochs of revolutionary crisis they anxiously conjure up the spirits of the past to their service and borrow from them names, battle slogans and costumes in order to present the new scene of world history in this time-honoured disguise and this borrowed language. Thus Luther donned the mask of the Apostle Paul, the Revolution of 1789 to 1814 draped itself alternately as the Roman Republic and the Roman Empire, and the Revolution of 1848 knew nothing better to do than to parody, in turn, 1789 and the revolutionary tradition of 1793 to 1795. In like manner the beginner who has learnt a new language always translates it back into his mother tongue, but he has assimilated the spirit of the new language and can produce freely in it only when he moves in it without remembering the old and forgets in it his ancestral tongue.

Consideration of this world-historical conjuring up of the dead reveals at once a salient difference. Camille Desmoulins, Danton, Robespierre, Saint-Just, Napoleon, the heroes, as well as the parties and the masses of the old French Revolution, performed the task of their time in Roman costume and with Roman phrases, the task of releasing and setting up modern *bourgeois* society. The first ones knocked the feudal basis to pieces and mowed off the feudal heads which had grown from it. The other created inside France the conditions under which free competition could first be developed, the parcelled landed property exploited, the unfettered productive power of the nation employed, and outside the French borders he everywhere swept the feudal formations away, so far as was necessary to furnish bourgeois society in France with a suitable up-to-date environment on the European Continent. The new social formation once established, the antediluvian Colossi disappeared and with them the resurrected Romans—the Brutuses, Cracchi, Publicolas, the tribunes, the senators and Caesar himself. Bourgeois society in its sober reality had begotten its true interpreters and mouthpieces in the Says, Cousins, Royer-Collards, Benjamin Constants and Guizots; its real military leaders sat behind the office desks, and the hogheaded Louis XVIII was its political chief. Wholly absorbed in the production of wealth and in the peaceful struggle of competition, it no longer comprehended that ghosts from the days of Rome had watched over its cradle. But unheroic as bourgeois society is, yet it had need of heroism, of sacrifice, of terror, of civil war and of national battles to bring it into being. And in the classically austere traditions of the Roman Republic its gladiators found the ideals and the art forms, the self-deceptions that they needed in order to conceal from themselves the bourgeois limitations of the content of their struggles and to keep their passion at the height of the great historical tragedy. Similarly, at another stage of development, a century earlier, Cromwell and the English people had borrowed speech, passions and illusions from the Old Testament for their bourgeois revolution.[2] When the real aim had been achieved, when the bourgeois transformation of English society had been accomplished, Locke supplanted Habakkuk.

The awakening of the dead in those revolutions therefore served the purpose of glorifying the new struggles, not of parodying the old; of magnifying the given tasks in imagination, not of taking flight from their solution in reality; of finding once more the spirit of revolution, not of making its ghost walk again.

From 1848 to 1851 only the ghost of the old revolution walked, from Marrast, the *republicain en gants jaunes*,[3] who disguised himself as the old Bailly, to the adventurer who hides his trivially repulsive features under the iron death mask of Napoleon. An entire people, which had imagined that by a revolution it had increased its power of action, suddenly finds itself set back into a dead epoch and, in order that no doubt as to the relapse may be possible, the old data again arise, the old chronology, the old names, the old edicts, which have long become a subject of antiquarian erudition, and the old henchmen, who had long seemed dead and decayed. The nation appears to itself like that mad Englishman in Bedlam, who fancies that he lives in the times of the ancient Pharaohs and daily bemoans the hard labour that he must perform in the Ethiopian mines as a gold digger, immured in this subterranean prison, a dimly burning lamp fastened to his head, the overseer of the slaves behind him with a long whip, and at the exits a confused mass of barbarian mercenaries, who understand neither the forced labourers in the mines nor one another, since they have no common speech. "And all this is expected of me," groans the mad Englishman, "of me, a free-born Briton, in order to make gold for the old Pharaohs." "In order to pay the debts of the Bonaparte family," sighs the French nation. The Englishman, so long as he was in his right mind, could not get rid of the fixed idea of making gold. The French, so long as they were engaged in revolution, could not get rid of the memory of Napoleon, as the election of December 10, 1848,[4] proved. From the perils of revolution their longings went back to the flesh-pots of Egypt, and December 2, 1851, was the

2. The bourgeoisie was allied with the new nobility against the monarchy, the feudal nobility, and the ruling church. [*Marx*]

3. Republican in yellow gloves.

4. The day Louis Bonaparte was elected president of the republic.

answer. They have not only a caricature of the old Napoleon, they have the old Napoleon himself, caricatured as he would inevitably appear in the middle of the nineteenth century.

The social revolution of the nineteenth century cannot draw its poetry from the past, but only from the future. It cannot begin with itself, before it has stripped off all superstition in regard to the past. Earlier revolutions required world-historical recollections in order to drug themselves concerning their own content. In order to arrive at its content, the revolution of the nineteenth century must let the dead bury their dead. There the phrase went beyond the content; here the content goes beyond the phrase.

The February Revolution was a sudden attack, a taking of the old society by *surprise*, and the people proclaimed this unhoped for *stroke* as a world-historic deed, opening the new epoch. On December 2 the February Revolution is conjured away by a card-sharper's trick, and what seems overthrown is no longer the monarchy; it is the liberal concessions that were wrung from it by century-long struggles. Instead of *society* having conquered a new content for itself, the *state* only appears to have returned to its oldest form, to the shamelessly simple domination of the sabre and the cowl. This is the answer to the *coup de main* of February 1848, given by the *coup de tête* of December 1851. Easy come, easy go. Meanwhile the interval has not passed by unused. During the years 1848 to 1851 French society has made up, and that by an abbreviated, because revolutionary, method, for the studies and experiences which, in a regular, so to speak, text-book development would have had to precede the February Revolution, if the latter was to be more than a disturbance of the surface. Society now seems to have fallen back behind its point of departure; it has in truth first to create for itself the revolutionary point of departure, the situation, the relationships, the conditions, under which modern revolution alone becomes serious.

Bourgeois revolutions, like those of the eighteenth century, storm more swiftly from success to success; their dramatic effects outdo each other; men and things seem set in sparkling brilliants; ecstasy is the everyday spirit: but they are short lived; soon they have attained their zenith, and a long depression lays hold of society before it learns soberly to assimilate the results of its storm and stress period. Proletarian revolutions, on the other hand, like those of the nineteenth century, criticise themselves constantly, interrupt themselves continually in their own course, come back to the apparently accomplished in order to begin it afresh, deride with unmerciful thoroughness the inadequacies, weaknesses and paltrinesses of their first attempts, seem to throw down their adversary only in order that he may draw new strength from the earth and rise again more gigantic before them, recoil ever and anon from the indefinite prodigiousness of their own aims, until the situation has been created which makes all turning back impossible, and the conditions themselves cry out:

Hic Rhodus, hic salta!
Hier ist die Rose, hier tanze![5]

For the rest, every fairly competent observer, even if he had not followed the course of French development step by step, must have had a presentiment that a terrible fiasco was in store for the revolution. It was enough to hear the self-complacent howl of victory with which Messieurs the Democrats congratulated each other on the gracious consequences of May 2, 1852.[6] In their minds May 2, 1852, had become a fixed idea, a dogma, like the day on which Christ should reappear and the millennium begin, in the minds of the Chiliasts.[7] As ever, weakness had taken refuge in a belief in miracles, had fancied the enemy overcome when he was only conjured away in imagination, and lost all understanding of the present in a passive glorification of the future that was in store for it and of the deeds it had *in petto*,[8] but merely did not want to carry out as yet. Those heroes, who seek to disprove their demonstrated incapacity by mutually offering each other their sympathy and getting together in a crowd, had tied up their bundles, collected their laurel wreaths in advance and were just then engaged in discounting on the exchange market the republics *in partibus*,[9] for which they had already thoughtfully organised the government personnel with all the calm of their unassuming disposition. December 2 struck them like a thunderbolt from a clear sky, and the peoples that in epochs of pusillanimous depression gladly let their inward apprehension be drowned by the loudest bawlers will perchance have convinced themselves that the times are past when the cackle of geese could save the Capitol.[1]

The Constitution, the National Assembly, the dynastic parties,[2] the blue and the red republicans,[3] the heroes of Africa,[4] the thun-

---

5. "Here is Rhodes, leap here! Here is the rose, dance here!" The words are from a fable by Aesop about a braggart who claimed he could produce witnesses to prove he had once made a remarkable leap in Rhodes, to which claim he received the reply: "Why cite witnesses if it is true? Here is Rhodes, leap here!" That is, "Show us right here what you can do." The German paraphrase of the Greek quotation (*Rhodus* means *rose*) was used by Hegel in the preface to his *Philosophy of Right*.
6. The day on which new presidential elections were to be held. Louis Bonaparte would have had to retire on this day, as the constitution did not permit anyone to be elected to the presidency for a second time, except after an interval of four years.
7. The adherents of an ancient Christian sect, who believed in the second coming of Christ and in the establishment of the millennium, a thousand years of paradise on earth.
8. In reserve.
9. *In partibus infidelium*: literally, "in the country of the infidels." An expression often used by Marx and Engels to describe émigré governments formed abroad without regard to the real situation in a country.

der from the platform, the sheet lightning of the daily press, the entire literature, the political names and the intellectual reputations, the civil law and penal code, the *liberté, egalité, fraternité* and the second of May 1852—all have vanished like a phantasmagoria before the spell of a man whom even his enemies do not make out to be a magician. Universal suffrage seems to have survived only for a moment, in order that with its own hand it may make its last will and testament before the eyes of all the world and declare in the name of the people itself: Everything that exists has this much worth, that it will perish.

It is not enough to say, as the French do, that their nation has been taken by surprise. A nation and a woman are not forgiven the unguarded hour in which the first adventurer that came along could violate them. The riddle is not solved by such terms of speech, but merely formulated in another way. It remains to be explained how a nation of thirty-six millions can be surprised and delivered unresisting into captivity by three high class swindlers.

Let us recapitulate in their general outlines the phases that the French Revolution has gone through from February 24, 1848, to December 1851.

Three main periods are unmistakable: the *February period*; the *period of the constituting of the republic or of the Constituent National Assembly*, May 4, 1848, to May 29, 1849; the *period of the constitutional republic or of the Legislative National Assembly*, May 29, 1849, to December 2, 1851.

The first period, from February 24, or the overthrow of Louis Philippe, to May 4, 1848, the meeting of the Constituent Assembly, the *February period proper*, may be described as the *prologue* of the Revolution. Its character was officially expressed in the fact that the government improvised by it declared itself to be *provisional* and, like the government, everything that was instigated, attempted or enunciated during this period, proclaimed itself to be *provisional*. Nothing and nobody ventured to lay claim to the right of existence and of real action. All the elements that had prepared or determined the Revolution, the dynastic opposition, the republican bourgeoisie, the democratic-republican petty bourgeoisie and the social-democratic workers, provisionally found their place in the February government.

It could not be otherwise. The February days originally intended

1. An old Roman story tells that once, when Rome was besieged, the sacred geese in the Roman fortress, the Capitol, wakened the garrison with their cackling; thanks to this, the garrison was able to beat off the attack of the enemies who had stolen up in the night.

2. The Legitimists, who supported the Bourbons, and the Orleanists.
3. The blue (bourgeois) and the red (socialist) republican parties.
4. This refers to the generals distinguished for their savage deeds in Africa during the conquest of Algeria (Cavaignac, Changarnier and others).

an electoral reform, by which the circle of the politically privileged among the possessing class itself was to be widened and the exclusive domination of the aristocracy of finance overthrown. When it came to the actual conflict, however, when the people mounted the barricades, the National Guard maintained a passive attitude, the army offered no serious resistance and the monarchy ran away, the republic appeared to be a matter of course. Every party construed it in its own sense. Having been won by the proletariat by force of arms, the proletariat impressed its stamp on it and proclaimed it to be a *social republic*. There was thus indicated the general content of the modern revolution, which stood in most singular contradiction to everything that, with the material at hand, with the degree of education attained by the masses, under the given circumstances and relationships, could be immediately realised in practice. On the other hand, the claims of all the remaining elements that had participated in the February Revolution were recognised by the lion's share that they obtained in the government. In no period do we therefore find a more confused mixture of high-flown phrases and actual uncertainty and clumsiness, of more enthusiastic striving for innovation and more deeply rooted domination of the old routine, of more apparent harmony of the whole society and more profound estrangement of its elements. While the Paris proletariat still revelled in the vision of the wide prospects that had opened before it and indulged in seriously-meant discussions on social problems, the old powers of society had grouped themselves, assembled, reflected and found an unexpected support in the mass of the nation, the peasants and petty bourgeois, who all at once stormed on to the political stage, after the barriers of the July monarchy had fallen.

The *second period*, from May 4, 1848, to the end of May 1849, is the period of the *constitution*, of the *foundation of the bourgeois republic*. Directly after the February days the dynastic opposition had not only been surprised by the republicans, the republicans by the socialists, but all France had been surprised by Paris. The National Assembly, which had met on May 4, 1848, having emerged from the national elections, represented the nation. It was a living protest against the presumptuous aspirations of the February days and was to reduce the results of the Revolution to the bourgeois scale. In vain the Paris proletariat, which immediately grasped the character of this National Assembly, attempted on May 15, a few days after it met, forcibly to deny its existence, to dissolve it, to disintegrate once more into its constituent parts the organic form in which the proletariat was threatened by the reactionary spirit of the nation. As is known, May 15 had no other result save that of removing Blanqui and his comrades, that is, the real leaders of the proletarian party [the revolutionary communists],[5] from the public stage for the entire duration of the cycle we are considering.

The *bourgeois monarchy* of Louis Philippe can only be followed by the *bourgeois republic*, that is, if a limited section of the bourgeoisie formerly ruled in the name of the king, the whole of the bourgeoisie will now rule in the name of the people. The demands of the Paris proletariat are utopian nonsense to which an end must be put. To this declaration of the Constituent National Assembly the Paris proletariat replied with the *June Insurrection*, the most colossal event in the history of European civil wars. The bourgeois republic triumphed. On its side stood the aristocracy of finance, the industrial bourgeoisie, the middle class, the petty bourgeois, the army, the *lumpenproletariat* organised as the Mobile Guard, the intellectual lights, the clergy, and the rural population. On the side of the Paris proletariat stood none but itself. More than three thousand insurgents were butchered after the victory, and fifteen thousand were transported without trial. With this defeat the proletariat passes into the background of the revolutionary stage. It attempts to press forward again on every occasion, as soon as the movement appears to make a fresh start, but with ever decreased expenditure of strength and always more insignificant results. As soon as one of the social strata situated above it gets into revolutionary ferment, it enters into an alliance with it and so shares all the defeats that the different parties suffer one after another. But these subsequent blows become steadily weaker, the more they are distributed over the entire surface of society. Its more important leaders in the Assembly and the press successively fall victims to the courts, and ever more equivocal figures come to the fore. In part it throws itself into *doctrinaire experiments, exchange banks and workers' associations, hence into a movement in which it renounces the revolutionising of the old world by means of its own great, combined resources, and seeks, rather, to achieve its salvation behind society's back, in private fashion, within its limited conditions of existence, and hence inevitably suffers shipwreck.* It seems to be unable either to rediscover revolutionary greatness in itself or to win new energy from the alliances newly entered into, until *all classes* with which it contended in June themselves lie prostrate beside it. But at least it succumbs with the honours of the great, world-historic struggle; not only France, but all Europe trembles at the June earthquake, while the ensuing defeats of the upper classes

5. Here and elsewhere the square brackets in the text denote passages of the first edition omitted in subsequent editions.

are so cheaply bought that they require bare-faced exaggeration by the victorious party to be able to pass for events at all and become the more ignominious the further the defeated party is removed from the proletariat.

The defeat of the June insurgents, to be sure, had now prepared and levelled the ground on which the bourgeois republic could be founded and built up, but it had shown at the same time that in Europe there are other questions involved than that of "republic or monarchy." It had revealed that here *bourgeois republic* signifies the unlimited despotism of one class over other classes. It had proved that in lands with an old civilisation, with a developed formation of classes, with modern conditions of production and with an intellectual consciousness into which all traditional ideas have been absorbed by the work of centuries, *the republic* signifies *in general only the political form of the revolution of bourgeois society* and not its *conservative form of life,* as, for example, in the United States of North America, where, though classes, indeed, already exist, they have not yet become fixed, but continually change and interchange their elements in a constant state of flux, where the modern means of production, instead of coinciding with a stagnant surplus population, rather supply the relative deficiency of heads and hands and where, finally, the feverishly youthful movement of material production, that has a new world to make its own, has left neither time nor opportunity for abolishing the old spirit world.

During the June days all classes and parties had united in the *Party of Order* against the proletarian class as the *party of anarchy,* of socialism, of communism. They had "saved" society from "*the enemies of society.*" They had given out the watchwords of the old society, "*property, family, religion, order,*" to their army as passwords and had proclaimed to the counter-revolutionary crusaders: "In this sign you will conquer!" From that moment, as soon as one of the numerous parties which had gathered under this sign against the June insurgents seeks to hold the revolutionary battlefield in its own class interests it goes down before the cry: "Property, family, religion, order." Society is saved just as often as the circle of its rulers contracts, as a more exclusive interest is maintained against a wider one. Every demand of the simplest bourgeois financial reform, of the most ordinary liberalism, of the most formal republicanism, of the most insipid democracy, is simultaneously castigated as an "attempt on society" and stigmatised as "socialism." And, finally, the high priests of "religion and order" themselves are driven wtih kicks from their Pythian tripods, hauled out of their beds in the darkness of night, put in prison-vans, thrown into dungeons or sent into exile; their temple is razed to the ground, their mouths are sealed, their pens broken, their law torn to pieces in the name of religion, of property, of family, of order. Bourgeois fanatics for order are shot down on their balconies by mobs of drunken soldiers, their domestic sanctuaries profaned, their houses bombarded for amusement—in the name of property, of family, of religion and of order. Finally the scum of bourgeois society forms *the holy phalanx of order* and the hero Crapulinsky[6] installs himself in the Tuileries[7] as the *"saviour of society."*

* * *

VII

On the threshold of the February Revolution, the *social republic* appeared as a phrase, as a prophecy. In the June days of 1848, it was drowned in the blood of the *Paris proletariat,* but it haunts the subsequent acts of the drama like a ghost. The *democratic republic* makes its appearance. On June 13, 1849, it is dissipated together with its *petty bourgeois,* who take to their heels, but in its flight it blows its own trumpet with redoubled boastfulness. The *parliamentary republic,* together with the bourgeoisie, takes possession of the entire stage; it lives out its existence to the full, but December 2, 1851, buries it to the accompaniment of the cry of terror of the royalists in coalition: "Long live the republic!"

The French bourgeoisie offered resistance to the domination of the working proletariat; it has brought the *lumpenproletariat* to domination, with the chief of the Society of December 10 at the head. The bourgeoisie kept France in breathless fear of the future terrors of red anarchy; Bonaparte discounted this future for it when, on December 4, he had the eminent bourgeois of the Boulevard Montmartre and the Boulevard des Italiens shot down at their windows by the army of order, whose enthusiasm was inspired by liquor. It apotheosised the sword; the sword rules it. It destroyed the revolutionary press; its own press has been destroyed. It placed public meetings under police supervision; its salons are under the supervision of the police. It disbanded the democratic National Guard; its own National Guard has been disbanded. It imposed the state of siege; the state of siege has been imposed on it. It supplanted the juries by military commissions; its juries are supplanted by military commissions; it subjected public education to the priests; the priests subject it to their own education. It transported people without

6. The hero of Heine's poem, *Two Knights*. In this character, Heine ridicules the spendthrift Polish nobleman ("Crapulinsky" comes from the French word *crapule*—gluttony, greediness). Here Marx means Louis Bonaparte.
7. The residence of the head of the government in France.

trial; it is transported without trial. It suppressed every stirring in society by means of the state power; every stirring in its society is repressed by means of the state power. Out of enthusiasm for its purse, it rebelled against its own politicians and men of letters; its politicians and men of letters are swept aside, but its purse is plundered now that its mouth has been gagged and its pen broken. The bourgeoisie never wearied of crying out to the revolution what Saint Arsenius cried out to the Christians: *"Fuge, tace, quiesce!"* Flee, be silent, keep quiet! Bonaparte cries to the bourgeoisie: *"Fuge, tace, quiesce!"* Flee, be silent, keep quiet!

The French bourgeoisie had long since found the solution to Napoleon's dilemma: *"Dans cinquante ans l'Europe sera républicaine ou cosaque."*[8] It had found the solution to it in the *"république cosaque."* No Circe, by means of black magic, has distorted that work of art, the bourgeois republic, into a monstrous shape. That republic has nothing but the semblance of respectability. The present-day France was contained in a finished state within the parliamentary republic. It only required a bayonet thrust for the bubble to burst and the monster to spring forth before our eyes.

[The immediate aim of the February Revolution was to overthrow the Orleans dynasty and the section of the bourgoisie that ruled during its reign. This aim was only attained on December 2, 1851. The immense possessions of the house of Orleans, the real basis of its influence, were now confiscated and what had been expected after the February Revolution came to pass after the December coup—prison, flight, dismissal, banishment, disarming, derision for the men who since 1830 had wearied France with their renown. But under Louis Philippe only a part of the commercial bourgeoisie ruled. Its other sections formed a dynastic and a republican opposition or were altogether disfranchised. Only the parliamentary republic accepted all sections of the commercial bourgeoisie into its sphere of state. Under Louis Philippe, moreover, the commercial bourgeoisie excluded the landowning bourgeoisie. Only the parliamentary republic set them side by side, with equal rights, married the July monarchy to the Legitimist monarchy and fused two epochs of property rule into one. Under Louis Philippe, the favoured section of the bourgeoisie concealed its rule under cover of the crown; in the parliamentary republic the rule of the bourgeoisie, after it had united all its elements and extended its realm to be the realm of its class, revealed its uncovered head. Thus the revolution itself had first to create the form in which the rule of the bourgeoisie could obtain its broadest, most general and final expression, and therefore could also be overthrown without being able to arise again.

8. "Within fifty years Europe will be republican or Cossack."

Only now was the judgment, passed in February, executed on the Orleanist bourgeoisie, that is, on the most vital section of the French bourgeoisie. Now it was defeated in its parliament, its bar, its commercial courts, its provincial representative bodies, its notaries, its university, its tribune and its tribunals, its press and its literature, its administrative revenues and its court fees, its army pay and its state incomes, in its mind and in its body. *Blanqui* had made the disbandment of the bourgeois guards the first demand on the revolution, and the bourgeois guards, who in February offered the revolution their hand in order to hinder its progress, vanished from the scene in December. The Pantheon itself becomes transformed into an ordinary church. With the final form of the bourgeois regime the spell is likewise broken which transfigured its initiators of the eighteenth century into saints.][9]

Why did not the Paris proletariat rise in revolt after December?

The overthrow of the bourgeoisie had as yet only been decreed; the decree had not been carried out. Any serious insurrection of the proletariat would at once have put fresh life into the bourgeoisie, would have reconciled it with the army and would have ensured a second June defeat for the workers.

On December 4 the proletariat was incited to fight by the bourgeois and the small shopkeepers. On the evening of that day several legions of the National Guard promised to appear, armed and uniformed, on the scene of action. For the bourgeois and the small shopkeepers had found out that in one of his decrees of December 2 Bonaparte abolished the secret ballot and enjoined them to record their "yes" or "no" in the official registers after their names. The resistance of December 4 intimidated Bonaparte. During the night he caused placards to be posted on all the street corners of Paris, announcing the restoration of the secret ballot. The bourgeois and the small shopkeepers believed that they had gained their end. Those who failed to appear next morning were the bourgeois and the small shopkeepers.

By a *coup de main* during the night of December 1 to 2, Bonaparte had robbed the Paris proletariat of its leaders, the barricade commanders. An army without officers, made disinclined to fight under the banner of the *Montagnards* by the memories of June 1848 and 1849 and May 1850, it left to its vanguard, the secret societies, the task of saving the insurrectionary honour of Paris, which the bourgeoisie had so spinelessly surrendered to the soldiers that, later on, Bonaparte could sneeringly give as his motive for disarming the National Guard—his fear that its arms would be turned against itself by anarchists!

9. The sentences in square brackets were omitted by Engels from the third German edition because of censorship restrictions.

"*C'est le triomphe complet et définitif du socialisme!*"[1]

Thus Guizot characterised December 2. But if the overthrow of the parliamentary republic contains within itself the germ of the triumph of the proletarian revolution, its immediate and obvious result was *the victory of Bonaparte over parliament, of the executive power over the legislative power, of force without phrases over the force of phrases*. In parliament the nation made its general will the law, that is, it made the law of the ruling class its general will. Before the executive power it renounces all will of its own and surrenders itself to the superior orders of something alien, of authority. The executive power, in contrast to the legislative power, expresses the heteronomy[2] of the nation, in contrast to its autonomy. France, therefore, seems to have escaped the despotism of a class only to fall back beneath the despotism of an individual and, what is more, beneath the authority of an individual without authority. The struggle seems to be settled in such a way that all classes, equally impotent and equally mute, fall on their knees before the club.

But the revolution is thorough-going. It is still in process of passing through purgatory. It does its work methodically. By December 2, 1851, it had completed one half of its preparatory work; it is now completing the other half. First it perfected the parliamentary power, in order to be able to overthrow it. Now that it has attained this, it perfects the *executive power*, reduces it to its purest expression, isolates it, sets it up against itself as the sole target, in order to concentrate all its forces of destruction against it. And when it has done this second half of its preliminary work, Europe will leap from her seat and exultantly exclaim: Well grubbed, old mole![3]

This executive power with its enormous bureaucratic and military organisation, with its artificial state machinery embracing wide strata, with a host of officials numbering half a million, besides an army of another half million, this appalling parasitic growth, which enmeshes the body of French society like a net and chokes all its pores, sprang up in the days of the absolute monarchy, with the decay of the feudal system, which it helped to hasten. The seigniorial privileges of the landowners and towns became transformed into so many attributes of the state power, the feudal dignitaries into paid officials and the motley pattern of conflicting mediæval plenary powers into the regulated plan of a state authority, whose work is divided and centralised as in a factory. The first French Revolution, with its task of breaking all local, territorial, urban and

1. "This is the complete and final triumph of socialism."   The actual words are: "Old mole! Canst work i' the earth so fast? A worthy pioneer!"
2. Dependence on foreign authority.
3. A reference to Shakespeare's *Hamlet*.

provincial independent powers in order to create the bourgeois unity of the nation, was bound to develop what the absolute monarchy had begun—centralisation, but at the same time the extent, the attributes and the agents of governmental authority. Napoleon perfected this state machinery. The Legitimist monarchy and the July monarchy added nothing but a greater division of labour, growing in the same measure that the division of labour within bourgeois society created new groups of interests, and, therefore, new material for state administration. Every *common* interest was straightaway severed from society, counter posed to it as a higher, *general* interest, snatched from the self-activity of society's members and made an object of governmental activity from the bridge, the school-house and the communal property of a village community to the railways, the national wealth and the national university of France. The parliamentary republic, finally, in its struggle against the revolution, found itself compelled to strengthen, along with the repressive measures, the resources and centralisation of governmental power. All the revolutions perfected this machine instead of smashing it. The parties that contended in turn for domination regarded the possession of this huge state edifice as the principal spoils of the victor.

But under the absolute monarchy, during the first revolution, and under Napoleon, bureaucracy was only the means of preparing the class rule of the bourgeoisie. Under the Restoration, under Louis Philippe and under the parliamentary republic, it was the instrument of the ruling class, however much it strove for power of its own.

Only under the second Bonaparte does the state seem to have made itself completely independent. As against bourgeois society, the state machine has consolidated its position so thoroughly that the chief of the Society of December 10 suffices for its head, an adventurer blown in from abroad, elevated on the shield by a drunken soldiery, which he has bought with liquor and sausages, and which he must continually ply with sausage anew. Hence the downcast despair, the feeling of most dreadful humiliation and degradation that oppresses the breast of France and makes her catch her breath. She feels herself dishonoured.

And yet the state power is not suspended in mid-air. Bonaparte represents a class, and the most numerous class of French society at that, the *small peasants.*

Just as the Bourbons were the dynasty of large landed property and just as the Orleans were the dynasty of money, so the Bonapartes are the dynasty of the peasants, that is, the mass of the French people. Not the Bonaparte who submitted to the bourgeois parliament, but the Bonaparte who dispersed it is the chosen of the peasantry. For three years the towns had succeeded in falsifying the meaning of the election of December 10 and in cheating the peasants out of the restoration of the Empire. The election of December 10, 1848, was consummated only by the *coup d'état* of December 2, 1851.

The small peasants form a vast mass, the members of which live in similar conditions, but without entering into manifold relations with one another. Their mode of production isolates them from one another, instead of bringing them into mutual intercourse. The isolation is increased by France's bad means of communication and by the poverty of the peasants. Their field of production, the small holding, admits of no division of labour in its cultivation, no application of science and, therefore, no multiplicity of development, no diversity of talents, no wealth of social relationships. Each individual peasant family is almost self-sufficient; it itself directly produces the major part of its consumption and thus acquires its means of life more through exchange with nature than in intercourse with society. The small holding, the peasant and his family; alongside them another small holding, another peasant and another family. A few score of these make up a village, and a few score of villages make up a Department. In this way, the great mass of the French nation is formed by simple addition of homologous magnitudes, much as potatoes in a sack form a sackful of potatoes. In so far as millions of families live under economic conditions of existence that divide their mode of life, their interests and their culture from those of the other classes, and put them in hostile contrast to the latter, they form a class. In so far as there is merely a local interconnection among these small peasants, and the identity of their interests begets no unity, no national union and no political organisation, they do not form a class. They are consequently incapable of enforcing their class interest in their own name, whether through a parliament or through a convention. They cannot represent themselves, they must be represented. Their representative must at the same time appear as their master, as an authority over them, as an unlimited governmental power that protects them against the other classes and sends them the rain and the sunshine from above. The political influence of the small peasants, therefore, finds its final expression in the executive power subordinating society to itself.

Historical tradition gave rise to the faith of the French peasants in the miracle that a man named Napoleon would bring all the glory back to them. And an individual was found who gives himself out as the man because he bears the name of Napoleon, in consequence of the *Code Napoléon*,[4] which lays down that *la recherche*

4. The French code of civil law, promulgated on March 31, 1804.

de la paternité est interdite.[5] After being a vagabond for twenty years and after a series of grotesque adventures, the legend finds fulfilment and the man becomes Emperor of the French. The fixed idea of the nephew was realised, because it coincided with the fixed idea of the most numerous class of the French people.

But, it may be objected, what about the peasant risings in half of France, the hounding of masses of peasants by the army, the mass incarceration and transportation of the peasants?

Since Louis XIV, France has experienced no similar persecution of the peasants "on account of demagogic intrigues."

But let there be no misunderstanding. The Bonaparte dynasty represents not the revolutionary, but the conservative peasant; not the peasant that strikes out beyond the condition of his social existence, the small holding, but rather the peasant who wants to consolidate it; not the country folk who want to overthrow the old order through their own energies linked up with the towns, but on the contrary those who, in stupefied bondage to this old order, want to see themselves with their small holding saved and favoured by the ghost of the empire. It represents not the enlightenment, but the superstition of the peasant; not his judgment, but his prejudice; not his future, but his past; not his modern Cevennes,[6] but his modern Vendée.[7]

The three years' rigorous rule of the parliamentary republic had freed a part of the French peasants from the Napoleonic illusion and had revolutionised them, even if only superficially, but the bourgoisie violently repressed them, as often as they set themselves in motion. Under the parliamentary republic the modern and the traditional consciousness of the French peasant contended for mastery. The contest proceeded in the form of an incessant struggle between the schoolmasters and the priests. The bourgeoisie struck down the schoolmasters. For the first time, the peasants made efforts to behave independently in the face of governmental activity. This was shown in the continual conflict between the mayors and the prefects. The bourgeoisie deposed the mayors. Finally, during the period of the parliamentary republic, the peasants of different localities rose against their own offspring, the army. The bourgeoisie punished them with states of siege and distraints on their goods. And this same bourgeoisie now cries out about the stupidity of the masses, the vile multitude, that has betrayed it to Bonaparte. It has itself forcibly strengthened the imperialism[8] of

---

5. Inquiry into fatherhood is forbidden.
6. In Cevennes (Southern France, Languedoc), at the beginning of the eighteenth century, there was an uprising of peasants under the slogans, "Down with taxes! Freedom of faith!"

7. The Vendée peasantry was the most politically backward at the time of the first French bourgeois revolution; it supported the royalist counter-revolution.
8. In the sense of imperial sentiments.

the peasant class, it held fast to the conditions that form the birth-place of this peasant religion. The bourgeoisie, to be sure, is bound to fear the stupidity of the masses, as long as they remain conservative, and the insight of the masses, as soon as they become revolutionary.

In the risings after the *coup d'état*, a part of the French peasants protested, arms in hand, against their own vote of December 10, 1848. The school they had gone through since 1848 had sharpened their wits. But they had made themselves over to the underworld of history; history held them to their word, and the majority was still so bound that in precisely the reddest Departments the peasant population voted openly for Bonaparte.[9] In its view, the National Assembly had hindered his progress. He had now merely broken the fetters that the town had imposed on the will of the countryside. In some parts the peasants even entertained the grotesque notion of a Convention[1] side by side with a Napoleon.

After the first revolution had transformed the peasants from semi-villeins into freeholders, Napoleon confirmed and regulated the conditions on which they could exploit undisturbed the soil of France which had only just come into their possession and slake their youthful passion for property. But what is now causing the ruin of the French peasant is his dwarf holding itself, the division of the land, the form of property which Napoleon consolidated in France. It is precisely the material conditions which made the feudal peasant into a small peasant and Napoleon into an emperor. Two generations have sufficed to produce the inevitable result: progressive deterioration of agriculture, progressive indebtedness of the agriculturist. The "Napoleonic" form of property, which at the beginning of the nineteenth century was the condition for the liberation and enrichment of the French country folk, has developed in the course of this century as the law of their enslavement and pauperisation. And it is just this law which is the first of the *"idées napoléoniennes"* which the second Bonaparte has to uphold. If he still shares with the peasants the illusion that the cause of their ruin is to be sought not in this small holding property itself but outside it in the influence of secondary causes, then his experiments will burst like soap bubbles when they come into contact with the relations of production.

The economic development of this small holding property has

9. In the plebiscite that ratified the *coup d'état*, by voting Bonaparte back as President with a huge majority.
1. The Convention. The revolutionary representative assembly of the first French bourgeois revolution. It was convened in September 1792, after the overthrow of the monarchy and the establishment of the republic. After the expulsion of the Girondins (May 31–June 2, 1893), the majority of its members were Jacobins—the representatives of the revolutionary petty bourgeoisie.

turned the relation of the peasants to the remaining classes of society completely upside down. Under Napoleon, the fragmentation of the land in the countryside supplemented free competition and the beginning of big industry in the towns. [Even the favouring of the peasant class was in the interest of the new bourgeois order. This newly-created class was the many sided extension of the bourgeois regime beyond the gates of the towns, its realisation on a national scale.][2] This class was the ubiquitous protest against the landed aristocracy which had just been overthrown.

[If it was favoured above all, it, above all, offered the point of attack for the restoration of the feudal lands.]

The roots that this small holding property struck in French soil deprived feudalism of all nutriment. Its landmarks formed the natural fortifications of the bourgeoisie against any *coup de main* on the part of its old overlords. But in the course of the nineteenth century the feudal lords were replaced by urban usurers; the feudal obligation that went with the land was replaced by the mortgage; aristocratic landed property was replaced by bourgeois capital. The small holding of the peasant is now only the pretext that allows the capitalist to draw profits, interest and rent from the soil, while leaving it to the tiller of the soil himself to see how he can extract his wages. The mortgage debt burdening the soil of France imposes on the French peasantry payment of an amount of interest equal to the annual interest on the entire British national debt. Small-holding property, in this enslavement by capital to which its development inevitably pushes forward, has transformed the mass of the French nation into troglodytes. Sixteen million peasants (including women and children) dwell in hovels, a large number of which have but one opening, others only two and the most favoured only three. And windows are to a house what the five senses are to the head. The bourgeois order, which at the beginning of the century set the state to stand guard over the newly arisen small holding and manured it with laurels, has become a vampire that sucks out its blood and marrow and throws them into the alchemistic cauldron of capital. The *Code Napoléon* is now nothing but a *codex* of distraints, forced sales and compulsory auctions. To the four million (including children, etc.) officially recognised paupers, vagabonds, criminals and prostitutes in France must be added five millions who hover on the margin of existence and either have their haunts in the countryside itself or, with their rags and their children, continually desert the countryside for the towns and the towns for the countryside. The interests of the peasants, therefore, are no longer,

2. The sentences in square brackets on this and the following pages were omitted by Engels from the third German edition because of censorship restrictions.

as under Napoleon, in accord with, but in opposition to the interests of the bourgeoisie, to capital. Hence the peasants find their natural ally and leader in the *urban proletariat*, whose task is the overthrow of the bourgeois order. But *strong and unlimited government* —and this is the second *"idée napoléonienne,"* which the second Napoleon has to carry out—is called upon to defend by force this "material" order. This "material order" also serves as the catchword in all Bonaparte's proclamations against the rebellious peasants.

Besides the mortgage which capital imposes on it, the small holding is burdened by *taxes*. Taxes are the source of life for the bureaucracy, the army, the priests and the court, in short, for the whole apparatus of the executive power. Strong government and heavy taxes are identical. By its very nature, small holding property forms a suitable basis for an all-powerful and innumerable bureaucracy. It creates a uniform level of relationships and persons over the whole surface of the land. Hence it also permits of uniform action from a supreme centre on all points of this uniform mass. It annihilates the aristocratic intermediate grades between the mass of the people and the state power. On all sides, therefore, it calls forth the direct interference of this state power and the intervention of its immediate organs. Finally, it produces an unemployed surplus population for which there is no place either on the land or in the towns, and which accordingly reaches out for state offices as a sort of respectable alms, and provokes the creation of state posts.

[Under Napoleon this numerous governmental personnel was not merely immediately productive, inasmuch as, through the means of compulsion of the state, it executed on behalf of the newly arisen peasantry, in the form of public works, etc., what the bourgeoisie could not yet accomplish by way of private industry. State taxes were a necessary means of compulsion to maintain exchange between town and country. Otherwise, the owner of a dwarf holding would in his rustic self-sufficiency have severed his connection with the townsman, as in Norway and a part of Switzerland.]

By the new markets which he opened at the point of the bayonet, and by the plundering of the Continent, Napoleon repaid the compulsory taxes with interest. These taxes were a spur to the industry of the peasant, whereas now they rob his industry of its last sources of aid and complete his powerlessness to resist pauperism. And an enormous bureaucracy, well-dressed and well-fed, is the *"idée napoléonienne"* which is most congenial of all to the second Bonaparte. How could it be otherwise, seeing that alongside the actual classes of society, he is forced to create an artificial caste, for which the maintenance of his regime becomes a bread-and-butter question? Accordingly, one of his first financial operations was the raising of officials' salaries to their old level again and the creation of new sinecures.

Another *"idée napoléonienne"* is the domination of the *priests* as a means of government. But if in its accord with society, in its dependence on natural forces and its subjection to the authority which protected it from above, the small holding that had newly come into being was naturally religious, the small holding that is ruined by debts, at odds with society and authority, and driven beyond its own limitations, naturally becomes irreligious. Heaven was quite a pleasing accessory to the narrow strip of land just won, more particularly as it makes the weather; it becomes an insult as soon as it is thrust forward as substitute for the small holding. The priest then appears as only the anointed bloodhound of the earthly police —another *"idée napoléonienne*[—whose mission under the second Bonaparte is to keep watch over, not the enemies of the peasant regime in the towns, as under Napoleon, but the enemies of Bonaparte in the country]. On the next occasion, the expedition against Rome will take place in France itself, but in a sense opposite to that of M. de Montalembert.[3]

Finally, the culminating point of the *"idées napoléoniennes"* is the preponderance of the *army*. The army was the *point d'honneur* of the peasants, it was they themselves transformed into heroes, defending their new possessions against the outer world, glorifying their recently won nationality, plundering and revolutionising the world. The uniform was their own state dress; war was their poetry; the small holding, extended and rounded off in imagination, was their fatherland, and patriotism the ideal form of the property sense. But the enemies against whom the French peasant has now to defend his property are not the Cossacks; they are the *hussiers*[4] and the tax collectors. The small holding lies no longer in the so-called fatherland, but in the register of mortgages. The army itself is no longer the flower of the peasant youth; it is the swamp-flower of the peasant *lumpenproletariat*. It consists in large measure of *remplaçants*, of substitutes, just as the second Bonaparte is himself only a *remplaçant*, the substitute for Napoleon. It now performs its deeds of valour by hounding the peasants in masses like chamois, by discharging *gendarme* duties, and when the internal contradictions of his system chase the chief of the Society of December 10 over the French border, his army, after some acts of brigandage, will reap, not laurels, but thrashings.

One sees: *all* idées napoléoniennes *are the ideas of the undeveloped small holding in the freshness of its youth*: for the small holding that has outlived its day they are an absurdity. They are only

3. Montalembert, the head of the militant Catholic Party, spoke, during the discussions on the repeal of universal suffrage, on the necessity of undertaking a Roman expedition "within" France—meaning support of the Roman Pope and the Catholic clergy. Marx, on the other hand, is speaking of an expedition against Rome in the sense of a struggle *against* the clergy.
4. Bailiffs.

the hallucinations of its death struggle, words that are reduced to phrases, spirits reduced to ghosts. But the parody of imperialism was necessary to free the mass of the French nation from the weight of tradition and to work out in pure form the opposition between the state power and society. With the progressive undermining of this small holding property, the state structure erected upon it collapses. The state centralisation that modern society requires arises only on the ruins of the military-bureaucratic governmental machinery which was forged in opposition to feudalism.

[The demolition of the state machine will not endanger centralisation. Bureaucracy is only the low and brutal form of a centralisation that is still afflicted with its opposite, with feudalism. On coming to despair of the Napoleonic Restoration, the French peasant parts with his belief in his small holding, the entire state edifice erected on this small holding falls to the ground and the *proletarian revolution* obtains *that chorus without which its solo song in all peasant nations becomes a swan song.*]

French peasant relationships provide us with the answer to the riddle of the general elections of December 20 and 21, which bore the second Napoleon up Mount Sinai, not to receive laws, but to give them.

[To be sure, on those fateful days the French nation committed a deadly sin against democracy, which is on its knees and prays daily: Holy universal suffrage, intercede for us! Naturally, the believers in universal suffrage do not want to renounce a miraculous power that has accomplished such great things in regard to themselves, which has transformed Bonaparte II into a Napoleon, a Saul into a Paul and a Simon into a Peter. The spirit of the people speaks to them through the ballot-box as the god of the prophet Ezekiel spoke to the marrowless bones: *"Haec dicit dominus deus ossibus suis: Ecce, ego intromittam in vos spiritum et vivetis."* "Thus saith the Lord God unto these bones: Behold, I will cause breath to enter into you, and ye shall live."]

Manifestly, the bourgeoisie had now no choice but to elect Bonaparte. [Despotism or anarchy. Naturally, it voted for despotism.] When the puritans at the Council of Constance complained of the dissolute lives of the popes and wailed about the necessity of moral reform, Cardinal Pierre d'Ailly thundered to them: "Only the devil in person can now save the Catholic Church, and you ask for angels." In like manner, after the *coup d'état*, the French bourgeoisie cried: Only the chief of the Society of December 10 can now save bourgeois society! Only theft can now save property; only perjury, religion; only bastardy, the family; only disorder, order!,

As the executive authority which has made itself an independent power, Bonaparte feels it to be his mission to safeguard "civil order." But the strength of this civil order lies in the middle class. He looks on himself, therefore, as the representative of the middle class and issues decrees in this sense. Nevertheless, he is somebody solely due to the fact that he has broken the political power of this middle class and daily breaks it anew. Consequently, he looks on himself as the adversary of the political and literary power of the middle class. But by protecting its material power, he generates its political power anew. The cause must accordingly be kept alive; but the effect, where it manifests itself, must be done away with. But this cannot pass off without slight confusions of cause and effect, since in their interaction both lose their distinguishing features. New decrees, that obliterate the border-line. At the same time, Bonaparte looks on himself as the representative of the peasants, and of the people in general, against the bourgeoisie, who wants to make the lower classes of the people happy within the frame of bourgeois society. New decrees, that cheat the "true socialists" of their statecraft in advance. But, above all, Bonaparte looks on himself as the chief of the Society of December 10, as the representative of the *lumpenproletariat* to which he himself, his *entourage*, his government and his army belong, and for which the prime consideration is to benefit itself and draw California lottery prizes from the state treasury. And he makes good his position as chief of the Society of December 10 with decrees, without decrees and despite decrees.

This contradictory task of the man explains the contradictions of his government, the confused groping hither and thither which seeks now to win, now to humiliate first one class and then another and arrays all of them uniformly against him, whose practical uncertainty forms a highly comical contrast to the imperious categorical style of the government decrees, a style which is copied obsequiously from the Uncle.

Industry and trade, hence the business affairs of the middle class, are to prosper in hot-house fashion under the strong government. Granting of innumerable railway concessions. But the Bonapartist *lumpenproletariat* is to enrich itself. Trickery with the railway concessions on the *Bourse* by those previously initiated. But no capital is forthcoming for the railways. Obligation of the Bank to make advances on railway shares. But, at the same time, the Bank is to be exploited for personal ends and therefore must be cajoled. Release of the Bank from the obligation to publish its report weekly. Leonine agreement[5] of the Bank with the government. The people are to be given employment. Inauguration of public works. But the public works increase the obligations of the people in respect of

5. Meaning an agreement by which one gets the lion's share.

taxes. Therefore, reduction of the taxes by an onslaught on the *rentiers*,[6] by conversion of the five per cent bonds to four-and-a-half per cent. But, once more, the middle class must receive a sop. Therefore doubling of the wine tax for the people, who buy it *en détail*,[7] and halving of the wine tax for the middle class, who drink it *en gros*.[8] Dissolution of the actual workers' associations, but promises of miracles of association in the future. The peasants are to be helped. Mortgage banks, that expedite their getting into debt and accelerate the concentration of property. But these banks are to be used to make money out of the confiscated estates of the house of Orleans. No capitalist wants to agree to this condition, which is not in the decrees, and the mortgage bank remains a mere decree, etc., etc.

Bonaparte would like to appear as the patriarchal benefactor of all classes. But he cannot give to one class without taking from another. Just as at the time of the Fronde it was said of the Duke of Guise that he was the most *obligeant* man in France because he had turned all his possessions into his partisans' obligations to him, so Bonaparte would fain be the most *obligeant* man in France and turn all the property, all the labour of France into a personal obligation to himself. He would like to steal the whole of France in order to be able to make a present of her to France or, rather, in order to be able to buy France anew with French money, for as the chief of the Society of December 10 he must needs buy what ought to belong to him. And all the state institutions, the Senate, the Council of State, the legislative body, the Legion of Honour, the soldiers' medals, the wash-houses, the public works, the railways, the *état major*[9] of the National Guard to the exclusion of privates, and the confiscated estates of the house of Orleans—all become parts of the institution of purchase. Every place in the army and in the government machine becomes a means for purchase. But the most important feature of this process, whereby France is taken in order to give to her, is the percentages that find their way to the head and the members of the Society of December 10 during the turnover. The witticism with which Countess L., the mistress of M. de Morny, characterised the confiscation of the Orleans estates: "*C'est le premier vol de l'aigle*,"[1] is applicable to every flight of the *eagle*, which is more like a *raven*. He himself and his adherents call out to one another daily like that Italian Carthusian admonishing the miser who, with boastful display, counted up the goods on which he could yet live for years to come: "*Tu fai conto sopra i beni,*

6. Persons drawing income from bonds and investments.
7. Retail.
8. Wholesale.

9. General Staff.
1. "It is the first flight (theft) of the eagle." *Vol* means flight and theft.

bisogna prima far il conto sopra gli anni."[2] Lest they make a mistake in the years, they count the minutes. At the court, in the ministries, at the head of the administration and the army, a crowd of fellows pushes forward, of the best of whom it can be said that no one knows whence he comes, a noisy, disreputable, rapacious Bohéme that dresses itself in gallooned coats with the same caricature of dignity as the high dignitaries of Soulouque. One can visualise clearly this upper stratum of the Society of December 10, if one reflects that *Veron-Crevel*[3] is its preacher of morals and *Granier de Cassagnac* its thinker. When Guizot, at the time of his ministry, utilised this Granier on a hole-and-corner newspaper against the dynastic opposition, he used to boast of him with the quip: "*C'est le roi des drôles,*" "he is the king of buffoons." One would do wrong to recall the Regency of Louis XV in connection with Louis Bonaparte's court and clique. For "often already, France has experienced a government of mistresses; but never before, a government of *hommes entretenus.*"[4]

Driven by the contradictory demands of his situation, and, at the same time, like a conjurer under the necessity of keeping the public gaze fixed on himself, as Napoleon's subsitute, by constant surprises, hence of executing a *coup d'état en miniature* every day, Bonaparte throws the entire bourgeois economy into confusion, lays hands on everything that seemed inviolable to the revolution of 1848, makes some tolerant of revolution, others desirous of revolution, and produces actual anarchy in the name of order, while at the same time he divests the whole state machine of its halo, profanes it and makes it at once loathsome and ridiculous. The cult of the Holy Coat of Treves[5] he duplicates at Paris in the cult of the Napoleonic imperial mantle. But if the imperial mantle finally falls on the shoulders of Louis Bonaparte, the iron statue of Napoleon will crash from the top of the Vendôme column.

2. Thou countest thy goods, thou shouldst first count thy years.
3. In his work, *La Cousine Bette*, Balzac delineates the thoroughly dissolute Parisian philistine in the character of Crevel, which he draws after the model of Dr. Veron, the proprietor of the *Constitutionnel*. [*Marx*]
4. Kept men. The words quoted are the words of Madame Girardin. [*Marx*]
5. One of the "sacred" relics ("the vestment of the Lord"), exhibited in the Treves cathedral in 1844 for public worship.

The Civil War in France

KARL MARX

This, the last of Marx's great political pamphlets, was composed during the Paris Revolution of September, 1870–May, 1871, and read by Marx to the General Council of the International Working Men's Association on May 30, 1871, only two days after the last resistance of the Paris Commune's fighters was overcome. In addition to providing an immensely vivid and trenchant account of the Commune and its fate, the Address was a major contribution to Marxist theory of the state and of the revolutionary process itself from the political point of view. It treated the Paris Commune as the short-lived but momentous first example in history of a "dictatorship of the proletariat." In preparing the document for publication as a separate pamphlet on the twentieth anniversary of the Paris Commune in 1891, Engels included in the publication two shorter addresses by Marx on the Franco-Prussian War, in which the Paris Revolution had its origin. Parts III and IV of the pamphlet are reprinted here.

Introduction

I did not anticipate that I would be asked to prepare a new edition of the Address of the General Council of the International on *The Civil War in France*, and to write an introduction to it. Therefore I can only touch briefly here on the most important points.

I am prefacing the longer work mentioned above by the two shorter Addresses of the General Council on the Franco-Prussian War. In the first place, because the second of these, which itself cannot be fully understood in full without the first, is referred to in *The Civil War*. But also because these two Addresses, likewise drafted by Marx, are, no less than *The Civil War*, outstanding examples of the author's remarkable gift, first proved in *The Eighteenth Brumaire of Louis Bonaparte*, for grasping clearly the character, the import and the necessary consequences of great historical events, at a time when these events are still in progress before our eyes or have only just taken place. And, finally, because today we in Germany are still having to endure the consequences which Marx predicted would follow from these events.

Has that which was declared in the first Address not come to pass· that if Germany's defensive war against Louis Bonaparte degenerated into a war of conquest against the French people, all the misfortunes which befell Germany after the so-called wars of liberation[1] would revive again with renewed intensity? Have we not had a further twenty years of Bismarck's rule, the Exceptional Law and Socialist-baiting taking the place of the prosecutions of demagogues, with the same arbitrary action of the police and with literally the same staggering interpretations of the law?

And has not the prediction been proved to the letter, that the annexation of Alsace-Lorraine would "force France into the arms of Russia," and that after this annexation Germany must either become the avowed servant of Russia, or must, after some short respite, arm for a new war, and, moreover, "a race war against the combined Slavonic and Roman races"? Has not the annexation of the French provinces driven France into the arms of Russia? Has not Bismarck for fully twenty years vainly wooed the favour of the tsar, wooed it with services even more lowly than those which little Prussia, before it became the "first Power in Europe," was wont to lay at Holy Russia's feet? And is there not every day still hanging over our heads the Damocles' sword of war, on the first day of which all the chartered covenants of princes will be scattered like chaff; a war of which nothing is certain but the absolute uncertainty of its outcome; a race war which will subject the whole of Europe to devastation by fifteen or twenty million armed men, and which is not raging already only because even the strongest of the great military states shrinks before the absolute incalculability of its final result?

All the more is it our duty to make again accessible to the German workers these brilliant proofs, now half-forgotten, of the farsightedness of international working-class policy in 1870.

What is true of these two Addresses is also true of *The Civil War in France*. On May 28, the last fighters of the Commune succumbed to superior forces on the slopes of Belleville; and only two days later, on May 30, Marx read to the General Council the work in which the historical significance of the Paris Commune is delineated in short, powerful strokes, but with such trenchancy, and above all such truth as has never again been attained in all the mass of literature on this subject.

Thanks to the economic and political development of France since 1789, Paris has been placed for the last fifty years in such a position that no revolution could break out there without assuming a proletarian character, that is to say, without the proletariat, which had bought victory with its blood, advancing its own

1. The wars against Napoleon I in 1813–15.

demands after victory. These demands were more or less unclear and even confused, corresponding to the state of development reached by the workers of Paris at the particular period, but in the last resort they all amounted to the abolition of the class antagonism between capitalists and workers. It is true that no one knew how this was to be brought about. But the demand itself, however indefinitely it still was couched, contained a threat to the existing order of society; the workers who put it forward were still armed; therefore, the disarming of the workers was the first commandment for the bourgeois, who were at the helm of the state. Hence, after every revolution won by the workers, a new struggle, ending with the defeat of the workers.

This happened for the first time in 1848. The liberal bourgeois of the parliamentary opposition held banquets for securing a reform of the franchise, which was to ensure supremacy for their party. Forced more and more, in their struggle with the government, to appeal to the people, they had gradually to yield precedence to the radical and republican strata of the bourgeoisie and petty bourgeoisie. But behind these stood the revolutionary workers, and since 1830 these had acquired far more political independence than the bourgeois, and even the republicans, suspected. At the moment of the crisis between the government and the opposition, the workers began street-fighting; Louis Philippe vanished, and with him the franchise reform; and in its place arose the republic, and indeed one which the victorious workers themselves designated as a "social" republic. No one, however, was clear as to what this social republic was to imply; not even the workers themselves. But they now had arms and were a power in the state. Therefore, as soon as the bourgeois republicans in control felt something like firm ground under their feet, their first aim was to disarm the workers. This took place by driving them into the insurrection of June 1848 by direct breach of faith, by open defiance and the attempt to banish the unemployed to a distant province. The government had taken care to have an overwhelming superiority of force. After five days' heroic struggle, the workers were defeated. And then followed a blood-bath among the defenceless prisoners, the like of which has not been seen since the days of the civil wars which ushered in the downfall of the Roman republic. It was the first time that the bourgeoisie showed to what insane cruelties of revenge it will be goaded the moment the proletariat dares to take its stand against the bourgeoisie as a separate class, with its own interests and demands. And yet 1848 was only child's play compared with the frenzy of the bourgeoisie in 1871.

Punishment followed hard at heel. If the proletariat was not yet able to rule France, the bourgeoisie could no longer do so. At least not at that period, when the greater part of it was still monarchically inclined, and it was divided into three dynastic parties and a fourth, republican party. Its internal dissensions allowed the adventurer Louis Bonaparte to take possession of all the commanding points—army, police, administrative machinery—and, on December 2, 1851, to explode the last stronghold of the bourgeoisie, the National Assembly. The Second Empire began—the exploitation of France by a gang of political and financial adventurers, but at the same time also an industrial development such as had never been possible under the narrow-minded and timorous system of Louis Philippe, with the exclusive domination of only a small section of the big bourgeoisie. Louis Bonaparte took the political power from the capitalists under the pretext of protecting them, the bourgeois, from the workers, and on the other hand the workers from them; but in return his rule encouraged speculation and industrial activity —in a word, the upsurgence and enrichment of the whole bourgeoisie to an extent hitherto unknown. To an even greater extent, it is true, corruption and mass thievery developed, clustering around the imperial court, and drawing their heavy percentages from this enrichment.

But the Second Empire was the appeal to French chauvinism, was the demand for the restoration of the frontiers of the First Empire, which had been lost in 1814, or at least those of the First Republic. A French empire within the frontiers of the old monarchy and, in fact, within the even more amputated frontiers of 1815—such a thing was impossible for any length of time. Hence the necessity for occasional wars and extensions of frontiers. But no extension of frontiers was so dazzling to the imagination of the French chauvinists as the extension to the German left bank of the Rhine. One square mile on the Rhine was more to them than ten in the Alps or anywhere else. Given the Second Empire, the demand for the restoration of the left bank of the Rhine, either all at once or piecemeal, was merely a question of time. The time came with the Austro-Prussian War of 1866; cheated of the anticipated "territorial compensation" by Bismarck and by his own over-cunning, hesitant policy, there was now nothing left for Napoleon but war, which broke out in 1870 and drove him first to Sedan, and thence to Wilhelmshöhe.[2]

The necessary consequence was the Paris Revolution of September 4, 1870. The empire collapsed like a house of cards, and the republic was again proclaimed. But the enemy was standing at the gates; the armies of the empire were either hopelessly encircled at

2. At Sedan, on September 2, 1870, the French army was defeated and captured together with the emperor. He was detained at Wilhelmshöhe, a Prussian castle near Kassel.

Metz or held captive in Germany. In this emergency the people allowed the Paris deputies to the former legislative body to constitute themselves into a "Government of National Defence." This was the more readily conceded, since, for the purposes of defence, all Parisians capable of bearing arms had enrolled in the National Guard and were armed, so that now the workers constituted a great majority. But very soon the antagonism between the almost completely bourgeois government and the armed proletariat broke into open conflict. On October 31, workers' battalions stormed the town hall and captured part of the membership of the government. Treachery, the government's direct breach of its undertakings, and the intervention of some petty-bourgeois battalions set them free again, and in order not to occasion the outbreak of civil war inside a city besieged by a foreign military power, the former government was left in office.

At last, on January 28, 1871, starved Paris capitulated. But with honours unprecedented in the history of war. The forts were surrendered, the city wall stripped of guns, the weapons of the regiments of the line and of the Mobile Guard were handed over, and they themselves considered prisoners of war. But the National Guard kept its weapons and guns, and only entered into an armistice with the victors. And these did not dare enter Paris in triumph. They only dared to occupy a tiny corner of Paris, which, into the bargain, consisted partly of public parks, and even this they only occupied for a few days! And during this time they, who had maintained their encirclement of Paris for 131 days, were themselves encircled by the armed workers of Paris, who kept a sharp watch that no "Prussian" should overstep the narrow bounds of the corner ceded to the foreign conqueror. Such was the respect which the Paris workers inspired in the army before which all the armies of the empire had laid down their arms; and the Prussian *Junkers*, who had come to take revenge at the home of the revolution, were compelled to stand by respectfully, and salute precisely this armed revolution!

During the war the Paris workers had confined themselves to demanding the vigorous prosecution of the fight. But now, when peace had come after the capitulation of Paris, now Thiers, the new supreme head of the government, was compelled to realise that the rule of the propertied classes—big landowners and capitalists—was in constant danger so long as the workers of Paris had arms in their hands. His first action was an attempt to disarm them. On March 18, he sent troops of the line with orders to rob the National Guard of the artillery belonging to it, which had been constructed during the siege of Paris and had been paid for by public subscription. The attempt failed: Paris mobilised as one man for resistance, and war between Paris and the French Government sitting at Versailles was declared. On March 26 the Paris Commune was elected and on March 28 it was proclaimed. The Central Committee of the National Guard, which up to then had carried on the government, handed in its resignation to the Commune after it had first decreed the abolition of the scandalous Paris "Morality Police." On March 30 the Commune abolished conscription and the standing army, and declared the sole armed force to be the National Guard, in which all citizens capable of bearing arms were to be enrolled. It remitted all payments of rent for dwelling houses from October 1870 until April, the amounts already paid to be booked as future rent payments, and stopped all sales of articles pledged in the municipal loan office. On the same day the foreigners elected to the Commune were confirmed in office, because "the flag of the Commune is the flag of the World Republic." On April 1 it was decided that the highest salary to be received by any employee of the Commune, and therefore also by its members themselves, was not to exceed 6,000 francs (4,800 marks). On the following day the Commune decreed the separation of the church from the state, and the abolition of all state payments for religious purposes as well as the transformation of all church property into national property; as a result of which, on April 8, the exclusion from the schools of all religious symbols, pictures, dogmas, prayers—in a word, "of all that belongs to the sphere of the individual's conscience"—was ordered and gradually put into effect. On the 5th, in reply to the shooting, day after day, of captured Commune fighters by the Versailles troops, a decree was issued for the imprisonment of hostages, but it was never carried into execution. On the 6th, the guillotine was brought out by the 137th battalion of the National Guard, and publicly burnt, amid great popular rejoicing. On the 12th, the Commune decided that the Victory Column on the *Place Vendôme*, which had been cast from captured guns by Napoleon after the war of 1809, should be demolished as a symbol of chauvinism and incitement to national hatred. This was carried out on May 16. On April 16 it ordered a statistical tabulation of factories which had been closed down by the manufacturers, and the working out of plans for the operation of these factories by the workers formerly employed in them, who were to be organised in co-operative societies, and also plans for the organisation of these co-operatives in one great union. On the 20th it abolished night work for bakers, and also the employment offices, which since the Second Empire had been run as a monopoly by creatures appointed by the police—labour exploiters of the first rank; these offices were transferred to the mayoralties of the twenty *arrondissements* of Paris. On April 30 it ordered the closing of the pawnshops, on the ground that they were a private exploitation of the workers, and were in contradiction with the right of the workers to their instruments of labour and to credit. On May 5 it ordered the razing of the Chapel of Atonement, which had been built in expiation of the execution of Louis XVI.

Thus from March 18 onwards the class character of the Paris movement, which had previously been pushed into the background by the fight against the foreign invaders, emerged sharply and clearly. As almost only workers, or recognised representatives of the workers, sat in the Commune, its decisions bore a decidedly proletarian character. Either these decisions decreed reforms which the republican bourgeoisie had failed to pass solely out of cowardice, but which proveded a necessary basis for the free activity of the working class—such as the realisation of the principle that *in relation to the state*, religion is a purely private matter—or the Commune promulgated decrees which were in the direct interest of the working class and in part cut deeply into the old order of society. In a beleaguered city, however, it was possible to make at most a start in the realisation of all this. And from the beginning of May onwards all their energies were taken up by the fight against the armies assembled by the Versailles government in ever-growing numbers.

On April 7 the Versailles troops had captured the Seine crossing at Neuilly, on the western front of Paris; on the other hand, in an attack on the southern front on the 11th they were repulsed with heavy losses by General Eudes. Paris was continually bombarded and, moreover, by the very people who had stigmatised as a sacrilege the bombardment of the same city by the Prussians. These same people now begged the Prussian government for the hasty return of the French soldiers taken prisoner at Sedan and Metz, in order that they might recapture Paris for them. From the beginning of May the gradual arrival of these troops gave the Versailles forces a decided superiority. This already became evident when, on April 23, Thiers broke off the negotiations for the exchange, proposed by the Commune, of the Archbishop of Paris and a whole number of other priests held as hostages in Paris, for only one man, Blanqui, who had twice been elected to the Commune but was a prisoner in Clairvaux. And even more from the changed language of Thiers; previously procrastinating and equivocal, he now suddenly became insolent, threatening, brutal. The Versailles forces took the redoubt of Moulin Saquet on the southern front, on May 3; on the 9th, Fort Issy, which had been completely reduced to ruins by gunfire; on the 14th, Fort Vanves. On the western front they advanced gradually, capturing the numerous villages and buildings which extended up to the city wall, until they reached the main defences; on the 21st, thanks to treachery and the carelessness of the National Guards stationed there, they succeeded in forcing their way into the city. The Prussians, who held the northern and eastern forts, allowed the Versailles troops to advance across the land north of the city, which was forbidden ground to them under the armistice, and thus to march forward, attacking on a wide front, which the Parisians naturally thought covered by the armistice, and therefore held only weakly. As a result of this, only a weak resistance was put up in the western half of Paris, in the luxury city proper; it grew stronger and more tenacious the nearer the incoming troops approached the eastern half, the working-class city proper. It was only after eight days' fighting that the last defenders of the Commune succumbed on the heights of Belleville and Menilmontant; and then the massacre of defenceless men, women and children, which had been raging all through the week on an increasing scale, reached its zenith. The breechloaders could no longer kill fast enough; the vanquished were shot down in hundreds by *mitrailleuse*[3] fire. The "Wall of the Federals" at the Père Lachaise cemetery, where the final mass murder was consummated, is still standing today, a mute but eloquent testimony to the frenzy of which the ruling class is capable as soon as the working class dares to stand up for its rights. Then, when the slaughter of them all proved to be impossible, came the mass arrests, the shooting of victims arbitrarily selected from the prisoners' ranks, and the removal of the rest to great camps where they awaited trial by courts-martial. The Prussian troops surrounding the northeastern half of Paris had orders not to allow any fugitives to pass; but the officers often shut their eyes when the soldiers paid more obedience to the dictates of humanity than to those of the Supreme Command; particular honour is due to the Saxon army corps, which behaved very humanely and let through many who were obviously fighters for the Commune.

If today, after twenty years, we look back at the activity and historical significance of the Paris Commune of 1871, we shall find it necessary to make a few additions to the account given in *The Civil War in France*.

The members of the Commune were divided into a majority, the Blanquists, who had also been predominant in the Central Committee of the National Guard; and a minority, members of the International Working Men's Association, chiefly consisting of adherents of the Proudhon school of socialism. The great majority of the Blanquists were at that time Socialists only by revolutionary, proletarian instinct; only a few had attained greater clarity on principles, through Vaillant, who was familiar with German scientific social-

3. *Mitrailleuse*: Machine-gun. *Wall of*   Wall of the Communards.
the Federals: Now usually called the

ism. It is therefore comprehensible that in the economic sphere much was left undone which, according to our view today, the Commune ought to have done. The hardest thing to understand is certainly the holy awe with which they remained standing respectfully outside the gates of the Bank of France. This was also a serious political mistake. The bank in the hands of the Commune—this would have been worth more than ten thousand hostages. It would have meant the pressure of the whole of the French bourgeoisie on the Versailles government in favour of peace with the Commune. But what is still more wonderful is the correctness of much that nevertheless was done by the Commune, composed as it was of Blanquists and Proudhonists. Naturally, the Proudhonists were chiefly responsible for the economic decrees of the Commune, both for their praiseworthy and their unpraiseworthy aspects; as the Blanquists were for its political commissions and omissions. And in both cases the irony of history willed—as is usual when doctrinaires come to the helm—that both did the opposite of what the doctrines of their school prescribed.

Proudhon, the Socialist of the small peasant and mastercraftsman, regarded association with positive hatred. He said of it that there was more bad than good in it; that it was by nature sterile, even harmful, because it was a fetter on the freedom of the worker; that it was a pure dogma, unproductive and burdensome, in conflict as much with the freedom of the worker as with economy of labour; that its disadvantages multiplied more swiftly than its advantages; that, as compared with it, competition, division of labour and private property were economic forces. Only in the exceptional cases —as Proudhon called them—of large-scale industry and large establishments, such as railways, was the association of workers in place. (See *General Idea of the Revolution*, 3rd sketch.)

By 1871, large-scale industry had already so much ceased to be an exceptional case even in Paris, the centre of artistic handicrafts, that by far the most important decree of the Commune instituted an organisation of large-scale industry and even of manufacture which was not only to be based on the association of the workers in each factory, but also to combine all these associations in one great union; in short, an organisation which, as Marx quite rightly says in *The Civil War*, must necessarily have led in the end to communism, that is to say, the direct opposite of the Proudhon doctrine. And, therefore, the Commune was the grave of the Proudhon school of socialism. Today this school has vanished from French working-class circles; here, among the Possibilists no less than among the "Marxists," Marx's theory now rules unchallenged. Only among the "radical" bourgeoisie are there still Proudhonists.

The Blanquists fared no better. Brought up in the school of conspiracy, and held together by the strict discipline which went with it, they started out from the viewpoint that a relatively small number of resolute, well-organised men would be able, at a given favourable moment, not only to seize the helm of state, but also by a display of great, ruthless energy, to maintain power until they succeeded in sweeping the mass of the people into the revolution and ranging them round the small band of leaders. This involved, above all, the strictest, dictatorial centralisation of all power in the hands of the new revolutionary government. And what did the Commune, with its majority of these same Blanquists, actually do? In all its proclamations to the French in the provinces, it appealed to them to form a free federation of all French Communes with Paris, a national organisation which for the first time was really to be created by the nation itself. It was precisely the oppressing power of the former centralised government, army, political police, bureaucracy, which Napoleon had created in 1798 and which since then had been taken over by every new government as a welcome instrument and used against its opponents—it was precisely this power which was to fall everywhere, just as it had already fallen in Paris.

From the very outset the Commune was compelled to recognise that the working class, once come to power, could not go on managing with the old state machine; that in order not to lose again its only just conquered supremacy, this working class must, on the one hand, do away with all the old repressive machinery previously used against it itself, and, on the other, safeguard itself against its own deputies and officials, by declaring them all, without exception, subject to recall at any moment. What had been the characteristic attribute of the former state? Society had created its own organs to look after its common interests, originally through simple division of labour. But these organs, at whose head was the state power, had in the course of time, in pursuance of their own special interests, transformed themselves from the servants of society into the masters of society. This can be seen, for example, not only in the hereditary monarchy, but equally so in the democratic republic. Nowhere do "politicians" form a more separate and powerful section of the nation than precisely in North America. "There, each of the two major parties which alternately succeed each other in power is itself in turn controlled by people who make a business of politics, who speculate on seats in the legislative assemblies of the Union as well as of the separate states, or who make a living by carrying on agitation for their party and on its victory are rewarded with positions. It is well known how the Americans have been trying for thirty years to shake off this yoke, which has become intolerable, and how in spite of it all they continue to sink ever deeper in this swamp of corruption. It is precisely in America that we see best how there takes place this process of the state power making itself independent in relation to society, whose mere instrument it was originally intended to be. Here there exists no dynasty, no nobility, no standing army, beyond the few men keeping watch on the Indians, no bureaucracy with permanent posts or the right to pensions. And nevertheless we find here two great gangs of political speculators, who alternately take possession of the state power and exploit it by the most corrupt means and for the most corrupt ends—and the nation is powerless against these two great cartels of politicians, who are ostensibly its servants, but in reality dominate and plunder it.

Against this transformation of the state and the organs of the state from servants of society into masters of society—an inevitable transformation in all previous states—the Commune made use of two infallible means. In the first place, it filled all posts—administrative, judicial and educational—by election on the basis of universal suffrage of all concerned, subject to the right of recall at any time by the same electors. And, in the second place, all officials, high or low, were paid only the wages received by other workers. The highest salary paid by the Commune to anyone was 6,000 francs. In this way an effective barrier to place-hunting and careerism was set up, even apart from the binding mandates to delegates to representative bodies which were added besides.

This shattering [*Sprengung*] of the former state power and its replacement by a new and truly democratic one is described in detail in the third section of *The Civil War*. But it was necessary to dwell briefly here once more on some of its features, because in Germany particularly the superstitious belief in the state has been carried over from philosophy into the general consciousness of the bourgeoisie and even of many workers. According to the philosophical conception, the state is the "realisation of the idea," or the Kingdom of God on earth, translated into philosophical terms, the sphere in which eternal truth and justice is or should be realised. And from this follows a superstitious reverence for the state and everything connected with it, which takes root the more readily since people are accustomed from childhood to imagine that the affairs and interests common to the whole of society could not be looked after otherwise than as they have been looked after in the past, that is, through the state and its lucratively positioned officials. And people think they have taken quite an extraordinarily bold step forward when they have rid themselves of belief in hereditary monarchy and swear by the democratic republic. In reality, however, the state is nothing but a machine for the oppression of one class by another, and indeed in the democratic republic no less than in the monarchy; and at best an evil inherited by the proletariat after its victorious struggle for class supremacy, whose worst sides the victorious proletariat, just like the Commune, cannot avoid having to lop off at once as much as possible until such time as a generation reared in new, free social conditions is able to throw the entire lumber of the state on the scrap heap.

Of late, the Social-Democratic philistine has once more been filled with wholesome terror at the words: Dictatorship of the Proletariat. Well and good, gentlemen, do you want to know what this dictatorship looks like? Look at the Paris Commune. That was the Dictatorship of the Proletariat.

Friedrich Engels

London, on the twentieth anniversary of the Paris Commune, March 18, 1891

* * *

III

On the dawn of the 18th of March, Paris arose to the thunderburst of "Vive la Commune!" What is the Commune, that sphinx so tantalising to the bourgeois mind?

"The proletarians of Paris," said the Central Committee in its manifesto of the 18th March, "amidst the failures and treasons of the ruling classes, have understood that the hour has struck for them to save the situation by taking into their own hands the direction of public affairs.... They have understood that it is their imperious duty and their absolute right to render themselves masters of their own destinies, by seizing upon the governmental power." But the working class cannot simply lay hold of the ready-made state machinery, and wield it for its own purposes.

The centralised State power, with its ubiquitous organs of standing army, police, bureaucracy, clergy, and judicature—organs wrought after the plan of a systematic and hierarchic division of labour,—originates from the days of absolute monarchy, serving nascent middle-class society as a mighty weapon in its struggles against feudalism. Still, its development remained clogged by all manner of mediaeval rubbish, seignorial rights, local privileges, municipal and guild monopolies and provincial constitutions. The gigantic broom of the French Revolution of the eighteenth century swept away all these relics of bygone times, thus clearing simultaneously the social soil of its last hindrances to the superstructure of the modern State edifice raised under the First Empire, itself the offspring of the coalition wars of old semi-feudal Europe against modern France. During the subsequent *régimes* the Government, placed under parliamentary control—that is, under the direct control of the propertied classes—became not only a hotbed of huge national debts and crushing taxes; with its irresistible allurements of place, pelf, and patronage, it became not only the bone of contention between the rival factions and adventurers of the ruling classes; but its political character changed simultaneously with the economic changes of society. At the same pace at which the progress of modern industry developed, widened, intensified the class antagonism between capital and labour, the State power assumed more and more the character of the national power of capital over labour, of a public force organised for social enslavement, of an engine of class despotism. After every revolution marking a progressive phase in the class struggle, the purely repressive character of the State power stands out in bolder and bolder relief. The Revolution of 1830, resulting in the transfer of Government from the landlords to the capitalists, transferred it from the more remote to the more direct antagonists of the working men. The bourgeois Republicans, who, in the name of the Revolution of February, took the State power, used it for the June massacres, in order to convince the working class that "social" republic meant the Republic ensuring their social subjection, and in order to convince the royalist bulk of the bourgeois and landlord class that they might safely leave the cares and emoluments of Government to the bourgeois "Republicans." However, after their one heroic exploit of June, the bourgeois Republicans had, from the front, to fall back to the rear of the "Party of Order"—a combination formed by all the rival fractions and factions of the appropriating class in their now openly declared antagonism to the producing classes. The proper form of their joint-stock Government was the *Parliamentary Republic*, with Louis Bonaparte for its President. Theirs was a *régime* of avowed class terrorism and deliberate insult toward the "vile multitude." If the Parliamentary Republic, as M. Thiers said, "divided them (the different fractions of the ruling class) least," it opened an abyss between that class and the whole body of society outside their spare ranks. The restraints by which their own divisions had under former *régimes* still checked the State power, were removed by their union; and in view of the threatening upheaval of the proletariat, they now used that State power mercilessly and ostentatiously as the national war-engine of capital against labour. In their uninterrupted crusade against the producing masses they were, however, bound not only to invest the executive with continually increased powers of repression, but at the same time to divest their own parliamentary stronghold —the National Assembly—one by one, of all its own means of defence against the Executive. The Executive, in the person of Louis Bonaparte, turned them out. The natural offspring of the "Party-of-Order" Republic was the Second Empire.

The empire, with the *coup d'état* for its certificate of birth, universal suffrage for its sanction, and the sword for its sceptre, professed to rest upon the peasantry, the large mass of producers not directly involved in the struggle of capital and labour. It professed to save the working class by breaking down Parliamentarism, and, with it, the undisguised subserviency of Government to the propertied classes. It professed to save the propertied classes by upholding their economic supremacy over the working class; and, finally, it professed to unite all classes by reviving for all the chimera of national glory. In reality, it was the only form of government possible at a time when the bourgeoisie had already lost, and the working class had not yet acquired, the faculty of ruling the nation. It was acclaimed throughout the world as the saviour of society. Under its sway, bourgeois society, freed from political cares, attained a development unexpected even by itself. Its industry and commerce expanded to colossal dimensions; financial swindling celebrated cosmopolitan orgies; the misery of the masses was set off by a shameless display of gorgeous, meretricious and debased luxury. The State power, apparently soaring high above society, was at the same time itself the greatest scandal of that society and the very hotbed of all its corruptions. Its own rottenness, and the rottenness of the society it had saved, were laid bare by the bayonet of Prussia, herself eagerly bent upon transferring the supreme seat of that *régime* from Paris to Berlin. Imperialism is, at the same time, the most prostitute and the ultimate form of the State power which nascent middle-class society had commenced to elaborate as a means of its own emancipation from feudalism, and which full-grown bourgeois society had finally transformed into a means for the enslavement of labour by capital.

The direct antithesis to the empire was the Commune. The cry of "social republic," with which the revolution of February was ushered in by the Paris proletariat, did but express a vague aspiration after a Republic that was not only to supersede the monarchical form of class-rule, but class-rule itself. The Commune was the positive form of that Republic.

Paris, the central seat of the old governmental power, and, at the same time, the social stronghold of the French working class, had risen in arms against the attempt of Thiers, and the Rurals to restore and perpetuate that old governmental power bequeathed to them by the empire. Paris could resist only because, in consequence of the siege, it had got rid of the army, and replaced it by a National Guard, the bulk of which consisted of working men. This fact was now to be transformed into an institution. The first decree of the Commune, therefore, was the suppression of the standing army, and the substitution for it of the armed people.

The Commune was formed of the municipal councillors, chosen by universal suffrage in the various wards of the town, responsible and revocable at short terms. The majority of its members were naturally working men, or acknowledged representatives of the working class. The Commune was to be a working, not a parliamentary, body, executive and legislative at the same time. Instead of continuing to be the agent of the Central Government, the police was at once stripped of its political attributes, and turned into the responsible and at all times revocable agent of the Commune. So were the officials of all other branches of the Administration. From the members of the Commune downwards, the public service had to be done at *workmen's wages*. The vested interests and the representation allowances of the high dignitaries of State disappeared along with the high dignitaries themselves. Public functions ceased to be the private property of the tools of the Central Government. Not only municipal administration, but the whole initiative hitherto exercised by the State was laid into the hands of the Commune.

Having once got rid of the standing army and the police, the physical force elements of the old Government, the Commune was anxious to break the spiritual force of repression, the "parson-power," by the disestablishment and disendowment of all churches as proprietary bodies. The priests were sent back to the recesses of private life, there to feed upon the alms of the faithful in imitation of their predecessors, the Apostles. The whole of the educational institutions were opened to the people gratuitously, and at the same time cleared of all interference of Church and State. Thus, not only was education made accessible to all, but science itself freed from the fetters which class prejudice and governmental force had imposed upon it.

The judicial functionaries were to be divested of that sham independence which had but served to mask their abject subserviency to all succeeding governments to which, in turn, they had taken, and broken, the oaths of allegiance. Like the rest of public servants, magistrates and judges were to be elective, responsible, and revocable.

The Paris Commune was, of course, to serve as a model to all the great industrial centres of France. The communal *régime* once established in Paris and the secondary centres, the old centralised

Government would in the provinces, too, have to give way to the self-government of the producers. In a rough sketch of national organisation which the Commune had no time to develop, it states clearly that the Commune was to be the political form of even the smallest country hamlet, and that in the rural districts the standing army was to be replaced by a national militia, with an extremely short term of service. The rural communes of every district were to administer their common affairs by an assembly of delegates in the central town, and these district assemblies were again to send deputies to the National Delegation in Paris, each delegate to be at any time revocable and bound by the *mandat impératif* (formal instructions) of his constituents. The few but important functions which still would remain for a central government were not to be suppressed, as has been intentionally mis-stated, but were to be discharged by Communal, and therefore strictly responsible agents. The unity of the nation was not to be broken, but, on the contrary, to be organised by the Communal Constitution and to become a reality by the destruction of the State power which claimed to be the embodiment of that unity independent of, and superior to, the nation itself, from which it was but a parasitic excrescence. While the merely repressive organs of the old governmental power were to be amputated, its legitimate functions were to be wrested from an authority usurping pre-eminence over society itself, and restored to the responsible agents of society. Instead of deciding once in three or six years which member of the ruling class was to misrepresent the people in Parliament, universal suffrage was to serve the people, constituted in the Communes, as individual suffrage serves every other employer in the search for the workmen and managers in his business. And it is well known that companies, like individuals, in matters of real business generally know how to put the right man in the right place, and, if they for once make a mistake, to redress it promptly. On the other hand, nothing could be more foreign to the spirit of the Commune that to supersede universal suffrage by hierarchic investiture.

It is generally the fate of completely new historical creations to be mistaken for the counterpart of older and even defunct forms of social life, to which they may bear a certain likeness. Thus, this new Commune, which breaks the modern State power, has been mistaken for a reproduction of the mediaeval Communes, which first preceded, and afterwards became the substratum of, that very State power. The Communal Constitution has been mistaken for an attempt to break up into a federation of small States, as dreamt of by Montesquieu and the Girondins, that unity of great nations which, if originally brought about by political force, has now become a powerful coefficient of social production. The antagonism of the Commune against the State power has been mistaken for an exaggerated form of the ancient struggle against over-centralisation. Peculiar historical circumstances may have prevented the classical development, as in France, of the bourgeois form of government, and may have allowed, as in England, to complete the great central State organs by corrupt vestries, jobbing councillors, and ferocious poor-law guardians in the towns, and virtually hereditary magistrates in the counties. The Communal Constitution would have restored to the social body all the forces hitherto absorbed by the State parasite feeding upon, and clogging the free movement of, society. By this one act it would have initiated the regeneration of France. The provincial French middle class saw in the Commune an attempt to restore the sway their order had held over the country under Louis Philippe, and which, under Louis Napoleon, was supplanted by the pretended rule of the country over the towns. In reality, the Communal Constitution brought the rural producers under the intellectual lead of the central towns of their districts, and these secured to them, in the working men, the natural trustees of their interests. The very existence of the Commune involved, as a matter of course, local municipal liberty, but no longer as a check upon the, now superseded, State power. It could only enter into the head of a Bismarck, who, when not engaged on his intrigues of blood and iron, always likes to resume his old trade, so befitting his mental calibre, of contributor to *Kladderadatsch* (the Berlin *Punch*), it could only enter into such a head, to ascribe to the Paris Commune aspirations after that caricature of the old French municipal organisation of 1791, the Prussian municipal constitution which degrades the town governments to mere secondary wheels in the police-machinery of the Prussian State. The Commune made that catchword of bourgeois revolutions, cheap government, a reality, by destroying the two greatest sources of expenditure—the standing army and State functionarism. Its very existence presupposed the non-existence of monarchy, which, in Europe at least, is the normal incumbrance and indispensable cloak of class-rule. It supplied the Republic with the basis of really democratic institutions. But neither cheap Government nor the "true Republic" was its ultimate aim; they were its mere concomitants.

The multiplicity of interpretations to which the Commune has been subjected, and the multiplicity of interests which construed it in their favour, show that it was a thoroughly expansive political form, while all previous forms of government had been emphatically repressive. Its true secret was this. It was essentially a working-class government, the produce of the struggle of the producing against the appropriating class, the political form at last discovered under which to work out the economic emancipation of labour.

Except on this last condition, the Communal Constitution would have been an impossibility and a delusion. The political rule of the producer cannot coexist with the perpetuation of his social slavery. The Commune was therefore to serve as a lever for uprooting the economical foundations upon which rests the existence of classes, and therefore of class-rule. With labour emancipated, every man becomes a working man, and productive labour ceases to be a class attribute.

It is a strange fact. In spite of all the tall talk and all the immense literature, for the last sixty years, about Emancipation of Labour, no sooner do the working men anywhere take the subject into their own hands with a will, than uprises at once all the apologetic phraseology of the mouthpieces of present society with its two poles of Capital and Wages Slavery (the landlord now is but the sleeping partner of the capitalist), as if capitalist society was still in its purest state of virgin innocence, with its antagonisms still undeveloped, with its delusions still unexploded, with its prostitute realities not yet laid bare. The Commune, they exclaim, intends to abolish property, the basis of all civilisation! Yes, gentlemen, the Commune intended to abolish that class-property which makes the labour of the many the wealth of the few. It aimed at the expropriation of the expropriators. It wanted to make individual property a truth by transforming the means of production, land and capital, now chiefly the means of enslaving and exploiting labour, into mere instruments of free and associated labour.—But this is Communism, "impossible" Communism! Why, those members of the ruling classes who are intelligent enough to perceive the impossibility of continuing the present system—and they are many—have become the obtrusive and full-mouthed apostles of co-operative production. If co-operative production is not to remain a sham and a snare; if it is to supersede the Capitalist system; if united co-operative societies are to regulate national production upon a common plan, thus taking it under their own control, and putting an end to the constant anarchy and periodical convulsions which are the fatality of Capitalist production—what else, gentlemen, would it be but Communism, "possible" Communism?

The working class did not expect miracles from the Commune. They have no ready-made utopias to introduce *par décret du peuple*. They know that in order to work out their own emancipation, and along with it that higher form to which present society is irresistibly tending by its own economical agencies, they will have to pass through long struggles, through a series of historic processes, transforming circumstances and men. They have no ideals to realise, but to set free the elements of the new society with which old collapsing bourgeois society itself is pregnant. In the full consciousness of their historic mission, and with the heroic resolve to act up to it, the working class can afford to smile at the coarse invective of the gentlemen's gentlemen with the pen and inkhorn, and at the didactic patronage of well-wishing bourgeois-doctrinaires, pouring forth their ignorant platitudes and sectarian crotchets in the oracular tone of scientific infallibility.

When the Paris Commune took the management of the revolution in its own hands; when plain working men for the first time dared to infringe upon the Governmental privilege of their "natural superiors," and, under circumstances of unexampled difficulty, performed their work modestly, conscientiously, and efficiently,— performed it at salaries the highest of which barely amounted to one-fifth of what, according to high scientific authority,[4] is the minimum required for a secretary to a certain metropolitan school board,—the old world writhed in convulsions of rage at the sight of the Red Flag, the symbol of the Republic of Labour, floating over the Hôtel de Ville.

And yet, this was the first revolution in which the working class was openly acknowledged as the only class capable of social initiative, even by the great bulk of the Paris middle class—shopkeepers, tradesmen, merchants—the wealthy capitalists alone excepted. The Commune had saved them by a sagacious settlement of that ever-recurring cause of dispute among the middle classes themselves—the debtor and creditor accounts.[5] The same portion of the middle class, after they had assisted in putting down the working men's insurrection of June, 1848, had been at once unceremoniously sacrificed to their creditors by the then Constituent Assembly. But this was not their only motive for now rallying round the working class. They felt that there was but one alternative—the Commune, or the Empire—under whatever name it might reappear. The Empire had ruined them economically by the havoc it made of public wealth, by the wholesale financial swindling it fostered, by the props it lent to the artificially accelerated centralisation of capital, and the concomitant expropriation of their own ranks. It had suppressed them politically, it had shocked them morally by its orgies, it had insulted their Voltairianism by handing over the education of their children to the frères Ignorantins, it had revolted their national feeling as Frenchmen by precipitating them headlong into a war which left

4. Professor Huxley. [Engels, German edition of 1871]
5. On April 18, the Commune promul-gated a decree postponing payments on debt obligations for three years.

only one equivalent for the ruins it made—the disappearance of the Empire. In fact, after the exodus from Paris of the high Bonapartist and capitalist *bohème*, the true midle-class Party of Order came out in the shape of the "Union Républicaine," enrolling themselves under the colours of the Commune and defending it against the wilful misconstruction of Thiers. Whether the gratitude of this great body of the middle class will stand the present severe trial, time must show.

The Commune was perfectly right in telling the peasants that "its victory was their only hope." Of all the lies hatched at Versailles and re-echoed by the glorious European penny-a-liner, one of the most tremendous was that the Rurals represented the French peasantry. Think only of the love of the French peasant for the men to whom, after 1815, he had to pay the milliard of indemnity. In the eyes of the French peasant, the very existence of a great landed proprietor is in itself an encroachment on his conquests of 1789. The bourgeois, in 1848, had burdened his plot of land with the additional tax of forty-five cents in the franc; but then he did so in the name of the revolution; while now he had fomented a civil war against the revolution, to shift on to the peasant's shoulders the chief load of the five milliards of indemnity to be paid to the Prussian. The Commune, on the other hand, in one of its first proclamations, declared that the true originators of the war would be made to pay its cost. The Commune would have delivered the peasant of the blood tax,—would have given him a cheap government, —transformed his present blood-suckers, the notary, advocate, executor, and other judicial vampires, into salaried communal agents, elected by, and responsible to, himself. It would have freed him of the tyranny of the *garde champêtre*, the gendarme, and the prefect; would have put enlightenment by the schoolmaster in the place of stultification by the priest. And the French peasant is, above all, a man of reckoning. He would find it extremely reasonable that the pay of the priest, instead of being extorted by the taxgatherer, should only depend upon the spontaneous action of the parishioners' religious instincts. Such were the great immediate boons which the rule of the Commune—and that rule alone—held out to the French peasantry. It is, therefore, quite superfluous here to expatiate upon the more complicated but vital problems which the Commune alone was able, and at the same time compelled, to solve in favour of the peasant, viz., the hypothecary debt, lying like an incubus upon his parcel of soil, the *prolétariat foncier* (the rural proletariat), daily growing upon it, and his expropriation from it enforced, at a more and more rapid rate, by the very development of modern agriculture and the competition of capitalist farming.

The French peasant had elected Louis Bonaparte president of the Republic; but the Party of Order created the Empire. What the French peasant really wants he commenced to show in 1849 and 1850, by opposing his *maire* to the Government's prefect, his schoolmaster to the Government's priest, and himself to the Government's gendarme. All the laws made by the Party of Order in January and February, 1850, were avowed measures of repression against the peasant. The peasant was a Bonapartist, because the great Revolution, with all its benefits to him, was, in his eyes, personified in Napoleon. This delusion, rapidly breaking down under the Second Empire (and in its very nature hostile to the Rurals), this prejudice of the past, how could it have withstood the appeal of the Commune to the living interests and urgent wants of the peasantry?

The Rurals—this was, in fact, their chief apprehension—knew that three months' free communication of Communal Paris with the provinces would bring about a general rising of the peasants, and hence their anxiety to establish a police blockade around Paris, so as to stop the spread of the rinderpest.

If the Commune was thus the true representative of all the healthy elements of French society, and therefore the truly national Government, it was, at the same time, as a working men's Government, as the bold champion of the emancipation of labour, emphatically international. Within sight of the Prussian army, that had annexed to Germany two French provinces, the Commune annexed to France the working people all over the world.

The Second Empire had been the jubilee of cosmopolitan black-legism, the rakes of all countries rushing in at its call for a share in its orgies and in the plunder of the French people. Even at this moment the right hand of Thiers is Ganesco, the foul Wallachian, and his left hand is Markovsky, the Russian spy. The Commune admitted all foreigners to the honour of dying for an immortal cause. Between the foreign war lost by their treason, and the civil war fomented by their conspiracy with the foreign invader, the bourgeoisie had found the time to display their patriotism by organising police-hunts upon the Germans in France. The Commune made a German working man its Minister of Labour. Thiers, the bourgeoisie, the Second Empire, had continually deluded Poland by loud professions of sympathy, while in reality betraying her to, and doing the dirty work of, Russia. The Commune honoured the heroic sons of Poland by placing them at the head of the defenders of Paris. And, to broadly mark the new era of history it was conscious of initiating, under the eyes of the conquering Prussians, on the one side, and of the Bonapartist army, led by Bonapartist generals, on the other, the Commune pulled down that colossal symbol of martial glory, the Vendôme column.

The great social measure of the Commune was its own working existence. Its special measures could but betoken the tendency of a government of the people by the people. Such were the abolition of the nightwork of journeymen bakers; the prohibition, under penalty, of the employers' practice to reduce wages by levying upon their work-people fines under manifold pretexts,—a process in which the employer combines in his own person the parts of legislator, judge, and executor, and filches the money to boot. Another measure of this class was the surrender, to associations of workmen, under reserve of compensation, of all closed workshops and factories, no matter whether the respective capitalists had absconded or preferred to strike work.

The financial measures of the Commune, remarkable for their sagacity and moderation, could only be such as were compatible with the state of a beseiged town. Considering the colossal robberies committed upon the city of Paris by the great financial companies and contractors, under the protection of Haussmann,[6] the Commune would have had an incomparably better title to confiscate their property than Louis Napoleon had against the Orleans family. The Hohenzollern and the English oligarchs, who both have derived a good deal of their estates from Church plunder, were, of course, greatly shocked at the Commune clearing but 8,000 f. out of secularisation.

While the Versailles Government, as soon as it had recovered some spirit and strength, used the most violent means against the Commune; while it put down the free expression of opinion all over France, even to the forbidding of meetings of delegates from the large towns; while it subjected Versailles and the rest of France to an espionage far surpassing that of the Second Empire; while it burned by its gendarme inquisitors all papers printed at Paris, and sifted all correspondence from and to Paris; while in the National Assembly the most timid attempts to put in a word for Paris were howled down in a manner unknown even to the *Chambre introuvable* of 1816; with the savage warfare of Versailles outside, and its attempts at corruption and conspiracy inside Paris—would the Commune not have shamefully betrayed its trust by affecting to keep up all the decencies and appearances of liberalism as in a time of profound peace? Had the Government of the Commune been

6. During the Second Empire, Baron Haussmann was Prefect of the Department of the Seine, that is, of the City of Paris. He introduced a number of changes in the layout of the city for the purpose of facilitating the crushing of workers' insurrections. [*V. I. Lenin, 1905 Russian translation*]

akin to that of M. Thiers, there would have been no more occasion to suppress Party-of-Order papers at Paris than there was to suppress Communal papers at Versailles.

It was irritating indeed to the Rurals that at the very same time they declared the return to the church to be the only means of salvation for France, the infidel Commune unearthed the peculiar mysteries of the Picpus nunnery, and of the Church of Saint Laurent. It was a satire upon M. Thiers that, while he showered grand crosses upon the Bonapartist generals in acknowledgement of their mastery in losing battles, signing capitulations, and turning cigarettes at Wilhelmshöhe, the Commune dismissed and arrested its generals whenever they were suspected of neglecting their duties. The explusion from, and arrest by, the Commune of one of its members who had slipped in under a false name, and had undergone at Lyons six days' imprisonment for simple bankruptcy, was it not a deliberate insult hurled at the forger, Jules Favre, then still the foreign minister of France, still selling France to Bismarck, and still dictating his orders to that paragon Government of Belgium? But indeed the Commune did not pretend to infallibility, the invariable attribute of all governments of the old stamp. It published its doings and sayings, it initiated the public into all its shortcomings.

In every revolution there intrude, at the side of its true agents, men of a different stamp; some of them survivors of and devotees to past revolutions, without insight into the present movement, but preserving popular influence by their known honesty and courage, or by the sheer force of tradition; others mere bawlers, who, by dint of repeating year after year the same set of stereotyped declamations against the Government of the day, have sneaked into the reputation of revolutionists of the first water. After the 18th of March, some such men did also turn up, and in some cases contrived to play pre-eminent parts. As far as their power went, they hampered the real action of the working class, exactly as men of that sort have hampered the full development of every previous revolution. They are an unavoidable evil: with time they are shaken off; but time was not allowed to the Commune.

Wonderful, indeed, was the change the Commune had wrought in Paris! No longer any trace of the meretricious Paris of the Second Empire. No longer was Paris the rendezvous of British landlords, Irish absentees, American ex-slaveholders and shoddy men, Russian ex-serf-owners, and Wallachian boyards. No more corpses at the morgue, no nocturnal burglaries, scarcely any robberies; in fact, for the first time since the days of February, 1848, the streets of Paris were safe, and that without any police of any kind. "We," said a member of the Commune, "hear no longer of assassination, theft and personal assault; it seems indeed as if the police had dragged along with it to Versailles all its Conservative friends." The *cocottes* had refound the scent of their protectors—the absconding men of family, religion, and, above all, of property. In their stead, the real women of Paris showed again at the surface—heroic, noble, and devoted, like the women of antiquity. Working, thinking, fighting, bleeding Paris—almost forgetful, in its incubation of a new society, of the cannibals at its gates—radiant in the enthusiasm of its historic intiative!

Opposed to this new world at Paris, behold the old world at Versailles—that assembly of the ghouls of all defunct *régimes*, Legitimists and Orleanists, eager to feed upon the carcass of the nation, —with a tail of antediluvian Republicans, sanctioning, by their presence in the Asssembly, the slaveholders' rebellion, relying for the maintenance of their Parliamentary Republic upon the vanity of the senile mountebank at its head, and caricaturing 1789 by holding their ghastly meetings in the *Jeu de Paume*.[7] There it was, this Assembly, the representative of everything dead in France, propped up to the semblance of life by nothing but the swords of the generals of Louis Bonaparte. Paris all truth, Versailles all lie; and that lie vented through the mouth of Thiers.

Thiers tells a deputation of the mayors of the Seine-et-Oise,— "You may rely upon my word, which I have *never* broken!" He tells the Assembly itself that "it was the most freely elected and most Liberal Assembly France ever possessed"; he tells his motley soldiery that it was "the admiration of the world, and the finest army France ever possessed"; he tells the provinces that the bombardment of Paris by him was a myth: "If some cannonshots have been fired, it is not the deed of the army of Versailles, but of some insurgents trying to make believe that they are fighting, while they dare not show their faces." He again tells the provinces that "the artillery of Versailles does not bombard Paris, but only cannonades it." He tells the Archbishop of Paris that the pretended executions and reprisals (!) attributed to the Versailles troops were all moonshine. He tells Paris that he was only anxious "to free it from the hideous tyrants who oppress it," and that, in fact, the Paris of the Commune was "but a handful of criminals."

The Paris of M. Thiers was not the real Paris of the "vile multitude," but a phantom Paris, the Paris of the *francs-fileurs*,[8] the Paris of the Boulevards, male and female—the rich, the capitalist, the gilded, the idle Paris, now thronging with its lackeys, its black-

7. The tennis court where the National Assembly of 1789 adopted its famous decisions. [*Engels, German edition of 1871*]

8. Absconders.

legs, its literary *bohême*, and its *cocottes* at Versailles, Saint-Denis, Rueil, and Saint-Germain; considering the civil war but an agreeable diversion, eyeing the battle going on through telescopes, counting the rounds of cannon, and swearing by their own honour and that of their prostitutes, that the performance was far better got up than it used to be at the Porte St. Martin. The men who fell were really dead; the cries of the wounded were cries in good earnest; and, besides, the whole thing was so intensely historical.

This is the Paris of M. Thiers, as the emigration of Coblenz was the France of M. de Calonne.

IV

The first attempt of the slaveholders' conspiracy to put down Paris by getting the Prussians to occupy it, was frustrated by Bismarck's refusal. The second attempt, that of the 18th of March, ended in the rout of the army and the flight to Versailles of the Government, which ordered the whole administration to break up and follow in its track. By the semblance of peace-negotiations with Paris, Thiers found the time to prepare for war against it. But where to find an army? The remnants of the line regiments were weak in number and unsafe in character. His urgent appeal to the provinces to succour Versailles, by their National Guards and volunteers, met with a flat refusal. Brittany alone furnished a handful of *Chouans* fighting under a white flag, every one of them wearing on his breast the heart of Jesus in white cloth, and shouting "*Vive le Roi!*" (Long live the King!) Thiers was, therefore, compelled to collect, in hot haste, a motley crew, composed of sailors, marines, Pontifical Zouaves, Valentin's gendarmes, and Pietri's *sergents-de-ville* and *mouchards*. This army, however, would have been ridiculously ineffective without the instalments of imperialist war-prisoners, which Bismarck granted in numbers just sufficient to keep the civil war a-going, and keep the Versailles Government in abject dependence on Prussia. During the war itself, the Versailles police had to look after the Versailles army, while the gendarmes had to drag it on by exposing themselves at all posts of danger. The forts which fell were not taken, but bought. The heroism of the Federals convinced Thiers that the resistance of Paris was not to be broken by his own strategic genius and the bayonets at his disposal.

Meanwhile, his relations with the provinces became more and more difficult. Not one single address of approval came in to gladden Thiers and his Rurals. Quite the contrary. Deputations and addresses demanding, in a tone anything but respectful, conciliation with Paris on the basis of the unequivocal recognition of the

Republic, the acknowledgement of the Communal liberties, and the dissolution of the National Assembly, whose mandate was extinct, poured in from all sides, and in such numbers that Dufaure, Thiers' Minister of Justice, in his circular of April 23 to the public prosecutors, commanded them to treat "the cry of conciliation" as a crime! In regard, however, of the hopeless prospect held out by his campaign, Thiers resolved to shift his tactics by ordering, all over the country, municipal elections to take place on the 30th of April, on the basis of the new municipal law dictated by himself to the National Assembly. What with the intrigues of his prefects, what with police intimidation, he felt quite sanguine of imparting, by the verdict of the provinces, to the National Assembly that moral power it had never possessed, and of getting at last from the provinces the physical force required for the conquest of Paris.

His banditti-warfare against Paris, exalted in his own bulletins, and the attempts of his ministers at the establishment, throughout France, of a reign of terror, Thiers was from the beginning anxious to accompany with a little by-play of conciliation, which had to serve more than one purpose. It was to dupe the provinces, to inveigle the middle-class element in Paris, and, above all, to afford the professed Republicans in the National Assembly the opportunity of hiding their treason against Paris behind their faith in Thiers. On the 21st of March, when still without an army, he had declared to the Assembly: "Come what may, I will not send an army to Paris." On the 27th March he rose again: "I have found the Republic an accomplished fact, and I am firmly resolved to maintain it." In reality, he put down the revolution at Lyons and Marseilles[9] in the name of the Republic, while the roars of his Rurals drowned the very mention of its name at Versailles. After this exploit, he toned down the "accomplished fact" into an hypothetical fact. The Orleans princes, whom he had cautiously warned off Bordeaux, were now, in flagrant breach of the law, permitted to intrigue at Dreux. The concessions held out by Thiers in his interminable interviews with the delegates from Paris and the provinces, although constantly varied in tone and colour, according to time and circumstances, did in fact never come to more than the prospective restriction of revenge to the "handful of criminals implicated in the murder of Lecomte and Clément Thomas," on the well-understood premise that Paris and France were unreservedly to accept M. Thiers himself as the best of possible Republics, as he, in 1830, had done with Louis Philippe. Even these concessions he not only took

9. A few days after March 18, 1871, revolutionary outbreaks occurred in Lyons and Marseilles aimed at the proclamation of Communes. The movement was crushed by the Thiers government.

care to render doubtful by the official comments put upon them in the Assembly through his Ministers. He had his Dufaure to act. Dufaure, this old Orleanist lawyer, had always been the justiciary of the state of siege, as now in 1871, under Thiers, so in 1839 under Louis Philippe, and in 1849 under Louis Bonaparte's presidency. While out of office he made a fortune by pleading for the Paris capitalists, and made political capital by pleading against the laws he had himself originated. He now hurried through the National Assembly not only a set of repressive laws which were, after the fall of Paris, to extirpate the last remnants of Republican liberty in France; he foreshadowed the fate of Paris by abridging the, for him, too slow procedure of courts-martial, and by a new-fangled, Draconic code of deportation. The Revolution of 1848, abolishing the penalty of death for political crimes, has replaced it by deportation. Louis Bonaparte did not dare, at least not in theory, to re-establish the *régime* of the guillotine. The Rural Assembly, not yet bold enough even to hint that the Parisians were not rebels, but assassins, had therefore to confine its prospective vengeance against Paris to Dufaure's new code of deportation. Under all these circumstances Thiers himself could not have gone on with his comedy of conciliation, had it not, as he intended it to do, drawn forth shrieks of rage from the Rurals, whose ruminating mind did neither understand the play, nor its necessities of hypocrisy, tergiversation, and procrastination.

In sight of the impending municipal elections of the 30th April, Thiers enacted one of his great conciliation scenes on the 27th April. Amidst a flood of sentimental rhetoric, he exclaimed from the tribune of the Assembly: "There exists no conspiracy against the Republic but that of Paris, which compels us to shed French blood. I repeat it again and again. Let those impious arms fall from the hands which hold them, and chastisement will be arrested at once by an act of peace excluding only the small number of criminals." To the violent interruption of the Rurals he replied: "Gentlemen, tell me, I implore you, am I wrong? Do you really regret that I could have stated the truth that the criminals are only a handful? Is it not fortunate in the midst of our misfortunes that those who have been capable to shed the blood of Clément Thomas and General Lecomte are but rare exceptions?"

France, however, turned a deaf ear to what Thiers flattered himself to be a parliamentary siren's song. Out of 700,000 municipal councillors returned by the 35,000 communes still left to France, the united Legitimists, Orleanists and Bonapartists did not carry 8,000. The supplementary elections which followed were still more decidedly hostile. Thus, instead of getting from the provinces the badly-needed physical force, the National Assembly lost even its last claim to moral force, that of being the expression of the universal suffrage of the country. To complete the discomfiture, the newly-chosen municipal councils of all the cities of France openly threatened the usurping Assembly at Versailles with a counter Assembly at Bordeaux.

Then the long-expected moment of decisive action had at last come for Bismarck. He peremptorily summoned Thiers to send to Frankfort plenipotentiaries for the definitive settlement of peace. In humble obedience to the call of his master, Thiers hastened to depatch his trusty Jules Favre, backed by Pouyer-Quertier. Pouyer-Quertier, an "eminent" Rouen cotton-spinner, a fervent and even servile partisan of the Second Empire, had never found any fault with it save its commercial treaty with England, prejudicial to his own shop-interest. Hardly installed at Bordeaux as Thiers' Minister of Finance, he denounced that "unholy" treaty, hinted at its near abrogation, and had even the effrontery to try, although in vain (having counted without Bismarck), the immediate enforcement of the old protective duties against Alsace, where, he said, no previous international treaties stood in the way. This man, who considered counter-revolution as a means to put down wages at Rouen, and the surrender of French provinces as a means to bring up the price of his wares in France, was he not *the one* predestined to be picked out by Thiers as the helpmate of Jules Favre in his last and crowning treason?

On the arrival at Frankfort of this exquisite pair of plenipotentiaries, bully Bismarck at once met them with the imperious alternative: Either the restoration of the Empire, or the unconditional acceptance of my own peace terms! These terms included a shortening of the intervals in which the war indemnity was to be paid and the continued occupation of the Paris forts by Prussian troops until Bismarck should feel satisfied with the state of things in France; Prussia thus being recognised as the supreme arbiter in internal French politics! In return for this he offered to let loose, for the extermination of Paris, the captive Bonapartist army, and to lend them the direct assistance of Emperor William's troops. He pledged his good faith by making payment of the first instalment of the indemnity dependent on the "pacification" of Paris. Such a bait was, of course, eagerly swallowed by Thiers and his plenipotentiaries. They signed the treaty of peace on the 10th of May, and had it endorsed by the Versailles Assembly on the 18th.

In the interval between the conclusion of peace and the arrival of the Bonapartist prisoners, Thiers felt the more bound to resume his comedy of conciliation, as his Republican tools stood in sore need of a pretext for blinking their eyes at the preparations for the carnage of Paris. As late as the 8th of May he replied to a deputation of middle-class conciliators: "Whenever the insurgents will make up their minds for capitulation, the gates of Paris shall be flung wide open during a week for all except the murderers of Generals Clément Thomas and Lecomte."

A few days afterwards, when violently interpellated on these promises by the Rurals, he refused to enter into any explanations; not, however, without giving them this significant hint. "I tell you there are impatient men amongst you, men who are in too great a hurry. They must have another eight days; at the end of these eight days there will be no more danger, and the task will be proportionate to their courage and to their capacities." As soon as MacMahon was able to assure him that he could shortly enter Paris, Thiers declared to the Assembly that "he would enter Paris with the *laws* in his hands, and demand a full expiation from the wretches who had sacrificed the lives of soldiers and destroyed public monuments." As the moment of decision drew near he said—to the Assembly, "I shall be pitiless!"—to Paris, that it was doomed; and to his Bonapartist banditti, that they had State licence to wreak vengeance upon Paris to their hearts' content. At last, when treachery had opened the gates of Paris to General Douay, on the 21st of May, Thiers, on the 22nd, revealed to the Rurals the "goal" of his conciliation comedy, which they had so obstinately persisted in not understanding. "I told you a few days ago that we were approaching *our goal*; today I come to tell you *the goal* is reached. The victory of order, justice and civilisation is at last won!"

So it was. The civilisation and justice of bourgeois order comes out in its lurid light whenever the slaves and drudges of that order rise against their masters. Then this civilisation and justice stand forth as undisguised savagery and lawless revenge. Each new crisis in the class struggle between the appropriator and the producer brings out this fact more glaringly. Even the atrocities of the bourgeois in June, 1848, vanish before the ineffable infamy of 1871. The self-sacrificing heroism with which the population of Paris—men, women and children—fought for eight days after the entrance of the Versaillese, reflects as much the grandeur of their cause, as the infernal deeds of the soldiery reflect the innate spirit of that civilisation of which they are the mercenary vindicators. A glorious civilisation, indeed, the great problem of which is how to get rid of the heaps of corpses it made after the battle was over!

To find a parallel for the conduct of Thiers and his blood-hounds we must go back to the times of Sulla and the two Triumvirates of Rome. The same wholesale slaughter in cold blood; the same disregard, in massacre, of age and sex; the same system of torturing prisoners; the same proscriptions, but this time of a whole class; the same savage hunt after concealed leaders, lest one might escape; the same denunciations of political and private enemies; the same indifference for the butchery of entire strangers to the feud. There is but this difference, that the Romans had no *mitrailleuses* for the despatch, in the lump, of the proscribed, and that they had not "the law in their hands," nor on their lips the cry of "civilisation."

And after those horrors, look upon the other, still more hideous, face of that bourgeois civilisation as described by its own press!

"With stray shots," writes the Paris correspondent of a London Tory paper, "still ringing in the distance, and untended wounded wretches dying amid the tombstones of Père la Chaise—with 6,000 terror-stricken insurgents wandering in an agony of despair in the labyrinth of the catacombs, and wretches hurried through the streets to be shot down in scores by the *mitrailleuse*—it is revolting to see the *cafés* filled with the votaries of absinthe, billiards, and dominoes; female profligacy perambulating the boulevards, and the sound of revelry disturbing the night from the *cabinets particuliers* of fashionable restaurants." M. Edouard Hervé writes in the *Journal de Paris*, a Versaillist journal suppressed by the Commune: "The way in which the population of Paris (!) manifested its satisfaction yesterday was rather more than frivolous, and we fear it will grow worse as time progresses. Paris has now a *fête* day appearance, which is sadly out of place; and, unless we are to be called the *Parisiens de la décadence*, this sort of thing must come to an end." And then he quotes the passage from Tacitus: "Yet, on the morrow of that horrible struggle, even before it was completely over, Rome—degraded and corrupt—began once more to wallow in the voluptuous slough which was destroying its body and polluting its soul—*alibi proelia et vulnera; alibi balnea popinaeque* (here fights and wounds, there baths and restaurants)." M. Hervé only forgets to say that the "population of Paris" he speaks of is but the population of the Paris of M. Thiers—the *francs-fileurs* returning in throngs from Versailles, Saint-Denis, Rueil and Saint-Germain—*the* Paris of the "Decline."

In all its bloody triumphs over the self-sacrificing champions of a new and better society, that nefarious civilisation, based upon the enslavement of labour, drowns the moans of its victims in a hue-and-cry of calumny, reverberated by a worldwide echo. The serene working men's Paris of the Commune is suddenly changed into a pandemonium by the bloodhounds of "order." And what does this tremendous change prove to the bourgeois mind of all countries? Why, that the Commune has conspired against civilisation! The Paris people die enthusiastically for the Commune in numbers unequalled in any battle known to history. What does that prove? Why, that the Commune was not the people's own government but the usurpation of a handful of criminals! The women of Paris joyfully give up their lives at the barricades and on the place of execution. What does this prove? Why, that the demon of the Commune has changed them into Megaeras and Hecates! The moderation of the Commune during two months of undisputed sway is equalled only by the heroism of its defence. What does that prove? Why, that for months the Commune carefully hid, under a mask of moderation and humanity, the blood-thirstiness of its fiendish instincts, to be let loose in the hour of its agony!

The working men's Paris, in the act of its heroic self-holocaust, involved in its flames buildings and monuments. While tearing to pieces the living body of the proletariat, its rulers must no longer expect to return triumphantly into the intact architecture of their abodes. The Government of Versailles cries, "Incendiarism!" and whispers this cue to all its agents, down to the remotest hamlet, to hunt up its enemies everywhere as suspect of professional incendiarism. The bourgeoisie of the whole world, which looks complacently upon the wholesale massacre after the battle, is convulsed by horror at the desecration of brick and mortar!

When governments give state-licences to their navies to "kill, *burn* and destroy," is that a licence for incendiarism? When the British troops wantonly set fire to the Capitol at Washington and to the summer palace of the Chinese Emperor, was that incendiarism? When the Prussians, not for military reasons, but out of the mere spite of revenge, burned down, by the help of petroleum, towns like Châteaudun and innumerable villages, was that incendiarism? When Thiers, during six weeks, bombarded Paris, under the pretext that he wanted to set fire to those houses only in which there were people, was that incendiarism?—In war, fire is an arm as legitimate as any. Buildings held by the enemy are shelled to set them on fire. If their defenders have to retire, they themselves light the flames to prevent the attack from making use of the buildings. To be burnt down has always been the inevitable fate of all buildings situated in the front of battle of all the regular armies of the world. But in the war of the enslaved against their enslavers, the only justifiable war in history, this is by no means to hold good! The Commune used fire strictly as a means of defence. They used it to stop up to the Versailles troops those long, straight avenues which Haussmann had expressly opened to artillery-fire; they used it to cover their retreat, in the same way as the Versaillese, in their advance, used their shells which destroyed at least as many buildings as the fire of the Commune. It is a matter of dispute, even now, which buildings were set fire to by the defence, and which by the attack. And the defence resorted to fire only then, when the Versaillese troops had already commenced their wholesale murdering of prisoners.—Besides, the Commune had, long before, given full public notice that, if driven to extremities, they would bury themselves under the ruins of Paris, and make Paris a second Moscow, as the Government of Defence, but only as a cloak for its treason, had promised to do. For this purpose Trochu had found them the petroleum. The Commune knew that its opponents cared nothing for the lives of the Paris people, but cared much for their own Paris buildings. And Thiers, on the other hand, had given them notice that he would be implacable in his vengeance. No sooner had he got his army ready on one side, and the Prussians shutting up the trap on the other, than he proclaimed: "I shall be pitiless! The expiation will be complete, and justice will be stern!" If the acts of the Paris working men were vandalism, it was the vandalism of defence in despair, not the vandalism of triumph, like that which the Christians perpetrated upon the really priceless art treasures of heathen antiquity; and even that vandalism has been justified by the historian as an unavoidable and comparatively trifling concomitant to the titanic struggle between a new society arising and an old one breaking down. It was still less the vandalism of Haussmann, razing historic Paris to make place for the Paris of the sightseer!

But the execution by the Commune of the sixty-four hostages, with the Archbishop of Paris at their head! The bourgeoisie and its army in June, 1848, re-established a custom which had long disappeared from the practice of war—the shooting of their defenceless prisoners. This brutal custom has since been more or less strictly adhered to by the suppressors of all popular commotions in Europe and India; thus proving that it constitutes a real "progress of civilisation!" On the other hand, the Prussians, in France, had re-established the practice of taking hostages—innocent men, who, with their lives, were to answer to them for the acts of others. When Thiers, as we have seen, from the very beginning of the conflict, enforced the humane practice of shooting down the Communal prisoners, the Commune, to protect their lives, was obliged to resort to the Prussian practice of securing hostages. The lives of the hostages had been forfeited over and over again by the continued shooting of prisoners on the part of the Versaillese. How could they be spared any longer after the carnage with which MacMahon's praetorians celebrated their entrance into Paris? Was even the last check upon the unscrupulous ferocity of bourgeois governments—the taking of hostages—to be made a mere sham of? The real murderer of Archbishop Darboy is Thiers. The Commune again and again had offered to exchange the archbishop, and ever so many priests in the bargain, against the single Blanqui, then in the hands of Thiers. Thiers obstinately refused. He knew that with Blanqui he would give to the Commune a head; while the archbishop would serve his purpose best in the shape of a corpse. Thiers acted upon the precedent of Cavaignac. How, in June, 1848, did not Cavaignac and his men of order raise shouts of horror by stigmatising the insurgents as the assassins of Archbishop Affre! They knew perfectly well that the archbishop had been shot by the soldiers of order. M. Jacquemet, the archbishop's vicar-general, present on the spot, had immediately afterwards handed them in his evidence to that effect.

All this chorus of calumny, which the Party of Order never fail, in their orgies of blood, to raise against their victims, only proves that the bourgeois of our days considers himself the legitimate successor to the baron of old, who thought every weapon in his own hand fair against the plebeian, while in the hands of the plebeian a weapon of any kind constituted in itself a crime.

The conspiracy of the ruling class to break down the Revolution by a civil war carried on under the patronage of the foreign invader —a conspiracy which we have traced from the very 4th of September down to the entrance of MacMahon's praetorians through the gate of St. Cloud—culminated in the carnage of Paris. Bismarck gloats over the ruins of Paris, in which he saw perhaps the first instalment of that general destruction of great cities he had prayed for when still a simple Rural in the Prussian *Chambre introuvable* of 1849. He gloats over the cadavers of the Paris proletariat. For him this is not only the extermination of revolution, but the extinction of France, now decapitated in reality, and by the French Government itself. With the shallowness characteristic of all successful statesmen, he sees but the surface of this tremendous historic event. Whenever before has history exhibited the spectacle of a conqueror crowning his victory by turning into, not only the gendarme, but the hired bravo of the conquered Government? There existed no war between Prussia and the Commune of Paris. On the contrary, the Commune had accepted the peace preliminaries, and Prussia had announced her neutrality. Prussia was, therefore, no belligerent. She acted the part of a bravo, a cowardly bravo, because incurring no danger; a hired bravo, because stipulating beforehand the payment of her blood-money of 500 millions on the fall of Paris. And thus, at last, came out the true character of the war, ordained by Providence as a chastisement of godless and debauched France by pious and moral Germany! And this unparalled breach of the law of nations, even as understood by the old-world lawyers, instead of arousing the "civilised" Governments of Europe to declare the felonious Prussian Government, the mere tool of the St. Petersburg Cabinet, an outlaw amongst nations, only incites them to consider whether the few victims who escape the double cordon around Paris are not to be given up to the hangman at Versailles!

That after the most tremendous war of modern times, the conquering and the conquered hosts should fraternise for the common massacre of the proletariat—this unparalleled event does indicate, not, as Bismarck thinks, the final repression of a new society upheaving, but the crumbling into dust of bourgeois society. The highest heroic effort of which old society is still capable is national war; and this is now proved to be a mere governmental humbug, intended to defer the struggle of classes, and to be thrown aside as soon as that class struggle bursts out into civil war. Class rule is no longer able to disguise itself in a national uniform; the national Governments are one as against the proletariat!

After Whit-Sunday, 1871, there can be neither peace nor truce possible between the working men of France and the appropriators of their produce. The iron hand of a mercenary soldiery may keep for a time both classes tied down in common oppression. But the battle must break out again and again in ever-growing dimensions, and there can be no doubt as to who will be the victor in the end, —the appropriating few, or the immense working majority. And the French working class is only the advanced guard of the modern proletariat.

While the European governments thus testify, before Paris, to the international character of class-rule, they cry down the International Working Men's Association—the international counter-organisation of labour against the cosmopolitan conspiracy of capital —as the head fountain of all these disasters. Thiers denounced it as the despot of labour, pretending to be its liberator. Picard ordered those abroad should be cut off; Count Jaubert, Thiers' mummified accomplice of 1835, declares it the great problem of all civilised that all communications between the French Internationals and governments to weed it out. The Rurals roar against it, and the whole European press joins the chorus. An honourable French writer, completely foreign to our Association, speaks as follows:— "The members of the Central Committee of the National Guard, as well as the greater part of the members of the Commune, are the most active, intelligent, and energetic minds of the International Working Men's Association; . . . men who are thoroughly honest, sincere, intelligent, devoted, pure, and fanatical in the *good* sense of the word." The police-tinged bourgeois mind naturally figures to itself the International Working Men's Association as acting in the manner of a secret conspiracy, its central body ordering, from time to time, explosions in different countries. Our Association is, in fact, nothing but the international bond between the most advanced working men in the various countries of the civilised world. Whenever, in whatever shape, and under whatever conditions the class struggle obtains any consistency, it is but natural that members of our Association should stand in the foreground. The soil out of which it grows is modern society itself. It cannot be stamped out by any amount of carnage. To stamp it out, the Governments would have to stamp out the despotism of capital over labour—the condition of their own parasitical existence.

Working men's Paris, with its Commune, will be for ever celebrated as the glorious harbinger of a new society. Its martyrs are enshrined in the great heart of the working class. Its exterminators history has already nailed to that eternal pillory from which all the prayers of their priests will not avail to redeem them.

On Imperialism in India

KARL MARX

Marx's way of analyzing the problems of an Asian society under European imperial rule is reflected in these two articles which he wrote in English for *The New York Daily Tribune* and which were printed in its issues of June 25 and August 8, 1853. Of special interest in the analysis is the conception he entertained of Oriental despotism as an antique form of class society with a ruling bureaucracy based on large-scale irrigation works. We may note, too, his assumption that it was the fate of non-Western societies like that of India to go the way of bourgeois development as seen in modern Europe.

The British Rule in India

London, Friday, June 10, 1853

Hindostan is an Italy of Asiatic dimensions, the Himalayas for the Alps, the Plains of Bengal for the Plains of Lombardy, the Deccan for the Appenines, and the Isle of Ceylon for the Island of Sicily. The same rich variety in the products of the soil, and the same dismemberment in the political configuration. Just as Italy has, from time to time, been compressed by the conqueror's sword into different national masses, so do we find Hindostan, when not under the pressure of the Mohammedan, or the Mogul, or the Briton, dissolved into as many independent and conflicting States as it numbered towns, or even villages. Yet, in a social point of view, Hindostan is not the Italy, but the Ireland of the East. And this strange combination of Italy and of Ireland, of a world of voluptuousness and of a world of woes, is anticipated in the ancient traditions of the religion of Hindostan. That religion is at once a religion of sensualist exuberance, and a religion of self-torturing asceticism; a religion of the Lingam and of the Juggernaut; the religion of the Monk, and of the Bayadere.

I share not the opinion of those who believe in a golden age of Hindostan, without recurring, however, like Sir Charles Wood, for the confirmation of my view, to the authority of Khuli-Khan. But take, for example, the times of Aurung-Zebe; or the epoch, when the Mogul appeared in the North, and the Portuguese in the South; or the age of Mohammedan invasion, and of the Heptarchy[1] in Southern India; or, if you will, go still more back to antiquity, take the mythological chronology of the Brahmin himself, who places the commencement of Indian misery in an epoch even more remote than the Christian creation of the world.

There cannot, however, remain any doubt but that the misery inflicted by the British on Hindostan is of an essentially different and infinitely more intensive kind than all Hindostan had to suffer before. I do not allude to European despotism, planted upon Asiatic despotism, by the British East India Company,[2] forming a more monstrous combination than any of the divine monsters startling us in the temple of Salsette.[3] This is no distinctive feature of British colonial rule, but only an imitation of the Dutch, and so much so that in order to characterise the working of the British East India Company, it is sufficient to literally repeat what Sir Stamford Raffles, the *English* Governor of Java, said of the old Dutch East India Company:

"The Dutch Company, actuated solely by the spirit of gain, and viewing their subjects with less regard or consideration than a West India planter formerly viewed a gang upon his estate, because the latter had paid the purchase money of human property, which the other had not, employed all the existing machinery of despotism to squeeze from the people their utmost mite of contribution, the last dregs of their labour, and thus aggravated the evils of a capricious and semi-barbarous Government, by working it with all the practised ingenuity of politicians, and all the monopolising selfishness of traders."

All the civil wars, invasions, revolutions, conquests, famines, strangely complex, rapid and destructive as the successive action in Hindostan may appear, did not go deeper than its surface. England has broken down the entire framework of Indian society, without

1. The conventional designation in English history of the seven Saxon Kingdoms (sixth to eighth century). Marx by analogy uses this term here to denote the feudal dismemberment of the Deccan before its conquest by the Moslems.
2. The British East India Company was organised in 1600 for the purpose of carrying on a monopoly trade with India. Under cover of the Company's "trading" operations the English capitalists conquered the country and governed it for decades. During the Indian uprising of 1857–1859 the Company was dissolved and the British Government began to rule India directly.
3. A cave temple situated on the island of that name near the city of Bombay. It contains a huge number of stone carvings.

any symptoms of reconstitution yet appearing. This loss of his old world, with no gain of a new one, imparts a particular kind of melancholy to the present misery of the Hindoo, and separates Hindostan, ruled by Britain, from all its ancient traditions, and from the whole of its past history.

There have been in Asia, generally, from immemorial times, but three departments of Government: that of Finance, or the plunder of the interior; that of War, or the plunder of the exterior; and, finally, the department of Public Works. Climate and territorial conditions, especially the vast tracts of desert, extending from the Sahara, through Arabia, Persia, India and Tartary, to the most elevated Asiatic highlands, constituted artificial irrigation by canals and waterworks the basis of Oriental agriculture. As in Egypt and India, inundations are used for fertilising the soil of Mesopotamia, Persia, etc.; advantage is taken of a high level for feeding irrigative canals. This prime necessity of an economical and common use of water, which, in the Occident, drove private enterprise to voluntary association, as in Flanders and Italy, necessitated, in the Orient where civilisation was too low and the territorial extent too vast to call into life voluntary association, the interference of the centralising power of Government. Hence an economical function devolved upon all Asiatic Governments the function of providing public works. This artificial fertilisation of the soil, dependent on a Central Government, and immediately decaying with the neglect of irrigation and drainage, explains the otherwise strange fact that we now find whole territories barren and desert that were once brilliantly cultivated, as Palmyra, Petra, the ruins in Yemen, and large provinces of Egypt, Persia and Hindostan; it also explains how a single war of devastation has been able to depopulate a country for centuries, and to strip it of all its civilisation.

Now, the British in East India accepted from their predecessors the department of finance and of war, but they have neglected entirely that of public works. Hence the deterioration of an agriculture which is not capable of being conducted on the British principle of free competition, of *laissez-faire* and *laissez-aller*. But in Asiatic empires we are quite accustomed to see agriculture deteriorating under one government and reviving again under some other government. There the harvests correspond to good or bad government, as they change in Europe with good or bad seasons. Thus the oppression and neglect of agriculture, bad as it is, could not be looked upon as the final blow dealt to Indian society by the British intruder, had it not been attended by a circumstance of quite different importance, a novelty in the annals of the whole Asiatic world. However changing the political aspect of India's past must appear, its social condition has remained unaltered since its remotest antiquity, until the first decennium of the 19th century. The hand-loom and the spinning-wheel, producing their regular myriads of spinners and weavers, were the pivots of the structure of that society. From immemorial times, Europe received the admirable textures of Indian labour, sending in return for them her precious metals, and furnishing thereby his material to the goldsmith, that indispensable member of Indian society, whose love of finery is so great that even the lowest class, those who go about nearly naked, have commonly a pair of golden ear-rings and a gold ornament of some kind hung round their necks. Rings on the fingers and toes have also been common. Women as well as children frequently wore massive bracelets and anklets of gold or silver, and statuettes of divinities in gold and silver were met with in the households. It was the British intruder who broke up the Indian hand-loom and destroyed the spinning wheel. England began with driving the Indian cottons from the European market; it then introduced twist into Hindostan and in the end inundated the very mother country of cotton with cottons. From 1818 to 1836 the export of twist from Great Britain to India rose in the proportion of 1 to 5,200. In 1824 the export of British muslins to India hardly amounted to 1,000,000 yards while in 1837 it surpassed 64,000,000 yards. But at the same time the population of Dacca decreased from 150,000 inhabitants to 20,000. This decline of Indian towns celebrated for their fabrics was by no means the worst consequence. British steam and science uprooted, over the whole surface of Hindostan, the union between agricultural and manufacturing industry.

These two circumstances—the Hindoo, on the one hand, leaving, like all Oriental peoples, to the central government the care of the great public works, the prime condition of his agriculture and commerce, dispersed, on the other hand over the surface of the country, and agglomerated in small centres by the domestic union of agricultural and manufacturing pursuits—these two circumstances had brought about, since the remotest times, a social system of particular features—the so-called *village system*, which gave to each of these small unions their independent organisation and distinct life. The peculiar character of this system may be judged from the following description, contained in an old official report of the British House of Commons on Indian affairs:

"A village, geographically considered, is a tract of country comprising some hundred or thousand acres of arable and waste lands; politically viewed it resembles a corporation or township. Its proper establishment of officers and servants consists of the following descriptions: the *potail*, or head inhabitant, who has generally the superintendence of the affairs of the village, settles the disputes of the inhabitants, attends to the police, and performs the duty of collecting the revenue within his village, a duty which his personal influence and minute acquaintance with the situation and concerns of the people render him the best qualified for this charge. The *kurnum* keeps the accounts of cultivation, and registers everything connected with it. The *Tallier* and the *totie*, the duty of the former of which consists in gaining information of crimes and offences, and in escorting and protecting persons travelling from one village to another; the province of the latter appearing to be more immediately confined to the village, consisting, among other duties, in guarding the crops and assisting in measuring them. The *boundary man*, who preserves the limits of the village, or gives evidence respecting them in cases of dispute. The Superintendent of Tanks and Watercourses distributes the water for the purposes of agriculture. The Brahmin, who performs the village worship. The school-master, who is seen teaching the children in a village to read and write in the sand. The calendar-Brahmin, or astrologer, etc. These officers and servants generally constitute the establishment of a village; but in some parts of the country it is of less extent; some of the duties and functions above described being united in the same person; in others it exceeds the above-named number of individuals. Under this simple form of municipal government, the inhabitants of the country have lived from time immemorial. The boundaries of the villages have been but seldom altered; and though the villages themselves have been sometimes injured, and even desolated by war, famine or disease, the same name, the same limits, the same interests, and even the same families, have continued for ages. The inhabitants gave themselves no trouble about the breaking up and divisions of kingdoms; while the village remains entire, they care not to what power it is transferred, or to what sovereign it devolves; its internal economy remains unchanged. The *potail* is still the head inhabitant, and still acts as the petty judge or magistrate, and collector or rentor of the village."

These small stereotype forms of social organism have been to the greater part dissolved, and are disappearing, not so much through the brutal interference of the British tax-gatherer and the British soldier, as to the working of English steam and English free trade. Those family-communities were based on domestic industry, in that peculiar combination of hand-weaving, hand-spinning and hand-tilling agriculture which gave them self-supporting power. English interference having placed the spinner in Lancashire and the weaver in Bengal, or sweeping away both Hindoo spinner and weaver, dissolved these small semi-barbarian, semi-civilised communities, by blowing up their economical basis, and thus produced the greatest, and, to speak the truth, the only *social* revolution ever heard of in Asia.

Now, sickening as it must be to human feeling to witness those myriads of industrious patriarchal and inoffensive social organisations disorganised and dissolved into their units, thrown into a sea of woes, and their individual members losing at the same time their ancient form of civilisation, and their hereditary means of subsistence, we must not forget that these idyllic village communities, inoffensive though they may appear, had always been the solid foundation of Oriental despotism, that they restrained the human mind within the smallest possible compass, making it the unresisting tool of superstition, enslaving it beneath traditional rules, depriving it of all grandeur and historical energies. We must not forget the barbarian egotism which, concentrating on some miserable patch of land, had quietly witnessed the ruin of empires, the perpetration of unspeakable cruelties, the massacre of the population of large towns, with no other consideration bestowed upon them than on natural events, itself the helpless prey of any aggressor who deigned to notice it at all. We must not forget that this undignified, stagnatory, and vegetative life, that this passive sort of existence evoked on the other part, in contradistinction, wild, aimless, unbounded forces of destruction and rendered murder itself a religious rite in Hindostan. We must not forget that these little communities were contaminated by distinctions of caste and by slavery, that they subjugated man to external circumstances instead of elevating man to be the sovereign of circumstances, that they transformed a self-developing social state into never changing natural destiny, and thus brought about a brutalising worship of nature, exhibiting its degradation in the fact that man, the sovereign of nature, fell down on his knees in adoration of *Hanuman*, the monkey, and *Sabbala*, the cow.

England, it is true, in causing a social revolution in Hindostan, was actuated only by the vilest interests, and was stupid in her manner of enforcing them. But that is not the question. The question is, can mankind fulfill its destiny without a fundamental revolution in the social state of Asia? If not, whatever may have been the crimes of England she was the unconscious tool of history in bringing about that revolution.

Then, whatever bitterness the spectacle of the crumbling of an ancient world may have for our personal feelings, we have the right, in point of history, to exclaim with Goethe:

> "Sollte diese Qual uns quälen,
> Da sie unsre Lust vermehrt,
> Hat nicht Myriaden Seelen
> Timur's Heerschaft aufgezehrt?"[4]

4. Should this torture then torment us
Since it brings us greater pleasure?
Were not through the rule of Timur
Souls devoured without measure?
(Goethe, *Westöstlicher Diwan.
An Suleika*)

The Future Results of British Rule in India

London, Friday, July 22, 1853

How came it that English supremacy was established in India? The paramount power of the Great Mogul was broken by the Mogul Viceroys. The power of the Viceroys was broken by the Mahrattas.[5] The power of the Mahrattas was broken by the Afghans, and while all were struggling against all, the Briton rushed in and was enabled to subdue them all. A country not only divided between Mohammedan and Hindoo, but between tribe and tribe, between caste and caste; a society whose framework was based on a sort of equilibrium, resulting from a general repulsion and constitutional exclusiveness between all its members. Such a country and such a society, where they not the predestined prey of conquest? If we knew nothing of the past history of Hindostan, would there not be the one great and incontestable fact, that even at this moment India is held in English thraldom by an Indian army maintained at the cost of India? India, then, could not escape the fate of being conquered, and the whole of her past history, if it be anything, is the history of the successive conquests she has undergone. Indian society has no history at all, at least no known history. What we call its history, is but the history of the successive intruders who founded their empires on the passive basis of that unresisting and unchanging society. The question, therefore, is not whether the English had a right to conquer India, but whether we are to prefer India conquered by the Turk, by the Persian, by the Russian, to India conquered by the Briton.

England has to fulfil a double mission in India: one destructive, the other regenerating—the annihilation of old Asiatic society, and the laying of the material foundations of Western society in Asia.

Arabs, Turks, Tartars, Moguls, who had successively overrun India, soon became *Hindooised*, the barbarian conquerors being, by an eternal law of history, conquered themselves by the superior civilisation of their subjects. The British were the first conquerors superior, and therefore, inaccessible to Hindoo civilisation. They destroyed it by breaking up the native communities, by uprooting the native industry, and by levelling all that was great and elevated in the native society. The historic pages of their rule in India report hardly anything beyond that destruction. The work of regeneration

5. A group of people in Central India who rose against the Mohammedans and in the beginning of the eighteenth century formed a confederation of feudal princedoms.

hardly transpires through a heap of ruins. Nevertheless it has begun.

The political unity of India, more consolidated, and extending farther than it ever did under the Great Moguls, was the first condition of its regeneration. That unity, imposed by the British sword, will now be strengthened and perpetuated by the electric telegraph. The native army, organised and trained by the British drill-sergeant, was the *sine qua non* of Indian self-emancipation, and of India ceasing to be the prey of the first foreign intruder. The free press, introduced for the first time into Asiatic society, and managed principally by the common offspring of Hindoo and Europeans, is a new and powerful agent of reconstruction. The *Zemindars* and *Ryotwar*[6] themselves, abominable as they are, involve two distinct forms of private property in land—the great *desideratum* of Asiatic society. From the Indian natives, reluctantly and sparingly educated at Calcutta, under English superintendence, a fresh class is springing up, endowed with the requirements for government and imbued with European science. Steam has brought India into regular and rapid communication with Europe, has connected its chief ports with those of the whole south-eastern ocean, and has revindicated it from the isolated position which was the prime law of its stagnation. The day is not far distant when, by a combination of railways and steam vessels, the distance between England and India, measured by time, will be shortened to eight days, and when that once fabulous country will thus be actually annexed to the Western world.

The ruling classes of Great Britain have had, till now, but an accidental, transitory and exceptional interest in the progress of India. The aristocracy wanted to conquer it, the moneyocracy to plunder it, and the millocracy to undersell it. But now the tables are turned. The millocracy have discovered that the transformation of India into a reproductive country has become of vital importance to them, and that, to that end, it is necessary, above all, to gift her with means of irrigation and of internal communication. They intend now drawing a net of railways over India. And they will do it. The results must be inappreciable.

It is notorious that the productive powers of India are paralysed by the utter want of means for conveying and exchanging its various produce. Nowhere, more than in India, do we meet with social destitution in the midst of natural plenty, for want of the means of exchange. It was proved before a Committee of the British House

1. *Zemindars*: New big landowners who were established by the British from among former tax collectors and merchant-usurers through the expropriation of the Indian peasantry. The zemindar system was widespread in Northeast India. *Ryotwar:* A system of renting land to peasants for an unlimited period of time. Introduced by the British in the South of India, it permitted them to let land to peasants on extremely onerous terms.

of Commons, which sat in 1848, that "when grain was selling from 6s. to 8s. a quarter at Kandeish, it was sold at 64s. to 70s. at Poonah, where the people were dying in the streets of famine, without the possibility of gaining supplics from Kandeish, because the clay-roads were impracticable."

The introduction of railways may be easily made to subserve agricultural purposes by the formation of tanks, where ground is required for embankment, and by the conveyance of water along the different lines. Thus irrigation, the *sine qua non* of farming in the East, might be greatly extended, and the frequently recurring local famines, arising from the want of water, would be averted. The general importance of railways, viewed under this head, must become evident, when we remember that irrigated lands, even in the district near Ghauts, pay three times as much in taxes, afford ten or twelve times as much employment, and yield twelve or fifteen times as much profit, as the same area without irrigation.

Railways will afford the means of diminishing the amount and the cost of the military establishments. Col. Warren, Town Major of the Fort St. William, stated before a Select Committee of the House of Commons:

"The practicability of receiving intelligence from distant parts of the country in as many hours as at present it requires days and even weeks, and of sending instructions with troops and stores, in the more brief period, are considerations which cannot be too highly estimated. Troops could be kept at more distant and healthier stations than at present, and much loss of life from sickness would by this means be spared. Stores could not to the same extent be required at the various dépôts, and the loss by decay, and the destruction incidental to the climate, would also be avoided. The number of troops might be diminished in direct proportion to their effectiveness."

We know that the municipal organisation and the economical basis of the village communities has been broken up, but their worst feature, the dissolution of society into stereotyped and disconnected atoms, has survived their vitality. The village isolation produced the absence of roads in India, and the absence of roads perpetuated the village isolation. On this plan a community existed with a given scale of low conveniences, almost without intercourse with other villages, without the desires and efforts indispensable to social advance. The British having broken up this self-sufficient *inertia* of the villlages, railways will provide the new want of communication and intercourse. Besides, "one of the effects of the railway system will be to bring into every village affected by it such knowledge of the contrivances and appliances of other countries, and such means of obtaining them, as will first put the hereditary and stipendiary village artisanship of India to full proof of its capabilities, and then supply its defects." (Chapman, *The Cotton and Commerce of India*.)

I know that the English millocracy intend to endow India with railways with the exclusive view of extracting at diminished expenses the cotton and other raw materials for their manufactures. But when you have once introduced machinery into the locomotion of a country, which possesses iron and coals, you are unable to withhold it from its fabrication. You cannot maintain a net of railways over an immense country without introducing all those industrial processes necessary to meet the immediate and current wants of railway locomotion, and out of which there must grow the application of machinery to those branches of industry not immediately connected with railways. The railway-system will therefore become, in India, truly the forerunner of modern industry. This is the more certain as the Hindoos are allowed by British authorities themselves to possess particular aptitude for accommodating themselves to entirely new labour, and acquiring the requisite knowledge of machinery. Ample proof of this fact is afforded by the capacities and expertness of the native engineers in the Calcutta mint, where they have been for years employed in working the steam machinery, by the natives attached to the several steam engines in the Hurdwar coal districts and by other instances. Mr. Campbell himself, greatly influenced as he is by the prejudices of the East India Company, is obliged to avow "that the great mass of the Indian people possesses a great *industrial energy*, is well fitted to accumulate capital, and remarkable for a mathematical clearness of head, and talent for figures and exact sciences." "Their intellects," he says, "are excellent." Modern industry, resulting from the railway-system, will dissolve the hereditary divisions of labour, upon which rest the Indian castes, those decisive impediments to Indian progress and Indian power.

All the English bourgeoisie may be forced to do will neither emancipate nor materially mend the social condition of the mass of the people, depending not only on the development of the productive powers, but on their appropriation by the people. But what they will not fail to do is to lay down the material premises for both. Has the bourgeoisie ever done more? Has it ever affected a progress without dragging individuals and peoples through blood and dirt, through misery and degradation?

The Indians will not reap the fruits of the new elements of society scattered among them by the British bourgeoisie, till in Great Britain itself the now ruling classes shall have been supplanted by the industrial proletariat, or till the Hindoos themselves shall have grown strong enough to throw off the English yoke altogether. At all events, we may safely expect to see, at a more or less remote period, the regeneration of that great and interesting country, whose gentle natives are, to use the expression of Prince Solty-kov, even in the most inferior classes, *"plus fins et plus adroits que les Italiens,"*[7] whose submission even is counterbalanced by a certain calm nobility, who, notwithstanding their natural languor, have astonished the British officers by their bravery, whose country has been the source of our languages, our religions, and who represent the type of the ancient German in the *Jat* and the type of the ancient Greek in the Brahmin.[8]

I cannot part with the subject of India without some concluding remarks.

The profound hypocrisy and inherent barbarism of bourgeois civilisation lies unveiled before our eyes, turning from its home, where it assumes respectable forms, to the colonies, where it goes naked. They are the defenders of property, but did any revolutionary party ever originate agrarian revolutions like those in Bengal, in Madras, and in Bombay? Did they not, in India, to borrow an expression of that great robber, Lord Clive himself, resort to atrocious extortion, when simple corruption could not keep pace with their rapacity? While they prated in Europe about the inviolable sanctity of the national debt, did they not confiscate in India the dividends of the *rajahs*, who had invested their private savings in the Company's own funds? While they combatted the French revolution under the pretext of defending "our holy religion," did they not forbid, at the same time, Christianity to be propagated in India, and did they not, in order to make money out of the pilgrims streaming to the temples of Orissa and Bengal, take up the trade in the murder and prostitution perpetrated in the temple of Juggernaut? These are the men of "Property, Order, Family, and Religion."

The devastating effects of English industry, when contemplated with regard to India, a country as vast as Europe, and containing 150 millions of acres, are palpable and confounding. But we must not forget that they are only the organic results of the whole system of production as it is now constituted. That production rests on the supreme rule of capital. The centralisation of capital is essential to the existence of capital as an independent power. The destructive influence of that centralisation upon the markets of the world does but reveal, in the most gigantic dimensions, the inherent organic laws of political economy now at work in every civilised town. The bourgeois period of history has to create the material basis of the new world—on the one hand the universal intercourse founded upon the mutual dependency of mankind, and the means of that intercourse; on the other hand the development of the productive powers of man and the transformation of material production into a

7. Marx quotes from A. D. Soltykov's book *Lettres sur l'Inde,* Paris, 1848.
8. *Jat*: A member of an agricultural caste in Northwest India. *Brahmin*: A member of the highest Hindu caste.

scientific domination of natural agencies. Bourgeois industry and commerce create these material conditions of a new world in the same way as geological revolutions have created the surface of the earth. When a great social revolution shall have mastered the results of the bourgeois epoch, the market of the world and the modern powers of production, and subjected them to the common control of the most advanced peoples, then only will human progress cease to resemble that hideous pagan idol, who would not drink the nectar but from the skulls of the slain.

On Social Relations in Russia

FRIEDRICH ENGELS

Russian radicals in the second half of the nineteenth century showed an increasingly intense interest in Marxism, and Marx noted in a letter of 1880 that in Russia "*Capital* is more read and appreciated than anywhere else." Until the 1890's, however, the Russian socialist movement was largely Populist (*narodnik*), believing that in pre-bourgeois Russia there could be an early socialist revolution based on peasant rather than proletarian masses and using the archaic village commune as the nucleus of a future Russian socialist society. Leading Russian Populists occasionally wrote to Marx and Engels, either to elicit their views on the Russian situation or to defend their own views. One of them, Pyotr Tkachov, wrote an "Open Letter" to Engels in 1874, and Engels' reply, "On Social Relations in Russia," is the fullest statement of his own and Marx's appraisal of Russian society in the late nineteenth century and the prospects for revolution there. Following the essay is a statement on the same subject from Marx's letter of March 8, 1881, to a Russian radical, Vera Zasulich.

On the subject matter proper, Mr. Tkachov tells the German workers that as regards Russia I possess not even a "little knowledge," possess nothing but "ignorance"; and he feels himself, therefore, obliged to explain to them the real state of affairs, and in particular the reasons why just at the present time a social revolution could be made in Russia with the greatest of ease, much more easily than in Western Europe.

"We have no urban proletariat, that is undoubtedly true; but, then, we also have no bourgeoisie; . . . our workers will have to fight only against the *political power*—the *power of capital* is with us still only in embryo. And you, sir, are undoubtedly aware that the fight against the former is much easier than against the latter."

The revolution which modern socialism strives to achieve is, briefly, the victory of the proletariat over the bourgeoisie, and the establishment of a new organisation of society by the destruction of all class distinctions. This requires not only a proletariat that carries out this revolution, but also a bourgeoisie in whose hands the productive forces of society have developed so far that they allow of the final destruction of class distinctions. Among savages and semi-savages there likewise often exist no class distinctions, and every people has passed through such a state. It could not occur to us to re-establish this state, for the simple reason that class distinctions necessarily emerge out of it as the productive forces of society develop. Only at a certain level of development of the productive forces of society, an even very high level for our modern conditions, does it become possible to raise production to such an extent that the abolition of class distinctions can be a real progress, can be lasting without bringing about stagnation or even decline in the mode of social production. But the productive forces have reached this level of development only in the hands of the bourgeoisie. The bourgeoisie, therefore, in this respect also is just as necessary a precondition of the socialist revolution as the proletariat itself. Hence a man who will say that this revolution can be more easily carried out in a country, because, *although* it has no proletariat, it has no bourgeoisie *either*, only proves that he has still to learn the ABC of socialism.

The Russian workers—and these workers are, as Mr. Tkachov himself says, "tillers of the soil and as such not proletarians but *owners*—have, therefore, an easier task because they do not have to fight against the power of capital, but "only against the political power," against the Russian state. And this state "appears only at a distance as a power; . . . it has no roots in the economic life of the people; it does not embody the interests of any particular estate. . . . In your country the state is no imaginary power. It stands four square on the basis of capital; it embodies in itself [!!] certain economic interests. . . . In our country the situation is just the reverse —the form of our society owes its existence to the state, to a state hanging in the air, so to speak, one that has nothing in common with the existing social order, and that has its roots in the past, but not in the present."

Let us waste no time over the confused notion that the economic interests need the state, which they themselves create, in order to acquire a *body*, or over the bold contention that the Russian "form of society (which, of course, must include also the communal property of the peasants) owes its existence to the state," or over the contradiction that this same state "has nothing in common" with the existing social order which is supposed to be its very own creation. Let us rather examine at once this "state hanging in the air," which does not represent the interests of even a single estate.

In European Russia the peasants possess 105 million dessiatins, the nobility (as I shall here term the big landowners for the sake of brevity) 100 million dessiatins of land, of which about half belong to 15,000 nobles, who consequently each possess on the average 3,-300 dessiatins. The land of the peasants is, therefore, only a trifle bigger than that of the nobles. So you see, the nobles have not the slightest interest in the existence of the Russian state, which protects them in the possession of half the country! To continue. The peasants, from their half, pay 195 million rubles land tax annually, the nobles—13 million! The lands of the nobles are on the average twice as fertile as those of the peasants, because during the settlement for the redemption of the *corvée* the state not only took the greater part but also the best part of the land from the peasants and gave it to the nobles, and for this worst land the peasants had to pay the nobility the price of the best. And the Russian nobility has no interest in the existence of the Russian state!

The peasants—taken in the mass—have been put by the redemption into a most miserable and wholly untenable position. Not only has the greatest and best part of their land been taken from them, so that in all the fertile parts of the country the peasant land is far too small—under Russian agricultural conditions—for them to be able to make a living from it. Not only were they charged an excessive price for it, advanced to them by the state and for which they now have to pay interest and instalments on the principal to the state. Not only is almost the whole burden of the land tax thrown upon them, while the nobility escapes almost scot-free—so that the land tax alone consumes the entire ground rent value of the peasant land and more, and all further payments which the peasant has to make and which we will speak of immediately are direct deductions from that part of his income which represents his wages. Then, in addition to the land tax, to the interest and amortisation payments on the money advanced by the state, since the recent introduction of local administration, there are the provincial and district imposts as well. The most essential consequence of this "reform" was fresh tax burdens for the peasant. The state retained its revenues in their entirety, but passed on a large part of its expenditure to the provinces and districts, which imposed new taxes to meet them, and in Russia it is the rule that the higher estates are almost tax exempt and the peasant pays almost everything.

Such a situation is as if specially created for the usurer, and with the almost unequalled talent of the Russians for trading on a lower level, for taking full advantage of favourable business situations and the swindling inseparable from this—Peter I long ago said that one Russian could get the better of three Jews—the usurer everywhere makes his appearance. When taxes are about to fall due, the usurer, the kulak—frequently a rich peasant of the same village community —comes along and offers his ready cash. The peasant must have the money at all costs and is obliged to accept the conditions of the usurer without demur. But this only gets him into a tighter fix, and he needs more and more ready cash. At harvest time the grain dealer arrives; the need for money forces the peasant to sell a part of the grain which he and his family require for their subsistence. The grain dealer spreads false rumours which lower prices, pays a low price and often even part of this in all sorts of high-priced goods; for the truck system is also highly developed in Russia. It is quite obvious that the great corn exports of Russia are based directly on the starvation of the peasant population. Another method of exploiting the peasant is the following: a speculator rents domain land from the government for a long term of years, and cultivates it himself as long as it yields a good crop without manure; then he divides it up into small plots and lets out the exhausted land at high rents to neighbouring peasants who cannot manage on the income from their allotment. Here we have exactly the Irish middlemen, just as above the English truck system. In short, there is no country in which, in spite of the pristine savagery of bourgeois society, capitalistic parasitism is so developed, so covers and entangles the whole country, the whole mass of the population, with its nets as in Russia. And all these bloodsuckers of the peasants are supposed to have no interest in the existence of the Russian state, whose laws and law courts protect their sleek and profitable practices!

The big bourgeoisie of Petersburg, Moscow, Odessa, which has developed with unheard-of rapidity during the last decade, chiefly due to the railways, and which cheerfully "went smash" along with the rest during the last swindle years, the grain, hemp, flax and tallow exporters, whose whole business is built up on the misery of the peasant, the entire Russian large-scale industry, which only exists thanks to the protective tariffs granted it by the state—have all these important and rapidly growing elements of the population no interest in the existence of the Russian state? To say nothing of the countless army of officials, which swarms over Russia and plunders it and here constitutes a real social estate. And when Mr. Tkachov assures us that the Russian state has "no roots in the economic life of the people," that "it does not embody the interests of any particular estate," that it "hangs in the air," methinks it is not the Russian state that hangs in the air, but rather Mr. Tkachov.

It is clear that the condition of the Russian peasants since the emancipation from serfdom has become intolerable and cannot be maintained much longer, and that for this reason alone if for no other a revolution is in the offing in Russia. The question is only: what can be, what will be the result of this revolution? Mr. Tkachov says it will be a social one. This is pure tautology. Every real revolution is a social one, in that it brings a new class to power and allows it to remodel society in its own image. But he wants to say it will be a socialist one, it will introduce into Russia the form of society aimed at by West European socialism, even before we in the West succeed in doing so—and that in a condition of society in which both proletariat and bourgeoisie appear only sporadically and at a low stage of development. And this is supposed to be possible because the Russians are, so to speak, the chosen people of socialism, and have artels and common ownership of land.

The artel, which Mr. Tkachov mentions only incidentally, but which we include here because since the time of Herzen it has played a mysterious role with many Russians—the artel in Russia is a widespread form of association, the simplest form of free co-operation, such as is to be found for hunting among hunting tribes. Word and content are not of Slavic but of Tatar origin. Both are to be found among the Kirghiz, Yakuts, etc., on the one hand, and among the Lapps, Samoyeds and other Finnish peoples, on the other.[1] That is why the artel developed originally in the North and East, by contact with Finns and Tatars, not in the South-West. The severe climate makes necessary industrial activity of various kinds, and so the lack of urban development and of capital is replaced, as far as possible, by this form of co-operation. One of the most characteristic features of the artel, the collective responsibility of its members for one another to third parties, was based originally on blood relationship, like the mutual liability [Gewere] of the ancient Germans, the blood vengeance, etc. Moreover, in Russia the word artel is used for every form of not only collective activity but also collective institution. The *Bourse* is also an artel. In workers' artels, an elder (*starosta, starshina*) is always chosen who fulfils the functions of treasurer, bookkeeper, etc., and of manager as far as necessary and receives a special salary. Such artels are formed:

1. For temporary enterprises, after the completion of which they dissolve;

2. For the members of one and the same trade, for instance, porters, etc.;

3. For permanent enterprises, industrial in the proper sense of the word.

They are established by a contract signed by all the members. Now if these members cannot bring together the necessary capital, as very often happens, for instance, in the case of cheeseries and fisheries (for nets, boats, etc.), the artel falls a prey to the usurer, who advances the amount lacking at high interest, and thereafter pockets

1. On the artel, compare *inter alia: Sbornik materialov ob artelyakh v Rossii* [Collection of Material on Ar- tels in Russia], St. Petersburg 1873, Part 1. [Engels]

the greater part of the income from work. Still more shamefully exploited, however, are the artels which hire themselves in a body to an employer as wage labourers. They direct their industrial activity themselves and thus save the capitalist the cost of supervision. The latter lets to the members huts to live in and advances them the means of subsistence, which in turn gives rise to the most disgraceful truck system. Such is the case with the lumbermen and tar distillers in the Archangel *gubernia*, and in many trades in Siberia, etc. (*Cf.* Flerovsky, *Polozheniye rabochevo klassa v Rossii.* [*The Condition of the Working Class in Russia*], St. Petersburg 1869.) Here then the artel serves to considerably *facilitate* the exploitation of the wage-worker by the capitalist. On the other hand, there are also artels which themselves employ wage-workers, who are *not* members of the association.

It is thus seen that the artel is a co-operative society which has arisen spontaneously and is, therefore, still very undeveloped, and as such neither exclusively Russian nor even Slavic. Such societies are formed wherever the need for them exists. For instance, in Switzerland among the dairy farmers, in England among the fishermen, where they even assume a great variety of forms. The Silesian navvies (Germans, not Poles), who built so many German railways in the forties, were organised in complete artels. The predominance of this form in Russia proves, it is true, the existence in the Russian people of a strong impulse to associate, but is far from proving their ability to jump, with the aid of this impulse, from the artel straight into the socialist order of society. For that, it is necessary above all that the artel itself should be capable of development, that it shed its primitive form, in which, as we saw, it serves the workers less than it does capital, and rise *at least* to the level of the West European co-operative societies. But if we are to believe Mr. Tkachov for once (which, after all that has preceded, is certainly more than risky), this is by no means the case. On the contrary, he assures us with a pride highly indicative of his standpoint: "As regards the co-operative and credit associations on the German [!] model, recently artificially transplanted to Russia, these have met with complete indifference on the part of the majority of our workers and have been a failure almost everywhere." The modern co-operative society has at least proved that it can run large-scale industry profitably on its own account (spinning and weaving in Lancashire). The artel is so far not only incapable of doing this; it must of necessity even be destroyed by big industry if it does not develop further.

The communal property of the Russian peasants was discovered about the year 1845 by the Prussian Government Councillor Haxthausen and trumpeted to the world as something absolutely wonderful, although Haxthausen could still have found survivals enough of it in his Westphalian homeland, and, as a government official, it was even part of his duty to know them thoroughly. It was from Haxthausen that Herzen, himself a Russian landowner, first learned that his peasants owned the land in common, and he made use of the fact to describe the Russian peasants as the true vehicles of socialism, as born Communists in contrast to the workers of the aging, decayed European West, who would first have to go through the ordeal of acquiring socialism artificially. From Herzen this knowledge came to Bakunin, and from Bakunin to Mr. Tkachov. Let us hear the latter:

"Our people . . . in its great majority . . . is permeated with the principles of common ownership; it is, if one may use the term, instinctively, traditionally communist. The idea of collective property is so closely interwoven with the whole world outlook [we shall see immediately how far the world of the Russian peasant extends] of the Russian people that today, when the government begins to understand that this idea is incompatible with the principles of a 'well-ordered' society, and in the name of these principles wishes to impress the idea of individual property on the consciousness and life of the people, it can succeed in doing so only with the help of the bayonet and the knout. It is clear from this that our people, despite its ignorance, is much nearer to socialism than the peoples of Western Europe, although the latter are more educated."

In reality communal ownership of the land is an institution which is to be found among all Indo-Germanic peoples on a low level of development, from India to Ireland, and even among the Malays, who are developing under Indian influence, for instance, in Java. As late as 1608, in the newly conquered North of Ireland, the legally established communal ownership of the land served the English as a pretext for declaring the land as ownerless and as escheated to the Crown. In India a whole series of forms of communal property has been in existence down to the present time. In Germany it was general; the communal lands still to be found here and there are a relic of it; and often still distinct traces of it, temporary divisions of the communal lands, etc., are also to be found, especially in the mountains. More exact references and details with regard to old German communal ownership may be consulted in the various writings of *Maurer*, which are classic on this question. In Western Europe, including Poland and Little Russia, at a certain stage in the social development, this communal ownership became a fetter, a brake on agricultural production, and was more and more eliminated. In Great Russia (that is, Russia proper), on the other hand, it has persisted until today, thereby proving in the first place that here agricultural production and the social condi-

tions in the countryside corresponding to it are still very undeveloped, as is actually the case. The Russian peasant lives and has his
being only in his village community; the rest of the world exists for
him only in so far as it interferes with his village community. This
is so much the case that in Russia the same word, *mir*, means, on
the one hand, "world" and, on the other, "peasant community."
Ves mir, the whole world, means to the peasant the meeting of the
community members. Hence, when Mr. Tkachov speaks of the
"*world outlook*" of the Russian peasants, he has obviously translated the Russian *mir* incorrectly. Such a complete isolation of the
individual communities from one another, which creates throughout
the country similar, but the very opposite of common, interests, is
the natural basis for *Oriental despotism*, and from India to Russia
this form of society, wherever it prevailed, has always produced it,
and always found its complement in it. Not only the Russian state
in general, but even its specific form, tsarist despotism, instead of
hanging in the air, is the necessary and logical product of Russian
social conditions with which, according to Mr. Tkachov, it has
"nothing in common"! Further development of Russia in a *bourgeois* direction would here also destroy communal property little by
little, without any need for the Russian government to intervene
with "bayonet and knout." And this all the more because the
communally owned land in Russia is not cultivated by the peasants
in common so that the product may then be divided, as is still the
case in some districts in India; on the contrary, from time to time
the land is divided up among the various heads of families, and
each cultivates his allotment for himself. Consequently, great differences in degree of prosperity are possible among the members of the
community, and actually exist. Almost everywhere there are a few
rich peasants among them—here and there millionaires—who play
the usurer and suck the blood of the mass of the peasants. No one
knows this better than Mr. Tkachov. While he wants the German
workers to believe that the "idea of collective ownership" can be
driven out of the Russian peasants, these instinctive, traditional
Communists, only by bayonet and knout, he writes on page 15 of
his Russian pamphlet: 'Among the peasants a class of *usurers*
(*kulaks*) is making its way, a class of people who *buy up* and *rent*
the lands of peasants and nobles—a muzhik aristocracy." These
are the same kind of bloodsuckers as we described more fully above.

What dealt the severest blow to communal ownership was again
the redemption of the *corvée*. The greater and better part of the
land was allotted to the nobility; for the peasant there remained
scarcely enough, often not enough, to live on. In addition the forests were given to the nobles; the wood for fuel, implements and
building, which the peasant formerly might fetch there for nothing,
he has now to buy. Thus the peasant has nothing now but his house

and the bare land, without means to cultivate it, and on the average without enough land to support him and his family from one harvest to the next. Under such conditions and under the pressure of taxes and usurers, communal ownership of the land is no longer a blessing; it becomes a fetter. The peasants often run away from it, with or without their families, to earn their living as migratory labourers, and leave their land behind them.[2]

It is clear that communal ownership in Russia is long past its period of florescence and to all appearances is moving towards its disintegration. Nevertheless, the possibility undeniably exists of raising this form of society to a higher one, if it should last until circumstances are ripe for that, and if it shows itself capable of development in such manner that the peasants no longer cultivate the land separately, but collectively;[3] of raising it to this higher form without it being necessary for the Russian peasants to go through the intermediate stage of bourgeois small holdings. This, however, can only happen if, before the complete break-up of communal ownership, a proletarian revolution is successfully carried out in Western Europe, creating for the Russian peasant the preconditions requisite for such a transition, particularly the material conditions which he needs if only to carry through the revolution necessarily connected therewith of his whole agricultural system. It is, therefore, sheer bounce for Mr. Tkachov to say that the Russian peasants, although "owners," are "nearer to socialism" than the propertyless workers of Western Europe. Quite the opposite. If anything can still save Russian communal ownership and give it a chance of growing into a new, really viable form, it is a proletarian revolution in Western Europe.

Mr. Tkachov treats the political revolution just as lightly as he does the economic one. The Russian people, he relates, "protests incessantly" against its enslavement, now in form of "religious sects ... refusal to pay taxes ... robber bands (the German workers will be glad to know that, accordingly, Schinderhannes[4] is the father of German Social-Democracy) ... incendiarism ... revolts ... and hence the Russian people may be termed an instinctive revolutionist." And thus Mr. Tkachov is convinced that "it is only necessary to evoke an outburst in a number of places at the same time of all the accumulated bitterness and discontent, which is always seeth-

---

2. On the position of the peasants compare *inter alia* the official report of the government commission on agricultural production (1873), and further, Skaldin, *V zakholustye i v stolitse* [*In the Backwoods and in the Capital*], St. Petersburg 1870; the latter publication by a liberal conservative. [*Engels*]
3. In Poland, particularly in the Grodno *gubernia*, where the nobility for the most part was ruined by the re-

bellion of 1863, the peasants now frequently buy or rent estates from the nobles and cultivate them unpartitioned and *on their collective account*. And these peasants have not had communal ownership for centuries and are not Great Russians, but Poles, Lithuanians and Byelorussians. [*Engels*]
4. *Schinderhannes*: nickname of Johann Bückler, a well-known German robber.

ing in the breast of our people." Then "the union of the revolutionary forces will come about *of itself*, and the fight . . . must end favourably for the people's cause. Practical necessity, the instinct of self-preservation," will then achieve quite of itself "a firm and indissoluble alliance among the protesting village communities."

It is impossible to conceive of a revolution on easier and more pleasant terms. One starts shooting, at three or four places simultaneously, and the "instinctive revolutionist," "practical necessity" and the "instinct of self-preservation" do the rest "of themselves." Being so dead easy, it is simply incomprehensible why the revolution has not long ago been made, the people liberated and Russia transformed into the model socialist country.

Actually, it is quite a different matter. The Russian people, this instinctive revolutionist, has, true enough, made numerous isolated peasant revolts against the *nobility* and against individual officials, but *never against the tsar*, except when *a false tsar* put himself at its head and claimed the throne. The last great peasant rising, under Catherine II, was only possible because Yemelyan Pugachov claimed to be her husband, Peter III, who allegedly had not been murdered by his wife, but dethroned and clapped in prison, and who had now escaped. The tsar is, on the contrary, the earth god of the Russian peasant: *Bog vysoko, tsar daleko*—God is on high and the tsar far away, is his cry in the hour of need. There is no doubt that the mass of the peasant population, especially since the redemption of the *corvée*, has been reduced to a condition which more and more forces on it a fight also against the government and the tsar; but Mr. Tkachov will have to try to sell his fairy-tale of the "instinctive revolutionist" somewhere else.

And then, even *if* the mass of the Russian peasants were ever so instinctively revolutionary, even *if* we imagined that revolutions could be made to order, just as one makes a piece of flowered calico or a teakettle—even then I ask, is it permissible for one over twelve years of age to imagine the course of a revolution in such an utterly childish manner as is the case here? And remember further that this was written after the first revolution made on this Bakunin model —the Spanish one of 1873—had so brilliantly failed. There, too, they let loose at several places simultaneously. There too it was calculated that practical necessity and the instinct of self-preservation would of themselves bring about a firm and indissoluble alliance between the protesting communities. And what happened? Every village community, every town only defended itself, there was no question of mutual assistance, and with only three thousand men Pavia overcame one town after another in a fortnight and put an end to the entire anarchist glory. (*Cf.* my *Bakuninists at Work*, where this is described in detail.)

Russia undoubtedly is on the eve of a revolution. Her financial affairs are in extreme disorder. Taxes cannot be screwed any higher, the interest on old state loans is paid by means of new loans, and every new loan meets with greater difficulties; money can now only be raised under the pretext of building railways! The administration, as of old, corrupt from top to bottom, the officials living more from theft, bribery and extortion than on their salaries. The entire agricultural production—by far the most essential for Russia—completely dislocated by the redemption settlement of 1861; the big landowners without sufficient labour power, the peasants without sufficient land, oppressed by taxation and sucked dry by usurers, agricultural production declining from year to year. The whole held together with great difficulty and only outwardly by an Oriental despotism whose arbitrariness we in the West simply cannot imagine; a despotism which not only from day to day comes into more glaring contradiction with the views of the enlightened classes and in particular with those of the rapidly developing bourgeoisie of the capital, but which, in the person of its present bearer, has lost its head, one day making concessions to liberalism and the next, frightened, cancelling them again and thus bringing itself more and more into disrepute. With all that a growing recognition among the enlightened strata of the nation concentrated in the capital that this position is untenable, that a revolution is impending, and the illusion that it will be possible to guide this revolution into a smooth, constitutional channel. Here all the conditions of a revolution are combined, of a revolution which, started by the upper classes of the capital, perhaps even by the government itself, must be rapidly carried further, beyond the first constitutional phase, by the peasants; of a revolution which will be of the greatest importance for the whole of Europe if only because it will destroy at one blow the last, so far intact, reserve of the entire European reaction. This revolution is surely approaching. Only two events could still delay it: a successful war against Turkey or Austria, for which money and firm alliances are necessary, or—a premature attempt at insurrection, which would drive the possessing classes back into the arms of the government.

Marx's Reply to Vera Zasulich

* * * the analysis given in *Capital* assigns no reasons for or against the vitality of the rural community, but the special research into this subject which I conducted, the materials for which I obtained from original sources, has convinced me that this community is the mainspring of Russia's social regeneration, but in order that it might function as such one would first have to eliminate the deleterious influences which assail it from every quarter and then to ensure the conditions normal for spontaneous development.

Europocentric World Revolution

The proletarian socialist revolution was to be a world revolution (a world market having taken shape under capitalism), and, as Marx said in *The Class Struggles in France*, "the social revolution of the nineteenth century." Europe's advanced capitalism made it appear the natural epicenter of world revolution. How would European revolution be affected by and affect developments elsewhere? A letter of October 8, 1858, to Engels reflected Marx's uneasiness on this score. A much later letter, from Engels to Karl Kautsky on September 12, 1882, voiced a more sanguine view in the suggestion that a socialist Europe and North America would lead the rest of the world to socialist revolution by force of example.

Marx to Engels

* * * The specific task of bourgeois society is the establishment of a world market, at least in outline, and of production based upon this world market. As the world is round, this seems to have been completed by the colonisation of California and Australia and the opening up of China and Japan. The difficult question for us is: on the Continent the revolution is imminent and will immediately assume a socialist character. Is it not bound to be crushed in this little corner, considering that in a far greater territory the movement of bourgeois society is still in the ascendant?

Engels to Karl Kautsky

* * * You ask me what the English workers think about colonial policy. Well, exactly the same as they think about politics in general: the same as the bourgeois think. There is no workers' party here, you see, there are only Conservatives and Liberal-Radicals, and the workers gaily share the feast of England's monopoly of the world market and the colonies. In my opinion the colonies proper, i.e., the countries occupied by a European population—Canada, the Cape, Australia—will all become independent; on the other hand, the countries inhabited by a native population, which are simply subjugated—India, Algeria, the Dutch, Portuguese and Spanish possessions—must be taken over for the time being by the proletariat and led as rapidly as possible towards independence. How this process will develop is difficult to say. India will perhaps, indeed very probably, make a revolution, and as a proletariat in process of self-emancipation cannot conduct any colonial wars, it would have to be allowed to run its course; it would not pass off without all sorts of destruction, of course, but that sort of thing is inseparable from all revolutions. The same might also take place elsewhere, e.g., in Algeria and Egypt, and would certainly be the best thing *for us.* We shall have enough to do at home. Once Europe is reorganized, and North America, that will furnish such colossal power and such an example that the semi-civilized countries will of themselves follow in their wake; economic needs, if anything, will see to that. But as to what social and political phases these countries will then have to pass through before they likewise arrive at socialist organization, I think we today can advance only rather idle hypotheses. One thing alone is certain: the victorious proletariat can force no blessings of any kind upon any foreign nation without undermining its own victory by so doing. Which of course by no means excludes defensive wars of various kinds. * * *

PART V

The Later Engels: Elaboration and Popularization

Speech at the Graveside of Karl Marx

FRIEDRICH ENGELS

Marx died on March 14, 1883. Three days later Engels delivered this graveside speech in English at Highgate Cemetery, London, where Marx was buried. Engels spoke in English. The speech appeared in a German paper in German translation, and has appeared in English only in retranslation from the German.

On the 14th of March, at a quarter to three in the afternoon, the greatest living thinker ceased to think. He had been left alone for scarcely two minutes, and when we came back we found him in his armchair, peacefully gone to sleep—but for ever.

An immeasurable loss has been sustained both by the militant proletariat of Europe and America, and by historical science, in the death of this man. The gap that has been left by the departure of this mighty spirit will soon enough make itself felt.

Just as Darwin discovered the law of development of organic nature, so Marx discovered the law of development of human history: the simple fact, hitherto concealed by an overgrowth of ideology, that mankind must first of all eat, drink, have shelter and clothing, before it can pursue politics, science, art, religion, etc.; that therefore the production of the immediate material means of subsistence and consequently the degree of economic development attained by a given people or during a given epoch form the foundation upon which the state institutions, the legal conceptions, art, and even the ideas on religion, of the people concerned have been evolved, and in the light of which they must, therefore, be explained, instead of *vice versa*, as had hitherto been the case.

But that is not all. Marx also discovered the special law of motion governing the present-day capitalist mode of production and the bourgeois society that this mode of production has created. The discovery of surplus value suddenly threw light on the problem, in trying to solve which all previous investigations, of both bourgeois economists and socialist critics, had been groping in the dark.

Two such discoveries would be enough for one lifetime. Happy the man to whom it is granted to make even one such discovery. But in every single field which Marx investigated—and he investigated very many fields, none of them superficially—in every field, even in that of mathematics, he made independent discoveries.

Such was the man of science. But this was not even half the man. Science was for Marx a historically dynamic, revolutionary force. However great the joy with which he welcomed a new discovery in some theoretical science whose practical application perhaps it was as yet quite impossible to envisage, he experienced quite another kind of joy when the discovery involved immediate revolutionary changes in industry, and in historical development in general. For example, he followed closely the development of the discoveries made in the field of electricity and recently those of Marcel Deprez.

For Marx was before all else a revolutionist. His real mission in life was to contribute, in one way or another, to the overthrow of capitalist society and of the state institutions which it had brought into being, to contribute to the liberation of the modern proletariat, which *he* was the first to make conscious of its own position and its needs, conscious of the conditions of its emancipation. Fighting was his element. And he fought with a passion, a tenacity and a success such as few could rival. His work on the first *Rheinische Zeitung* (1842), the Paris *Vorwärts*[1] (1844), the *Deutsche Brüsseler Zeitung* (1847), the *Neue Rheinische Zeitung* (1848–49), the *New York Tribune* (1852–61), and in addition to these a host of militant pamphlets, work in organisations in Paris, Brussels and London, and finally, crowning all, the formation of the great International Working Men's Association—this was indeed an achievement of which its founder might well have been proud even if he had done nothing else.

And, consequently, Marx was the best hated and most calumniated man of his time. Governments, both absolutist and republican, deported him from their territories. Bourgeois, whether conservative or ultra-democratic, vied with one another in heaping slanders upon him. All this he brushed aside as though it were cobweb, ignoring it, answering only when extreme necessity compelled him. And he died beloved, revered and mourned by millions of revolutionary fellow workers—from the mines of Siberia to California, in all parts of Europe and America—and I make bold to say that though he may have had many opponents he had hardly one personal enemy.

His name will endure through the ages, and so also will his work!

1. *Vorwarts* (*Forward*): A radical newspaper of the German Socialists in emigration, one of whose contributors was Karl Marx. It appeared in German at Paris in 1844.

Socialism: Utopian and Scientific

FRIEDRICH ENGELS

Engels' polemical work *Herr Eugen Dühring's Revolution in Science*, better known as *Anti-Dühring*, came out in 1878. At the request of his friend Paul Lafargue, Engels arranged three general chapters of *Anti-Dührung* as a pamphlet dealing with the origins of Marxism and summarizing its view of history. Originally published in French in 1880, *Socialism: Utopian and Scientific* soon appeared in many other languages and became, along with the *Communist Manifesto*, the most influential popular presentation of the Marxist position in the late nineteenth century. The text given here is that of the authorized English edition of 1892.

I

Modern socialism is, in its essence, the direct product of the recognition, on the one hand, of the class antagonism existing in the society of today between proprietors and non-proprietors, between capitalists and wage-workers; on the other hand, of the anarchy existing in production. But, in its theoretical form, modern socialism originally appears ostensibly as a more logical extension of the principles laid down by the great French philosophers of the eighteenth century. Like every new theory, modern socialism had, at first, to connect itself with the intellectual stock-in-trade ready to its hand, however deeply its roots lay in material economic facts.

The great men, who in France prepared men's minds for the coming revolution, were themselves extreme revolutionists. They recognised no external authority of any kind whatever. Religion, natural science, society, political institutions—everything was subjected to the most unsparing criticism: everything must justify its existence before the judgement-seat of reason or give up existence. Reason became the sole measure of everything. It was the time when, as Hegel says, the world stood upon its head;[1] first in the

1. This is the passage on the French Revolution: "Thought, the concept of law, all at once made itself felt, and against this the old scaffolding of wrong could make no stand. In this conception of law, therefore, a constitution has now been established, and henceforth everything must be based upon this. Since the sun had been in the firmament, and the planets circled round him, the sight had never been seen of man standing upon his

sense that the human head, and the principles arrived at by its thought, claimed to be the basis of all human action and associations; but by and by, also, in the wider sense that the reality which was in contradiction to these principles had, in fact, to be turned upside down. Every form of society and government then existing, every old traditional notion was flung into the lumber-room as irrational; the world had hitherto allowed itself to be led solely by prejudices; everything in the past deserved only pity and contempt. Now, for the first time, appeared the light of day, the kingdom of reason; henceforth superstition, injustice, privilege, oppression, were to be superseded by eternal truth, eternal Right, equality based on Nature and the inalienable rights of man.

We know today that this kingdom of reason was nothing more than the idealised kingdom of the bourgeoisie; that this eternal Right found its realisation in bourgeois justice; that this equality reduced itself to bourgeois equality before the law; that bourgeois property was proclaimed as one of the essential rights of man; and that the government of reason, the Contrat Social of Rousseau, came into being, and only could come into being, as a democratic bourgeois republic. The great thinkers of the eighteenth century could, no more than their predecessors, go beyond the limits imposed upon them by their epoch.

But, side by side with the antagonism of the feudal nobility and the burghers, who claimed to represent all the rest of society, was the general antagonism of exploiters and exploited, of rich idlers and poor workers. It was this very circumstance that made it possible for the representatives of the bourgeoisie to put themselves forward as representing not one special class, but the whole of suffering humanity. Still further. From its origin the bourgeoisie was saddled with its antithesis: capitalists cannot exist without wage-workers, and, in the same proportion as the mediaeval burgher of the guild developed into the modern bourgeois, the guild journeyman and the day-labourer, outside the guilds, developed into the proletarian. And although, upon the whole, the bourgeoisie, in their struggle with the nobility, could claim to represent at the same time the interests of the different working classes of that period, yet in every great bourgeois movement there were independent outbursts

---

head—*i.e.*, on the Idea—and building reality after this image. Anaxagoras first said that the Nous, reason, rules the world; but now, for the first time, had man come to recognise that the Idea must rule the mental reality. And this was a magnificent sunrise. All thinking beings have participated in celebrating this holy day. A sublime emotion swayed men at that time, an enthusiasm of reason pervaded the world, as if now had come the reconciliation of the Divine Principle with the world." [Hegel: *Philosophy of History*, 1840, p. 535.] Is it not high time to set the anti-Socialist law in action against such teachings, subversive and to the common danger, by the late Professor Hegel? [*Engels*]

of that class which was the forerunner, more or less developed, of the modern proletariat. For example, at the time of the German Reformation and the Peasants' War, the Anabaptists and Thomas Munzer; in the great English Revolution, the Levellers; in the great French Revolution, Babeuf.

There were theoretical enunciations corresponding with these revolutionary uprisings of a class not yet developed; in the sixteenth and seventeenth centuries, Utopian pictures of ideal social conditions;[2] in the eighteenth, actual communistic theories (Morelly and Mably). The demand for equality was no longer limited to political rights; it was extended also to the social conditions of individuals. It was not simply class privileges that were to be abolished, but class distinctions themselves. A communism, ascetic, denouncing all the pleasures of life, Spartan, was the first form of the new teaching. Then came the three great Utopians: Saint-Simon, to whom the middle-class movement, side by side with the proletarian, still had a certain significance; Fourier; and Owen, who in the country where capitalist production was most developed, and under the influence of the antagonisms begotten of this, worked out his proposals for the removal of class distinction systematically and in direct relation to French materialism.

One thing is common to all three. Not one of them appears as a representative of the interests of that proletariat which historical development had, in the meantime, produced. Like the French philosophers, they do not claim to emancipate a particular class to begin with, but all humanity at once. Like them, they wish to bring in the kingdom of reason and eternal justice, but this kingdom, as they see it, is as far as heaven from earth, from that of the French philosophers.

For, to our three social reformers, the bourgeois world, based upon the principles of these philosophers, is quite as irrational and unjust, and, therefore, finds its way to the dust-hole quite as readily as feudalism and all the earlier stages of society. If pure reason and justice have not, hitherto, ruled the world, this has been the case only because men have not rightly understood them. What was wanted was the individual man of genius, who has now arisen and who understands the truth. That he has now arisen, that the truth has now been clearly understood, is not an inevitable event, following of necessity in the chain of historical development, but a mere happy accident. He might just as well have been born 500 years earlier, and might then have spared humanity 500 years of error, strife, and suffering.

We saw how the French philosophers of the eighteenth century,

---

the forerunners of the Revolution, appealed to reason as the sole judge of all that is. A rational government, rational society, were to be founded; everything that ran counter to eternal reason was to be remorselessly done away with. We saw also that this eternal reason was in reality nothing but the idealised understanding of the eighteenth century citizen, just then evolving into the bourgeois. The French Revolution had realised this rational society and government.

But the new order of things, rational enough as compared with earlier conditions, turned out to be by no means absolutely rational. The state based upon reason completely collapsed. Rousseau's Contrat Social had found its realisation in the Reign of Terror, from which the bourgeoisie, who had lost confidence in their own political capacity, had taken refuge first in the corruption of the Directorate, and, finally, under the wing of the Napoleonic despotism. The promised eternal peace was turned into an endless war of conquest. The society based upon reason had fared no better. The antagonism between rich and poor, instead of dissolving into general prosperity, had become intensified by the removal of the guild and other privileges, which had to some extent bridged it over, and by the removal of the charitable institutions of the Church. The "freedom of property" from feudal fetters, now veritably accomplished, turned out to be, for the small capitalists and small proprietors, the freedom to sell their small property, crushed under the overmastering competition of the large capitalists and landlords, to these great lords, and thus, as far as the small capitalists and peasant proprietors were concerned, became "freedom *from* property." The development of industry upon a capitalistic basis made poverty and misery of the working masses conditions of existence of society. Cash payment became more and more, in Carlyle's phrase, the sole nexus between man and man. The number of crimes increased from year to year. Formerly, the feudal vices had openly stalked about in broad daylight; though not eradicated, they were now at any rate thrust into the background. In their stead, the bourgeois vices, hitherto practised in secret, began to blossom all the more luxuriantly. Trade became to a greater and greater extent cheating. The "fraternity" of the revolutionary motto was realised in the chicanery and rivalries of the battle of competition. Oppression by force was replaced by corruption; the sword, as the first social lever, by gold. The right of the first night was transferred from the feudal lords to the bourgeois manufacturers. Prostitution increased to an extent never heard of. Marriage itself remained, as before, the legally recognised form, the official cloak of prostitution, and, moreover, was supplemented by rich crops of adultery.

In a word, compared with the splendid promises of the philosophers, the social and political institutions born of the "triumph of reason" were bitterly disappointing caricatures. All that was wanting was the men to formulate this disappointment, and they came with the turn of the century. In 1802 Saint-Simon's Geneva letters appeared; in 1808 appeared Fourier's first work, although the groundwork of his theory dated from 1799; on January 1, 1800, Robert Owen undertook the direction of New Lanark.

At this time, however, the capitalist mode of production, and with it the antagonism between the bourgeoisie and the proletariat, was still very incompletely developed. Modern industry, which had just arisen in England, was still unknown in France. But modern industry develops, on the one hand, the conflicts which make absolutely necessary a revolution in the mode of production, and the doing away with its capitalistic character—conflicts not only between the classes begotten of it, but also between the very productive forces and the forms of exchange created by it. And, on the other hand, it develops, in these very gigantic productive forces, the means of ending these conflicts. If, therefore, about the year 1800, the conflicts arising from the new social order were only just beginning to take shape, this holds still more fully as to the means of ending them. The "have-nothing" masses of Paris, during the Reign of Terror, were able for a moment to gain the mastery, and thus to lead the bourgeois revolution to victory in spite of the bourgeoisie themselves. But, in doing so, they only proved how impossible it was for their domination to last under the conditions then obtaining. The proletariat, which then for the first time evolved itself from these "have-nothing" masses as the nucleus of a new class, as yet quite incapable of independent political action, appeared as an oppressed, suffering order, to whom, in its incapacity to help itself, help could, at best, be brought in from without or down from above.

This historical situation also dominated the founders of socialism. To the crude conditions of capitalistic production and the crude class conditions corresponded crude theories. The solution of the social problems, which as yet lay hidden in undeveloped economic conditions, the Utopians attempted to evolve out of the human brain. Society presented nothing but wrongs; to remove these was the task of reason. It was necessary, then, to discover a new and more perfect system of social order and to impose this upon society from without by propaganda, and wherever it was possible, by the example of model experiments. These new social systems were foredoomed as Utopian; the more completely they were worked out in detail, the more they could not avoid drifting off into pure phantasies.

These facts once established, we need not dwell a moment longer upon this side of the question, now wholly belonging to the past. We can leave it to the literary small fry to solemnly quibble over these phantasies, which today only make us smile, and to crow over the superiority of their own bald reasoning, as compared with such "insanity." For ourselves, we delight in the stupendously grand thoughts and germs of thought that everywhere break out through their phantastic covering, and to which these Philistines are blind.

Saint-Simon was a son of the great French Revolution, at the outbreak of which he was not yet thirty. The Revolution was the victory of the third estate, *i.e.*, of the great masses of the nation, *working* in production and in trade, over the privileged *idle* classes, the nobles and the priests. But the victory of the third estate soon revealed itself as exclusively the victory of a small part of this "estate," as the conquest of political power by the socially privileged section of it, *i.e.*, the propertied bourgeoisie. And the bourgeoisie had certainly developed rapidly during the Revolution, partly by speculation in the lands of the nobility and of the Church, confiscated and afterwards put up for sale, and partly by frauds upon the nation by means of army contracts. It was the domination of these swindlers that, under the Directorate, brought France to the verge of ruin, and thus gave Napoleon the pretext for his *coup d'état*.

Hence, to Saint-Simon the antagonism between the third estate and the privileged classes took the form of an antagonism between "workers" and "idlers." The idlers were not merely the old privileged classes, but also all who, without taking any part in production or distribution, lived on their incomes. And the workers were not only the wage-workers, but also the manufacturers, the merchants, the bankers. That the idlers had lost the capacity for intellectual leadership and political supremacy had been proved, and was by the Revolution finally settled. That the non-possessing classes had not this capacity seemed to Saint-Simon proved by the experiences of the Reign of Terror. Then, who was to lead and command? According to Saint-Simon, science and industry, both united by a new religious bond, destined to restore that unity of religious ideas which had been lost since the time of the Reformation—a necessarily mystic and rigidly hierarchic "new Christianity." But science, that was the scholars; and industry, that was, in the first place, the working bourgeois, manufacturers, merchants, bankers. These bourgeois were, certainly, intended by Saint-Simon to transform themselves into a kind of public officials, of social trustees; but they were still to hold, *vis-à-vis* of the workers, a commanding and economically privileged position. The bankers especially were to be called upon to direct the whole of social production by the regulation of credit. This conception was in exact keeping with a time in which modern industry in France and, with it, the chasm between bourgeoisie and proletariat was only just coming into existence. But what Saint-Simon especially lays stress upon is this: what interests him first, and above all other things, is the lot of the class that is the most numerous and the most poor ("*la classe la plus nombreuse et la plus pauvre*").

Already in his Geneva letters, Saint-Simon lays down the proposition that "all men ought to work." In the same work he recognises also that the Reign of Terror was the reign of the non-possessing masses. "See," says he to them, "what happened in France at the time when your comrades held sway there: they brought about a famine." But to recognise the French Revolution as a class war, and not simply one between nobility and bourgeoisie, but between nobility, bourgeoisie, and the non-possessors, was, in the year 1802, a most pregnant discovery. In 1816, he declares that politics is the science of production, and foretells the complete absorption of politics by economics. The knowledge that economic conditions are the basis of political institutions appears here only in embryo. Yet what is here already very plainly expressed is the idea of the future conversion of political rule over men into an administration of things and a direction of processes of production—that is to say, the "abolition of the state," about which recently there has been so much noise.

Saint-Simon shows the same superiority over his contemporaries, when in 1814, immediately after the entry of the allies into Paris, and again in 1815, during the Hundred Days' War, he proclaims the alliance of France with England, and then of both these countries with Germany, as the only guarantee for the prosperous development and peace of Europe. To preach to the French in 1815 an alliance with the victors of Waterloo required as much courage as historical foresight.

If in Saint-Simon we find a comprehensive breadth of view, by virtue of which almost all the ideas of later Socialists that are not strictly economic are found in him in embryo, we find in Fourier a criticism of the existing conditions of society, genuinely French and witty, but not upon that account any the less thorough. Fourier takes the bourgeoisie, their inspired prophets before the Revolution, and their interested eulogists after it, at their own word. He lays bare remorselessly the material and moral misery of the bourgeois world. He confronts it with the earlier philosophers' dazzling promises of a society in which reason alone should reign, of a civilisation in which happiness should be universal, of an illimitable human perfectibility, and with the rose-coloured phraseology of the bourgeois ideologists of his time. He points out how everywhere the most pitiful reality corresponds with the most high-sounding phrases, and he overwhelms this hopeless fiasco of phrases with his mordant sarcasm.

Fourier is not only a critic; his imperturbably serene nature makes him a satirist, and assuredly one of the greatest satirists of all time. He depicts, with equal power and charm, the swindling speculations that blossomed out upon the downfall of the Revolution, and the shopkeeping spirit prevalent in, and characteristic of, French commerce at that time. Still more masterly is his criticism of the bourgeois form of the relations between the sexes, and the position of woman in bourgeois society. He was the first to declare that in any given society the degree of woman's emancipation is the natural measure of the general emancipation.

But Fourier is at his greatest in his conception of the history of society. He divides its whole course, thus far, into four stages of evolution—savagery, barbarism, the patriarchate, civilisation. The last is identical with the so-called civil, or bourgeois, society of today— i.e., with the social order that came in with the sixteenth century. He proves "that the civilised stage raises every vice practised by barbarism in a simple fashion into a form of existence, complex, ambiguous, equivocal, hypocritical"—that civilisation moves in "a vicious circle," in contradictions which it constantly reproduces without being able to solve them; hence it constantly arrives at the very opposite to that which it wants to attain, or pretends to want to attain, so that, e.g., "under civilisation poverty is born of superabundance itself."

Fourier, as we see, uses the dialectic method in the same masterly way as his contemporary, Hegel. Using these same dialectics, he argues against the talk about illimitable human perfectibility, that every historical phase has its period of ascent and also its period of descent, and he applies this observation to the future of the whole human race. As Kant introduced into natural science the idea of the ultimate destruction of the earth, Fourier introduced into historical science that of the ultimate destruction of the human race.

Whilst in France the hurricane of the Revolution swept over the land, in England a quieter, but not on that account less tremendous, revolution was going on. Steam and the new tool-making machinery were transforming manufacture into modern industry, and thus revolutionising the whole foundation of bourgeois society. The sluggish march of development of the manufacturing period changed into a veritable storm and stress period of production. With constantly increasing swiftness the splitting-up of society into large capitalists and non-possessing proletarians went on. Between these, instead of the former stable middle class, an unstable mass of artisans and small shopkeepers, the most fluctuating portion of the population, now led a precarious existence.

The new mode of production was, as yet, only at the beginning of its period of ascent; as yet it was the normal, regular method of production—the only one possible under existing conditions. Nevertheless, even then it was producing crying social abuses—the herding together of a homeless population in the worst quarters of the large towns; the loosening of all traditional moral bonds, of patriarchal subordination, of family relations; overwork, especially of women and children, to a frightful extent; complete demoralisation of the working class, suddenly flung into altogether new conditions, from the country into the town, from agriculture into modern industry, from stable conditions of existence into insecure ones that changed from day to day.

At this juncture there came forward as a reformer a manufacturer 29 years old—a man of almost sublime, childlike simplicity of character, and at the same time one of the few born leaders of men. Robert Owen had adopted the teaching of the materialistic philosophers: that man's character is the product, on the one hand, of heredity; on the other, of the environment of the individual during his lifetime, and especially during his period of development. In the industrial revolution most of his class saw only chaos and confusion, and the opportunity of fishing in these troubled waters and making large fortunes quickly. He saw in it the opportunity of putting into practice his favourite theory, and so of bringing order out of chaos. He had already tried it with success, as superintendent of more than five hundred men in a Manchester factory. From 1800 to 1829, he directed the great cotton mill at New Lanark, in Scotland, as managing partner, along the same lines, but with greater freedom of action and with a success that made him a European reputation. A population, originally consisting of the most diverse and, for the most part, very demoralised elements, a population that gradually grew to 2,500, he turned into a model colony, in which drunkenness, police, magistrates, lawsuits, poor laws, charity, were unknown. And all this simply by placing the people in conditions worthy of human beings, and especially by carefully bringing up the rising generation. He was the founder of infant schools, and introduced them first at New Lanark. At the age of two the children came to school, where they enjoyed themselves so much that they could scarcely be got home again. Whilst his competitors worked their people thirteen or fourteen hours a day, in New Lanark the working-day was only ten and a half hours. When a crisis in cotton stopped work for four months, his workers received their full wages all the time. And with all this the business more than doubled in value, and to the last yielded large profits to its proprietors.

In spite of all this, Owen was not content. The existence which he secured for his workers was, in his eyes, still far from being worthy of human beings. "The people were slaves at my mercy." The relatively favourable conditions in which he had placed them were still far from allowing a rational development of the character and of the intellect in all directions, much less of the free exercise of all their faculties. "And yet, the working part of this population of 2,500 persons was daily producing as much real wealth for society as, less than half a century before, it would have required the working part of a population of 600,000 to create. I asked myself, what became of the difference between the wealth consumed by 2,500 persons and that which would have been consumed by 600,000?"[3]

The answer was clear. It had been used to pay the proprietors of the establishment 5 per cent on the capital they had laid out, in addition to over £300,000 clear profit. And that which held for New Lanark held to a still greater extent for all the factories in England. "If this new wealth had not been created by machinery, imperfectly as it has been applied, the wars of Europe, in opposition to Napoleon, and to support the aristocratic principles of society, could not have been maintained. And yet this new power was the creation of the working class."[4] To them, therefore, the fruits of this new power belonged. The newly-created gigantic productive forces, hitherto used only to enrich individuals and to enslave the masses, offered to Owen the foundations for a reconstruction of society; they were destined, as the common property of all, to be worked for the common good of all.

Owen's communism was based upon this purely business foundation, the outcome, so to say, of commercial calculation. Throughout, it maintained this practical character. Thus, in 1823, Owen proposed the relief of the distress in Ireland by communist colonies, and drew up complete estimates of costs of founding them, yearly expenditure, and probable revenue. And in his definite plan for the future, the technical working out of details is managed with such practical knowledge—ground plan, front and side and bird's-eye views all included—that the Owen method of social reform once accepted, there is from the practical point of view little to be said against the actual arrangement of details.

His advance in the direction of communism was the turning-point in Owen's life. As long as he was simply a philanthropist, he was rewarded with nothing but wealth, applause, honour, and glory. He was the most popular man in Europe. Not only men of his own class, but statesmen and princes listened to him approvingly. But when he came out with his communist theories that was quite another thing. Three great obstacles seemed to him especially to block the path to social reform: private property, religion, the pres-

---

3. From "The Revolution in Mind and Practice," p. 21, a memorial addressed to all the "red Republicans, Communists and Socialists of Europe," and sent to the provisional government of France, 1848, and also "to Queen Victoria and her responsible advisers." [*Engels*]

4. Note, *l.c.*, p. 22. [*Engels*]

ent form of marriage. He knew what confronted him if he attacked these—outlawry, excommunication from official society, the loss of his whole social position. But nothing of this prevented him from attacking them without fear of consequences, and what he had foreseen happened. Banished from official society, with a conspiracy of silence against him in the press, ruined by his unsuccessful communist experiments in America, in which he sacrificed all his fortune, he turned directly to the working class and continued working in their midst for thirty years. Every social movement, every real advance in England on behalf of the workers links itself on to the name of Robert Owen. He forced through in 1819, after five years' fighting, the first law limiting the hours of labour of women and children in factories. He was president of the first Congress at which all the Trade Unions of England united in a single great trade association. He introduced as transition measures to the complete communistic organisation of society, on the one hand, co-operative societies for retail trade and production. These have since that time, at least, given practical proof that the merchant and the manufacturer are socially quite unnecessary. On the other hand, he introduced labour bazaars for the exchange of the products of labour through the medium of labour-notes, whose unit was a single hour of work; institutions necessarily doomed to failure, but completely anticipating Proudhon's bank of exchange of a much later period, and differing entirely from this in that it did not claim to be the panacea for all social ills, but only a first step towards a much more radical revolution of society.

The Utopians' mode of thought has for a long time governed the socialist ideas of the nineteenth century, and still governs some of them. Until very recently all French and English Socialists did homage to it. The earlier German communism, including that of Weitling, was of the same school. To all these socialism is the expression of absolute truth, reason and justice, and has only to be discovered to conquer all the world by virtue of its own power. And as absolute truth is independent of time, space, and of the historical development of man, it is a mere accident when and where it is discovered. With all this, absolute truth, reason, and justice are different with the founder of each different school. And as each one's special kind of absolute truth, reason, and justice is again conditioned by his subjective understanding, his conditions of existence, the measure of his knowledge and his intellectual training, there is no other ending possible in this conflict of absolute truths than that they shall be mutually exclusive one of the other. Hence, from this nothing could come but a kind of eclectic, average socialism, which, as a matter of fact, has up to the present time dominated the minds of most of the socialist workers in France and England. Hence, a mish-mash allowing of the most manifold shades of opinion; a mish-mash of such critical statements, economic theories, pictures of future society by the founders of different sects, as excite a minimum of opposition; a mish-mash which is the more easily brewed the more the definite sharp edges of the individual constituents are rubbed down in the stream of debate, like rounded pebbles in a brook.

To make a science of socialism, it had first to be placed upon a real basis.

II

In the meantime, along with and after the French philosophy of the eighteeenth century had arisen the new German philosophy, culminating in Hegel. Its greatest merit was the taking up again of dialectics as the highest form of reasoning. The old Greek philosophers were all born natural dialecticians, and Aristotle, the most encyclopaedic intellect of them, had already analysed the most essential forms of dialectic thought. The newer philosophy, on the other hand, although in it also dialectics had brilliant exponents (e.g., Descartes and Spinoza), had, especially through English influence, become more and more rigidly fixed in the so-called metaphysical mode of reasoning, by which also the French of the eighteenth century were almost wholly dominated, at all events in their special philosophical work. Outside philosophy in the restricted sense, the French nevertheless produced masterpieces of dialectics. We need only call to mind Diderot's *Le Neveu de Rameau* and Rousseau's *Discours sur l'origine et les fondements de l'inégalité parmi les hommes.* We give here, in brief, the essential character of these two modes of thought.

When we consider and reflect upon Nature at large or the history of mankind or our own intellectual activity, at first we see the picture of an endless entanglement of relations and reactions, permutations and combinations, in which nothing remains what, where and as it was, but everything moves, changes, comes into being and passes away. We see, therefore, at first the picture as a whole, with its individual parts still more or less kept in the background; we observe the movements, transitions, connections, rather than the things that move, combine and are connected. This primitive, naïve but intrinsicially correct conception of the world is that of ancient Greek philosophy, and was first clearly formulated by Heraclitus: everything is and is not, for everything is fluid, is constantly changing, constantly coming into being and passing away.

But this conception, correctly as it expresses the general character of the picture of appearances as a whole, does not suffice to explain the details of which this picture is made up, and so long as we do not understand these, we have not a clear idea of the whole picture. In order to understand these details we must detach them from their natural or historical connection and examine each one separately, its nature, special causes, effects, etc. This is, primarily, the task of natural science and historical research: branches of science which the Greeks of classical times, on very good grounds, relegated to a subordinate position, because they had first of all to collect materials for these sciences to work upon. A certain amount of natural and historical material must be collected before there can be any critical analysis, comparison, and arrangement in classes, orders, and species. The foundations of the exact natural sciences were, therefore, first worked out by the Greeks of the Alexandrian period,[5] and later on, in the Middle Ages, by the Arabs. Real natural science dates from the second half of the fifteenth century, and thence onward it has advanced with constantly increasing rapidity. The analysis of Nature into its individual parts, the grouping of the different natural processes and objects in definite classes, the study of the internal anatomy of organic bodies in their manifold forms—these were the fundamental conditions of the gigantic strides in our knowledge of Nature that have been made during the last four hundred years. But this method of work has also left us as legacy the habit of observing natural objects and processes in isolation, apart from their connection with the vast whole; of observing them in repose, not in motion; as constants, not as essentially variables; in their death, not in their life. And when this way of looking at things was transferred by Bacon and Locke from natural science to philosophy, it begot the narrow, metaphysical mode of thought peculiar to the last century.

To the metaphysician, things and their mental reflexes, ideas, are isolated, are to be considered one after the other and apart from each other, are objects of investigation fixed, rigid, given once for all. He thinks in absolutely irreconcilable antitheses. "His communication is 'yea, yea; nay, nay'; for whatsoever is more than these cometh of evil." For him a thing either exists or does not exist; a thing cannot at the same time be itself and something else. Positive and negative absolutely exclude one another; cause and effect stand in a rigid antithesis one to the other.

At first sight this mode of thinking seems to us very luminous, because it is that of so-called sound common sense. Only sound com-

5. The *Alexandrian period* of the development of science comprises the period extending from the third century B.C. to the seventh century A.D. It derives its name from the town of Alexandria in Egypt, which was one of the most important centres of international economic intercourse at that time. In the Alexandrian period, mathematics (Euclid and Archimedes), geography, astronomy, anatomy, physiology, etc., attained considerable development.

mon sense, respectable fellow that he is, in the homely realm of his own four walls, has very wonderful adventures directly he ventures out into the wide world of research. And the metaphysical mode of thought, justifiable and necessary as it is in a number of domains whose extent varies according to the nature of the particular object of investigation, sooner or later reaches a limit, beyond which it becomes one-sided, restricted, abstract, lost in insoluble contradictions. In the contemplation of individual things, it forgets the connection between them; in the contemplation of their existence, it forgets the beginning and end of that existence; of their repose, it forgets their motion. It cannot see the wood for the trees.

For everyday purposes we know and can say, e.g., whether an animal is alive or not. But, upon closer inquiry, we find that this is, in many cases, a very complex question, as the jurists know very well. They have cudgelled their brains in vain to discover a rational limit beyond which the killing of the child in its mother's womb is murder. It is just as impossible to determine absolutely the moment of death, for physiology proves that death is not an instantaneous, momentary phenomenon, but a very protracted process.

In like manner, every organic being is every moment the same and not the same; every moment it assimilates matter supplied from without, and gets rid of other matter; every moment some cells of its body die and others build themselves anew; in a longer or shorter time the matter of its body is completely renewed, and is replaced by other molecules of matter, so that every organic being is always itself, and yet something other than itself.

Further, we find upon closer investigation that the two poles of an antithesis, positive and negative, e.g., are as inseparable as they are opposed, and that despite all their opposition, they mutually interpenetrate. And we find, in like manner, that cause and effect are conceptions which only hold good in their application to individual cases; but as soon as we consider the individual cases in their general connection with the universe as a whole, they run into each other, and they become confounded when we contemplate that universal action and reaction in which causes and effects are eternally changing places, so that what is effect here and now will be cause there and then, and *vice versa*.

None of these processes and modes of thought enters into the framework of metaphysical reasoning. Dialectics, on the other hand, comprehends things and their representations, ideas, in their essential connection, concatenation, motion, origin, and ending. Such processes as those mentioned above are, therefore, so many corroborations of its own method of procedure.

Nature is the proof of dialectics, and it must be said for modern science that it has furnished this proof with very rich materials increasing daily, and thus has shown that, in the last resort, Nature works dialectically and not metaphysically; that she does not move in the eternal oneness of a perpetually recurring circle, but goes through a real historical evolution. In this connection Darwin must be named before all others. He dealt the metaphysical conception of Nature the heaviest blow by his proof that all organic beings, plants, animals, and man himself, are the products of a process of evolution going on through millions of years. But the naturalists who have learned to think dialectically are few and far between, and this conflict of the results of discovery with preconceived modes of thinking explains the endless confusion now reigning in theoretical natural science, the despair of teachers as well as learners, of authors and readers alike.

An exact representation of the universe, of its evolution, of the development of mankind, and of the reflection of this evolution in the minds of men, can therefore only be obtained by the methods of dialectics with its constant regard to the innumerable actions and reactions of life and death, of progressive or retrogressive changes. And in this spirit the new German philosophy has worked. Kant began his career by resolving the stable solar system of Newton and its eternal duration, after the famous initial impulse had once been given, into the result of a historic process, the formation of the sun and all the planets out of a rotating nebulous mass. From this he at the same time drew the conclusion that, given this origin of the solar system, its future death followed of necessity. His theory half a century later was established mathematically by Laplace, and half a century after that the spectroscope proved the existence in space of such incandescent masses of gas in various stages of condensation.

This new German philosophy culminated in the Hegelian system. In this system—and herein is its great merit—for the first time the whole world, natural, historical, intellectual, is represented as a process, i.e., as in constant motion, change, transformation, development; and the attempt is made to trace out the internal connection that makes a continuous whole of all this movement and develop ment. From this point of view the history of mankind no longer appeared as a wild whirl of senseless deeds of violence, all equally condemnable at the judgement-seat of mature philosophic reason and which are best forgotten as quickly as possible, but as the process of evolution of man himself. It was now the task of the intellect to follow the gradual march of this process through all its devious ways, and to trace out the inner law running through all its apparently accidental phenomena.

That the Hegelian system did not solve the problem it propounded is here immaterial. Its epoch-making merit was that it propounded the problem. This problem is one that no single individual will ever be able to solve. Although Hegel was—with Saint-Simon —the most encyclopaedic mind of his time, yet he was limited, first, by the necessarily limited extent of his own knowledge and, second, by the limited extent and depth of the knowledge and conceptions of his age. To these limits a third must be added. Hegel was an idealist. To him the thoughts within his brain were not the more or less abstract pictures of actual things and processes, but, conversely, things and their evolution were only the realised pictures of the "Idea," existing somewhere from eternity before the world was. This way of thinking turned everything upside down, and completely reversed the actual connection of things in the world. Correctly and ingeniously as many individual groups of facts were grasped by Hegel, yet, for the reasons just given, there is much that is botched, artificial, laboured, in a word, wrong in point of detail. The Hegelian system, in itself, was a colossal miscarriage—but it was also the last of its kind. It was suffering, in fact, from an internal and incurable contradiction. Upon the one hand, its essential proposition was the conception that human history is a process of evolution, which, by its very nature, cannot find its intellectual final term in the discovery of any so-called absolute truth. But, on the other hand, it laid claim to being the very essence of this absolute truth. A system of natural and historical knowledge, embracing everything, and final for all time, is a contradiction to the fundamental law of dialectic reasoning. This law, indeed, by no means excludes, but, on the contrary, includes the idea that the systematic knowledge of the external universe can make giant strides from age to age.

The perception of the fundamental contradiction in German idealism led necessarily back to materialism, but, *nota bene*, not to the simply metaphysical, exclusively mechanical materialism of the eighteenth century. Old materialism looked upon all previous history as a crude heap of irrationality and violence; modern materialism sees in it the process of evolution of humanity, and aims at discovering the laws thereof. With the French of the eighteenth century, and even with Hegel, the conception obtained of Nature as a whole, moving in narrow circles, and for ever immutable, with its eternal celestial bodies, as Newton, and unalterable organic species, as Linnaeus, taught. Modern materialism embraces the more recent discoveries of natural science, according to which Nature also has its history in time, the celestial bodies, like the organic species that, under favourable conditions, people them, being born and perishing. And even if Nature, as a whole, must still be said to move in recurrent cycles, these cycles assume infinitely larger dimensions. In both aspects, modern materialism is essentially dialectic, and no longer requires the assistance of that sort of philosophy which, queen-like, pretended to rule the remaining mob of sciences. As soon as each special science is bound to make clear its position in the great totality of things and of our knowledge of things, a special science dealing with this totality is superfluous or unnecessary. That which still survives of all earlier philosophy is the science of thought and its laws—formal logic and dialectics. Everything else is subsumed in the positive science of Nature and history.

Whilst, however, the revolution in the conception of Nature could only be made in proportion to the corresponding positive materials furnished by research, already much earlier certain historical facts had occurred which led to a decisive change in the conception of history. In 1831, the first working-class rising took place in Lyons; between 1838 and 1842, the first national working-class movement, that of the English Chartists, reached its height. The class struggle between proletariat and bourgeoisie came to the front in the history of the most advanced countries in Europe, in proportion to the development, upon the one hand, of modern industry, upon the other, of the newly-acquired political supremacy of the bourgeoisie. Facts more and more strenuously gave the lie to the teachings of bourgeois economy as to the identity of the interests of capital and labour, as to the universal harmony and universal prosperity that would be the consequence of unbridled competition. All these things could no longer be ignored, any more than the French and English socialism, which was their theoretical, though very imperfect, expression. But the old idealist conception of history, which was not yet dislodged, knew nothing of class struggles based upon economic interests, know nothing of economic interests; production and all economic relations appeared in it only as incidental, subordinate elements in the "history of civilisation."

The new facts made imperative a new examination of all past history. Then it was seen that *all* past history, with the exception of its primitive stages, was the history of class struggles; that these warring classes of society are always the products of the modes of production and of exchange—in a word, of the *economic* conditions of their time; that the economic structure of society always furnishes the real basis, starting from which we can alone work out the ultimate explanation of the whole superstructure of juridical and political institutions as well as of the religious, philosophical, and other ideas of a given historical period. Hegel had freed history from metaphysics—he had made it dialectic; but his conception of history was essentially idealistic. But now idealism was driven from its last refuge, the philosophy of history; now a materialistic treatment of history was propounded, and a method found of explaining man's "knowing" by his "being," instead of, as heretofore, his "being" by his "knowing."

From that time forward socialism was no longer an accidental discovery of this or that ingenious brain, but the necessary outcome of the struggle between two historically developed classes—the proletariat and the bourgeoisie. Its task was no longer to manufacture a system of society as perfect as possible, but to examine the historico-economic succession of events from which these classes, and their antagonism had of necessity sprung, and to discover in the economic conditions thus created the means of ending the conflict. But the socialism of earlier days was as incompatible with this materialistic conception as the conception of Nature of the French materialists was with dialectics and modern natural science. The socialism of earlier days certainly criticised the existing capitalistic mode of production and its consequences. But it could not explain them, and, therefore, could not get the mastery of them. It could only simply reject them as bad. The more strongly this earlier socialism denounced the exploitation of the working class, inevitable under capitalism, the less able was it clearly to show in what this exploitation consisted and how it arose. But for this it was necessary—(1) to present the capitalistic method of production in its historical connection and its inevitableness during a particular historical period, and therefore, also, to present its inevitable downfall; and (2) to lay bare its essential character, which was still a secret. This was done by the discovery of *surplus value*. It was shown that the appropriation of unpaid labour is the basis of the capitalist mode of production and of the exploitation of the worker that occurs under it; that even if the capitalist buys the labour power of his labourer at its full value as a commodity on the market, he yet extracts more value from it than he paid for; and that in the ultimate analysis this surplus value forms those sums of value from which are heaped up the constantly increasing masses of capital in the hands of the possessing classes. The genesis of capitalist production and the production of capital were both explained.

These two great discoveries, the materialistic conception of history and the revelation of the secret of capitalistic production through surplus value, we owe to Marx. With these discoveries socialism became a science. The next thing was to work out all its details and relations.

III

The materialist conception of history starts from the proposition that the production of the means to support human life and, next to production, the exchange of things produced, is the basis of all social structure; that in every society that has appeared in history, the manner in which wealth is distributed and society divided into

classes or orders is dependent upon what is produced, how it is produced, and how the products are exchanged. From this point of
view the final causes of all social changes and political revolutions
are to be sought, not in men's brains, not in men's better insight
into eternal truth and justice, but in changes in the modes of production and exchange. They are to be sought not in the *philosophy*,
but in the *economics* of each particular epoch. The growing perception that existing social institutions are unreasonable and unjust,
that reason has become unreason and right wrong,[6] is only proof
that in the modes of production and exchange changes have silently
taken place with which the social order, adapted to earlier economic
conditions, is no longer in keeping. From this it also follows that
the means of getting rid of the incongruities that have been brought
to light must also be present, in a more or less developed condition,
within the changed modes of production themselves. These means
are not to be invented by deduction from fundamental principles,
but are to be discovered in the stubborn facts of the existing system
of production.

What is, then, the position of modern socialism in this connection?

The present structure of society—this is now pretty generally
conceded—is the creation of the ruling class of today, of the bourgeoisie. The mode of production peculiar to the bourgeoisie, known,
since Marx, as the capitalist mode of production, was incompatible
with the feudal system, with the privileges it conferred upon individuals, entire social ranks and local corporations, as well as with
the hereditary ties of subordination which constituted the framework
of its social organisation. The bourgeoisie broke up the feudal
system and built upon its ruins the capitalist order of society, the
kingdom of free competition, of personal liberty, of the equality,
before the law, of all commodity owners, of all the rest of the capitalist blessings. Thenceforward the capitalist mode of production
could develop in freedom. Since steam, machinery, and the making
of machines by machinery transformed the older manufacture into
modern industry, the productive forces evolved under the guidance
of the bourgeoisie developed with a rapidity and in a degree
unheard of before. But just as the older manufacture, in its time,
and handicraft, becoming more developed under its influence, had
come into collision with the feudal trammels of the guilds, so now
modern industry, in its more complete development, comes into collision with the bounds within which the capitalistic mode of production holds it confined. The new productive forces have already
outgrown the capitalistic mode of using them. And this conflict
between productive forces and modes of production is not a conflict

6. Mephistopheles, in Goethe's *Faust*.

engendered in the mind of man, like that between original sin and divine justice. It exists, in fact, objectively, outside us, independently of the will and actions even of the men that have brought it on. Modern socialism is nothing but the reflex, in thought, of this conflict in fact; its ideal reflection in the minds, first, of the class directly suffering under it, the working class.

Now, in what does this conflict consist?

Before capitalistic production, i.e., in the Middle Ages, the system of petty industry obtained generally, based upon the private property of the labourers in their means of production; in the country, the agriculture of the small peasant, freeman or serf; in the towns, the handicrafts organised in guilds. The instruments of labour—land, agricultural implements, the workshop, the tool— were the instruments of labour of single individuals, adapted for the use of one worker, and, therefore, of necessity, small, dwarfish, circumscribed. But, for this very reason they belonged, as a rule, to the producer himself. To concentrate these scattered, limited means of production, to enlarge them, to turn them into the powerful levers of production of the present day—this was precisely the historic role of capitalist production and of its upholder, the bourgeoisie. In the fourth section of *Capital*[7] Marx has explained in detail how since the fifteenth century this has been historically worked out through the three phases of simple co-operation, manufacture and modern industry. But the bourgeoisie, as is also shown there, could not transform these puny means of production into mighty productive forces without transforming them, at the same time, from means of production of the individual into *social* means of production only workable by a collectivity of men. The spinning-wheel, the hand-loom, the blacksmith's hammer, were replaced by the spinning-machine, the power-loom, the steam-hammer; the individual workshop, by the factory implying the co-operation of hundreds and thousands of workmen. In like manner, production itself changed from a series of individual into a series of social acts, and the products from individual to social products. The yarn, the cloth, the metal articles that now came out of the factory, were the joint product of many workers, through whose hands they had successively to pass before they were ready. No one person could say of them; "I made that; this is *my* product."

But where, in a given society, the fundamental form of production is that spontaneous division of labour which creeps in gradually and not upon any preconceived plan, there the products take on the form of *commodities*, whose mutual exchange, buying and selling, enable the individual producers to satisfy their manifold wants. And this was the case in the Middle Ages. The peasant, e.g., sold to the

7. See pp. 384–403, above. [*R. T.*]

artisan agricultural products and bought from him the products of handicraft. Into this society of individual producers, of commodity producers, the new mode of production thrust itself. In the midst of the old division of labour, grown up spontaneously and upon *no definite plan*, which had governed the whole of society, now arose division of labour upon a *definite* plan, as organised in the factory; side by side with *individual* production appeared *social* production. The products of both were sold in the same market, and, therefore, at prices at least approximately equal. But organisation upon a definite plan was stronger than spontaneous division of labour. The factories working with the combined social forces of a collectivity of individuals produced their commodities far more cheaply than the individual small producers. Individual production succumbed in one department after another. Socialised production revolutionised all the old methods of production. But its revolutionary character was, at the same time, so little recognised that it was, on the contrary, introduced as a means of increasing and developing the production of commodities. When it arose, it found ready-made, and made liberal use of, certain machinery for the production and exchange of commodities: merchants' capital, handicraft, wage-labour. Socialised production thus introducing itself as a new form of the production of commodities, it was a matter of course that under it the old forms of appropriation remained in full swing, and were applied to its products as well.

In the mediaeval stage of evolution of the production of commodities, the question as to the owner of the product of labour could not arise. The individual producer, as a rule, had, from raw material belonging to himself, and generally his own handiwork, produced it with his own tools, by the labour of his own hands or of his family. There was no need for him to appropriate the new product. It belonged wholly to him, as a matter of course. His property in the product was, therefore, based *upon his own labour*. Even where external help was used, this was, as a rule, of little importance, and very generally was compensated by something other than wages. The apprentices and journeymen of the guilds worked less for board and wages than for education, in order that they might become master craftsmen themselves.

Then came the concentration of the means of production and of the producers in large workshops and manufactories, their transformation into actual socialised means of production and socialised producers. But the socialised producers and means of production and their products were still treated, after this change, just as they had been before, i.e., as the means of production and the products of individuals. Hitherto, the owner of the instruments of labour had himself appropriated the product, because, as a rule, it was his own product and the assistance of others was the exception. Now the owner of the instruments of labour always appropriated to himself the product, although it was no longer *his* product but exclusively the product of the *labour of others*. Thus, the products now produced socially were not appropriated by those who had actually set in motion the means of production and actually produced the commodities, but by the *capitalists*. The means of production, and production itself, had become in essence socialised. But they were subjected to a form of appropriation which presupposes the private production of individuals, under which, therefore, everyone owns his own product and brings it to market. The mode of production is subjected to this form of appropriation, although it abolishes the conditions upon which the latter rests.[8]

This contradiction, which gives to the new mode of production its capitalistic character, *contains the germ of the whole of the social antagonisms of today*. The greater the mastery obtained by the new mode of production over all important fields of production and in all manufacturing countries, the more it reduced individual production to an insignificant residuum, *the more clearly was brought out the incompatibility of socialised production with capitalistic appropriation.*

The first capitalists found, as we have said, alongside of other forms of labour, wage-labour ready-made for them on the market. But it was exceptional, complementary, accessory, transitory wage-labour. The agricultural labourer, though, upon occasion, he hired himself out by the day, had a few acres of his own land on which he could at all events live at a pinch. The guilds were so organized that the journeyman of today became the master of tomorrow. But all this changed as soon as the means of production became socialised and concentrated in the hands of capitalists. The means of production, as well as the product, of the individual producer became more and more worthless; there was nothing left for him but to turn wage-worker under the capitalist. Wage-labour, aforetime the exception and accessory, now became the rule and basis of all production; aforetime complementary, it now became the sole remaining function of the workers. The wage-worker for a time became a wage-worker for life. The number of these permanent wage-workers was further enormously increased by the breaking-up of the feudal

8. It is hardly necessary in this connection to point out that, even if the *form* of appropriation remains the same, the *character* of the appropriation is just as much revolutionised as production is by the changes described above. It is, of course, a very different matter whether I appropriate to myself my own product or that of another. Note in passing that wage-labour, which contains the whole capitalistic mode of production in embryo, is very ancient; in a sporadic, scattered form it existed for centuries alongside of slave-labour. But the embryo could duly develop into the capitalistic mode of production only when the necessary historical preconditions had been furnished. [*Engels*]

system that occurred at the same time, by the disbanding of the retainers of the feudal lords, the eviction of the peasants from their homesteads, etc. The separation was made complete between the means of production concentrated in the hands of the capitalists, on the one side, and the producers, possessing nothing but their labour-power, on the other. *The contradiction between socialised production and capitalistic appropriation manifested itself as the antagonism of proletariat and bourgeoisie.*

We have seen that the capitalistic mode of production thrust its way into a society of commodity-producers, of individual producers, whose social bond was the exchange of their products. But every society based upon the production of commodities has this peculiarity: that the producers have lost control over their own social inter-relations. Each man produces for himself with such means of production as he may happen to have, and for such exchange as he may require to satisfy his remaining wants. No one knows how much of his particular article is coming on the market, nor how much of it will be wanted. No one knows whether his individual product will meet an actual demand, whether he will be able to make good his costs of production or even to sell his commodity at all. Anarchy reigns in socialised production.

But the production of commodities, like every other form of production, has its peculiar, inherent laws inseparable from it; and these laws work, despite anarchy, in and through anarchy. They reveal themselves in the only persistent form of social inter-relations, i.e., in exchange, and here they affect the individual producers as compulsory laws of competition. They are, at first, unknown to these producers themselves, and have to be discovered by them gradually and as the result of experience. They work themselves out, therefore, independently of the producers, and in antagonism to them, as inexorable natural laws of their particular form of production. The product governs the producers.

In mediaeval society, especially in the earlier centuries, production was essentially directed towards satisfying the wants of the individual. It satisfied, in the main, only the wants of the producer and his family. Where relations of personal dependence existed, as in the country, it also helped to satisfy the wants of the feudal lord. In all this there was, therefore, no exchange; the products, consequently, did not assume the character of commodities. The family of the peasant produced almost everything they wanted: clothes and furniture, as well as means of subsistence. Only when it began to produce more than was sufficient to supply its own wants and the payments in kind to the feudal lord, only then did it also produce commodities. This surplus, thrown into socialised exchange and offered for sale, became commodities.

The artisans of the towns, it is true, had from the first to produce for exchange. But they, also, themselves supplied the greatest part of their own individual wants. They had gardens and plots of land. They turned their cattle out into the communal forest, which, also, yielded them timber and firing. The women spun flax, wool, and so forth. Production for the purpose of exchange, production of commodities, was only in its infancy. Hence, exchange was restricted, the market narrow, the methods of production stable; there was local exclusiveness without, local unity within; the Mark in the country; in the town, the guild.

But with the extension of the production of commodities, and especially with the introduction of the capitalist mode of production, the laws of commodity production, hitherto latent, came into action more openly and with greater force. The old bonds were loosened, the old exclusive limits broken through, the producers were more and more turned into independent, isolated producers of commodities. It became apparent that the production of society at large was ruled by absence of plan, by accident, by anarchy; and this anarchy grew to greater and greater height. But the chief means by aid of which the capitalist mode of production intensified this anarchy of socialised production was the exact opposite of anarchy. It was the increasing organisation of production, upon a social basis, in every individual productive establishment. By this, the old, peaceful, stable condition of things was ended. Wherever this organisation of production was introduced into a branch of industry, it brooked no other method of production by its side. The field of labour became a battle-ground. The great geographical discoveries, and the colonisation following upon them, multiplied markets and quickened the transformation of handicraft into manufacture. The war did not simply break out between the individual producers of particular localities. The local struggles begot in their turn national conflicts, the commercial wars of the seventeenth and eighteenth centuries.

Finally, modern industry and the opening of the world market made the struggle universal, and at the same time gave it an unheard-of virulence. Advantages in natural or artificial conditions of production now decide the existence or non-existence of individual capitalists, as well as of whole industries and countries. He that falls is remorselessly cast aside. It is the Darwinian struggle of the individual for existence transferred from Nature to society with intensified violence. The conditions of existence natural to the animal appear as the final term of human development. The contradiction between socialised production and capitalistic appropriation now presents itself as *an antagonism between the organisation of production in the individual workshop and the anarchy of production in society generally.*

The capitalistic mode of production moves in these two forms of the antagonism immanent to it from its very origin. It is never able to get out of that "vicious circle" which Fourier had already discovered. What Fourier could not, indeed, see in his time is that this circle is gradually narrowing; that the movement becomes more and more a spiral, and must come to an end, like the movement of the planets, by collision with the centre. It is the compelling force of anarchy in the production of society at large that more and more completely turns the great majority of men into proletarians; and it is the masses of the proletariat again who will finally put an end to anarchy in production. It is the compelling force of anarchy in social production that turns the limitless perfectibility of machinery under modern industry into a compulsory law by which every individual industrial capitalist must perfect his machinery more and more, under penalty of ruin.

But the perfecting of machinery is making human labour superfluous. If the introduction and increase of machinery means the displacement of millions of manual by a few machine-workers, improvement in machinery means the displacement of more and more of the machine-workers themselves. It means, in the last instance, the production of a number of available wage-workers in excess of the average needs of capital, the formation of a complete industrial reserve army, as I called it in 1845, available at the times when industry is working at high pressure, to be cast out upon the street when the inevitable crash comes, a constant dead weight upon the limbs of the working class in its struggle for existence with capital, a regulator for the keeping of wages down to the low level that suits the interests of capital. Thus it comes about, to quote Marx, that machinery becomes the most powerful weapon in the war of capital against the working class; that the instruments of labour constantly tear the means of subsistence out of the hands of the labourer; that the very product of the worker is turned into an instrument for his subjugation. Thus it comes about that the economising of the instruments of labour becomes at the same time, from the outset, the most reckless waste of labour power, and robbery based upon the normal conditions under which labour functions; that machinery, "the most powerful instrument for shortening labour time, becomes the most unfailing means for placing every moment of the labourer's time and that of his family at the disposal of the capitalist for the purpose of expanding the value of his capital." (*Capital*, English edition, p. 406.)[9] Thus it comes

9. See p. 406, above. [*R. T.*]

about that the overwork of some becomes the preliminary condition for the idleness of others, and that modern industry, which hunts after new consumers over the whole world, forces the consumption of the masses at home down to a starvation minimum, and in doing thus destroys its own home market. "The law that always equilibrates the relative surplus population, or industrial reserve army, to the extent and energy of accumulation, this law rivets the labourer to capital more firmly than the wedges of Vulcan did Prometheus to the rock. It establishes an accumulation of misery, corresponding with accumulation of capital. Accumulation of wealth at one pole is, therefore, at the same time, accumulation of misery, agony of toil, slavery, ignorance, brutality, mental degradation, at the opposite pole, i.e. on the side of the class that produces *its own product in the form of capital.*" (*Capital*, p. 661.)[1] And to expect any other division of the products from the capitalistic mode of production is the same as expecting the electrodes of a battery not to decompose acidulated water, not to liberate oxygen at the positive, hydrogen at the negative pole, so long as they are connected with the battery.

We have seen that the ever-increasing perfectibility of modern machinery is, by the anarchy of social production, turned into a compulsory law that forces the individual industrial capitalist always to improve his machinery, always to increase its productive force. The bare possibility of extending the field of production is transformed for him into a similar compulsory law. The enormous expansive force of modern industry, compared with which that of gases is mere child's play, appears to us now as a *necessity* for expansion, both qualitative and quantitative, that laughs at all resistance. Such resistance is offered by consumption, by sales, by the markets for the products of modern industry. But the capacity for extension, extensive and intensive, of the markets is primarily governed by quite different laws that work much less energetically. The extension of the markets cannot keep pace with the extension of production. The collision becomes inevitable, and as this cannot produce any real solution so long as it does not break in pieces the capitalist mode of production, the collisions become periodic. Capitalist production has begotten another "vicious circle."

As a matter of fact, since 1825, when the first general crisis broke out, the whole industrial and commercial world, production and exchange among all civilised peoples and their more or less barbaric hangers-on, are thrown out of joint about once every ten years. Commerce is at a standstill, the markets are glutted, products accumulate, as multitudinous as they are unsaleable, hard cash disappears, credit vanishes, factories are closed, the mass of the workers are in want of the means of subsistence, because they have pro-

1. See p. 431, above. [*R. T.*]

duced too much of the means of subsistence; bankruptcy follows upon bankruptcy, execution upon execution. The stagnation lasts for years; productive forces and products are wasted and destroyed wholesale, until the accumulated mass of commodities finally filters off, more or less depreciated in value, until production and exchange gradually begin to move again. Little by little the pace quickens. It becomes a trot. The industrial trot breaks into a canter, the canter in turn grows into the headlong gallop of a perfect steeplechase of industry, commercial credit, and speculation which finally, after breakneck leaps, ends where it began—in the ditch of a crisis. And so over and over again. We have now, since the year 1825, gone through this five times, and at the present moment (1877) we are going through it for the sixth time. And the character of these crises is so clearly defined that Fourier hit all of them off when he described the first as *"crise pléthorique,"* a crisis from plethora.

In these crises, the contradiction between socialised production and capitalist appropriation ends in a violent explosion. The circulation of commodities is, for the time being, stopped. Money, the means of circulation, becomes a hindrance to circulation. All the laws of production and circulation of commodities are turned upside down. The economic collision has reached its apogee. *The mode of production is in rebellion against the mode of exchange.*

The fact that the socialised organisation of production within the factory has developed so far that it has become incompatible with the anarchy of production in society, which exists side by side with and dominates it, is brought home to the capitalists themselves by the violent concentration of capital that occurs during crises, through the ruin of many large, and a still greater number of small, capitalists. The whole mechanism of the capitalist mode of production breaks down under the pressure of the productive forces, its own creations. It is no longer able to turn all this mass of means of production into capital. They lie fallow, and for that very reason the industrial reserve army must also lie fallow. Means of production, means of subsistence, available labourers, all the elements of production and of general wealth, are present in abundance. But "abundance becomes the source of distress and want" (Fourier), because it is the very thing that prevents the transformation of the means of production and subsistence into capital. For in capitalistic society the means of production can only function when they have undergone a preliminary transformation into capital, into the means of exploiting human labour power. The necessity of this transformation into capital of the means of production and subsistence stands like a ghost between these and the workers. It alone prevents the coming together of the material and personal levers of production;

it alone forbids the means of production to function, the workers to work and live. On the one hand, therefore, the capitalistic mode of production stands convicted of its own incapacity to further direct these productive forces. On the other, these productive forces themselves, with increasing energy, press forward to the removal of the existing contradiction to the abolition of their quality as capital, to the *practical recognition of their character as social productive forces.*

This rebellion of the productive forces, as they grow more and more powerful, against their quality as capital, this stronger and stronger command that their social character shall be recognised, forces the capitalist class itself to treat them more and more as social productive forces, so far as this is possible under capitalist conditions. The period of industrial high pressure, with its unbounded inflation of credit, not less than the crash itself, by the collapse of great capitalist establishments, tends to bring about that form of the socialisation of great masses of means of production which we meet with in the different kinds of joint-stock companies. Many of these means of production and of distribution are, from the outset, so colossal that, like the railways, they exclude all other forms of capitalistic exploitation. At a further stage of evolution this form also becomes insufficient. The producers on a large scale in a particular branch of industry in a particular country unite in a trust, a union for the purpose of regulating production. They determine the total amount to be produced, parcel it out among themselves, and thus enforce the selling price fixed beforehand. But trusts of this kind, as soon as business becomes bad, are generally liable to break up, and on this very account compel a yet greater concentration of association. The whole of the particular industry is turned into one gigantic joint-stock company; internal competition gives place to the internal monopoloy of this one company. This has happened in 1890 with the English alkali production, which is now, after the fusion of 48 large works, in the hands of one company, conducted upon a single plan, and with a capital of £6,000,000.

In the trusts, freedom of competition changes into its very opposite—into monopoly; and the production without any definite plan of capitalistic society capitulates to the production upon a definite plan of the invading socialistic society. Certainly this is so far still to the benefit and advantage of the capitalists. But in this case the exploitation is so palpable that it must break down. No nation will put up with production conducted by trusts, with so barefaced an exploitation of the community by a small band of dividend-mongers.

In any case, with trusts or without, the official representative of capitalist society—the state—will ultimately have to undertake the direction of production.[2] This necessity for conversion into state property is felt first in the great institutions for intercourse and communication—the post office, the telegraphs, the railways.

If the crises demonstrate the incapacity of the bourgeoisie for managing any longer modern productive forces, the transformation of the great establishments for production and distribution into joint-stock companies, trusts and state property shows how unnecessary the bourgeoisie are for that purpose. All the social functions of the capitalist are now performed by salaried employees. The capitalist has no further social function than that of pocketing dividends, tearing off coupons, and gambling on the Stock Exchange, where the different capitalists despoil one another of their capital. At first the capitalistic mode of production forces out the workers. Now it forces out the capitalists, and reduces them, just as it reduced the workers, to the ranks of the surplus population, although not immediately into those of the industrial reserve army.

But the transformation, either into joint-stock companies and trusts, or into state ownership, does not do away with the capitalistic nature of the productive forces. In the joint-stock companies and trusts this is obvious. And the modern state, again, is only the organisation that bourgeois society takes on in order to support the external conditions of the capitalist mode of production against the encroachments as well of the workers as of individual capitalists. The modern state, no matter what its form, is essentially a capitalist machine, the state of the capitalists, the ideal personification of the total national capital. The more it proceeds to the taking over of productive forces, the more does it actually become the national capitalist, the more citizens does it exploit. The workers remain wage-workers—proletarians. The capitalist relation is not done away with. It is rather brought to a head. But, brought to a head, it top-

2. I say "have to." For only when the means of production and distribution have *actually* outgrown the form of management by joint-stock companies, and when, therefore, the taking them over by the state has become *economically* inevitable, only then—even if it is the state of today that effects this—is there an economic advance, the attainment of another step preliminary to the taking over of all productive forces by society itself. But of late, since Bismarck went in for state ownership of industrial establishments, a kind of spurious socialism has arisen, degenerating, now and again, into something of flunkeyism, that without more ado declares *all* state ownership, even of the Bismarckian sort, to be socialistic. Certainly, if the taking over by the state of the tobacco industry is socialistic, then Napoleon and Metternich must be numbered among the founders of socialism. If the Belgian state, for quite ordinary political and financial reasons, itself constructed its chief railway lines; if Bismarck, not under any economic compulsion, took over for the state the chief Prussian lines, simply to be the better able to have them in hand in case of war, to bring up the railway employees as voting cattle for the government, and especially to create for himself a new source of income independent of parliamentary votes—this was, in no sense, a socialistic measure, directly or indirectly, consciously or unconsciously. Otherwise, the Royal Maritime Company, the Royal porcelain manufacture, and even the regimental tailor shops of the Army would also be socialistic institutions, or even, as was seriously proposed by a sly dog in Frederick William III's reign, the taking over by the state of the brothels. [*Engels*]

ples over. State ownership of the productive forces is not the solution of the conflict, but concealed within it are the technical conditions that form the elements of that solution.

This solution can only consist in the practical recognition of the social nature of the modern forces of production, and therefore in the harmonising of the modes of production, appropriation, and exchange with the socialised character of the means of production. And this can only come about by society openly and directly taking possession of the productive forces which have outgrown all control except that of society as a whole. The social character of the means of production and of the products today reacts against the producers, periodically distrupts all production and exchange, acts only like a law of Nature working blindly, forcibly, destructively. But with the taking over by society of the productive forces, the social character of the means of production and of the products will be utilised by the producers with a perfect understanding of its nature, and instead of being a source of disturbance and periodical collapse, will become the most powerful lever of production itself.

Active social forces work exactly like natural forces: blindly, forcibly, destructively, so long as we do not understand, and reckon with, them. But when once we understand them, when once we grasp their action, their direction, their effects, it depends only upon ourselves to subject them more and more to our own will, and by means of them to reach our own ends. And this holds quite especially of the mighty productive forces of today. As long as we obstinately refuse to understand the nature and the character of these social means of action—and this understanding goes against the grain of the capitalist mode of production and its defenders—so long these forces are at work in spite of us, in opposition to us, so long they master us, as we have shown above in detail.

But when once their nature is understood, they can, in the hands of the producers working together, be transformed from master demons into willing servants. The difference is as that between the destructive force of electricity in the lightning of the storm, and electricity under command in the telegraph and the voltaic arc; the difference between a conflagration, and fire working in the service of man. With this recognition, at last, of the real nature of the productive forces of today, the social anarchy of production gives place to a social regulation of production upon a definite plan, according to the needs of the community and of each individual. Then the capitalist mode of appropriation, in which the product enslaves first the producer and then the appropriator, is replaced by the mode of appropriation of the products that is based upon the nature of the modern means of production; upon the one hand, direct social appropriation, as means to the maintenance and extension of production—on the other, direct individual appropriation, as means of subsistence and of enjoyment.

Whilst the capitalist mode of production more and more completely transforms the great majority of the population into proletarians, it creates the power which, under penalty of its own destruction, is forced to accomplish this revolution. Whilst it forces on more and more the transformation of the vast means of production, already socialised, into state property, it shows itself the way to accomplishing this revolution. *The proletariat seizes political power and turns the means of production into state property.*

But, in doing this, it abolishes itself as proletariat, abolishes all class distinctions and class antagonisms, abolishes also the state as state. Society thus far, based upon class antagonisms, had need of the state. That is, of an organisation of the particular class which was *pro tempore* the exploiting class, an organisation for the purpose of preventing any interference from without with the existing conditions of production, and, therefore, especially, for the purpose of forcibly keeping the exploited classes in the condition of oppression corresponding with the given mode of production (slavery, serfdom, wage-labour). The state was the official representative of society as a whole; the gathering of it together into a visible embodiment. But it was this only in so far as it was the state of that class which itself represented, for the time being, society as a whole: in ancient times, the state of slaveowning citizens; in the Middle Ages, the feudal lords; in our own time, the bourgeoisie. When at last it becomes the real representative of the whole of society, it renders itself unnecessary. As soon as there is no longer any social class to be held in subjection; as soon as class rule, and the individual struggle for existence based upon our present anarchy in production, with the collisions and excesses arising from these, are removed, nothing more remains to be repressed, and a special repressive force, a state, is no longer necessary. The first act by virtue of which the state really constitutes itself the representative of the whole of society—this is, at the same time, its last independent act as a state. State interference in social relations becomes, in one domain after another, superfluous, and then dies out of itself; the government of persons is replaced by the administration of things, and by the conduct of processes of production. The state is not "abolished." *It dies out.* This gives the measure of the value of the phrase *"a free state,"* both as to its justifiable use at times by agitators, and as to its ultimate scientific insufficiency; and also of the demands of the so-called anarchists for the abolition of the state out of hand.

Since the historical appearance of the capitalist mode of production, the appropriation by society of all the means of production has often been dreamed of, more or less vaguely, by individuals, as well as by sects, as the ideal of the future. But it could become possible, could become a historical necessity, only when the actual conditions for its realisation were there. Like every other social advance, it becomes practicable, not by men understanding that the existence of classes is in contradiction to justice, equality, etc., not by the mere willingness to abolish these classes, but by virtue of certain new economic conditions. The separation of society into an exploiting and an exploited class, a ruling and an oppressed class, was the necessary consequence of the deficient and restricted development of production in former times. So long as the total social labour only yields a product which but slightly exceeds that barely necessary for the existence of all; so long, therefore, as labour engages all or almost all the time of the great majority of the members of society—so long, of necessity, this society is divided into classes. Side by side with the great majority, exclusively bond slaves to labour, arises a class freed from directly productive labour, which looks after the general affairs of society: the direction of labour, state business, law, science, art, etc. It is, therefore, the law of division of labour that lies at the basis of the division into classes. But this does not prevent this division into classes from being carried out by means of violence and robbery, trickery and fraud. It does not prevent the ruling class, once having the upper hand, from consolidating its power at the expense of the working class, from turning its social leadership into an intensified exploitation of the masses.

But if, upon this showing, division into classes has a certain historical justification, it has this only for a given period, only under given social conditions. It was based upon the insufficiency of production. It will be swept away by the complete development of modern productive forces. And, in fact, the abolition of classes in society presupposes a degree of historical evolution at which the existence, not simply of this or that particular ruling class, but of any ruling class at all, and, therefore, the existence of class distinction itself has become an obsolete anachronism. It presupposes, therefore, the development of production carried out to a degree at which appropriation of the means of production and of the products, and, with this, of political domination, of the monopoly of culture, and of intellectual leadership by a particular class of society, has become not only superfluous but economically, politically, intellectually, a hindrance to development.

This point is now reached. Their political and intellectual bankruptcy is scarcely any longer a secret to the bourgeoisie themselves. Their economic bankruptcy recurs regularly every ten years. In every crisis, society is suffocated beneath the weight of its own productive forces and products, which it cannot use, and stands helpless, face to face with the absurd contradiction that the producers have nothing to consume, because consumers are wanting. The expansive force of the means of production bursts the bonds that the capitalist mode of production had imposed upon them. Their deliverance from these bonds is the one precondition for an unbroken, constantly accelerated development of the productive forces, and therewith for a practically unlimited increase of production itself. Nor is this all. The socialised appropriation of the means of production does away, not only with the present artificial restrictions upon production, but also with the positive waste and devastation of productive forces and products that are at the present time the inevitable concomitants of production, and that reach their height in the crises. Further, it sets free for the community at large a mass of means of production and of products, by doing away with the senseless extravagance of the ruling classes of today and their political representatives. The possibility of securing for every member of society, by means of socialised production, an existence not only fully sufficient materially, and becoming day by day more full, but an existence guaranteeing to all the free development and exercise of their physical and mental faculties—this possibility is now for the first time here, but *it is here*.[3]

With the seizing of the means of production by society, production of commodities is done away with, and, simultaneously, the mastery of the product over the producer. Anarchy in social production is replaced by systematic, definite organisation. The struggle for individual existence disappears. Then for the first time man, in a certain sense, is finally marked off from the rest of the animal kingdom, and emerges from mere animal conditions of existence into really human ones. The whole sphere of the conditions of life which environ man, and which have hitherto ruled man, now comes under the dominion and control of man, who for the first time becomes the real, conscious lord of Nature, because he has now become master of his own social organisation. The laws of his own social action, hitherto standing face to face with man as laws of Nature foreign to, and dominating him, will then be used with full understanding, and so mastered by him. Man's own social organisation, hitherto confronting him as a necessity imposed by Nature and history, now becomes the result of his own free action. The extraneous objective forces that have hitherto governed history pass under the control of man himself. Only from that time will man

3. A few figures may serve to give an approximate idea of the enormous expansive force of the modern means of production, even under capitalist pressure. According to Mr. Giffen, the total wealth of Great Britain and Ireland amounted, in round numbers in

1814 to £2,200,000,000.
1865 to £6,100,000,000.
1875 to £8,500,000,000.

As an instance of the squandering of means of production and of products during a crisis, the total loss in the German iron industry alone, in the crisis 1873–78, was given at the second German Industrial Congress (Berlin, February 21, 1878) as £22,750,000. [*Engels*]

himself, more and more consciously, make his own history—only from that time will the social causes set in movement by him have, in the main and in a constantly growing measure, the results intended by him. It is the ascent of man from the kingdom of necessity to the kingdom of freedom.

Let us briefly sum up our sketch of historical evolution.

I. *Mediaeval Society.* Individual production on a small scale. Means of production adapted for individual use; hence primitive, ungainly, petty, dwarfed in action. Production for immediate consumption, either of the producer himself or of his feudal lord. Only where an excess of production over this consumption occurs is such excess offered for sale, enters into exchange. Production of commodities, therefore, only in its infancy. But already it contains within itself, in embryo, *anarchy in the production of society at large.*

II. *Capitalist Revolution.* Transformation of industry, at first by means of simple co-operation and manufacture. Concentration of the means of production, hitherto scattered, into great workshops. As a consequence, their transformation from individual to social means of production—a transformation which does not, on the whole, affect the form of exchange. The old forms of appropriation remain in force. The capitalist appears. In his capacity as owner of the means of production, he also appropriates the products and turns them into commodities. Production has become a *social* act. Exchange and appropriation continue to be *individual* acts, the acts of individuals. *The social product is appropriated by the individual capitalist.* Fundamental contradiction, whence arise all the contradictions in which our present-day society moves, and which modern industry brings to light.

A. Severance of the producer from the means of production. Condemnation of the worker to wage-labour for life. *Antagonism between the proletariat and the bourgeoisie.*

B. Growing predominance and increasing effectiveness of the laws governing the production of commodities. Unbridled competition. *Contradiction between socialised organisation in the individual factory and social anarchy in production as a whole.*

C. On the one hand, perfecting of machinery, made by competition compulsory for each individual manufacturer, and complemented by a constantly growing displacement of labourers. *Industrial reserve army.* On the other hand, unlimited extension of production, also compulsory under competition, for every manufacturer. On both sides, unheard-of development of productive forces, excess of supply over demand, over-production, glutting of the markets, crises every ten years, the vicious circle: excess here, of means of production and products—excess there, of labourers, without employment and without means of existence. But these two levers of production and of social well-being are unable to work together, because the capitalist form of production prevents the productive forces from working and the products from circulating, unless they are first turned into capital—which their very superabundance prevents. The contradiction has grown into an absurdity. *The mode of production rises in rebellion against the form of exchange.* The bourgeoisie are convicted of incapacity further to manage their own social productive forces.

D. Partial recognition of the social character of the productive forces forced upon the capitalists themselves. Taking over of the great institutions for production and communication, first by joint-stock companies, later on by trusts, then by the state. The bourgeoisie demonstrated to be a superfluous class. All its social functions are now performed by salaried employees.

III. *Proletarian Revolution.* Solution of the contradictions. The proletariat seizes the public power, and by means of this transforms the socialised means of production, slipping from the hands of the bourgeoisie, into public property. By this act, the proletariat frees the means of production from the character of capital they have thus far borne, and gives their socialised character complete freedom to work itself out. Socialised production upon a predetermined plan becomes henceforth possible. The development of production makes the existence of different classes of society thenceforth an anachronism. In proportion as anarchy in social production vanishes, the political authority of the state dies out. Man, at last the master of his own form of social organisation, becomes at the same time the lord over Nature, his own master—free.

To accomplish this act of universal emancipation is the historical mission of the modern proletariat. To thoroughly comprehend the historical conditions and thus the very nature of this act, to impart to the new oppressed proletarian class a full knowledge of the conditions and of the meaning of the momentous act it is called upon to accomplish, this is the task of the theoretical expression of the proletarian movement, scientific socialism.

On the Division of Labour in Production

FRIEDRICH ENGELS

This selection from Engels' work of 1878, *Anti-Dühring*, shows that the dehumanizing nature of the division of labour was a central theme in the thought of Marx and Engels, linking their early philosophical communism with *Capital* and other later writings in an unbroken line of continuity. The socialism of Marx and Engels, unlike that of some other socialist theorists of their time and after, placed principal emphasis upon production rather than distribution. Its central concern was with the individual as a producer and the conditions of his productive activity. It saw the division of labour in production as an enslaving situation that had been characteristic of all hitherto existing modes of production—capitalism particularly—and looked to future socialism as a mode of production in which the division of labour would be, so far as technically possible, abolished.

* * * Distribution, in so far as it is governed by purely economic considerations, is regulated by the interests of production, and production is most encouraged by a mode of distribution which allows *all* members of society to develop, maintain and exert their capacities in all possible directions. It is true that, to the mode of thought of the educated classes which Herr Dühring has inherited, it must seem monstrous that in time to come there will no longer be any professional porters or architects, and that the man who for half an hour gives instructions as an architect will also push a barrow for a period, until his activity as an architect is once again required. It is a fine sort of socialism which perpetuates the professional porter!

* * * In every society in which production has developed spontaneously—and our present society is of this type—the situation is not that the producers control the means of production, but that the means of production control the producers. In such a society each new lever of production is necessarily transformed into a new means for the subjection of the producers to the means of production. This is most of all true of that lever of production which, prior to the introduction of modern industry, was by far the most

718

powerful—the division of labour. The first great division of labour, the separation of town and country, condemned the rural population to thousands of years of mental torpidity, and the people of the towns each to subjection to his own individual trade. It destroyed the basis of the intellectual development of the former and the physical development of the latter. When the peasant appropriates his land, and the townsman his trade, his land appropriates the peasant and his trade the townsman to the very same extent. In the division of labour, man is also divided. All other physical and mental faculties are sacrificed to the development of one single activity. This stunting of man grows in the same measure as the division of labour, which attains its highest development in manufacture. Manufacture splits up each trade into its separate partial operations, allots each of these to an individual labourer as his life calling, and thus chains him for life to a particular detail function and a particular tool. "It converts the labourer into a crippled monstrosity, by forcing his detail dexterity at the expense of a world of productive capabilities and instincts. . . . The individual himself is made the automatic motor of a fractional operation" (Marx)[1]—a motor which in many cases is perfected only by literally crippling the labourer physically and mentally. The machinery of modern industry degrades the labourer from a machine to the mere appendage of a machine. "The life-long speciality of handling one and the same tool, now becomes the lifelong speciality of serving one and the same machine. Machinery is put to a wrong use, with the object of transforming the workman, from his very childhood, into a part of a detail-machine" (Marx).[2] And not only the labourers, but also the classes directly or indirectly exploiting the labourers are made subject, through the divison of labour, to the tool of their function: the empty-minded bourgeois to his own capital and his own insane craving for profits; the lawyer to his fossilized legal conceptions, which dominate him as an independent power; the "educated classes" in general to their manifold species of local narrow-mindedness and one-sidedness, to their own physical and mental short-sightedness, to their stunted growth due to their narrow specialized education and their being chained for life to this specialized activity—even when this specialized activity is merely to do nothing.

The utopians were already perfectly clear in their minds as to the effects of the division of labour, the stunting on the one hand of the labourer, and on the other of the labour function, which is restricted to the lifelong, uniform, mechanical repetition of one and the same operation. The abolition of the antithesis between town and country was demanded by Fourier, as by Owen, as the first

1. See *Capital*, p. 398, above. [R. T.]   2. See *Capital*, p. 408, above. [R. T.]

prerequisite for the abolition of the old division of labour altogether. Both of them thought that the population should be scattered through the country in groups of sixteen hundred to three thousand persons; each group was to occupy a gigantic palace, with a household run on communal lines, in the centre of their area of land. It is true that Fourier occasionally refers to towns, but these were to consist in turn of only four or five such palaces situated near each other. Both writers would have each member of society occupied in agriculture as well as in industry; with Fourier, industry covers chiefly handicrafts and manufacture, while Owen assigns the main role to modern industry and already demands the introduction of steam-power and machinery in domestic work. But within agriculture as well as industry both of them also demand the greatest possible variety of occupation for each individual, and in accordance with this, the training of the youth for the utmost possible all-round technical functions. They both consider that man should gain universal development through universal practical activity and that labour should recover the attractiveness of which the division of labour has despoiled it, in the first place through this variation of occupation, and through the correspondingly short duration of the "sitting"—to use Fourier's expression—devoted to each particular kind of work. Both Fourier and Owen are far in advance of the mode of thought of the exploiting classes inherited by Herr Dühring, according to which the antithesis between town and country is inevitable in the nature of things; the narrow view that a number of "entities" must in any event be condemned to the production of *one single* article, the view that desires to perpetuate the "economic species" of men distinguished by their way of life—people who take pleasure in the performance of precisely this and no other thing, who have therefore sunk so low that they *rejoice* in their own subjection and one-sidedness. In comparison with the basic conceptions even of the "idiot" Fourier's most recklessly bold fantasies; in comparison even with the paltriest ideas of the "crude, feeble, and paltry" Owen—Herr Dühring, himself still completely dominated by the division of labour, is no more than an impertinent dwarf.

In making itself the master of all the means of production to use them in accordance with a social plan, society puts an end to the former subjection of men to their own means of production. It goes without saying that society cannot free itself unless every individual is freed. The old mode of production must therefore be revolutionized from top to bottom, and in particular the former division of labour must disappear. Its place must be taken by an organization of production in which, on the one hand, no individual can throw on the shoulders of others his share in productive labour, this natural condition of human existence; and in which, on the other hand, productive labour, instead of being a means of subjugating men, will become a means of their emancipation, by offering each individual the opportunity to develop all his faculties, physical and mental, in all directions and exercise them to the full—in which, therefore, productive labour will become a pleasure instead of being a burden.

Today this is no longer a fantasy, no longer a pious wish. With the present development of the productive forces, the increase in production that will follow from the very fact of the socialization of the productive forces, coupled with the abolition of the barriers and disturbances, and of the waste of products and means of production, resulting from the capitalist mode of production, will suffice, with everybody doing his share of work, to reduce the time required for labour to a point which, measured by our present conceptions, will be small indeed.

Nor is the abolition of the old division of labour a demand which could only be carried through to the detriment of the productivity of labour. On the contrary. Thanks to modern industry it has become a condition of production itself. "The employment of machinery does away with the necessity of crystallizing this distribution after the manner of Manufacture, by the constant annexation of a particular man to a particular function. Since the motion of the whole system does not proceed from the workman, but from the machinery, a change of persons can take place at any time without an interruption of the work. . . . Lastly, the quickness with which machine work is learnt by young people does away with the necessity of bringing up for exclusive employment by machinery, a special class of operatives."[3] But while the capitalist mode of employment of machinery necessarily perpetuates the old division of labour with its fossilized specialization, although it has become superfluous from a technical standpoint, the machinery itself rebels against this anachronism. The technical basis of modern industry is revolutionary. "By means of machinery, chemical processes and other methods, it is continually causing changes not only in the technical basis of production, but also in the functions of the labourer, and in the social combinations of the labour process. At the same time, it thereby also revolutionizes the division of labour within the society, and incessantly launches masses of capital and of workpeople from one branch of production to another. Modern industry, by its very nature, therefore necessitates variation of labour, fluency of function, universal mobility of the labourer. . . . We have seen how this absolute contradiction . . . vents its rage . . .

3. See *Capital*, p. 408, above. [R. T.]

in the incessant human sacrifices from among the working class, in the most reckless squandering of labour-power, and in the devastation caused by social anarchy. This is the negative side. But, if, on the one hand, variation of work at present imposes itself after the manner of an overpowering natural law, and with the blindly destructive action of a natural law that meets with resistance at all points, modern industry, on the other hand, through its catastrophes imposes the necessity of recognizing, as a fundamental law of production, variation of work, consequently fitness of the labourer for varied work, consequently the greatest possible development of his varied aptitudes. It becomes a question of life and death for society to adapt the mode of production to the normal functioning of this law. Modern industry, indeed, compels society, under penalty of death, to replace the detail-worker of today, crippled by lifelong repetition of one and the same trivial operation, and thus reduced to the mere fragment of a man, by the fully developed individual, fit for a variety of labours, ready to face any change of production, and to whom the different social functions he performs, are but so many modes of giving free scope to his own natural and acquired powers" (Marx, *Capital*).[4]

Modern industry, which has taught us to convert the movement of molecules, something more or less universally feasible, into the movement of masses for technical purposes, has thereby to a considerable extent freed production from restrictions of locality. Water-power was local; steam-power is free. While water-power is necessarily rural, steam-power is by no means necessarily urban. It is capitalist utilization which concentrates it mainly in the towns and changes factory villages into factory towns. But in so doing it at the same time undermines the conditions under which it operates. The first requirement of the steam-engine, and a main requirement of almost all branches of production in modern industry, is relatively pure water. But the factory town transforms all water into stinking manure. However much therefore urban concentration is a basic condition of capitalist production, each individual industrial capitalist is constantly striving to get away from the large towns necessarily created by this concentration, and to transfer his plant to the countryside. This process can be studied in detail in the textile industry districts of Lancashire and Yorkshire; modern capitalist industry is constantly bringing new large towns into being there by constant flight from the towns into the country. The situation is similar in the metal-working districts where, in part, other causes produce the same effects.

Once more, only the abolition of the capitalist character of

4. See pp. 413–414, above. [*R. T.*]

modern industry can bring us out of this new vicious circle, can resolve this contradiction in modern industry, which is constantly reproducing itself. Only a society which makes it possible for its productive forces to dovetail harmoniously into each other on the basis of one single vast plan can allow industry to be distributed over the whole country in the way best adapted to its own development, and to the maintenance and development of the other elements of production.

Accordingly, abolition of the antithesis between town and country is not merely possible. It has become a direct necessity of industrial production itself, just as it has become a necessity of agricultural production and, besides, of public health. The present poisoning of the air, water and land can be put an end to only by the fusion of town and country; and only such fusion will change the situation of the masses now languishing in the towns, and enable their excrement to be used for the production of plants instead of for the production of disease.

Capitalist industry has already made itself relatively independent of the local limitations arising from the location of sources of the raw materials it needs. The textile industry works up, in the main, imported raw materials. Spanish iron ore is worked up in England and Germany and Spanish and South-American copper ores, in England. Every coal-field now supplies fuel to an industrial area beyond its own borders, an area which is widening every year. Along the whole of the European coast steam engines are driven by English and to some extent also by German and Belgian coal. Society liberated from the barriers of capitalist production can go much further still. By generating a race of producers with an all-round training who understand the scientific basis of industrial production as a whole, and each of whom has had practical experience in a whole series of branches of production from start to finish, this society will bring into being a new productive force which will abundantly compensate for the labour required to transport raw materials and fuel from great distances.

The abolition of the separation of town and country is therefore not utopian, also, in so far as it is conditioned on the most equal distribution possible of modern industry over the whole country. It is true that in the huge towns civilization has bequeathed us a heritage which it will take much time and trouble to get rid of. But it must and will be got rid of, however protracted a process it may be. Whatever destiny may be in store for the German Empire of the Prussian nation, Bismarck can go to his grave proudly aware that the desire of his heart is sure to be fulfilled: the great towns will perish.

And now see how puerile Herr Dühring's notions are—that

society can take possession of all means of production in the aggregate without revolutionizing from top to bottom the old method of production and first of all putting an end to the old division of labour; that everything will be in order once "natural aptitudes and personal capabilities are taken into account"—that therefore whole masses of entities will remain, as in the past, subjected to the production of *one single* article; whole "populations" will be engaged in a single branch of production, and humanity continue divided, as in the past, into a number of different crippled "economic species," for there still are "porters" and "architects." Society is to become master of the means of production as a whole, in order that each individual may remain the slave of his means of production, and have only a choice as to *which* means of production are to enslave him. And see also how Herr Dühring considers the separation of town and country as "inevitable in the nature of things," and can find only a tiny palliative in schnaps-distilling and beet-sugar manufacturing—two, in their connection specifically Prussian, branches of industry; how he makes the distribution of industry over the country dependent on certain future inventions and on the *necessity* of associating industry directly with the procurement of raw materials—raw materials which are already used at an ever increasing distance from their place of origin! And Herr Dühring finally tries to cover his retreat by assuring us that in the long run social wants will carry through the union between agriculture and industry even *against* economic considerations, as if this would be some economic sacrifice!

Certainly, to be able to see that the revolutionary elements, which will do away with the old division of labour, along with the separation of town and country, and will revolutionize the whole of production; see that these elements are already contained in embryo in the productive conditions of modern large-scale industry and that their development is hindered by the existing capitalist mode of production—to be able to see these things, it is necessary to have a somewhat wider horizon than the sphere of jurisdiction of the Prussian *Landrecht,* than the country where production of schnaps and beet-sugar are the key industries, and where commercial crises can be studied on the book market. To be able to see these things it is necessary to have some knowledge of real large-scale industry in its historical growth and in its present actual form, especially in the one country where it has its home and where alone it has attained its classical development. Then no one will think of attempting to vulgarize modern scientific socialism and to degrade it into Herr Dühring's *specifically Prussian socialism*.

On Morality

FRIEDRICH ENGELS

Value judgments resting on moral convictions abound in Marx and Engels. Thus they not only analyze exploitation and the division of labour in society, but morally condemn these phenomena as evil. Yet, there is almost no abstract discussion of ethics in their voluminous writings. An exception is this passage from *Anti-Dühring*, frequently cited as an authoritative statement of the view of Marx and Engels on the nature of morality. The mode of reasoning seems more distinctively characteristic of Engels' mind, however, than of Marx's.

---

* * * If, then, we have not made much progress with truth and error, we can make even less with good and evil. This opposition manifests itself exclusively in the domain of morals, that is, a domain belonging to the history of mankind, and it is precisely in this field that final and ultimate truths are most sparsely sown. The conceptions of good and evil have varied so much from nation to nation and from age to age that they have often been in direct contradiction to each other.

But all the same, someone may object, good is not evil and evil is not good; if good is confused with evil there is an end to all morality, and everyone can do as he pleases. This is also, stripped of all oracular phrases, Herr Dühring's opinion. But the matter cannot be so simply disposed of. If it were such an easy business there would certainly be no dispute at all over good and evil; everyone would know what was good and what was bad. But how do things stand today? What morality is preached to us today? There is first Christian-feudal morality, inherited from earlier religious times; and this is divided, essentially, into a Catholic and a Protestant morality, each of which has no lack of subdivisions, from the Jesuit-Catholic and Orthodox-Protestant to loose "enlightened" moralities. Alongside these we find the modern-bourgeois morality and beside it also the proletarian morality of the future, so that in the most advanced European countries alone the past, present and future provide three great groups of moral theories which are in force simultaneously and alongside each other. Which, then, is the true one? Not one of them, in the sense of absolute finality; but certainly that morality contains the maximum elements promising permanence which, in the present, represents the overthrow of the present, represents the future, and that is proletarian morality.

But when we see that the three classes of modern society, the feudal aristocracy, the bourgeoisie and the proletariat, each have a morality of their own, we can only draw the one conclusion: that men, consciously or unconsciously, derive their ethical ideas in the last resort from the practical relations on which their class position is based—from the economic relations in which they carry on production and exchange.

But nevertheless there is quite a lot which the three moral theories mentioned above have in common—is this not at least a portion of a morality which is fixed once and for all? These moral theories represent three different stages of the same historical development, have therefore a common historical background, and for that reason alone they necessarily have much in common. Even more. At similar or approximately similar stages of economic development moral theories must of necessity be more or less in agreement. From the moment when private ownership of movable property developed, all societies in which this private ownership existed had to have this moral injunction in common: Thou shalt not steal. Does this injunction thereby become an eternal moral injunction? By no means. In a society in which all motives for stealing have been done away with, in which therefore at the very most only lunatics would ever steal, how the preacher of morals would be laughed at who tried solemnly to proclaim the eternal truth: Thou shalt not steal!

We therefore reject every attempt to impose on us any moral dogma whatsoever as an eternal, ultimate and forever immutable ethical law on the pretext that the moral world, too, has its permanent principles which stand above history and the differences between nations. We maintain on the contrary that all moral theories have been hitherto the product, in the last analysis, of the economic conditions of society obtaining at the time. And as society has hitherto moved in class antagonisms, morality has always been class morality; it has either justified the domination and the interests of the ruling class, or, ever since the oppressed class became powerful enough, it has represented its indignation against this domination and the future interests of the oppressed. That in this process there has on the whole been progress in morality, as in all other branches of human knowledge, no one will doubt. But we have not yet passed beyond class morality. A really human morality which stands above class antagonisms and above any recollection of them becomes possible only at a stage of society which has not only overcome class antagonisms but has even forgotten them in practical life. And now one can gauge Herr Dühring's presumption in advancing his claim, from the midst of the old class society and on the eve of a social revolution, to impose on the future classless society an eternal morality independent of time and changes in reality. Even assuming—what we do not know up to now—that he understands the structure of the society of the future at least in its main outlines. * * *

Versus the Anarchists

FRIEDRICH ENGELS

The issue between Marxism and Anarchism has often been defined in terms of two opposing beliefs as to the grand strategy of socialist revolution—with Marxists taking the position that state power must be seized and employed for the transformation of society and Anarchists (such as Bakunin) holding that state power must be destroyed in the very process of the revolution. Underlying that important disagreement, as Engels made plain in this letter of January 24, 1872, to Theodor Cuno, is a still more fundamental theoretical divergence that turns on differing definitions of what is to be regarded as the "main evil" in society—capital or state power.

Bakunin, who up to 1868 had intrigued against the International, joined it after he had suffered a fiasco at the Berne Peace Congress[1] and at once began to conspire *within it* against the General Council. Bakunin has a peculiar theory of his own, a medley of Proudhonism and communism, the chief point of which is, in the first place, that he does not regard capital—and therefore the class antagonism between capitalists and wage-workers which has arisen through social development—but the *state* as the main evil to be abolished. While the great mass of the Social-Democratic workers hold our view that the state power is nothing more than the organisation with which the ruling classes—landlords and capitalists—have provided themselves in order to protect their social privileges, Bakunin maintains that it is the *state* which has created capital, that the capitalist has his capital *only by the grace of the state*. As, therefore, the state is the chief evil, it is above all the state which must be done away with and then capitalism will go to blazes of itself. We, on the contrary, say: Do away with capital, the concentration of all means of production in the hands of the few, and the state will fall of itself. The difference is an essential one: Without a previous social revolution the abolition of the state is

1. The reference is to the Berne Congress of the bourgeois League of Peace and Freedom, in which Bakunin took a leading part until October 1868.

nonsense; the abolition of capital *is* precisely the social revolution and involves a change in the whole mode of production. Now then, inasmuch as to Bakunin the state is the main evil, nothing must be done which can maintain the existence of the state, that is, of any state, whether it be a republic, a monarchy or anything else. Hence *complete abstention from all politics.* To commit a political act, and especially to take part in an election, would be a betrayal of principle. The thing to do is to carry on propaganda, heap abuse upon the state; organise, and when ALL the workers are won over, that is, the majority, depose all the authorities, abolish the state and replace it by the organisation of the International. This great act, with which the millennium begins, is called *social liquidation.*

All this sounds extremely radical, and is so simple that it can be learnt by heart in five minutes; that is why this theory of Bakunin's has speedily found favour in Italy and Spain among young lawyers, doctors and other doctrinaires. But the mass of the workers will never allow itself to be persuaded that the public affairs of their countries are not also their own affairs, they are by nature *political* and whoever tries to make out to them that they should leave politics alone will in the end be left alone. To preach to the workers that they should in all circumstances abstain from politics is to drive them into the arms of the priests or the bourgeois republicans.

Now, as the International, according to Bakunin, was not formed for political struggle but in order that it may at once replace the old state organisation as soon as social liquidation takes place, it follows that it must come as near as possible to the Bakuninist ideal of the society of the future. In this society there will above all be no *authority,* for authority=state=an absolute evil. (Indeed, how these people propose to run a factory, operate a railway or steer a ship without having in the last resort one deciding will, without single management, they of course do not tell us.) The authority of the majority over the minority also ceases. Every individual and every community is autonomous; but as to how a society, even of only two people, is possible unless each gives up some of his autonomy, Bakunin again maintains silence. * * *

On Authority

FRIEDRICH ENGELS

In this article written in October, 1872, and originally published in Italian in the collection *Almanacco Repubblicano* for 1874, Engels continued the debate against the Anarchists. Of special note is his argument that revolution itself is "certainly the most authoritarian thing there is," and his further contention, which seems inconsistent with some of what we know of the thinking of Marx, that machine industry is inherently "despotic" in relation to the workers.

A number of Socialists have latterly launched a regular crusade against what they call the *principle of authority*. It suffices to tell them that this or that act is *authoritarian* for it to be condemned. This summary mode of procedure is being abused to such an extent that it has become necessary to look into the matter somewhat more closely. Authority, in the sense in which the word is used here, means: the imposition of the will of another upon ours; on the other hand, authority presupposes subordination. Now, since these two words sound bad and the relationship which they represent is disagreeable to the subordinated party, the question is to ascertain whether there is any way of dispensing with it, whether—given the conditions of present-day society—we could not create another social system, in which this authority would be given no scope any longer and would consequently have to disappear. On examining the economic, industrial and agricultural conditions which form the basis of present-day bourgeois society, we find that they tend more and more to replace isolated action by combined action of individuals. Modern industry with its big factories and mills, where hundreds of workers supervise complicated machines driven by steam, has superseded the small workshops of the separate producers; the carriages and wagons of the highways have been substituted by railway trains, just as the small schooners and sailing feluccas have been by steam-boats. Even agriculture falls increasingly under the dominion of the machine and of steam, which slowly but relentlessly put in the place of the small proprietors big capitalists, who with the aid of hired workers cultivate vast stretches of land. Everywhere combined action, the complication of processes dependent upon each other, displaces independent action by individuals. But whoever mentions combined action speaks of organisation; now, is it possible to have organisation without authority?

Supposing a social revolution dethroned the capitalists, who now exercise their authority over the production and circulation of wealth. Supposing, to adopt entirely the point of view of the anti-authoritarians, that the land and the instruments of labour had become the collective property of the workers who use them. Will authority have disappeared or will it only have changed its form? Let us see.

Let us take by way of example a cotton spinning mill. The cotton must pass through at least six successive operations before it is reduced to the state of thread, and these operations take place for the most part in different rooms. Furthermore, keeping the machines going requires an engineer to look after the steam engine, mechanics to make the current repairs, and many other labourers whose business it is to transfer the products from one room to another, and so forth. All these workers, men, women and children, are obliged to begin and finish their work at the hours fixed by the authority of the steam, which cares nothing for individual autonomy. The workers must, therefore, first come to an understanding on the hours of work; and these hours, once they are fixed, must be observed by all, without any exception. Thereafter particular questions arise in each room and at every moment concerning the mode of production, distribution of materials, etc., which must be settled at once on pain of seeing all production immediately stopped; whether they are settled by decision of a delegate placed at the head of each branch of labour or, if possible, by a majority vote, the will of the single individual will always have to subordinate itself, which means that questions are settled in an authoritarian way. The automatic machinery of a big factory is much more despotic than the small capitalists who employ workers ever have been. At least with regard to the hours of work one may write upon the portals of these factories: *Lasciate ogni autonomia, voi che entrate!*[1] If man, by dint of his knowledge and inventive genius, has subdued the forces of nature, the latter avenge themselves upon him by subjecting him, in so far as he employs them, to a veritable despotism independent of all social organisation. Wanting to abolish authority in large-scale industry is tantamount to wanting to abolish industry itself, to destroy the power loom in order to return to the spinning wheel.

Let us take another example—the railway. Here too the co-opera-

1. "Leave, ye that enter in, all autonomy behind!"

tion of an infinite number of individuals is absolutely necessary, and this co-operation must be practised during precisely fixed hours so that no accidents may happen. Here, too, the first condition of the job is a dominant will that settles all subordinate questions, whether this will is represented by a single delegate or a committee charged with the execution of the resolutions of the majority of persons interested. In either case there is very pronounced authority. Moreover, what would happen to the first train dispatched if the authority of the railway employees over the Hon. passengers were abolished?

But the necessity of authority, and of imperious authority at that, will nowhere be found more evident than on board a ship on the high seas. There, in time of danger, the lives of all depend on the instantaneous and absolute obedience of all to the will of one.

When I submitted arguments like these to the most rabid antiauthoritarians the only answer they were able to give me was the following: Yes, that's true, but here it is not a case of authority which we confer on our delegates, *but of a commission entrusted!* These gentlemen think that when they have changed the names of things they have changed the things themselves. This is how these profound thinkers mock at the whole world.

We have thus seen that, on the one hand, a certain authority, no matter how delegated, and, on the other hand, a certain subordination, are things which, independently of all social organisation, are imposed upon us together with the material conditions under which we produce and make products circulate.

We have seen, besides, that the material conditions of production and circulation inevitably develop with large-scale industry and large-scale agriculture, and increasingly tend to enlarge the scope of this authority. Hence it is absurd to speak of the principle of authority as being absolutely evil, and of the principle of autonomy as being absolutely good. Authority and autonomy are relative things whose spheres vary with the various phases of the development of society. If the autonomists confined themselves to saying that the social organisation of the future would restrict authority solely to the limits within which the conditions of production render it inevitable, we could understand each other; but they are blind to all facts that make the thing necessary and they passionately fight the word.

Why do the anti-authoritarians not confine themselves to crying out against political authority, the state? All Socialists are agreed that the political state, and with it political authority, will disappear as a result of the coming social revolution, that is, that public functions will lose their political character and be transformed into the simple administrative functions of watching over the true interests of society. But the anti-authoritarians demand that the authoritarian political state be abolished at one stroke, even before the social conditions that gave birth to it have been destroyed. They demand that the first act of the social revolution shall be the abolition of authority. Have these gentlemen ever seen a revolution? A revolution is certainly the most authoritarian thing there is; it is the act whereby one part of the population imposes its will upon the other part by means of rifles, bayonets and cannon—authoritarian means, if such there be at all; and if the victorious party does not want to have fought in vain, it must maintain this rule by means of the terror which its arms inspire in the reactionaries. Would the Paris Commune have lasted a single day if it had not made use of this authority of the armed people against the bourgeois? Should we not, on the contrary, reproach it for not having used it freely enough?

Therefore, either one of two things: either the anti-authoritarians don't know what they are talking about, in which case they are creating nothing but confusion; or they do know, and in that case they are betraying the movement of the proletariat. In either case they serve the reaction.

The Origin of the Family, Private Property, and the State

FRIEDRICH ENGELS

In *Ancient Society, or Researches in the Lines of Human Progress from Savagery Through Barbarism to Civilization* (1877), the American anthropologist Lewis H. Morgan propounded a matrilineal theory of the origins of human society. His account of a stateless primitive society founded on communal property appeared to Marx and Engels to have (as Engels later put it) the same significance for the history of primitive society as Darwin's theory of evolution had for biology and Marx's theory of surplus value had for political economy. Marx planned to write a study based on Morgan's researches, and made extensive extracts from and notes on *Ancient Society* for this purpose.* Using Marx's materials as well as the original sources, and occasionally even interpolating Marx's marginalia, Engels in 1884 wrote his monograph on *The Origin of the Family, Private Property, and the State*, from which this selection is taken. The two subtitles have been added by the editor of this reader.

The Family: Its Past, Present and Future

* * *

* * * The evolution of the family in prehistoric times consisted in the continual narrowing of the circle—originally embracing the whole tribe—within which marital community between the two sexes prevailed. By the successive exclusion, first of closer, then of ever remoter relatives; and finally even of those merely related by marriage; every kind of group marriage was ultimately rendered practically impossible; and in the end there remained only the one, for the moment still loosely united, couple, the molecule, with the dissolution of which marriage itself completely ceases. This fact alone shows how little individual sex love, in the modern sense of

---

* Now available in *The Ethnological* and edited by Laurence Krader *Notebooks of Karl Marx*, transcribed (Assen: Van Gorcum, 1972).

the word, had to do with the origin of monogamy. The practice of all peoples in this stage affords still further proof of this. Whereas under previous forms of the family men were never in want of women but, on the contrary, had a surfeit of them, women now became scarce and were sought after. Consequently with pairing marriage begins the abduction and purchase of women— widespread *symptoms,* but nothing more of a much more deeply-rooted change that had set in. * * *

The pairing family, itself too weak and unstable to make an independent household necessary, or even desirable, did not by any means dissolve the communistic household transmitted form earlier times. But the communistic household implies the supremacy of women in the house, just as the exclusive recognition of a natural mother, because of the impossibility of determining the natural father with certainty, signifies high esteem for the women, that is, for the mothers. That woman was the slave of man at the commencement of society is one of the most absurd notions that have come down to us from the period of Enlightenment of the eighteenth century. Woman occupied not only a free but also a highly respected position among all savages and all barbarians of the lower and middle stages and partly even of the upper stage. Let Arthur Wright, missionary for many years among the Seneca Iroquois, testify what her place still was in the pairing family: "As to their family system, when occupying the old long houses [communistic households embracing several families] . . . it is probable that some one clan [gens] predominated, the women taking husbands from other clans [gentes]. . . . Usually the female portion ruled the house; the stores were in common; but woe to the luckless husband or lover who was too shiftless to do his share of the providing. No matter how many children or whatever goods he might have in the house, he might at any time be ordered to pack up his blanket and budge; and after such orders it would not be healthful for him to attempt to disobey. The house would be too hot for him; and he had to retreat to his own clan [gens]; or, as was often done, go and start a new matrimonial alliance in some other. The women were the great power among the clans [gentes], as everywhere else. They did not hesitate, when occasion required, to knock off the horns, as it was technically called, from the head of the chief and send him back to the ranks of the warriors." * * *

* * *

* * * As wealth increased, it, on the one hand, gave the man a more important status in the family than the woman, and, on the other hand, created a stimulus to utilise this strengthened position in order to overthrow the traditional order of inheritance in favour of his children. But this was impossible as long as descent accord-

ing to mother right prevailed. This had, therefore, to be overthrown, and it was overthrown; and it was not so difficult to do this as it appears to us now. For this revolution—one of the most decisive ever experienced by mankind—need not have disturbed one single living member of a gens. All the members could remain what they were previously. The simple decision sufficed that in future the descendants of the male members should remain in the gens, but that those of the females were to be excluded from the gens and transferred to that of their father. The reckoning of descent through the female line and the right of inheritance through the mother were hereby overthrown and male lineage and right of inheritance from the father instituted. We know nothing as to how and when this revolution was effected among the civilised peoples. It falls entirely within prehistoric times. That it was actually *effected* is more than proved by the abundant traces of mother right which have been collected, especially by Bachofen. How easily it is accomplished can be seen from a whole number of Indian tribes, among whom it has only recently taken place and is still proceeding, partly under the influence of increasing wealth and changed methods of life (transplantation from the forests to the prairies), and partly under the moral influence of civilisation and the missionaries. Of eight Missouri tribes, six have male and two still retain the female lineage and female inheritance line. Among the Shawnees, Miamis and Delawares it has become the custom to transfer the children to the father's gens by giving them one of the gentile names obtaining therein, in order that they may inherit from him. "Innate human causuistry to seek to change things by changing their names! And to find loopholes for breaking through tradition within tradition itself, wherever a direct interest provided a sufficient motive!" (Marx.) As a consequence, hopeless confusion arose; and matters could only be straightened out, and partly were straightened out, by the transition to father right. "This appears altogether to be the most natural transition." (Marx) As for what the experts on comparative law have to tell us regarding the ways and means by which this transition was effected among the civilised peoples of the Old World—almost mere hypotheses, of course—see M. Kovalevsky, *Outline of the Origin and Evolution of the Family and Property*, Stockholm, 1890.

The overthrow of mother right was the *world-historic defeat of the female sex*. The man seized the reins in the house also, the woman was degraded, enthralled, the slave of the man's lust, a mere instrument for breeding children. This lowered position of women, especially manifest among the Greeks of the Heroic and still more of the Classical Age, has become gradually embellished and dissembled and, in part, clothed in a milder form, but by no means abolished.

The first effect of the sole rule of the men that was now established is shown in the intermediate form of the family which now emerges, the patriarchal family. Its chief attribute is not polygamy —of which more anon—but "the organisation of a number of persons, bond and free, into a family under the paternal power of the head of the family. In the Semitic form, this family chief lives in polygamy, the bondsman has a wife and children, and the purpose of the whole organisation is the care of flocks and herds over a limited area." The essential features are the incorporation of bondsmen and the paternal power; the Roman family, accordingly, constitutes the perfected type of this form of the family. The word *familia* did not originally signify the ideal of our modern Philistine, which is a compound of sentimentality and domestic discord. Among the Romans, in the beginning, it did not even refer to the married couple and their children, but to the slaves alone. *Famulus* means a household slave and *familia* signifies the totality of slaves belonging to one individual. Even in the time of Gaius the *familia, id est patrimonium* (that is, the inheritance) was bequeathed by will. The expression was invented by the Romans to describe a new social organism, the head of which had under him wife and children and a number of slaves, under Roman paternal power, with power of life and death over them all. "The term, therefore, is no older than the ironclad family system of the Latin tribes, which came in after field agriculture and after legalised servitude, as well as after the separation of the Greeks and (Aryan) Latins." To which Marx adds: "The modern family contains in embryo not only slavery (*servitus*) but serfdom also, since from the very beginning it is connected with agricultural services. It contains within itself in *miniature* all the antagonisms which later develop on a wide scale within society and its state."

Such a form of the family shows the transition of the pairing family to monogamy. In order to guarantee the fidelity of the wife, that is, the paternity of the children, the woman is placed in the man's absolute power; if he kills her, he is but exercising his right.

* * *

We are confronted with this new form of the family in all its severity among the Greeks. While, as Marx observes, the position of the goddesses in mythology represents an earlier period, when women still occupied a freer and more respected place, in the Heroic Age we already find women degraded owing to the predominance of the man and the competition of female slaves. One may read in the *Odyssey* how Telemachus cuts his mother short and enjoins silence upon her. In Homer the young female captives become the objects of the sensual lust of the victors; the military chiefs, one after the other, according to rank, choose the most beautiful ones for themselves. The whole of the *Iliad*, as we know, revolves around the quarrel between Achilles and Agamemnon over such a female slave. In connection with each Homeric hero of importance mention is made of a captive maiden with whom he shares tent and bed. These maidens are taken back home, to the conjugal house, as was Cassandra by Agamemnon in Aeschylus. Sons born of these slaves receive a small share of their father's estate and are regarded as freemen. Teukros was such an illegitimate son of Telamon and was permitted to adopt his father's name. The wedded wife is expected to tolerate all this, but to maintain strict chastity and conjugal fidelity herself. True, in the Heroic Age the Greek wife is more respected than in the period of civilisation; for the husband, however, she is, in reality, merely the mother of his legitimate heirs, his chief housekeeper, and the superintendent of the female slaves, whom he may make, and does make his concubines at will. It is the existence of slavery side by side with monogamy, the existence of beautiful young slaves who belong to the *man* with all they have, that from the very beginning stamped on monogamy its specific character as monogamy *only for the woman*, but not for the man. And it retains this character to this day.

* * *

* * * In Euripides, the wife is described as *oikurema*, a thing for housekeeping (the word is in the neuter gender), and apart from the business of bearing children, she was nothing more to the Athenian than the chief housemaid. The husband had his gymnastic exercises, his public affairs, from which the wife was excluded; in addition, he often had female slaves at his disposal and, in the heyday of Athens, extensive prostitution, which was viewed with favour by the state, to say the least. It was precisely on the basis of this prostitution that the sole outstanding Greek women developed, who by their *esprit* and artistic taste towered as much above the general level of ancient womanhood as the Spartiate women did by virtue of their character. That one had first to become a *hetaera* in order to become a woman is the strongest indictment of the Athenian family.

In the course of time, this Athenian family became the model upon which not only the rest of the Ionians, but also all the Greeks of the mainland and of the colonies increasingly moulded their domestic relationships. But despite all seclusion and surveillance the Greek women found opportunities often enough for deceiving their husbands. The latter, who would have been ashamed to evince any love for their own wives, amused themselves with *hetaerae* in all kinds of amours. But the degradation of the women recoiled on the men themselves and degraded them too, until they sank into the perversion of boy-love, degrading both themselves and their gods by the myth of Ganymede.

This was the origin of monogamy, as far as we can trace it among the most civilised and highly-developed people of antiquity. It was not in any way the fruit of individual sex love, with which it had absolutely nothing in common, for the marriages remained marriages of convenience, as before. It was the first form of the family based not on natural but on economic conditions, namely, on the victory of private property over original, naturally developed, common ownership. The rule of the man in the family, the procreation of children who could only be his, destined to be the heirs of his wealth—these alone were frankly avowed by the Greeks as the exclusive aims of monogamy. For the rest, it was a burden, a duty to the gods, to the state and to their ancestors, which just had to be fulfilled. In Athens the law made not only marriage compulsory, but also the fulfilment by the man of a minimum of the so-called conjugal duties.

Thus, monogamy does not by any means make its appearance in history as the reconciliation of man and woman, still less as the highest form of such a reconciliation. On the contrary, it appears as the subjection of one sex by the other, as the proclamation of a conflict between the sexes entirely unknown hitherto in prehistoric times. In an old unpublished manuscript, the work of Marx and myself in 1846,[1] I find the following: "The first division of labour is that between man and woman for child breeding." And today I can add: The first class antagonism which appears in history coincides with the development of the antagonism between man and woman in monogamian marriage, and the first class oppression with that of the female sex by the male. Monogamy was a great historical advance, but at the same time it inaugurated, along with slavery and private wealth, that epoch, lasting until today, in which every advance is likewise a relative regression, in which the well-being and development of the one group are attained by the misery and repression of the other. It is the cellular form of civilised society, in which we can already study the nature of the antagonisms and contradictions which develop fully in the latter.

* * * With the rise of property differentiation—that is, as far back as the upper stage of barbarism—wage labour appears sporadically alongside of slave labour; and simultaneously, as its necessary correlate, the professional prostitution of free women appears side by side with the forced surrender of the female slave. Thus, the heritage bequeathed to civilisation by group marriage is double-sided, just as everything engendered by civilisation is double-sided, dou-

---

1. The reference is to *The German Ideology*.

ble-tongued, self-contradictory and antagonistic: on the one hand, monogamy, on the other, hetaerism, including its most extreme form, prostitution. Hetaerism is as much a social institution as any other; it is a continuation of the old sexual freedom—in favour of the men. Although, in reality, it is not only tolerated but even practised with gusto, particularly by the ruling classes, it is condemned in words. In reality, however, this condemnation by no means hits the men who indulge in it, it hits only the women: they are ostracised and cast out in order to proclaim once again the absolute domination of the male over the female sex as the fundamental law of society.

A second contradiction, however, is hereby developed within monogamy itself. By the side of the husband, whose life is embellished by hetaerism, stands the neglected wife. And it is just as impossible to have one side of a contradiction without the other as it is to retain the whole of an apple in one's hand after half has been eaten. Nevertheless, the men appear to have thought differently, until their wives taught them to know better. Two permanent social figures, previously unknown, appear on the scene along with monogamy—the wife's paramour and the cuckold. The men had gained the victory over the women, but the act of crowning the victor was magnanimously undertaken by the vanquished. Adultery —proscribed, severely penalised, but irrepressible—became an unavoidable social institution alongside of monogamy and hetaerism. The assured paternity of children was now, as before, based, at best. on moral conviction; and in order to solve the insoluble contradiction, Article 312 of the *Code Napoléon* decreed: *"L'enfant conçu pendant le mariage a pour père le mari,"* "a child conceived during marriage has for its father the husband." This is the final outcome of three thousand years of monogamy.

Thus, in the monogamian family, in those cases that faithfully reflect its historical origin and that clearly bring out the sharp conflict between man and woman resulting from the exclusive domination of the male, we have a picture in miniature of the very antagonisms and contradictions in which society, split up into classes since the commencement of civilisation, moves, without being able to resolve and overcome them. Naturally, I refer here only to those cases of monogamy where matrimonial life really takes its course according to the rules governing the original character of the whole institution, but where the wife rebels against the domination of the husband. That this is not the case with all marriages no one knows better than the German Philistine, who is no more capable of ruling in the home than in the state, and whose wife, therefore, with full justification, wears the breeches of which he is unworthy. But in consolation he imagines himself to be far superior to his

French companion in misfortune, who, more often than he, fares far worse.

* * *

Although monogamy was the only known form of the family out of which modern sex love could develop, it does not follow that this love developed within it exclusively, or even predominantly, as the mutual love of man and wife. The whole nature of strict monogamian marriage under male domination ruled this out. Among all historically active classes, that is, among all ruling classes, matrimony remained what it had been since pairing marriage—a matter of convenience arranged by the parents. And the first form of sex love that historically emerges as a passion, and as a passion in which any person (at least of the ruling classes) has a right to indulge, as the highest form of the sexual impulse—which is precisely its specific feature—this, its first form, the chivalrous love of the Middle Ages, was by no means conjugal love. On the contrary, in its classical form, among the Provençals, it steers under full sail towards adultery, the praises of which are sung by their poets. The "*Albas*," in German *Tagelieder*, are the flower of Provençal love poetry. They describe in glowing colours how the knight lies with his love—the wife of another—while the watchman stands guard outside, calling him at the first faint streaks of dawn (*alba*) so that he may escape unobserved. The parting scene then constitutes the climax. The Northern French as well as the worthy Germans, likewise adopted this style of poetry, along with the manners of chivalrous love which corresponded to it; and on this same suggestive theme our own old Wolfram von Eschenbach has left us three exquisite Songs of the Dawn, which I prefer to his three long heroic poems.

Bourgeois marriage of our own times is of two kinds. In Catholic countries the parents, as heretofore, still provide a suitable wife for their young bourgeois son, and the consequence is naturally the fullest unfolding of the contradiction inherent in monogamy—flourishing hetaerism on the part of the husband, and flourishing adultery on the part of the wife. The Catholic Church doubtless abolished divorce only because it was convinced that for adultery, as for death, there is no cure whatsoever. In Protestant countries, on the other hand, it is the rule that the bourgeois son is allowed to seek a wife for himself from his own class, more or less freely. Consequently, marriage can be based on a certain degree of love which, for decency's sake, is always assumed, in accordance with Protestant hypocrisy. In this case, hetaerism on the part of the men is less actively pursued, and adultery on the woman's part is not so much the rule. Since, in every kind of marriage, however, people remain what they were before they married, and since the citizens of Protestant countries are mostly Philistines, this Protestant monogamy leads merely, if we take the average of the best cases, to a wedded life of leaden boredom, which is described as domestic bliss. The best mirror of these two ways of marriage is the novel; the French novel for the Catholic style, and the German novel for the Protestant. In both cases "he gets it": in the German novel the young man gets the girl; in the French, the husband gets the cuckold's horns. Which of the two is in the worse plight is not always easy to make out. For the dullness of the German novel excites the same horror in the French bourgeois as the "immorality" of the French novel excites in the German Philistine, although lately, since "Berlin is becoming a metropolis," the German novel has begun to deal a little less timidly with hetaerism and adultery, long known to exist there.

In both cases, however, marriage is determined by the class position of the participants, and to that extent always remains marriage of convenience. In both cases, this marriage of convenience often enough turns into the crassest prostitution—sometimes on both sides, but much more generally on the part of the wife, who differs from the ordinary courtesan only in that she does not hire out her body, like a wage-worker, on piecework, but sells it into slavery once for all. And Fourier's words hold good for all marriages of convenience: "Just as in grammar two negatives make a positive, so in the morals of marriage, two prostitutions make one virtue." Sex love in the relation of husband and wife is and can become the rule only among the oppressed classes, that is, at the present day, among the proletariat, no matter whether this relationship is officially sanctioned or not. But here all the foundations of classical monogamy are removed. Here, there is a complete absence of all property, for the safeguarding and inheritance of which monogamy and male domination were established. Therefore, there is no stimulus whatever here to assert male domination. What is more, the means, too, are absent; bourgeois law, which protects this domination, exists only for the propertied classes and their dealings with the proletarians. It costs money, and therefore, owing to the worker's poverty has no validity in his attitude towards his wife. Personal and social relations of quite a different sort are the decisive factors here. Moreover, since large-scale industry has transferred the woman from the house to the labour market and the factory, and makes her, often enough, the bread-winner of the family, the last remnants of male domination in the proletarian home have lost all foundation—except, perhaps, for some of that brutality towards women which became firmly rooted with the establishment of monogamy. Thus, the proletarian family is no longer monogamian in the strict sense, even in cases of the most passionate love and strictest faithfulness of the two parties, and despite all spiritual and worldly benedictions which may have been received. The two eternal adjuncts of monogamy—hetaerism and adultery—therefore, play an almost negligible role here; the woman has regained, in fact, the right of separation, and when the man and woman cannot get along they prefer to part. In short, proletarian marriage is monogamian in the etymological sense of the word, but by no means in the historical sense.

Our jurists, to be sure, hold that the progress of legislation to an increasing degree removes all cause for complaint on the part of the woman. Modern civilised systems of law are recognising more and more, first, that, in order to be effective marriage must be an agreement voluntarily entered into by both parties; and secondly, that during marriage, too, both parties must be on an equal footing in respect to rights and obligations. If, however, these two demands were consistently carried into effect, women would have all that they could ask for.

This typical lawyer's reasoning is exactly the same as that with which the radical republican bourgeois dismisses the proletarian. The labour contract is supposed to be voluntarily entered into by both parties. But it is taken to be voluntarily entered into as soon as the law has put both parties on an equal footing *on paper*. The power given to one party by its different class position, the pressure it exercises on the other—the real economic position of both—all this is no concern of the law. And both parties, again, are supposed to have equal rights for the duration of the labour contract, unless one or the other of the parties expressly waived them. That the concrete economic situation compels the worker to forego even the slightest semblance of equal rights—this again is something the law cannot help.

As far as marriage is concerned, even the most progressive law is fully satisfied as soon as the parties formally register their voluntary desire to get married. What happens behind the legal curtains, where real life is enacted, how this voluntary agreement is arrived at —is no concern of the law and the jurist. And yet the simplest comparison of laws should serve to show the jurist what this voluntary agreement really amounts to. In countries where the children are legally assured of an obligatory share of their parents' property and thus cannot be disinherited—in Germany, in the countries under French law, etc.—the children must obtain their parents' consent in the question of marriage. In countries under English law, where parental consent to marriage is not legally requisite, the parents have full testatory freedom over their property and can, if they so desire, cut their children off with a shillling. It is clear, therefore, that despite this, or rather just because of this, among those classes which have something to inherit, freedom to marry is not one whit greater in England and America than in France or Germany.

The position is no better with regard to the juridical equality of man and woman in marriage. The equality of the two before the law, which is a legacy of previous social conditions, is not the cause but the effect of the economic oppression of women. In the old communistic household, which embraced numerous couples and their children, the administration of the household, entrusted to the women, was just as much a public, a socially necessary industry as the providing of food by the men. This situation changed with the patriarchal family, and even more with the monogamian individual family. The administration of the household lost its public character. It was no longer the concern of society. It became a *private service*. The wife became the first domestic servant, pushed out of participation in social production. Only modern large-scale industry again threw open to her—and only to the proletarian woman at that—that avenue to social production; but in such a way that, when she fulfils her duties in the private service of her family, she remains excluded from public production and cannot earn anything; and when she wishes to take part in public industry and earn her living independently, she is not in a position to fulfil her family duties. What applies to the woman in the factory applies to her in all the professions, right up to medicine and law. The modern individual family is based on the open or disguised domestic enslavement of the woman; and modern society is a mass composed solely of individual families as its molecules. Today, in the great majority of cases the man has to be the earner, the bread-winner of the family, at least among the propertied classes, and this gives him a dominating position which requires no special legal privileges. In the family, he is the bourgeois; the wife represents the proletariat. In the industrial world, however, the specific character of the economic oppression that weighs down the proletariat stands out in all its sharpness only after all the special legal privileges of the capitalist class have been set aside and the complete juridical equality of both classes is established. The democratic republic does not abolish the antagonism between the the two classes; on the contrary, it provides the field on which it is fought out. And, similarly, the peculiar character of man's domination over woman in the modern family, and the necessity, as well as the manner, of establishing real social equality between the two, will be brought out into full relief only when both are completely equal before the law. It will then become evident that the first premise for the emancipation of women is the reintroduction of the entire female sex into public industry; and that this again demands that the quality possessed by the individual family of being the economic unit of society be abolished.

* * *

We have, then, three chief forms of marriage, which, by and large, conform to the three main stages of human development. For savagery—group marriage; for barbarism—pairing marriage; for civilisation—monogamy, supplemented by adultery and prostitution. In the upper stage of barbarism, between pairing marriage and monogamy, there is wedged in the dominion exercised by men over female slaves, and polygamy.

As our whole exposition has shown, the advance to be noted in this sequence is linked with the peculiar fact that while women are more and more deprived of the sexual freedom of group marriage, the men are not. Actually, for men, group marriage exists to this day. What for a woman is a crime entailing dire legal and social consequences, is regarded in the case of a man as being honourable or, at most, as a slight moral stain that one bears with pleasure. The more the old traditional hetaerism is changed in our day by capitalist commodity production and adapted to it, and the more it is transformed into unconcealed prostitution, the more demoralising are its effects. And it demoralises the men far more than it does the women. Among women, prostitution degrades only those unfortunates who fall into its clutches; and even these are not degraded to the degree that is generally believed. On the other hand, it degrades the character of the entire male world. Thus, in nine cases out of ten, a long engagement is practically a preparatory school for conjugal infidelity.

We are now approaching a social evolution in which the hitherto existing economic foundations of monogamy will disappear just as certainly as will those of its supplement—prostitution. Monogamy arose out of the concentration of considerable wealth in the hands of one person—and that a man—and out of the desire to bequeath this wealth to this man's children and to no one else's. For this purpose monogamy was essential on the woman's part, but not on the man's; so that this monogamy of the woman in no way hindered the overt or covert polygamy of the man. The impending social revolution, however, by transforming at least the far greater part of permanent inheritable wealth—the means of production—into social property, will reduce all this anxiety about inheritance to a minimum. Since monogamy arose from economic causes, will it disappear when these causes disappear?

One might not unjustly answer: far from disappearing, it will only begin to be completely realised. For with the conversion of the means of production into social property, wage labour, the proletariat, also disappears, and therewith, also, the necessity for a certain —statistically calculable—number of women to surrender themselves for money. Prostitution disappears; monogamy, instead of declining, finally becomes a reality—for the men as well.

At all events, the position of the men thus undergoes considerable change. But that of the women, of *all* women, also undergoes important alteration. With the passage of the means of production into common property, the individual family ceases to be the economic unit of society. Private housekeeping is transformed into a social industry. The care and education of the children becomes a public matter. Society takes care of all children equally, irrespective of whether they are born in wedlock or not. Thus, the anxiety about the "consequences," which is today the most important social factor—both moral and economic—that hinders a girl from giving herself freely to the man she loves, disappears. Will this not be cause enough for a gradual rise of more unrestrained sexual intercourse, and along with it, a more lenient public opinion regarding virginal honour and feminine shame? And finally, have we not seen that monogamy and prostitution in the modern world, although opposites, are nevertheless inseparable opposites, poles of the same social conditions? Can prostitution disappear without dragging monogamy with it into the abyss?

Here a new factor comes into operation, a factor that, at most, existed in embryo at the time when monogamy developed, namely individual sex love.

No such thing as individual sex love existed before the Middle Ages. That personal beauty, intimate association, similarity in inclinations, etc., aroused desire for sexual intercourse among people of opposite sexes, that men as well as women were not totally indifferent to the question of with whom they entered into this most intimate relation is obvious. But this is still a far cry from the sex love of our day. Throughout antiquity marriages were arranged by the parents; the parties quietly acquiesced. The little conjugal love that was known to antiquity was not in any way a subjective inclination, but an objective duty; not a reason for but a correlate of marriage. In antiquity, love affairs in the modern sense occur only outside official society. The shepherds, whose joys and sorrows in love are sung by Theocritus and Moschus, or by Longus's *Daphnis and Chloë* are mere slaves, who have no share in the state, the sphere of the free citizen. Except among the slaves, however, we find love affairs only as disintegration products of the declining ancient world; and with women who are also beyond the pale of official society, with *hetaerae*, that is, with alien or freed women; in Athens beginning with the eve of its decline, in Rome at the time of the emperors. If love affairs really occurred between free male and female citizens, it was only in the form of adultery. And sex love in our sense of the term was so immaterial to that classical love poet of antiquity old Anacreon, that even the sex of the beloved one was a matter of complete indifference to him.

Our sex love differs materially from the simple sexual desire, the *eros*, of the ancients. First, it presupposes reciprocal love on the part of the loved one; in this respect, the woman stands on a par with the man; whereas in the ancient *eros*, the woman was by no means always consulted. Secondly, sex love attains a degree of intensity and permanency where the two parties regard non-possession or separation as a great, if not the greatest, misfortune; in order to possess each other they take great hazards, even risking life itself—what in antiquity happened, at best, only in cases of adultery. And finally, a new moral standard arises for judging sexual intercourse. The question asked is not only whether such intercourse was legitimate or illicit, but also whether it arose from mutual love or not. It goes without saying that in feudal or bourgeois practice this new standard fares no better than all the other moral standards—it is simply ignored. But it fares no worse, either. It is recognized in theory, on paper, like all the rest. And more than this cannot be expected for the present.

Where antiquity broke off with its start towards sex love, the Middle Ages began, namely, with adultery. We have already described chivalrous love, which gave rise to the Songs of the Dawn. There is still a wide gulf between this kind of love, which aimed at breaking up matrimony, and the love destined to be its foundation, a gulf never completely bridged by the age of chivalry. Even when we pass from the frivolous Latins to the virtuous Germans, we find, in the *Nibelungenlied,* that Kriemhild—although secretly in love with Siegfried every whit as much as he is with her—nevertheless, in reply to Gunther's intimation that he has plighted her to a knight whom he does not name, answers simply: "You have no need to ask; as you command, so will I be forever. He whom you, my lord, choose for my husband, to him will I gladly plight my troth." It never occurs to her that her love could possibly be considered in this matter. Gunther seeks the hand of Brunhild without ever having seen her, and Etzel does the same with Kriemhild. The same occurs in the *Gudrun,* where Sigebant of Ireland seeks the hand of Ute the Norwegian, Hetel of Hegelingen that of Hilde of Ireland; and lastly, Siegfried of Morland, Hartmut of Ormany and Herwig of Seeland seek the hand of Gudrun; and here for the first time it happens that Gudrun, of her own free will, decides in favour of the last named. As a rule, the bride of a young prince is selected by his parents; if these are no longer alive, he chooses her himself with the counsel of his highest vassal chiefs, whose word carries great weight in all cases. Nor can it be otherwise. For the knight, or baron, just as for the prince himself, marriage is a political act, an opportunity for the accession of power through new alliances; the interests of the *House* and not individual inclination are the decisive factor. How can love here hope to have the last word regarding marriage?

It was the same for the guildsman of the medieval towns. The very privileges which protected him—the guild charters with their special stipulations, the artificial lines of demarcation which legally separated him from other guilds, from his own fellow guildsmen and from his journeymen and apprentices—considerably restricted the circle in which he could hope to secure a suitable spouse. And the question as to who was the most suitable was definitely decided under this complicated system, not by individual inclination, but by family interest.

Up to the end of the Middle Ages, therefore, marriage, in the overwhelming majority of cases, remained what it had been from the commencement, an affair that was not decided by the two principal parties. In the beginning one came into the world married, married to a whole group of the opposite sex. A similar relation probably existed in the later forms of group marriage, only with an ever-increasing narrowing of the group. In the pairing family it is the rule that the mothers arrange their children's marriages; and here also, considerations of new ties of relationship that are to strengthen the young couple's position in the gens and tribe are the decisive factor. And when, with the predominance of private property over common property, and with the interest in inheritance, father right and monogamy gain the ascendancy, marriage becomes more than ever dependent on economic considerations. The *form* of marriage by purchase disappears, the transaction itself is to an ever-increasing degree carried out in such a way that not only the woman but the man also is appraised, not by his personal qualities but by his possessions. The idea that the mutual inclinations of the principal parties should be the overriding reason for matrimony had been unheard-of in the practice of the ruling classes from the very beginning. Such things took place, at best, in romance only, or—among the oppressed classes, which did not count.

This was the situation found by capitalist production when, following the era of geographical discoveries, it set out to conquer the world through world trade and manufacture. One would think that this mode of matrimony should have suited it exceedingly, and such was actually the case. And yet—the irony of world history is unfathomable—it was capitalist production that had to make the decisive breach in it. By transforming all things into commodities, it dissolved all ancient traditional relations, and for inherited customs and historical rights it substituted purchase and sale, "free" contract. And H. S. Maine, the English jurist, believed that he made a colossal discovery when he said that our entire progress in comparison with previous epochs consists in our having evolved from status to contract, from an inherited state of affairs to one voluntarily contracted—a statement which, in so far as it is correct, was contained long ago in the *Communist Manifesto*.

But the closing of contracts presupposes people who can freely dispose of their persons, actions and possessions, and who meet each other on equal terms. To create such "free" and "equal" people was precisely one of the chief tasks of capitalist production. Although in the beginning this took place only in a semiconscious manner, and in religious guise to boot, nevertheless, from the time of the Lutheran and Calvinistic Reformation it became a firm principle that a person was completely responsible for his actions only if he possessed full freedom of the will when performing them, and that it was an ethical duty to resist all compulsion to commit unethical acts. But how does this fit in with the previous practice of matrimony? According to bourgeois conceptions, matrimony was a contract, a legal affair, indeed the most important of all, since it disposed of the body and mind of two persons for life. True enough, formally the bargain was struck voluntarily; it was not done without the consent of the parties; but how this consent was obtained, and who really arranged the marriage was known only too well. But if real freedom to decide was demanded for all other contracts, why not for this one? Had not the two young people about to be paired the right freely to dispose of themselves, their bodies and its organs? Did not sex love become the fashion as a consequence of chivalry, and was not the love of husband and wife its correct bourgeois form, as against the adulterous love of the knights? But if it was the duty of married people to love each other, was it not just as much the duty of lovers to marry each other and nobody else? And did not the right of these lovers stand higher than that of parents, relatives and other traditional marriage brokers and matchmakers? If the right of free personal investigation unceremoniously forced its way into church and religion, how could it halt at the intolerable claim of the older generation to dispose of body and soul, the property, the happiness and unhappiness of the younger generation?

These questions were bound to arise in a period which loosened all the old social ties and which shook the foundations of all traditional conceptions. At one stroke the size of the world had increased nearly tenfold. Instead of only a quadrant of a hemisphere the whole globe was now open to the gaze of the West Europeans who hastened to take possession of the other seven quadrants. And the thousand-year-old barriers set up by the medieval prescribed mode of thought vanished in the same way as did the old, narrow barriers of the homeland. An infinitely wider horizon opened up both to man's outer and inner eye. Of what avail were the good intentions of respectability, the honoured guild privileges handed down through the generations, to the young man who was allured by India's riches, by the gold and silver mines of Mexico and Potosi? It was the knight-errant period of the bourgeoisie; it had its romance also, and its love dreams, but on a bourgeois basis and, in the last analysis, with bourgeois ends in view.

Thus it happened that the rising bourgeoisie, particularly in the Protestant countries, where the existing order was shaken up most of all, increasingly recognized freedom of contract for marriage also and carried it through in the manner described above. Marriage remained class marriage, but, within the confines of the class, the parties were accorded a certain degree of freedom of choice. And on paper, in moral theory as in poetic description, nothing was more unshakably established than that every marriage not based on mutual sex love and on the really free agreement of man and wife was immoral. In short, love marriage was proclaimed a human right; not only as man's right (*droit de l'homme*) but also, by way of exception, as woman's right (*droit de la femme*).

But in one respect this human right differed from all other so-called human rights. While, in practice, the latter remained limited to the ruling class, the bourgeoisie—the oppressed class, the proletariat, being directly or indirectly deprived of them—the irony of history asserts itself here once again. The ruling class continues to be dominated by the familiar economic influences and, therefore, only in exceptional cases can it show really voluntary marriages; whereas, as we have seen, these are the rule among the dominated class.

Thus, full freedom in marriage can become generally operative only when the abolition of capitalist production, and of the property relations created by it, has removed all those secondary economic considerations which still exert so powerful an influence on the choice of a partner. Then, no other motive remains than mutual affection.

Since sex love is by its very nature exclusive—although this exclusiveness is fully realised today only in the woman—then marriage based on sex love is by its very nature monogamy. We have seen how right Bachofen was when he regarded the advance from group marriage to individual marriage chiefly as the work of the women; only the advance from pairing marriage to monogamy can be placed to the men's account, and, historically, this consisted essentially in a worsening of the position of women and in facilitating infidelity on the part of the men. With the disappearance of the economic considerations which compelled women to tolerate the customary infidelity of the men—the anxiety about their own livelihood and even more about the future of their children—the equality of woman thus achieved will, judging from all previous experience, result far more effectively in the men becoming really monogamous than in the women becoming polyandrous.

What will most definitely disappear from monogamy, however, is all the characteristics stamped on it in consequence of its having arisen out of property relationships. These are, first, the dominance of the man, and secondly, the indissolubility of marriage. The predominance of the man in marriage is simply a consequence of his economic predominance and will vanish with it automatically. The indissolubility of marriage is partly the result of the economic conditions under which monogamy arose, and partly a tradition from the time when the connection between these economic conditions and monogamy was not yet correctly understood and was exaggerated by religion. Today it has been breached a thousandfold. If only marriages that are based on love are moral, then, also, only those are moral in which love continues. The duration of the urge of individual sex love differs very much according to the individual, particularly among men; and a definite cessation of affection, or its displacement by a new passionate love, makes separation a blessing for both parties as well as for society. People will only be spared the experience of wading through the useless mire of divorce proceedings.

Thus, what we can conjecture at present about the regulation of sex relationships after the impending effacement of capitalist production is, in the main, of a negative character, limited mostly to what will vanish. But what will be added? That will be settled after a new generation has grown up: a generation of men who never in all their lives have had occasion to purchase a woman's surrender either with money or with any other means of social power, and of women who have never been obliged to surrender to any man out of any consideration other than that of real love, or to refrain from giving themselves to their beloved for fear of the economic consequences. Once such people appear, they will not care a rap about what we today think they should do. They will establish their own practice and their own public opinion, conformable therewith, on the practice of each individual—and that's the end of it.

* * *

The Origin of the State

* * * Above we discussed separately each of the three main forms in which the state was built up on the ruins of the gentile constitution. Athens represented the purest, most classical form. Here the state sprang directly and mainly out of the class antagonisms that developed within gentile society. In Rome gentile society became an exclusive aristocracy amidst numerous plebs, standing outside of it, having no rights but only duties. The victory of the plebs burst the old gentile constitution asunder and erected on its ruins the state, in which both the gentile aristocracy and the plebs were soon wholly absorbed. Finally, among the German vanquishers of the Roman Empire, the state sprang up as a direct result of the conquest of large foreign territories, which the gentile constitution had no means of ruling. As this conquest did not necessitate either a serious struggle with the old population or a more advanced division of labour, and as conquered and conquerors were almost at the same stage of economic development and thus the economic basis of society remained the same as before, therefore, the gentile constitution could continue for many centuries in a changed, territorial form, in the shape of a Mark constitution, and even rejuvenate itself for a time in enfeebled form in the noble and patrician families of later years, and even in peasant families, as in Dithmarschen.[2]

The state is, therefore, by no means a power forced on society from without; just as little is it "the reality of the ethical idea," "the image and reality of reason," as Hegel maintains. Rather, it is a product of society at a certain stage of development; it is the admission that this society has become entangled in an insoluble contradiction with itself, that it is cleft into irreconcilable antagonisms which it is powerless to dispel. But in order that these antagonisms, classes with conflicting economic interests, might not consume themselves and society in sterile struggle, a power seemingly standing above society became necessary for the purpose of moderating the conflict, of keeping it within the bounds of "order"; and this power, arisen out of society, but placing itself above it, and increasingly alienating itself from it, is the state.

In contradistinction to the old gentile organisation, the state, first, divides its subjects *according to territory*. As we have seen, the old gentile associations, built upon and held together by ties of blood, became inadequate, largely because they presupposed that the members were bound to a given territory, a bond which had long ceased to exist. The territory remained, but the people had become mobile. Hence, division according to territory was taken as the point of departure, and citizens were allowed to exercise their public rights and duties wherever they settled, irrespective of gens and tribe. This organisation of citizens according to locality is a feature common to all states. That is why it seems natural to us; but we have seen what long and arduous struggles were needed before it could replace, in Athens and Rome, the old organisation according to gentes.

The second is the establishment of a *public power* which no longer directly coincided with the population organising itself as an armed force. This special public power is necessary, because a self-acting armed organisation of the population has become impossible since the cleavage into classes. The slaves also belonged to the population; the 90,000 citizens of Athens formed only a privileged class as against the 365,000 slaves. The people's army of the Athenian democracy was an aristocratic public power against the slaves, whom it kept in check; however, a gendarmerie also became necessary to keep the citizens in check, as we related above. This public power exists in every state; it consists not merely of armed people but also

2. The first historian who had at least an approximate idea of the nature of the gens was Niebuhr, thanks to his knowledge of the Dithmarschen families—to which, however, he also owes the errors he mechanically copied from there. [*Engels*]

of material adjuncts, prisons and institutions of coercion of all kinds, of which gentile society knew nothing. It may be very insignificant, almost infinitesimal, in societies where class antagonisms are still undeveloped and in out-of-the-way places as was the case at certain times and in certain regions in the United States of America. It grows stronger, however, in proportion as class antagonisms within the state become more acute, and as adjacent states become larger and more populated. We have only to look at our present-day Europe, where class struggle and rivalry in conquest have screwed up the public power to such a pitch that it threatens to devour the whole of society and even the state.

In order to maintain this public power, contributions from the citizens become necessary— *taxes*. These were absolutely unknown in gentile society; but we know enough about them today. As civilisation advances, these taxes become inadequate; the state makes drafts on the future, contracts loans, *public debts*. Old Europe can tell a tale about these, too.

In possession of the public power and of the right to levy taxes, the officials, as organs of society, now stand *above* society. The free, voluntary respect that was accorded to the organs of the gentile constitution does not satisfy them, even if they could gain it; being the vehicles of a power that is becoming alien to society, respect for them must be enforced by means of exceptional laws by virtue of which they enjoy special sanctity and inviolability. The shabbiest police servant in the civilised state has more "authority" than all the organs of gentile society put together; but the most powerful prince and the greatest statesman, or general, of civilisation may well envy the humblest gentile chief for the uncoerced and undisputed respect that is paid to him. The one stands in the midst of society, the other is forced to attempt to represent something outside and above it.

As the state arose from the need to hold class antagonisms in check, but as it arose, at the same time, in the midst of the conflict of these classes, it is, as a rule, the state of the most powerful, economically dominant class which, through the medium of the state, becomes also the politically dominant class, and thus acquires new means of holding down and exploiting the oppressed class. Thus, the state of antiquity was above all the state of the slave owners for the purpose of holding down the slaves, as the feudal state was the organ of the nobility for holding down the peasant serfs and bondsmen, and the modern representative state is an instrument of exploitation of wage labour by capital. By way of exception, however, periods occur in which the warring classes balance each other so nearly that the state power, as ostensible mediator, acquires, for the moment, a certain degree of independence of both. Such was the absolute monarchy of the seventeenth and eighteenth centuries, which held the balance between the nobility and the class of burghers; such was the Bonapartism of the First, and still more of the Second French Empire, which played off the proletariat against the bourgeoisie and the bourgeoisie against the proletariat. The latest performance of this kind, in which ruler and ruled appear equally ridiculous, is the new German Empire of the Bismarck nation: the capitalists and workers are balanced against each other and equally cheated for the benefit of the impoverished Prussian cabbage Junkers.

In most of the historical states, the rights of citizens are, besides, apportioned according to their wealth, thus directly expressing the fact that the state is an organisation of the possessing class for its protection against the non-possessing class. It was so already in the Athenian and Roman classification according to property. It was so in the mediaeval feudal state, in which the alignment of political power was in conformity with the amount of land owned. It is seen in the electoral qualifications of the modern representative states. Yet this political recognition of property distinctions is by no means essential. On the contrary, it marks a low stage of state development. The highest form of the state, the democratic republic, which under our modern conditions of society is more and more becoming an inevitable necessity, and is the form of state in which alone the last decisive struggle between proletariat and bourgeoisie can be fought out—the democratic republic officially knows nothing any more of property distinctions. In it wealth exercises its power indirectly, but all the more surely. On the one hand, in the form of the direct corruption of officials, of which America provides the classical example; on the other hand, in the form of an alliance between government and Stock Exchange, which becomes the easier to achieve the more the public debt increases and the more joint-stock companies concentrate in their hands not only transport but also production itself, using the Stock Exchange as their centre. The latest French republic as well as the United States is a striking example of this; and good old Switzerland has contributed its share in this field. But that a democratic republic is not essential for this fraternal alliance between government and Stock Exchange is proved by England and also by the new German Empire, where one cannot tell who was elevated more by universal suffrage, Bismarck or Bleichröder. And lastly, the possessing class rules directly through the medium of universal suffrage. As long as the oppressed class, in our case, therefore, the proletariat, is not yet ripe to emancipate itself, it will in its majority regard the existing order of society as the only one possible and, politically, will form the tail of the capitalist class, its extreme Left wing. To the extent, however, that this class matures for its self-emancipation, it constitutes itself as its own party and elects its own representatives, and not those of the capitalists. Thus, universal suffrage is the gauge of the maturity of the working class. It cannot and never will be anything more in the present-day state; but that is sufficient. On the day the thermometer of universal suffrage registers boiling point among the workers, both they and the capitalists will know what to do.

The state, then, has not existed from all eternity. There have been societies that did without it, that had no conception of the state and state power. At a certain stage of economic development, which was necessarily bound up with the cleavage of society into classes, the state became a necessity owing to this cleavage. We are now rapidly approaching a stage in the development of production at which the existence of these classes not only will have ceased to be a necessity, but will become a positive hindrance to production. They will fall as inevitably as they arose at an earlier stage. Along with them the state will inevitably fall. The society that will organise production on the basis of a free and equal association of the producers will put the whole machinery of state where it will then belong: into the Museum of Antiquities, by the side of the spinning wheel and the bronze axe.

Thus, from the foregoing, civilisation is that stage of development of society at which division of labour, the resulting exchange between individuals, and commodity production, which combines the two, reach their complete unfoldment and revolutionise the whole hitherto existing society.

Production at all former stages of society was essentially collective and, likewise, consumption took place by the direct distribution of the products within larger or smaller communistic communities. This production in common was carried on within the narrowest limits, but concomitantly the producers were masters of their process of production and of their product. They knew what became of the product: they consumed it, it did not leave their hands; and as long as production was carried on on this basis, it could not grow beyond the control of the producers, and it could not raise any strange, phantom powers against them, as is the case regularly and inevitably under civilisation.

But, slowly, division of labour crept into this process of production. It undermined the collective nature of production and appropriation, it made appropriation by individuals the largely prevailing rule, and thus gave rise to exchange between individuals—how, we examined above. Gradually, the production of commodities became the dominant form.

With the production of commodities, production no longer for one's own consumption but for exchange, the products necessarily pass from hand to hand. The producer parts with his product in the course of exchange; he no longer knows what becomes of it. As soon as money, and with it the merchant, steps in as a middleman between the producers, the process of exchange becomes still more complicated, the ultimate fate of the product still more uncertain. The merchants are numerous and none of them knows what the other is doing. Commodities now pass not only from hand to hand, but also from market to market. The producers have lost control of the aggregate production of the conditions of their own life, and the merchants have not acquired it. Products and production become the playthings of chance.

But chance is only one pole of an interrelation, the other pole of which is called necessity. In nature, where chance also seems to reign, we have long ago demonstrated in each particular field the inherent necessity and regularity that asserts itself in this chance. What is true of nature holds good also for society. The more a social activity, a series of social processes, becomes too powerful for conscious human control, grows beyond human reach, the more it seems to have been left to pure chance, the more do its peculiar and innate laws assert themselves in this chance, as if by natural necessity. Such laws also control the fortuities of the production and exchange of commodities; these laws confront the individual producer and exchanger as strange and, in the beginning, even as unknown powers, the nature of which must first be laboriously investigated and ascertained. These economic laws of commodity production are modified at the different stages of development of this form of production; on the whole, however, the entire period of civilisation has been dominated by these laws. To this day, the product is master of the producer; to this day, the total production of society is regulated, not by a collectively thought-out plan, but by blind laws, which operate with elemental force, in the last resort in the storms of periodic commercial crises.

We saw above how human labour power became able, at a rather early stage of development of production, to produce considerably more than was needed for the producer's maintenance, and how this stage, in the main, coincided with that of the first appearance of the division of labour and of exchange between individuals. Now, it was not long before the great "truth" was discovered that man, too, may be a commodity; that human power may be exchanged and utilised by converting man into a slave. Men had barely started to engage in exchange when they themselves were exchanged. The active became a passive, whether man wanted it or not.

With slavery, which reached its fullest development in civilisation, came the first great cleavage of society into an exploiting and an exploited class. This cleavage has continued during the whole period of civilisation. Slavery was the first form of exploitation, peculiar to the world of antiquity; it was followed by serfdom in the Middle Ages, and by wage labour in modern times. These are the three great forms of servitude, characteristic of the three great epochs of civilisation; open, and, latterly, disguised slavery, are its steady companions.

The stage of commodity production, with which civilisation began, is marked economically by the introduction of 1) metal money and, thus, of money capital, interest and usury; 2) the merchants acting as middlemen between producers; 3) private ownership of land and mortgage; 4) slave labour as the prevailing form of production. The form of the family corresponding to civilisation and under it becoming the definitely prevailing form is monogamy, the supremacy of the man over the woman, and the individual family as the economic unit of society. The cohesive force of civilised society is the state, which in all typical periods is exclusively the state of the ruling class, and in all cases remains essentially a machine for keeping down the oppressed, exploited class. Other marks of civilisation are: on the one hand fixation of the contrast between town and country as the basis of the entire division of social labour; on the other hand, the introduction of wills, by which the property holder is able to dispose of his property even after his death. This institution, which was a direct blow at the old gentile constitution, was unknown in Athens until the time of Solon; in Rome it was introduced very early, but we do not know when.[3] Among the Germans it was introduced by the priests in order that the good honest German might without hindrance bequeath his property to the Church.

With this constitution as its foundation civilisation has accomplished things with which the old gentile society was totally unable to cope. But it accomplished them by playing on the most sordid instincts and passions of man, and by developing them at the expense of all his other faculties. Naked greed has been the moving spirit of civilisation from the first day of its existence to the present time; wealth, more wealth and wealth again; wealth, not of society, but of this shabby individual was its sole and determining aim. If, in the pursuit of this aim, the increasing development of science and

3. Lassalle's *Das System der erworbenen Rechte* (*System of Acquired Rights*) turns, in its second part, mainly on the proposition that the Roman testament is as old as Rome itself, that in Roman history there was never "a time when testaments did not exist": that the testament arose rather in pre-Roman times out of the cult of the dead. As a confirmed Hegelian of the old school, Lassalle derived the provisions of the Roman law not from the social conditions of the Romans, but from the "speculative conception" of the will, and thus arrived at this totally unhistoric assertion. This is not to be wondered at in a book that from the same speculative conception draws the conclusion that the transfer of property was purely a secondary matter in Roman inheritance. Lassalle not only believes in the illusions of Roman jurists, especially of the earlier period, but he even excels them. [*Engels*]

repeated periods of the fullest blooming of art fell into its lap, it was only because without them the ample present-day achievements in the accumultion of wealth would have been impossible.

Since the exploitation of one class by another is the basis of civilisation, its whole development moves in a continuous contradiction. Every advance in production is at the same time a retrogression in the condition of the oppressed class, that it, of the great majority. What is a boon for the one is necessarily a bane for the other; each new emancipation of one class always means a new oppression of another class. The most striking proof of this is furnished by the introduction of machinery, the effects of which are well known today. And while among barbarians, as we have seen, hardly any distinction could be made between rights and duties, civilisation makes the difference and antithesis between these two plain even to the dullest mind by assigning to one class pretty nearly all the rights, and to the other class pretty nearly all the duties.

But this is not as it ought to be. What is good for the ruling class should be good for the whole of the society with which the ruling class identifies itself. Therefore, the more civilisation advances, the more it is compelled to cover the ills it necessarily creates with the cloak of love, to embellish them, or to deny their existence; in short, to introduce conventional hypocrisy—unknown both in previous forms of society and even in the earliest stages of civilisation —that culminates in the declaration: The exploiting class exploits the oppressed class solely and exclusively in the interest of the exploited class itself; and if the latter fails to appreciate this, and even becomes rebellious, it thereby shows the basest ingratitude to its benefactors, the exploiters.[4]

And now, in conclusion, Morgan's verdict on civilisation: "Since the advent of civilisation, the outgrowth of property has been so immense, its forms so diversified, its uses so expanding and its management so intelligent in the interests of its owners that it *has become*, on the part of the people, *an unmanageable power. The human mind stands bewildered in the presence of its own creation.* The time will come, nevertheless, when human intelligence will rise to the mastery over property, and define the relations of the state to the property it protects, as well as the obligations and the limits of the rights of its owners. The interests of society are paramount to individual interest, and the two must be brought into just and har-

---

4. I had intended at the outset to place the brilliant critique of civilisation, scattered through the works of Fourier, by the side of Morgan's and my own. Unfortunately, I cannot spare the time. I only wish to remark that Fourier already considered monogamy and property in land as the main characteristics of civilisation, and that he described it as a war of the rich against the poor. We also find already in his work the deep appreciation of the fact that in all imperfect societies, those torn by conflicting interests, the individual families (*les familles incohérentes*) are the economic units. [*Engels*]

monious relation. A mere property career is not the final destiny of mankind, if progress is to be the law of the future as it has been of the past. The time which has passed away since civilisation began is but a fragment of the past duration of man's existence; and but a fragment of the ages yet to come. The dissolution of society bids fair to become the termination of a career of which property is the end and aim, because such a career contains the elements of self-destruction. Democracy in government, brotherhood in society, equality in rights and privileges, and universal education, foreshadow the next higher plane of society to which experience, intelligence and knowledge are steadily tending. *It will be a revival, in a higher form, of the liberty, equality and fraternity of the ancient gentes.*" (Morgan, *Ancient Society*, p. 552.)

Letters on Historical Materialism

FRIEDRICH ENGELS

Because of his preoccupation with *Capital* and for other reasons, Marx in his later years failed to produce a detailed and comprehensive formulation of the materialist conception of history. Engels attempted to make good this deficiency with the sketch of the conception presented in *Socialism: Utopian and Scientific*, and by offering clarifications on important particular points in these letters. Of special note are his discussions of ideology and his effort to guard against an oversimplified interpretation of the doctrine of economic determinism in history.

To Joseph Bloch

London, September 21–22, 1890

According to the materialist conception of history, the *ultimately* determining element in history is the production and reproduction of real life. More than this neither Marx nor I have ever asserted. Hence if somebody twists this into saying that the economic element is the *only* determining one, he transforms that proposition into a meaningless, abstract, senseless phrase. The economic situation is the basis, but the various elements of the superstructure: political forms of the class struggle and its results, to wit: constitutions established by the victorious class after a successful battle, etc., juridical forms, and then even the reflexes of all these actual struggles in the brains of the participants, political, juristic, philosophical theories, religious views and their further development into systems of dogmas, also exercise their influence upon the course of the historical struggles and in many cases preponderate in determining their *form*. There is an interaction of all these elements in which, amid all the endless host of accidents (that is, of things and events, whose inner connection is so remote or so impossible of proof that we can regard it as non-existent, as negligible) the economic movement finally asserts itself as necessary. Otherwise the application of the theory to any period of history one chose would be easier than the solution of a simple equation of the first degree.

We make our history ourselves, but, in the first place, under very definite assumptions and conditions. Among these the economic ones are ultimately decisive. But the political ones, etc., and indeed even the traditions which haunt human minds also play a part, although not the decisive one. The Prussian state also arose and developed from historical, ultimately economic causes. But it could scarcely be maintained without pedantry that among the many small states of North Germany, Brandenburg was specifically determined by economic necessity to become the great power embodying the economic, linguistic and, after the Reformation, also the religious difference between North and South, and not by other elements as well (above all by its entanglement with Poland, owing to the possession of Prussia, and hence with international political relations—which were indeed also decisive in the formation of the Austrian dynastic power). Without making oneself ridiculous it would be a difficult thing to explain in terms of economics the existence of every small state in Germany, past and present, or the origin of the High German consonant shifts, which widened the geographical wall of partition, formed by the mountains from the Sudetic range to the Taunus, to the extent of a regular fissure across all Germany.

In the second place, however, history is made in such a way that the final result always arises from conflicts between many individual wills, of which each again has been made what it is by a host of particular conditions of life. Thus there are innumerable intersecting forces, an infinite series of parallelograms of forces which give rise to one resultant—the historical event. This may again itself be viewed as the product of a power which works as a whole, *unconsciously* and without volition. For what each individual wills is obstructed by everyone else, and what emerges is something that no one willed. Thus past history proceeds in the manner of a natural process and is essentially subject to the same laws of motion. But from the fact that individual wills—of which each desires what he is impelled to by his physical constitution and external, in the last resort economic, circumstances (either his own personal circumstances or those of society in general)—do not attain what they want, but are merged into a collective mean, a common resultant, it must not be concluded that their value is equal to zero. On the contrary, each contributes to the resultant and is to this degree involved in it.

I would furthermore ask you to study this theory from its original sources and not at second-hand; it is really much easier. Marx hardly wrote anything in which it did not play a part. But especially *The Eighteenth Brumaire of Louis Bonaparte* is a most excellent example of its application. There are also many allusions in *Capital*. Then may I also direct you to my writings: *Herr Eugen Dühring's Revolution in Science* and *Ludwig Feuerbach and the End of Classical German Philosophy*, in which I have given the most detailed account of historical materialism which, as far as I know, exists.

Marx and I are ourselves partly to blame for the fact that the younger people sometimes lay more stress on the economic side than is due to it. We had to emphasise the main principle *vis-à-vis* our adversaries, who denied it, and we had not always the time, the place or the opportunity to allow the other elements involved in the interaction to come into their rights. But when it was a case of presenting a section of history, that is, of a practical application, it was a different matter and there no error was possible. Unfortunately, however, it happens only too often that people think they have fully understood a new theory and can apply it without more ado from the moment they have mastered its main principles, and even those not always correctly. And I cannot exempt many of the more recent "Marxists" from this reproach, for the most amazing rubbish has been produced in this quarter, too.

* * *

The reaction of the state power upon economic development can be one of three kinds: it can run in the same direction, and then development is more rapid; it can oppose the line of development, in which case nowadays state power in every great people will go to pieces in the long run; or it can cut off the economic development from certain paths, and prescribe certain others. This case ultimately reduces itself to one of the two previous ones. But it is obvious that in cases two and three the political power can do great damage to the economic development and result in the squandering of great masses of energy and material.

Then there is also the case of the conquest and brutal destruction of economic resources, by which, in certain circumstances, a whole local or national economic development could formerly be ruined. Nowadays such a case usually has the opposite effect, at least among great peoples: in the long run the vanquished often gains more economically, politically and morally than the victor.

Similarly with law. As soon as the new division of labour which creates professional lawyers becomes necessary, another new and independent sphere is opened up which, for all its general dependence on production and trade, still has also a special capacity for reacting upon these spheres. In a modern state, law must not only correspond to the general economic condition and be its expression, but must also be an *internally coherent* expression which does not, owing to inner contradictions, reduce itself to nought. And in order to achieve this, the faithful reflection of economic conditions suffers increasingly. All the more so the more rarely it happens that a code of law is the blunt, unmitigated, unadulterated expression of the domination of a class—this in itself would offend the "conception of right." Even in the *Code Napoléon* the pure, consistent conception of right held by the revolutionary bourgeoisie of 1792–96 is already adulterated in many ways, and, in so far as it is embodied there, has daily to undergo all sorts of attenuations owing to the rising power of the proletariat. Which does not prevent the *Code Napoléon* from being the statute book which serves as a basis for every new code of law in every part of the world. Thus to a great extent the course of the "development of right" only consists, first, in the attempt to do away with the contradictions arising from the direct translation of economic relations into legal principles, and to establish a harmonious system of law, and then in the repeated breaches made in this system by the influence and pressure of further economic development, which involves it in further contradictions. (I am speaking here only of civil law for the moment.)

The reflection of economic relations as legal principles is necessarily also a topsy-turvy one: it goes on without the person who is acting being conscious of it; the jurist imagines he is operating with *a priori* propositions, whereas they are really only economic reflexes; so everything is upside down. And it seems to me obvious that this inversion, which, so long as it remains unrecognised, forms what we call *ideological conception*, reacts in its turn upon the economic basis and may, within certain limits, modify it. The basis of the law of inheritance —assuming that the stages reached in the development of the family are equal—is an economic one. Nevertheless, it would be difficult to prove, for instance, that the absolute liberty of the testator in England and the severe restrictions imposed upon him in France are only due in every detail to economic causes. Both react back, however, on the economic sphere to a very considerable extent, because they influence the distribution of property.

As to the realms of ideology which soar still higher in the air, religion, philosophy, etc., these have a prehistoric stock, found already in existence by, and taken over in, the historic period, of what we should today call bunk. These various false conceptions of nature, of man's own being, of spirits, magic forces, etc., have for the most part only a negative economic basis; the low economic development of the prehistoric period is supplemented and also partially conditioned and even caused by the false conceptions of nature. And even though economic necessity was the main driving force of the progressive knowledge of nature and becomes ever more so, it would surely be pedantic to try and find economic causes for all this primitive nonsense. The history of science is the history of the gradual clearing away of this nonsense or of its replacement by fresh but always less absurd nonsense. The people who attend to this belong in their turn to special spheres in the division of labour and appear to themselves to be working in an independent field. And to the extent that they form an independent group within the social division of labour, their productions, including their errors, react back as an influence upon the whole development of society, even on its economic development. But all the same they themselves are again under the dominating influence of economic development. In philosophy, for instance, this can be most readily proved for the bourgeois period. Hobbes was the first modern materialist (in the eighteenth century sense) but he was an absolutist in a period when absolute monarchy was at its height throughout the whole of Europe and when the fight of absolute monarchy versus the people was beginning in England. Locke, both in religion and politics, was the child of the class compromise of 1688. The English deists and their more consistent continuators, the French materialists, were the true philosophers of the bourgeoisie, the French even of the bourgeois revolution. The German Philistine runs through German philosophy from Kant to Hegel, sometimes positively and sometimes negatively. But the philosophy of every epoch, since it is a definite sphere in the division of labour, has as its presupposition certain definite thought material handed down to it by its predecessors, from which it takes its start. And that is why economically backward countries can still play first fiddle in philosophy: France in the eighteenth century compared with England, on whose philosophy the French based themselves, and later Germany relatively to both. But in France as well as Germany philosophy and the general blossoming of literature at that time were the result of a rising economic development. I consider the ultimate supremacy of economic development established in these spheres too, but it comes to pass within the conditions imposed by the particular sphere itself: in philosophy, for instance, through the operation of economic influences (which again generally act only under political, etc., disguises) upon the existing philosphic material handed down by predecessors. Here economy creates nothing anew, but it determines the way in which the thought material found in existence is altered and further developed, and that too for the most part indirectly, for it is the political, legal and moral reflexes which exercise the greatest direct influence upon philosophy.

About religion I have said what was most necessary in the last section on Feuerbach.[1]

1. Paul Barth, author of *Hegel's Philosophy of History and the Hegelians* *Up to Marx and Hartmann* (Leipzig, 1890).

If therefore Barth supposes that we deny any and every reaction of the political, etc., reflexes of the economic movement upon the movement itself, he is simply tilting at windmills. He has only got to look at Marx's *Eighteenth Brumaire*, which deals almost exclusively with the *particular* part played by political struggles and events; of course, within their *general* dependence upon economic conditions. Or *Capital*, the section on the working day, for instance, where legislation, which is surely a political act, has such a trenchant effect. Or the section on the history of the bourgeoisie. (Chapter XXIV.) Or why do we fight for the political dictatorship of the proletariat if political power is economically impotent? Force (that is, state power) is also an economic power!

But I have no time to criticise the book now. I must first get volume III[2] out and besides I think that Bernstein, for instance, could deal with it quite effectively.

What these gentlemen all lack is dialectics. They always see only here cause, there effect. That this is a hollow abstraction, that such metaphysical polar opposites exist in the real world only during crises, while the whole vast process goes on in the form of interaction—though of very unequal forces, the economic movement being by far the strongest, most primeval, most decisive—that here everything is relative and nothing absolute—this they never begin to see. Hegel has never existed for them.

To Franz Mehring

London, July 14, 1893

Today is my first opportunity to thank you for the *Lessing Legend* you were kind enough to send me. I did not want to reply with a bare formal acknowledgement of receipt of the book but intended at the same time to tell you something about it, about its contents. Hence the delay.

I shall begin at the end—the appendix on historical materialism,[3] in which you have lined up the main things excellently and for any unprejudiced person convincingly. If I find anything to object to it is that you give me more credit than I deserve, even if I count in everything which I might possibly have found out for myself—in time—but which Marx with his more rapid *coup d'œil*[4] and wider vision discovered much more quickly. When one has the good fortune to work for forty years with a man like Marx, one does

2. A reference to Volume Three of Marx's *Capital*.
3. Mehring's article "Über den historischen Materialismus" ("On Historical Materialism") was printed in 1893 as an appendix to his book *Die Lessing Legende (The Lessing Legend)*.
4. Grasp.

not usually get the recognition one thinks one deserves during his lifetime. Then, if the greater man dies, the lesser easily gets over-rated and this seems to me to be just my case at present; history will set all this right in the end and by that time one will have qui-etly turned up one's toes and not know anything any more about anything.

Otherwise there is only one point lacking, which, however, Marx and I always failed to stress enough in our writings and in regard to which we are all equally guilty. That is to say, we all laid, and *were bound* to lay, the main emphasis, in the first place, on the *deriva-tion* of political, juridical and other ideological notions, and of actions arisng through the medium of these notions, from basic eco-nomic facts. But in so doing we neglected the formal side—the ways and means by which these notions, etc., come about—for the sake of the content. This has given our adversaries a welcome opportunity for misunderstandings and distortions, of which Paul Barth is a striking example.

Ideology is a process accomplished by the so-called thinker con-sciously, it is true, but with a false consciousness. The real motive forces impelling him remain unknown to him; otherwise it simply would not be an ideological process. Hence he imagines false or seeming motive forces. Because it is a process of thought he derives its form as well as its content from pure thought, either his own or that of his predecessors. He works with mere thought material, which he accepts without examination as the product of thought, and does not investigate further for a more remote source independ-ent of thought; indeed this is a matter of course to him, because, as all action is *mediated* by thought, it appears to him to be ulti-mately *based* upon thought.

The ideologist who deals with history (history is here simply meant to comprise all the spheres—political, juridical, philosophical, theological—belonging to *society* and not only to nature) thus pos-sesses in every sphere of science material which has formed itself independently out of the thought of previous generations and has gone through its own independent process of development in the brains of these successive generations. True, external facts belonging to one or another sphere may have exercised a codetermining influ-ence on this development, but the tacit presupposition is that these facts themselves are also only the fruits of a process of thought, and so we still remain within that realm of mere thought, which appar-ently has successfully digested even the hardest facts.

It is above all this appearance of an independent history of state constitutions, of systems of law, of ideological conceptions in every separate domain that dazzles most people. If Luther and Calvin "overcome" the official Catholic religion or Hegel "overcomes" Fichte and Kant or Rousseau with his republican *contrat social* indirectly overcomes the constitutional Montesquieu, this is a process which remains within theology, philosophy or political science, represents a state in the history of these particular spheres of thought and never passes beyond the sphere of thought. And since the bourgeois illusion of the eternity and finality of capitalist production has been added as well, even the overcoming of the mercantilists by the physiocrats and Adam Smith is accounted as a sheer victory of thought; not as the reflection in thought of changed economic facts but as the finally achieved correct understanding of actual conditions subsisting always and everywhere—in fact, if Richard Coeur de Lion and Philip Augustus had introduced free trade instead of getting mixed up in the crusades we should have been spared five hundred years of misery and stupidity.

This aspect of the matter, which I can only indicate here, we have all, I think, neglected more than it deserves. It is the old story: form is always neglected at first for content. As I say, I have done that too and the mistake has always struck me only later. So I am not only far from reproaching you with this in any way—as the older of the guilty parties I certainly have no right to do so; on the contrary. But I would like all the same to draw your attention to this point for the future.

Hanging together with this is the fatuous notion of the ideologists that because we deny an independent historical development to the various ideological spheres which play a part in history we also deny them any *effect upon history*. The basis of this is the common undialectical conception of cause and effect as rigidly opposite poles, the total disregarding of interaction. These gentlemen often almost deliberately forget that once a historic element has been brought into the world by other, ultimately economic causes, it reacts, can react on its environment and even on the causes that have given rise to it. * * *

To H. Starkenburg

London, January 25, 1894

* * *

* * * Men make their history themselves, but not as yet with a collective will according to a collective plan or even in a definite, delimited given society. Their aspirations clash, and for that very reason all such societies are governed by *necessity*, the complement and form of appearance of which is *accident*. The necessity which here asserts itself athwart all accident is again ultimately economic necessity. This is where the so-called great men come in for treatment. That such and such a man and precisely that man arises at a particular time in a particular country is, of course, pure chance. But cut him out and there will be a demand for a substitute, and this substitute will be found, good or bad, but in the long run he will be found. That Napoleon, just that particular Corsican, should have been the military dictator whom the French Republic, exhausted by its own warfare, had rendered necessary, was chance; but that, if a Napoleon had been lacking, another would have filled the place, is proved by the fact that the man was always found as soon as he became necessary: Caesar, Augustus, Cromwell, etc. While Marx discovered the materialist conception of history, Thierry, Mignet, Guizot and all the English historians up to 1850 are evidence that it was being striven for, and the discovery of the same conception by Morgan proves that the time was ripe for it and that it simply *had* to be discovered.

So with all the other accidents, and apparent accidents, of history. The further the particular sphere which we are investigating is removed from the economic sphere and approaches that of pure abstract ideology, the more shall we find it exhibiting accidents in its development, the more will its curve run zigzag. But if you plot the average axis of the curve, you will find that this axis will run more and more nearly parallel to the axis of economic development the longer the period considered and the wider the field dealt with.

* * *

Bibliographic Note

The literature on classical Marxism and its founders is very large and constantly growing. Many new studies have appeared in recent years as a result of the discovery of the early Marx and the controversy over the place of "original Marxism" in the development of Marx's thought and, more broadly, in intellectual history. This note makes no pretense to being an exhaustive guide even to the books available in English on classical Marxism. It is a small personal selection of studies that may be useful for further reading. The final part lists some works by major Marxist thinkers after Marx and Engels. (Books marked with an asterisk are available as paperbacks; the name of the paperback publisher is given in parentheses.)

BIOGRAPHICAL

The standard Marxist biography of Marx is *Franz Mehring, *Karl Marx: The Story of His Life* (New York, 1957) (Michigan). The comparable biography of Engels is Gustav Mayer, *Friedrich Engels: A Biography* (New York, 1936). See also Steven Marcus, *Engels, Manchester and the Working Class* (New York, 1971). Other biographical studies of Marx include: Otto Rühle, *Karl Marx: His Life and Work* (London, 1929); *Isaiah Berlin, *Karl Marx: His Life and Environment* (New York, 1959) (Oxford); *Leopold Schwarzschild, *The Red Prussian* (New York, 1958) (Grosset & Dunlap); *Boris Nicolaevsky and O. Mänchen-Helfen, *Karl Marx: Man and Fighter* (New York, 1975) (Penguin); and *M. Rubel and M. Mamale, *Marx Without Myth: A Chronological Study of His Life and Work* (New York, 1975) (Harper & Row).

SOCIALIST THOUGHT BEFORE MARXISM

On classical Marxism's background in earlier modern socialist theories: G. D. H. Cole, *History of Socialist Thought*, Volume I, *The Forerunners 1789–1850* (New York, 1953); *J. L. Talmon, *The Origins of Totalitarian Democracy* (New York, 1970) (Norton); *George Lichtheim, *The Origins of Socialism* (New York, 1969) (Praeger); *Martin Buber, *Paths in Utopia* (Boston, 1949) (Beacon); and *Frank E. Manuel, *The Prophets of Paris: Turgot, Condorcet, Saint-Simon, Fourier, Comte* (New York, 1965) (Harper & Row).

THE EARLY MARX

On Marxism's background in German philosophy, the interpretation of the early Marx, and the alienation theme in Marxism: *Louis Dupré, *The Philosophical Foundations of Marxism* (New York, 1966) (Harcourt Brace Jovanovich); *Herbert Marcuse, *Reason and Revolution: Hegel and the Rise of Social Theory* (Boston, 1960) (Beacon); William J. Brazill, *The Young Hegelians* (New Haven, 1970); Eugene Kamenka, *The Philosophy of Ludwig Feuerbach* (New York, 1970); *Erich Fromm, *Marx's Concept of Man* (New York, 1961) (Unger); *Shlomo Avineri, *The Social and Political Thought of Karl Marx* (New York, 1968) (Cambridge); *Sidney Hook, *From Hegel to Marx: Studies in the Intellectual Development of Karl Marx* (New York, 1950) (Michigan); *N. Lobkowicz, ed., *Marx and the Western World* (South Bend, Ind., 1967) (Notre Dame); *Louis Althusser, *For Marx* (New York, 1970) (Vintage); and *Robert C. Tucker, *Philosophy and Myth in Karl Marx*, revised edition (New York, 1972) (Cambridge); *Bertell Ollman, *Alienation: Marx's Conception of Man in Capitalist Society* (New York, 1972) (Cambridge); and *Istvan Mcszaros, *Marx's Theory of Alienation* (New York, 1972) (Harper & Row).

HISTORICAL MATERIALISM

On classical Marxist theory in its development from 1848: G. D. H. Cole, *History of Socialist Thought*, Vol. II, *Marxism and Anarchism 1850–1890* (New York, 1954); *George Lichtheim, *Marxism: An Historical and Critical Study* (New York, 1961) (Praeger); *M. M. Bober, *Karl Marx's Interpretation of History* (New York, 1950) (Norton); *Ralf Dahrendorf, *Class and Class Conflict in Industrial Society* (Stanford, Calif., 1959) (Stanford); *Edwin R. A. Seligman, *The Economic Interpretation of History* (New York, 1907) (Columbia); Karl Korsch, *Karl Marx* (London, 1938); Norman Levine, *The Tragic Deception: Marx Contra Engels* (Oxford, England, 1975); *Robert C. Tucker, *Philosophy and Myth in Karl Marx*, revised edition (New York, 1972) (Cambridge); and *The Marxian Revolutionary Idea* (New York, 1969) (Norton).

THE REVOLUTIONARY POLITICS OF MARX AND ENGELS

On revolutionary strategy and tactics according to classical Marxism, the relations of Marxism and anarchism, and the involvement of Marx and Engels in the socialist and revolutionary politics of the middle and later nineteenth century: G. D. H. Cole, *History of Socialist Thought*, Vol. II, *Marxism and Anarchism 1850–1890* (New York, 1954); J. Hampden Jackson, *Marx, Proudhon and European Socialism* (London, 1957); *Arthur Rosenberg, *Democracy and Socialism* (Boston, 1965) (Beacon); *George Lichtheim, *Marxism: An Historical and Critical Study* (New York, 1961) (Praeger); *Robert C. Tucker, *The Marxian Revolutionary Idea* (New York, 1969) (Norton); Hal Draper, *Marx's Theory of Revolution*, 2 vols. (New York, 1977); and R. Hunt, *The Political Ideas of Marx and Engels*, Vol. I (Pittsburgh, 1974).

MARX'S ECONOMICS

A. D. Lindsay, *Karl Marx's Capital: An Introductory Essay* (London, 1947); Paul C. Roberts and Matthew A. Stephenson, *Marx's Theory of Exchange, Alienation and Crisis* (Stanford, Calif., 1973); M. Movishima, *Marx's Economics* (Cambridge, England, 1973); M. C. Howard and J. E. King, *The Political Economy of Marx* (New York, 1975); R. L. Meek, *Studies in the Labour Theory of Value* (London, 1956); S. De Brunhof, *Marx on Money* (New York, 1976); Ernest Mandel, *The Formation of the Economic Thought of Karl Marx* (New York, 1971); M. Desai, *Marxian Economic Theory* (London, 1974); I. I. Rubin, *Essays on Marx's Theory of Value* (Detroit, 1972); and *Paul Sweezy, *The Theory of Capitalist Development* (New York, 1956) (Monthly Review).

SOME LATER WORKS OF MARXISM

Significant later contributions to Marxist thought include: *Karl Kautsky, *The Class Struggle* (New York, 1971) (Norton) and *The Dictatorship of the Proletariat* (Ann Arbor, 1964) (Michigan); *Eduard Bernstein, *Evolutionary Socialism* (New York, 1961) (Schocken); Rosa Luxemburg, *The Accumulation of Capital* (London, 1951), *Reform or Revolution* (New York, 1970) (Pathfinder), and *The Russian Revolution and Leninism or Marxism?* (Ann Arbor, 1961) (Michigan); Lenin, *What Is to Be Done?*, *The State and Revolution*, and other works, in *The Lenin Anthology*, ed. Robert C. Tucker (New York, 1975) (Norton); *Leon Trotsky, *The New Course* (Ann Arbor, 1965) (Michigan) and *The Revolution Betrayed* (New York, 1937) (Pathfinder); I. V. Stalin, *Problems of Leninism* (Moscow, many editions); Georg Lukacs, *History and Class Consciousness* (Cambridge, Mass., 1968); *Gajo Petrovic, *Marx in the Mid-Twentieth Century: A Yugoslav Philosopher Reconsiders Karl Marx's Writings* (Garden City, N.Y., 1967) (Anchor); Mihailo Markovic, *The Contemporary Marx: Essays on Humanist Communism* (London, 1974) and *From Affluence to Praxis* (Ann Arbor, 1974) (Michigan); *Svetozar Stoianovic, *Between Ideals and Reality: A Critique of Socialism and Its Future* (New York, 1973) (Oxford); *Leszek Kolakowski, *Toward a Marxist Humanism* (New York, 1968) (Grove); and *Andre Gorz, *Socialism and Revolution* (Garden City, N.Y., 1973) (Anchor).

Index

Abstraction (thinking essence), 110–11, 121–24, 125
Accumulated labour
  in bourgeois society, 480
  capital and, 98, 207–10, 211–12, 224
  in Communist society, 485
Activity, 85–86, 89–90
Actuality, 120
"Address of the Central Committee to the Communist League" (Marx and Engels), 501–19
Adultery, 740, 741, 742, 743, 745, 746, 747
Aeschylus, 57
Agriculture, 347
  Asian, 655–56
  as basic economic category, 242–43
  capitalist accumulation and, 434–35
  decline of Roman Empire and, 152–53
  feudal, 153
  liberation and development of, 169
  modern industry and, 415–17
  Roman conquests and, 152
Aiken, 184
Ailly, Pierre d', 614
Alexander the Great, 180
Alienated labour, see Labour, alienated
Alienation, 96, 221
  class and, 133–35
  economic, 85
  religion and, 72, 74, 78, 85
Allgemeine Augsburger Zeitung, 4
Allgemeine Literatur-Zeitung, 68n, 107n
Alsace-Lorraine, 564, 619
Althusser, Louis, 136n
Amalfi, 187
Amsterdam, Marx's speech in (1872), 522–24
Anarchists, 542, 547, 728–29
Ancient Society (Morgan), 734
Anecdotis (Ruge), 68, 107
Animals, 75–76
Annenkov, P. V., 136
Annulment, 120–25
Anti-Corn Law League, 176
Anti-Dühring (Engels), 683–727
Antipatros, 406
Appearance, 10–11, 120
  philosophy opposed to, 11
Apprentices, feudal, 153
  patriarchal relationship between masters and, 177
Aristocracy
  democracy and, 160
  French, 174
  honor and loyalty under, 173
Aristotle, 9, 92, 333n–334n, 406, 694

Art, 8
  ethical mind and, 120
  as mode of production, 85
  religion and, 109, 119
  social development and, 245–46
  timeless character of, 221, 246
Asiatic mode of production, 5
Atelier, 536
Atheism
  communism and, 85, 92–93
  humanism and, 120–21
  as mediation, 92–93
  and the state, 36
Australia, 6
Austria, 61, 570
Austro-Prussian War (1866), 621–23
Authority, 730–33
Automation, capitalism and, 221, 278–90
Avignon, 394

Babeuf, François Nöel, 497, 685
Bachofen, 736, 750
Bacon, Francis, 695
Baking industry, 368–70, 375
Bakunin, Mikhail, 542–48, 671, 728–29
Banks, 184
Barbarians, 152–53
Barbès, Armand, 577
Barbon, Nicholas, 303n, 304n, 305
Barrot, Odilon, 572
Barter, 451, 460
Barth, Paul, 765
Bastiat, Frédéric, 223, 246
Bauer, Bruno, 8n, 67n, 68n, 146
  on dialectic, 106–7
  on Jewish question, 26–32, 35, 37–38, 40, 42, 47, 49, 51
  on nature, 134, 170
  polemic against, 133–35
Beaumont, Gustave de, 31n, 39
Bebel, August, 549, 566
Being
  becoming as, 124
  essence and, 122
  natural and species-, 116
  objective, 116
  other-, 118
  thinking and, 86
Belgium, 570
Bernstein, Eduard, 549, 764
Big industry
  abolition of private property and, 190
  capital determined by, 186
  class created by, 185–86
  communications and, 185
  contradiction between means of production and private property in, 189–90

771